Xunzi

Xunzi

荀子

THE COMPLETE TEXT

TRANSLATED AND WITH AN INTRODUCTION BY
Eric L. Hutton

PRINCETON UNIVERSITY PRESS
PRINCETON AND OXFORD

Third printing, first paperback printing, 2016

Cloth ISBN 978-0-691-16104-4
Paper ISBN: 978-0-691-16931-6
Library of Congress Control Number: 2014933937

British Library Cataloging-in-Publication Data is available

This book has been composed in Baskerville 10 Pro

Printed on acid-free paper. ∞

Printed in the United States of America

5 7 9 10 8 6

弟子通利則思師

When the disciple has achieved success and profit,
then he gratefully thinks of his teacher.

—*Xunzi*, chap. 14

*This book is dedicated to P. J. Ivanhoe,
my mentor and friend.*

CONTENTS

Acknowledgments   ix

Introduction   xi

A Traditional Timeline of Early Chinese History   xxxi

CHAPTER 1: An Exhortation to Learning   1

CHAPTER 2: Cultivating Oneself   9

CHAPTER 3: Nothing Improper   16

CHAPTER 4: On Honor and Disgrace   23

CHAPTER 5: Against Physiognomy   32

CHAPTER 6: Against the Twelve Masters   40

CHAPTER 7: On Confucius   47

CHAPTER 8: The Achievements of the *Ru*   52

CHAPTER 9: The Rule of a True King   68

CHAPTER 10: Enriching the State   83

CHAPTER 11: The True King and the Hegemon   99

CHAPTER 12: The Way to Be a Lord   117

CHAPTER 13: The Way to Be a Minister   133

CHAPTER 14: On Attracting Men of Worth   141

CHAPTER 15: A Debate on Military Affairs   145

CHAPTER 16: The Strong State   163

CHAPTER 17: Discourse on Heaven   175

CHAPTER 18: Correct Judgments   183

CHAPTER 19: Discourse on Ritual   201

CHAPTER 20: Discourse on Music   218

CHAPTER 21: Undoing Fixation   224

CHAPTER 22: Correct Naming   236

CHAPTER 23: Human Nature Is Bad   248

CHAPTER 24: The Gentleman   258

CHAPTER 25: Working Songs   262

CHAPTER 26: *Fu*   277

CHAPTER 27: The Grand Digest   288

CHAPTER 28: The Right-Hand Vessel   318

CHAPTER 29: The Way to Be a Son   325

CHAPTER 30: The Proper Model and Proper Conduct   330

CHAPTER 31: Duke Ai   333

CHAPTER 32: Yao Asked   339

APPENDIX 1: Important Terms and Names   344

APPENDIX 2: Cross-Reference List   347

Textual Notes   359

Bibliography   385

Index   387

ACKNOWLEDGMENTS

I began this translation project in 1996. Over the eighteen years that I have worked on it, it has benefited from the insights and suggestions of a tremendous number of people, including my teachers, students, classmates, colleagues, friends, and fellow scholars. I hereby most gratefully acknowledge their help and hope that they will be pleased with the final product.

I would like to extend special recognition to the following individuals and institutions. Early on, significant portions of this work were published as part of *Readings in Classical Chinese Philosophy* (Hackett, 2003), and the manuscript was greatly improved by comments from the editors, Bryan Van Norden and P. J. Ivanhoe. In the time since then, P. J. has also given me invaluable feedback on every portion of this text, and to him I owe gratitude beyond all words. At points along the way, I have spent many enjoyable hours dissecting the Chinese text in the company of Jack Kline, Michael Nylan, Hui-chieh Loy, and Eirik Harris, hours that have contributed immensely to my understanding of the *Xunzi* and to this translation. Also, discussions with Aaron Stalnaker, Miranda Brown, David Elstein, Eric Schwitzgebel, Mark Csikszentmihalyi, Ted Slingerland, Justin Tiwald, Erin Cline, and Bryan Van Norden have likewise enriched this work. When a substantial portion of the translation had been completed, Gordon Mower read through the lengthy draft and identified many places where it could be improved. In 2008, Stephen Angle and Michael Slote used selected chapters from the manuscript in their NEH summer seminar on Confucianism and contemporary virtue ethics, and I received very helpful suggestions from them and the seminar participants. During the 2009–10 academic year, I was able to make significant progress toward finishing the manuscript thanks to support from the University of Utah in the form of a Virgil C. Aldrich Research Fellowship from the Tanner Humanities Center and a Faculty Fellow Award from the University Research Committee.

I also wish to express my gratitude to a number of people involved in the last stages leading to this publication. In particular, I thank Rob Tempio at Princeton University Press for his tremendous support, as well as three anonymous reviewers for the press who offered encouraging and helpful feedback. Deborah Mower and Rochelle Beiersdorfer enthusiastically advocated for this translation, which I appreciated very much. I visited Berkeley in the summer of 2013, and Mark Csikszentmihalyi provided some crucial research assistance during that period. Toni Lee Capossela read through the whole manuscript and offered many suggestions that have made it more readable. To Deborah Wilkes at Hackett Publishing I am likewise indebted for her invaluable assistance with matters of copyright and other technical issues concerning publishing.

Finally, I would like to thank my mother for nurturing me and encouraging my scholarly endeavors from the time I was a child to the present. I would also like to thank my wife, Sophia, for her love and patient support during the many years over which this project was completed.

INTRODUCTION

Without a doubt, the *Xunzi* is one of the most philosophically interesting and sophisticated texts in the Confucian tradition. It covers a wide variety of topics—education, ritual, music, language, psychology, history, religion, ethics, politics, and warfare, to name just a few—and it provides quite thoughtful treatments of all these subjects. Indeed, despite being a very old text, many of its insights still ring true in the present. It is thus a text that amply rewards study, and not only for those seeking to understand ancient Chinese views in particular, but also for anyone reflecting on these important aspects of human life in general.

THE PURPOSE AND FEATURES OF THIS TRANSLATION

Although the *Xunzi* is a very rich text, study of the *Xunzi* was relatively neglected for many centuries in China, due in large part to the greater popularity of another early Confucian text with rival ideas, the *Mencius* (also called the *Mengzi*). As a result, the *Xunzi* was initially also rather neglected by many Western students of Chinese thought. Fortunately, this situation is slowly being rectified, and study of the *Xunzi* has begun to flourish again both inside and outside China in recent years. Nevertheless, the evidence of long neglect is still apparent in various ways, one of which is that there was no complete English translation of the *Xunzi* available before the work of John Knoblock appeared during the years 1988–94. Since one of the most important means for promoting the study of Chinese thought in the West is by making primary sources available to readers through translations, this was a major step forward for the field.

Yet, while Knoblock has undeniably made a great contribution to study of the *Xunzi*, in various ways his translation is not well suited for use in teaching undergraduates. For one thing, he provides a tremendous amount of explanatory material and endnotes that far exceed the needs of the typical undergraduate reader, which makes his translation a massive work and contributed to its being unfortunately priced well beyond what is reasonable for textbook adoptions. (Moreover, at the time of writing this, the original version has gone out of print. A bilingual reprint from mainland China is currently available for purchase, but is still quite expensive and omits all of Knoblock's explanatory material and endnotes, thereby leaving students with no aids whatsoever for understanding the more difficult parts of the text.) Also, in striving to be precise and literal, Knoblock produced prose that is frequently difficult to follow for undergraduate readers. More seriously, there are some substantial inaccuracies and technical flaws in the translation that have been pointed out in published reviews of it, which I will not rehearse here.

As an alternative to using Knoblock's translation for teaching undergraduates, there exists a widely available, older translation of the *Xunzi* by Burton Watson, which is often more readable and more accurate and has been priced more affordably than Knoblock's work. It is thus better suited to serve the needs of the undergraduate classroom, and hence has continued to be the preferred edition for many instructors, even after the appearance of Knoblock's translation. Yet, because Watson's translation is abridged, it omits many chapters that are both historically and philosophically very significant, and which can markedly impact one's interpretation of the text. Instructors teaching from Watson's text but wishing to cover parts of the *Xunzi* not included in it have therefore been faced with the choice of supplementing Watson's work either by undertaking the time-consuming task of translating the other parts themselves—if they have the requisite linguistic competence in Chinese at all—or by borrowing sections from Knoblock or other partial translations, a practice that is likewise not ideal, since different translators adopt different conventions in rendering various terms, concepts, and so on, which can make it difficult to combine them in any straightforward manner.

The present translation is intended to fill a gap that has thus been left by the work of Knoblock and Watson, as well as other partial English translations, by providing a new and complete English translation of the *Xunzi* that will be well suited for use in teaching undergraduates. While the translation is thus not designed primarily for the edification of graduate students or specialists in Chinese thought, the work as a whole and certain features of it in particular may perhaps still prove useful for their research. If so, I would find that gratifying. Nonetheless, more advanced readers should bear in mind that the translation aims primarily to serve a different audience, and hence there are features that they might find desirable, but that I have purposely omitted, because it is rather considerations about undergraduate readers and their needs, based on my own experience in teaching, that have driven many choices I have made in the course of producing the work.

First, as with any translation, I have been very concerned with accuracy, but because my target is the undergraduate classroom, I have also made certain compromises. The Chinese text of the *Xunzi* was written with great erudition, which I have tried to reflect in the translation. However, to make the text accessible to undergraduates, I also have tried very hard to make it easy to read, that is, to have it sound learned to a modern ear without being stodgy. In some cases this has required adopting renderings that are not very literal translations of the Chinese, including, for instance, simplifying some of the long lists of nearly synonymous terms that one often finds in the *Xunzi*, which make for extremely cumbersome English if each and every item is translated. Likewise, on a number of occasions the *Xunzi* gives names of minerals, plants, and (sometimes mythical) animals for which—if the named item can be reliably identified at all—there is no common equivalent in English, or for which the common equivalent is unfamiliar or meaningless to most urban-dwelling college students. For many such cases, I have opted simply to give the name used by the *Xunzi* in romanization, rather than trying to supply an exact English equivalent. In these and other instances, I have taken such steps only when it seems that no especially significant philosophical point will be sacrificed by the use of transliterations or less literal translations.

Second, since most undergraduate students are likely to encounter the *Xunzi* as part of a larger course on Chinese thought, I have tried to make the translation friendly to such use in certain ways. For one thing, students in these courses are often required to read several works, each of which has been done by a different translator. If, as mentioned earlier, the various translators each render key terms very differently, it then becomes difficult for students to grasp and keep sight of the fact that these different texts are all employing and debating a shared set of Chinese terms. This problem arises from the fact that there is not an overwhelming scholarly consensus about how to translate a number of Chinese words. Nevertheless, among many English translators there is a tradition of rendering certain Chinese terms with particular English words, and for the sake of cross-compatibility with existing translations, I have largely followed this tradition, even when there might be reasons for adopting different translations if the terms were to be considered in complete isolation from both other texts and other terms in this text (e.g., I follow convention in rendering *zhuhou* 諸侯 as "feudal lords," even though the ancient Chinese political system may have been "feudal" in only a very tenuous sense at best). Readers should therefore keep in mind that the English words used as translations here are intended as stand-ins and approximations for Chinese terms, whose actual meanings must always be grasped through observing their use in context—the English terms are *not* to be taken as precise equivalents for the Chinese words.

For a very small number of important philosophical terms, however, such as *ren* 仁 and *yi* 義, for which any choice of translation is especially contentious, and whose varying usages in the text make it quite difficult to adopt any rendering in a completely consistent manner, I have opted to leave them untranslated and instead simply written them in romanization. Since this book is intended for the classroom, I am anticipating that students reading the *Xunzi* as part of a course will be introduced to these terms in some fashion (or via some translation) by their instructor. The choice to leave these words untranslated is intended to allow readers to track with great clarity exactly where the terms appear and how they are deployed, and thereby to assess for themselves how best to understand what the words mean in the context of the *Xunzi*. For readers without the aids of an instructor and classroom, or who have no prior exposure to Chinese thought, I have provided explanations of these terms in the footnotes and in appendix 1 that should give them a basic understanding of these concepts, and I have also provided a very brief overview of important ideas in the text in the third section of this introduction.

A third way in which this translation is tailored for undergraduate students is that I have limited notes on technical matters to an absolute minimum, since such notes are relevant mostly to readers with advanced skills in classical Chinese, which few undergraduate students possess at this time. The technical notes are indicated with superscript letters and can be found at the end of the book. I have generally indicated only those instances where my reading differs from that found in the major premodern commentaries on the text. So, for example, when I have followed emendations or variant readings suggested by the major premodern commentaries (especially those cited in Wang Xianqian's *Xunzi Jijie* 荀子集解, which is my base text), I usually have not noted this. In those cases, scholars looking for justifications for particular renderings are encouraged to consult Wang's book and the other works I have used in preparing this translation, which are listed in the bibliography. Overall, I have taken a fairly conservative stance toward the text, and have generally adopted emendations only when it seems to me necessary in order to make sense of it.

Compared with explanations of technical matters, I have provided many more notes on matters of historical background and other supplementary information, but in this case also I have tried to limit the explanations to what is most essential for understanding the *Xunzi* or to what I think will be most useful for undergraduate students. With regard to the former kind of explanation, important names and terms are generally explained in the notes when they first appear in the text, and the index lists in bold type the pages where these introductory accounts are given, for easy reference afterward. Readers requiring more detailed information about people and events mentioned by the *Xunzi* are encouraged to consult Knoblock's work, which contains copious explanations and references. With regard to the latter kind of material, since the translation may be used as a part of a general course on Chinese thought, I have indicated in the notes a number of places where comparisons with other early Chinese texts are illuminating, with the hope that these citations will encourage students to undertake such comparisons on their own.

Two further features of the translation deserve mention here. The first is the numbering system I have deployed. Unlike a number of other early Chinese texts such as the *Analects*, the *Mencius*, and the *Daodejing*, for which there exist standard numbering systems that facilitate ease and precision of references, there is no standard numbering system for the text of the *Xunzi*. There are two concordances that many scholars use as the basis for their references, but since these texts are in Chinese only, they are not accessible to those who cannot read the language. Knoblock numbered the paragraphs of his translation, but the way that his numbering is done can sometimes misleadingly suggest discontinuities in the text's discussions. Moreover, the matter of how to divide the text into paragraphs is itself uncertain and occasionally quite controversial. (My own paragraph divisions mostly follow those of other editions, but in some cases depart from common practice, sometimes for the convenience of English readers.) As an alternative way to facilitate scholarly references, I have provided line numbers for my translation. I have also provided an appendix to aid students who may be trying to track down references in secondary literature on the *Xunzi* based on the Chinese concordances, or who wish to compare this translation with others. In the notes and appendixes, references to my translation are given in the form "chapter number.line number" to enable readers to locate the indicated passages quickly and precisely.

The other feature of this translation that warrants comment is the handling of rhymed lines. The *Xunzi* contains numerous rhymed passages. A number of these are quotations from the *Odes*, which is an ancient collection of poems—or more accurately, songs—that the *Xunzi* treats as a repository of wisdom, and which it cites to illustrate and support its claims. Many other rhymed passages appear to be original to the *Xunzi*. (I say "appear" because it is always possible that in particular cases the text is quoting, without attribution, from some source now lost to us, but it is doubtful that all of the unattributed passages come from some other source.) Some of these other rhyming passages are probably modeled after the *Odes*, and some or even all of the rhymed passages may likewise have been intended to be sung aloud, perhaps with the purpose of making the lessons they teach more memorable. However, these rhymes that are not quoted from the *Odes* have not always been noted in previous translations of the *Xunzi*. Both Watson and Knoblock often overlook them, as do many translations of the *Xunzi* into modern Chinese and Japanese and Korean.

The function of these rhymed sections and their significance for understanding the *Xunzi* are substantial issues that merit lengthy discussion more appropriate for an article or book than this introduction, but I consider the presence of these rhymes a feature of the text that is sufficiently noteworthy to deserve being reflected conspicuously in the translation. Since the rhyming sections can easily be overlooked (especially by students) if they are indicated merely in footnotes or with offsetting, I have chosen to make them conspicuous by translating rhymed passages in Chinese with rhymed sections of English, *except* when I felt it beyond my ability or when the constraints imposed by translating in rhyme would necessitate obscuring or misrepresenting something I thought to be of special significance. In such cases, I have left the English text unrhymed and instead resorted to indicating the rhymes in the notes and/or with offset lines.[1] For the rhymes in English, I have tried to follow the original rhyme pattern used in the Chinese where possible, but where that made the task of rhyming the English too difficult, I have not followed the Chinese rhymes, on the grounds that I think it more important to convey to students *that* the text is rhymed than exactly *how* it is rhymed, as the latter issue is mostly of interest to specialists. For the same reason, I have not noted the original Chinese words that rhyme. The identification of the rhymes in the Chinese text requires detailed knowledge of ancient phonology that I lack, and so I have relied on published studies of rhymes in the *Xunzi* by other scholars. Since their analyses may have missed some of the rhyming passages, and since there is ongoing scholarly debate about how to reconstruct the sounds of ancient Chinese in the first place, I do not claim to have identified every instance of rhyme in the text, but I do hope to have surpassed previous translations in highlighting this feature of the *Xunzi*.

The rhymed sections of the *Xunzi*, both the quotations from the *Odes* and the unattributed rhymes, generally display an additional feature, namely fixed line lengths. That is to say, usually the lines are all composed of the same number of Chinese characters, or alternate in the number of characters according to some pattern, which would normally translate to a fixed number of syllables per line if spoken. Awareness of this aspect is important for appreciating the artistry involved in the composition of ancient Chinese verse, for it thus required meeting two distinct challenges, namely getting the lines to rhyme and doing so within the constraint of fixed line lengths. In order to represent the latter feature of the Chinese text, when translating the rhymed passages with English rhymes, in most cases I have

---

[1] In those instances, I have not provided explanations for why I chose not to translate those passages with rhyming English. Suffice it to say that when readers encounter passages that are noted as rhyming in the original, but do not rhyme in the translation, they may simply take it that I felt a rhyming translation at that point would have forced an unacceptably large sacrifice of accuracy.

adopted lines with fixed numbers of syllables. Since many English words are polysyllabic, however, it is not possible to match the number of syllables in the Chinese lines exactly, so case by case I have picked a limit for the syllables in the English lines, based on what seemed to be the minimum for rendering the Chinese into English with reasonable accuracy.

Through translating the rhymed sections in a fashion that simulates the constraints faced by the original composers, I hope to have approximated—not equaled—the artistry that appears in the Chinese text of the *Xunzi*. Although the great scholar of Chinese thought D. C. Lau once claimed that the *Xunzi* displays "an indifferent literary style,"[2] I respectfully disagree with his assessment. Even if the *Xunzi* does not display the imaginative fancy of some early texts, such as the *Zhuangzi*, the style of writing in the *Xunzi* is extremely powerful and elegant. While I cannot match this power and elegance in English, I hope that what I have done can in some small measure convey to the English reader a bit of the beauty of the *Xunzi*'s Chinese text and its mastery of multiple forms of presentation, and that this effect can compensate for the occasional, slight departures from literal accuracy involved in producing the rhymed translations.

Last, it is by now a well-worn cliché that "every translation is an act of interpretation." Like any other scholar, I have my own particular views about how best to interpret the text, but in general, I have tried not to inject too many of my own particular readings into the translation, especially where these would be highly idiosyncratic. Readers who compare this work with other translations and commentaries will find that, by and large, I am in agreement with traditional interpretations of the text. Nonetheless, part of my aim has also been to present a reading of the *Xunzi* that is philosophically coherent, and so in some cases this has meant departing from the consensus view when it has seemed to me that the traditional readings have not done full justice to the content of the text. In most cases, I have discussed these departures in the textual notes or footnotes. Along the way, I have also tried to improve on the efforts of previous translators such as Knoblock and Watson, by consulting published criticisms of their work and taking care to avoid problems pointed out by the critics, when I could agree that their criticisms were justified. I have tried to have good reasons for all the decisions I have made in the course of translating the *Xunzi*, but since the present work is intended to offer primarily a translation and not a full-scale commentary on the text, I have not attempted to explain all those decisions in this book. No doubt, some readers will question or disagree with the choices I have made, and likely some will rightly identify places where I myself

[2] Lau (1970, p. 8).

could and should have done better. Even so, if this translation serves to instill in students an appreciation of the *Xunzi* and a desire to study it further, its purpose will be fulfilled.

XUNZI: TEXT AND PERSON

The received text of the *Xunzi* is divided into thirty-two sections, which I refer to as "chapters." These chapters (or parts of them) likely circulated as freestanding pieces in ancient China, and probably were never intended to be read in a particular order in the form of a single book, as we now have it. Rather, our received text was first compiled by Liu Xiang (77–6 BCE), who states in his preface that he started with 322 sections of text, which he reduced to our current text of thirty-two chapters, after eliminating "duplicates" and performing other editing.[3] The sources from which Liu worked are now lost to us, and while future archaeological work may recover pieces of the text that predate Liu's work, we are not at present in a position to know for sure what might have been lost, added, or changed in the process of his editing.

This history of the text has certain implications for how to approach it.[4] For one thing, in attempting to understand its philosophical content, little significance can be attached to the order of the chapters, since Liu Xiang was apparently the first to combine them in a set, which necessitated giving them some order. Indeed, over the centuries, editors of the *Xunzi* have felt free to rearrange the chapters on various grounds, and so the arrangements tell us more about the editors' views than about the meaning of the chapters in their original context. The arrangement in this translation follows that of the Tang dynasty edition (818 CE) of Yang Liang, which is the basis for most copies of the *Xunzi* in print today. A point similar to the first one also applies to the organization of content *within* the chapters. In particular, some chapters offer rather choppy discussions of a single theme or seem to combine discussions of unrelated topics, but these features of the text may simply be artifacts of Liu's editing, rather than reflecting how the content was originally supposed to be read. Hence, such organization (or as it may be, disorganization) can bear little weight in interpreting the philosophical content or assessing the authenticity of the chapters. The same must be said about the titles

---

[3] Despite Liu's remark about eliminating duplicates, there are still various places in the text where a passage appears verbatim or nearly verbatim in one or more chapters. I have noted these instances in the translation for purposes of aiding comparisons across chapters.

[4] A number of points in this paragraph are taken from Knoblock (1988, vol. 1, pp. 123–24, 128).

of the chapters as well. Some works in ancient China circulated without titles, and there are no records prior to Liu Xiang's edition of the *Xunzi* of any of the chapter titles of the *Xunzi* listed by Liu, so he may well have added them himself.

Our title for the whole collection of chapters, the *Xunzi*—which also is most likely an addition by editors—comes from the name of the person, Xunzi, whose thought it purports to record.[5] In turn, the name "Xunzi" (literally, "Master Xun") is an honorific title for the man Xun Kuang 荀況. As is the case for so many other early Chinese thinkers, little is known for sure about his life. There is no firm evidence for his dates of birth and death, and hence scholars have made varying proposals on the matter. To give just a small sample illustrating the diversity of opinions, Qian Mu 錢穆 estimates Xunzi's dates as 340 to 245 BCE, the authors of the Beijing University Philosophy Department commentary as ca. 325 to ca. 235 BCE, You Guo'en 游國恩 as 314 to 217 BCE, and John Knoblock as ca. 315 to ca. 215 BCE.[6] While there is thus disagreement about the exact span of his life, there is a fairly strong consensus that Xunzi was active in the latter half of the Warring States period (403–221 BCE). At that time, the power of the nominal ruling dynasty, the Zhou dynasty, was in steep decline, and what was then Chinese territory was divided into several states that were engaged in a violent struggle among themselves for overall supremacy. As can be seen from some of the above estimates of Xunzi's life that favor later dates, he may have lived long enough to see the momentous end of this period, when the state of Qin finished off the last of its rivals to become the sole ruling power in 221 BCE. Indeed, according to early accounts, two of Xunzi's students, Han Feizi and Li Si, were important agents in Qin's rise to dominance, but given Qin's brutal government practices, this association wound up bringing disrepute to Xunzi's name in later history. Judging by the content of the *Xunzi*, however, he himself apparently would not have approved of Li Si's and Han Feizi's methods.

During his lifetime, as with most other intellectuals of his day, Xunzi moved from state to state, seeking to persuade a ruler to employ him and put his teachings into practice. Over the years, he managed to become a fairly prominent figure. In the state of Qi, for example, he was thrice given the high honor of being the ritual "libationer" for the group of distinguished people the king had assembled at Jixia. Xunzi also succeeded in obtaining political office. He was magistrate of Lanling in the state of Chu twice, and in the

---

[5] Since there have been many alternate names for Xunzi, the text has likewise had a number of different titles over time. See note 7 below.

[6] See Qian (2008, p. 688), Beida Zhexuexi (1979, pp. 613–19), You (1982), and Knoblock (1982–83).

interim between those positions, he was given the title of "Minister" (*qing* 卿) in the state of Zhao, which is why he is also known as Xun Qing.[7] However, during his time in office, he was unable to bring about the grand reforms envisioned in the writings attributed to him, perhaps in part because of political intrigues against him and his rulers. In 238 BCE, his lord in Chu was assassinated, and Xunzi lost his post for the last time. Early sources report that he then lived out the rest of his life in retirement from office in Lanling, writing and teaching. His tradition of scholarship was very influential for a long period after his life, especially in the early years of the Han dynasty that followed the short reign of Qin. Much later, the Tang dynasty thinker Han Yu (768–824 CE) famously criticized Xunzi's thought as having "impurities," and this appraisal became very influential during the Song dynasty (960–1279 CE) and thereafter. The *Mencius* came to be preferred by many Confucian thinkers, while Xunzi came to be regarded as a "heterodox" Confucian. This view persists in some quarters even today, though, as noted earlier, a greater appreciation for the *Xunzi* is now growing.

The relation between the person Xunzi and the text *Xunzi* is a complicated issue. To start with a general point, archaeological finds and historical research have led many scholars now to believe that a number of ancient Chinese texts that tradition attributes to a single author, such as the *Daodejing* and the *Zhuangzi*, are in fact composite texts, written by different authors, whose work perhaps spans a long period of time. To that extent, the respective traditional ascriptions of these texts to single figures such as Laozi and Zhuangzi are incorrect; Laozi and Zhuangzi may never even have existed as persons, or if they did, they may not have thought, said, or written any of the things attributed to them. For this reason, some scholars want to avoid any reference to Laozi and Zhuangzi at all, preferring to speak only of "what the *Daodejing* says" or "what the *Zhuangzi* says," and so forth.

When it comes to the *Xunzi*, there are indications in the text that not all of it was written by a single person, and hence that not all of it was written by Xunzi himself. For example, some chapters contain dialogues in which Xunzi appears as an interlocutor, but in which he is called Xun Qingzi ("Master Xun Qing") or other titles that it would be extremely unlikely for a Chinese writer to employ in referring to himself. At minimum, such instances seem to be evidence of

---

[7] In addition, the family name Xun 荀 in "Xunzi" appears in some early texts as Sun 孫. As a result, Xunzi is sometimes referred to as Sun Qing 孫卿, and sometimes the appellation *zi* 子 ("Master") is added to the "Qing" to yield "Xun Qingzi" or "Sun Qingzi." Since our text is named after the person, the text has likewise been called by these alternate names at points in time. For discussion of Xunzi's family name, see Knoblock (1988, vol. 1, pp. 233–39).

editing by someone other than Xunzi, and many scholars consider it likely that these sections were originally written by his disciples, who were recording (or maybe inventing) the words of their teacher. Also, the last six chapters in the present arrangement of the text display both a piecemeal quality and a use of didactic vignettes, differing significantly from the essays that constitute the bulk of the first twenty-four chapters. For this reason, many have likewise suspected the material of the last six chapters of being a compilation made by Xunzi's students, rather than the writings of Xunzi himself. A further relevant point is that a number of passages in the *Xunzi* that are not explicitly attributed to any other source appear verbatim or nearly verbatim—and without any mention of Xunzi or the *Xunzi*—in early texts such as the *Hanshi Waizhuan* 韓詩外傳, *Liji* 禮記, *Kongzi Jiayu* 孔子家語, and so on. The existence of these parallel passages raises difficult questions about whether these texts are incorporating sections from the *Xunzi* or the *Xunzi* is incorporating sections from them, or whether all of them are incorporating sections from some earlier, now lost source.[8] To the extent that either of the latter two scenarios is the case, the *Xunzi* would contain many more elements that Xunzi did not write.

Given these indications that various sections of the *Xunzi* were not all written by a single person, one might then wonder how much of it really was written by Xunzi after all. Since we have little information about Xunzi's life, and since most of the information we do have comes from sources whose veracity and accuracy are not fully reliable, it is impossible to say for sure that the historical Xunzi is responsible for any of the text that now bears his name. Nevertheless, few scholars seem inclined to doubt the existence of Xunzi as a real person, and few seem inclined to take the position that the *Xunzi* does not at all reflect the views of the historical Xunzi. Between the position that Xunzi is responsible for all of our text and the position that he is responsible for none of it, there is a wide range of possibilities, over which scholars have argued at length. Their positions and arguments are so varied and numerous that I will not rehearse them here. Instead, I simply note that most scholars seem to agree that chapters 1 to 26 in the present arrangement are more likely to contain material that comes directly from Xunzi, though this still leaves much room for disagreement. Ultimately, most scholars could probably agree that from a strict historical perspective, it is safest to speak of "what

---

[8] In this translation, I do not indicate the passages that overlap with other early texts, on the grounds that tracing the overlaps, comparing the parallels, and assigning authorship are issues mainly of interest to graduate students and specialists, rather than beginning students and those reading simply for philosophical content. Readers interested in the textual overlaps are advised to consult Knoblock's translation, which contains quite extensive discussions of the matter.

the *Xunzi* says," while claims about "what Xunzi says" or "what Xunzi thinks" must be regarded as somewhat tentative.

However, the historical perspective is not the only perspective through which one can read and discuss the text, and from a philosophical perspective in particular, these worries about the composition of the text are less pressing. If we are interested in the ideas in the text, the coherence among them, and whether there are any lessons we can learn from it for ourselves about how we should think and live nowadays, then it matters little whether Xunzi himself is actually responsible for the content of the *Xunzi*. Likewise, from such a perspective, it matters little whether the text was written by a single person or by many people over time. For neither does it follow from the mere fact that a single person writes a text that it will be consistent or insightful, nor does it follow from the mere fact that a text is written by a multitude of people that it will be inconsistent or unenlightening. Hence, for example, even if chapters 27 to 32 of the *Xunzi* were produced by a wholly different set of persons than the author(s) of rest of the work, that fact does not by itself entail that these last six chapters do not "belong" with the rest of the *Xunzi* in the sense of forming a coherent whole—that is a matter that can be assessed only by examining the content of those chapters. Some scholars have suggested that the material of chapters 27 to 32, though not composed by Xunzi, was used by him in teaching his students, who then recorded, collected, and preserved it after his death. If such were the case, then we might actually *expect* a fairly good fit between the ideas of those chapters and the rest (and in my view that is what we find when we examine them). We cannot be sure whether the chapters really came about in this way, but the important point is that historical facts about the origins of the text will not suffice to answer every question one might be interested in asking about it.

Furthermore, from a philosophical perspective, when one is trying to assess what one might learn from a text, one wants to know not just what it says, but moreover *how* to think with it. That is to say, one wants to know what it is like to think from the point of view of someone who holds the beliefs propounded by the text (insofar as a coherent point of view can be distilled from it), in order to see how well such a way of thinking can answer questions, respond to challenges, and so on. If the text is said to be written by a certain named individual, then for the sake of discussion it will be quite natural to label this point of view with the person's name, and thus to speak of it in terms of the person's claims and thoughts. Such a manner of speaking is philosophical, not historical,[9] for the primary referent of such

---

[9] For other examples of such nonhistorical ways of speaking, compare discussions of fictional characters. Since Sherlock Holmes is not a real person, claims such as

discussion is the point of view, rather than the actual person, who may or may not in fact have had that point of view, and may or may not even have existed. If the text turns out to be a composite work—or even if it is known to be such from the outset—then it is perhaps somewhat less likely (though not impossible) that this point of view was ever in fact held by any particular individual. Yet, even this fact about the text would not entail that one cannot hypothesize an individual with such a point of view for the purposes of philosophical inquiry, nor would it preclude giving this hypothetical individual and point of view a name for the sake of discussion, including, as before, the name(s) of the text's supposed author(s).

In such a philosophical manner, then, one can speak of "what Xunzi says" and "what Xunzi thinks," based on what appears in the text, while leaving open the question of the extent to which this "Xunzi" and his views correspond to those of the actual person Xunzi and/or other people responsible for the content of the *Xunzi*. (A similar approach can likewise be taken with Laozi and Zhuangzi and other Warring States figures.) I do not mean to claim that this approach is to be preferred over all others, but since I approach the text primarily from a philosophical perspective, this is how I will be speaking when I talk of Xunzi and his views from here on.[10]

XUNZI'S THOUGHT: ITS BACKGROUND AND SALIENT FEATURES

During the Warring States period, alongside the rivalry among political powers, there was also a lively competition among ideas. One of these competitors was the emerging tradition that we now call "Confucianism," which as an English label suggests that the tradition originates with Confucius. However, the thinkers in this tradition—including Confucius himself, at least as he is depicted in our primary source for knowledge about him, the *Analects*—viewed themselves as

---

"Sherlock Holmes is a genius" are false, if taken as historical claims about a real person. However, such claims are usually neither offered nor received as historical claims. Anyone who would completely bar such ways of speaking on the grounds that they are historically inaccurate is insisting on the priority of the historical perspective in all cases, which is obviously an extreme position requiring substantial arguments to make it even remotely plausible.

[10] Some might worry that this manner of speaking may still encourage historically inaccurate views. Here is not the appropriate place to engage in lengthy discussion of the matter, so on this occasion I reply merely by noting that any manner of speaking has the potential to be misunderstood in one way or another. Which sorts of misunderstanding are more important to try to prevent and the lengths to which one should go to try to prevent them will depend upon one's purposes, audience, etc., and per the previous footnote, it is hardly obvious that avoiding false views about historical matters should always have the highest priority.

belonging to an older tradition of thought and practice that they believed stretched far back in time to long before their own day. They credited the origins of this tradition to a series of sages (*sheng ren* 聖人) and sage kings (*sheng wang* 聖王), such as the founding rulers of the Zhou dynasty, namely King Wen, King Wu, and the Duke of Zhou, and even earlier kings such as Yao, Shun, Yu, and Tang.[11] As part of the belief that they were upholding this ancient tradition, these Warring States thinkers tended to identify themselves using the label *ru* 儒, which originally meant simply a "cultivated person" or "learned person," but over centuries of association with these thinkers and their later followers came to be the name for their whole group, which we now translate as "Confucians."[12]

A very concise summary of their ideas might be given as follows. These *ru* thinkers believed that what the ancient sages and sage kings practiced and taught—and hence what they themselves likewise practiced and taught—was the Way (*dao* 道), that is, the proper way to live and to organize society. They believed that knowledge of the Way was preserved in certain "classic" texts, which they accordingly treated as revered objects of study. In turn, to live according to this Way required practicing certain rituals (*li* 禮) and exercising certain virtues. The most important of these virtues are *ren* 仁, which includes caring for others as a central element, and *yi* 義, which involves a devotion to what is right.[13] On their view, in embodying the Way to the highest degree, one becomes a gentleman (*junzi* 君子) or even a sage. Furthermore, they believed that such cultivated people possess a kind of moral charisma (*de* 德, translated in this volume as "virtue")[14] that makes others friendly and supportive to them. The combination of these factors, the *ru* thought, explained why the ancient sage kings were able to be great leaders who brought peace and prosperity to the whole world, and hence these thinkers hoped to put an end to the chaos and suffering of the Warring States era by practicing moral cultivation and by getting others, especially rulers, to cultivate themselves.

---

[11] Archaeological findings seem to confirm the existence of King Wen, King Wu, and the Duke of Zhou, but not necessarily their status as moral paragons. As yet, there is no archaeological support for the existence of Yao, Shun, Yu, and Tang, who are now generally viewed as mythical, though many early Chinese people believed them to be real, historical persons.

[12] The *Xunzi*'s use of *ru* largely conforms to the word's earlier sense, and there are places where rendering it as "Confucian" would conflict with the context, so I have left it untranslated.

[13] My description here is intentionally vague, to accommodate various differences in early texts. More explanation of these and other concepts mentioned here is provided in appendix 1.

[14] In this introductory section, however, I use "virtue" to refer just to morally good traits, rather than as a translation for *de*.

At the same time this *ru* tradition was taking form, however, it was also challenged on many fronts. Rival thinkers claimed that the *ru* had the wrong understanding of the Way, and hence that their approach to individual moral behavior as well as their views of government were mistaken or, even worse, positively harmful to individuals and society. To give just a few examples, Laozi and Zhuangzi rejected the *ru* ideals as being, in a sense, a highly artificial way of life for human beings.[15] Against this, they proposed what they considered to be a more natural form of life. On the other hand, Mozi and his followers (the Mohists) criticized many of the rituals prized by the *ru* as a mere waste of resources and time; they advocated a fairly austere form of life and government instead. Yet others questioned the *ru* insistence that political power must be wedded to moral excellence in the form of having a sage king on the throne. In early China, certain rulers had been militarily and politically quite successful without conforming to the moral ideals of the *ru*, and these rulers, called *ba* 霸 ("hegemons"), presented an alternative model for governing that apparently some found less demanding and more practicable, and hence more attractive.[16]

In relation to this background, Xunzi firmly believes in the main elements of the *ru* position as described above, and many of his discussions are aimed at elucidating and defending it against challenges such as the ones just mentioned, while also criticizing his rivals' views. For Xunzi, however, there is an additional worry. Although he regards Confucius as a sage and a true inheritor of the Way as taught by the sages of yore, there are others who came after Confucius and who claimed to be *ru,* but whom Xunzi considers to be misrepresenting the authentic teachings and practices of the ancient sages and of Confucius. Xunzi therefore tries to combat these views as well, and does not shy away from singling out fellow *ru* thinkers by name for criticism.

Perhaps the most famous—or one might say, infamous—case of the latter sort of criticism is that which appears in chapter 23. There Xunzi argues that human nature is bad and explicitly attacks the claim of Mencius that human nature is good (a criticism that led later

---

[15] Per the previous section, the extent to which we can attribute views to particular named figures in early China is highly subject to question from the standpoint of historical accuracy. Nevertheless, in presenting the ideas of Xunzi (as explained earlier) here and below I retain the reference to particular individuals, because that is how Xunzi views the matter—he treats them as the views of particular *people*, and I am speaking from his perspective.

[16] Xunzi does not name anyone as favoring the hegemon ideal, but proposals that would come close to it (at least to his ears) can be found in texts such as the *Han Feizi* and the *Shangjun Shu (Book of Lord Shang)*, and such a view may have been favored by many actual rulers and government officials in the Warring States period.

ru to belittle the *Xunzi* when the *Mencius* gained in popularity, as mentioned previously). Xunzi thinks not only that there is no good evidence for Mencius's view, but moreover that it threatens to undermine the *ru* tradition instead of supporting it. If people somehow naturally knew the Way and were naturally inclined to follow it, Xunzi reasons, then there would be little need for them to seek guidance from the ancient sages and their wisdom as handed down in the classic texts; they could simply look within themselves for the answers instead. However, encouraging people to trust in their own individual judgments, if they do not in fact naturally conform to the Way, will likely result in chaos and disaster, and so is a very dangerous idea from Xunzi's perspective.

By the same token, even though Mencius is his explicit target, Xunzi's contention that human nature is bad also serves as a response to Laozi and Zhuangzi. For it amounts to the claim that, contrary to what they propose, living in a more "natural" manner would not be better for people, but would in fact make them worse off. In sharp contrast to these other figures, Xunzi exalts *wei* 偽. The word *wei* originally connotes what is "artificial" in a negative sense, but in Xunzi's hands it becomes a technical term (rendered here as "deliberate effort") for ways of behaving that do not arise from human nature and may even be contrary to it, and that thus provide a way to avoid the misdeeds and troubles to which human nature would otherwise lead us. Xunzi's rejection of these rival views is also reflected in his choice of analogies. Whereas the *Mencius* frequently compares the proper course of human development to that of the natural growth of plants, and the *Daodejing* analogizes the ideal human state to wood in its unhewn and original condition, Xunzi most frequently illustrates his view of proper human development with examples from crafts, such as the bending of wood, in which human artifice transforms raw natural materials into things that are useful and beautiful.

As for the questions of exactly what Xunzi means in claiming that human nature is bad, whether this claim is really opposed to the claim that human nature is good in the sense that the *Mencius* depicts Mencius as believing it, and whether either claim is correct—these are issues about which there has been tremendous scholarly debate stretching over centuries. This introduction is not the place to try to settle any of those matters.[17] One point is very clear, though, which is that although Xunzi thinks that human nature is bad, he also believes that through deliberate effort, people have the potential to overcome their natures and become good—indeed, to become sages. Accord-

---

[17] Very helpful discussions of these questions can be found in Kline and Ivanhoe (2000).

ingly, one of the most commonly repeated themes of his remarks is to urge people to become as good as possible, both for their own sakes, and for the sake of peace and order in the world at large.

In this process of becoming good, ritual plays an especially important role in Xunzi's view. As he conceives them, the rituals constitute a set of standards for proper behavior that were created by the past sages and should govern virtually every aspect of a person's life.[18] These rituals are not inviolable rules: Xunzi allows that people with developed moral judgment may need to depart from the strict dictates of ritual on some occasions, but he thinks those just beginning the process of moral learning need to submit completely to the requirements of ritual. Of the many important roles played by the rituals in making people good on Xunzi's view, three particularly deserve mention here. First, the rituals serve to *display* certain attitudes and emotions. The ritually prescribed actions in the case of mourning, for instance, exhibit grief over the loss of a loved one, whether or not the ritual practitioner actually feels sadness. Second, even if the ritual practitioner does not actually feel the particular attitude or emotion embodied in the ritual, Xunzi believes that repeated performance of the ritual can, when done properly, serve to *cultivate* those attitudes and emotions in the person. To use a modern example, toddlers who do not know to be grateful when given a gift may be taught to say "thank you" and may do so without any understanding of its meaning or a feeling of gratitude. With repetition, time, and a more mature understanding of the meaning of the phrase, many of these children grow into adults who not only feel gratitude upon receiving gifts but also say "thank you" as a conscious expression of that feeling. Similarly, on Xunzi's view, rituals serve to inculcate attitudes and feelings, such as caring and respect, that are characteristic of virtue, and then serve to express a person's virtue once it is fully developed. A third important function of the rituals is to allot different responsibilities, privileges, and goods to different individuals, and thereby help to prevent conflict over these things among people.

In Xunzi's thought, these features of ritual help both to solve the problem posed by the badness of human nature and to respond to challenges such as those posed by Mozi. Xunzi thinks that certain impulses that are part of human nature cannot be eliminated or wholly suppressed. The rituals provide a way of giving expression to these impulses, and hence they help to satisfy certain human needs, but at

---

[18] Despite his devotion to these rituals, Xunzi often omits the details on what they require, perhaps because he thinks his audience already knows or can easily discover these details. Some bodies of ritual lore from early China have come down to us in three texts, the *Liji* 禮記, the *Zhouli* 周禮, and the *Yili* 儀禮, but it is unclear to what extent the rituals as Xunzi conceives them are the same as what is described in those texts.

the same time they constrain, shape, and channel these impulses to result in behaviors that are peaceful, orderly, and beneficial, whereas these impulses would otherwise lead mostly to strife, chaos, and harm. In this manner, ritual serves as a key part of the cure for the badness of human nature, and the badness of human nature thus helps justify adherence to ritual.[19] At the same time, many aspects of ritual that Mozi criticized turn out on this view not to be wasteful or useless for ordering society, but rather to be quite reasonable and even necessary for that purpose. For as Xunzi sees it, creating a stable, well-functioning society depends upon satisfying but also managing various elements of human psychology in ways that only ritual can do.[20]

This last point in response to Mozi also forms the basis of Xunzi's answer to those tempted by the figure of the hegemon, whom even Xunzi acknowledges to be a strong and successful ruler. On Xunzi's analysis, the hegemon has these achievements because he manifests a degree of self-restraint and even virtue, namely trustworthiness (*xin* 信), which enables him to build relationships with his ministers and subjects that result in an effective government and military. Since the hegemon is virtuous to this limited extent, he is better than vicious tyrants who, through greed, arrogance, and folly, bring destruction upon themselves, but the hegemon nevertheless still ranks second behind the fully virtuous sage king in Xunzi's view. The hegemon is inferior, he thinks, because the hegemon is not committed to moral cultivation of himself or those he rules, and without such cultivation, the kind of relationship between ruler and ruled will be neither as strong nor as stable as that which obtains in the case of a sage king. In contrast, the sage king as Xunzi portrays him is someone who not only strives for utmost virtue in himself, but also aims to teach his people and reform their bad natures, and hence both sides will share the same moral standards, and the ruled will admire and love the ruler for embodying those standards to the highest degree. As before, ritual plays a key role in this picture by serving as the means to inculcate these shared moral standards in both the ruler and his people, as well as providing for their expression in action, such that the ruler comes to be recognized by his subjects as a moral paragon.

---

[19] This view, however, also leaves many puzzles. As one example, Xunzi maintains that the sages had the same bad nature as everyone else does, so it is reasonable to wonder how they ever overcame their bad nature to create the rituals in the first place. Xunzi never gives a clear answer to the question himself, and scholars have debated what he could or should have said. For a provocative and stimulating suggestion on this topic, see Nivison (1996).

[20] Of course, one can still question whether Xunzi is really right about this point, and whether Mozi's views really fail in this regard.

It is noteworthy that in focusing on these social and psychological effects of ritual on both the ritual practitioner and those around him, Xunzi rejects the idea that rituals have any supernatural powers. For instance, Heaven (*tian* 天, lit. "sky") was regarded by many in early China as a deity with awareness, intentions, and a tendency to intervene in the world to reward the virtuous and punish the vicious. In keeping with such a view, some rituals sought to enlist Heaven's aid or avoid its wrath. Xunzi, however, espouses an understanding of Heaven as much more like what we might call "Nature," namely an impersonal force in the world that is responsible for various phenomena and does not react to human virtue or vice, or supplication (chap. 17). Hence, human performance of rituals can have no power to affect Heaven, and Xunzi takes a similar view of other rituals that purport to influence other beings such as ghosts and spirits, about whose existence he seems skeptical. While not believing in the supposed supernatural efficacy of such rituals, neither does Xunzi advocate abandoning them. Rather, in his view they are to remain part of the practice of even cultivated people, whom he expects to understand that the rituals lack supernatural efficacy but are still valuable for their psychological and social effects. Thus, though it may sound strange to a modern ear, Xunzi presents ritual practice as involving "a sophisticated form of pretending" (as one scholar nicely puts it)[21] that is undertaken neither for the sake of deceiving self or others nor for the sake of manipulating supernatural forces, but rather for the ways in which it can structure, beautify, and even elevate human life.

Apart from its relation to his view of ritual, Xunzi's conception of Heaven as described in the previous paragraph is significant for other reasons that also deserve comment here. In particular, the view of Heaven as an impersonal, amoral force does not seem to originate with Xunzi. Rather, that idea seems to have first been proposed in the *Daodejing* and the *Zhuangzi*. There it is used to undermine *ru* thinkers as well as the Mohists, who had both appealed to a more theological conception of Heaven as supporting their moral and political programs; all agreed that humans ought to model themselves after Heaven, but if Heaven is an impersonal, amoral force, then following its model actually leads one away from the *ru* and Mohist ideals. Strikingly, Xunzi adopts nearly the same conception of Heaven as one sees in the *Daodejing* and the *Zhuangzi*, but then argues that precisely because Heaven is so different from human beings, it should *not* be our model for behavior, and instead there is a unique role for human beings to play in the world with its own distinct set of moral standards. In this manner, Xunzi takes this notion of Heaven bor-

---

[21] See Berkson (2014).

rowed from others, turns it around, and uses it to attack his rivals while defending the *ru* tradition.

This brings us to a final noteworthy feature of Xunzi's thought, namely his engagement with competing views. Besides his conception of Heaven, his use of the terms "emptiness," "single-mindedness," and "stillness" in chapter 21 and the analogy there between the heart and a mirror are further examples of his incorporating into his own view ideas that seem to have originated among rival thinkers. More generally, it is clear from the text that Xunzi is familiar with nearly all the major intellectual currents of the Warring States era. He learns from them, even from thinkers vehemently opposed to the *ru*, yet he is not hesitant to attack what he thinks is wrong, though it sometimes means criticizing a fellow member of his own tradition. In this respect, Xunzi presents an admirable model for philosophical activity, even in today's setting.

A Traditional Timeline of Early Chinese History

(Most dates before 221 BCE are unconfirmed.)

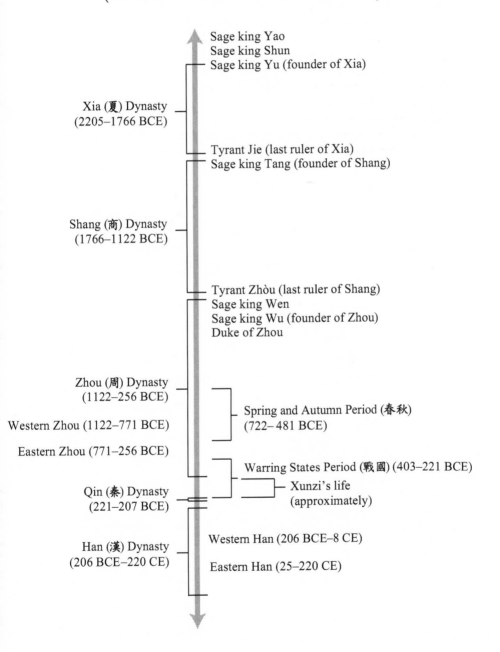

Sage king Yao
Sage king Shun
Sage king Yu (founder of Xia)

Xia (夏) Dynasty
(2205–1766 BCE)

Tyrant Jie (last ruler of Xia)
Sage king Tang (founder of Shang)

Shang (商) Dynasty
(1766–1122 BCE)

Tyrant Zhòu (last ruler of Shang)
Sage king Wen
Sage king Wu (founder of Zhou)
Duke of Zhou

Zhou (周) Dynasty
(1122–256 BCE)

Spring and Autumn Period (春秋)
(722– 481 BCE)

Western Zhou (1122–771 BCE)

Eastern Zhou (771–256 BCE)

Warring States Period (戰國) (403–221 BCE)

Xunzi's life
(approximately)

Qin (秦) Dynasty
(221–207 BCE)

Western Han (206 BCE–8 CE)

Han (漢) Dynasty
(206 BCE–220 CE)

Eastern Han (25–220 CE)

CHAPTER 1

An Exhortation to Learning

The gentleman says: Learning must never stop. Blue dye derives from the indigo plant, and yet it is bluer than the plant. Ice comes from water, and yet it is colder than water. Through steaming and bending, you can make wood as straight as an ink-line[1] into a wheel. And after its curve conforms to the compass, even when parched under the sun it will not become straight again, because the steaming and bending have made it a certain way. Likewise, when wood comes under the ink-line, it becomes straight, and when metal is brought to the whetstone, it becomes sharp.[2] The gentleman learns broadly and examines himself thrice daily,[3] and then his knowledge is clear and his conduct is without fault.

And so if you never climb a high mountain, you will not know the height of Heaven.[4] If you never visit a deep ravine, you will not know the depth of the Earth. If you never hear the words passed down from the former kings,[5] you will not know the magnificence of learning. The children of the Han, Yue, Yi, and Mo[6] peoples all cry with the same sound at birth, but when grown they have different customs, because teaching makes them thus.[7] The *Odes* says:[8]

> O harken, all ye gentlemen,
> Don't always be at ease and rest!
> Perform your office steadfastly.
> Love what's correct and upright best.

[1] A carpenter's tool used for marking straight lines.

[2] See 23.19–22 and 23.205–7. See also Gaozi's remarks in *Mencius* 6A1.

[3] See also *Analects* 1.4.

[4] Many early Chinese treated Heaven (*tian* 天, lit. "sky") like a deity. In Xunzi's thought, however, it is less a deity and more an impersonal force, like what we might call "Nature." See the discussion of Heaven at 17.1–5.

[5] The "former kings" were sages who, according to Xunzi, brought peace and prosperity to the world, but it is unclear exactly whom he has in mind. The set likely includes the early Zhou dynasty leaders King Wen, King Wu, and the Duke of Zhou. See chapter 3, note 20.

[6] These are the names of "barbarian" states and tribes.

[7] See also *Analects* 17.2.

[8] The *Odes* is a collection of poems (originally songs) that Xunzi views as a classic and quotes often. For more on the *Odes*, see appendix 1. References here are according to the arrangement in the Mao version of the *Odes*. The quote that follows is from poem 207.

The spirits will thus hear of this,
And they will make you greatly bless'd.[9]

25   No spirit-like state is greater than having transformed oneself with the Way.[10] No blessing is superior to being without misfortunes.

I once spent the whole day pondering, but it was not as good as a moment's worth of learning.[11] I once stood on my toes to look far away, but it was not as good as the broad view from a high place. If

30   you climb to a high place and wave, you have not lengthened your arms, but you can be seen from further away. If you shout from upwind, you have not made your voice stronger, but you can be heard more clearly. One who makes use of a chariot and horses has not thereby improved his feet, but he can now go a thousand *li*.[12] One

35   who makes use of a boat and oars has not thereby become able to swim, but he can now cross rivers and streams. The gentleman is exceptional not by birth, but rather by being good at making use of things.

In the south there is a bird called the *meng jiu*.[13] It makes its nest

40   from feathers, weaving it together with hair, and attaches it to the slender branch of a reed. When the wind comes along, the branch snaps, the eggs break, and its young perish. This happens not because the nest itself is flawed, but rather because of what it is attached to. In the west there is a plant called the *ye gan*. Its stem is four inches

45   long, and it grows on the top of high mountains, so that it overlooks ravines a hundred yards deep. It has this view not because its stem can grow long, but rather because of where it stands.

Likewise, when the *peng* vine grows among hemp plants, it goes up straight without being stood upright. The root of the *lan huai* plant

50   is sweet-smelling angelica, but if you soak it in foul water then the gentleman will not draw near it, and the common people will not wear it. This happens not because the original material is not fra-

---

[9] Mei (1961) notes that the words *zheng* 正 ("correct") and *zhi* 直 ("upright") in this poem also mean "straight," and hence connect with the prior images of shaping wood. The point is to urge people both to reform themselves and to value others who have done so.

[10] The term *shen* 神 can mean "spirit," as in the poem, but Xunzi also frequently uses it as a kind of quality (rendered in this translation as "spirit-like"). In such cases it connotes great power that works invisibly. See 17.45–46. Xunzi often associates this power with virtue (*de* 德), because in his view virtue also has a transformative effect on others that works invisibly. See lines 82–85 below and 3.120–23.

[11] See *Analects* 15.31.

[12] A Chinese measurement of distance, equivalent to roughly one-third of a mile.

[13] These remarks about the *meng jiu* 蒙鳩 may be parodying chap. 1 of the *Zhuangzi*, especially its story of the *xue jiu* 學鳩 bird. See Kjellberg (1996, pp. 17–18) for a useful discussion.

grant, but rather because of what it is soaked in. Therefore, the gentleman is sure to select carefully the village where he dwells, and he is sure to associate with well-bred men when he travels. This is how he avoids corruption and draws near to what is correct.

> All the things and the kinds that come about
> Surely have a point from which they start out.
> Honor or disgrace that comes unto you
> Surely reflects your degree of virtue.
> In rotten meat bugs are generated.
> In fish that's spoiled maggots are created.
> Lazy, haughty men who forget their place
> Shall have misfortune and ruin to face.
> Rigid things get themselves used for bracing.
> Pliant things get themselves used for lacing.ᵃ
> If with corruption your person is filled,
> It's this upon which hate toward you will build.

You may spread out firewood as though all of the same kind, but fire will still seek out the dry pieces.¹⁴ You may level the earth so that it appears all even, but water will still seek out the wet places. Wherever grasses and trees grow together, birds and beasts will flock. This is because each thing follows its own class. For this reason, wherever an archery target is set out, bows and arrows will follow. Wherever wood grows in abundance, axes and hatchets will go. Wherever trees create shade, flocks of birds will rest. Wherever something turns sour, flies will gather. Likewise, there are words that summon misfortune, and there is conduct that beckons disgrace, so the gentleman is careful about where he takes his stand.

If you accumulate enough earth to form a mountain, then wind and rain will arise from it. If you accumulate enough water to form a deep pool, then dragons will come to live in it. If you accumulate enough goodness to achieve virtue, then you will naturally attain to spirit-like powers and enlightenment, and the heart of a sage is complete therein. And so,

> Without accumulating tiny steps,
> You have no way to go a thousand *li*.
> Without accumulating little streams,
> You have no way to form river or sea.
> Let the horse Qi Ji¹⁵ take a single leap;

---

¹⁴ Wording nearly identical to this and the next sentence also appears at 27.631–33.
¹⁵ The horse Qi Ji was famous for his ability to go a thousand *li* in a single day.

It still would go no farther than ten strides.
Yet old nags ridden ten days equal him;
Not giving up is where success resides.

95 If you start carving and give up, you will not be able to break even rotten wood, but if you start carving and do not give up, then you can engrave even metal and stone. The earthworm does not have sharp teeth and claws, nor does it have strong bones and muscles. Yet, it eats of the earth above, and it drinks from the Yellow Springs below,[16] because it acts with single-mindedness. In contrast, the crab has six 100 legs and two pincers. Yet were it not for the abandoned holes of water snakes and eels, it would have no place to lodge, because it is frenetic-minded. For this reason,

If you do not first have somber intention,
No brilliant understanding can there be.
105 If you do not first have determined effort,
No glorious achievements will you see.
One walking both forks of a road goes nowhere.
One serving two lords is not viewed welcomely.
Eyes focused on two things at once are not sharp.
110 Ears tuned to two things at once don't hear clearly.
Though footless, the *teng* snake moves quick as flying,
Yet five limbs give the *wu* rodent no safety.[b]

The *Odes* says:

The *shi jiu* bird is on the mulberry.
115 Seven is the number of its offspring.
As for the noble man and gentleman,
Their standard is one and unwavering.
Their standard is one and unwavering
Like their hearts were tied to it by binding.[17]

120 Thus is the gentleman bound to one thing.[18]

---

[16] The Yellow Springs were thought to be deep underground and were believed to house the spirits of the dead.

[17] Mao #152. The poem says that the standard of the noble man and gentleman is *yi* 一, which literally means "one." Here I translate it as "one and unwavering" to highlight the idea of consistency, following commentators' reading of the line in its original context. However, this is also the same word rendered as "single-mindedness" elsewhere in this chapter, and Xunzi may intend the line to be read with that sense as well (or instead).

[18] I.e., the Way. See lines 209–12 below. This sentence contains the same ambiguous use of *yi* 一 ("one," rendered here as "one thing") discussed in the previous note.

In ancient times, Hu Ba played the lute, and the swimming fish came up to listen. Bo Ya played the zither, and the six kinds of horses all raised up their heads from grazing. There is no sound so small as not to be heard. There is no action so subtle as not to be manifest. Where there is jade in a mountain, the vegetation is lush, and where a pool begets pearls, its banks do not dry out. If you do good, will it not accumulate? How could it be that none hear of it?

Where does learning begin? Where does learning end? I say: Its order begins with reciting the classics, and ends with studying ritual. Its purpose begins with becoming a well-bred man, and ends with becoming a sage. If you truly accumulate effort for a long time, then you will advance. Learning proceeds until death and only then does it stop. And so, the order of learning has a stopping point, but its purpose cannot be given up for even a moment. To pursue it is to be human, to give it up is to be a beast.[19] Thus:

The *Documents* is the record of government affairs.[20]
The *Odes* is the repository of balanced sound.
Rituals are the great divisions in the model for things.
Outlines of things' proper classes are in the rituals found.

And so, learning comes to ritual and then stops, for this is called the ultimate point in pursuit of the Way and virtue. In the reverence and refinement of ritual, the balance and harmony of music, the broad content of the *Odes* and *Documents*, the subtleties of the *Spring and Autumn Annals*,[21] all things between Heaven and Earth are complete.[c]

The learning of the gentleman enters through his ears, fastens to his heart, spreads through his four limbs, and manifests itself in his actions. His slightest word, his most subtle movement, all can serve as a model for others.[22] The learning of the petty person enters through his ears and passes out his mouth. From mouth to ears is only four inches—how could it be enough to improve a whole body much larger than that? Students in ancient times learned for their own sake, but the students of today learn for the sake of impressing others.[23] Thus the learning of the gentleman is used to improve his

---

[19] This remark may not be meant literally. Cf. 4.58–60 on calling others "beasts."

[20] The *Documents* is a text purporting to record the speeches of ancient sage kings. Like the *Odes*, Xunzi treats it as a source of wisdom. For more on the *Documents*, see appendix 1.

[21] The *Spring and Autumn Annals* is a history of the state of Lu during the eighth to fifth centuries BCE. Like the *Odes* and *Documents*, Xunzi considers it a very important text that deserves careful study. For more on the *Spring and Autumn Annals*, see appendix 1.

[22] See also the use of this sentence at 13.214–15.

[23] See *Analects* 14.24.

own person, while the learning of the petty man is used like gift
155 oxen.[24] To speak without being asked is what people call being presumptuous, and to speak two things when asked only one is what
people call being wordy. Being presumptuous is wrong, and being
wordy is wrong. The gentleman is simply like an echo.[25]

In learning, nothing is more expedient than to draw near to the
160 right person. Rituals and music provide proper models but give no
precepts. The *Odes* and *Documents* contain ancient stories but no explanation of their present application. The *Spring and Autumn Annals*
is terse and cannot be quickly understood. However, if you imitate
the right person in his practice of the precepts of the gentleman, then
165 you will come to honor these things for their comprehensiveness, and
see them as encompassing the whole world. Thus, in learning, nothing is more expedient than to draw near to the right person.[d]

Of the paths to learning, none is quicker than to like the right
person, and exalting ritual comes second. If at best you cannot like
170 the right person, and at worst you cannot exalt ritual, then you will
simply be learning haphazard knowledge and focusing your intentions on blindly following the *Odes* and *Documents*. If so, then to the
end of your days you cannot avoid being merely a vulgar *ru*.[26] If you
are going to take the former kings as your fount and make *ren* and *yi*
175 your root,[27] then rituals are exactly the highways and byways for you.[e]
It will be like the action of turning up your fur collar by simply curl-
ing your five fingers and pulling on it—it goes smoothly numberless
times.[f] If you do not take the regulations of ritual as your way, but
instead go at it with just the *Odes* and *Documents*, then it will be like
180 trying to measure the depth of a river with your finger, or trying to
pound millet with a halberd, or trying to eat out of a pot with an
awl—you simply will not succeed at it. And so if you exalt ritual, then
even if you are not brilliant, you will still be a man of the proper
model. If you do not exalt ritual, then even if you are an acute de-
185 bater, you will be only a dissolute *ru*.

Do not answer one who asks about something improper. Do not
ask questions of one who speaks on something improper. Do not
listen to one who tries to persuade you of something improper. Do

---

[24] In ancient China, animals were given as gifts to superiors and honored guests.
Xunzi's point is that the petty man flaunts his learning to win favor with others.

[25] The basis of the analogy is that there is no echo without a preceding sound, and an
echo lasts only a short time. Likewise, the gentleman does not show off his learning
by speaking out of place, or by droning on about matters for which a shorter discussion will suffice.

[26] The word *ru* 儒 originally meant something like "a cultivated person" or "a scholar."
In later times, it came to mean more narrowly "a Confucian scholar." Xunzi himself
does not understand it so narrowly, though there are hints of this usage in the text
(see 6.219–29). See also the discussion at the beginning of chapter 8, note 9.

[27] *Ren* and *yi* are two central virtues in Xunzi's thought. See appendix 1 for discussion.

not debate with a person of combative demeanor. Only if people approach you in the proper way should you receive them. If they do not 190
approach you in the proper way, then avoid them. And so, only if
they follow ritual and are reverent should you discuss the methods of
the Way with them. Only if their speech is calm should you discuss
the pattern of the Way with them. Only if their countenance is agreeable should you discuss the culmination of the Way with them. To 195
discuss these things with those unfit to discuss them is called being
presumptuous. Not to discuss these things with those fit to discuss
them is called being secretive. To discuss these things without first
observing the person's manner and countenance is called being
blind.[28] The gentleman is neither presumptuous nor secretive nor 200
blind; he carefully acts according to the other person's character. The
Odes says:

> The gentlemen are not indolent or haughty.
> Rewarded by the Son of Heaven shall they be.[29]

This expresses my meaning. 205
    One who misses a single shot out of a hundred does not deserve to
be called good at archery. One who falls short of going a thousand *li*
by the distance of even a half step does not deserve to be called good
at chariot driving. One who does not fully comprehend the proper
kinds and classes of things, or who is not single-minded in pursuit of 210
ren and *yi*, does not deserve to be called good at learning. Learning
is precisely learning to pursue them single-mindedly. To depart from
it in one affair and adhere to it in another is to be such as common
people. To have in oneself little that is good and much that is not
good is to be such as the tyrants Jie and Zhòu and Robber Zhi.[30] Per- 215
fect it and complete it,[31] and only then is one truly a learned person.

---

[28] Compare *Analects* 16.6.
[29] See Mao #222. The quote here differs from the Mao text. "Son of Heaven" is the
title for Zhou dynasty kings. The Son of Heaven claimed authority over the whole
world, and so for early Chinese the title came to represent a supreme ruler, akin to
"emperor." Accordingly, in the *Xunzi*, the title "Son of Heaven" is sometimes projected backward to describe pre-Zhou rulers with supreme authority. (Later Chinese emperors considered themselves to occupy this same position, but more commonly used another title, *Huangdi* 皇帝, most often translated as "emperor" in
English. That title does not appear in the *Xunzi*, but part of it, *di* 帝, is sometimes
rendered here as "emperor" to convey a similar sense.)
[30] Jie was the last ruler of the Xia dynasty. He was overthrown by the virtuous king
Tang, who established the Shang (also called Yin) dynasty. Zhòu was the last ruler
of the Shang. He was overthrown by King Wu, who established the Zhou dynasty.
(To avoid confusion, the tyrant's name will be spelled as "Zhòu" to distinguish it
from the name of the dynasty.)
[31] The "it" here refers to learning and its moral content such as *ren* and *yi*.

The gentleman knows that whatever is imperfect and unrefined does not deserve praise. And so he repeatedly recites his learning in order to master it, ponders it in order to comprehend it, makes his
220 person so as to dwell in it, and eliminates things harmful to it in order to nourish it. He makes his eyes not want to see what is not right, makes his ears not want to hear what is not right, makes his mouth not want to speak what is not right, and makes his heart not want to deliberate over what is not right.[32] He comes to the point where he
225 loves it, and then his eyes love it more than the five colors, his ears love it more than the five tones, his mouth loves it more than the five flavors, and his heart considers it more profitable than possessing the whole world.[33] For this reason, power and profit cannot sway him, the masses cannot shift him, and nothing in the world can shake him.[34]
230 He lives by this, and he dies by this. This is called the state in which virtue has been grasped.

When virtue has been grasped, only then can one achieve fixity.[35] When one can achieve fixity, only then can one respond to things. To be capable both of fixity and of responding to things—this is called
235 the perfected person. Heaven shows off its brilliance, Earth shows off its breadth, and the gentleman values his perfection.[36,g]

[32] See *Analects* 12.1.
[33] As before, the five instances of "it" here refer to the content of the gentleman's learning, i.e., what is right.
[34] See *Mencius* 3B2.
[35] The Chinese word translated here as "fixity" is *ding* (定), which is distinct from and etymologically unrelated to the Chinese word *bi* (蔽) that is translated as "fixation" in chapter 21 and elsewhere. The former word connotes stability and is generally, as seen here, a positive trait for Xunzi, whereas the latter word connotes a failure of understanding (that comes from or leads to an excessive and improper concern for something) and is hence a negative trait.
[36] This hints at Xunzi's conception of the "triad" formed by Heaven, Earth, and the virtuous person. See 17.33–37.

CHAPTER 2

Cultivating Oneself

When you observe goodness in others, then inspect yourself, desirous of cultivating it.[a] When you observe badness in others, then examine yourself, fearful of discovering it.[1] If you find goodness in your person, then commend yourself, desirous of holding firm to it. If you find badness in your person, then reproach yourself, regarding it as 5 calamity. And so, he who rightly criticizes me acts as a teacher toward me,[2,b] and he who rightly supports me acts as a friend toward me, while he who flatters and toadies to me acts as a villain toward me.[3] Accordingly, the gentleman exalts those who act as teachers toward him and loves those who act as friends toward him, so as to utterly 10 hate those who act as villains toward him. He loves goodness tirelessly, and can receive admonitions and take heed. Even if he had no desire to improve, how could he avoid it? The petty man is the opposite. He is utterly disorderly, but hates for people to criticize him. He is utterly unworthy, but wishes for people to consider him worthy. 15 His heart is like that of a tiger or wolf, and his conduct like that of beasts, but he hates for people to consider him a villain. To those who flatter and toady to him he shows favor, while those who would admonish him he keeps at a distance. Those who cultivate correctness he considers laughable, and those truly loyal to him he considers 20 villains. Even though he does not wish to perish, how could he avoid it? The *Odes* says:

> These men conspire and practice slander.
> This is a matter for great sorrow!
> To any plan that's worth adopting, 25
> Complete resistance is what they show.
> But as for plans not worth adopting,
> These they completely wish to follow![4]

[1] See *Analects* 4.17.

[2] Here and elsewhere, although Xunzi uses first-person words such as "I," "me," and "my," they do not refer to Xunzi himself, but are instead intended in an impersonal sense.

[3] The term *zei* 賊 connotes a bad action or actor. It can refer merely to thievery, but often in ancient texts it also refers to murder in particular. Here it is rendered as "villain" to preserve the range of wrongdoing it covers as well as the sense of condemnation it conveys. See also the discussion below, lines 65–66.

[4] Mao #195.

This expresses my meaning.

30   The measure for goodness in all things is this:

> Use it to control your *qi*[5] and nourish your life,
> Then you will live longer than Peng Zu.[6]
> Use it to cultivate yourself and achieve fame,
> Then you'll be equal to Yao and Yu.[7,c]
35   It is fitting in times of prosperity.
> It is useful in facing adversity

—truly such is ritual.

> If your exertions of blood, *qi*, intention, and thought accord with ritual, they will be ordered and effective.[8] If they do not
40   accord with ritual, they will be disorderly and unproductive. If your meals, clothing, dwelling, and activities accord with ritual, they will be congenial and well-regulated. If they do not accord with ritual, you will encounter dangers and illnesses. If your countenance, bearing, movements, and stride
45   accord with ritual, they will be graceful. If they do not accord with ritual, they will be barbaric, obtuse, perverse, vulgar, and unruly.

Hence,

> If their lives are without ritual,
> Then people cannot survive.
50   If affairs are without ritual,
> In them success does not thrive.
> If state and clan are without ritual,
> For them peace does not arrive.[9]

---

[5] *Qi* 氣 is an energy or force that was thought to circulate through the universe and to be a component of all material things. Health and illness were often explained in terms of a person's *qi*, the state of which was thought to affect moral behavior as well, so theorists proposed ways of improving one's *qi* to achieve long life and/or virtue (e.g., *Mencius* 2A2).

[6] Peng Zu was reputed to have lived seven hundred years.

[7] Yao and Yu were sage kings. According to traditional stories, Yu founded the Xia dynasty.

[8] The five sentences after this one are rhymed, and some scholars suggest that originally this sentence was part of that rhyming group, but became corrupted and so no longer rhymes. Since its grammatical structure is closely parallel to the sentences that follow, I have offset it with the rest of the rhymed lines.

[9] A near-identical rhyme appears at 27.246–51. Chap. 39 of the *Daodejing* and the "Jie Lao" chapter of the *Han Feizi* employ similar rhymes, but use them to describe "oneness" and the Way, respectively, in contrast with Xunzi's emphasis here on ritual.

The *Odes* says: 55

> Ritual and ceremony have right measure completely.
> Laugh and speak only in complete accord with propriety.[10]

This expresses my meaning.

To lead others along in what is good is called "teaching." To harmonize with others in what is good is called "proper compliance." To   60
lead others along in what is bad is called "flattery." To harmonize with others in what is bad is called "toadying." To endorse what is right and condemn what is wrong is called "wisdom." To endorse what is wrong and condemn what is right is called "stupidity." To attack a good person is called "slander." To injure a good person is   65
called "villainy." To call the right as right and the wrong as wrong is called "uprightness." To steal goods is called "thievery." To conceal one's actions is called "deceptiveness." To speak too easily of things is called "boastfulness." To be without fixity in one's likes and dislikes is called "lacking constancy." To abandon *yi* in favor of profit is called   70
"utmost villainy." To have heard many things is called "broadness."[11] To have heard few things is called "shallowness." To have seen many things is called "erudition." To have seen few things is called "boorishness."[12] To have difficulty in progressing is called "indolence." To forget things easily is called "leakiness." For one's actions   75
to be few and well ordered is called "being controlled." For one's actions to be many and disorderly is called "being wasteful."

The methods for controlling the *qi* and nourishing the heart: For unyielding blood and *qi*, soften them with harmoniousness. For overly deep thinking, simplify it with easy goodness. For overly fero-   80
cious courage, reform it with proper compliance. For expedience-seeking hastiness, restrain it with regulated movements. For small-minded narrowness, broaden it with expansiveness. For excessive humility, sluggishness, or greed for profit, resist it with lofty intentions. For vulgarity or dissoluteness, expunge it with teachers and   85
friends. For indolence or profligacy, illuminate it with the prospect of

---

[10] Mao #209. These lines are also quoted at 19.198–99. In their original context, they describe people ("Their ritual . . . / They laugh . . ."). Without that context, here the lines are ambiguous, and I have rendered them to fit this context best.

[11] In this and the next three sentences, the "things" in question are probably best understood as the teachings and/or practices of the sages.

[12] "Boorishness" (*lou* 陋) is an important term for Xunzi. It is the uncultivated state in which a person has not yet been shown the greatest goods in life (i.e., the way of the sages), and so does not properly appreciate them. See 4.197–213. See also *Analects* 9.14.

disasters. For simple-minded rectitude or scrupulous honesty,[13] make
it suitable with ritual and music, and enlighten it with reflection.[d] In
90   each method of controlling the *qi* and nourishing the heart, nothing
is more direct than following ritual, nothing is more important than
having a good teacher, and nothing works with greater spirit-like efficacy than liking it with single-minded devotion. These are called the
methods for controlling the *qi* and nourishing the heart.

95   If one's intentions are cultivated, then one will disregard wealth
and nobility. If one's concern for the Way and *yi* is great, then one will
take kings and dukes lightly. It is simply that one examines oneself
on the inside, and thus external goods carry little weight. A saying
goes, "The gentleman makes things his servants. The petty man is
100   servant to things."[14] This expresses my meaning. If an action tires
your body but puts your heart at ease, do it. If it involves little profit
but much *yi*, do it. Being successful in the service of a lord who creates chaos is not as good as simply being compliant in the service of
an impoverished lord. And so, a good farmer does not fail to plant
105   because of drought, a good merchant does not fail to open shop because of losses, and the well-bred man and the gentleman are not lax
in their pursuit of the Way because of poverty.

       If your bearing is reverent and respectful and your heart is
       loyal and trustworthy, if your method is ritual and *yi* and
110   your disposition is concern for others, then you may wander
       across the whole world, and even if you become trapped
       among barbarians, no one will fail to value you.[15] If you are
       eager to take the lead in laborious matters, if you can give
       way in pleasant matters, and if you show scrupulousness,
115   honesty, integrity, trustworthiness, self-control, and meticu-
       lousness, then you may wander across the whole world, and
       even if you become trapped among barbarians, no one will
       fail to employ you. If your bearing is arrogant and obtuse
       and your heart is stubborn and deceitful, if your method is to
120   follow Mozi and your truest essence is polluted and corrupt,
       then you may wander across the whole world, and even if you

---

[13] In most other places in the text, *duan que* 端愨 ("scrupulous honesty" or "scrupulousness and honesty") is presented as something good, with no sense that there is
anything deficient about it. Insofar as it is treated here as being in need of modifica-
tion through ritual, music, and reflection, perhaps Xunzi has in mind a case where
it becomes an excessive moral fastidiousness, something that he warns against in
other places (e.g., 4.23–24).

[14] See also Xunzi's discussion 22.365–407. Similar advice about not becoming subser-
vient to things appears in the *Zhuangzi*, which encourages "treating things as [mere]
things" (*wu wu* 物物) in chapters 11 and 20.

[15] The Chinese text of this and the next three sentences contains rhymed sections.

reach every corner of it, no one will fail to consider you base.[16]
If you try to put off or wriggle out of laborious matters, if
you are grasping and will not yield in pleasant matters, if you
are perverse and dishonest, if you are not meticulous in work,   125
then you may wander across the whole world, and even if you
reach every corner of it, no one will fail to reject you.

He walks with his arms clasped before him, but not because he
fears dirtying his sleeves with mud. He walks with his head bowed,
but not because he fears tripping over something. When he exchanges   130
glances with another he bows first, but not because he is afraid.
Rather, the well-bred man wishes only to cultivate his person, and
does not use this to offend common people.

The horse Qi Ji could go a thousand *li* in a day, but with ten days
of riding an old nag can also go that far. If you attempt to exhaust the   135
inexhaustible or pursue the limitless, then you can break your bones
and rupture your tendons trying, but to the end of your life you will
not succeed.[17] If you have some stopping point, then even though a
thousand *li* is far, whether slow or fast, first or last, how could you not
reach it? Will those who do not understand how to walk along the   140
Way attempt to exhaust the inexhaustible and pursue the limitless?
Or will they think to have a stopping point? As for investigations into
hardness and whiteness, difference and sameness, things with thickness and things without thickness,[18] it is not that these are not matters
of acute investigation. However, the gentleman does not debate   145
about such things, because he stops at such a point.[19] As for unusual
and grandiose feats, it is not that these are not difficult to do. However, the gentleman does not do them, because he stops at such a
point. And so one who learns rightly says, "I may be slow, but it[20]
stops and awaits me, and I go and approach it.ᵉ So whether slow or   150
fast, first or last, how could I not likewise arrive there?"

And so, going step by step without stopping, even a lame turtle
can go a thousand *li*. If you pile up earth without ceasing, then hills
and mountains will majestically arise. If you plug up their sources
and open up their channels, then even the great rivers can be drained. 155

---

[16] Mozi (also known as Mo Di) was a thinker who had harshly criticized Confucianism and argued against the value of ritual and music. Xunzi criticizes him very
often (see chapters 6, 10, 17, 20, 21). Here, "following Mozi" most likely refers specifically to rejecting ritual.

[17] Compare the beginning of chap. 3 of the *Zhuangzi*.

[18] This is a reference to the "paradoxes" and other strange claims propounded by
thinkers such as Gongsun Long, Hui Shi, and Deng Xi.

[19] Compare Xunzi's remarks about having a stopping point at 21.375–78. See also
3.1–13.

[20] That is, the object of one's study—in this case, the Way.

If one horse advances, another retreats, another goes left, and another goes right, then even a team of six thoroughbreds will not get anywhere. As for the disparity between different people's endowments and natures, how could it be as great as that between the lame
160 turtle's feet and those of the six thoroughbreds? That the lame turtle can get there while the six thoroughbreds cannot, is for no other reason than that he works at it, but they do not. And so even if the way is short, if you do not proceed along it, you will not arrive anywhere. Even if a matter is small, if you do not work at it, it will not be
165 completed. If your character is such as to take holidays frequently, then your comings and goings will not take you very far.

He who likes the right model and carries it out is a well-bred man. He who focuses his intentions upon it and embodies it is a gentleman. He who completely understands it and practices it without tir-
170 ing is a sage. If a person lacks the proper model, then he will act recklessly. If he has the proper model but does not fix his intentions on its true meaning, then he will act too rigidly. If he relies on the proper model and also deeply understands its categories, only then will he act with comfortable mastery of it.

175 Ritual is that by which to correct your person. The teacher is that by which to correct your practice of ritual.[21] If you are without ritual, then how will you correct your person? If you are without a teacher, how will you know that your practice of ritual is right? When ritual is so, and you are also so, then this means your disposition accords
180 with ritual. When the teacher explains thus, and you also explain thus, then this means your understanding is just like your teacher's understanding. If your disposition accords with ritual, and your understanding is just like your teacher's understanding, then this is to be a sage. And so, to contradict ritual is to be without a proper model,
185 and to contradict your teacher is to be without a teacher. If you do not concur with your teacher and the proper model but instead like to use your own judgment, then this is like relying on a blind person to distinguish colors, or like relying on a deaf person to distinguish sounds. You will accomplish nothing but chaos and recklessness.
190 And so in learning, ritual is your proper model, and the teacher is one whom you take as the correct standard and whom you aspire to accord with. The *Odes* says, "While not knowing, not understanding, he follows the principles of Shang Di."[22] This expresses my meaning.

If he is scrupulous, honest, properly compliant, and a good
195 younger brother, then he can be called a good youth. If he has in addition to these a love of learning, amenability, and a keen mind, then

---

[21] That is, the teacher shows one both the right rituals to practice and how to practice them correctly.

[22] Mao #241. Shang Di (lit. the "Lord on High") was the main deity worshipped by the Shang dynasty.

he will have talents equal to those to whom none are superior, and he may use them to become a true gentleman. If he is lazy and cowardly, if he is shameless and cares only for food and drink, then he can be called a bad youth. If he has in addition to these a fierce disobedience 200 and a dangerous, villainous lack of respect for his elder brothers, then he can be called an inauspicious youth, and he may even fall so far as to suffer capital punishment.

If a person treats the old as befits the old, then those who are in their prime will come to him. If a person does not afflict those who 205 are already in extreme difficulty, then those who are successful will gather by him. If a person works in obscurity and practices kindness without seeking recompense, then the worthy and the unworthy will unanimously follow him. If a person has these three kinds of conduct, then even if he were to commit some great error, Heaven would 210 not cast him down!

In seeking profit, the gentleman acts with restraint. In averting harms, he acts early. In avoiding disgrace, he acts fearfully. In carrying out the Way, he acts courageously. Even if living in poverty, the gentleman's intentions are still grand. Even if wealthy and honored, 215 his demeanor is reverent. Even if living at ease, his blood and *qi* are not lazy. Even if weary from toil, his countenance is not disagreeable. When angry he is not excessively harsh, and when happy he is not excessively indulgent. The gentleman retains grand intentions even in poverty, because he exalts *ren*. He maintains a reverent demeanor 220 even when wealthy and honored, because he takes contingent fortune lightly. His blood and *qi* do not become lazy when at ease, because he is heedful of good order. His countenance is not disagreeable even when weary from toil, because he is fond of good relations. He is neither excessively harsh when angry nor excessively indulgent when 225 happy, because his adherence to the proper model overcomes any personal capriciousness. The *Documents* says:

> Do not create new likes.
> Follow the kings' way.
> Do not create new dislikes. 230
> On the kings' path stay.[23]

This is saying that through avoidance of prejudice and through *yi* the gentleman overcomes capricious personal desires.[24]

---

[23] See *Shujing*, "Hongfan" ("The Great Plan"), translated in Waltham (1971, p. 128). Xunzi quotes these lines again at 17.264–67.

[24] "Avoidance of prejudice" translates *gong* 公, a virtue opposite to prejudice in favor of oneself (i.e., selfishness) or others (i.e., one-sidedness). Stated positively, it combines both public-spiritedness and impartiality. See 3.175–86. See also *Han Feizi*, chap. 49.

CHAPTER 3

Nothing Improper

In matters of conduct, the gentleman does not esteem feats that are difficult but improper. In matters of argument, he does not esteem improper inquiries. In matters of reputation, he does not esteem improper fame. Only what is proper does he esteem. To cast oneself into a river while clutching a heavy stone is a difficult thing to do, but Shentu Di could do it.[1] However, the gentleman does not esteem such conduct, because it does not accord with ritual and *yi*. Claims such as "Mountains and valleys are level," "Heaven and Earth lie even," "Qi and Qin are adjacent,"[2] "It enters the ears and comes out the mouth," "Women have whiskers," "Eggs have feathers"—these are difficult arguments to propound, but Hui Shi and Deng Xi could do it. However, the gentleman does not esteem such arguments, because they do not accord with ritual and *yi*. Robber Zhi was terrifying enough to make people stutter,[a] but his reputation is widely known like the sun and moon and is ceaselessly handed down together with that of the sages Shun and Yu.[3] However, the gentleman does not esteem such reputation, because it does not accord with ritual and *yi*. And so I say: In matters of conduct, the gentleman does not esteem feats that are difficult but improper. In matters of argument, he does not esteem improper inquiries. In matters of reputation, he does not esteem improper fame. Only what is proper does he esteem. The *Odes* says:

> He does have many a good thing,
> But only with the right timing.[4]

This expresses my meaning.

---

[1] Little is known about Shentu Di, but according to other early Chinese accounts, he drowned himself as a form of protest against political and social ills.

[2] Qin was the state farthest west, and Qi was the state farthest east, separated by states in between, so this statement would seem paradoxical to an early Chinese reader.

[3] Shun was originally a minister to Yao. He succeeded to the throne after Yao and distinguished himself as a sage king. Likewise, Yu was originally Shun's minister and eventually took over ruling after Shun.

[4] Mao #170. The quote here differs from the received text of the *Odes* in a way that makes the quoted lines support the present point more clearly than the received version does.

The gentleman is easy to get to know,[5] but difficult to become intimate with. He is easily made apprehensive,[6] but difficult to intimidate. He fears troubles, but will not avoid dying when it is for the
sake of what is *yi*. He desires what is beneficial, but will not do what
he considers wrong. In associating with others, he is friendly but not   30
cliquish. In speaking, he argues well but does not play games with
words. How great is the difference between his manners and those of
the rest of the world!

If the gentleman is talented, he is likeable, and if he is untalented,
he is still likeable. If the petty man is talented, he is repulsive, and if   35
he is untalented, he is still repulsive. If the gentleman is talented,
then with broad-minded patience and easygoing uprightness he edu-
cates and guides other people. If he is untalented, then with respect
and modesty he carefully serves other people. If the petty man is
talented, then with arrogance and perversity he takes pride in sur-   40
passing other people. If he is untalented, then with jealousy and slanderous complaints he tries to ruin other people. And so I say: If the
gentleman is talented, then people consider it an honor to learn from
him. If he is untalented, then people are happy to instruct him. If the
petty man is talented, then people consider it base to learn from him.   45
If he is untalented, then people are ashamed to instruct him. This is
the difference between the gentleman and the petty man.

The gentleman is tolerant yet not lax, principled yet not oppres-
sive.[7] He debates but is not quarrelsome, investigates keenly but does
not aim to astound. He stands alone without being superior, and is   50
strong without being violent. He is flexible and yielding yet not un-
scrupulous. He is respectful and cautious yet congenial. This is called
utmost good form. The *Odes* says, "Warm and respectful of others,
virtue alone is his foundation."[8] This expresses my meaning.

When the gentleman exalts another's virtue or praises another's   55
excellence, it is not flattery or toadying. When he points out another's
faults with straight talk and direct accusation, it is not slander or
calumny. When he speaks of how his own excellence is like that of
Shun and Yu and forms a triad with Heaven and Earth,[9] it is not bragging or boasting. When he bends and straightens with the occasion,   60

---

[5] Compare 18.39.
[6] This remark is perhaps best understood as describing the gentleman's sensitivity to
   problematic situations even in their incipient stages, in contrast with others who are
   slow to recognize worrisome signs and so face greater troubles later on. See 2.212–
   13.
[7] See 5.207–13.
[8] Mao #256. This quotation differs slightly from the received text of the *Odes*. These
   same lines are quoted at 6.196–7 and 12.322–23.
[9] See 17.33–37.

flexible and yielding like a reed, it is not cowardice or timidity. When he shows unyielding strength and ferocious determination, bending in nothing, it is not arrogance or violent temper. Through *yi*, he changes and adapts to circumstances, because he knows when it is
65 appropriate to bend and straighten. The *Odes* says:

> On the right, on the right,
> The gentleman does what is fitting.
> On the left, on the left,
> The gentleman has things in hand.[10]

70 This speaks of how, through *yi*, the gentleman bends and straightens, changing and adapting to circumstances.

The gentleman is the opposite of the petty man. If the gentleman is great-hearted then he reveres Heaven and follows the Way. If he is small-hearted then he cautiously adheres to *yi* and regulates himself.[11]
75 If he is smart, then with enlightened comprehension he acts according to the proper categories of things. If he is unlearned, then with scrupulous honesty he follows the proper model. If he is heeded,[12] then he is reverent and reserved. If he is disregarded, then he is respectful and controlled. If he is happy then he is harmonious and
80 well-ordered.[13] If he is troubled, then he is calm and well-ordered. If he is successful, then he is refined and enlightened. If he is unsuccessful, then he is restrained and circumspect.

The petty man is not so. If great-hearted, then he is arrogant and violent. If small-hearted, then he is perverse and dissolute. If he is
85 smart, then he is a greedy thief and works by deception. If he is unlearned, then as a poisonous villain he creates chaos. If he is heeded, then he is avaricious and arrogant. If he is disregarded, then he is resentful and dangerous. If he is happy, then he is flippant and capricious.[14] If he is worried, then he is frustrated and cowardly. If he is
90 successful, then he is haughty and one-sided. If he is unsuccessful, then he is downcast and despondent. A saying goes, "In both cases the gentleman advances. In both cases the petty man falters." This expresses my meaning.

[10] Mao #214. The lines partly rhyme in the original.

[11] Though it may sound bad, being "small-hearted" is not likely intended as a derogatory label here, given that it is used to describe the gentleman. Since being "great-hearted" likely refers to a combination of lofty ambition and a high level of self-confidence, being "small-hearted" is probably best understood by contrast as a combination of more mundane ambition and a more ordinary level of self-confidence.

[12] That is, heeded by people in power.

[13] From this sentence to the end of the paragraph, the Chinese text is rhymed.

[14] Based on parallels with the corresponding section of the previous paragraph, Long Yuchun (1963) argues that this sentence and the three after it also rhyme originally.

The gentleman puts in good order what is orderly.[15] He does not put in good order what is chaotic. What does this mean? I say: Ritual and *yi* are called orderly. What is not ritual and *yi* is called chaotic. So, the gentleman is one who puts in good order the practice of ritual and *yi*. He does not put in good order what is not ritual and *yi*. That being so, if the state is in chaos will the gentleman not put it in good order? I say: Putting a chaotic state in good order does not mean making use of the chaos to put it in order. One gets rid of the chaos and replaces it with order. Bringing cultivation to a corrupt person does not mean making use of his corruption in order to cultivate him. One gets rid of the corruption and supplants it with cultivation. So, the gentleman gets rid of chaos and does not put chaos in good order. He gets rid of corruption and does not cultivate corruption. The proper use of the term "put in good order" is as when one says that the gentleman "does what is orderly and does not do what is chaotic, does what is cultivated and does not do what is corrupt." The gentleman refines his arguments, and those of a like mind will accord with him. He makes his words good, and those of a like kind will respond to him. So, when one horse neighs and another responds to it, they do not act from wisdom, but rather because their natural inclination is so. So, those who have just bathed shake out their clothes, and those who have just washed their hair dust off their caps. This is the natural disposition of people. Who can endure pollution from others when one's own self is pure?[16]

For the gentleman's cultivation of his heart, nothing is better than integrity.[17] When you have achieved integrity, there is nothing more to do than to cling to *ren* and to carry out *yi*. If you cling to *ren* with a heart of integrity, then you will come to embody it. If you embody it, then you will have spirit-like power. With this spirit-like power, you can then transform things. If you carry out *yi* with a heart of integrity, then you will become well-ordered. If you are well-ordered,

95

100

105

110

115

120

---

[15] This passage plays on the fact that the word *zhi* 治 can mean both "to order" something and "to be a master" of or at something. The rendering here as "put in good order" is intended to try to capture both these senses.

[16] The point of this last part of the paragraph may be difficult to see, but it continues the thought of the previous lines. Namely, just as someone freshly bathed does not want to get dirty, so the gentleman in ordering the state will rely on only what is orderly, and not what is chaotic. Accordingly, the lines about cultivating his speech seem to describe the way he will order the state, i.e., by refining himself and relying on his virtue to bring others in line.

[17] "Integrity" is a translation for *cheng* 誠, which is a difficult term to explain. In other contexts, it means something like "sincerity," "truthfulness," or even "being true to oneself." However, judging by how Xunzi employs it here, it seems closer to a kind of consistency or unwavering devotion, and thus I have rendered it as "integrity." So understood, *cheng* should be compared with the virtue of "single-mindedness" discussed in chapters 1 and 21.

125   then you will become enlightened. When you are enlightened, then
you can adapt to things. To transform and adapt in succession is
called Heavenly virtue.

Heaven does not speak, but people infer its height. Earth does not
speak, but people infer its thickness. The four seasons do not speak,
130   but the common people anticipate them. These things have such constancy because they have utmost integrity. The gentleman is the ultimate in virtue. He makes himself understood without speaking. He
is loved without yet bestowing favor. He inspires awe without showing anger. His orders are obeyed with such diligence because he is
135   vigilantly steadfast.

The way that goodness works is such that if you do not have integrity, then you will not be steadfast. If you are not steadfast, then you
will not embody goodness. If you do not embody it, then even if it is
at work in your heart, appears on your countenance, and comes out
140   in your words, the people will not follow you, and even if they do
follow they are sure to be suspicious of you.

Heaven and Earth are most vast, but without integrity they could
not transform the myriad things. The sage is most wise, but without
integrity he could not transform the myriad people. Father and son
145   are most intimate, but without integrity they will become estranged.
Lords and superiors are most exalted, but without integrity they will
be debased.

Integrity is what the gentleman clings to, and is the basis for government affairs. He dwells in it alone so that others of his kind will
150   come to him. If you grasp it, then you will attain it. If you let it go,
then you will lose it. If you grasp and attain it, then it will become
easy. When it becomes easy, then you will act steadfastly. If you act
steadfastly and do not let it go, then you will improve. If you improve and fully develop your endowment, moving forward for a
155   long time and not returning to your beginnings,[18] then you will be
transformed.

The gentleman's position is honored but his intentions are reverent. His heart is little but his Way is great.[19] He listens and looks to
what is nearby, but hears and sees what is far away. Why is this? It is
160   because of the method he grasps. So to him, the dispositions of a
thousand or ten thousand people are the same as those of a single

[18] "Beginnings" seems to be a reference to human nature. Xunzi's belief that human
nature is bad (see chapter 23) explains why he would advise people to move away
from these "beginnings" and not return to them.

[19] As before (note 11), the description of the gentleman as having a "small heart" is not
intended negatively. Here it seems to refer literally to the physical size of the human
heart, in contrast to the (metaphorical) largeness of the Way. Compare the remark
at the end of the paragraph about a small carpenter's square serving as a worldwide
standard.

person, the beginning of Heaven and Earth is the same as today, and the Way of the hundred kings is the same as that of the later kings.[20] The gentleman examines the Way of the later kings and then discusses events prior to the hundred kings as easily as clasping his 165 hands and debating in court. He extends the controlling influence of ritual and *yi*, marks out the divisions between right and wrong, gathers into hand the crucial affairs of the world, and orders the masses within the four seas, all as though employing a single person. Thus, his grasp is quite restricted, but his deeds are quite grand. A five-inch 170 carpenter's square is an exhaustive standard for all right angles in the world. And so, the gentleman does not descend from his hall, but the facts about how everything within the region of the four seas is disposed are gathered here before him, because of the method he grasps.

There are men of comprehensive goodness, there are men without 175 prejudice, there are upright men, there are honest men, and there are petty men:

One kind of man is able to honor his lord above, and is able to show concern for the people below. When things come, he adapts to them. When situations arise, he discerns the proper response. One 180 who is like this can be called a man of comprehensive goodness.

Another kind of man does not conspire with those below to deceive his superiors, nor does he collaborate with his superiors to afflict those below. When there is divisive contention over something, he does not harm the situation through selfish interests. One who is 185 like this can be called a man without prejudice.

For another kind of man, even if his superiors are unaware of his talents, he does not on this account betray his lord. Even if his superiors are unaware of his faults, he does not accept rewards for them. He ornaments neither his talents nor his faults, but rather presents 190 himself in accordance with the true disposition of his abilities. One who is like this can be called an upright man.

Another kind of man strives to be trustworthy in every word, and strives to be conscientious in every action. He is afraid to follow corrupt customs, but does not dare to be self-righteous about what he 195 holds to steadfastly. One who is like this can be called an honest man.

---

[20] Xunzi never makes clear exactly who is included among the "hundred kings" versus "later kings." Generally, the "later kings" seem to be kings of the Zhou dynasty, though it is still somewhat unclear whether he intends this to refer just to the founding Zhou rulers (King Wen, King Wu, and the Duke of Zhou), or whether it includes Zhou kings after these. The "hundred kings," by contrast, would apparently include all the pre-Zhou sage kings, going at least as far back as Yao, Shun, and Yu. See 5.122–38. Xunzi's term "the former kings" sometimes refers to this set, namely when it is used in contrast with the "later kings," but otherwise it seems to include all sage kings from Yao to the Duke of Zhou (and possibly beyond). Context often makes it clear which Xunzi has in mind.

Another kind of man has words that are never trustworthy, and his actions have no constant standard. Whenever there is a chance for profit, there is nothing to which he will not stoop. One who is like this can be called a petty man.

Being without prejudice results in clear understanding. One-sidedness results in delusion.[21] Scrupulousness and honesty result in success. Deception and artifice result in coming to dire straits. Integrity and trustworthiness result in spirit-like power. Exaggeration and boastfulness result in bewilderment. These six results are what the gentleman is careful about, and what distinguishes Yu from Jie.

On weighing between the desirable and the undesirable, between that worth adopting and that worth rejecting: When you see something that may be desirable, be sure to consider forward and backward what may be undesirable in it. When you see something that may be beneficial, be sure to consider forward and backward what may be harmful in it. Weigh both sides and reckon them thoroughly, and only then decide whether it is desirable or undesirable, worth adopting or worth rejecting. If you proceed thus, then you will reliably avoid falling into trouble. In most cases, people's problems are due to their own one-sidedness harming them. They see what may be desirable in something, but then do not consider what may be undesirable in it; they see what may be beneficial in it, but then do not look to what may be harmful in it. Thus, when they move on it they are sure to fall into trouble, and when they act on it they are sure to encounter disgrace. These are the problems that occur when one-sidedness harms a person.[22]

I hate what other people hate, but categorically disdaining the wealthy and noble while seeking to succor the poor and lowly is not the true disposition of the person of *ren*. This is the means by which vile people will steal a reputation for themselves from a benighted age. There is nothing more dangerous. So I say: stealing a reputation is worse than stealing goods, and Tian Zhong and Shi Qiu are worse than robbers.[23]

---

[21] Compare this with Xunzi's remarks on the problem of "fixation" at 21.1–26. Cf. also 4.230–31.

[22] Compare Xunzi's remarks on weighing up the good and the bad at 22.335–49.

[23] See the remarks about these two men at 6.13–21. It is unclear exactly what they did to incur Xunzi's criticism, but from what other early texts tell us, both appear to have had a reputation for uncompromising moral scrupulousness. Xunzi is apparently worried that their particular form of scrupulousness is merely a simulacrum of virtue, not the real thing, and so may mislead people to a false conception of what true goodness is.

CHAPTER 4

On Honor and Disgrace

Arrogance and haughtiness are the downfall of people, but reverence and restraint can halt even the five weapons, for the sharpness of spears and lances is not as good as the keenness of reverence and restraint.[1] Thus, giving someone kind words is more warming than hemp-cloth and silk,[2] while hurtful words cut people more deeply than spears and halberds. So if there is some place on the broad, flat earth where you cannot tread, it is not because the ground itself is not safe. Rather, it is entirely your own words that endanger your step and leave you nowhere to tread. On the great roads people will jostle each other, and the small roads are dangerous, so that even if you desire to be indiscreet, still there are certain words that are not to be employed.

Uncontrolled rage will cause you to perish, even though you are full of life. Jealousy will cause you to be maimed, even though you have keen intelligence. Slandering others will cause you to face impasses, even though you are broadly learned. An uncontrolled mouth will cause you to be stained all the more, even though you try to purify yourself.[3] Indiscriminate associations will cause you to starve all the more, even though you try to fatten yourself. Being combative will cause you to be unpersuasive, even though you argue well. An attitude of superiority will cause you not to be recognized, even though you take an upright stance. Oppressiveness will cause you not to be honored, even though you are principled. Greediness will cause you not to be feared, even though you are courageous. Inflexibility will cause you not to be respected, even though you are trustworthy. These things are what the petty man works at, but what the gentleman will not do.

A man who engages in brawling[4] is someone who has forgotten his own person, forgotten his family, and forgotten his lord. When carry-

---

[1] Except for the last part of this sentence, the whole of this paragraph originally rhymes.

[2] Compare Xunzi's remarks on good words at 5.183–84.

[3] Wording similar to the opening of this paragraph also appears at 27.722–25.

[4] The word here is *dou* 鬭, which basically means "fight" and can refer to many different types of fighting, with positive, neutral, or negative connotations. In this case, Xunzi seems to have in mind fights among private individuals (rather than, say, soldiers at war). The connotation of the term is clearly negative here, so I have ren-

ing out a moment's rage will result in losing your only body, to do it nevertheless is to have forgotten your own person. When your kin will straightaway be maimed and your parents will not escape punishment and execution, to do it nevertheless is to have forgotten your
35 family.[5] When it is what your lord and superior hates, and what his laws and punishments greatly prohibit, to do it nevertheless is to have forgotten your lord. To forget your own person below, to forget your family in the middle, and to forget your lord above—this is something the laws and punishments will not pardon, something the
40 sage king will not accept. A nursing sow will charge a tiger, and a nursing dog will not wander far from her pups, because they do not forget their family. If someone forgets his own person below, forgets his family in the middle, and forgets his lord above, then this is a human being who is not even as good as pigs and dogs!
45   Every person who engages in brawling is sure to think himself right and the other person wrong. If he thinks himself resolutely right and the other person resolutely wrong, then this is to consider himself a gentleman and the other a petty man, and to use the enmity between gentleman and petty man to harm and kill others. He forgets
50 his own person below, forgets his family in the middle, and forgets his lord above. Is this not a grave fault! Such people are "using a prized Gu Fu lance to slice cow dung." Do they think it is wise? There is no greater stupidity. Do they think it is beneficial? There is nothing more harmful. Do they think it is honorable? There is nothing more
55 disgraceful. Do they think it is safe? There is nothing more dangerous. Oh why do people engage in brawling? I would classify them as mad, confused, or ill, but I cannot, because the sage kings nevertheless punish them. I would classify them as birds, rodents, or beasts, but I cannot, because their form is nevertheless human, and their
60 likes and dislikes are mostly the same as those of humans. Oh why do people engage in such brawling? I loathe it utterly.
    There is the courage of dogs and pigs, the courage of merchants and robbers, the courage of petty men, and the courage of well-bred men and gentlemen.[6] To struggle over food and drink, to have no
65 restraint or shame, to be ignorant of right and wrong, to be heedless of injury and death, to have no fear of superior numbers or greater strength, ravenously seeing only the benefit of food and drink—such is the courage of dogs and pigs. To strive for benefit in all affairs, to struggle over goods and wealth, to have no deference or yielding, to
70 act from brazen daring, to commit brutality from ferocious greed,

---

dered *dou* as "brawling" to try to convey this negative sense (and likewise for similar cases later in the text).
[5] In Xunzi's day, some states had laws that mandated punishment not only for the person who committed a crime, but for the offender's family as well.
[6] Compare this discussion of courage with 23.338–363.

ravenously seeing only benefit—such is the courage of merchants and robbers. To commit violence from disdain of death—such is the courage of petty men. Wherever *yi* lies, not to be swayed by power, nor to focus on benefit, not even changing his glance when offered the whole state in bribery, to uphold *yi* unswervingly while yet taking death seriously—such is the courage of well-bred men and gentlemen. 75

The *chou qiao* is a fish that floats on the water's surface, near to the sun. When it becomes trapped on the sand then it longs for the water, but it is simply too late. To be hung up in troubles and then wish to 80 be careful is also simply of no use. Those who know themselves do not complain against others, and those who understand fate do not complain against Heaven. Those who complain against others are bankrupt, and those who complain against Heaven lack proper intentions. The fault is with themselves, but instead they seek it in others. 85 How far off the mark they are!

On the great division between honor and disgrace, and the reliable sources of safety and danger, benefit and harm: Those who put *yi* first and benefit second will attain honor. Those who put benefit first and *yi* second will attain disgrace. Those honored will reliably advance, 90 while those disgraced will reliably be thwarted. Those who advance will reliably get to regulate others, and those who are thwarted will reliably be regulated by others. This is the great division between honor and disgrace. Those who are humble and honest will reliably have safety and benefit. Those who are unrestrained and vicious will 95 reliably face danger and harm. Those who have safety and benefit will reliably be happy and at ease. Those who face danger and harm will reliably be troubled and alarmed. Those who are happy and at ease will reliably have great longevity. Those who are troubled and alarmed will reliably be cut off early in life. These are the reliable sources of 100 safety and danger, benefit and harm.

Heaven gave birth to the multitude of people, and there is a way to obtain them.[7] Making one's thoughts and intentions extremely cultivated, making one's practice of virtue extremely abundant, making one's knowledge and deliberations extremely enlightened—these 105 are the means by which the Son of Heaven obtains all under Heaven.

Making one's government lawful, making one's policies timely, hearing and deciding cases without prejudice, complying with the orders of the Son of Heaven above, guarding the common people below—these are the means by which the feudal lords[8] obtain their 110 states.

---

[7] "Obtain" here means both to "get" the people on one's side and to rule them.
[8] "Feudal lords" is the conventional translation for *zhuhou* 諸侯. These were regional rulers who controlled states that were established by grants from the Son of Heaven.

Making one's intentions and conduct cultivated, fulfilling one's official post in accordance with proper order, complying with one's superiors above, guarding one's position below—these are the means
115 by which the officers and grand ministers obtain their landholdings.

Adhering to the laws, standards, punishments, and written records, not fully understanding their purpose but carefully guarding their arrangement, being cautious and not daring to subtract from or add to them, handing them down from father to son in support of the
120 kings and dukes, so that even after the passing of three generations, the same order and law still exist—these are the means by which the officials and functionaries obtain their salaries and stations.

Being a good son and younger brother, conscientious and honest, restrained and hardworking, carrying out one's tasks without daring
125 to be lazy or arrogant—these are the means by which the common people obtain warm clothing, plentiful food, and long life, avoiding punishment and execution.

Ornamenting perverse teachings, adorning vile doctrines, performing deviant acts, being boastful, rapacious, unrestrained, vi-
130 cious, arrogant and brutal, so as to live basely and perversely in a chaotic world—these are the means by which vile people obtain danger, disgrace, and execution. Their deliberations about these things are not deep, their choices of these things are not carefully made, and their decisions about what to adopt and reject are crude and careless.
135 These are the means by which they endanger themselves.

With regard to endowment, nature, intelligence, and capabilities, the gentleman and the petty man are one and the same. Both like honor and hate disgrace. Both like what is beneficial and hate what is harmful. In this the gentleman and the petty man are the same, but
140 they differ in the means by which they seek these things. The petty man works at boasting but wishes others to trust him. He works at deceiving people but wishes others to love him. His conduct is that of wild beasts, but he wishes others to consider him good. He can hardly figure out whatever he deliberates on, can hardly find safety in
145 whatever he carries out, and can hardly establish whatever he supports. In the end, he is sure not to get what he likes, but is sure to meet with what he hates.

On the other hand, the gentleman himself is trustworthy, and wishes others to trust him. He himself is loyal, and wishes others to
150 love him. He himself is cultivated and well-ordered, and wishes others to consider him good. He easily figures out whatever he deliber-

---

The political system (both in theory and practice) was highly different from feudalism as practiced in medieval Europe, so little weight should be attached to the label "feudal." The description here is the expression of an ideal, rather than historical fact: by the time of the Warring States era, these rulers nominally owed allegiance to the Son of Heaven, but mostly operated as de facto independent sovereigns.

ates on, easily finds safety in whatever he carries out, and easily establishes whatever he supports. In the end, he is sure to get what he likes, and sure not to meet with what he hates. For this reason, if he is thwarted, he is not obscured,[9] and if he succeeds, then he shines greatly. Even if he dies, his reputation becomes only brighter. The petty men all stretch their necks and stand on their toes to look at him, saying, "In his endowment, nature, intelligence, and capabilities, he originally had what it takes to be a worthy." They do not know that there is no difference between themselves and him. It is only that the gentleman refines these things to a fitting end, and the petty man refines these things to the wrong end.

So, if you thoroughly investigate the intelligence and capabilities of the petty man, you will know that he has them in abundance and can do everything the gentleman does. It is like the way the people of Yue are at home in Yue, and the people of Chu are at home in Chu—the gentleman is at home in what is graceful. They differ not because of endowment, nature, intelligence, and capabilities, but rather because of the measures by which they train and refine themselves. *Ren*, *yi*, and virtuous conduct are reliable means to safety, but that does not mean that one will never encounter danger. Corruption, carelessness, and rapaciousness are reliable means to danger, but that does not mean one will never have any safety. The gentleman chooses his way according to what is reliable, but the petty man chooses his way according to what is the exception.

All people share one thing in common: when hungry they desire to eat, when cold they desire warmth, when tired they desire rest, they like what is beneficial and hate what is harmful. This is something people have from birth; it is not something one awaits to become so. This is something in which Yu and Jie were the same. The eyes distinguish between light and dark, beautiful and ugly. The ears distinguish between noises and notes, high and low sounds. The mouth distinguishes between sour and salty, sweet and bitter. The nose distinguishes between fragrant and foul-smelling. The bones and flesh distinguish between cold and hot, pain and itch. These are also what people always have from birth, things which one does not await to become so, things in which Yu and Jie were the same. You can use them to become Yao or Yu. You can use them to become Jie or Robber Zhi. You can use them to become a laborer or craftsman. You can use them to become a farmer or merchant. It all rests in how you grasp the accumulated results of refinement and training.[a] If you become Yao or Yu, then you will reliably have safety and honor. If you become Jie and Zhi, then you will reliably face danger and disgrace.

[9] I.e., even if his political efforts fail, his good character is still manifest to all around him.

If you become Yao and Yu then you will reliably have joy and ease. If
195 you become a laborer, craftsman, farmer, or merchant, then you will
reliably have worry and toil.

Nonetheless, people work at becoming one of the latter and expend little effort on becoming one of the former. Why is this? I say:
it is because of boorishness.[10] Yao and Yu were not born perfect. They
200 began by changing their original substance and perfected themselves
through cultivation. Cultivation is such that one must await its culmination and only then is one complete. By birth, people are originally petty people.[11] Without a teacher or the proper model, they will
seek only benefit.[12] By birth, people are originally petty people, and
205 if they meet with a chaotic age and acquire chaotic customs, then this
is to add pettiness to pettiness, to get chaos from chaos. If the gentleman does not have power, then he will have no way to get inside
them. What do people's mouths and bellies know of ritual and *yi*?
What do they know of deference and yielding? What do they know
210 of principled shame and concentrated accumulation of effort?
Munching and chomping, the mouth chews. Gurgling and burbling,
the belly becomes full. Without a teacher or the proper model, people's hearts are nothing beyond their mouths and bellies.

Now if a person lived without ever having seen meats and fine rice
215 but had seen only vegetables and rice dregs, he would think that
complete sufficiency consisted in these latter things. If someone suddenly came to him bearing meats and fine rice beautifully cooked,
then with a surprised expression he would look at them and say,
"What are these strange things?" If when he smelled them they were
220 pleasing to his nose, and if when he tasted them they were sweet in
his mouth, and if when he ate them they were comforting to his body,
then no one would fail to choose these foods and to give up the earlier ones.[13] Now how about the way of the former kings and the ordering influence of *ren* and *yi*, and how these make for communal life,
225 mutual support, mutual adornment, and mutual security? And how
about the way of Jie and Robber Zhi? How could the distance between them simply be no greater than that separating meats and fine
rice from vegetables and rice dregs!

Nonetheless, people work at the latter and expend little effort on
230 the former. Why is this? I say: boorishness. Boorishness is the com-

---

[10] See the explanation of this term at 2.73–74.

[11] Compare chapter 23.

[12] More literally, this sentence says that uncultivated people "see" (*jian* 見) only benefit. The implication seems to be that they evaluate things only on the basis of
benefit and harm, whereas the cultivated person has a distinctive way of "seeing"
the world that involves evaluations in terms other than solely benefit and harm,
e.g., *yi* versus not-*yi*.

[13] Compare *Mencius* 6A7.

mon problem for all under Heaven.[14] It is the great downfall of people, a great harm to them. And so I say, the person of *ren* likes to instruct and demonstrate to people. He instructs them and demonstrates to them, refines them and urges them on, guides them and works repeatedly on them. Then, the uncomprehending will quickly come to understand, the boorish will quickly become learned, and the stupid will quickly become wise. If this is not done, then even if Tang and Wu were in power, what good could they do? Even if Jie and Zhòu were in power, what further harm could they do? If Tang and Wu preserve this, then all under Heaven will follow them and be ordered. If Jie and Zhòu preserve this, then all under Heaven will follow them and be chaotic. Is this not because people's dispositions can surely become like either the former or the latter!

    The natural disposition of people is that for food they want meats, for clothes they want embroidered garments, for travel they want chariots and horses, and moreover they want the riches of surplus wealth and accumulated goods. Even if provided these things, to the end of their years they would never be satisfied; this is also the natural disposition of people. Now for their livelihood, people know how to raise chickens, dogs, and pigs, and moreover they raise cows and sheep, but for their food they do not dare to have wine and meat. They save up money and have stockpiles and storehouses, but for their clothes they do not dare to have silk fabrics. Those who are thrifty have caches in cabinets and chests, but for their travels they do not dare to have chariots and horses. Why is this? It is not because they do not want them. Can it be for any other reason than that considering the long run and reflecting on the consequences they fear they would have no way to continue in these things? Therefore, they live frugally and constrain their desires, and they store up and stockpile things in order to continue in them. Is not consideration of the long run and reflecting on consequences thus best for oneself? Those who live basely and those of shallow knowledge do not understand even this. Their consumption of food is extravagant, and they do not reflect on the consequences, so that they suddenly find themselves reduced to poverty. This is why they cannot avoid freezing and starving. Clutching a beggar's satchel and ladle, they wind up as emaciated corpses in ditches beside the roads.

    How much more important are the way of the former kings, the ordering influence of *ren* and *yi*, and the proper social divisions as contained in the *Odes* and *Documents* and in the rituals and music! These are originally the greatest considerations under Heaven. For the sake of all the populace under Heaven, they consider the long run and reflect on consequences in order to protect them for ten thousand

235

240

245

250

255

260

265

270

[14] Cf. 3.201–22 and 21.1–26.

ages. Their effects stretch over a long time. Their power to comfort is
275 abundant. Their accomplishments fill up even remote and distant
places. No one but a thoroughly cultivated gentleman can understand them.[15] And so I say:

> With a bucket-rope that is too short,
> One cannot reach to a deep well's springs.
280 > With those who have but little knowledge,
> One cannot plumb the sages' sayings.[16]

For the social divisions contained in the *Odes* and *Documents* and in
the rituals and music are not something an ordinary person will understand. Thus I say: study them once, and you will find them worth
285 studying again. Take them in hand, and you can use them for a long
time. Broaden them, and you will be able to apply them everywhere.
Ponder them, and you will be able to rest at ease in them. Repeatedly
follow and investigate them, and you will find them even more likeable. If you use them to order your natural dispositions, then you will
290 gain benefit. If you use them to found your reputation then you will
gain honor. If you use them to live in community then there will be
harmony. If you use them to stand alone then you will be self-suffi-
cient. Is this not a delight to think about?
    To be as noble as the Son of Heaven and to be so rich as to possess
295 the whole world—these are what the natural dispositions of people
are all alike in desiring. However, if you followed along with people's
desires, then their power could not be accommodated, and goods
could not be made sufficient.[17] Accordingly, for their sake the former
kings established ritual and *yi* in order to divide the people up and
300 cause there to be the rankings of noble and base, the distinction between old and young, and the divisions between wise and stupid and
capable and incapable. All these cause each person to carry out his
proper task and each to attain his proper place. After that, they cause
the amount and abundance of their salaries to reach the proper bal-
305 ance. This is the way to achieve community life and harmonious
unity. So, when a person of *ren* is in power, the farmers devote all
their strength to their fields, the merchants devote all their cleverness
to their earnings, and the hundred craftsmen devote all their skillful-
ness to their products. From the officers and high ministers up to the
310 dukes and marquises, no one fails to devote all his *ren*, generosity,
intelligence, and capabilities to fulfilling his official position. This is
called the utmost balance. And so, one man takes the world as his

---

[15] See 19.350–58.
[16] See the similar analogies at 18.253–56.
[17] See 9.67–83.

salary but does not consider it much. Another man guards the gates, steers the army, secures the passes, or sounds the alarms, but does not consider it little. And so it is said: "cut apart and yet even, crooked and yet aligned, different and yet one."[18] Such is called the proper gradation of people. The *Odes* says: 315

> Jade *gong* tokens large and small were accepted by the king,
> And he became protector for the states then submitting.[19]

This expresses my meaning.   320

---

[18] This same line is quoted again at 13.262–63.

[19] See Mao #304; the Mao text is slightly different from this. The king mentioned here is the sage Tang. The relevance of the quote here seems to lie in the idea that having a system in which "large and small" are distinguished, i.e., a hierarchy with well-defined roles, is part of what made Tang a great king. Compare the end of chapter 13.

CHAPTER 5

Against Physiognomy

Physiognomizing people is something that the ancients would not embrace, something that a learned person does not take as his way.[a] In ancient times there was Gubu Ziqing, and in the present age there is Tang Ju of Liang. They have physiognomized people's outer form and facial features to know whether they would have good or ill fortune. Vulgar people praise this, but it is something that the ancients would not embrace, something that a learned person does not take as his way. Physiognomizing a person's outer form is not as good as judging his heart, and judging his heart is not as good as ascertaining his chosen course. The outer form is not superior to the heart, and the heart is not superior to its chosen course. Once the chosen course is set, the heart follows it. So even though one's outer form is bad, it will pose no impediment to becoming a gentleman if one's heart and chosen course are good. Even if one's outer form is good, it will pose no impediment to becoming a petty man if one's heart and chosen course are bad. Becoming a gentleman is called good fortune. Becoming a petty man is called ill fortune. And so, being tall or short, having a good or a bad outer form—these do not determine good or ill fortune. That is something that the ancients would not embrace, something that a learned person does not take as his way.

Lord Yao was tall, but Lord Shun was short. King Wen was tall, but the Duke of Zhou was short.[1] Confucius was tall, but Zigōng[2] was short. In the past, Duke Ling of Wey had a minister named Gongsun Lü.[3] His body was seven *chi* tall. His face was three *chi* long, and three *cun* wide.[4] His nose, ears, and eyes were all fully formed, and his repu-

---

[1] King Wen was the father of King Wu, founder of the Zhou dynasty. The Duke of Zhou was King Wu's brother, who acted as regent for King Wu's young son (King Cheng) after King Wu died. All three are regarded as sages by Xunzi. See the story of the Duke of Zhou at the beginning of chapter 8.

[2] This Zigōng 子弓 is to be distinguished from Confucius's well-known disciple Zigong 子貢, who appears later in the text of the *Xunzi*. It is not known exactly who Zigōng is, but the most plausible view seems to be that he is another disciple of Confucius, Ran Yong.

[3] Here and in the rest of this translation, I romanize the name of the state 衛 as "Wey" in order to distinguish it from the state 魏, which is romanized as "Wei."

[4] The *cun* and *chi* are ancient units of measurement, sometimes called a "Chinese inch" and "Chinese foot," respectively. The *cun* was around 2.3 centimeters in length, and ten *cun* equaled one *chi* (i.e., about 23 centimeters), so by these measurements the person would have had an extremely long and narrow face. Elsewhere in this translation, *cun* is simply rendered as "inch" for the convenience of American readers.

tation stirred the whole world. Sunshu Ao of Chu was a rustic from Qi Si. He was bald, with his left leg longer than his right, and he stood lower than the crossbar on a chariot, but using Chu he established a hegemony.[5] Duke Zigao of Ye had a slight frame and a short spine. When he walked it was as though he could almost not support   30
his clothing. However, during the chaos created by Duke Bai, when Lingyin Zixi and Sima Ziqi both died, Duke Zigao of Ye entered and took over Chu, executed Duke Bai, and settled the state of Chu, as easily as just turning over his hand.[6] His display of *ren* and *yi* and his accomplishments and reputation are still praised by later genera-   35
tions. And so, in considering affairs one does not measure a person's length, reckon his size, or weigh his weight, but only what his intentions are. How could the height, size, or beauty of a person's outer form be worth judging?

Moreover, the appearance of King Yan of Xu[7] was such that his   40
eyes were as big as a horse's.[b] Confucius's appearance was such that his face looked like an ugly mask. The Duke of Zhou's appearance was such that his body looked like a broken tree trunk. Gao Yao's[8] appearance was such that his color looked like that of a peeled melon. Hong Yao's[9] appearance was such that no skin was visible on his face.[10]   45
Fu Yue's[11] appearance was such that his body looked like it had a raised fin. Yi Yin's[12] appearance was such that his face had no beard or eyebrows. Yu hobbled about, and Tang leaned on one side. Yao and Shun were cross-eyed. Will you, my followers, judge their thoughts and intentions and compare their culture and learning? Or   50
will you only differentiate the tall and the short, distinguish the beautiful and the ugly, and so deceive and snub one another?

Among the ancients, Jie and Zhòu were tall, stout, and beautiful; they were the most outstanding in the world. In their physical strength, they were energetic and powerful; each was a match for a   55

[5] More precisely, Sunshu Ao made the king of Chu a hegemon. "Hegemons" (*ba* 霸) were lords who, as the Zhou dynasty's strength waned, made their states the new dominant powers. The Zhou ruler granted them the title *ba* as a recognition of their power, while still reserving the title "king" for himself. By Xunzi's time the Zhou and its system of titles were basically defunct, and Xunzi uses *ba* to refer simply to any ruler who strengthens his state to the point of dominating all others. Xunzi views the hegemon as better than a tyrant, but not by much. See chapters 7, 9, 11.

[6] Duke Bai instituted a rebellion against the ruling house of the state of Chu. Lingyin Zixi and Sima Ziqi were high-ranking members of the government.

[7] Little is known about this king, but some accounts portray him as extremely virtuous.

[8] According to legend, Gao Yao was a sagely minister who served Shun.

[9] A virtuous minister who supposedly tried to reform the tyrant Zhòu.

[10] Because it was covered with hair, according to commentators.

[11] A sagely minister of King Wuding of the Shang dynasty.

[12] A legendary minister of the sage king Tang at the founding of the Shang dynasty.

hundred men. Nevertheless, they were put to death and their states perished. They became the greatest disgraces in the world, and discussions by subsequent generations about badness are sure to mention them.[13] This was not due to a fault in their appearance, but was rather because their understanding was deficient, and their judgments were base.[14]

Now none of the disorderly lords of this vulgar age and the wily rascals of the countryside fail to be handsome and charming.[15] They wear exotic clothing and effeminate ornaments, and their temperament and bearing resemble that of a woman. The ladies all want them as husbands, and the young girls all want them as suitors—crowding each other shoulder to shoulder, they abandon their homes and families, wishing to elope with them. However, ordinary lords are ashamed to have such men as ministers, ordinary fathers are ashamed to have them as sons, ordinary elder brothers are ashamed to have them as younger brothers, and ordinary citizens are ashamed to have them as friends. When these [bad] men suddenly find themselves restrained by the authorities and facing execution in the great markets, then none of them fail to cry to Heaven, weeping and wailing, bitterly lamenting their present state and regretting their past.

This is not due to a fault in their appearance, but is rather because their understanding is deficient, and their judgments are base. That being the case, which aspect will you approve of?

There are three inauspicious traits of a person: to be young but unwilling to serve one's elders; to be lowly but unwilling to serve the noble; to be lacking in talent but unwilling to serve the worthy. These are the three inauspicious traits for a person to have. There are three cases in which a person is sure to suffer dire consequences. If, as a superior, he cannot love his subordinates, or if, as a subordinate, he likes to malign his superiors—this is the first case in which a person is sure to suffer dire consequences. If he is courteous toward others when face to face with them,[c] but then slanders them when their backs are turned—this is the second case in which a person is sure to suffer dire consequences. If his understanding is shallow and his con-

---

[13] See the nearly identical wording at 18.132–34.

[14] Xunzi's claim that all the sages and worthies had deformities is remarkably reminiscent of the *Zhuangzi*, which frequently depicts people with physical defects as superior to others, but Xunzi goes beyond the *Zhuangzi* in then portraying the most evil tyrants as outwardly perfect. The *Zhuangzi* is probably mocking views like those of Mencius (see *Mencius* 7A21), and Xunzi may have the same intent here.

[15] From here down to the words "their past," the text rhymed in the original.

duct base, and if his views on the crooked and the upright are far from correct, but the person of *ren* cannot move him, and knowledgeable men cannot enlighten him[d]—this is the third case in which a person is sure to suffer dire consequences. If a person engages in   95
these three kinds of various practices, then as a superior he is sure to face danger, and as a subordinate he is sure to be destroyed. The *Odes* says:

> Even when rain and snow have fallen heavily,
> Still they will melt away when the sun shines brightly.   100
> But none of these men consent to step down and yield,
> So they keep showing arrogance repeatedly.[16]

This expresses my meaning.

What is that by which humans are human?[17] I say: it is because they have distinctions. Desiring food when hungry, desiring warmth when   105
cold, desiring rest when tired, liking the beneficial and hating the harmful—these are things people have from birth. These one does not have to await, but are already so. These are what Yu and Jie both share. However, that by which humans are human is not because they are special in having two legs and no feathers,[e] but rather because   110
they have distinctions. Now the ape's form is such that it also has two feet and no feathers. However, the gentleman sips ape soup and eats ape meat. Thus, that by which humans are human is not because they are special in having two legs and no feathers, but rather because they have distinctions. The birds and beasts have fathers and sons but not   115
the intimate relationship of father and son. They have the male sex and the female sex but no differentiation between male and female. And so for human ways, none is without distinctions. Of distinctions, none are greater than social divisions, and of social divisions, none are greater than rituals, and of rituals, none are greater than those of   120
the sage kings.

But there are a hundred sage kings—which of them shall one take as one's model? And so I say: culture persists for a long time and then expires; regulations persist for a long time and then cease. The authorities in charge of preserving models and arrangements do their   125
utmost in carrying out ritual but lose their grasp. And so I say: if you wish to observe the tracks of the sage kings, then look to the most clear among them. Such are the later kings. The later kings were lords of the whole world. To reject the later kings and take one's way from furthest antiquity is like rejecting one's own lord and serving another's lord. And so I say: If you wish to observe a thousand years' time,   130

---

[16] See Mao #223. The quotation here is not exactly the same as the Mao text.
[17] Compare this with 9.316–19.

then reckon upon today's events. If you wish to understand ten thousand or one-hundred thousand, then examine one and two. If you wish to understand the ancient ages, then examine the way of the
135 Zhou.[18] If you wish to understand the way of the Zhou, then examine the gentlemen whom their people valued. Thus it is said: Use the near to know the far; use the one to know the ten thousand; use the subtle to know the brilliant. This expresses my meaning.

The reckless person says, "The dispositions of [the world in] an-
140 cient times and the present are different, so they require different ways for ordering chaos."[19] The masses are misled by this, for they are foolish and have no arguments, are boorish and have no proper measure. They can be deceived about what they see before them—how much more so in the case of reports about a thousand ages past!
145 Those reckless people can be deceived about what is within their own homes—how much more so in the case of what happened beyond a thousand ages past! How is it that the sage is not deceived? I say: it is because the sage is one who makes himself a measure. And so, he uses his person to measure other people. He uses his dispositions to
150 measure the dispositions of others. He uses his class to measure things of the same class. He uses words to measure accomplishments. He uses the Way to observe all completely. There is one measure for ancient times and the present. So long as one does not contravene the proper classes of things, then even though a long time has passed, the
155 same order obtains. Hence, one may face what is devious and twisted without being confused, and one may observe a jumble of things without being misled, because one measures them thus.

There are no reports of people from before the five lords, but that is not because there were no worthies then, but rather because a long
160 time has passed. There are no reports of government in the times of the five lords,[20] but that is not because they lacked good government, but rather because a long time has passed. There are reports of the government of Yu and Tang, but they are not as exact as those concerning the Zhou. That is also not because they lacked good govern-
165 ment, but rather because a long time has passed. When the report is from long ago, then its discussion is scanty. When it is from closer times, then its discussion is detailed. If scanty, it brings up large

---

[18] This argument may be intended as a response to attempts by rival thinkers to ground their views in claims about sages who supposedly preceded even Yao and Shun. One sometimes sees such appeals in the *Zhuangzi* and other texts hostile to Confucian ideas.

[19] Compare the "Five Vermin" chapter of the *Han Feizi*, which argues for this sort of view.

[20] Xunzi never says exactly who is included among the five, and various ancient texts give different lists, so it is impossible to be sure exactly who he has in mind.

points. If detailed, it brings up small points.[21] When the foolish hear what is scanty they do not comprehend the details, and when they hear the details they do not comprehend the larger points. Thus: 170

Culture persists for a long time and then is extinguished;
Regulations persist for a long time and then cease.[22]

Whatever words do not agree with the former kings or do not accord with ritual and *yi* are to be called vile words. Even if they are keenly argued, the gentleman will not listen to them. A person who 175 models himself on the former kings, accords with ritual and *yi*, and befriends men of learning, but nevertheless does not enjoy or delight in speaking out, is surely not a true well-bred man. And so, the gentleman's attitude toward right words is that he enjoys them in his thoughts, takes comfort in putting them into practice, and delights 180 in speaking them. Hence, the gentleman is sure to engage in argument.[23] Everyone enjoys speaking about what he considers good, and the gentleman is especially so. And so, to present to others right words is a weightier gift than gold, gems, pearls, or jade.[24] To display to others right words is more beautiful than embroidered emblems or 185 patterns. To sound to others right words is more musical than bells, drums, lutes, or zithers. Thus, the gentleman never tires of speaking out. The crude person is the opposite of this; he likes only right substance and cares nothing about right form. And so to the end of his days, he cannot avoid being lowly and vulgar. Thus, the *Book of* 190 *Changes* says, "A closed bag deserves neither blame nor praise."[25] This describes just such degenerate *ru*.

The difficulties of persuasion lie in using what is extremely lofty to encounter what is extremely base, and using what is extremely orderly to encounter what is extremely chaotic. In such cases, one can- 195 not approach things directly. But if one raises remote parallels, then

[21] Given that approximately seven hundred years had passed since the period of King Wen, King Wu, and the Duke of Zhou, if Xunzi means to include their regimes as times about which many details can be known, his view is incredibly optimistic.

[22] This sentence rhymes in the original. The close parallel earlier at lines 123–24 does not rhyme; some scholars claim that it once had the same rhyme but became corrupted, and so suggest emending the text to restore the rhyme.

[23] This sentence seems a clear indication that the whole passage is intended as an assault on Mencius, who disclaims any fondness for argument (*bian* 辯; see *Mencius* 3B9). The attack is continued further below. Compare Xunzi's proposed remedy for "boorishness" at 4.197–213.

[24] See 4.4–7.

[25] This quotation comes from the commentary to the second hexagram, *kun* 坤. As Xunzi uses it here, the "closed bag" represents the person who does not promote the Way by speaking out about it.

one risks being misunderstood, and if one cites^f closer events, then one risks being crude.[26] One who is good at it falls between these two; he is sure to raise remote parallels without being misunderstood, and
200 cites closer events without being crude. He shifts with the occasions and bends with the times, slowing down or speeding up, expanding or being restrained, bending as though there were a water channel or wood-shaping frame[27] constraining him. He achieves completely what he wants to express, but does so without causing hurt. Thus, in
205 measuring himself, the gentleman uses an ink-line, but in dealing with others, he uses lenience.^g He measures himself with an ink-line, and so he can be a model and standard for all under Heaven. He uses lenience in dealing with others, and so he can be tolerant and respond to their needs, and thereby accomplish the greatest affairs in
210 the world. Hence, the gentleman is worthy but can tolerate the sluggish. He is wise but can tolerate the foolish. He is broadly learned but can tolerate the shallow. He is refined but can tolerate the impure. This is called the method of inclusiveness.[28] The *Odes* says:

215
We have now integrated the region of Xu.
To the Son of Heaven's merit this is due.[29]

This expresses my meaning.
The method of persuasive speaking: practice it[30] with respect and dignity, live it with honesty and integrity, uphold it with firmness and strength, explain it with divisions and differentiations, illustrate it
220 with analogies and examples, and present it with joyfulness and sweetness. Treasure it, cherish it, value it, treat it as spirit-like. If you do so, then rarely will your persuasions fail to be accepted, and even if you do not succeed in persuading people, no one will fail to value you. This is called being able to ennoble what one values.[31] A saying
225 goes, "Only the gentleman can ennoble what he values." This expresses my meaning.

---

[26] I.e., the indirect means used to persuade a tyrant must neither be so vague that he misses the point, nor so close to home that he sees through it as a thinly veiled criticism. The latter fault differs little from direct confrontation and is thus crude.

[27] Xunzi's favorite analogy. See 1.3–7, 23.19–20, and 23.205–207.

[28] See 3.48–49.

[29] Mao #263. Xunzi's point seems to be that just as the king's merit has won over the rebellious state of Xu, so the gentleman's virtue helps to bring others over to his side. In the original context of the *Odes*, however, it is less clear that the poem interprets Xu's submission this way.

[30] Here "it" refers to one's view of what is right.

[31] In a word play difficult to translate, Xunzi uses *gui* 貴 to mean both valuing something and making something valuable, i.e., ennobling it.

The gentleman is sure to engage in argument. Everyone enjoys speaking about what they consider good, and the gentleman is especially so. Hence, when the petty man argues he speaks of dangerous things, and when the gentleman argues he speaks of *ren*. If one's speech does not accord with *ren*, then speaking is not as good as being silent, and arguing keenly is not as good as speaking clumsily. If one's speech accords with *ren*, then those who like right speech will come forth, and those who do not like right speech will withdraw. Thus, words of *ren* are great indeed! When they originate among superiors as a means to guide their subordinates, they are proper commands, and when they originate among subordinates as a means of expressing loyalty to their superiors, they are counsels and admonishments. Thus, the gentleman never tires of practicing *ren*. He enjoys it in his thoughts, takes comfort in putting it into practice, and delights in speaking of it. Hence I say, the gentleman is sure to engage in argument. Arguing about minor matters is not as good as perceiving the starting points of affairs, and perceiving the starting points of affairs is not as good as perceiving how to adhere to one's station. To be able to argue about minor matters with acuteness, to perceive the starting points of affairs and understand them, and to adhere to one's station with good order—in this the station of the sage, well-bred man, and gentleman are complete.

There is the argumentation of the petty man, the argumentation of the well-bred man, and the argumentation of the sage. One sort of person does not ponder beforehand or plan ahead of time. He simply puts it forth and it is appropriate, achieving good form and systematic order. In formulating measures he shifts and alters, adapting to changes without end—such is the argumentation of the sage.

Another sort of person has to ponder beforehand and plan ahead of time, but even when speaking on a moment's notice his words are still worth heeding. He achieves good form yet is extremely practical. He is broadly learned but speaks what is correct—such is the argumentation of the well-bred man and gentleman.

With respect to yet another sort of person, if one listens to his words, his arguments are niggling and without unifying order. If one employs him, then he is full of deception and without accomplishment. Above, he is incapable of following the enlightened kings. Below, he is incapable of harmonizing the people. Nevertheless, the smoothness of his tongue is such that his chattering has a certain measure to it, so that he is capable of becoming one of those who engage in strange exaggerations and bold haughtiness—such a one is called the vile person's hero. When sage kings arise, these are the ones they first execute, and then come robbers and villains. For robbers and villains can be changed, but these people cannot be changed.

CHAPTER 6

Against the Twelve Masters[1]

In the current era, there are people who ornament perverse doctrines and embellish vile teachings, such that they disturb and disorder the whole world. Their exaggerated, twisted, and overly subtle arguments cause all under Heaven to be muddled and not know wherein
5   right and wrong and order and disorder are contained.

Some of these men give rein to their inborn dispositions and nature. They are at ease in license and arrogance and have the conduct of beasts. They are incapable of bringing about accordance with proper form or creating comprehensive rule. Nevertheless, they can
10   cite evidence for maintaining their views, and they achieve a reasoned order in their explanations, so that it is enough to deceive and confuse the foolish masses. Just such men are Tuo Xiao and Wei Mou.[2]

Some of these men resist their inborn dispositions and nature. They go to great extremes and look upon what is deviant as benefi-
15   cial. With impropriety, they take distinguishing themselves from other people as supreme. They are incapable of coordinating the great masses or of making clear the great divisions of society. Nevertheless, they can cite evidence for maintaining their views, and they achieve a reasoned order in their explanations, so that it is enough to
20   deceive and confuse the foolish masses. Just such men are Chen Zhong and Shi Qiu.[3]

Some of these men do not understand the proper scales for unifying the world and establishing states and families. They elevate concrete results and usefulness, and they extol frugality and restraint.
25   But they have disdain for ranks and classes, and so they have never been able to accept distinctions and differences, or to discriminate between lord and minister. Nevertheless, they can cite evidence for maintaining their views, and they achieve a reasoned order in their explanations, so that it is enough to deceive and confuse the foolish
30   masses. Just such men are Mo Di and Song Xing.[4]

---

[1] The "twelve masters" are Tuo Xiao, Wei Mou, Chen Zhong, Shi Qiu, Mo Di (Mozi), Song Xing, Shen Dao, Tian Pian, Hui Shi, Deng Xi, Zisi, and Meng Ke (Mencius). Here, Xunzi groups them by pairs into six "doctrines" and criticizes them successively.

[2] Nothing is known about Tuo Xiao, and while a little is known about Wei Mou, it is not enough to make clear exactly what Xunzi is criticizing him for.

[3] Chen Zhong is another name for Tian Zhong. He and Shi Qiu are also criticized at 3.223–29.

[4] None of Song Xing's work survives apart from references in Xunzi and other texts. For some aspects of his views that Xunzi found unacceptable, see 18.454–587 and

Some of these men exalt law but follow no model. They look down on cultivation and are fond of innovation. Above, they obtain the ear of their superiors; below, they obtain a following among the vulgar. They speak all day long with good form and elegance, but if you re-peatedly scrutinize their words and investigate them, they are eccen- 35 tric and lack foundation, and cannot be used to set straight the state or fix proper social divisions. Nevertheless, they can cite evidence for maintaining their views, and they achieve a reasoned order in their explanations, so that it is enough to deceive and confuse the foolish masses. Just such men are Shen Dao and Tian Pian.[5] 40

Some of these men do not take the former kings as their model, nor do they take ritual and *yi* to be right. They like to master strange arguments and to play with unusual expressions. They investigate things with extreme acuteness but without any beneficent intent, and they debate matters but provide no useful results. They meddle in 45 many affairs but have few accomplishments, and they cannot be made the binding thread of good order. Nevertheless, they can cite evidence for maintaining their views, and they achieve a reasoned order in their explanations, so that it is enough to deceive and con-fuse the foolish masses. Just such men are Hui Shi and Deng Xi. 50

Some of these men only roughly model themselves on the former kings and do not understand their overall system. Nevertheless, their talents are many and their intentions grand. What they have seen and heard is broad and haphazard, and following the old past they create new doctrine, calling it the Five Conducts. This doctrine is extremely 55 deviant and does not accord with the proper categories of things. It is murky and has no proper arguments. It is esoteric and has no proper explanation. They accordingly embellish their phrases and treat the doctrine with deferential respect, saying, "These are truly the words of those former gentlemen." Zisi sings the lead, and Meng Ke 60 chimes in with him.[6] The stupid *ru* of this vulgar age yammer all

---

22.148–55, though it is not clear that he has in mind here exactly the same points he criticizes in those chapters.

[5] Shen Dao's thought survives in fragments. As Xunzi notes here, he was very con-cerned with rule by law, as opposed to governing by ritual or virtue, and this is the basis for Xunzi's dislike for him. See the criticism of him at 17.251–52 and 21.105–6. Little is known about Tian Pian, other than that he was a very persuasive rhetori-cian.

[6] Zisi was the grandson of Confucius and supposedly authored the famous Confucian text *Zhongyong* ("The Doctrine of the Mean"). Meng Ke is the full name of Mencius. The Five Conducts doctrine does not appear in either of the works attributed to them, but based on recently excavated Chinese texts, it seems probable that the Five Conducts are *ren, yi*, ritual, wisdom, and sageliness. Even with the excavated texts, though, it is still unclear exactly what Xunzi finds objectionable about this, since he himself espouses the same values in one way or another. Perhaps, given his criticism of Mencius in chapter 23 for espousing that human nature is good, there was some-

about this and do not know the error they are committing. Consequently, they accept the doctrine and pass it on, thinking the gift of
Confucius and Zigōng to later generations to consist in this. Such is
65 the crime of Zisi and Meng Ke.

Other men are able to combine the various arts and strategies, to
make their words and deeds match each other, and to have a unified
understanding of the overall system and proper categories of things.
They bring together the most valiant and talented men under Heaven,
70 inform them of the ancient past, and teach them how to comply fully
with what is right. Within their dwellings, within the very space of the
mats where they sit, the patterns and forms of the sage kings are all
gathered together compactly, and the customs that could bring peace
to the whole world arise from there with lively form. The six mis-
75 guided doctrines cannot enter into these men, nor can the twelve
masters win their affection.[7] Even though they do not possess so
much as a spade's worth of land, kings and dukes cannot compete
with their fame.[8] If they had occupied even so much as a grand minister's position, then no single lord could keep them, and no single
80 state could contain them. They would accomplish fame greater than
the feudal lords, and no one would fail to want them as ministers.
These men are sages who do not obtain power, and just such men
were Confucius and Zigōng.

Other men unify all under Heaven and use the ten thousand things
85 as their resources. They raise and nourish the people, and bring benefit to the whole world. None of the regions to which people have
penetrated will fail to submit and follow them. Views such as the six
misguided doctrines are immediately extinguished, and men such as
the twelve masters are transformed. This is what happens in the case
90 of sages who obtain power, and just such men were Shun and Yu.

Now what does the person of *ren* strive for? At his greatest, he
models himself on the controlling order of Shun and Yu, and at the
least, he models himself on the *yi* of Confucius and Zigōng, and he
thereby strives to extinguish the teachings of the twelve masters. If
95 one manages to do this, then the harm to the world will be eliminated, the work of the person of *ren* will be completed, and the accomplishments of the sage king will be made manifest.

To trust in what is trustworthy is trustworthiness. To doubt what
is doubtful is also trustworthiness.[9] To honor those who are worthy is

---

thing about the Five Conducts doctrine that implied they were inborn, and that is
what provoked Xunzi's criticism. However, at this point the matter awaits further
scholarly investigation.

[7] See note 1 in this chapter.

[8] Wording nearly identical to this and the next few sentences appears at 8.359–64.

[9] I take Xunzi's point to be that trustworthiness, understood as living up to one's
word, involves knowing both what one can trust oneself to accomplish, i.e., what

ren. To treat as lowly those who are unworthy is also *ren*. When one   100
speaks and it is fitting, this is wisdom. When one is silent and it is
fitting, this is also wisdom. Thus, knowing when to be silent is just as
good as knowing when to speak. And so, he who speaks much but
whose words match the proper categories of things is a sage.[10] He
who speaks little but conforms to the proper model in everything is   105
a gentleman. He who does not follow the proper model regardless of
how much or little he speaks, and whose words are perverse and
murky, even if he argues keenly, is nothing but a petty man.

Thus, to exert one's physical strength in a way that does not fit
with the proper tasks of the people is called doing vile works. To   110
exert one's understanding in a way that does not match with the former kings is called having a vile heart. When one's arguments, persuasions, and explanations are hasty, opportunistic, and not in conformity with ritual and *yi*, this is called making vile speech. These
three vilenesses are behaviors that the sage kings prohibited.   115

Some men are smart but dangerous, and they can work harm with
spirit-like efficacy. They are clever at artifice and deceit. Their words
are useless, but they argue for them forcefully. Their arguments are
not beneficial to people, but they investigate them keenly. Such men
are a great calamity for good government. They are firm in carrying   120
out deviant acts and are fond of adorning what is wrong. Their practices are vile and slick, and their words are argumentative and aberrant. Such men were severely prohibited in ancient times. They are
clever but lack the proper model. They are bold but lack proper fear.
They argue keenly, but their behavior is deviant and perverse. If   125
someone were to admire and employ these men, then they would indulge their taste for vileness and spread it to the masses. Yet, as rulers
they would be like one who gets lost while seeking the easy path for
his feet, or who collapses while trying to carry a heavy stone, and so
these are men whom the whole world would abandon.   130

The heart that can make the whole world submit is one wherein, if
the person occupies a high position or is honored and noble, he does
not use these to treat others arrogantly. If he is brilliant or has sagely
wisdom, he does not use these to reduce others to dire straits. If he is
swift or comprehends things quickly, he does not strive to surpass   135
others. If he is steadfastly valiant or courageous and daring, he does
not use these to harm others. If he does not know something, then he
asks others about it. If he is unable to do something, then he learns
how to do it. Or even if he is already capable, he is sure to be deferential. Only then does he have virtue. When he encounters his lord,   140

---

one is capable of, and what it is doubtful that one can do, i.e., what one is not capable of.

[10] A nearly identical passage appears at 27.686–90.

then he enacts the *yi* of a minister and subordinate. When he encounters his fellow-villager, then he enacts the *yi* of an elder or junior. When he encounters his seniors, then he enacts the *yi* of a son or younger brother. When he encounters his friends, then he enacts the
145 *yi* of ritual restraint and deference. When he encounters those who are lowly or who are young, then he enacts the *yi* of being guiding and tolerant. There are none for whom he does not feel concern. There are none to whom he does not show respect. On no occasion does he contend with others, but rather he is broad and open just like the way
150 Heaven and Earth encompass the myriad things. If one is like this, then those who are worthy will honor you, and even those who are unworthy will favor you. When one is like this, those who still do not submit can be called unnatural and devious men. Even if they happen to be among your sons or younger brothers, it is fitting for them
155 to suffer punishment. The *Odes* says:

> Shang Di is not to blame for these evil days.
> You Shang have not followed your old ways.
> Even if there were no elders to guide you,
> Good models and laws do still remain.
160 > But since you will not heed their refrain,
> The great Mandate you will not retain.[11]

This expresses my meaning.

In ancient times, what was called being "a well-bred man in office" was being one who was kind and generous, and who brought people
165 together in community. He delighted in wealth and noble rank, and delighted in sharing and bestowing gifts. He stayed far from offenses and crimes, worked at the proper order of affairs, and was ashamed of being wealthy alone. Nowadays, what is called being "a well-bred man in office" is being one who is corrupt and haughty, who is vil-
170 lainous and creates disorder, who is unrestrained and arrogant, and is greedy for profit. He is unlawful and defiant, and lacks all ritual and *yi*, and has a taste only for power.

In ancient times, what was called being "a well-bred man in retirement" was being one whose virtue was abundant, who was able to
175 achieve stillness,[12] who cultivated correctness, who understood fate,

[11] In the poem (Mao #255) from which this quote comes, these words are spoken by King Wen, who warns the Shang ruler that he will lose his reign because of his viciousness. Xunzi may be playing on the fact that the word *ming* 命 ("mandate") can also mean "life," so that this serves as a general warning even for those who are not rulers that they, too, will suffer punishment if they fail to be virtuous or refuse to submit to virtuous people.

[12] It is unclear exactly what Xunzi has in mind by "stillness" (*jing* 靜) here, but it may be connected with his use of the term at 21.171–85. Read in light of that discussion, the point here would be to stress the person's clear view of affairs.

and who made clear what was right. Nowadays, what is called being "a well-bred man in retirement" is being one who has no ability but says he is capable, who has no knowledge but says he knows, and who has an unquenchable thirst for profit in his heart but pretends to desire nothing. His conduct is false, perilous, and odious, but he insists on lofty doctrines, cautiousness, and honesty. He takes what is unusual as his personal custom, and though he avoids ordinary licentiousness, he still proceeds to slander others.[a]

What the well-bred man and gentleman can and cannot do: The gentleman can make himself honorable, but he cannot ensure that others will honor him.[13] He can make himself trustworthy, but cannot ensure that others will trust him. He can make himself useful, but cannot ensure that others will employ him. And so, the gentleman is ashamed of not being cultivated; he is not ashamed of being maligned. He is ashamed of not being trustworthy; he is not ashamed of not being trusted. He is ashamed of being incapable; he is not ashamed of not being employed. Thus, he is not tempted by good reputation, nor is he intimidated by slander. He follows the Way as he goes, strictly keeping himself correct, and he does not deviate from it for the sake of material goods. Such a one is called the true gentleman. The *Odes* says, "Warm and respectful of others, virtue alone is his foundation."[14] This expresses my meaning.

The appearance of the well-bred man and gentleman: His cap is forward, his clothes are worn snugly,[b] and his countenance is glad. He is imposing and robust, calm and tolerant. He is broad and encompassing, radiant and energetic. Such is the appearance of a proper father or older brother.

His cap is forward, his clothes are worn snugly, and his countenance is honest. He is reserved and attentive, helpful and upright. He is thoughtful and considerate and accommodating, deferentially averting his gaze. Such is the appearance of a proper son or younger brother.

I will tell you the appearance of degeneracy in a scholar. His cap slants forward, his chin-strap and belt are slack, and his countenance is casual and lackadaisical. He is full of himself, perverse, hollow, and smug. He stares at things, looking fixedly and wide-eyed. When there is wine, food, and the delights of sound and sight to be had, he is as though overcome with pleasure. When there are ritual affairs to be performed, he is hasty and critical of others. When there is laborious and bitter work to be done, he is sluggish and avoidant. He tries to put it off and disappears,[c] and lacking all shame, he is

---

[13] Wording nearly identical to this sentence and the second sentence after it also appears at 27.726–28.

[14] Mao #256. Compare the use of this quotation at 3.53–54 and 12.322–23.

willing to endure the disparagements of others. This is degeneracy in a scholar.

220   They arrange and prettify their caps. They amplify and aggrandize their words.[d] They try to walk like Yu and run like Shun—such are the base *ru* in the school of Zizhang.[15]

  They make correct their caps and clothing. They keep in order the expressions on their faces. As though holding something in their mouths, they say nothing all day long—such are the base *ru* in the
225   school of Zixia.

  They are lazy and afraid of work. They have no shame, but do have a taste for drinking and eating. They are sure to say, "The gentlemen certainly never employs his physical strength." Such are the base *ru* in the school of Ziyou.

230   The true gentleman is not so. He relaxes without becoming indolent, and works hard without delaying. He follows the true fount[16] to adapt to changes, and in everything obtains what is fitting. When he is thus, only then is he a sage.

---

[15] Zizhang, along with Zixia and Ziyou, who are mentioned below, were all disciples of Confucius. Thus, Xunzi is here criticizing rival Confucian sects. Note also that this is one case where *ru* seems to refer more specifically to Confucian scholars. Zixia appears in a more positive light at 27.620–627.

[16] I.e., the Way.

CHAPTER 7

On Confucius

Among the disciples of Confucius, even the young lads considered it shameful to speak in praise of the five hegemons. How can this be the case?[1] I say: It is indeed so—to praise them is truly worthy of shame. Duke Huan of Qi was the most successful of the five hegemons, but among his early deeds he killed his elder brother and seized the state. 5 In conducting internal family matters, there were seven of his sisters and aunts whom he did not marry off. Within his private chambers he indulged in extravagant entertainments and music. He was presented with the whole state of Qi as his portion, but he did not consider it sufficient. In foreign affairs, he deceived Zhu and ambushed 10 Ju, and he annexed thirty-five states. Such was the impetuousness, corruption, perversion, and extravagance of his affairs and conduct. Simply how could he be worthy of praise in the school of the great gentleman![2]

Even though he was like that, how is it that he did not perish but 15 on the contrary became a hegemon? I say: Ah, Duke Huan of Qi adopted the greatest measures in the world. Who could have made him perish? At a glance, he saw that Guan Zhong's ability was sufficient to entrust him with the state—this was the greatest wisdom in the world.[3] The Duke let rest and forgot his anger at Guan Zhong, 20 and he cast out and forgot their enmity. He thereupon established him as "Uncle"[4]—this was the greatest decision in the world.

> The Duke established him as "Uncle," and none of the royal relatives dared envy him.[5] The Duke gave him a position equal to that of the Gao and Guo families, and none of the 25 original court ministers dared to hate him. The Duke gave

---

[1] The question is ambiguous between asking how it can be shameful to praise the hegemon and how it can be that the disciples of Confucius refrained from such praise. In the response that follows, the former question is answered first, and that explanation is treated as sufficient to answer the latter question as well, at the end.

[2] Although here the hegemons are portrayed quite negatively, in chapters 9 and 11 they are presented in a more positive light.

[3] Guan Zhong originally served Duke Huan's elder brother, and during the conflict between the two brothers, Guan Zhong narrowly missed killing Duke Huan with an arrow. After his lord died, according to custom Guan Zhong should have committed suicide, but he did not and instead went on to serve Duke Huan, proving to be a very wise advisor. The Chinese text *Guanzi* purports to record Guan Zhong's views.

[4] This was an official title given to Guan Zhong.

[5] This and the next two sentences are rhymed in the original.

him a holding of three hundred altar districts,[6] and none among the wealthy dared to spurn him.

30 The noble and the lowly, elders and the youth alike, all with due order followed Duke Huan in honoring and respecting him. These were the greatest measures in the world. If a feudal lord were to take just one such measure, then no one could make him perish. Duke Huan combined all these measures and had them complete. How, indeed, could he have perished? It was fitting that he become a hegemon! That was 35 not because of luck. Rather, that was due to the number of things he did right.[7]

Nevertheless, among the disciples of Confucius, even the young lads considered it shameful to speak in praise of the five hegemons. How can this be the case? I say: It is indeed so. For the hegemons did 40 not base themselves on government through education.[8] They did not strive to become exalted and lofty. They did not pursue the extremes of culture and good order. They did not make people's hearts submit willingly. They inclined to tactics and stratagems, paid attention to fatigue and rest for troops, accumulated stores and fostered 45 their men's fighting skills, and so they were able to topple their rivals. They used deceitful hearts in order to achieve victory, and used deference as a cover for conflict. They relied on the appearance of being *ren*, but walked the path of obtaining profit. They are heroes for petty men. Simply how could they be worthy of praise in the school of the 50 great gentleman!

A true king is not like that. He is most worthy, and can use this to save those who are unworthy. He is most strong, and can use this to be kind to those who are weak. In battle, he is surely able to defeat his opponents, but considers it shameful to brawl with them. Hum-55 bly, he achieves proper form. He displays this to all under Heaven, and violent states accordingly transform of themselves. Only when there are disastrous or perverse states does he launch a punitive campaign. King Wen launched four punitive campaigns.[9] King Wu launched two. The Duke of Zhou finished their work, and by the time

---

[6] According to ancient sources, an "altar district" (*she* 社) contained twenty-five households. As Guan Zhong's holdings, these households paid taxes to him and so provided him with income. With three hundred altar districts, the income would have been quite substantial indeed.

[7] Here we are not given a complete categorization of the right measures taken by Duke Huan, but one can identify at least four distinct elements of the Duke's behavior that Xunzi approves: (1) recognizing a person as having talent (the "greatest wisdom"), (2) employing that person as a minister (the "greatest decision"), (3) showing respect for that person, and (4) giving that person material rewards. Compare 12.16–27 and 12.386–400.

[8] Compare this and the following few sentences to 11.72–77.

[9] Wording nearly identical to this and the next two sentences appears 27.397–400.

of King Cheng all was peaceful, with no one left to punish. Thus, 60
how could it be that the Way does not work? King Wen had a territory of only a hundred *li*, and yet the whole world became unified
under him. The tyrants Jie and Zhòu abandoned it,[10] and though they
possessed the most abundant power under Heaven, they did not even
get to live to old age as peasants.[11] And so, if one makes good use of 65
it, even a state of a hundred *li* is enough to stand alone. If one does
not make good use of it, then even with the state of Chu's six thousand *li*, one will still become a servant to one's enemies. Thus, for a
ruler not to work at obtaining the Way and instead strive to possess
great power is the means by which he will endanger himself. 70

The method for occupying an official position and handling royal
favor, such that to the end of one's days one never becomes hated: If
the ruler honors and values you, then be reverent, respectful, and
modest. If the ruler trusts and cherishes you, then be circumspect,
cautious, and humble. If the ruler employs you exclusively, then care- 75
fully maintain your office and be thorough in your work. If the ruler
feels safe with you and draws near to you, then be wary of becoming
cliquish and do not let yourself go astray. If the ruler puts you at a
distance, then be whole-heartedly and single-mindedly devoted, and
do not betray him. If the ruler disparages or demotes you, be fearful 80
and apprehensive but not resentful. Be honored without becoming
boastful. Be trusted without engaging in dubious acts. Undertake
heavy responsibilities without daring to monopolize affairs. When
wealth and profit come, then treat them as good, but also as though
you do not deserve them. Be sure to carry out completely the *yi* of 85
deference and refusing, and only then accept them. When good fortune arrives, then be harmonious and well-ordered. When misfortune
arrives, be calm and well-ordered. When rich, be broadly generous.
When poor, restrict your expenditures. Be such that you can be made
noble or be made lowly, can be made rich or can be made poor, can 90
be killed but cannot be made to do what is vile. This is the method
for occupying an official position and handling royal favor, such that
to the end of one's days one never becomes hated. Be such that even
in circumstances of poverty and homelessness[a] you take your model
from this. One who is such is called an auspicious person. The *Odes* 95
says:

> Since they have adoration for this one man,
> May he watch over his virtue carefully,

---

[10] The "it" here most likely refers to the Way.

[11] I.e., one potential scenario is that a ruler who loses power would still be able to
enjoy his natural life span, living out his remaining years with the status of a lowly
peasant, but Jie and Zhòu were executed, and so did not get even the benefit of a
complete lifetime.

        May he always be filial in his thoughts,
100   And maintain his ancestors' work splendidly![12]

This expresses my meaning.

In seeking to fulfill a position of heavy responsibility well, to set in good order important affairs, or to hold favor in a state of ten thousand chariots,[13] there is a method for making sure one has no later
105 worries: nothing is as good as liking and cooperating with the right people. Aid the worthy and be broadly generous. Eliminate resentments and do no harm to others. If you are capable and are equal to your responsibilities, then carefully put into practice this way. If you are capable but are not equal to your responsibilities, and moreover
110 are afraid of losing favor, then nothing is as good as cooperating with the right people early. Recommend those who are worthy, defer to those who are capable, and quietly follow behind them. If you do this, then if you hold favor, it is sure to be truly joyful, and even if you lose favor, you are sure to be blameless. This is the most precious
115 thing for one serving a lord, and is the method for making sure one has no later worries. Thus, the way that the wise person conducts affairs is that when he is most successful, then he takes thought for humility. When there is calm, then he takes thought for hazards. When there is safety, then he takes thought for danger. He makes
120 comprehensive and abundant preparation, as though fearful of encountering disaster, and for this reason in a hundred acts he never meets with a downfall. Confucius said, "Those who are clever but fond of proper measure are sure to be well regulated. Those who are brave but fond of cooperating are sure to be victorious. Those who
125 are knowledgeable but fond of humility are sure to be worthy." This expresses my meaning.

The foolish person is the opposite of this. When he occupies a position of heavy responsibility or holds power, then he is fond of monopolizing affairs and is jealous of those who are worthy and ca-
130 pable. He oppresses those who have true meritorious accomplishments, and persecutes those who have committed errors. His intentions are set on being arrogant and self-satisfied, and he takes lightly old resentments against him. He holds to stinginess and does not

[12] Mao #243. In the original context, the "one man" is either King Wu or King Cheng.
[13] In ancient China, a state's military strength was often described in terms of the number of chariots it could field in battle. (In the Warring States era, the actual practice of fighting shifted away from chariot-based warfare, but the earlier ways of speaking persisted.) Horses were expensive, usually the chariots carried more than one person, and often each chariot was accompanied by a number of foot soldiers. So, a state that could field ten thousand chariots would have to be very wealthy and populous, and the expression "a state of ten thousand chariots" became a byword for a large and powerful state.

practice generous ways. He hails his superiors as important, but gathers power for himself from his subordinates, so as to harm others.[b] 135
Even if he wanted to live without danger, how could he succeed? Thus, if his position is elevated, he is sure to be endangered. If his responsibilities are heavy, he is sure to be removed from office. If he holds favor, he is sure to be disgraced. These are things one can simply stand by and wait for, things that will be over in the space of a 140
breath.[c] Why is this? It is simply that those who would cast him down will be many, while those who would support him will be few.

There is a method most effective in all the world. Use it to serve your lord, and you are sure to be successful. Use it to practice *ren*, and you are sure to achieve sagehood. That is: set up the exalted standard[14] 145
and do not depart from it. Then use respect and reverence to advance it, use loyalty and trustworthiness to unify it, use diligence and caution to practice it, and use scrupulousness and honesty to preserve it. In times of difficulty then follow it up with vigorous effort in order to extend and redouble it. Even if your lord does not appreciate you, let 150
your heart be without resentment and hatred. Even if your meritorious deeds are great, let not your countenance boast of your virtue. Have few requests, but many meritorious deeds. Be respectful and caring without tiring. If you are thus, then things will always go smoothly for you. Use it to serve your lord, and you are sure to be 155
successful. Use it to practice *ren*, and you are sure to achieve sagehood. This is called the most effective method in all the world.

For the young to serve their elders, for the lowly to serve the noble, for the unworthy to serve the worthy—these are *yi* for all under Heaven. If there is a person whose position is not above others, and 160
who is ashamed to be below others, then this is the heart of a vile person. If one's intentions cannot avoid such a vile heart, one's actions cannot avoid vile ways. If one should then seek to have the reputation of a gentleman or sage, then to draw an analogy for it, this would be like trying to lick Heaven by bending down, or trying to 165
save someone from hanging to death by pulling on their feet. Such a proposition is sure not to succeed, and the harder one works at it, the further off one gets.[15] Thus, the gentleman is such that when the times are restrictive, he bends with them, and when the times are more expansive, then he extends with them. 170

[14] I.e., the Way.
[15] Compare the identical wording at 16.208–12.

CHAPTER 8

The Achievements of the *Ru*

The achievements of a great *ru*: When King Wu had fallen in death and King Cheng was still a youth,[1] the Duke of Zhou put aside King Cheng and took up from King Wu in order to keep the empire subordinate, because he hated that the empire should betray the Zhou.[a]

5   He carried out the station of the Son of Heaven and heard the empire's cases for judgment with as much ease as if he had originally possessed it, but the empire did not proclaim him greedy in this. He killed Guan Shu[2] and emptied out the Shang capital, but the empire did not proclaim him violent in this. He controlled the empire wholly

10   and established seventy-one fiefdoms, with fifty-three members of the Ji clan[3] each occupying one alone, but the empire did not proclaim him one-sided in this. He educated and guided King Cheng to make him understand the Way and be able to follow in the tracks of King Wen and King Wu. The Duke of Zhou then returned the Zhou state

15   and gave back to King Cheng the station of Son of Heaven, and the empire did not stop serving the Zhou. Thereafter, the Duke of Zhou paid him court, facing north as a subject.[4] The position of Son of Heaven cannot be filled by a minor, and it cannot be discharged by a proxy.[5] If he is capable, then the empire will return to him. If he is

20   incapable, then the empire will abandon him. Thus, the Duke of Zhou put aside King Cheng and took up from King Wu, because he hated that the empire should desert the Zhou. When King Cheng was capped as an adult[6] and the Duke of Zhou returned to him the Zhou state and gave back his station, it made clear that what is *yi* is not

---

[1]   According to traditional stories, King Wu died shortly after he overthrew the Shang dynasty and established the Zhou dynasty. Since the heir to the throne, his son King Cheng, was young and inexperienced, it was a perilous time for the fledgling dynasty.

[2]   Guan Shu, younger brother of King Wu and elder brother of the Duke of Zhou, was inciting the remaining people of the Shang dynasty to rebel.

[3]   The Ji clan was the clan of Kings Wen and Wu and the Duke of Zhou.

[4]   Ritual prescribed that, at court, the ruler should be positioned to the north of his subjects (an arrangement also seen in the layout of ancient Chinese cities). "Facing north" thus came to represent the status of a subject, and "facing south" represented being a ruler.

[5]   Although the reasons for excluding rule by proxy are not clarified here, this exclusion explains why the Duke of Zhou had to act as the Son of Heaven himself, rather than leaving King Cheng on the throne and acting as his representative.

[6]   An ancient Chinese rite of passage.

destroying the main line of succession.[7] The Duke of Zhou no longer   25
held the empire. The reason that he held it in the past, but did not
hold it now, is not because he abdicated it.[8] The reason that King
Cheng did not hold it in the past, but held it now, is not because he
wrested it away. Rather, this sequence in the change of power accorded with the proper measure. Thus, a branch clan substituted for   30
the main line, but it was not an overstepping of proper bounds. A
younger brother executed his older brother, but it was not savagery.
The lord and minister traded places, but it was not disobedience. And
even though these were deviations—namely, the ways he pursued harmony for the empire, followed up the works of Kings Wen and Wu,   35
and made clear what is *yi* for branch clan and main line—nonetheless
the empire remained peaceful as though united in one. None but a
sage could do so. This is called the achievement of a great *ru*.[9]

King Zhao of Qin questioned Xunzi,[10] saying, "The *ru* are of no benefit to a person's state."   40
    Xunzi said, "The *ru* model themselves on the former kings, they
exalt ritual and *yi*. They are diligent in being sons and ministers, and
they most value their superiors. If the ruler should use them, then
their position will be in the court, and they will act appropriately. If
the ruler does not use them, then they withdraw to the ranks of the   45
common people and remain honest. They are sure to be compliant
subordinates. Even if they should be in difficult times, freezing, or
starving, they are sure not to become corrupt with perverse ways.
Though they lack even so much land as to plant an awl in, still they

---

[7] The Son of Heaven's throne was normally supposed to pass to his eldest son born
    from his principal wife (as opposed to a son born from his concubines): this consti-
    tuted the "main line" of succession. Since the Duke of Zhou was the younger brother
    of King Wu, he was part of a "branch clan" relative to the "main line" of succession
    leading from King Wen to King Wu to King Cheng. Had the Duke kept power for
    himself, he would have destroyed this "main line," which would have been unethical
    and contrary to *yi* in particular.
[8] I.e., since he never formally assumed power, relinquishing it was not an abdication,
    and therefore was not an abnormal transfer of power.
[9] It is worth noting that here the Duke of Zhou is called a *ru*, but since he preceded
    Confucius by centuries, *ru* cannot be translated here as "Confucian." Also, here is
    one place where *ru* seems to mean something more like "a very cultivated person" in
    general, as opposed to "a scholar," since according to this the Duke was not particu-
    larly involved in studying and preserving the Confucian classics. See the discussion
    of this term in chapter 1, note 26.
[10] The name given in the text is actually "Sun Qingzi" (孫卿子), which is an alternate,
    honorific way of referring to Xunzi. To avoid any confusion for readers, though, I
    have simply substituted "Xunzi" here. The use of the honorific title implies that this
    section was at least edited by someone other than Xunzi, and perhaps the conversa-
    tion was originally recorded by one of his followers, which would likewise account
    for the honorific.

50   understand the great *yi* of maintaining the altars of soil and grain.[11] Though they call out and none can respond to them properly,[12] nevertheless they still comprehend the key principles for making use of the ten thousand things and nurturing the common people. If their position is above others, then they have the materials for becoming

55   kings or dukes. If their position is below others, then they are ministers devoted to the altars of soil and grain, and they are treasures for their lord. Even if they should be hidden away in poor neighborhoods and leaky huts, no one will fail to value them, because the Way is truly preserved in them. When Confucius was about to become

60   Minister of Justice,[13] Shen You no longer dared to give his sheep water in the morning, Gong Shen expelled his wife, Shen Gui crossed the borders and moved away, and those selling cattle and horses in Lu no longer deceived people about the prices.[14] This is because Confucius made sure early on to act correctly in his dealings with people.

65   When he lived in Quedang, there was nothing that the sons and younger brothers of Quedang did not share,[b] and those with parents still alive were given more. This is because he used filial piety and being a good younger brother to transform them. When the *ru* are in the court, they improve the government. When they are in subordi-

70   nate positions, then they improve the state's customs. This is how the *ru* are as subordinates."

The king said, "If that is so, then how are they as people's superiors?"

Xunzi said, "As people's superiors they are great indeed! Their

75   intentions and thoughts are set properly within them. Ritual and proper regulation are cultivated in the court. Laws, standards, and measures are kept straight among the officials. Loyalty, trustworthiness, concern, and beneficence are manifested toward those who are subordinate. Even if they could obtain the whole world by perform-

80   ing a single act that goes against *yi* or by killing a single innocent

[11] The altars of soil and grain were the sites of important sacrifices that (in traditional belief) were considered crucial for preserving the state, and so "the altars of soil and grain" became a byword for the state itself. Hence, the point of Xunzi's remark is that the *ru* understand well the heavy responsibilities ("the great *yi*") involved in maintaining the state.

[12] I.e., the *ru* call for social and government reform, but are not given official positions that would enable them to implement the reforms.

[13] Traditional stories claim that Confucius served for a short period as Minister of Justice in his home state, Lu, and some editions of the *Xunzi* explicitly add "in Lu" at this juncture.

[14] According to other sources, Shen You's giving his sheep water in the morning was part of a scheme to deceive buyers in the market (perhaps by making the sheep heavier than they normally were), Gong Shen's wife was involved in "uncontrolled licentiousness," and Shen Gui was guilty of "extravagances" that exceeded the bounds of law.

person, they would not do it. Thus, the *yi* of the lord is trusted among the people. When this trust spreads throughout the four seas, then all under Heaven will respond to him as though with a single shout. Why is this? It is because when one values having a reputation that is pure, then all under Heaven become well-ordered. Thus, singing 85
and chanting, those who are nearby will delight in him.[15] Exhausted and stumbling, those who are far away will run to him. All within the four seas will become like one family, and all the men of understanding will willingly submit. This is called being the teacher of the people. The *Odes* says: 90

> From the west and from the east,
> From the south and from the north,
> All submit as they come forth.[16]

This expresses my meaning. Thus, when the *ru* are people's subordinates, it is like what I described before, and when they are people's 95
superiors, it is like what I have just said. How can you say they are of no benefit to a person's state?"

King Zhao said, "Well spoken!"

The Way of the former kings consists in exalting *ren*. One must cleave to what is central in carrying it out. What do I mean by "what is cen- 100
tral"? I say: it is ritual and *yi*. The Way is not the way of Heaven, nor is it the way of Earth. It is that whereby humans make their way, and that which the gentleman takes as his way. What the gentleman calls being worthy is not the ability of doing everything which people are able to do. What the gentleman calls being wise is not the ability of 105
knowing everything which people know. What the gentleman calls being skilled in argument is not the ability of arguing everything which people argue. What the gentleman calls being keen in investigation is not the ability of investigating everything which people investigate. Rather, there is something that is proper to him. 110

When it comes to sizing up high and low ground, inspecting for rich or poor soil, and arranging planting of the five seeds, the gentleman is not as good as the farmer. When it comes to transporting wealth and goods, sizing up good and bad quality, and distinguishing high and low value, the gentleman is not as good as the merchant. 115
When it comes to applying the compass and square, laying out the ink-line, and providing equipment and utensils, the gentleman is not as good as the craftsman. When it comes to disregarding the true

---

[15] The Chinese text beginning from this sentence on down to the line after the quotation of the *Odes* also appears in an almost identical passage at 15.327–37.

[16] Mao #244. These lines are also quoted at 11.324–26 and 15.334–36.

disposition of right and wrong and so and not so in order to degrade
120   and humiliate others,[17] the gentleman is not as good as Hui Shi and
Deng Xi. When it comes to assessing people's virtue and assigning
them ranks, measuring people's abilities and giving them official positions, so that the worthy and unworthy each obtain their proper
places, the capable and the incapable each receive their proper of-
125   fices, the myriad things all get what is appropriate for them, and
changes in affairs are each met with the proper response, so that Shen
Dao and Mozi have nowhere to advance their doctrines, so that Hui
Shi and Deng Xi do not dare to smuggle in their investigations, and
so that people's words always fit with good order and their work is
130   always directed to appropriate tasks—this, at last, is what the gentleman excels in.

For every kind of work and practice, if it is of benefit to good order,
establish it. If it is of not benefit to good order, discard it. This is
called making one's affairs conform to what is central. For every kind
135   of learning and doctrine, if it is of benefit to good order, proceed with
it. If it is of no benefit to good order, abandon it. This is called making one's doctrines conform to what is central. Works and practices
that lose what is central are called vile affairs. Learning and doctrines
that lose what is central are called vile ways. Vile affairs and vile ways
140   are what an ordered age rejects, and what a chaotic age follows and
obeys.

As for the problems of how fullness and emptiness mutually replace each other, or the distinctions between the hard and the white,
the similar and the dissimilar,[18] these are things that a keen ear cannot
145   listen to, things that a sharp eye cannot look into, things that a skilled
arguer cannot speak of. Even if one should have the wisdom of a
sage, one could not comprehensively point out answers for them.[c] To
be ignorant of these things does no harm to becoming a gentleman.
To know them is no impediment to becoming a petty person. If a
150   craftsman does not know them, it does no harm to his making artful
productions. If a gentleman does not know them, it does no harm to
his bringing about order. If kings and dukes are fond of these things,
it will disorder the laws. If the common people are fond of these
things, it will disorder their work. Then reckless, confused, stupid,
155   and ignorant men will begin to lead their groups of disciples, argue

[17] The reference here is to the paradoxes propounded by Hui Shi and Deng Xi (for
examples, see 3.7–11). Xunzi's point is that they arrived at these claims only by
blatantly disregarding how things truly are, and moreover that they did so for de-
spicable purposes. His subsequent remark that the gentleman is not as skilled as
they are in these matters is clearly not meant as an admission of any genuine shortcoming on the gentleman's part.
[18] This is again a reference to various paradoxes propounded by Gongsun Long, Hui
Shi, and others.

over their doctrines, and expound their peculiar terminology. Even as they become old and see their sons become grown men, they will not understand the wrong they are doing. This is called the highest foolishness, and to make a name for oneself in this way is not even as good as doing it by physiognomizing chickens and dogs.[19] The *Odes* says: 160

> If either you were a ghost or you were a *yu*,[20]
> Getting at you would be impossible to do.
> But you possess a shameful human face and eyes,
> And you show others a lack of correctness, too.   165
> So I have now created this good song I sing,
> To correct your ways, which are faithless and untrue.[21,d]

This expresses my meaning.

If I want to go from being lowly to being noble, from being foolish to being wise, from being poor to being rich, is it possible? I say: 170
Only through learning! If one carries out such learning, then one is called a well-bred man. If one is enthusiastic and devoted to it, then one is a gentleman. If one truly comprehends it, then one is a sage. At the best one can become a sage, and at the least one can become a well-bred man or gentleman—who could prevent me from this? In   175
the past, one was a muddled man on the street. Suddenly, one is equal to Yao and Yu. Is this not a case of going from being lowly to being noble? In the past, when judging arguments in one's home, one was muddled and could not decide them. Suddenly, one can trace out the source of *ren* and *yi*, divide up right and wrong, take   180
measure of the whole world and roll it around in one's palm, distinguishing black and white. Is this not a case of going from being foolish to being wise? In the past, one was a pauper. Suddenly, all the great instruments for ordering the world are here before one. Is this not a case of going from being poor to being rich?   185

Now suppose there were a person here who had carefully concealed a treasure worth a thousand *yi** on his person.[22] Even if he had to beg in order to eat, people would still call him rich. If that treasure were such that one could not eat it, could not wear it, and could not even sell it off quickly, people would nevertheless still call him rich.   190
Why? Is it not because the instrument of achieving great riches is truly here with him? Thus, to be a magnificent person is also to be a rich man. Hence, the gentleman is noble without holding a title, and

---

[19] For Xunzi's contempt for physiognomy, see the beginning of chapter 5.

[20] According to legend, the *yu* was a kind of monster that lived in water and would spit sand with enough force to kill people.

[21] Mao #199. Compare the appearance of this poem at 22.259–64.

[22] An *yi** was an ancient measure for gold.

rich without receiving a salary. He is trustworthy without yet having
195 spoken, and is awe-inspiring without yet having gotten angry. He
dwells in poverty but is glorious, lives in seclusion but is joyful. Is
this not because the conditions for utmost honor, utmost riches, utmost importance, and utmost authority are all collected here in him?
Thus I say: A noble reputation cannot be grabbed by means of
200 cliquish associations. It cannot be had by means of bragging and
boasting. It cannot be extorted by means of great power. One must
truly have those other things, and only then will it be accomplished.
If one tries to grab it, one will lose it. If one lets it go, then it will
come. If one follows the Way, it will accumulate. If one boasts and
205 brags, it will dissipate. Hence, the gentleman cultivates what is on the
inside, and lets go of those things on the outside. He works at accumulating virtue in his person, and manages things by following the
Way. If he is like this, then a noble reputation will arise as brightly as
the sun and moon, and the whole world will respond to him with a
210 noise like a thunderclap. Thus it is said: the gentleman is hidden away
but eminent, his movements are subtle but illustrious, he defers and
gives way but conquers. The *Odes* says, "The crane cries out in the
Nine Marshes. Its voice resounds to Heaven."[23] This expresses my
meaning.
215 The crude person is the opposite of this. He engages in cliquish
associations, but praise for him only decreases. He crudely grabs for
it, but his reputation is only the more disgraced. He labors seeking
safety and benefit, but his person is only the more endangered. The
Odes says:

220 Those men who lack any decency
View one another resentfully.
Striving to get rank and salary,
They perish by acting unyieldingly.[24]

This expresses my meaning. Thus, a person of few abilities who tries
225 to take on a great task is like a person of little strength who tries to
carry a heavy burden: aside from breaking his bones and tearing his
tendons, he will get nowhere. An unworthy person who feigns being
worthy is like a hunchbacked person who straightens himself up and
likes to make himself look tall: those who point out his hump will
230 only be all the more numerous. Hence, the enlightened ruler judges
people's virtue and appoints them to official positions, and this is the
way he avoids disorder. The loyal minister makes sure he is truly ca-

---

[23] Mao #184.

[24] Mao #223. Many commentators understand the last two lines very differently in the
original context of the *Odes*.

pable and only then does he dare accept his office, and this is the way
he avoids over-stretching himself. When allotments[25] are not disordered above, and abilities are not over-stretched below, this is the   235
height of good order and proper distinction. The *Odes* says, "Left and
right, all is balanced. Thus does everyone follow."[26] This speaks of
how neither superiors nor subordinates bring disorder to the other.

To take following customs as being good, to take material goods
and money as treasures, to take maintaining one's life as one's ulti-   240
mate way—this is common people's virtue. If a person is most firm in
acting according to the proper model and does not allow selfish desires to disorder what he has learned, such a one can be called a well-
bred man who is resolute. If a person is most firm in acting according
to the proper model and likes to cultivate and practice what he has   245
learned, in order to straighten out and ornament his inborn dispositions and nature—if his doctrines are mostly right, but he does not
yet fully fathom them, if his practices are mostly right, but he does
not yet feel fully at ease in them, if his deliberations are mostly right,
but he is not yet all-encompassing and totally thorough in them—if   250
above he can show the greatness of that which he exalts, and below
can educate and guide those who are not as good as himself—such a
one can be called a generous and devoted gentleman. If a person
cultivates the models of the hundred kings as simply as distinguishing black and white, and if he can adapt to changes in the current   255
times as easily as counting one and two—if he practices ritual and
holds to proper regulation and feels as much at ease in these as he
does with his four limbs, and if his skill for grasping opportunities
and making accomplishments is as constant as the coming of the four
seasons[e]—if his goodness in peaceably governing and harmonizing   260
the people is such that masses of millions are unified as though they
were a single person—such a one can be called a sage.

> How precisely he holds to good order![27] How strictly he
> makes himself worthy of respect! How carefully he follows
> beginning through to end! How securely he is able to per-   265
> sist! How joyfully he upholds the Way without tiring! How
> brilliantly he uses his intelligence! How refinedly he applies
> the gradations in the overall categories of things! How prop-
> erly he holds to culture and good form! How magnanimously

---

[25] The word here is *fen* 分, which literally means "divide" or "division." It is an important term for Xunzi, who uses it to refer to an ideal system of social divisions (and
I have rendered it as "social divisions" in many places), but there are some contexts
such as this where "allot" and "allotment" are more natural and less confusing in
English.

[26] Mao #222.

[27] From here down to the words "people's wrongdoing," the original text is rhymed.

270   he takes joy in people's goodness! How apprehensively he
       fears people's wrongdoing!

Such a one can be called a sage, and that is because his way comes
from being single-minded.
       What do I mean by "single-minded"? I say: it is to take up the
275 spirit-like state and be firm in it. What do I mean by "the spirit-like
state"? I say: to achieve the utmost in goodness and to uphold proper
order is called the spirit-like state. [What do I mean by "being firm"?][28]
To be such that none of the ten thousand things can overturn you is
called being firm. One who is both spirit-like and firm in this state is
280 called a sage. The sage is the pitch pipe of the Way. The pitch pipe of
the Way for all people under Heaven rests in him. The ways of the
hundred kings are unified in him. Thus, the principles of the *Odes*,
Documents, *Rituals*, and *Music* are summed up in him. The *Odes* tells
of his intentions. The *Documents* tells of his works. The *Rituals* tells of
285 his conduct.[f] The *Music* tells of his harmoniousness. The *Spring and
Autumn Annals* tells of his subtlety. And so, the reason why the *Feng*[29]
do not go to excess is because they have him to regulate them. The
reason why the "Lesser *Ya*" are the "Lesser *Ya*" is because they have
him to ornament them. The reason why the "Greater *Ya*" are the
290 "Greater *Ya*" is because they have him to illuminate them. The reason
why the *Song* are the utmost[30] is because they have him to perfect
them. The Way for all people under Heaven rests in him.

       Those who turn to him will be preserved.[31]
       Those who turn away from him will perish.

295 From ancient times down to the present, there have never been any
who turned to him and were not preserved, nor have there been any
who turned away from him and did not perish.

A guest claimed, "Confucius said, 'Was not the Duke of Zhou magnificent? Though his person was honored, he was all the more rever-
300 entially submissive. Though his house was wealthy, he was all the
more sparing. Though he defeated his enemies, he was all the more
on guard.'"

---

[28] This sentence is not in the original text, but commentators suggest adding it, and it
     is clearly the concern that is answered by the next few sentences in the main text.
[29] The *Feng* (風 "Airs"), *Ya* (雅 "Elegies"), and *Song* (頌 "Hymns") are different sections
     of the *Odes*.
[30] The text is vague about the sense in which the *Song* are "the utmost." Many com-
     mentators take the point as being that the *Song* are utmost with respect to (repre-
     senting) virtue.
[31] This sentence and the next one are rhymed in the original.

I responded, "I am afraid that such was not the conduct of the Duke of Zhou, nor were those the words of Confucius. When King Wu had fallen in death and King Cheng was still a youth, the Duke of Zhou put aside King Cheng and took up from King Wu. He occupied the position of the Son of Heaven, sat with his back to the *yi** screen, and the feudal lords hastened to the foot of his hall.[32,g] At that time, who was being reverentially submissive?

"He controlled the empire wholly and established seventy-one fiefdoms, with fifty-three members of the Ji clan each occupying one alone among those. All of the sons and grandsons of the Zhou, except for those who were mad or deluded, became most eminent feudal lords in the empire. Who would say that the Duke of Zhou was sparing?

"When King Wu launched his punitive campaign against the tyrant Zhòu, the day he set out was inauspicious for military affairs. When they faced east, they were greeted by the great Year-star.[33] When they reached the banks of the Si, the waters were flooding. When they reached Huai, their boats were broken up. When they reached the top of Gong, there was a mountain landslide. Huo Shu[34] was frightened and said, 'We have been gone only three days and already five omens of disaster have arrived. Is this not because we are doing something impermissible?' The Duke of Zhou said, 'Bi Gan has been eviscerated and Jizi[35] has been imprisoned. Fei Lian and Wu Lai[36] are in charge of governing. What more could be impermissible?' Thereupon King Wu arranged his horses and advanced. In the morning, he ate at Qi,[37] and in the evening, he lodged at Hundred Springs. He lay in wait for the dawn on the shepherd's plain, and then when he drummed his troops forward, the soldiers of the tyrant Zhòu turned about and changed their direction. He thereupon rode the tide of the Shang people to attack the tyrant Zhòu. Accordingly, it was not any of the Zhou people who killed the tyrant Zhòu, but rather it was due to the Shang people themselves. Therefore, there was no capturing of prisoners or taking of heads as trophies,[38] and there was no rewarding of charges into danger. King Wu returned home. He put away the three

[32] According to commentators, the *yi** was a screen used only in the Son of Heaven's audience chamber, and only the Son of Heaven turned his back to it, while all visitors faced it. See the similar wording at 18.318–19.

[33] I.e., the planet Jupiter. According to tradition, it was inadvisable to attack in the direction where this heavenly body lay.

[34] A younger brother of King Wu who apparently accompanied him on the campaign.

[35] Bi Gan and Jizi were virtuous ministers who tried to remonstrate with Zhòu and get him to reform his ways, but Zhòu became angry and punished them.

[36] Fei Lian and Wu Lai were bad ministers who encouraged Zhòu in his evil-doing.

[37] This Qi (戚) is not the same as the state of Qi (齊).

[38] In ancient China, victorious soldiers and generals often used the severed heads of their vanquished enemies to prove their achievements in battle to their superiors.

types of armors and laid to rest the five types of weapons. He brought together all people under Heaven and established song and music. Thus, the *Wu* and the *Xiang*[39] came to be, and the *Shao* and *Hu*[40] were 340 put aside. Within the four seas, everyone changed their hearts and adjusted their deliberations so as to be transformed and follow him. Therefore, his outer gates were never closed, and he could walk across the whole world without encountering any boundaries. At that time, who was being on guard?"

345 Zao Fu was the best driver in the whole world, but without a chariot and horses, he would have had nowhere to display his abilities. Yi was the best archer in the world, but without a bow and arrows, he would have had nowhere to display his skill. The great *ru* is one who is good at aligning and unifying the whole world, but without a territory of 350 a hundred *li*, he will have nowhere to display his merit. If the chariot is sturdy and the horses are of select quality but the man cannot use them to go as far as a thousand *li* in a single day, then he is not a Zao Fu.[h] If the bow is properly adjusted and the arrows are straight but the man cannot use them to hit a fine point shooting from far away, 355 then he is not an Yi. If the man has use of a territory of a hundred *li* but cannot use it to align and unify the whole world and put a stop to violence and tyranny, then he is not a great *ru*.

The great *ru* is such that even if he is hidden away in a poor neighborhood and a leaky hut, lacking even so much land as to plant an 360 awl in, kings and dukes cannot compete with his fame.[41] If he were to occupy even so much as a grand minister's position, then no single lord could keep him, and no single state could contain him. He would accomplish fame greater than the feudal lords, and no one would fail to want him as a minister. If he were to have use of a territory of a 365 hundred *li*, then no state of a thousand *li* could compete with him for victory in battle. He would thrash the tyrannical states, bring concord and unity to the whole world, and no one could overthrow him. Such is the mark of a great *ru*.

His words accord with the proper categories of things, and his ac- 370 tions accord with ritual. In managing affairs, he leaves nothing to regret. In handling dangers and responding to changes, he does everything appropriately. He shifts and moves with the times. He bends and straightens with the age. Throughout a thousand acts and ten thousand changes, his way remains one and the same. Such is the test 375 of a great *ru*.

The enemies' ears (being smaller and more transportable than whole heads) were sometimes also used for this purpose.
[39] The *Wu* and *Xiang* were pieces of music associated with King Wu.
[40] The *Shao* and *Hu* were pieces of music associated with Shun and Tang, respectively.
[41] Wording nearly identical to this and the next few sentences appears at 6.76–81.

When he is in difficult circumstances, vulgar *ru* will mock him.[42] When he is successful, then heroes and outstanding men will be transformed to follow him. Men of twisted and petty behavior will flee him. Men of perverse doctrines will fear him. The masses will be ashamed before him.   380

When successful, then he unifies the whole world. When in difficult circumstances, then on his own he establishes a noble reputation for himself. Heaven cannot make it die. Earth cannot bury it. The ages of Jie and Robber Zhi cannot pollute it. None but a great *ru* can establish such a reputation. Just such men were Confucius and Zigōng.   385

Thus, there are vulgar men, vulgar *ru*, refined *ru*, and great *ru*. One sort of person does not study or question. He has no correctness or *yi*. He takes wealth and profit as his exalted standards. Such a person is a vulgar man.

Another sort of person wears large clothing with a slack belt. He   390 wears his cap looking like split-open fruit.[43,i] He only sketchily models himself on the former kings, but is capable enough to disorder the ways of the world. His learning is erroneous and his actions are haphazard. He does not know to model himself on the later kings and to pursue their regulations and measures single-mindedly. He does not   395 know to exalt ritual and *yi* and to put the *Odes* and *Documents* second. His clothing, cap, and practice of deliberate effort are already the same as the vulgar customs of the age, but he does not recognize his own badness. His arguments and speech are already the same as Mozi, but his own understanding cannot see the difference. He calls   400 upon the former kings so as to deceive the ignorant and seek clothing and food from them. If he gets enough provisions to stuff his mouth, then he is overjoyed. He follows his superiors, serves their attendants and favorites, and respects higher-ranking retainers in a manner like a contented lifelong slave who dares not have any other intentions.   405 Such a person is a vulgar *ru*.

Another sort of person models himself on the later kings. He pursues their regulations and measures single-mindedly. He exalts ritual and *yi* and puts the *Odes* and *Documents* second. His words and practices already hold to the grand model, but his own understanding   410 cannot make them match up completely. Cases which the model and teachings do not cover, or where his experience does not reach, his own knowledge is unable to bring into conformity with the proper categories of things. If he knows, then he says he knows. If he does not know, then he says he does not know.[44] On the inside, he does not   415

---

[42] This sentence and the five that follow it are rhymed in the original.
[43] The text here is difficult, and the translation is tentative.
[44] Compare *Analects* 2.17.

delude himself about himself. On the outside, he does not deceive others about himself. In this manner, he honors the worthy, fearfully holds to the proper model, and dares not be lazy or arrogant. Such a person is a refined *ru*.

420 Another sort of person models himself on the later kings. He gathers in himself all their rituals and *yi*. He pursues their regulations and measures single-mindedly. He uses what is shallow to manage what is broad, uses what is ancient to manage what is current, and uses what is one to manage what is myriad. As for the categories of *ren* and
425 *yi*, even if he were dwelling among birds and beasts, he could distinguish them as easily as black and white. If at some point there suddenly arise deviant things and unusual changes that have never been heard of or seen before, then he takes up the comprehensive categories of things and responds to them without any hesitation or misgiv-
430 ings. He sets out the proper model and measures them, and then his response fits just like bringing together two halves of a tally. Such a person is a great *ru*.

Thus, if a ruler of men employs vulgar men, then even a state of ten thousand chariots will perish. If he employs vulgar *ru*, then a state
435 of ten thousand chariots can be made to survive. If he employs refined *ru*, then a state of a thousand chariots can be made secure. If he employs great *ru*, then even a territory of just a hundred *li* can be preserved for a long time, and after several years, all people under Heaven will be unified under him, and the feudal lords will be his
440 ministers. If he should have use of a state of ten thousand chariots, then with a few orders all will be settled, and in a single day he will become renowned.

Not having heard of it is not as good as having heard of it.[45] Having heard of it is not as good as having seen it. Having seen it is not
445 as good as knowing it. Knowing it is not as good as putting it into practice. Learning arrives at putting it into practice and then stops, because to put it into practice is to understand it, and to understand it is to be a sage. The sage bases himself on *ren* and *yi*, hits exactly on what is right and wrong, and makes his words and practices
450 match up completely, all without the slightest misstep. There is no other way to this than simply to stop at putting it into practice. Thus, if you have heard of it but have not seen it, then even if you are broadly learned, you are sure to be mistaken. If you have seen it but do not know it, then even though you can recognize it, you are
455 sure to act recklessly. If you know it but do not put it into practice, then even if you are thoroughly familiar with it, you are sure to find yourself trapped. If you have neither heard of it nor seen it, then even though you hit on what is fitting, that is not *ren*; such a way

[45] Here and in what follows, the "it" most probably refers to ritual or the Way.

fails a hundred times for every hundred actions. And so, if people lack teachers and proper models, then the clever among them will 460 surely engage in robbery, and the bold among them will surely engage in villainy. The capable among them will surely engage in chaotic behavior, the perceptive among them will surely engage in strange contentions, and the deft arguers among them will surely engage in deceit. If people have teachers and proper models, then 465 the clever among them will quickly achieve comprehension, and the bold among them will quickly achieve awe-inspiring status. The capable among them will quickly become perfected, the perceptive among them will quickly come to full right understanding, and the deft arguers among them will quickly come to judge things cor- 470 rectly. Thus, having teachers and proper models is the greatest treasure for mankind, and lacking teachers and proper models is the greatest calamity for mankind.

If people have no teachers or proper models, then they will take human nature as their exalted standard. If they have teachers and 475 proper models, then they will take accumulated effort as their exalted standard. Following teachers and proper models is something one gets from one's dispositions, not something one receives from human nature, because it is insufficient to stand on its own and be well-ordered.ʲ Human nature is something I cannot remake, but it can be 480 transformed.[46] The dispositions are something I do not have complete grasp of, but they can be remade.[47],ᵏ Practice and habituation are the means to transform human nature. Being devoted to one thing and not departing from it are the means to bring about accumulated effort. Habituation changes your intentions, and being able 485 to take comfort in such things and persist in them changes your substance. If you are devoted to the one right thing and do not depart from it, then you will reach to spirit-like power and understanding and take your place in the triad with Heaven and Earth.

Thus, if you accumulate soil, you will form a mountain. If you ac- 490 cumulate water, you will form a sea. The accumulation of dawns and dusks is called a year. The highest thing is called Heaven, and the lowest thing is called Earth. The six directions in the world are called the extremes. If ordinary men in the street and the common people

---

[46] The point is that one cannot alter the fundamental impulses constituting human nature (e.g., one cannot make it so that one has no desire for food when one is hungry—see Xunzi's discussion of human nature at 23.51–52), but the expression of these impulses can be "transformed" in various ways so as to produce civilized and well-ordered behavior.

[47] That is, one cannot simply choose whether to experience emotions like anger, sorrow, etc., but through training and habituation, one can alter one's dispositions to feel them, so that one experiences them on the proper occasions, and does not experience them when they would be inappropriate.

495 accumulate goodness and make it whole and complete, they are
called sages. They must seek it and only then will they obtain it. They
must work at it and only then will they achieve it. They must accumulate it and only then will they be lofty. They must make it complete
and only then are they sages. So, the sage is the product of people's
500 accumulated efforts.

If people accumulate experience in weeding and plowing, they
become farmers. If they accumulate experience in chopping and
carving, they become craftsmen. If they accumulate experience in
selling and vending, they become merchants. If they accumulate ex-
505 perience in ritual and *yi*, they become gentlemen. The sons of craftsmen all continue their fathers' work, and the people of a state are
comfortably accustomed to the clothing of that area—if they live in
Chu they follow the style of Chu, if they live in Yue they follow the
style of Yue, and if they live in Xia, they follow the style of Xia. This
510 is not because of their Heavenly-given nature, but rather because accumulation and polishing have made it so.

Hence, if people know to be diligent about practice, be careful
about habituation, and esteem accumulation and polishing, then
they become gentlemen. If they give in to their inborn dispositions
515 and nature and do not sufficiently question and study, then they become petty men. He who becomes a gentleman has constant security
and glory. He who becomes a petty man faces constant danger and
disgrace. Everyone wants security and glory and dislikes danger and
disgrace, and so only the gentleman is able to obtain what he likes,
520 while the petty man each day invites what he dislikes. The *Odes* says:

> It is only these truly decent people
> Who are neither sought nor advanced by the lord.
> It is only those having cruel hearts within
> Whom he will care for and whom he will reward.
525 > The people thus desire to create chaos;
> Bitter, poisonous deeds are what they lean toward.[48]

This expresses my meaning.

On the classes of people: Some do not avoid being twisted and
selfish in their intentions, yet they hope others will consider them
530 public-spirited. They do not avoid corruption and arrogance in their
conduct, yet they hope others will consider them cultivated. They are
extremely foolish, ignorant, stupid, and dense, yet they hope others

---

[48] Mao #257. The "chaos" and "bitter, poisonous deeds" here apparently refer not to
misdeeds by the people toward each other, but rather to misdeeds against the ruler,
i.e., acts of rebellion.

will consider them wise. Such are the masses of people. Others must resist selfishness in their intentions, and only then can they be public-spirited. In their conduct they must resist their inborn dispositions 535 and nature, and only then can they be cultivated. In their under-standing they must like to inquire about things, and only then are they capable. One who is public-spirited, cultivated, and capable may be called a lesser *ru*. Others are fully at ease in being public-spirited in their intentions. In their conduct they are fully at ease in 540 being cultivated. In their understanding they thoroughly grasp the unifying categories of things. One who is like this may be called a great *ru*. A great *ru* is fit to be the Son of Heaven or one of the three dukes. A lesser *ru* is fit to be a feudal lord, a grand minister, or a func-tionary. The masses of people are fit to be craftsmen, farmers, and 545 merchants. Ritual is that which the ruler of men uses as the yardstick and test for his various subjects, and then the classes of people are marked out completely.

"For his words, the gentleman has a foundation and roof. For his conduct, he has levees and depth markers.[49] For his way, he has one 550 exalted standard." This means that what he requires of people's ways and virtue goes no lower than security and preservation for people. It means that what he requires of people's intentions and thoughts goes no lower than becoming a well-bred man. It means that what he requires of people's ways and virtue does not deviate from the later 555 kings. If a person's way goes back beyond the Three Dynasties, he calls it reckless. If a person's model deviates from the later kings, he calls it unrefined. Whether one elevates him or demotes him, belittles him or makes him a minister, he does not go outside these bounds. That is how the gentleman exercises his intentions and thoughts 560 within a foundation, roof, and halls. Thus, if the feudal lords ask him about government but do not touch upon security and preservation for people, he does not answer them. If commoners ask him about learning but do not touch upon becoming well-bred men, he does not teach them. If the doctrines of the hundred schools do not touch 565 upon the later kings, he does not listen to them. This is what is meant by "For his words, the gentleman has a foundation and roof. For his conduct, he has levees and depth markers."

[49] Compare 17.238–41.

CHAPTER 9

The Rule of a True King

Let us inquire into how to conduct the government. I say: Promote the worthy and the capable without waiting for them to rise through the ranks. Dismiss the unfit and the incapable without waiting for even a single moment. Execute those who incite others to bad deeds
5 without waiting to teach them.[1] Transform the ordinary people without waiting for government controls. If social divisions are not yet set, then take control of illuminating the proper bonds.[a] Even the sons and grandsons of kings, dukes, gentry, and grand ministers, if they cannot submit to ritual and *yi*, should be assigned the status of
10 commoners. Even the sons and grandsons of commoners, if they accumulate culture and learning, correct their person and conduct, and can submit to ritual and *yi*, should be assigned the status of prime minister, gentry, or grand ministers. And so, for those engaging in vile teachings, vile doctrines, vile works, and vile skills,[2] and for those
15 among the common people who are rebellious and perverse, give them each an occupation and teach them, and take a while to wait for them. Encourage them with accolades and rewards, and discipline them with punishments and penalties. If they rest secure in their occupations, then nurture them. If they do not rest secure in their oc-
20 cupations, then abandon them. The five types of handicapped people should be received by their superiors and nurtured, put to work according to their talents. Employ and feed and clothe them. Cover all of them without any omissions. Those who in their talents and conduct go against the times should die without pardon. This is called
25 Heavenly virtue,[3] the government of a true king.
    On the great division to be made in judging government affairs: If you use ritual to treat those who come bearing goodness, and use punishment to treat those who come bearing badness, then the worthy and unworthy will not be jumbled up, and what is right and what
30 is wrong will not be confused. If the worthy and unworthy are not jumbled up, then heroes and outstanding men will come. If what is right and what is wrong are not confused, then the state and family will be well ordered. If things are like this, then your reputation will daily become more renowned, all people under Heaven will esteem
35 you, what you order will be carried out, what you prohibit will come

---

[1] Compare 5.260–70.
[2] See the discussion of "vileness" at 6.109–15.
[3] Compare "Heavenly virtue" at 3.126–27.

to a stop, and the work of a true king will be complete. In every case of judging such affairs, if you are strict and harsh and show no fondness for those trying to lend you their ways, then your inferiors will be fearful and will not draw near. They will be secretive, closed, and will not fully exert themselves. If things are like this, then important 40 matters will be in danger of being handled loosely and minor affairs will be in danger of being let slip. If, on the other hand, you are easygoing and accommodating and show fondness for those trying to lend you their ways, but have no stop on them, then vile teachings will also all come, and speculative doctrines will proliferate sharply. 45 If things are like this, then judging affairs will become too complex, and work will become laborious. This will also harm governing. Thus, if one follows a model but does not debate over it, then cases where the model does not reach will surely be botched. If one holds a position but is not open-minded about things, then cases which one's 50 assigned position does not cover are sure to be let slip. Thus, to follow a model and debate over it, and hold a position while being open-minded about it, so that there is no secret plotting, no goodness left undone, and out of a hundred affairs no errors are made—none but the gentleman is capable of this. And so, public-spiritedness and 55 evenhandedness are one's scales in holding a position, and balance and harmoniousness are one's plumb line in judging affairs. In cases for which there is a model, act according to the model.[4] In cases for which there is no model, handle them according to their proper category. This is the utmost way of judging affairs. To be biased, partisan, and have no guiding principle is a perverted way of judging affairs. Thus, there are indeed cases where having a good model still results in chaos.[5] But from ancient times down to the present, a case where having a gentleman in charge results in chaos is unheard of. There is a saying, "Order is born from the gentleman. Chaos is born 65 from the petty man." This expresses my meaning.

If divisions of goods are all even, then they cannot be made ample enough.[6] If people's authority is all equal, then they cannot be unified. If all the masses are equal in status, then they cannot be put to use. However, just as there is Heaven and Earth, there is a difference 70 between above and below. An enlightened king must first arise and then he can arrange the state so that it has established order. As for the fact that two nobles cannot serve each other, and two base men cannot employ each other, this is the Heavenly order of things. If people's authority and position are equal and their desires and dis- 75 likes the same, then goods cannot be made sufficient for them, and

[4] This and the following sentence also appear at 27.324–27.
[5] Compare 12.1–16.
[6] Compare 4.294–320.

they will certainly struggle. If they struggle then there will certainly be chaos, and if there is chaos then they will be impoverished. The former kings hated this chaos, and so they established ritual and *yi* in order to divide up mankind, so as to cause ranking of poor and rich and noble and base, so that they might take charge of them. This is the basis for nourishing all under Heaven. The *Documents* says, "Total equality is not order."[7] This expresses my meaning.

If the horses are uneasy with the chariot, then the gentleman will not feel secure in riding the chariot. If the common people are uneasy with the government, then the gentleman will not feel secure in holding his position. When the horses are uneasy with the chariot, then nothing works better than calming them. When the common people are uneasy with the government, then nothing works better than treating them generously. Pick out those who are worthy and good. Raise high those who are dedicated and respectful. Promote those who are filial and act as good younger brothers. Take in those who are orphaned or widowed. Assist those who are poor and in dire straits. If you do this, then the common people will feel at ease with the government. When the common people feel at ease with the government, only then will the gentleman feel at ease in holding his position. There is a saying, "The lord is the boat. The common people are the water. The water can support the boat. The water can also overturn the boat." This expresses my meaning. Thus, if the lord of men wishes to be secure, then nothing works better than governing evenhandedly and showing concern for the people. If he wishes to have glory, then nothing works better than exalting ritual and respecting well-bred men. If he wishes to have accomplishments, then nothing works better than elevating the worthy and employing the capable. These are the great regulations in being the lord of men. If you abide by these three regulations, then the rest of your acts will all happen fittingly. If you do not abide by these three regulations, then even if the rest of your acts all happen fittingly, it will be of no benefit. Confucius says, "He who is right on the great regulations and right on the lesser regulations is a superior lord. He who is right on the great regulations, but who departs from the lesser regulations in some things while clinging to them in others, is a middling lord. For him who is wrong on the great regulations, even if he is right on the lesser regulations, I simply cannot see him having any further acts at all."

Marquis Cheng and Duke Si were both lords who amassed income and calculated about the order of things, but they never went as far

---

[7] See *Shujing, Lüxing* ("The Marquis of Lü on Punishment"), translated in Waltham (1971, p. 235), though Xunzi seems to be using the sentence very much out of line with its original context, so the translation here is very different.

as winning over the people. Zichan was a person who won over the people, but he never went as far as making government work. Guan Zhong was a person who made government work, but he never went   120
as far as cultivating ritual. Thus:

> He who cultivates ritual becomes a true king.
> He who makes government work becomes strong.
> He who wins over the people will be secure.
> He who amasses income will not last long.   125

And so, the true king enriches the people. The hegemon enriches the gentry. The state which barely survives enriches its grand ministers. The state which perishes enriches its coffers and fills up its treasuries. When the coffers are rich and the treasuries are full, but the common people are destitute, this is called "overflowing at the top but leaking   130
at the bottom." At home one cannot protect oneself, and abroad one cannot wage war, and so being overthrown or being destroyed are affairs one can simply stand by and wait for. Hence:

> If I amass goods then I cannot last long.[8]
> My enemy uses this chance to grow strong.   135

Amassing income is the path to summoning invaders, fattening one's enemy, destroying one's state, and imperiling one's person. Therefore, the enlightened ruler does not tread upon it.

He who seeks to become a true king seizes upon the right people. He who seeks to become a hegemon seizes upon good relations. He   140
who seeks to rule by brute strength seizes upon territory. He who seizes upon the right people will make the feudal lords his ministers. He who seizes upon good relations will make the feudal lords his friends. He who seizes upon territory will make the feudal lords his enemies. He who can make the feudal lords his ministers is a true   145
king. He who can make the feudal lords his friends is a hegemon. He who makes the feudal lords his enemies is endangering himself. In using brute strength, when another person defends his cities or comes out to do battle, and I use sheer force to overcome him, then the harm done to his people will surely be great. If the harm done to his people   150
is great, then his people are sure to have great hatred for me. If his people have great hatred for me, then daily they will wish all the more to fight against me. On the other hand, when another person defends his cities or comes out to do battle, and I use sheer force to overcome

---

[8] Here and elsewhere, although Xunzi uses first-person words such as "I," "me," and "my," they do not refer to Xunzi himself, but are instead intended in an impersonal sense.

155   him, then the harm done to my own people will surely be great. If the harm done to my own people is great, then my own people are sure to have great hatred for me. If my own people have great hatred for me, then daily they will wish all the less to fight for me. When his people daily wish all the more to fight against me, and my own peo-

160   ple daily wish all the less to fight for me, then this is why those who try to rule by brute strength on the contrary only become weaker. The territory may come to them, but the people will abandon them. They may have accumulated much, but they will have accomplished little.[b] So even though the land they have to defend is increased, their means

165   to defend it are reduced, and this is why those who hold to enlarging themselves on the contrary only become diminished.

    All the feudal lords remember past dealings and keep resentments and do not forget their enemies. They look for holes in the big and strong state, and they take advantage of the big and strong state's

170   errors. That is a dangerous time for the big and strong state. He who truly understands how to be big and strong does not work at being strong. He deliberates with a view to obtaining the kingly mandate. He keeps his strength undivided and solidifies his virtue. Since he keeps his strength undivided, then the feudal lords cannot weaken

175   him. Since he solidifies his virtue, the feudal lords cannot diminish him. If there is no true king or hegemonic ruler in the world, then he will always be victorious. Such is one who understands the way of being strong.

    The hegemon is not so: He opens up farmland, fills up his grana-

180   ries, and makes ready supplies. He then carefully recruits and selects by review men of talent and skill. Thereafter, he advances honors and rewards in order to encourage them, and he makes strict penalties and punishments in order to restrain them. He preserves those about to perish and reinstates lineages which have been broken off. He

185   protects the weak and suppresses the violent. If he does this all without a heart bent on taking over others, then the feudal lords will have affection for him. If he cultivates a way of befriending his rivals, and treats the feudal lords with reverence, then the feudal lords will delight in him. The reason they have affection for him is that he does

190   not try to take them over. If there should be any appearance of taking them over, then the feudal lords will distance themselves from him. The reason they delight in him is that he befriends his rivals. If there should be any appearance of making them subjects, then the feudal lords will abandon him. Hence, he makes clear to them that his con-

195   duct really does not aim at taking over others, and he gets them to trust that his way really is to befriend his rivals. If there is no true king or hegemonic ruler in the world, then he will always be victorious. King Min was destroyed by the five states, and Duke Huan was coerced by Duke Zhuang of Lu. These things happened for no other

reason than that they did not follow this way and instead deliberated   200
with a view to becoming king.

The true king is not so: His *ren* towers over the world. His *yi* towers
over the world. His awe-inspiring authority towers over the world.
His *ren* towers over the world, and so no one in the world fails to have
affection for him. His *yi* towers over the world, and so no one in the   205
world fails to honor him. His awe-inspiring authority towers over the
world, and so no one in the world dares to oppose him. He uses this
unopposed awe-inspiring authority to assist his way of making people submit, and so he is victorious without engaging in battle, and
makes gains without attacking people. Without labors of weapons   210
and armor, the whole world submits to him. Such is one who understands the way of a true king. For one who understands these two
means,[9] if he wishes to become a true king, then he becomes a true
king. If he wishes to become a hegemon, then he becomes a hegemon. If he wishes to be strong, then he is strong.   215

The character of a true king is that he ornaments his every move
with ritual and *yi*. He hears and decides cases in accordance with their
proper kinds. He holds up for clear inspection the fine points of
things. His policies adapt to changes endlessly. This is called having
a proper source [of action]. Such is the character of a true king.   220

The rule of a true king is such that his ways do not go back beyond
the Three Dynasties, and his models do not deviate from the later
kings. If a person's way goes back beyond the Three Dynasties, he
calls it reckless. If a person's model deviates from the later kings, he
calls it unrefined. His clothing and garments are properly regulated.   225
His palaces and homes have their proper measure. His followers have
their proper order. In funerals and sacrifices, the implements all accord with rank and proper position. As for music, everything that is
not refined music is discarded. As for sights, everything that is not the
patterns of old is discontinued. As for implements, everything that is   230
not the equipment of old is destroyed. This is called recovering the
ancient ways. Such is the rule of a true king.

The judgments of a true king are such that those without virtue are
not honored, those without ability are not given office, those without
meritorious accomplishment are not rewarded, and those without   235
criminal trespass are not punished. In the court, no one obtains their
position through luck. Among the people, no one obtains a livelihood through luck.[10] He elevates the worthy and employs the capable, and no ranks and positions are left unattended. He cuts off false

---

[9] The text does not make it clear exactly what the "two means" are, but they might be
the ruler's invincible authority and his method of making people submit. Some editions of the *Xunzi* have "three means" here instead, in which case the "three" would
likely be the means for becoming a king, becoming a hegemon, or being strong.

[10] See 10.97–99.

240 shows of virtue[c] and prohibits brutality, but his punishments and penalties are not excessive. The common people then all clearly understand that if they do good deeds among their family they will receive rewards in the court, and if they do bad deeds in secret they will suffer punishment in the open. This is called having fixed judgments.

245 Such are the judgments of a true king.

On the graduated taxation and governmental actions of a true king: He uses the myriad things as resources, and this is his means to nourish the people. He only takes one-tenth of the produce from the fields. The mountain passes and markets are overseen but no fees are

250 collected. The exploitation of mountain forests and dammed marshes is not taxed, but is prohibited in certain seasons. He measures up the quality of the land and adjusts his government policies accordingly. He reckons upon the distance of the route and requires contributions accordingly. He causes resources, goods, and grain to circulate with-

255 out delays and causes each to move to its appropriate place, so that the region within the four seas becomes like a single family. Thus, those nearby do not hide their abilities, and those far away are not troubled by the required labor. Among the isolated and remote states, all quickly send envoys and take comfort and delight in him.[11] This is

260 called being the teacher of the people. Such is the model of a true king. In the area of the northern sea, there are swift-running horses and barking dogs. However, the central states get to raise and employ them. In the area of the southern sea, there are bright feathers, ivory, tough hides, bronze, and beautiful stones. However, the central states

265 get to use them as resources. In the area of the eastern sea, there are purple fabrics, fish, and salt. However, the central states get to use them for clothing and food. In the area of the western sea, there are hide armors and patterned banners. However, the central states get to use them. Thus, people in the marshes are provided sufficiently

270 with wood, and people in the mountains are provided sufficiently with fish. The farmers neither carve wood nor craft ceramics, but they are provided sufficiently with tools. The craftsmen and merchants do not plow fields, but they are provided sufficiently with vegetables and grains. And so, although the tiger and leopard are ferocious animals,

275 the gentleman nevertheless has them skinned and makes use of them. Thus, all the areas covered by Heaven and all the areas supported by Earth produce their finest goods and contribute them for use. Above, they decorate good and worthy men. Below, they nourish the common people and bring them comfort and joy. This is called great

280 spirit-like power.[12] The *Odes* says:

---

[11] This same sentence appears at 15.329–30, where the idea of the "teacher of the people" is also mentioned.

[12] As I understand it, this statement is supposed to describe the true (sage) king, in virtue of the fact that his government policies bring about the situation described

Heaven made the high mountain.
The Great King opened the land.
These works were completed,
And King Wen made them more grand.[13]

This expresses my meaning.   285

Use the proper categories to manage muddled cases, and use the
one right standard manage the myriad situations, beginning and then
ending, ending and then beginning again, just like the way that a
jade loop has no endpoints. If you abandon these things, then the
whole world will consequently fall into decline. Heaven and Earth   290
are the beginning of life. Ritual and *yi* are the beginning of order. The
gentleman is the beginning of ritual and *yi*. Practicing them, habitu-
ating oneself in them, accumulating great regard for them, making
oneself fond of them—these are the beginning of becoming a gentleman. Thus, Heaven and Earth give birth to the gentleman, and the   295
gentleman brings order to Heaven and Earth. The gentleman is a
third partner to Heaven and Earth, a supervisor for the myriad things,
and mother and father to the people. If there were no gentleman,
then Heaven and Earth would not be properly ordered, and ritual
and *yi* would be without a unifying guide. Above, there would be no   300
lords or teachers, and below, there would be no fathers and sons.
Such a state is called utmost chaos. When the positions of lord and
minister, father and son, older brother and younger brother, husband
and wife all begin and then end, end and then begin again;[14] when
they are part of the same order with Heaven and Earth, and persist as   305
long as the myriad generations—this is called the great root.[15] And so,
funerals, sacrifices, court appearances, royal greetings, and military
matters all proceed by this one standard. Ennobling and degrading,
killing and giving birth, and bestowing and taking all proceed by this
one standard. To treat the lord as lord, the minister as minister, the   310

---

in the lines that precede this remark. Regarding "spirit-like power" (*shen* 神), see
chapter 1, note 10.

[13] Mao #270. The Great King is King Wen's grandfather, Gu Gong Danfu. According
to traditional stories, he moved the Zhou people to the Qishan area of what is now
Shaanxi province and founded a city there. This quotation seems intended to illustrate how the true king arranges for optimal use of human products and natural
resources. Compare the citation of this poem at 17.103–6.

[14] The Chinese at this juncture is ambiguous. As I understand it, here the cycle of
"beginning and ending and beginning again" refers primarily to the way that these
various roles, and especially the proper relations between them, can be maintained
over time by different people faithfully carrying out these positions. (E.g., in one
sense, the pact of marriage between a husband and wife ends when one of them
dies, but when their child weds and exchanges vows with his or her spouse, another
marriage begins.) The point is that such relations *should* be so maintained, as the
text goes on to say, over "myriad generations."

[15] I.e., the great root of social order, which is the foundation for all other goods in life.

father as father, the son as son, the elder brother as elder brother, and the younger brother as younger brother all proceed by this one standard.[16] To treat the farmer as farmer, the officer as officer, the craftsman as craftsman, and the merchant as merchant all proceed by this
315 one standard.

Water and fire have *qi* but are without life. Grasses and trees have life but are without awareness. Birds and beasts have awareness but are without *yi*. Humans have *qi* and life and awareness, and moreover they have *yi*.[17] And so they are the most precious things under Heaven.
320 They are not as strong as oxen or as fast as horses, but oxen and horses are used by them. How is this so? I say it is because humans are able to form communities while the animals cannot. Why are humans able to form communities? I say it is because of social divisions. How can social divisions be put into practice? I say it is because of
325 *yi*. And so if they use *yi* in order to make social divisions, then they will be harmonized. If they are harmonized, then they will be unified. If they are unified, then they will have more force. If they have more force, then they will be strong. If they are strong, then they will be able to overcome the animals. And so they can get to live in homes
330 and palaces. Thus, the reason why humans can order themselves with the four seasons, control the myriad things, and bring benefit to all under Heaven is none other than that they are able to get these social divisions and *yi*. And so human life cannot be without community. If humans form communities but are without social divisions, then they
335 will struggle. If they struggle, then there will be chaos.[18] If there is chaos then they will disband. If they disband then they will be weak. If they are weak then they cannot overcome the animals. And so they will not get to live in homes and palaces. This is the meaning of saying that "one must not let go of ritual and *yi* for even a moment."
340 One who can use these to serve his parents is called filial. One who can use these to serve his elder brother is called a proper younger brother. One who can use these to serve his superiors is called properly compliant. One who can use these to employ his subordinates is called a proper lord. The true lord is one who is good at forming
345 community.[19] When the way of forming community is properly practiced, then the myriad things will each obtain what is appropriate for them, the six domestic animals will each obtain their proper growth, and all the various living things will obtain their proper life spans.

[16] Compare *Analects* 12.11.
[17] Compare 5.104–21.
[18] Compare 10.105–8.
[19] Here Xunzi is playing upon that fact that the words "lord" (*jun* 君) and "community" (*qun* 群) were very similar in both pronunciation and written form during ancient times (a similarity that one can still perceive in their present pronunciations and written forms).

And so, when nurturing accords with the proper times, then the six domestic animals will multiply. When reaping accords with the 350 proper times, then the grasses and trees will flourish. If government commands accord with the proper times, then the common people will be united, and good and worthy men will submit and obey.

These are the regulations of a sage king: When the grasses and trees are flowering and abundant, then axes and hatchets are not to 355 enter the mountains and forests, so as not to cut short their life, and not to break off their growth. When the turtles and crocodiles, fish and eels are pregnant and giving birth, then nets and poisons are not to enter the marshes, so as not to cut short their life, and not to break off their growth. Plow in the spring, weed in the summer, harvest in 360 the fall, and store in the winter. These four activities are not to miss their proper times, and then the five grains will not be depleted, and the common people will have a surplus to eat. Be vigilant in the seasonal prohibitions concerning ponds, rivers, and marshes, and then turtles and fish will be fine and plentiful, and the common people will 365 have a surplus to use. Cutting and nurturing are not to miss their proper times, and then the mountains and forests will not be barren, and the common people will have surplus materials.[20]

This is the way a sage king operates: He observes Heaven above, and applies this knowledge on Earth below. He arranges completely 370 everything between Heaven and Earth and spreads beneficence over the myriad things.

> His actions are subtle, yet they are shining.
> Though they are brief, their results are long-lasting.
> Their scope is narrow; their impact, wide-ranging. 375

He has spirit-like powers of intelligence that are broad and vast, yet work by the utmost restraint. Thus it is said: the person who by even the slightest movements always does what is right is called a sage.[21]

The Proper Order for Officials: The Master of Cups oversees the arrangements of sacrificial animals for hosting guests, for making of- 380 ferings, and for banquets. The Director of Workers oversees the arrangements of the hundred ancestral clans, of building city walls, and of provision of implements. The Director of Cavalry oversees the arrangements of military campaigns, of weapons and armor, and of chariots and foot troops. The work of the Music Master is to cultivate 385 government regulations and orders, to keep watch over poetry and artistic form, to prohibit perverse music, and to smoothly cultivate these tasks at the appropriate times, so as to prevent barbarian, vul-

---

[20] Compare this paragraph with *Mencius* 1A3.
[21] The text of this paragraph is very difficult, and the translation is tentative.

gar, and deviant tunes from daring to disorder the refined pieces. The
390 work of the Director of Public Works is to repair dikes and bridges,
to open up gutters and ditches, to make water drainages flow, to
make water reservoirs secure, and to dam these up or release them at
the appropriate times, so that even if the year is poor due to flooding
or drought, the farmers still to have something to reap. The work of
395 the Overseer of Fields is to size up high and low ground, to inspect
for rich or poor soil, to arrange the five seeds, to assess agricultural
endeavors, to keep careful watch over harvesting and storing, and to
smoothly cultivate these tasks at the appropriate times, so that the
farmers are dedicated in their work and restrict their efforts in other
400 areas. The work of the Master of Provisions is to cultivate the regulations concerning burn-off, to nurture the mountains, forests, marshes,
trees, grasses, fish, turtles, and the hundred necessities, and to prohibit collecting these or to open them up at the appropriate times, so
that the state and families have sufficient supplies for their uses, but
405 resources and goods are not depleted. The work of the Village Master
is to make districts and neighborhoods harmonious, to demarcate
dwellings, to nurture the six domestic animals, to train people in
horticulture, to encourage transformative teaching, to foster filial
piety and good brotherly behavior, and to smoothly cultivate these
410 tasks at the appropriate times, so that the common people will comply with orders and peacefully and happily dwell in their villages. The
work of the Master of Craftsmen is to judge the hundred craftsmen,
to keep watch over the seasonal tasks, to distinguish between success
and failure, to honor perfection and usefulness, and to prepare equip-
415 ment and materials so that people do not dare to make up ways of
carving, polishing, and patterning by themselves at home. The work
of the hunchbacked shamans and lame-footed seers is to assess the
yin and the *yang*, to divine the omens and portents, to drill the tor-
toise-shells and lay out the hexagrams,[22] to preside over ceremonies
420 for warding off ills, selecting lucky days, and the five prognostica-
tions, and to know good and bad fortune, the auspicious and the
inauspicious. The work of the Overseer of Cities is to cultivate clean-
ing, to make the roads easy to pass, to watch out for robbers and
murderers, to keep the prices of lodging fair,[d] and to cultivate these
425 tasks at the appropriate times, so that guests and travelers will be
secure and goods and wealth will flow. The work of the Director of
Justice is to strike down false shows of virtue[e] and prohibit brutality,
to prevent licentiousness and eliminate perversity, and to discipline
such behavior with the five punishments, so that violent, brutal peo-

---

[22] This is a reference to ancient practices of divination. The "hexagrams" are the series
of broken and unbroken lines that make up the main portion of the *Yijing*, or *Book
of Changes*.

ple are reformed, and vile, perverse people do not appear. The work 430
of the Grand Overseer is to lay the grounds for government by education, to set straight the laws and standards, to hear all sorts of cases
and at the appropriate times to supervise [the laws], to measure people's accomplishments, to judge rewards and penalties, and to carefully cultivate these tasks at the appropriate times, so that the hun- 435
dred administrators are completely diligent and their many underlings
are not lazy. The work of the Grand Duke is to judge rituals and
music, to make correct his personal conduct, to broaden the transformative influence of teaching, to beautify the customs of the state, and
to superintend all these things and harmonize and unify them. The 440
work of the Heavenly King is to make perfect his practice of the Way
and virtue, to achieve a lofty and elevated state, to reach the utmost
in proper form and good order, to unify the whole world, and to set
aright even the smallest matters, so that the whole world compliantly
sides with him and submits to following him. Thus, if governmental 445
affairs are chaotic, it is the fault of the Grand Overseer. If the states
and great clans lack their proper customs, it is the fault of the Grand
Duke. If the world is not unified, and if the feudal lords make rebelling their custom, then the one occupying the position of Heavenly
King is not the right person. 450

When one has prepared the means to become a true king, one will
become a true king. Or when one has prepared the means to become
a hegemon, one will become a hegemon. Or when one has prepared
the means to barely survive, one will barely survive. Or when one has
prepared the means to perish, one will perish. The person who uses a 455
state of ten thousand chariots is the one who causes its strength to be
established, its reputation to be fine, and its rivals to yield before it.
Control over whether or not the state is secure or endangered,
whether it is well run or badly run, all rests here with him, not with
others. Control over whether I become a true king, or become a he- 460
gemon, or barely survive securely, or live in danger, or am destroyed,
all rests in me, not with others. If one's strength is not sufficient to
intimidate one's neighbors and rivals, and if one's reputation is not
sufficient to hang over the whole world,[23] then this is because one's
state cannot yet stand on its own, and so how could one avoid being 465
tied up with troubles? When the world is threatened by violent states
and my allies do what I myself do not want in these circumstances,
then even though daily I share in the acts and the conduct of a Jie,
this does no harm to my becoming a Yao.[24] For those things are not
wherein merit and reputation accrue, not wherein survival or destruc- 470

---

[23] I.e., to hold sway over everyone.
[24] From here to the chapter's end, in many places the text is difficult and likely corrupt, so the translation is tentative.

tion, security or danger fall. What merit and reputation accrue to, and where survival and destruction, security and danger fall to, will surely be that wherein my joy and pain,[f] my true heart, are located. He who truly makes his state the place of a true king will become a
475 true king. He who makes his state a place of danger and destruction will be endangered and destroyed.

On the day when one has things aright,[g] accordingly one will stand neutral, without leaning to one side and engaging in the affairs of the Vertical and Horizontal alliances.[25] Calmly one will halt one's mili-
480 tary and remain still, and instead watch the violent states finish each other off. Accordingly, one will make one's government and education evenhanded, inspect one's regulations, and hone the common people, and on the day when one accomplishes this, then one's military will dominate as the mightiest in all the world. Accordingly, one
485 will cultivate *ren* and *yi*, achieve an exalted and lofty character, set straight laws and standards, pick out good and worthy men, and nourish the common people. On the day when one accomplishes this, then one's reputation will dominate as the finest in all the world. When one's power is weighty, one's soldiers mighty, and one's reputa-
490 tion fine, then not even Yao and Shun, in the way they unified the world, could add anything to this. When people who scheme after power and plot overthrows are withdrawn from court, then, accordingly, men who are good and worthy, wise and sagely, will naturally come forward. When one's punishments and government are even-
495 handed, when the common people are compliant, when the state's customs are well-regulated, then one's soldiers will be mighty and one's city walls secure. Accordingly, rival states will naturally yield. When one works at the fundamental tasks,[26] accumulates wealth and goods, and does not recklessly indulge or waste, this will cause one's
500 various ministers and the common people all to proceed according to proper order and due measure. Then wealth and goods will accumulate, and accordingly the state will naturally become rich. When one has embodied these three things,[27] then the whole world will submit. Accordingly, the lord of a violent state will naturally not be able to
505 use his military against me. Why is this? Because he will have no one to come with. Those who might come with him would surely be his own people. But his people's love for me will be like the joy they take in their own parents. Their fondness for me will be like the way they

[25] The "Vertical" (north-south) alliance was an alliance of states formed to combat the rising power of the state of Qin. The "Horizontal" (east-west) alliance was an alliance of states formed to support Qin. The two sides were involved in various political intrigues against each other.

[26] I.e., agriculture.

[27] I.e., getting good people in government, making one's rivals yield, and enriching the state.

are attracted to the fragrance of orchids or sesame. Looking back, they will regard their own superiors like the punishments of branding and tattooing, or like mortal enemies. Even though the people's disposition and nature were the same as Jie or Robber Zhi, how would they be willing to do what they hate in order to do villainy to those whom they like? I will already have seized them.[28] Thus, among the ancients there were people who could take over the whole world with only a single state. This was not because they traveled about to do this. Rather, they cultivated and governed their own places, and so everyone longed for them. When they did this, then they could punish the violent and prohibit brutality. Thus, when the Duke of Zhou led his punitive campaign to the south, the northern states complained, "Oh why does he not come here only?" When he led his punitive campaign to the east, the western states complained, "Oh why does he put us alone last?" Who could fight with such a one? Accordingly, one who uses his state to do these things will become a true king.

Or, on the day when one has things aright, accordingly one will still one's military and rest one's subjects, and take loving care of the common people. One will open up fields and grasslands, fill up the granaries, and make ready supplies. Accordingly, one will carefully recruit and select by review men of talent and skill. Thereafter, one will advance honors and rewards in order to encourage them, and make strict penalties and punishments in order to prevent them from doing wrong. One will select men who understand affairs and cause them to lead and control each other. Then one will engage in ample storing up and repairing, and goods and supplies will become sufficient. While others are daily exposing and breaking their weapons, armor, and materiel on the central plains, I will be repairing mine, resting them, and keeping them covered in my storehouses. While others are daily dissipating and wasting their goods, wealth, and grain in the central grasslands, I will be storing and collecting mine in my granaries. While others are daily using up their men of skill and talent, their top aides, their strong and brave men who fight tooth and nail, through clashing and breaking them against the enemy, I will be drawing them to my side, reviewing and incorporating them, and honing them in my court. When things are thus, then the others will daily accumulate faults, and I will daily accumulate perfections. The others will daily accumulate poverty, and I will daily accumulate wealth. The others will daily accumulate toils, and I will daily accumulate ease. While through harshness the relation between lord and ministers, superiors and subordinates will daily become more es-

510

515

520

525

530

535

540

545

550

---

[28] I.e., The virtuous ruler will have captured their hearts before any conflict could begin.

tranged and hateful among the others, through kindness it will become more close and loving on my side. I will use these things to face against their faults. Accordingly, one who uses his state to do these things will become a hegemon.

555 Or, in establishing one's character, one may follow vulgar customs. In carrying out affairs, one will accord with vulgar reasons. In promoting and demoting people, ennobling and debasing them, one will elevate vulgar men. The way such a person interacts with the common people below is to treat them with vulgar kindness. Such a one 560 will barely survive securely.

Or, in establishing one's character, one may be flippant and crude. In carrying out affairs, one will work at promulgating dubious schemes. In promoting and demoting people, ennobling and debasing them, one will elevate silver-tongued and crafty men. The way 565 such a person interacts with the common people below is to be fond of taking from them and invading and stealing from them. Such a one will be endangered.

Or, in establishing one's character, one may be arrogant and violent. In carrying out affairs, one will engage in overthrows. In pro- 570 moting and demoting people, ennobling and debasing them, one will elevate dark and dangerous men, men who are deceitful and act for ulterior motives. The way such a person interacts with the common people below is to be fond of using their dying efforts, but to be slow in recognizing their labors and merit. He is fond of using their tax 575 revenues, but forgets about their fundamental works. Such a one will be destroyed.

One must carefully choose from among these five grades. For they are the means for becoming a true king, or becoming a hegemon, or barely surviving securely, or living in danger, or being destroyed. He 580 who chooses well from among them will control others. He who does not choose well from among them will be controlled by others. He who chooses well from among them will become a true king. He who does not choose well from among them will be destroyed.[29] The distance between being king and being destroyed, between controlling others and being controlled by others—is it not great indeed!

---

[29] Here, in an untranslatable pun, Xunzi plays on the fact that during ancient times the terms for "become king" (王) and "be destroyed" (亡) were very close in pronunciation and rhymed with each other; in contemporary Mandarin, both now have the same pronunciation, *wang*.

CHAPTER 10

Enriching the State

The myriad things share the same cosmos and have different bodies. They have no intrinsic fittingness but are useful for humans. This is simply the arrangement of the world. Various grades of people live together. They share the same pursuits but have different ways. They share the same desires but have different understandings. This is sim- ply the way they are born. Everyone approves of something, and in this the wise and the stupid are the same. Yet, what they approve of differs, and this is what divides the wise from the stupid.[1] If people's authority is equal but they understand things differently, if they act for selfish gain and do not fear disaster, if they let their desires run wild without end, then the people's hearts will be stirred up and can- not be appeased. If the situation is thus, then the wise will not get controlling power. If the wise do not get controlling power, then no recognition of merit will be made. If no recognition of merit is made, then there will be no distinction among the masses. If there is no distinction among the masses, then the positions of lord and minister will not be established. If there is no lord to regulate ministers, no superior to regulate inferiors, then all under Heaven will suffer harm from letting their desires run wild.

People all desire the same things and all hate the same things. But while their desires are many, the things to satisfy them are few, and since they are few, people are sure to struggle over them. Thus, the products of the hundred crafts are means to nurture a person, but even the most capable cannot engage in every craft, nor can people each fill every official post. If they live apart and do not help each other, then they will be impoverished. If they live together but have no social divisions, then they will struggle with each other. Poverty is a catastrophe, and struggle is a disaster. If you wish to save them from catastrophe and eliminate disaster, then nothing is better than to make clear social divisions and so employ the masses. If the strong threaten the weak, if the wise terrorize the stupid, if the people below disregard their superiors, if the young bully their elders, if you do not govern by virtue—if it is like this, then the old and the weak will face the worry of losing their means of nurture, and those in their prime will face the disaster of divisive struggle. Work and labor are what people dislike, and merit and profit are what they are fond of. But if there is no division of occupations, then people will face the catastro-

5

10

15

20

25

30

35

---

[1] For more on the notion of "approval," see 22.275–300.

phe of trying to complete their work by themselves and the calamity of struggling over merit. If the concord between male and female and
40   the division between husband and wife are without rituals for introduction, betrothal, and marriage, then people will face the worry of losing concord and the disaster of struggling over mates. And so, the wise person makes divisions for these things.

The way to ensure sufficiency for the state is to keep expenditures
45   frugal, to enrich the people, and to store up well any surplus. One keeps expenditures frugal through ritual, and one enriches the people through government. When one enriches the people, then there will be great surplus. For when one enriches the people, then the people will be wealthy. When the people are wealthy, then the fields
50   will be fat and well maintained. When the fields are fat and well maintained, then their yield will be a hundred times greater. Those above take from this according to the proper model, and those below keep their expenditures of it frugal according to ritual. The surplus will then pile up like hills and mountains. If one does not occasionally
55   burn some of it up, one will have no place to store it. So, what worry would the gentleman have about lacking a surplus? Thus, one who knows how to keep expenditures frugal and to enrich the people is sure to have a reputation for being *ren* and *yi*, for being sagely and good, and he will moreover have an accumulated wealth like hills and
60   mountains. There is no other reason for these things; they are produced from keeping expenditures frugal and enriching the people.

If one does not know to keep expenditures frugal and to enrich the people, then the people will be poor. When the people are poor, then the fields will be starved and failing. When the fields are starved and
65   failing, then their yield will not even reach half of what is normal. Then, even should those above be fond of taking from the people and invading and stealing from them, they will still have a paltry harvest, and some will even try to keep expenditures frugal without ritual. As a result, they will have a reputation for being greedy for profit and
70   rapacious, and their true income will be empty and depleted. There is no other reason for these things than not understanding how to keep expenditures frugal and how to enrich the people. The "Announcement to the Prince of Kang" says, "How vastly all-covering is Heaven! Accord with virtue and you will enrich your person."[2] This
75   expresses my meaning.

In ritual, noble and lowly have their proper ranking, elder and youth have their proper distance, poor and rich, humble and emi-

---

[2] The "Announcement to the Prince of Kang" is a chapter in the *Documents*. See Waltham (1971, p. 148). Xunzi's quotation differs from the received version of the *Documents* and seems to convey a somewhat different point.

nent, each have their proper weights.[3] Thus, the Son of Heaven wears a red dragon-robe and a high ceremonial cap. The feudal lords wear black dragon-robes and high ceremonial caps. The grand officers wear lesser robes and high ceremonial caps. The regular officers wear fur caps and plain robes. One's virtue must have a matching position, one's position must have a matching salary, and one's salary must have matching uses. The officers on up must be regulated by ritual and music. The masses and the commoners must be controlled by legal arrangements. One surveys the territory and then establishes the state. One calculates the benefits and then raises one's people. One measures people's strengths and then assigns tasks. One makes it so that the people are sure to be equal to their tasks, their tasks are sure to issue in benefit, and the benefits will be sufficient to nurture the people. One makes it so that in every case the incomes and expenditures of clothing, food, and miscellaneous goods fit each other, and then one makes sure to store up any excess in a timely manner. This is called a "balanced arrangement." And so, one extends this from the Son of Heaven down to the commoners, no matter how great or how little their tasks, no matter how many or how few their tasks. Thus it is said, "In the court, no one obtains their position through luck. Among the people, no one obtains a livelihood through luck."[4] This expresses my meaning. Lighten taxes on the fields, make fair the tariffs at markets and passes, lower the numbers of merchants, rarely raise *corvée* labor parties, and do not drag people away during the times for agricultural work.[5] If one does these things, then the state will be rich. This is called enriching the people through government.

In order for people to live, they cannot be without community. If they form communities but lack social divisions then they will struggle with each other. If they struggle with each other then there will be chaos, and if there is chaos they will be impoverished.[6] Thus, to lack social divisions is the greatest harm to people, and to have social divisions is the root benefit for the whole world. And the lord of men is the pivot and crucial point in controlling social divisions. Thus, to adorn them is to adorn the root for the whole world. To make them secure is to secure the root for the whole world. To honor them is to honor the root for the whole world. In ancient times, the former kings divided up people and differentially ranked them. Thus, they caused some to be praised and others disdained, some to be generously pro-

---

[3] Compare 19.20–23. The wording of the next few sentences after this one is very similar to a passage at 27.27–31.

[4] See 9.236–38.

[5] Compare 11.681–84.

[6] See 9.333–35.

vided for and others thinly provided for, some to live in ease and leisure, others to live in labor and toil. They did not do this to gain a reputation for perversity, arrogance, and self-aggrandizement.

120 Rather, they did it in order to make clear the proper forms for *ren*, and in order to promote the smooth operations of *ren*. Thus, they created carving and inlay, insignias and patterns. They caused them to be sufficient to distinguish noble and lowly, and that is all. They did not seek to make them eye-catching. They created percussion in-

125 struments, stringed instruments, and wind instruments. They caused them to be sufficient to distinguish auspicious and inauspicious, to bring people together in joy, and establish harmony, and that is all. They did not seek anything more. They created palaces and homes, terraces and pavilions. They caused them to be sufficient to give shel-

130 ter from dry heat and wetness, to nurture people's virtue,[7] and to distinguish humble and eminent, and that is all. They did not seek anything beyond this. The *Odes* says:

> His emblems are made with fine carving.
> Gold and jade are used in their crafting.
135 > Spirited, spirited is my king!
> The whole world he is rectifying.[8]

This expresses my meaning.

As for being able to wear clothes of many colors, to eat foods of many flavors, to control many resources and goods, to bring together

140 everyone under Heaven and be lord over them—one has these things not so that one can engage in perversity and arrogance, but rather they are originally for the purpose of reigning as a true king over everyone under Heaven. In attempting to bring order to the myriad changes, to make use of the myriad things, to nurture the myriad

145 people, and to control all under Heaven, nothing is as good for doing this as the goodness of the person who is *ren*. This is because his wisdom and deliberations are sufficient to order people, his generosity is sufficient to comfort them, and his virtuous reputation is sufficient to transform them. If you obtain him, then there will be order. If you

150 lose him, then there will be chaos. The common people truly rely on his wisdom. Thus, they lead each other in toiling laboriously so they can give him ease, in order to nurture his wisdom. They truly admire his generosity. Thus, they will march out to die so that they can protect and save him, in order to nurture his generosity. They truly ad-

---

[7] The exact meaning of "virtue" (*de* 德) here is uncertain. In this context the word is perhaps best read in its root sense of "power," i.e., as a person's life force, the idea being that these architectural inventions help people survive.

[8] Mao #238. This quotation differs slightly from the received version. In its original context, this passage describes King Wen.

mire his virtue. Thus, they will make carving and inlay, insignias and   155
patterns so that they can adorn him, in order to nurture his virtue.
And so, when a person of *ren* serves as superior, then the common
people will honor him like Shang Di, they will love him like their own
parents, and they will happily march out to die for him.[9] There is no
other reason for this than that what they deem commendable in him   160
is truly fine, what they obtain from him is truly great, and the ways
they benefit from him are truly multitudinous. The *Odes* says:

> We shouldered loads, used our hands to pull carts,
> Filled wagons, and used oxen for hauling.
> Since our work here is finally complete,   165
> To our homes we shall now be returning.[10]

This expresses my meaning.

And so I say: The gentleman relies on virtue. The petty man relies
on strength.[11] Strength is the servant of virtue. The strength of the
common people awaits [the gentleman] and only then does it have   170
accomplishments. The community of the common people awaits him
and only then is it harmonious. The wealth of the common people
awaits him, and only then does it pile up. The circumstances of the
common people await him and only then are they comfortable. The
life span of the common people awaits him, and only then is it long.   175
Without him, relations between father and son will not be close.
Without him, relations between brothers will not be smooth.[12] Without him, relations between man and woman will not be happy.

> Through him, the young grow and mature.
> Through him, the old obtain nurture.   180

Thus it is said, "Heaven and Earth produce them, but the sage completes them." This expresses my meaning.

The current age is not like that.

> The superiors make hefty collections of money and so snatch
> away the people's wealth. They impose heavy taxes on the   185

---

[9] Compare the similar wording at 16.28–31.

[10] Mao #227. According to commentaries, this poem describes the feelings of men returning home after building a camp at the behest of their (sagely) rulers. Commentators on the *Xunzi* offer varying opinions about its relevance in this context, but
Yang Liang suggests very plausibly that the point is to illustrate how the common
people will work hard for a good superior.

[11] Given the lines that follow, "petty man" here is best understood in its political
sense, as the "lesser person," i.e., the commoner.

[12] Wording similar to this and the next few sentences appears at 27.200–6.

fields and so snatch away the people's food. They charge severe tariffs at passes and markets and so make difficulties for the people's affairs.[13]

190

And that is not all. They also engage in practicing entrapment, relying on deception, scheming after power, and plotting overthrows in order to completely delude and topple each other.[14] The common people all clearly recognize that they are corrupt, arrogant, and violent and will be greatly endangered and perish. Thus, some ministers assassinate their lords, and some subordinates kill their superiors;

195 they sell out their cities, betray their superior's regulations, and refuse to die in their service. These things happen for no other reason than that the ruler of men brings it upon himself. The *Odes* says, "No words will go unanswered. No virtue will go unrequited."[15] This expresses my meaning.

200 The way to provide universal sufficiency for all under Heaven rests with making clear social divisions. Irrigating the land and marking out plots,[a] cutting down weeds and planting grains, fertilizing often and fattening up the fields—these are the works of the farmers and the mass of commoners. Keeping watch over the seasons and putting

205 the people's strength to work, advancing projects and fostering accomplishments, harmonizing and organizing the common people, not letting them be lazy—these are the works of generals and leaders. Ensuring that high areas are not too dry and low-lying areas are not too wet, keeping cold and heat harmoniously regulated so that the

210 five grains ripen at the appropriate times—these are the works of Heaven. Universally keeping watch over the people, universally caring for them, universally ordering them, so that even when the year's harvest is ruined by drought or flood they will not face the disasters of freezing or starving—these are the works of sagely lords and their

215 worthy prime ministers.

In his teachings, Mozi worries very conspicuously about insufficiency for the whole world. However, insufficiency is not the common disaster facing the world. That is only Mozi's individual worry and erroneous reckoning. Now the way this soil gives birth to the five

220 grains is such that if people tend it well, a single *mu* of land will yield several bushels, and within a single year one can have two harvests. Beyond these, the melons, peaches, dates, and plums are such that from a single plant one may count the yield in bushels and drums. Beyond these, the greens and vegetables can grow so as to fill up

[13] These sentences are rhymed in the original.
[14] Compare the nearly identical wording at 15.225–26.
[15] Mao #256. These lines are rhymed in the original. Compare the use of this same quotation at 14.124.

whole swamps. Beyond these, in a single season the six domestic ani- 225
mals and other beasts can become [so numerous] as to fill up every
available cart. If the turtles, lizards, fish, and eel give birth at the
proper times, then in a single season they can form whole swarms.
Beyond these, the flying birds, ducks, and swans can become [so numerous as to be] like billows of smoke in the sky. Beyond these, the 230
insects and other myriad creatures live in the remaining space. Among
all these, there are countless that are edible. So, the way Heaven and
Earth give birth to the myriad things is such that there is originally
an abundance sufficient to feed people. The fibrous plants and silk
and the feathers, fur, teeth, and shells of the animals are originally in 235
abundance sufficient to clothe people. So, the question of abundance
or insufficiency is not the common disaster facing the world. That is
only Mozi's individual worry and erroneous reckoning.

Instead, the common disaster facing the world is that chaos harms
it. Why don't we inquire together into who it is that makes it chaotic? 240
I take it that Mozi's rejection of music will cause the world to be chaotic, and Mozi's advocacy of frugal expenditure will cause the world
to be impoverished. This is not an attempt to slander him. It is simply
that his teachings cannot avoid these results. If at his greatest Mozi
had possession of the whole world, or if at the least he had possession 245
of a single state, he would have people uncomfortably wearing coarse
clothes and eating bad food, and though they might be sad, he would
deny them music. If it were like this, then the state would be starved.
If the state were starved, then it could not provide satisfaction for
people's desires, and if it could not provide satisfaction for people's 250
desires, then rewards would not work. If at his greatest Mozi had
possession of the whole world, or if at the least he had possession of
a single state, he would reduce personnel and decrease the number of
officials. He would put foremost and regard with merit toils that are
laborious and bitter, dividing up the work evenly with the common- 255
ers and making equal all merit for labors. If it were like this, then the
state would not inspire awe, and if it did not inspire awe, then punishments would not work. If rewards do not work, then the worthy cannot be gotten to advance, and if punishments do not work, then the
unworthy cannot be gotten to withdraw. If the worthy cannot be 260
gotten to advance and the unworthy cannot be gotten to withdraw,
then the capable and incapable cannot be accorded their proper offices. If it were like this, then the myriad things would lose what is
appropriate to them, and when there were changes in circumstances,
one would lose out on the appropriate response. Above one would 265
lose out on Heaven's seasons, below one would lose out on Earth's
benefits, and in the middle one would lose harmony among mankind.
In that case, the whole world would be as though burned up or
scorched. Then, even if Mozi were to try to do something about it by

270 wearing crude garments, using a rope for a belt, eating only bean soup, and drinking only water, how could he make things sufficient? He would have already hacked away at the root of things and dried up their source, so that the whole world was scorched.

For these reasons, the former kings did not do things like this.
275 They understood that in the matter of being a lord and superior to others, to lack beautiful things and ornaments will leave one incapable of uniting the people, to lack wealth and generous endowments will leave one incapable of managing one's subordinates, and to lack strength and the power to inspire awe will leave one incapable of
280 stopping those who are violent and overcoming those who are brutal. Thus, the former kings were sure to strike great bells, beat sounding drums, blow on reeds and pipes, and play lyres and zithers, in order to fill up their ears. They were sure to have carving, polishing, engraving, and inlay, insignias and ornaments, in order to fill up their eyes.
285 They were sure to have fine meats and good grains, the five flavors and various spices, in order to fill up their mouths. Only afterward did they increase their personnel, set up official posts, promote rewards, and make strict punishments, in order to make the people's hearts watchful. They thereby caused all the people in the world to
290 know that what they wished for and desired lay here with the kings. Thus, their rewards worked. They caused the people to know that what they feared and dreaded lay here with the kings. Thus, their punishments inspired awe. When rewards work and punishments inspire awe, then the worthy can be gotten to advance and the unwor-
295 thy can be gotten to withdraw, and the capable and incapable can be accorded their proper offices. When it is like this, then the myriad things will obtain what is appropriate to them. When there are changes in circumstances, one will obtain the appropriate response. Above one will obtain the aid of Heaven's seasons, below one will
300 obtain Earth's benefits, and in the middle one will obtain harmony among mankind. Then, wealth and goods will flow forth as if from a spring, surge like rivers or seas, and pile up like hills and mountains, so that if one does not burn some of them from time to time, one will have no place to store them. What problems of insufficiency would
305 the world have?

Thus, if the methods of the *ru* are truly put into practice, then all under Heaven will be peaceful and prosperous. Put to work, the people will accomplish great things. Striking bells and beating drums, they will be harmonized. The *Odes* says:

310   *Huang huang*! Bells and drums play sonorously!
    Qiang qiang! Pipes and chimes sound resonantly!
    There is a rain of blessings in plenty.
    There is a rain of blessings tremendous.

Our decorum has been meticulous.
Having become drunk, having become full,[16]   315
Blessings and fortune are bestowed to us.[17]

This expresses my meaning.

On the other hand, if the methods of Mozi are truly put into practice, then all under Heaven will exalt frugality but will become only   320
poorer. The people will denounce fighting but will only struggle with
one another more each day. They will engage in laborious and bitter
toils, bent over and exhausted, but will only increasingly fail to have
accomplishments. Melancholy and sorrowful, they will denounce
music but will grow only less harmonious each day. The *Odes* says:
                                                                          325

Heaven is raining ills from the sky.
Great is the chaos, and many die.
No friendly words do the people cry.
Will you not repent or even sigh?[18]

This expresses my meaning.   330

If one neglects important tasks to nurture the common people,
coddling and babying them, making gruel for them in the winter and
giving them melons and porridge in the summer, in order to steal a
brief moment's praise from them, this is a thieving way.[19] In this manner, one can briefly obtain the vile common people's praise, but it is   335
not a way one can persist in for a long time. Important tasks are sure
not to be completed, and accomplishments are sure not to hold up,
for these are vile methods for governing. If one harshly works the
common people and rushes them to accord with the seasons, advancing tasks and developing achievements, taking bad reputation lightly   340
and being content with losing the people's affection, then tasks will
indeed be advanced, but the commoners will hate it. This also cannot
work, because it is merely stealing in another one-sided manner. It
moves toward self-destruction, falls into collapse and is, on the con-

---

[16] The Chinese does not indicate who is drunk and full. In its original context, the
subject is likely the spirits, who have partaken of the sacrificial offerings and so
bestow blessings. In the present context, the line might instead be taken as referring to the people performing the sacrifice, which would fit with the idea presented
earlier that the former kings partook of certain indulgences and thereby achieved a
well-ordered society (a "blessing").

[17] Mao #274. Xunzi's quotation differs slightly from the received version of the *Odes*.

[18] Mao #191. In their original context, these words are directed to a government official as criticism, and the penultimate line is understood by commentators as referring to complaints by the common people against this same official. Here it is imag-
ined that the common people will have no friendly words for Mozi's government,
and the last line is directed to him.

[19] Compare the end of 3.223–29.

trary, sure to result in no achievements. And so, neglecting important
tasks to nurture one's reputation cannot work, and pursuing achievements while forgetting about the people cannot work, because they
are both vile ways.

Thus, the ancients did not do things like this. They ensured that
the common people did not succumb to the heat in the summer and
that they did not freeze from cold in winter. They ensured that when
they hurried the common people, it was not to the point of harming
their strength, and when they allowed the common people to proceed slowly, they did not fall behind the seasons. Important tasks
were accomplished and their achievements were firmly established,
both superiors and subordinates were enriched, and the commoners
all felt affection for their superiors. The fact that people turned to
their leaders like water flowing down, loved them with the same
kind of delight they had for their own parents, and happily marched
out to die for them was for no other reason than that the superiors
had achieved the ultimate in loyalty, trustworthiness, harmoniousness, and evenhandedness.

And so, if the ruler of the state and leader of the people wishes to
keep up with the seasons and pursue achievements, then harmonious
adjustment, adding to the people's work and relieving them from it,
is more effective than rushing and hurrying them; practicing loyalty,
trustworthiness, and evenhandedness is more persuasive than offering them rewards and prizes; and making sure first to correct what
lies within oneself and only then slowly reprimand what lies with
others is more awe-inspiring than threatening them with penalties
and punishments. When these three virtues are truly present among
the superiors, then the subordinates will respond to them like a
shadow or echo. Even if those above desired neither glory nor success, could they avoid it? The *Documents* says, "Let you make greatly
brilliant those qualities which cause others to submit. Then the people will put their strength to work, acting harmoniously and with
speed."[20] This expresses my meaning.

And so, if one does not teach the people but simply executes them
[when they do wrong], then punishments will be abundant but perversity will not be overcome. If one simply teaches the people but
does not execute them [when they do wrong], then the vile people
among them will not be chastened. If one simply executes the people
[when they do wrong] but never rewards them [when they do good],
then the people who cleave to hard work will not be encouraged. If

---

[20] See *Shujing, Kanggao* ("The Announcement to the Prince of K'ang"), translated in
Waltham (1971, p. 148). Xunzi's quotation is slightly different from the received edition of the *Documents*, and he seems to be quoting these remarks without regard to
their original context, so the translation here is very different from the way most
commentators construe the passage as it appears in the *Documents*.

executions and punishments are not applied to the proper kinds of people, then subordinates will be confused about how to act, general custom will become unstable, and the common people will not be unified.

Hence, the former kings made clear ritual and *yi* in order to unify the people, cultivated loyalty and trustworthiness in order to make them love their superiors, elevated the worthy and employed the capable in order to cause proper gradations among them, and made gifts of positions, emblems, and other rewards in order to make them exert themselves and redouble their efforts. The former kings made the people's works accord with the times and lightened their burdens, in order to regulate them and bring them into line. Their broad concern included and covered all the people, and they nurtured and raised them, as though caring for a newborn. Since it was like this, vile and perverse people did not appear, robbery and villainy did not arise, and those who were transformed with goodness were encouraged. How was this possible? The ways of the former kings were easy for people to follow, the lessons with which they filled the people's hearts were solid, their government and orders were unified, and their levees and depth markers were clear.[21] Thus it is said, "When the superiors are of one mind, then the subordinates will be of one mind. When the superiors are of two minds, the subordinates will be of two minds." This expresses my meaning.

To profiteer from the people without profiting them is not as profitable as first profiting the people and then profiteering from them.[22] To work the people without showing them care does not produce as great achievements as first showing them care and then working them. To profit the people first and then profiteer from them is not as profitable as profiting the people and not profiteering from them. To show the people care first and then work them does not produce as great accomplishments as showing them care and not working them. He who can profit the people and not profiteer from them, show the people care and not work them, will win over all under Heaven. He who first profits the people and then profiteers from them, first shows them care and then works them, will preserve his altars of soil and grain. He who uses the people without profiting them, works them without showing them care, will endanger his state and clan.

---

21 "Levees and depth markers" appears to be a reference to rituals. See 17.238–41. See also 8.549–50.

22 In a word play that cannot be rendered easily in English, this paragraph makes use of the fact that the Chinese word *li* 利 can function as an adjective meaning "beneficial, profitable," a verb meaning "to bring benefit or profit to someone," or a verb meaning "to use, employ" (in either a negative or positive sense). I have translated the last usage as "to profiteer from" in order to reflect that the same word is being used throughout and to convey the negative tone it carries here.

In observing whether a state is well-ordered or chaotic, in good shape or not, when one arrives at the territorial boundaries the signs are already apparent. If the watchmen and patrols are sparse and the government controls at borders and passes involve extensive investi-
425 gations, this is simply the sign of a chaotic state. When one has entered the borders, if the fields are in poor condition and the urban areas are exposed to attack, this is simply the sign of a greedy ruler. If one observes the court and finds that the nobles are not worthy, if one observes the official staff and finds that those in charge are not
430 capable, if one observes the ruler's favorites and finds that those trusted are not honest, this is simply the sign of a benighted ruler. If everyone from the ruler to the prime minister to the officials on down to the various functionaries are exacting and extremely careful when it comes to the giving, receiving, and tallying of goods and wealth,
435 and their practice of ritual, *yi*, and proper regulations is lax and withered, this is simply the sign of a disgraced state.

If those doing the plowing delight in their fields, the soldiers are at ease in facing difficulties, the various functionaries are fond of the proper model, the court exalts ritual, and the high ministers investi-
440 gate and debate, this is simply the sign of a well-ordered state. If one observes the court and finds that the nobles are worthy, if one observes the official staff and finds that those in charge are capable, if one observes the ruler's favorites and finds that those trusted are honest, this is simply the sign of an enlightened ruler. If everyone from
445 the ruler to the prime minister to the officials on down to the various functionaries are generous and easygoing when it comes to the giving, receiving, and tallying of goods and wealth, and their practice of ritual, *yi*, and proper regulations is stringent and extremely careful, this is simply the sign of a glorious state. If, when those who are wor-
450 thy are all on a par, the ruler's relatives among them are first to be ennobled; if, when those who are capable are all on a par, the ruler's old friends among them are first to be given official positions; if among the ministers and various functionaries, those who are corrupt are all transformed and become cultivated, those who are brutal are
455 all transformed and become mild, and those who are conniving are all transformed and become honest, these are simply the signs of the accomplishments of an enlightened ruler.

In observing whether a state will be strong or weak, poor or rich, there are indicators and evidence to look for. If the superiors do not
460 exalt ritual, then the military will be weak. If the superiors do not care for the common people, then the military will be weak. If promises that have been made are not trustworthy, then the military will be weak. If prizes and rewards are not given out, then the military will be weak. If generals and leaders are not capable, then the military
465 will be weak. If the superiors are fond of engaging in offensive cam-

paigns and crave magnificent accomplishments, then the state will be poor. If the superiors are fond of profit, then the state will be poor. If there are great numbers of nobles and grand ministers, then the state will be poor.[23] If there are great numbers of craftsmen and merchants, the state will be poor.[24] If there are no regulations on quanti-   470
ties and no standards for measures, then the state will be poor. If those below are poor, then the superiors will be poor. If those below are rich, then the superiors will be rich.

And so, the fields and countryside are the starting point for wealth. Warehouses and granaries are the end point for wealth. Having the   475
common people harmonize with the seasons and having their work proceed in proper order is the fount from which goods come. Making assessments, collecting taxes, and putting them in storehouses are the channels by which goods flow away. An enlightened ruler is sure to be careful in nurturing harmony with the seasons, restricting the flow   480
of goods, opening up their fount, and pouring forth from it only at the appropriate times. Far and wide he causes all under Heaven to be sure of having surplus, and so superiors do not worry about insufficiency. When it is like this, then those above and those below are rich together, and for both there is no place to store all the goods—this is   485
the ultimate in knowing how to plan for the state. Thus, there were ten years of floods during the time of Yu, and there were seven years of drought during the time of Tang, and during those periods there was nothing[25] with the color of vegetation anywhere under Heaven, but after the tenth year,[26] the annual harvest of grain ripened again,   490
and when set out and piled up there was a surplus. There is no other reason for this—it is called understanding the starting point and the ending point, the fount and the flow of goods.

Thus, if the fields are bare but the state's granaries are full, and if the common people are drained but the state's storehouses are   495
packed, this is called a teetering state. When a state obliterates the starting point for goods, dries up their fount, and gathers them all at

---

23 Nobility and high-ranking government officials did not pay taxes, but instead received income from taxes on the common people, so the more nobility and officials there were, the less money was left for the common people and the state.

24 Xunzi's concern here seems to be that if craftsmen and merchants (who do not produce raw materials, but only rework them or trade them) outnumber the farmers (who do produce the raw materials), then the state will lack the basic resources it needs.

25 Many commentators read this instead as ". . . there was *nobody* with a green complexion [i.e., a complexion of illness due to starvation]." This is possible, but seems to fit less well with the contrasting point that immediately after the floods there was a surplus.

26 The commentator Gu Qianli suspects that there is a gap in the text here, and that it originally read "after the tenth year [in the one case], *and after the seventh year* [in the other case]. . . ." This seems likely to be right.

their ending point, but the ruler and prime minister nevertheless do not know that this is bad, then one can simply stand by and wait for
500 it be overthrown and destroyed. When one has the whole state as one's means of support but it is still insufficient to accommodate one's person, this is called utmost greediness. Such is the utmost foolish ruler. He seeks wealth but winds up losing his state. He seeks profit but winds up endangering his person. In ancient times there
505 were ten thousand states. Nowadays there are a few more than ten left among them. There is no other reason for this—the cause by which the others were lost is one and the same. May the lords of men be conscious of this! Even a state of merely a hundred *li* is sufficient to stand alone.
510   In all cases of those who launch offensive campaigns against others, if they are not acting for the sake of a good reputation, then they are acting for the sake of profit, or if for neither of those reasons, then it is because they are angry at those whom they attack. As for the way that a person of *ren* uses the state, he will cultivate his intentions and
515 thoughts, correct his person and conduct, achieve an exalted and lofty character, make himself loyal and trustworthy, and align himself with good form and proper order. If a man with only coarse clothes and roughly woven sandals were truly to do this, then even if he were to live in a poor neighborhood in a house with a leaky roof, kings and
520 dukes could not compete with him for a good reputation, and if he had the whole state to back him,[27] then no one in the world could obscure him. When the situation is like this, then those acting for the sake of a good reputation will not attack.
        The person of *ren* will open up farmland, fill up his granaries, and
525 make ready supplies. Then those above and those below will be of one mind, and the three armies will be united in strength. To vigorously pursue war far away against such a one will not work. His holdings within the borders are firmly guarded. When he sees that the time is right, he will meet the opposing army and strip it of its general
530 as easily as husking cooked grains. Even if the invader succeeds, it will not be enough to mend his injuries and make up for his losses. Such men jealously protect their claws and teeth and fear their enemies, so when the situation is like this, those acting for the sake of profit will not attack.
535   The person of *ren* will cultivate what is *yi* with respect to great and small states, strong and weak states, and maintain it carefully. His practice of ritual and proper regulation will display good form, his jade tablets and disks will be magnificent,[28] and his greeting gifts will

---

[27] I.e., if he were the lord of a state.
[28] According to ritual protocol, emissaries to a foreign state brought jades to give as tokens of good will.

be generous. The person whom he sends to persuade another lord will surely be a gentleman with refinement, good form, skill in argu- 540 ing, and great intelligence. If that lord has any human feelings in him at all, who would get angry at such a person? When the situation is like this, then those who get angry will not attack.

When those acting for the sake of good reputation will not attack, and those acting for the sake of profit will not attack, and those acting 545 for the sake of anger will not attack, then the state will be more solid than a great boulder and more long-lived than Ji and Yi.[29] Others will all be chaotic. I alone will be well-ordered. Others will all be endangered. I alone will be secure. Others will all lose their states. I alone will then rise up and take control of them. Thus, the way that a per- 550 son of *ren* uses the state is such that he will not merely hold on to what he possesses—he will also come to take in other people's states. The *Odes* says:

> As for the noble man and gentleman,
> Their standard does not err or deviate.[30]   555
> Their standard does not err or deviate.
> On all four sides they correct every state.[31]

This expresses my meaning.

On the hard way and the easy way to maintain a state: "To serve a violent state is hard, but to make a violent state serve oneself is easy." 560 If one serves it with goods and treasures, then one's goods and treasures will be depleted, and one's relations will still not be secure. If one signs treaties with it in good faith or makes covenants with it sealed by oaths, then even though the treaty is set, hardly a day will pass before it is violated. If one cuts off some measure of one's own 565 territory in order to bribe such a state, then even though the loss of territory is set, its greed will still not be satisfied. The more pains one goes to in serving it, the more it will encroach upon one. The situation will surely come to the point where one's resources are depleted and one's whole state is offered up, and only then will it stop. Even if 570 he had Yao as his advisor on the left and Shun as his advisor on the right, there has never been anyone who could escape from these things by following such a way. You can compare it to what would

---

[29] Ji and Yi were the names of stars.

[30] The basic meaning of the word *te* 忒 is "deviate," where this can refer simply to "change" from some previous state or, more particularly, to deviating from what is correct. Both senses are relevant here, but the latter seems primary for this context, so *te* is rendered as "err or deviate" to convey both the correctness and the constancy of the noble man and gentleman.

[31] Mao #152. The "four sides" are the four directions (north, south, east, west). Compare the use of this same quotation at 15.374–77 and 24.121–24.

happen if a maiden clasping precious pearls, wearing precious jade,
575 and carrying gold were to meet a bandit in the mountains. Even if she
averted her gaze from him, went with bowed waist and bent knee,
and acted compliantly like a household concubine, it still would not
be sufficient for her to escape him. Thus, this is not the way to hold
onto even a single person, and simply fearfully serving the violent
580 with ingratiating manner and politeness is not sufficient to maintain
a state or make one's person secure. For this reason, the enlightened
ruler does not follow this path.

Instead, he will surely cultivate ritual in order to set straight his
court. He will rectify his models for conduct in order to set straight
585 his officials. He will make his government evenhanded in order to set
straight the common people. Only then will the regulations be set
straight in his court, the hundred tasks set straight among his officials, and the masses set straight below. When the situation is like
this, then those close by will vie to draw near to him, and those far
590 away will send notice of their wish to submit to him. Those above and
those below will share one heart, and the three armies will merge their
strengths. His reputation will be enough to blaze over other states,
and his authority and strength will be enough to thrash them. He
need merely stand with hands clasped together and give directions,
595 and then none of the strong and violent states will fail to hurry in
doing his bidding.[32] One can compare it with what would happen if
Wu Huo[33] were to wrestle with a dwarf. Thus it is said, "To serve a violent state is hard, but to make a violent state serve oneself is easy."
This expresses my meaning.

[32] Compare the nearly identical wording at 15.201–3.
[33] A famous strongman from the state of Qin.

CHAPTER 11

The True King and the Hegemon

The state is the most efficacious instrument in the world, and to be ruler of men is the most efficacious power in the world. If you take the Way to hold onto these, then you will have great security and great honor—they will be a wellspring of accumulated goods. If you do not take the Way to hold onto them, then you will face great dan-   5
ger and great ignominy—it would be better not to have them. And in the most extreme circumstances, though you seek to finish your days as a commoner, you cannot get even that. Such was the case with King Min of Qi and King Xian of Song. Thus, although being ruler of men is the most efficacious power in the world, it is not secure of   10
itself. One who is to be secure in it must take hold of the Way.

So in using the state, if *yi* is established as your foundation, then you will be a true king. If trustworthiness is established as your foundation, then you will be a hegemon. If intrigues and schemes are established as your foundation, then you will perish. These three are   15
what the enlightened ruler carefully chooses among, and what the person of *ren* works to get clear about. He takes hold of the state so as to call forth ritual and *yi*, and does nothing to harm them. To perform one act contrary to *yi* or kill one innocent person and thereby gain the whole world is something that the person of *ren* would not   20
do. Like a stone—such is the fortitude with which he holds onto his heart and his state.

Those men with whom he collaborates in conducting the government are all men of *yi*. The punishments and laws he sets out for state and clan are all laws in accordance with *yi*. Those things which the   25
ruler is extremely vigorous in leading his various ministers to turn their heads to are all *yi* intentions. When it is like this, then those below will look up to those above for being *yi*. This is a case where the fundamental things are firmly settled. When the fundamental things are firmly settled, then the state will be firmly settled, and   30
when the state is firmly settled, then all under Heaven will be firmly settled.

Confucius lacked even so much land as to plant an awl in, but he sincerely cultivated *yi* in his thoughts and intentions, attached *yi* to his person and conduct, and made it clear in his words. From the days   35
he had perfected it, he has not been obscure in the world, and his name has been passed down to later generations. Now take also the most eminent feudal lord in the world. Let him sincerely cultivate *yi* in his thoughts and intentions, attach *yi* to his laws, standards, and

40   measures, make it clear in his governmental affairs, and accordingly
extend and reinforce it in the way he elevates some and lowers others,
executes some and lets others live, so that the end of one affair and
the beginning of the next are as though united seamlessly in it. When
it is like this, then the way his good reputation and fame will grow
45   and spread through all the space between Heaven and Earth will be
just like the light of sun and moon, or the sound of thunder, will it
not?

Hence it is said, "If one takes the state and aligns it with *yi*, then in
a single day one will become illustrious." Such was the case with Tang
50   and Wu. Tang used Bo, and King Wu used Hao—these were both
territories of merely a hundred *li* in size. But the world became united
under them, the feudal lords were their servants, and among those of
penetrating intelligence, none failed to submit and to follow. There is
no reason for this other than that they achieved perfection in *yi*. This
55   is what I mean by saying, "If *yi* is established as your foundation, then
you will be a true king."

There are some who, even though virtue is not yet completed in
them and *yi* is not yet perfected in them, nevertheless order and control for all under Heaven advances under them. Their punishments
60   and rewards and their promises to allow or not to allow things are
trusted by all under Heaven. Their ministers and subordinates all
clearly know that one can make pacts with them. When governmental
orders have been put forth, then even though they see opportunities
for gain or loss, they will not cheat their people. When covenants
65   have been settled upon, then even though they see opportunities for
gain or loss, they will not cheat their allies.

When it is like this, then their soldiers will be energetic and their
city walls solidly defended, and rival states will fear them. Their own
state will be united and its fundamental standards clear, and their
70   allied states will trust them. Then, even though they may reside in a
remote and backward state, their power to inspire awe will shake the
whole world. Such was the case with the five hegemons. They did not
base themselves on government through education.[1] They did not
strive to become exalted and lofty. They did not pursue the extremes
75   of culture and good order. They did not make people's hearts submit
willingly. They inclined to tactics and stratagems, paid attention to
fatigue and rest for troops, were careful to store up provisions, and
prepared the equipment necessary for war. Those above and those
below had mutual trust as tight as the way one's upper and lower
80   teeth come together, and no one under Heaven dared stand up to
them. Thus, Duke Huan of Qi, Duke Wen of Jin, King Zhuang of
Chu, King Helü of Wu, and King Goujian of Yue were all from re-

---

[1] Compare this and the following few sentences to 7.39–43.

mote and backward states, but their power to inspire awe shook the whole world, and their strength threatened the central states.[2] There is no other reason for this than that they mastered trustworthiness. 85 This is what I mean by saying, "If trustworthiness is established as your foundation, then you will be a hegemon."

There are some who take hold of the state so as to call forth personal accomplishments and profit. They do not work at developing yi or getting trustworthiness in order—they seek only profit. Within the 90 state, they are not afraid to deceive their people and obtain meager profits thereby. Outside the state, they are not afraid to deceive their allies and obtain great profits thereby. Within the state, they do not cultivate and set straight what they already hold, but they frequently desire the holdings of others. 95

When it is like this, the ministers, subordinates, and common people will all use deceptive hearts in dealing with their superiors. When superiors deceive their subordinates and subordinates deceive their superiors, then this is a case where superiors and subordinates are divided. When it is like this, then rival states will look down on them, 100 and allied states will be suspicious of them. Their intrigues and schemes may advance daily, but the state cannot avoid being endangered or having its territory diminished, and at the most extreme it will be destroyed. Such was the case with what happened between King Min of Qi and the Duke of Xue. Thus, in his activities to 105 strengthen Qi, the king did not act for the sake of cultivating ritual and yi, he did not act for the sake of government through education, and he did not act for the sake of uniting all under Heaven. Instead, he took as his constant task rushing envoys abroad continuously to form pacts and draw in others. Hence, Qi's strength was sufficient to 110 break Chu in the south, to bend back Qin in the west, to defeat Yan in the north, and to upturn Song in the center. But when the states were roused by Yan and Zhao to attack Qi together, it was like shaking a withered tree. The king of Qi perished and his state was destroyed, punished by all under Heaven. When later generations speak 115 of bad men, they are sure to mention him. There is no other reason for this than that he simply did not follow out ritual and yi, and instead followed out intrigues and schemes.

These three options are what the enlightened ruler carefully chooses among, and what the person of ren works to get clear about. 120 Those who choose well among them will control others, but those who do not choose well among them will be controlled by others.

The state is the greatest implement in the world, and the heaviest responsibility. You must be good at choosing a place for it and then positioning it there. If you put it in an unsafe position, then you will 125

---

[2] See the similar description of Qin at 16.268–69.

be endangered. You must be good at choosing a way for it and then guiding it along that way. If the path is overgrown and impassable then you will be blocked up. In you are in a dangerous place and blocked up there, then you will perish. In speaking of "the placing of 130 the state," the establishment of its boundaries is not what is meant.[3]

What models should one take as one's way? Which people[4] should one have as one's compatriots? So, he who takes for his way the models that make one a true king, and who runs the state together with people who are such as to make one a true king, will also become a 135 true king. He who takes for his way the models that make one a hegemon, and who runs the state together with people who are such as to make one a hegemon, will also become a hegemon. He who takes for his way the models that make a state perish, and who runs the state together with people who are such as to make a state perish, will 140 also perish. These three options are what the enlightened ruler carefully chooses among, and what the person of *ren* works to get clear about.

Thus, the state is a heavy responsibility to bear. If one does not use what has been accumulated[5] to support it, then it will not stand. 145 [Perhaps someone might ask:][6] But the state is such that what it relies upon to support it is new with each generation. That way of doing things would be to reject change fearfully.[a] "With a change in throne comes a change in tone."[7] Thus, for a single dawn there is just this sun, and for a single day there are just these people. That being the 150 case, how can there be any state that securely remains firm for a thousand years? I say: Take hold of a model that is trustworthy for a thousand years to support it, and then run the state together with men who are trustworthy for a thousand years.

[Perhaps someone might ask:] But people do not even have lon-155 gevity of a hundred years, so how could there be men who are trust-

---

[3] I.e., the "position" Xunzi is discussing is not its literal, physical location, but rather its political situation. Given the placement of this sentence, and the fact that it states something that seems fairly obvious, it might be an early commentary that was erroneously copied into the main text.

[4] The word here is *zi* 子, which also commonly means "Master," the respectful title for a teacher, as in Xunzi's own name, "Master Xun." Thus, Xunzi's question may also mean more particularly which teacher, i.e., which school of thought, one should follow in running the government.

[5] The exact referent of "what has been accumulated" is a bit vague here, but it seems most plausibly understood as referring to the accumulated wisdom and experience of the sages as embodied in the models and rituals that have been passed down.

[6] This passage is very difficult, and the text may be corrupt, so the translation is tentative. Commentators agree that Xunzi is engaging in a question-and-answer exchange with a (perhaps imaginary) interlocutor, though it is not clear exactly where the questions begin and end.

[7] This was apparently a common saying in early China.

worthy for a thousand years? I say: Those who use a model that is trustworthy for a thousand years to support themselves are men who are trustworthy for a thousand years. And so, if one runs the state together with gentlemen who have accumulated cultivation in ritual and *yi*, then one will become a true king. If one runs the state together 160 with men who practice uprightness with integrity and who have perfected trustworthiness, then one will become a hegemon. If one runs the state together with men who engage in intrigues and schemes, then one will perish.

These three options are what the enlightened ruler carefully 165 chooses among, and what the person of *ren* works to get clear about. One who chooses well among them will control other people, and one who does not choose well among them will be controlled by other people.

One who is going to uphold the state surely cannot do so alone. 170 Thus, whether the state is strong and firm, and whether it has glory or disgrace, rests in choosing the right prime minister. When the ruler himself is capable and his prime minister is capable, then one such as this will reign as a true king. When the ruler himself is not capable, but knows to worry about this and seek someone who is capable, then 175 one such as this will be strong. When the ruler himself is not capable, but does not know to worry about this and seek someone who is capable, and instead accordingly employs only those whom he favors, those close to him, and those who ingratiate themselves to him, then such a one will be endangered and have his state diminished, and 180 taken to the extreme, he will perish.

As for the state, he who makes great use of it will be great, and he who makes petty use of it will be petty. At the extreme of greatness, one will reign as a true king, and at the extreme of pettiness, one will perish.[8] One who departs from both the great and the petty[9] will 185 manage to survive. One who makes great use of the state puts *yi* first and profit second. Accordingly, he seeks only for those who are truly capable, without regard for closeness or distance of relationship, and without regard to noble or lowly status—this is called making great use of the state. One who makes petty use of the state puts profit first 190 and *yi* second. Accordingly, he employs only those whom he favors and those who ingratiate themselves to him, without regard to right and wrong, and without regard to crookedness and uprightness—this is called making petty use of the state. To make great use of the state is like the former, and to make petty use of the state is like the latter, 195

[8] As elsewhere, here Xunzi is playing on the fact that "king" (王) and "perish" (亡) were very close in pronunciation during ancient times.

[9] I.e., one who occupies a midway position between true king and tyrant, which in this case is the hegemon.

and one who departs from both the great and the petty is both like the former in one respect, and like the latter in one respect.[10] Thus it is said: "He who possesses them[11] purely will be a true king, he who possesses them in adulterated form will be a hegemon, and he who
200　does not have even a single one of them will perish."[12] This expresses my meaning.

If the state lacks ritual, then it will not be set straight. As for the way ritual sets straight the state, one can compare it to the relation of scales to the heavy and the light, the relation of the ink-line to the
205　curved and the straight, and the relation of compass and square to the round and the rectangular. When they have been set out properly, then no one can deceive you about these things. The *Odes* says:

> It is like a vast expanse of frost and snow.
> It is like the sun and moon's radiant glow.

210　If you practice this, you will survive, but if you do not practice it, you will perish.[13] This expresses my meaning.

Where the state is endangered, there will be no joyful lord. Where the state is secure, there will be no worried common people. If there is chaos, the state will be endangered. If there is order, the state will
215　be secure. Accordingly, if the lord of men hastens to pursue his own joy, but is slow in ordering the state, is his error not great indeed? You may compare it to one who likes beautiful sights and sounds but is content to lack eyes and ears. Is that not sad?

As for people's natural dispositions, their eyes desire the utmost in
220　sights, their ears desire the utmost in sounds, their mouths desire the utmost in flavors, their noses desire the utmost in smells, and their bodies[b] desire the utmost in comfort. These "five utmosts" are something the natural dispositions of people cannot avoid desiring. For nurturing these "five utmosts," there are certain tools. Without these
225　tools, the "five utmosts" cannot be obtained.

---

[10] I.e., he is good to some degree, and bad to some degree.

[11] The thing that is possessed purely is not explicitly stated here, but judging from the context, it would seem to be "good traits" or the like.

[12] This same saying is quoted at 16.325–28 and 26.10–13.

[13] Some commentators include this sentence in the quotation from the *Odes*. Since the quoted ode is not found in the received text, there is no way to be sure exactly where the quote ends. On the one hand, it does rhyme with the previous two sentences in the original, and the statement "This expresses my meaning" usually comes at the end of a quotation in the *Xunzi*, which would support including this sentence in the quotation. On the other hand, the subject matter of this sentence has no clear connection to quoted lines, the grammar seems unlike what is typical of the *Odes*, and the lines are of very different lengths from the previous ones, so there are also grounds for not including it.

To possess a state capable of fielding ten thousand chariots can be called great and vast wealth. Next, add to it the way that brings order, proper distinctions, strength, and firmness. If things are like this, then one will be content and happy and lack fears and troubles. Only then will the tools for nurturing the "five utmosts" be complete. Thus, the hundred joys are born from what orders the state, while worries and fears are born from what disorders the state. One who hastens to pursue his own joy but is slow in ordering the state is not a person who understands how to achieve joy. 230

And so, an enlightened lord will be sure first to order his state, and only then will the hundred joys be obtained therein. A benighted lord will be sure to hasten in pursuing his own joy while being slow to order the state. Accordingly, his worries and fears will be innumerable. He is sure to come to the point where he himself dies and his state is destroyed, and only then will he stop. Is this not sad? He will think that in this way he will have joy, but instead he will get worries from it. He will think that in this way he will have safety, but instead he will get dangers from it. He will think that in this way he will have good fortune, but instead he will get death and destruction from it. Is this not sad? Alas! May the lords of men look into these words of mine! 235 240 245

And so, there is a way to order the state. The ruler of men has a proper occupation. As for spending day after day setting in order detailed matters, with the whole of each day consumed in arranging them completely, this is what one employs the officials and hundred functionaries to do. It is not worth disturbing the lord's enjoyment of ease and relaxation over these things. As for choosing the one right prime minister to lead all the others, and making sure that the ministers and hundred functionaries all abide by the Way and aim at what is correct in their work, *this* is the proper occupation for the ruler of men. 250 255

When it is like this, then he will unify all under Heaven, and his fame will match that of Yao and Yu. For such a ruler as this, in what he watches over he acts with the utmost restraint, yet all the details are taken care of. In what he works at he experiences the utmost ease, yet he has great accomplishments.[14] He lets his clothing hang loose[15] and does not get down from his seat, but all the common people within the four seas want to have him as their sovereign and king. This is called the utmost restraint, and there is no greater joy than this. 260

The ruler of men is one who is judged capable because of his officials, but a commoner is one who is judged capable because of what he himself is capable of. For a ruler of men can employ people to do things for him, but a commoner has no one onto whom to shift his 265

---

[14] See the similar wording at 16.317–20.
[15] A sign of relaxation.

burdens—he is given a hundred *mu* of land to watch over by himself, because that task exhausts what can be done without having another onto whom to shift one's burdens.

Now if you set a single person to hear cases for all under Heaven, but his days contain spare time and the affairs to be set in order do not fill them up completely, that is because he appropriately employs people to do things for him. At his greatest, such a person may take hold of the whole world, or at the least he may take hold of a single state. On the other hand, if one must do things oneself and only then are they acceptable, then there is no more bitter, grueling, and exhausting labor than governing. If things are like that, then even a lowly servant would not be willing to exchange places and tasks with the Son of Heaven. But if one is going to use such a lofty position° to manage all under Heaven and unify the lands within the four seas, then for what reason must one do everything oneself? Doing everything oneself is the way of a servant, yet that is what Mozi teaches! Judging people's virtue, making use of their abilities, and then rewarding them with official position is the way of the sage kings, and this is what the *ru* carefully preserve.[16]

A saying goes: When the farmers are allotted their fields and then plow them, when the merchants are allotted their goods and then sell them, when the hundred craftsmen are allotted their tasks and then set to work, when the grand ministers and officers are allotted their assignments and then hear their cases, when the rulers who preside over states bestowed upon them as feudal lords are allotted their land and then guard it, when the three dukes collect together various proposed methods for governing and debate over them—then the Son of Heaven need merely keep himself in a reverent state and that is all. If both inside and outside the palace things are like this, then everything under Heaven will be peaceful and even, and everyone will be well ordered and live in accordance with the proper distinctions. This is something in which the hundred kings were the same, and such is the great division of society brought about by rituals and proper models.

To say that with a territory of only a hundred *li* one can obtain the whole world is not an empty claim. The difficult part rests in whether the ruler of men understands how to do it. By "obtaining the whole world," I do not mean making others come carrying their soil and attaching it to one's own.[17] Rather, it is for one's way to be sufficient

---

[16] Since Xunzi elsewhere thinks of some *ru* as "dissolute" and "degenerate" (see 6.219–29), this remark here is probably best taken as referring to the ideal or "true" *ru*.

[17] In early China, rulers of weak or conquered states would send samples of soil from their territories to a dominant state as a "gift" of territory, which signaled submission and tribute.

to unite people with oneself, and that is all. If people are united with me, then how would their land leave me and go to another? Thus, even with a territory of only a hundred *li*, the state's ranks and salaries are sufficient to accommodate all the worthy men in the world. Its 310 official positions and official tasks are sufficient to accommodate all the men of ability in the world. If, in following its old models for government, you pick the best among them and then highlight and employ them, they are sufficient to make people who are fond of benefit submit compliantly. When worthy men are united in a state, 315 men of ability are employed as officials there, and common people fond of benefit submit to it—when all three conditions are met, then there will be absolutely no one under Heaven who is outside it. Thus, a territory of only a hundred *li* is sufficient to win all power. Achieving loyalty and trustworthiness and manifesting *ren* and *yi* are suffi- 320 cient to win all people. When these two things are combined,[18] then the whole world is obtained. Those among the feudal lords who delay joining in are the first to be endangered.[19] The *Odes* says:

> From the west and from the east,
> From the south and from the north, 325
> All submit as they come forth.[20]

This is speaking of what it is like when one unifies people.

Yi and Peng Men were men who were good at getting archers to submit to them. Wang Liang and Zao Fu were men who were good at getting charioteers to submit to them. A bright and perceptive gentle- 330 man is one who is good at getting people in general to submit to him. When people submit to a man, then power will attach to him. When people do not submit to a man, then power will depart from him. Thus, being a true king rests in getting people to submit to oneself.

So, if the ruler of men wishes to get people who are good at shoot- 335 ing and can hit small targets from far away, nothing is as good as having Yi and Peng Men. If he wishes to get people who are good at driving and can rapidly go a great distance, nothing is as good as having Wang Liang and Zao Fu. If he wishes to be able to harmonize and unify all under Heaven and keep Qin and Chu in check, then 340 nothing is as good as having a bright and perceptive gentleman. When such a gentleman exercises his understanding, he is never stumped, when he is engaged in action, he does not become worn out, and his accomplishments and reputation are grand. He is very

---

[18] I.e., winning all power and winning all people to one's side.
[19] It is not clear exactly what Xunzi is thinking of here, but perhaps he has in mind the idea that the subjects of such "recalcitrant" feudal lords will rise up against them.
[20] Mao #244. These lines are also quoted at 8.91–93 and 15.334–36.

345 easy to get along with and is most delightful. Hence, an enlightened lord regards him as a treasure, but a foolish lord regards him as a troublemaker.

To be so noble as to be Son of Heaven; to be so rich as to possess the whole world; to have a reputation as being a sage king; to control
350 all others while not being controlled by any other—these are what people's natural dispositions are the same in desiring, but a true king is the only one who has all these. To wear clothes of many colors; to eat food of many flavors; to control wealth and goods of many kinds; to bring together all under Heaven and be lord over them; to have
355 abundant food and drink; to have grand music; to have lofty terraces and pavilions; to have vast gardens and parks; to employ the feudal lords as one's ministers; to unify all under Heaven—these are also what people's natural dispositions are the same in desiring, but only the rituals and regulations pertaining to the Son of Heaven are such
360 as to be like this. When regulations and measures have been set and when government orders have been taken up, then if an official neglects something crucial, he is punished with death, and if a duke or feudal lord neglects ritual propriety, he is relegated to obscurity;[21] if any state within the four corners displays a dissolute and rebellious
365 spirit, then it is surely destroyed; to have fame as bright as the sun and moon; to have accomplishments as great as Heaven and Earth; to have all the people under Heaven respond to one like a shadow or echo—these are also what people's natural dispositions are the same in desiring, but a true king is the only one who has all these.
370 Thus, people's natural disposition is such that their mouths like good flavors, and there are no finer flavors than the ones enjoyed by a true king. People's ears like good sounds, and there are no greater sounds than the music he enjoys. People's eyes like good sights, and none are more numerous than the exquisite decorations and the
375 women he enjoys. People's bodies like ease, and there is no greater comfort than the safety, stability, leisure, and peace he enjoys. People's hearts like profit, and there is no income more abundant than the one he enjoys. Combine what everyone under Heaven is the same in wishing for—he possesses all these things. He reigns over all under
380 Heaven and controls them just like controlling his children and grandchildren.

How could anyone who is not crazy, confused, stupid, or ignorant look upon such a life and not be filled with delight? Rulers who want this have succeeded one another as closely as though they were stand-
385 ing shoulder to shoulder, and men who are capable of bringing this

[21] Xunzi's meaning here is rather vague. Some commentators take "obscurity" as referring to imprisonment, while others take it as meaning that the person is demoted and another promoted to take his place.

about for them have never been absent in any generation, but for a thousand years these two sides have not come together. Why? I say: It is because the rulers of men have not been free of prejudice, and their ministers have not been loyal. As for the rulers of men, they have kept worthy men outside their inner circle and promoted others in a 390
biased fashion. As for their ministers, they have fought over official posts and been jealous of worthy men. This is the reason why the two sides have not come together.

Why are the rulers of men not more broad-minded? Let them pay no heed to closeness or distance of relationship, and show no bias 395
toward noble or lowly, but seek only those who are truly capable. If things were like this, then their ministers would set less store by official posts, yield to worthy men, and contentedly follow behind them. If things were thus, then a Shun or Yu would again arrive, and the works of a true king would again arise. His accomplishments 400
would unite all under Heaven, and his fame would equal Shun and Yu. Is there anything so fine as to be more delightful than this? Alas! May the lords of men look into these words of mine! Yang Zhu[22] wept upon coming to a point where the road divided. He said, "Is this not a case where one may take a half step wrong only to discover later 405
that one has gone astray by a thousand *li*?" So he wept sadly. This matter[23] is also exactly the point that divides honor and disgrace, safety and danger, and survival and destruction. There is more that is worthy of sorrow in this than in a mere divided road. Alas! How sad! For a thousand years the lords of men have not discovered this. 410

Every state has models of government that make for good order. Every state also has models of government that make for chaos. Every state has worthy men. Every state also has worthless men. Every state has honest people. Every state also has violent people. Every state has fine customs. Every state also has bad customs. When both types 415
are present in equal measure, then the state will go on existing. When the state inclines to the superior kinds, then it will exist and be secure.[d] When it inclines to the inferior kinds, then it will be in danger. If the superior kinds become the one and only type in the state, then you will rule as a true king. If the inferior kinds become the one 420
and only type in the state, then you will perish.[24]

And so, when the models of government make for good order, the ruler's aides are worthy men, the people are honest, the customs are

---

[22] Yang Zhu was a famous thinker of the Warring States period who seems to have lived sometime shortly after Mozi. There is little reliable evidence concerning his thought, but Mencius (3B9) says that he advocated a doctrine of "egoism" (*wei wo* 為我) that attracted a large number of adherents at one time.

[23] I.e., of choosing ministers.

[24] Again, Xunzi is playing on the similarity of pronunciation for "king" (王) and "perish" (亡) during ancient times.

fine, and all four of these things are uniformly present, this is called
425 making the superior kinds the one and only type. If things are like
this, then you will conquer without going into battle, and win without attacking. Your weapons and armor will not be put to work, yet
the whole world will submit. Tang used Bo, and King Wu used Hao—
these were both territories of merely a hundred *li* in size, but the
430 world became united under them, the feudal lords were their servants, and among those of penetrating intelligence, none failed to
submit and to follow. There is no reason for this other than that these
four superior kinds were uniformly present. The tyrants Jie and Zhòu
held the rank of those with power over the whole world, but when
435 they sought to live as common folk they could not achieve even that.
There is no reason for this other than that these four superior kinds
were all absent.

Thus, even though the models of government among the hundred
kings were not identical, their fundamentals were in this manner one
440 and the same:[25] superiors all had utmost concern for their subordinates and regulated them by means of ritual. The way superiors
treated their subordinates was as though caring for a newborn. Articulating government orders and standards and measures were the
means by which they interacted with the common folk and all the
445 people under Heaven, but if anything among those was not well ordered, even something very small, they surely would not apply it to
the people, even orphans, widows, and widowers. Therefore, as for
the way that subordinates loved their superiors, they delighted in
them as in their own parents, and they could be killed but could not
450 be made disobedient. Lords and ministers, superiors and subordinates, noble and lowly, old and young, all the way down to the commoners—everyone took this as their exalted standard of correctness.
After this, each inspected himself within so as to diligently fulfill his
allotted place. This is that in which the hundred kings were the same,
455 and this is the crucial element in the rituals and proper models.

After this, when the farmers were allotted their fields and then
plowed them, when the merchants were allotted their goods and then
sold them, when the hundred craftsmen were allotted their tasks and
then set to work, when the grand ministers and officers were allotted
460 their assignments and then heard their cases, when the rulers who
presided over states bestowed upon them as feudal lords were allotted their land and then guarded it, when the three dukes collected
together various proposed methods for governing and debated over

[25] Many commentators group this sentence with the preceding paragraph, in which
case the "fundamentals" to which it refers would be having only the four "superior
types" in their states. Also, compare Xunzi's remarks about the "binding thread"
among the hundred kings at 17.226–27.

them—then the Son of Heaven needed merely to keep himself in a reverent state and that is all. Since both inside and outside the palace things were like this, then everything under Heaven was peaceful and even, and everyone was well ordered and lived in accordance with the proper distinctions. This is something in which the hundred kings were the same, and such is the great division of society brought about by rituals and proper models.

As for day-to-day managing ordinary affairs, measuring things and seeing to it that they match one's uses, ensuring that clothing is properly regulated, that palaces and buildings have their proper measure, that personnel are in proper number, and that the equipment for funerals and sacrifices is sorted according to ranks and properly prepared, and on the basis of these uses gathering items from among the myriad things, proceeding only when the units of size are all in accordance with the regulations for numbers and the measures for quantity—these are affairs for the officials and functionaries. They are not worth recounting one by one in front of the great gentleman.[26]

And so, if the lord of men establishes a lofty standard of correctness in setting the fundamentals for his court and does so rightly, and if the person whom he employs to direct the hundred tasks is truly a man of *ren*, then the lord will be at ease and the state will be well-ordered. His accomplishments will be great and his reputation will be fine. At his greatest, he can become a true king, and at the least he can become a hegemon. If the lord of men establishes a lofty standard of correctness in setting the fundamentals for his court but does not do so rightly, and if the person whom he employs to direct the hundred tasks is not a man of *ren*, then the lord will be worn out and his state will be in chaos. His accomplishments will be a waste and his reputation will be disgraced. His altars of soil and grain are sure to be endangered. This matter[27] is the crucial point for the ruler of men.

And so, if he can hit upon the one right person, then he can gain the whole world. If he fails to hit upon the one right person, then his altars of soil and grain will be endangered. And there is no way of persuading people that one could somehow not be able to hit upon the one right person in this case, yet hit upon a hundred or thousand right people otherwise. When one is able to hit upon the one right person, then what labor would one have to undertake? One merely lets one's clothing hang loose, and the whole world is settled.

Thus, Tang employed Yi Yin. King Wen employed Lü Shang.[28] King Wu employed the Duke of Shao. King Cheng employed the

---

[26] I.e., the ruler.
[27] I.e., establishing the correct standards and finding the right prime minister.
[28] For more on Lü Shang (also known as the Grand Duke), see chapter 12, note 34.

505 Duke of Zhou. And as for lesser cases, there are the five hegemons. Within his private chambers, Duke Huan of Qi set up musical entertainments and other extravagances, cultivating only his own amusement. He is not called a cultivated person by anyone under Heaven. Nevertheless, nine times he convened a meeting of the feudal lords,

510 he brought the whole world in line, and he was foremost among the five hegemons. This is for no other reason than that he knew to entrust the entire government to Guan Zhong. This is the important point for the lord of men to watch over. Those who understand this will easily put their efforts toward this end, and their accomplish-

515 ments and fame will be extremely great. If one abandons this, then what else is worth doing?

And so, those of the ancients who had great accomplishments and fame were surely those who took this as their way. Those who lost their states and endangered themselves were surely those who did the

520 opposite of this. Hence, Confucius said, "The understanding of those who are wise certainly grasps many things, but they use it to watch over only a few things, so how could they be without keen insight? The understanding of those who are foolish certainly grasps only a few things, but they use it to watch over many things, so how can they

525 not act recklessly?" This expresses my meaning.

In ordering the state, when the hierarchical divisions are set, then the ruler, the prime minister, the subordinate ministers, and the various functionaries will each stick carefully to what they are supposed to hear, and will not work at listening to what they are not supposed

530 to hear.[29] They will each stick carefully to what they are supposed to oversee, and will not work at looking into what they are not supposed to oversee. When what they hear and what they oversee are truly set straight in this manner, then even among those living in isolated and obscure places, none of the common people will dare not to respect

535 their allotted places and settle into following the regulations, such that they will be transformed by their superiors. This is the sign of an ordered state.

In the way of a true ruler, one controls what is nearby, and does not try to control what is far away. One controls what is prominent,

540 and does not try to control what is obscure. One controls what is primary, and does not try to control what is secondary. If the ruler can control what is nearby, then what is far away will be well ordered. If the ruler can control what is prominent, then what is obscure will be transformed. If the ruler can be correct with respect to what is

545 primary, then the hundred affairs will turn out right. As for the case where one manages all under Heaven, but the days are in abundance

---

[29] As elsewhere, "hearing" in this instance most likely refers to hearing and judging legal cases.

and the matters needing decisions are not sufficient to fill them up, when things are like this, it is the height of good government.

When one is already able to control what is near, but then more- 550 over works at controlling what is far away; when one is already able to control what is prominent, but then moreover works at controlling what is obscure; when one is already able to be correct with respect to what is primary, but then moreover works at making the hundred affairs turn out right—this is going too far. Going too far is just like 555 not going far enough. One can compare it to planting a tree upright and then seeking to make its shadow crooked. If one is not able to control what is nearby, but then moreover works at controlling what is far away; if one is not able to discern what is prominent, but then moreover works at overseeing what is obscure; if one is not able to be correct with respect to what is primary, but then moreover works at 560 making the hundred affairs turn out right, this is doing things back- ward. One can compare it to planting a tree crooked and then seeking to make its shadow upright.

Thus, the enlightened ruler is fond of what is essential, and the benighted ruler is fond of the minor details. If the ruler is fond of 565 what is essential, then the hundred affairs will be taken care of down to their minor details, but if the ruler is fond of the minor details, then the hundred affairs will be neglected. A true lord is one who judges the one right prime minister, sets out the one right model, and makes clear the one right directive, so as to cover all, illuminate all, 570 and then observes things flourish. A true prime minister judges and arranges the heads of the hundred offices, and grasps the essentials in managing the hundred affairs, so as to elaborate the hierarchical divi- sions for the court's subordinate ministers and hundred functionar- ies. He measures their efforts and achievements, judges the commen- 575 dations and rewards, and at the end of the year takes their successful achievements and presents them to the lord. If he does this appropri- ately, then he is acceptable. If he does not do this appropriately, then he is discarded. Thus, the lord of men works hard in seeking him, but rests easy in employing him. 580

In the matter of using the state, he who gets the people to work for him will be rich, he who gets the people to die for him will be strong, and he who gets the people to praise him will be renowned. When all three of these achievements are complete, then all under Heaven will side with him, but if these three achievements are lacking, then all 585 under Heaven will abandon him. For all under Heaven to side with one is called being a true king, and for all under Heaven to abandon one is called destruction.

Tang and Wu followed the proper way, engaged in proper practice of yi, gave rise to benefits shared by all under Heaven, and eliminated 590 harms shared by all under Heaven, and so all under Heaven sided with them. Thus, Tang and Wu made great their reputations for virtue so as to stand at the forefront of the people.[30] They made clear ritual and *yi* so as to guide the people. They made themselves loyal and trustworthy so as to make the people care for them. They elevated the worthy and employed the capable so as to order the people in ranks. They made gifts of positions, emblems, and other rewards in order to make the people exert themselves and redouble their efforts. They made the people's works accord with the times and lightened their burdens, in order to regulate them and bring them into line. Their broad concern included and covered all the people, and they nurtured and raised them, as though caring for a newborn. In managing the people's livelihood, they caused them to be amply supplied. In employing the people, they caused them to be extremely well ordered. Articulating government orders and standards and measures were the means by which they interacted with the common folk and all the people under Heaven, but if anything among those was not well ordered, even something very small, they surely would not apply it to the people, even orphans, widows, and widowers. For this reason, the common folk honored them like Shang Di, loved them as their own fathers and mothers, and marched out to die for them without hesitation, and that was for no reason other than the fact that the kings' way and virtue were truly glorious, and the benefit and kindness they bestowed upon the people were truly generous.

A disordered age is not like this. In corruption, arrogance, cruelty, and robbery, the rulers stand at the forefront of the people. With schemes for power and plots to overthrow others they set an example for the people. Through granting the requests of their entertainers, dwarves, and women, they throw the people into disarray. They employ the foolish to order around the wise, and employ the unworthy to oversee the worthy. In managing the people's livelihood, they cause them to be pinched and destitute. In employing the people, they cause them to engage in extremely bitter toil and be exhausted. For this reason, the common folk look down upon them as if they were witches, and hate them as if they were ghosts. Every day the common folk desire to find an opening to cast down their rulers, trample them, and drive them out. In the end, there are incidents of bandits and other troublemakers. The rulers still look to the common folk to die on their behalf, but they cannot get them to do it, and no persuasion will win them over to it. Confucius said, "I am careful about how I go to meet people, because it creates a match in how people come to meet me."[e] This expresses my meaning.

---

[30] The text from this sentence down to the word "newborn" at line 602 below also appears in nearly identical form at 15.493–501.

What is it that harms the state? I say: To raise a petty man over the common people and give him authority, to use one's station inappropriately to take from the people and do so with skill—these are great calamities that harm the state. If there is a ruler whose state is large, but who is fond of seeing petty profits, this harms the state. If his attitude toward sights and sounds, terraces and pavilions, parks and gardens is that the more he is provided with these things, the more he desires new ones, this harms the state. If he does not follow up on and set straight that by which he has these things,[31] but always hungrily desires what others have, this harms the state. When these three evils are within his breast, and moreover on the outside he is fond of using men who engage in schemes for power and plots to overthrow others to decide matters for him—if things are like this, then his power will be diminished and his reputation will be disgraced, and his altars of soil and grain will surely be endangered. This is something that harms the state.

If there is a ruler whose state is large, and who does not treat fundamental good conduct as most lofty and does not respect the old models of government, but instead is fond of deception and contrivance—if he is like this, then the assembled ministers of his court will also follow along and become accustomed to not treating ritual and *yi* as lofty, and will rather be fond of overthrowing others. If the customs of the assembled ministers of his court are like this, then the masses and the common folk will also follow along and become accustomed to not treating ritual and *yi* as lofty, and will rather be fond of greed for profit. If the customs of the ruler, ministers, superiors, and subordinates are all like this, then even if the state has broad lands, its power is sure to be diminished. Even if its people are numerous, its soldiers are sure to be weak. Even if it imposes copious legal punishments, government orders will not be carried out below— this is called endangering the state, and this is something that harms the state.

A *ru* does not do things like this—he will surely implement proper distinctions completely. In the court, he will surely treat ritual and *yi* as lofty, and he will be careful about the difference between the noble and the lowly. If he is like this, then the officers and grand ministers will all respect proper regulation and die to uphold standards. The hundred officials will then set in order their standards and measures and treat their official posts with great seriousness. If they are like this, then the hundred functionaries will all fear the laws and follow what is straight. Passes and markets will be overseen but not taxed.

---

[31] I.e., he neglects to cultivate good character, which in Xunzi's view is the only real way to get and retain power.

Materials will be controlled and forbidden items will be stopped, but
675 this will not be done in a one-sided manner. If things are like this,
then the merchants will all be earnest, honest, and without deception.
The hundred craftsmen will chop wood and gather materials in accordance with the proper times, they will not rush their productions,
and they will hone the skillful performance of their jobs. If things are
680 like this, then the hundred craftsmen will all be loyal, trustworthy,
and not do shoddy work. The officials for the countryside will lighten
taxes on the fields, reduce collections of money, rarely raise *corvée*
labor parties, and will not drag people away during the times for
agricultural work.[32] If they are like this, then the farmers will all put
685 forward honest effort and reduce the number of other endeavors they
undertake.

When the officers and grand ministers work to maintain proper
regulation and will die to uphold standards, then the state's soldiers
will fight vigorously. When the hundred functionaries fear the laws
690 and follow what is straight, only then will the state never suffer chaos.
When the merchants are earnest, honest, and without deception, then
merchants and travelers will feel secure about their wares and will
make goods flow, and the needs of the state will be provided for.
When the hundred craftsmen are loyal, trustworthy, and do not do
695 shoddy work, then vessels and utensils will be skillfully made and
easy to use, and goods will not be lacking. When the farmers put
forward honest effort and reduce the number of other endeavors they
undertake, then above they will not miss out on the seasons of
Heaven, below they will not miss out on the advantages of the Earth,
700 in the middle they will obtain harmonious cooperation among people, and the hundred tasks will not be neglected. This is called having
effective government and fine customs. Use it for defense, and you
will be firm. Use it to attack, and you will be strong. When remaining
at rest, you will have great fame, and when engaged in action, you
705 will have great accomplishments. This is what the *ru* call implementing proper distinctions completely.

[32] Compare 10.99–102.

CHAPTER 12

The Way to Be a Lord

There are chaotic lords; there are no states chaotic of themselves. There are men who create order; there are no rules[1] creating order of themselves. The rules of Archer Yi have not perished, but not every age has an Archer Yi who hits the target precisely. The rules of Yu still survive, but not every age has a Xia dynasty to reign as true kings. Thus, rules cannot stand alone, and categories cannot implement themselves. If one has the right person, then they will be preserved. If one loses the right person, then they will be lost. The rules are the beginning of order, and the gentleman is the origin of the rules. And so, with the gentleman present, even if the rules are sketchy, they are enough to be comprehensive. Without the gentleman, even if the rules are complete, one will fail to apply them in the right order and will be unable to respond to changes in affairs, and thus they can serve to create chaos. One who tries to correct the arrangements of the rules without understanding their meaning, even if he is broadly learned, is sure to create chaos when engaged in affairs. And so, the enlightened ruler hastens to obtain the right person. The deluded ruler hastens to obtain power. If one hastens to obtain the right person, then one can rest at ease and the state will be ordered. One's accomplishments will be grand and one's reputation will be fine. At the greatest, one can become a true king, and at the least, one can become a hegemon. If one does not hasten to obtain the right person but instead hastens to obtain power, then one can work laboriously and the state will still be chaotic. One's accomplishments will be wasted and one's reputation will be disgraced. One's altars of soil and grain are sure to be endangered. Thus, the true lord of men labors to find the right person, and relaxes in employing him. The *Documents* says, "Only King Wen was respectful and cautious; he chose the one right man."[2] This expresses my meaning.

---

[1] The word here is *fa* 法, which generally connotes a rule-like standard for doing things. As such, it can also mean a "method" or "model" or "law." Here I have used "rules" to try to cover all these senses, but I have usually rendered it elsewhere as "model."

[2] See *Shujing, Kanggao* ("The Announcement to the Prince of K'ang"), translated in Waltham (1971, p. 151). The received text of the *Documents* differs from Xunzi's quotation here.

30   Breaking tallies into halves and matching up halves of tallies are
means by which to establish trust,[3] but if the superior is fond of
schemes for power, then his ministers below, the hundred functionaries, and deceitful people will take advantage of this to engage in trickery. Drawing lots and tossing coins[4] are means by which to establish
35   lack of prejudice, but if the superior is fond of crookedness and selfish interest, then his ministers below and the hundred functionaries
will take advantage of this to engage in one-sidedness. Setting up
scales and measuring out weights are means to establish what is balanced, but if the superior is fond of overthrowing people, then his
40   ministers below and the hundred functionaries will take advantage of
this to act precariously.[5] Measuring by pecks and bushels and leveling off the tops of containers are means by which to establish what is
equitable,[6] but if the superior is fond of greed for profit, then his
ministers below and the hundred functionaries will take advantage of
45   this to enlarge collections and cut back on distributions, taking from
the people without limit.

    And so, proper use of such equipment and measures is what flows
from good order—it is not the fount of good order. The gentleman is
the fount of good order. The officials keep watch over the measures,
50   and the gentleman nurtures the fount. If the fount is pure, what flows
on from it will be pure. If the fount is muddied, what flows on from
it will be muddied. Thus, if the superior is fond of ritual and *yi*, if he
elevates the worthy and employs the capable, if he is without a heart
that is greedy for profit, then his subordinates will go to the utmost
55   in yielding and deference, will achieve the height of loyalty and trustworthiness, and will be diligent in serving as ministers. If they are like
this, then even the lowliest of the common people will be trustworthy
without waiting for the breaking and matching of tallies, will show
lack of prejudice without waiting to draw lots or toss coins, will be
60   balanced without waiting to set up scales and measure out weights,

---

[3] In ancient China, contracts and other kinds of agreements would be written on
pieces of bamboo or wood, which would then be divided in two, with each party
keeping one half as proof of the agreement. Only when the halves were reunited
could the agreement be read, thereby preventing fraudulent alteration of the contract.

[4] The text literally says "tossing hooks." However, the exact meaning of that expression is not known. Some commentators suggest it refers to another form of drawing
lots. Whatever its exact meaning, the basic idea is the same, namely a method of
choosing, the outcome of which is random and thus impartial. In the absence of a
clear understanding of the Chinese, the English idiom of "tossing coins" is conve-
niently similar enough in phrasing and meaning to convey the general point.

[5] I.e., in an unbalanced and unfair fashion.

[6] In ancient China, there were standard volumes used as measures for collecting grain
as tax and for doling out grain in times of famine, and this practice is what Xunzi is
most likely referring to with his talk of "collections" and "distributions" here.

and will be equitable without waiting to measure by pecks and bushels and level off the tops of containers.

Thus, the people will work hard without the use of rewards, and they will obey without the use of punishments. Affairs will be put in order without those in charge working laboriously, and the state will have fine customs without a profusion of government orders. None of the common folk will dare fail to comply with their superior's laws, to fulfill his intentions, and to work hard on his tasks, but rather all will feel at ease and delight in following him. And so, in handing over taxes they will not worry about paying, in undertaking work projects they will not worry about hard labor, and in dealing with bandits and other trouble-makers they will not worry about dying. The city walls will be solid without waiting for them to be enhanced, and the blades of weapons will be keen without waiting to be honed. Rival states will submit without waiting to be subdued, and all people within the four seas will be unified without waiting to be given orders. This is called utmost peace.[7] The *Odes* says:

> When the king's plan was a true success,
> The lands of Xu came to acquiesce.[8]

This expresses my meaning.

"May I inquire about how to be a person's lord?"[9] I say: Make divisions and distributions according to ritual. Be evenhanded, inclusive, and not one-sided.

"May I inquire about how to be a person's minister?" I say: Serve your lord according to ritual. Be loyal, compliant, and not lazy.

"May I inquire about how to be a person's father?" I say: Be broadminded, kind, and follow the dictates of ritual.

"May I inquire about how to be a person's son?" I say: Be respectful, loving, and have utmost good form.

"May I inquire about how to be a person's elder brother?" I say: Be compassionate, loving, and display friendliness.

"May I inquire about how to be a person's younger brother?" I say: Be respectful, acquiescent, and do nothing improper.

"May I inquire about how to be a person's husband?" I say: Be extremely hardworking and do not stray. Be extremely watchful and follow proper distinctions.

---

[7] The word for "peace" here is *ping* 平, which was translated earlier as "balanced." Throughout this section, Xunzi is playing on these two senses of the term in a way not easily captured in English.

[8] Mao #263. These same lines are also quoted at 15.538–39. The poem from which the quotation comes describes how the land of Xu is attacked and brought to submission by king Xuan of the Zhou dynasty.

[9] Here and below, Xunzi engages with an imaginary questioner.

"May I inquire about the proper way to be a person's wife?" I say: If your husband follows the dictates of ritual, then compliantly obey him and wait upon him attentively. If your husband does not
100 follow the dictates of ritual, then be apprehensive but keep yourself respectful.[10]

If these ways are established in a one-sided manner,[11] then there will be chaos, but if they are established in a comprehensive manner, there will be order, so this matter is worth keeping watch over.[12]
105 "May I inquire about what to do in order to be capable of maintaining them all?" I say: Exercise vigilance over them through ritual. In ancient times, the former kings were vigilant over ritual as they traveled everywhere under Heaven, and none of their actions failed to hit the mark. And so, the gentleman is reverent without being in-
110 timidated, and is respectful without being frightened. In poverty and desperate circumstances, he is not distressed, and in wealth and honor, he is not arrogant. He encounters every change in circumstances without being at a loss for how to respond, because he exercises vigilance over these things through ritual.
115 And so, the gentleman's approach to ritual is that he respects and finds comfort in it. His approach to work is that he is swift, but does not neglect things. His approach to people is that he complains little and is broadminded and generous, but does not toady to others. The way he conducts himself is to be diligent in cultivation and self-im-
120 provement, but without being precarious.[13] The way he adapts to changing conditions is prompt and quick, but without becoming confused. His approach to Heaven, Earth, and the myriad things is that he does not work at explaining why they are as they are, but rather is extremely good at making use of the resources they provide.[14]
125 His approach to the work of the hundred officials and to men of skill and art is that he does not try to compete with their abilities, but rather is extremely good at making use of their accomplishments.[15] In serving his superiors he is loyal, compliant, and not lazy. In employing his subordinates, he is evenhanded, inclusive, and not one-sided.
130 In going about and traveling, he follows *yi* and accords with the proper categories for things. In dwelling in his village and neighbor-

---

[10] Instead of "but keep yourself respectful," the last part of this sentence might also be translated as "and keep yourself fearfully alert." It is unclear exactly which sense Xunzi intends.

[11] E.g., the son acts as he should, but the father does not.

[12] Alternatively, this last part of the line might be translated as ". . . and this can be proven."

[13] To be "precarious" is to have an "unsteady" grip on morality, so that one has to force oneself to act correctly, instead of doing so with ease. Compare Xunzi's discussion of "precariousness" at 21.250–314.

[14] Compare 17.78–84.

[15] Compare 8.111–131 and 21.235–42.

hood, he is easygoing and not disorderly. For this reason, even if he is poor, he is sure to have great fame, and if he is successful, he is sure to have great accomplishments. His *ren* is so abundant as to cover everyone under Heaven without strain. His intelligence is so far-   135 reaching as to make use of Heaven and Earth and bring order to the myriad changes without perplexity. His blood and *qi* are harmonious and balanced.[16] His thoughts and intentions are broad and great. His practice of *yi* fills up the space between Heaven and Earth.[17] He is the height of *ren* and wisdom. This is called being a sage, and it is due to   140 exercising vigilance over these things through ritual.

"May I inquire about how to run the state?" I answer: I have heard of cultivating one's person, but have never heard about "running the state."[18] The lord is a sundial. [The common people are the shadow.][19] If the sundial is straight, then the shadow will be straight.[20] The lord   145 is a basin. [The common people are the water.] If the basin is round, then the water will be round. The lord is a bowl. If the bowl is square, the water will be square. If the lord practices archery, his ministers will wear *jue* rings.[21] King Zhuang of Chu[22] liked slender waists, and so his court was full of starved-looking people. That is why I said, "I   150 have heard of cultivating one's person, but have never heard about 'running the state.'"

The lord is the fount for the people. If the fount is pure, what flows on from it will be pure. If the fount is muddied, what flows on from it will be muddied. Thus, if someone possessing altars of soil and   155 grain is not able to care for the people and is not able to benefit the people, yet seeks for the people to love and care for him, he cannot obtain this. If the people neither love nor care for him, yet he seeks that they will labor on his behalf and will die on his behalf, he cannot obtain this. If the people will neither labor on his behalf nor die on   160 his behalf, yet he seeks that his soldiers be vigorous and his city walls be firm, he cannot obtain this. If his soldiers are not vigorous and his city walls are not firm, yet he seeks that his rivals not come calling, he

---

[16] Compare 2.30–94.

[17] Compare Mencius's discussion of "flood-like *qi*" and its relation to righteousness in 2A2.

[18] As becomes clear from the contrast that follows, "running the state" here seems to refer to a purely technical, amoral approach to effective government, much like what was proposed by Han Feizi and others like him in early China.

[19] Some editions of the *Xunzi* do not contain the sentences bracketed here, but they seem required to make good sense of Xunzi's point.

[20] See 16.370–73 and 18.2–7 for similar imagery.

[21] According to commentators, these rings were accoutrements for archers. They were worn on the thumb, with a hook to help in drawing back a bowstring. The point of the reference is that if the lord practices archery, so will his ministers.

[22] In other texts of this period, this story is attributed to King Ling of Chu, so the attribution to King Zhuang here may be an error.

cannot obtain this. If his rivals come calling, yet he seeks to avoid
165 being endangered, having his territory reduced, or being destroyed,
he cannot obtain this. When the conditions for being endangered,
having his territory reduced, or being destroyed are all gathered here
before him, yet he still seeks comfort and joy—this is a person who
lives recklessly, and one who lives recklessly will not have to wait even
170 a moment before getting burned.[a]
And so, if the ruler of men desires strength, security, comfort, and
joy, then nothing is as good as going back to the source of these
things in the people. If he wishes to win the allegiance of his subordinates and unify the people, then nothing is as good as going back
175 to the source of these things in the government. If he wishes to cultivate the government and improve the state, then nothing is as good
as seeking the right person. As for those men who are such that someone nurturing and gathering them would thereby succeed in all these
things—those men are not absent in any age.
180 That "right person" is such that he lives in the world of today, but
his intentions are set on the ways of ancient times.[23] If no kings and
dukes in the world are fond of those ways, then nevertheless he will
be fond of them by himself. If no other people in the world desire
those ways, then nevertheless he will practice them by himself. Even
185 if people who are fond of those ways suffer poverty, and people who
practice them face dire straits, nevertheless he will still practice them
by himself, without stopping for even a moment. He alone understands clearly why past kings succeeded or failed, and he knows what
will make a state safe or endangered or good or bad, as plainly as
190 differentiating white from black. Such is "the right person."
If a ruler employs him in a great position, then all under Heaven
will become united, and the feudal lords will become his ministers. If
the ruler employs him in a minor position, then he will inspire awe
among his neighbors and rival states. Even if the ruler cannot employ
195 him in an official position, so long as the ruler sees to it that he does
not leave the borders of the state, then to the end of the ruler's days
the state will suffer no serious incidents. And so, if the lord of men
cares for the people, then he will be safe. If he is fond of well-bred
men, then he will have glory. However, if he lacks both of these traits,
200 then he will perish. The *Odes* says:

From the great man comes your palisade.
From the masses are your ramparts made.[24]

This expresses my meaning.

[23] Compare 31.4–7.
[24] Mao #254. The original context of the poem is one person warning another, possibly a king, against the dangers of governing badly. These lines are also quoted at
16.229–30.

What is the Way? I say: It is the way of a true lord. Who is a true lord? I say: It is one who is able to create community.[25] Who is able create community? I say: It is one who is good at keeping people alive and nurturing them, good at organizing and ordering people, good at elevating and employing people, and good at beautifying and ornamenting people. When one is good at keeping people alive and nurturing them, they will love him. When one is good at organizing and ordering people, they will feel comfortable with him. When one is good at elevating and employing people, they will delight in him. When one is good at beautifying and ornamenting people, they will give him glory. When all four key factors are possessed completely, then everyone under Heaven will side with him. This is called being able to create community.

When one is not able to keep people alive and nurture them, they will not love him. When one is not able to organize and order people, they will not feel comfortable with him. When one is not able to elevate and employ people, they will not delight in him. When one is not able to beautify and ornament people, they will not give him glory. When all four key factors are completely lacking, then everyone under Heaven will abandon him. This is called being reduced to a commoner. And so I say: When the Way is preserved, the state is preserved, and when the Way is lost, the state is lost.

Reducing the number of craftsmen and merchants while increasing the number of farmers, prohibiting robbery and villainy and rooting out vileness and perversion—this is how to keep people alive and nurture them. Letting the Son of Heaven have the three dukes, letting the feudal lords each have a prime minister, letting the grand ministers control their official positions and the officers maintain their posts, and having all model themselves after the proper measures and be without prejudice—this is how to organize and order people. Assigning rank by judging virtue, awarding official positions by assessing ability, and in each case making it so that the right person undertakes the right tasks and each gets what is proper for him,[26] with the highest worthies employed as the three dukes, the next worthiest employed as feudal lords, and the lowest worthies employed as grand ministers and officers—this is how to elevate and employ people. Arranging it so that caps and clothing, emblems and patterns, carving and inlay are all according to proper gradations—this is how to beautify and ornament people. Thus, from the Son of Heaven down to the ordinary folk, all will exhaust their abilities, achieve their

---

[25] As before (see chapter 9, note 19), here Xunzi is playing upon the close similarity between the words "lord" (*jun* 君) and "community" (*qun* 群) in both pronunciation and written form during ancient times.

[26] See the similar wording at 18.271–74.

intentions, and find comfort and joy in their tasks. This is something
245 in which they will all be the same. Their clothes will be warm and
their food will be filling, their dwellings will be comfortable and their
travels will be joyful, and their work will be timely, their responsibilities clear, and their supplies sufficient. This is also something in which
they will all be the same.
250   As for piling up colors to create fancy clothing patterns and piling
up flavors to create exquisite food preparations, these things are regarded as embellishments. A sage king takes such embellishments as
resources in order to make clear distinctions and differences. Above,
he uses them to ornament the worthy and the good and make clear the
255 distinction between noble and the lowly. Below, he uses them to ornament elders and juniors and make clear the distinction between closer
and more distant relations. Above in the court of the king and his
dukes, and below among the families of the common people, everyone
under Heaven understands clearly that he does this not for the sake of
260 having unique things, but rather in order to make clear social divisions, achieve order, and protect ten thousand generations. Thus, the
Son of Heaven and the feudal lords will have no excessive or wasteful
expenditures. The grand ministers and officers will have no deviant or
foul conduct. The hundred functionaries and officials will have no
265 cases of laziness or indolence. The ordinary masses and common people will have no vile or perverse customs, and will be free of the crimes
of robbery and villainy. Thus one can call this a case where *yi* is universal. And so it is said, "When there is order, embellishments reach
even to the common people. When there is disorder, then insufficiency
270 reaches even to kings and dukes." This expresses my meaning.
On the grand embodiment of the ultimate Way:[27]

Exalt ritual, set out proper models,
Then in the state there will be constancy.
Elevate worthies, employ the capable,
275   Commoners then will be pointed rightly.
Gather judgments, inspect without prejudice,[28]
Commoners then will not think doubtingly.

[27] In the remarks that follow, the text plays on two senses of the compound *da xing* 大
形 in a way that is difficult to capture in English. The first word, *da* 大, means
"large" or "great." The second word, *xing* 形, most literally means "shape" or "form,"
and is often used to refer to the "taking shape" or "manifestation" of something,
but it also often refers to a person's "physical form," or in other words, the "body."
Thus, when the text speaks of the *da xing* of the Way, it simultaneously refers to the
large-scale manifestation of the Way, and to a *great body* constituted by many people
following the Way. I have used "grand embodiment" here to try to capture both of
these senses.
[28] Here and below "without prejudice" and "unprejudiced" are used as translations
for *gong* 公. For more on this concept, see chapter 2, note 24.

Reward the successful, punish those slacking,
Commoners then will not act lazily.
Broadly hear cases, display perfect insight,   280
Then the whole world will be siding with thee.

After that, if you

Make clear people's allotments, their responsibilities,
Assign to people proper works, arrange activities,
Use those having talents, grant office for abilities,   285
So none are not well ordered, nor have improprieties,

Then

Unprejudiced ways will enjoy success,
And selfish approaches make no progress.
Unprejudiced *yi* will shine bright and clear,   290
And selfish pursuits wholly disappear.

When it is like this, then

Glib persuaders are made to stop;
Men rich in virtue are promoted.
The straight and principled rise up;   295
Those profit-greedy are demoted.

The *Documents* says, "Those who act before the proper time will be
killed without pardon. Those who fall behind the proper time will be
killed without pardon."[29] People will each practice their tasks and
become firmly settled in them, and people's performance of the hun-   300
dred tasks will be just like the way that the ears, eyes, nose, and mouth
cannot be borrowed to perform one another's office. And so, when

---

[29] See *Shujing, Yinzheng* ("The Punitive Expedition of Yin"), translated in Waltham
(1971, p. 61). The received text of the *Documents* differs from Xunzi's quotation here.
In its original context, the quoted remarks are made in reference to the punishment
of two officials who failed to keep watch over the timing of astronomical events.
Commentators suggest that in this context "proper time" is probably meant to be
taken as the time at which orders are given by the ruler, i.e., acting before the ruler
orders something and delaying to act once orders are issued both amount to in-
fringements of the ruler's power that are selfish (hence the relevance of the quote
here). The mention of execution here seems a little overly harsh for Xunzi's normal
attitude toward wrongdoers. The word *sha* 殺 is here translated as "kill," which is its
most common meaning and its sense in the original context, but Xunzi elsewhere
uses it to mean "make lower in rank," and it is possible that he intended it to be
taken in this weaker sense here, since he is quoting the lines from the *Documents*
somewhat out of context. However, compare also 9.23–24.

responsibilities have been allotted, then the people will not reach for what is outside their scope. When ranks have been fixed, then matters
305 of precedence will not become disordered. When one broadly hears cases and displays perfect insight, then the hundred tasks will not be neglected.

When it is like this, then from one's subordinate ministers and the hundred functionaries down to the ordinary people, all of them dare
310 to rest secure in their positions only after first cultivating themselves, and dare to accept responsibilities only when they are truly capable. The common people reform their customs, petty men change their hearts, and those who are adherents of what is vile and perverse return to honest ways. This is called the height of government through
315 education. And so, the Son of Heaven

> Sees clearly without having to look.
> Hears keenly without having to listen.
> Knows without having to deliberate.
> Achieves without having to stir.[30]

320 Tranquilly, he sits by himself, and all under Heaven follow him as if they were a single body, just as the four limbs follow the heart. This is called the grand embodiment. The *Odes* says, "Warm and respectful of others, virtue alone is his foundation."[31] This expresses my meaning.

Those who are rulers of men all desire strength and dislike weak-
325 ness, desire safety and dislike danger, desire honor and dislike disgrace—this is something in which Yu and Jie were the same. For securing these three objects of desire and warding off these three objects of dislike, just what way is there to do so expediently? I say: The key lies in carefully choosing one's prime minister. There is simply no
330 more direct way than this. Thus, if the man is intelligent but not *ren*, he is not acceptable. If he is *ren* but not intelligent, then he is not acceptable. When he is both intelligent and *ren*, then this sort of person is a treasure for the ruler of men, and the true assistant of kings and hegemons. If one does not hasten to seek such a man, one is not intel-
335 ligent. If one obtains such a man but does not put him to use, one is not *ren*. To be lacking such a man yet seek by luck to have his accomplishments—nothing is more stupid than this.

Now there are the following great errors[b] that the ruler of men may make: employing worthy people to do things but then consulting
340 with unworthy people in regulating them, employing wise people to deliberate on things but then consulting with foolish people in judg-

---

[30] This quartet of lines is rhymed in the original. For further explanation of such seemingly supernatural power, see below, lines 463–87. Compare also *Daodejing* chap. 47.

[31] Mao #256. Compare the use of this same citation at 3.53–54 and 6.196–7.

ing them, employing cultivated, well-bred men to implement things but then consulting with corrupt and perverse people so as to suspect them. Even though such a ruler wishes to succeed, how could he achieve it? You can compare this to setting up a straight board and 345 then worrying that its shadow might be crooked. Nothing is more confused than this.

A saying goes, "The looks of a beautiful woman are considered a disaster by the ugly ones. A man unprejudiced and upright is considered a festering sore by the vulgar masses. A person who follows the 350 Way is considered a villain by those who are corrupt and perverse." Now if one employs corrupt, perverse people to judge those whom they consider hateful villains and yet asks them to be impartial, how could one achieve this? You can compare this to setting up a crooked board and then seeking for its shadow to be straight. Nothing is more 355 chaotic than this.

And so, the men of ancient times did not do things like this. There was a way behind how they chose people, and there was a model for how they employed people. The way behind how they chose people was to gauge them with ritual. The model for how they employed 360 people was to constrain them with gradations of status. As for people's practice of *yi* and their comportment, they measured them with ritual. As for people's wisdom, deliberations, and choices of what to accept and reject, they assessed them by what they achieved. As days and months accumulated and grew to a long time, they examined 365 them according to the greatness of their accomplishments. Thus, those who were inferior were not put in a position to supervise those who were grand, those who were insubstantial were not put in a position to lord over those with real substance, and those who were stupid were not put in a position to dictate plans to those who were wise. 370 For this reason, their myriad undertakings were free from error.

And so, examine people through practice of ritual, and observe whether they are able to rest secure in respectfulness. Give them conditions where men's behaviors are unstable and shifting, and observe whether they are able to adapt to the changes. Give them conditions 375 of security and comfort, and observe whether they are able to avoid straying into licentiousness. Present them with beautiful sounds and sights, power and profit, resentment and anger, worry and danger, and observe whether they are able to avoid departing from what they maintain. Then, those who truly have what is required will be distin- 380 guished from those who truly lack what is required as clearly as white is distinguished from black. How could they possibly remain twisted up? Thus, Bo Le could not be deceived with regard to horses,[32] and

---

[32] According to traditional accounts, Bo Le was skilled in physiognomizing horses and was thus an expert judge of them.

the gentleman cannot be deceived with regard to people. This is the
385 way of an enlightened king.

If the ruler of men desires to obtain good archers, who can hit a
small target while shooting from far away, then he will dangle an offer
of noble rank and weighty rewards in order to attract them. Within
his family, he may not favor his sons and younger brothers. Outside
390 his family, he may not ignore someone from a faraway place. If the
person can hit the target, then one picks him. How could this not be
a sure way to obtain good archers? Even a sage cannot alter this.

If the ruler of men desires to obtain good chariot drivers, who can
travel great distances at high speed, going a thousand *li* in a single
395 day, then he will dangle an offer of noble rank and weighty rewards
in order to attract them. Within his family, he may not favor his sons
and younger brothers. Outside his family, he may not ignore someone from a faraway place. If the person can travel the distance, then
one picks him. How could this not be a sure way to obtain good
400 chariot drivers? Even a sage cannot alter this.

As for those who desire to order the state, steer the people, and
coordinate and unify superiors and subordinates, within the state
they will use these things to solidify its fortifications, and outside the
state they will use these things to ward off troubles. If there is order,
405 then they will have control over others, and others will not be able to
get control over them. If there is chaos, then danger, disgrace, and
destruction for them are things one can simply stand by and await.[33]
Nevertheless, in the way that they go about seeking premiers, prime
ministers, counselors, and assistants, only in this matter do they not
410 match up to their unprejudiced approach in the previous cases. Instead, they employ only their favorites and others who ingratiate
themselves. Is this not a great error?

And so, those who possess altars of soil and grain all desire
strength, but quickly they become weak. They all desire safety, but
415 quickly they become endangered. They all desire to be preserved, but
quickly they come to perish. In ancient times, there were ten thousand states, but nowadays those remaining from among them number only in the tens. There is no other reason for this than that all
have missed the mark on this matter.

420 Thus, enlightened rulers in some cases bestow personal favor on
people with gifts of precious metals and stones, pearls and jades, but
in no case do they bestow personal favor on people with gifts of official position or responsibilities. Why is this? I say: It is because

---

[33] The sentences that compose the paragraph up to this point fit together rather
strangely, and some commentators suggest that the text might be corrupt. The
translation reflects my best attempt to make sense of the flow of thought here, but
remains tentative.

doing otherwise is fundamentally not beneficial to those whom one personally favors. If the person is not capable but the ruler employs 425
him anyway, then the ruler is benighted. If a minister is not capable but boasts that he is capable anyway, then the minister is engaging in deceit. When the ruler is benighted in his position above, and ministers engage in deceit in their positions below, the day of destruction will be at hand, and so this is a way that leads to harm for both. 430

As for King Wen, it was not the case that he had no valued relatives. It was not the case that he had no sons or younger brothers. It was not the case that he had no favorites. In an extraordinary act, he raised the Grand Duke above his countrymen and employed him.[34] How would 435
that have been an instance of bestowing personal favor! Perhaps you think he did this because they were related? But the Zhou rulers were surnamed Ji, and that man was surnamed Jiang. Perhaps you think he did this because they were longtime acquaintances? But they had never known each other previously. Perhaps you think he did this because he was fond of good looks? But that man had passed seventy- 440
two years, and he was bald and his teeth had fallen out.[c]

The reason that he nevertheless employed the man was that King Wen desired to establish a noble way and to make shine a noble reputation in order to show kindness to all under Heaven, but he could not do it alone. Were it not for that man, then no one would have 445
sufficed to be raised to the position. And so, King Wen raised him up and employed him, and thereupon his noble way was indeed established, and his noble reputation indeed became brilliantly apparent. He controlled all under Heaven in an encompassing manner. He established seventy-one states, and there were fifty-three for which men 450
surnamed Ji had sole responsibility. Among the sons and grandsons of the Zhou lineage, all except those who were reckless or misguided became feudal lords most eminent throughout the world. To achieve this sort of situation is to be able to take care of people. And so, King Wen held to the greatest way in the world, he established the greatest 455
accomplishment in the world,[35] and only then did he practice generosity toward those whom he pitied and those for whom he cared. Even those below him in the clan were still able to become feudal lords most eminent throughout the world. Thus it is said, "Only an enlightened ruler can take care of those for whom he cares. A be- 460

---

[34] This remark refers to an incident in which, according to traditional stories, King Wen recognized great virtue and talent in a lowly fisherman named Lü Shang and made him prime minister, and this man was later known as the Grand Duke. Here the title "Grand Duke" is applied retrospectively: Lü Shang was not already Grand Duke when King Wen raised him above his peers.

[35] These first two segments of the sentence refer to King Wen's unprejudiced approach to choosing his prime minister and his resulting success in obtaining the Grand Duke for the position.

nighted ruler will surely endanger those for whom he cares." This expresses my meaning.

One's eyes cannot see what lies behind a wall, and one's ears cannot hear what lies beyond the distance of a *li*, but as for what the ruler
465 of men has responsibility to watch over, at its furthest it includes the whole world, and at its nearest it includes the area within the boundaries of a single state, and he cannot afford to know only sketchily what goes on. Among the changes that take place throughout the world, and even the events that take place within the borders of a
470 single state, there will be affairs that are neglected and affairs that go astray, and if the ruler of men has no way to know of them, then this is the starting point whence he may become hemmed in, subject to threat, and blocked up.[36] So narrow are the boundaries for the acuity of one's eyes and ears! So vast are the boundaries of what the ruler of
475 men has responsibility to watch over! So great is the danger—he cannot afford not to know what goes on in between these two!

Since it is like this, then how will the ruler of men know these things? I say: The ruler's favorites and members of his immediate circle are the gates and windows by which he observes what is far
480 away and receives the masses.[37] He cannot afford not to equip himself with them early.

And so, the ruler of men must have favorites and members of his immediate circle who can be trusted, and only then are they acceptable. Their wisdom and intelligence must suffice for employing them
485 to measure things, and their uprightness and integrity must suffice for employing them to determine things, and only then are they acceptable. Such people are called the precious equipment of the state.

Just as the ruler of men cannot do without periods where he travels around leisurely and goes sightseeing and periods where he feels se-
490 cure and comfortable, so it is unavoidable that he will experience changes in his condition such as illness or impairment.[38] If we draw a comparison for the state, things come at it as if pouring forth continuously from a spring, and if even a single thing does not receive a proper response, then this is the starting point of chaos. And so I say:
495 The ruler of men must not go it alone. The ruler's premier, prime

---

[36] As the passage goes on to make clear, the last part of this sentence refers primarily to the danger of ministers manipulating the ruler and usurping his power. "Blocked up" here connotes his being "cut off" from reliable sources of information and guidance, as well as having his exercise of authority "obstructed" by interference from others.

[37] The metaphor here picks up on the idea from the beginning of the previous paragraph: the eyes cannot see through a wall, but by putting doors and windows in it, things that lie behind the wall become open to view and, by coming through the door, can draw closer and be known.

[38] Commentators explain that the last word of this sentence is really a euphemism for death.

minister, counselors, and assistants are the foundation on which he stands and the staff he leans upon to walk. He cannot afford not to equip himself with them early.

And so, the ruler of men must have a premier, prime minister, counselors, and assistants who can be given responsibilities, and only 500 then are they acceptable. Their virtuous reputations must suffice to calm and soothe the common people, and their wisdom and deliberations must suffice to respond to and meet myriad changes in circumstances, and only then are they acceptable. Such people are called the precious equipment of the state. 505

Interactions with the feudal lords who border the four sides of one's state are something in which one cannot avoid involvement. However, those interactions will not necessarily be mutually genial. And so, the ruler of men must have people who will suffice for being employed in far away places to make clear his intentions and resolve 510 uncertainties, and only then are they acceptable. Their demonstrations and persuasions must suffice to dissolve worries. Their wisdom and deliberations must suffice to resolve uncertainties. Their swiftness and decisiveness must suffice to ward off disasters. They must not circumvent protocols or act confrontationally toward other lords, 515 but nevertheless their response to derogatory treatment and their defense against troubles must suffice to uphold the state's altars of soil and grain.[d] Only then are they acceptable. Such people are called the precious equipment of the state.

And so, if the ruler of men has no favorites and members of his 520 immediate circle who can be trusted, he is called "benighted." If he has no premier, prime minister, counselors, or assistants who can be given responsibilities, then he is called "alone." If those whom he has sent as emissaries to the feudal lords bordering the four sides of his state are not the right kind of people, then he is called "abandoned." 525 If he is abandoned, alone, and benighted, then he is called "endangered." Even if his state still exists, the ancients would call it "perished." The *Odes* says, "So impressively refined and numerous were the well-bred men! King Wen used them to bring about peace."[39] This expresses my meaning. 530

On classifying people according to their material: Being conscientious, honest, restrained, and hardworking, calculating meticulously and sparingly, not daring to lose or waste anything—this is the material for being an official, scribe, or functionary.

Being cultivated, careful, upright, and correct, someone who ex- 535 alts the proper model and respects his allotted station, devoid of any inclination to go astray in his heart; someone who keeps watch over his responsibilities and follows through on his assigned tasks, not

[39] Mao #235.

daring to add to or subtract from them; someone to whom can be
540 handed on the work of the preceding generation, but who cannot be
made to trespass upon and seize what does not belong to his position—this is the material for being a well-bred man, a grand minister,
or an overseer of officials.

Understanding that the way to revere one's lord is through exalt-
545 ing ritual and *yi*; understanding that the way to achieve a fine reputation is through being fond of well-bred men; understanding that the
way to bring peace to the state is through caring for the common
people; understanding that the way to unify their customs is through
having a constant model; understanding that the way to develop ac-
550 complishments is through elevating the worthy and employing the
capable; understanding that the way to increase resources is through
working at fundamental tasks while prohibiting insignificant pursuits; understanding that the way to achieve expediency in affairs is
through avoiding struggles with subordinates over small matters of
555 profit; understanding that the way to avoid having affairs become
bogged down is through making clear regulations and measures and
assessing things to ensure that they match their intended uses—this
is the material for being a premier, prime minister, counselor, or assistant, but it does not yet amount to the way of a lord.

560 Being able to judge people who are among these three kinds of
material, and then being able to put them in official positions, without missing the appropriate ranking for them—this is called the way
of a ruler. When there is someone like this, he himself will enjoy ease
and his state will be ordered. His accomplishments will be great and
565 his reputation will be fine. At the greatest, he can become a true king,
and at the very least, he can become a hegemon. This is the crucial
point for the ruler of men to keep watch over.

If the ruler of men is not able to judge people who are among these
three kinds of material, and if he does not take the above way as his
570 way, then instead he will simply wind up debasing his authority while
putting forth exhausting efforts. Putting aside delights for his eyes
and ears, he will personally spend day after day setting in order detailed matters. He will consume the whole of each day in comprehensively distinguishing things, as he deliberates how to contest with his
575 ministers and subordinates over trifling investigations and how to
display specialized expertise. From ancient times to the present there
has never been a situation like this that does not result in chaos. It is
what is called "inspecting that which one is not to look into, listening
after that which one is not to hear, and pursuing that which one is not
580 to accomplish." This expresses my meaning.

CHAPTER 13

The Way to Be a Minister

THE GRADES OF MINISTERS

There are fawning ministers, usurping ministers, meritorious ministers, and sagely ministers:

One sort of minister is such that at home, he cannot be employed to unify the people. Abroad, he cannot be employed to avert crises. 5
The common people have no affection for him, and the feudal lords do not trust him. However, with his clever words and flattering speech, he is good at obtaining favor from his superiors. Such is the fawning minister.

One sort of minister is such that he is not loyal to his lord above, 10 but he is good at obtaining repute among the people below. He cares nothing for the Way and *yi* that encompass all, and instead forms factions and cliques. He takes deceiving the ruler and plotting personal gain as his task. Such is the usurping minister.

One sort of minister is such that at home, he can be employed to 15 unify the people. Abroad, he can be employed to avert crises. The common people have affection for him, and well-bred men trust him. Above, he is loyal to his lord. Below, his concern for the common people is tireless. Such is the meritorious minister.

One sort of minister is such that he can revere his lord above while 20 also being able to care for the people below. His governmental orders and educational influence take form among his subordinates like a shadow following a body. He adapts completely to unexpected occurrences and changes as quickly as echo following a sound. He knows how to extend categories and connect types in order to handle 25 cases without a precedent. In every area, he brings about the phenomena of order. Such is the sagely minister.

And so,

> If you employ sagely ministers, you will be a true king.
> If you use meritorious ones, your might will be daunting. 30
> If you use usurping ministers, you will be endangered.
> If you use fawning ministers, you will soon be perishing.

If the fawning minister is employed, one is sure to die. If the usurping minister is employed, one is sure to be endangered. If the meritorious minister is employed, one is sure to attain honor. If the sagely minister 35 is employed, one is sure to be revered. Thus, Su Qin of Qi, Zhou

Hou of Chu, and Zhang Yi of Qin can be called fawning ministers. Zhang Quji of Han, Feng Yang of Zhao, and Meng Chang of Qi can be called usurping ministers. Guan Zhong of Qi, Jiu Fan of Jin, and Sunshu Ao of Chu can be called meritorious ministers. Yi Yin of the Shang dynasty and the Grand Duke of the Zhou dynasty can be called sagely ministers.

These are the grades of ministers. They are the extremes of auspicious and inauspicious, worthy and unworthy men. One must diligently focus one's intentions on this matter and carefully choose from among them, and the preceding will suffice to examine them.

To follow orders and thereby benefit one's lord is called "being properly compliant." To follow orders but not thereby benefit one's lord is called "flattering." To go against orders yet thereby benefit one's lord is called "being loyal." To go against orders but not thereby benefit one's lord is called "usurping." To care nothing for whether one's lord is honored or disgraced, to care nothing for whether the state is well off or not, and to behave in a lazily cooperative and improperly accommodating manner for the sole purpose of maintaining one's salary and nurturing those with whom one is connected—this is called "being a villain toward the state."

When the lord makes erroneous plans or takes erroneous actions, these are arrangements that will endanger the state and its clans and destroy the altars of soil and grain. If there is someone among the senior ministers, or even the lord's own father or elder brothers, who is able to present advice to the lord, and who is such that if his advice is taken, things will turn out all right, but if it is not taken, he will take his leave, this is called "remonstrating." If there is someone who is able to present advice to the lord, and who is such that if his advice is taken, things will turn out all right, but if it is not taken, he will die trying to change his lord's mind, this is called "contesting." If there is someone who is able to gather together knowledgeable people and combine their strength, then lead the assembled ministers and hundred functionaries and together with them threaten the lord and forcibly get hold of him, so that even if the lord is uncomfortable, he cannot but listen to them, and as a result a great problem for the state is resolved or a great harm to the state is eliminated, and they succeed in keeping the lord honored and the state safe—this is called "guiding." If there is someone who is able to resist his lord's orders, steal his lord's authority,[1] and oppose his lord's efforts, so as to render dangers to the state harmless and eliminate things that threaten disgrace for his lord, and whose accomplishments and victories are sufficient to bring about great benefit for the state—this is called "restraining."

---

[1] This may sound strange, but see note 6 below.

Thus, people who engage in remonstrating, contesting, guiding, 80
and restraining are true ministers of the altars of soil and grain, and
treasures for the lord of a state. They are the sort of people whom
enlightened lords honor and treat generously, but who are regarded
by benighted rulers and misguided lords as behaving villainously
toward them. And so, those whom an enlightened lord rewards are 85
those whom a benighted lord punishes, and those whom a benighted
lord rewards are those whom an enlightened lord executes. The behavior of Yi Yin[2] and Jizi[3] can be called "remonstrating." The behavior of Bi Gan and Zixu[4] can be called "contesting." The behavior of
Lord Pingyuan in relation to Zhao can be called "guiding."[5] The be- 90
havior of Lord Xinling in relation to Wei can be called "restraining."[6]
A proverb states, "Follow the Way, not your lord."[7] This expresses my
meaning.

[2] Although Yi Yin is usually known as a minister of Tang, founder of the Shang dynasty, some texts (see *Mencius* 6B6) report that he also served the tyrant Jie, whom
Tang overthrew. Furthermore, commentators suggest that in fact Tang sent Yi Yin to
serve Jie to reform him and thereby try to avoid the need to overthrow him, but this
strategy was not successful, so Yi Yin returned to Tang. It is most likely such stories
that Xunzi has in mind here.

[3] The mention of Jizi here is somewhat problematic. The explanation of "remonstrating" earlier in the text states that when the minister's advice is not taken, he will *qu*
去, which literally means "leave," and that would seem to be the sense that applies
to Yi Yin. However, most early stories about Jizi (and all other references to the Jizi
story in the *Xunzi*) claim that when the tyrant Zhòu did not heed his criticisms, Jizi
feigned madness and Zhòu imprisoned him, so he could not have "left" in the literal
sense. On the other hand, one source (the *Han Shu*) states that Jizi did actually flee
from Zhòu and went elsewhere. Since Xunzi provides no details here, it is unclear
which story is being referenced. I have therefore rendered *qu* 去 as "take his leave"
to permit a more literal or a less literal understanding (e.g., leaving off one's service
to the lord) of how Jizi fits the model.

[4] Wu Zixu was an important general in the state of Wu who garnered several victories
for that state. He warned King Fuchai of Wu about the dangers posed by state of
Yue, but he was not heeded, and ultimately the king ordered him to commit suicide,
which he did (ca. 486 BCE). Later, Yue indeed invaded, King Fuchai was killed, and
Wu was destroyed.

[5] According to various stories, the Lord Pingyuan, a member of the royal family of
Zhao, played an important role in saving Zhao from an attack by the state of Qin
(ca. 257 BCE). However, those descriptions of his involvement do not fit well with
the details of what Xunzi here labels as "guiding," so it is unclear what events Xunzi
has in mind.

[6] Lord Xinling was a member of the royal family of Wei. During the attack on Zhao
mentioned in the previous note, Wei initially sent troops to aid Zhao, but under
threat from Qin, the Wei king ordered his soldiers to halt their march. Lord Xinling
repeatedly begged the king to proceed with the attack, but the king refused. Lord
Xinling then stole the king's tally used to command the troops and led them to defeat Qin and save Zhao (which presumably Xunzi also regards as protecting Wei
from Qin's threat).

[7] This proverb is quoted again at 29.23–24. In general, the view expressed here in
these two paragraphs is similar to the view expressed in the opening paragraphs of
that chapter.

And so, if ministers who abide by what is correct and *yi* are put in place, then the court will not be toppled. If people who engage in remonstrating, contesting, guiding, and restraining are trusted, then the lord will not go far astray. If men who will fight as fangs and claws for the state are deployed, then enemies will not appear. If ministers for the borders are appropriately positioned, then territory will not be lost. Thus, the enlightened ruler is fond of having people collaborate with him, but the benighted ruler is fond of ruling alone. The enlightened ruler elevates the worthy, employs the capable, and celebrates their magnificence. The benighted ruler is jealous of the worthy, fears the capable, and destroys their meritorious achievements. To punish those who are truly loyal while rewarding those who treat you villainously is called utmost benightedness, and it is how Jie and Zhòu came to be destroyed.

In serving a sagely lord, engage in listening and following, and do not engage in remonstrating and contesting. In serving a mediocre lord, engage in remonstrating and contesting, and do not engage in flattery and toadying. In serving a violent lord, engage in patching over and mending up his deficiencies, and do not engage in forcibly getting hold of and restraining him.[8]

When you are forcibly constrained by a chaotic age and are reduced to dwelling in a violent state, and there is no way to avoid it, then extol what is fine about it, praise what is good in it, treat as taboo what is bad in it, and conceal its failures: speak of its strong points, and do not mention its shortcomings.[9] Make this your established custom. The *Odes* says:

> The state faces a momentous fate
> This must not be told to others.
> Guard your person.[10]

This expresses my meaning.

Being reverent, respectful, and obliging; hearing and obeying with haste; not daring to make decisions or choices according to selfish interests; not daring to take or give things according to selfish interests; having compliance with one's superiors as one's intention—these are what is *yi* in the service of a sagely lord.

---

[8] This remark may appear odd, but Xunzi's view seems to be that with a violent lord, strong-arm approaches will not work, and instead a more gentle approach is required.

[9] Wording nearly identical to this also appears at 27.717–20.

[10] This poem does not appear in the received text of the *Odes*. The lines are rhymed in the original. Commentators suggest that the sentiment in this paragraph is similar to *Analects* 14.3.

Being loyal and trustworthy but not toadying; engaging in remonstrating and contesting but not flattery; with a forceful manner, being 130 resolute, criticizing directly, and making one's intentions upright, without any deviation or swaying in one's heart; saying of what is right that it is right, and saying of what is wrong that it is wrong—these are what is *yi* in the service of a mediocre lord.

Being accommodating, yet not to the point of becoming unscru- 135 pulous; being flexible, yet not to the point of simply caving in; being tolerant, yet not to the point of allowing chaos; holding firm to the ultimate Way with a clear understanding, yet being accommodating and harmonious in all things; being able to exert transformative influence, and at the appropriate times to win him over—these are what 140 is *yi* in the service of a violent lord.

Treat him like riding an unbroken horse, like caring for a newborn, like feeding a starving person.[11] And so, take advantage of his fearful moods to correct his mistakes. Take advantage of his worried moods to scrutinize his habits. Take advantage of his joyful moods to rein in 145 his ways.[a] Take advantage of his angry moods to eliminate his offenses. Then in every case you will have just the thing to say to him. The *Documents* says:[12] "He followed orders and did not forcibly restrain [the king]. He subtly remonstrated without tiring. As a superior, he was enlightened. As a subordinate, he was obliging."[13] This 150 expresses my meaning.

If there is someone who serves others and yet is not found agreeable by those he serves, it is because he is someone who is not diligent. If there is someone who is diligent and yet is not found agreeable by those he serves, it is because he is someone who does not 155 show respect. If there is someone who shows respect and yet is not found agreeable by those he serves, it is because he is someone who does not display loyalty. If there is someone who displays loyalty and yet is not found agreeable by those he serves, it is because he is someone who lacks accomplishments. If there is someone who has accom- 160 plishments and yet is not found agreeable by those he serves, it is because he is someone who lacks virtue. Thus, the way that lack of virtue works is such that it harms one's diligence, topples one's ac-

[11] I.e., these are all cases where one cannot rush things and must proceed with extreme care, and so too for dealing with a violent lord, as per the earlier remarks in this chapter.

[12] The quotation from the *Documents* here does not closely match anything in the received text. Some commentators consider it an alternate version of some lines in the chapter *Yi Xun* ("The Instructions of I," see translation in Waltham 1971, p. 75), but the discrepancies are so large that others regard it as coming from some different, now-lost chapter. Here I follow the former view partially and with hesitation.

[13] In the context of the *Yi Xun* chapter, the "he" refers to the sage king Tang. Xunzi is perhaps speaking of the time when Tang still served the tyrant Jie.

complishments, and destroys one's laborious efforts.[14] Therefore, the
165   gentleman does not behave like that.

There are some who have the greatest kind of loyalty. There are
some who have the next best kind of loyalty. There are some who
have the lowest kind of loyalty. There are some who are villains toward the state.

170   To use one's virtue to envelop one's lord and thereby transform
him is the greatest kind of loyalty. To use one's virtue to temper one's
lord and thereby patch up his faults is the next best kind of loyalty.
To use what is right to remonstrate against what is wrong and thereby
anger him is the lowest kind of loyalty. To care nothing for whether
175   one's lord is honored or disgraced, to care nothing for whether the
state is well off or not, and to behave in a lazily cooperative and improperly accommodating manner for the sole purpose of maintaining
one's salary and nurturing those with whom one is connected—this is
to be a villain toward the state.

180   The way that the Duke of Zhou behaved toward King Cheng can
be called the greatest kind of loyalty. The way that Guan Zhong behaved toward Duke Huan can be called the next best kind of loyalty.
The way that Wu Zixu behaved toward King Fuchai can be called the
lowest kind of loyalty. The way that Cao Chulong behaved toward
185   the tyrant Zhòu can be called being a villain toward the state.

The person of *ren* is sure to show respect for others. In every case,
if a person is not a worthy, then accordingly he is someone unworthy.
If a person is a worthy and one does not treat him with respect, then
this is to be a beast. If a person is unworthy and one does not treat
190   him with respect, then this is to offend a tiger. If one acts like a beast,
then there will be chaos, and if one offends a tiger, then one will be
in danger. Either way, disaster will come upon one's person. The *Odes*
says:

Dare not toward tigers be harassing,
195   Nor on the *He* to go trespassing.[15]
Such kinds of danger, all people know.
Yet no grasp of others do they show.
Proceed with caution and with dread,
As though a chasm lies ahead,
200   As though upon thin ice you tread![16]

This expresses my meaning.

[14] I.e., lack of virtue wipes out any *credit* in the eyes of one's superiors that one would
otherwise normally get for these meritorious things.
[15] The *He* River (or, as it is better known, the Yellow River) can be quite dangerous to
cross at certain times and places.
[16] Mao #195.

Thus, the person of *ren* is sure to show respect for others. There is a proper way to show respect for others. If they are worthy, then one values them and shows them respect. If they are unworthy, then one fears them and shows them respect. If they are worthy, one draws   205
near to them and shows them respect. If they are unworthy, one keeps them at a distance and shows them respect. There is to be respect for one and all, but the dispositions involved are of two kinds. Being loyal, trustworthy, scrupulous, honest, and not hurtful, and never failing to practice these things in one's interactions with others—this   210
is the substance of the person of *ren*. He has loyalty and trustworthiness for his substance, scrupulousness and honesty as his guiding principles, ritual and *yi* as his form, and the proper classes and categories as his pattern. His slightest word, his most subtle movement, all can serve as a model for others.[17] The *Odes* says, "Be neither aber-   215
rant nor villainous, and then few will not regard you as a model."[18] This expresses my meaning.

To be reverent and respectful makes for ritual propriety. To be accommodating and harmonious makes for musicality. To be careful and cautious makes for benefit. To go brawling and raging makes for   220
harm.[19] And so, the gentleman rests in ritual propriety and musicality, employs carefulness and caution, and avoids brawling and raging. For this reason, in a hundred actions he commits no errors. The petty man is the opposite of this.

The compliance that comes from thoroughly grasping loyalty, the   225
peace that comes from counterbalancing dangers, the echoing that attends upon disaster and chaos: none but an enlightened ruler is capable of knowing these three things.

> Despite a struggle with his lord,
> Still a good man he remains.   230
> Though defying those above him,
> Great accomplishments he gains.
> Completely without selfishness,
> Marching off to die he goes.
> While staying free of prejudice,   235
> Proven loyalty he shows.

This is called the compliance that comes from thoroughly grasping loyalty. Lord Xinling was like this.

> Despite moving to seize power,
> Still he counts as being *yi*.   240

---

[17] Compare the use of this sentence at 1.147–48.
[18] Mao #256.
[19] See 4.14–61.

Though he has engaged in killing,
Yet a man of *ren* is he.
The ruling order was reversed,
But he acted faithfully.
245 With the works of Heaven and Earth
His deeds form a trinity,
And all people benefited
From his generosity.

This is called the peace that comes from counterbalancing dangers.
250 Such were Tang and Wu.

He shares the disposition
Of others who go astray.
In his seeking harmony,
No standard does he obey.
255 Caring naught for right or wrong,
Straight or bent he does not weigh.ᵇ
Improper acquiescence
Is just what his deeds display.
For those who live recklessly[20]
260 He brings further disarray.

This is called the echoing that attends upon disaster and chaos. Such were Fei Lian and Wu Lai. A proverb says, "cut apart and yet even, crooked and yet aligned, different and yet one."[21] The *Odes* says:

Jade *qiu* tokens large and small were accepted by the king,
265 And he became a standard for the states then submitting.[22]

This expresses my meaning.

---

[20] See 12.166–70.

[21] See the earlier quotation of this line at 4.315–16. Here it seems to have a different point. The earlier occurrence was used to sum up the idea that having a hierarchy with divisions of labor and goods can actually promote social cohesion. Here it seems to be used to sum up the idea that subordinates who occasionally resist their rulers are truly loyal, whereas subordinates who simply cater to the ruler's wishes are not, in fact, good followers.

[22] Mao #304. The king referred to here is the sage Tang. The relevance of the quotation to the preceding remarks is not entirely clear, but perhaps the mention of accepting both the "large and small" is meant to echo the idea that a wise ruler values subordinates who are not "uniform," i.e., subordinates who may disagree with him and act in other ways that are not conventionally regarded as loyal, but who are in fact truly loyal. See also 4.318–319, which quotes the next stanza of this poem.

CHAPTER 14

On Attracting Men of Worth

THE METHOD OF HEARING CASES EVENLY, EXPOSING
THOSE CONCEALING THINGS, FAVORING THOSE ENLIGHTENED,
REPELLING THOSE VILE, AND ADVANCING THOSE GOOD

The gentleman does not listen to words of praise from those who
form parties and cliques. He does not make use of criticisms from   5
those who defame and vilify others. He does not become close with
people who are jealous or fixated. He does not grant requests accompanied by goods, money, or gift animals. He is careful of all
perverse teachings, perverse doctrines, perverse works, perverse
plans, perverse praise, and perverse censure—in short, whatever is   10
baseless or comes in an oblique manner. He listens to what he hears
and with understanding decides its proper class.[a] When he has determined what is appropriate and an appropriate case occurs,[b] only
then does he employ[c] punishments and rewards to repay it in kind.
When it is thus, no one will attempt vile teachings, vile doctrines,   15
vile works, vile plans, vile praise, or vile censure. No one will fail to
master loyal teachings, loyal doctrines, loyal works, loyal plans,
loyal praise, and loyal censure, and they will engage in them everywhere in order to do their utmost for their superior. This is called
the method of hearing cases evenly, exposing those concealing   20
things, favoring those enlightened, repelling those vile, and advancing those good.[1]
 Wherever the rivers and waterways are deep, fish and turtles will
settle there. Wherever the mountains and forests are luxuriant, birds
and beasts will settle there. Wherever punishments and government   25
regulations are evenhanded, the common people will settle there.
Wherever the practice of ritual and *yi* is perfected, the gentleman will
settle there. And so, when the practice of ritual reaches to one's person, then one's conduct is cultivated, and when the practice of *yi*
reaches to the state, then there is enlightened government. As for one   30
who is able to hold himself according to ritual and whose noble reputation is pure, everyone under Heaven will long for him, what he
commands will be carried out, and what he prohibits will be stopped,
and in this the work of a true king is complete! The *Odes* says, "Show

---

[1] This passage seems to be corrupt and the translation is tentative.

35   kindness to the central realm, in order to soothe the four corners."[2]
     This expresses my meaning.
        The rivers and waterways are where fish and dragons dwell. The
     mountains and forests are where birds and beasts dwell. The state and
     family are where well-bred men and common people dwell. If the riv-
40   ers and waterways dry up, the fish and dragons will abandon them.
     If the mountains and forests are despoiled, the birds and beasts will
     abandon them. If the state and family lose their proper governance,
     the well-bred men and common people will abandon them. Without
     land, there is nowhere for people to dwell securely. Without people,
45   the land will not be guarded. Without the Way and the proper mod-
     els, people will not come. Without the gentleman, the Way will not
     be upheld. Thus, as for the way that land goes together with people,
     and the Way goes together with proper models, these are the funda-
     mental makings of the state and family. The gentleman is crucial for
50   the Way and the proper models, and one cannot lack him for even a
     moment. If one obtains him, there will be order. If one loses him,
     there will be chaos. If one obtains him, there will be security. If one
     loses him, there will be danger. If one obtains him, there will be
     preservation.[3] If one loses him, there will be destruction. Thus, there
55   have been instances of chaos even where there are good models, but
     from ancient times to the present it is unheard of to have chaos where
     the gentleman is in charge. A saying goes, "Order is born from the
     gentleman. Chaos is born from the petty man." This expresses my
     meaning.

60   Obtaining the affection of the masses moves Heaven.
          Living with fine thoughts extends one's years.
          Integrity and trustworthiness bring one spirit-like powers.
          Boasting and deception make an outcast of one's own soul.[4]

        The problem with rulers of men is not that they do not speak of em-
65   ploying the worthy, but rather that they do not honestly make sure to
     employ the worthy. As for speaking of employing the worthy, this is
     due to one's mouth, but driving the worthy away is due to one's con-
     duct. When one's mouth and one's conduct are at odds with each
     other, but one still wishes that those worthy will come and those un-
70   worthy will withdraw, is this not quite difficult to achieve? For those

---

[2] Mao #253.
[3] In this and the following sentence, it is not entirely clear what will be preserved or
    destroyed. The most likely candidate is the state.
[4] These four lines are rhymed in the Chinese. They do not seem to fit with the context,
    and commentators suspect that they originally belonged somewhere else. The first
    line seems incompatible with the view of Heaven proposed in chapter 17 (cf. 17.1–5),
    so perhaps the entire section is an interpolation.

who hunt cicadas with firelight, the task rests in making their fire bright and shaking the trees, and that is all. If the fire is not bright, then even if one shakes the trees, it will be of no use. Now if among the rulers of men there were one who could make bright his virtue, then everyone under Heaven would be drawn to him just as cicadas   75
are drawn to bright fire.

In managing affairs and interacting with the people, to change and adapt with *yi*; to be kind, generous, and broadly accepting; to be reverent and respectful in order to lead them—this is the starting point for government. Only afterward does one investigate matters   80
and decide cases with evenhandedness and harmoniousness, in order to guide them—this is the high point for government. Only afterward does one advance some and dismiss others, punish some and reward others—this is the final matter for government. Thus, in the first year one gives them the starting point, and after three years one gives   85
them the final matter. If one uses the final matter as the starting point, then government orders will not be effective, there will be resentment and hatred among superiors and subordinates, and chaos appears on its own from this. The *Documents* says:

> Even when it is in accordance with *yi* to punish or kill people,   90
> have no haste to do so. You are to say only, "I have not yet
> been able to make matters go smoothly."[5]

This is saying that one is to use teaching first.

Scales are a standard for goods, and ritual is a standard for proper regulation. One uses scales in order to establish the quantity of   95
things, and one uses ritual in order to set the proper grades of people. One grants status on the basis of people's virtue and awards official positions on the basis of their ability. In following proper regulation, seek always to be stringent, and when dealing with the people, seek always to be kind. When one follows proper regulation stringently,   100
one will have good form, and when the people are treated kindly, they will be at ease in their lives. When superiors have good form and the people are at ease in their lives, this is the height of accomplishment and fame, and there is nothing that can be added.

The lord occupies the most exalted position in the state, and the   105
father occupies the most exalted position in the family. When the

---

[5] No section of the received text of the *Documents* matches this quote exactly, but a passage in the *Kanggao* chapter is fairly close and is the likely source of Xunzi's quotation (see Waltham 1971, p. 149). In that context, the speaker is the Duke of Zhou, addressing a younger brother of his who is being entrusted with a certain territory. His remark seems to counsel cultivating humility by laying the blame for people's misdeeds first on oneself. A nearly identical version of this quotation from the *Documents* and the sentence about teaching that follows it also appear at 28.70–73.

most exalted position is held by one person alone, there will be order, but if held by two people, there will be chaos. From ancient times to the present there has not yet been a case where two people who both 110 occupy the most exalted position and contend for greater authority can last for long.

Among the skills for being a proper teacher there are four elements, but being broadly learned is not a part of them. If one is dignified, stern, and inspires awe, one can be a teacher. If at the age of fifty 115 or sixty one has proven oneself trustworthy, one can be a teacher. If one can recite and explain things without ever violating them oneself, one can be a teacher. If one's understanding is subtle and properly ordered, one can be a teacher. Thus, among the skills for being a proper teacher there are four elements, but being broadly learned is 120 not a part of them.

When flowing water reaches a deep place, it curls backward. What falls from the tree fertilizes the roots. When the disciple has achieved success and profit, then he gratefully thinks of his teacher. The *Odes* says, "No words will go unanswered. No virtue will go unrequited."[6] 125 This expresses my meaning.

In rewarding people, one does not want to be overly indulgent, and in punishing people, one does not want to be indiscriminate. If one is overly indulgent when rewarding people, then the benefits one bestows will extend even to the petty man. If one is indiscriminate 130 when punishing people, then the harms one inflicts will extend even to the gentleman.[7] If, through unfortunate circumstances, one commits an error, it is preferable to be overly indulgent and not act indiscriminately at all. For when compared with harming the good, it is better to benefit the perverse.

---

[6] Mao #256. These lines are rhymed in the original. Compare the use of this quotation at 10.197–98.

[7] An implicit premise of this argument seems to be that the petty man (because he is bad) does not deserve any benefits, whereas the gentleman (because he is good) does not deserve any harms, and that underserved treatment of either sort is to be avoided.

CHAPTER 15

A Debate on Military Affairs

Lord Linwu and Xunzi held a debate on military affairs before King Xiaocheng of Zhao.[1] The king said, "May I ask about the crucial points in military affairs?"

Lord Linwu said, "Above, obtain the right season from Heaven. Below, obtain beneficial terrain from Earth. Observe the enemy's changes and movements. Wait for them to set out, but arrive at the battlefield before them. This is the crucial method in using military forces."

Xunzi said, "Not so! I have heard that in the way of the ancients, the fundamental task for all use of military forces and offensive warfare lies with unifying the people. If the bow and arrow are not properly adjusted, then even Archer Yi could not hit a small target. If the six horses do not work in harmony, then even Zao Fu could not drive very far. Without the affection and adherence of well-bred men and the common people, even Tang and Wu could not achieve certain victory. And so, the person who is good at obtaining the people's adherence is the person who is good at using military forces. Thus, the crucial point in military affairs is to be good at obtaining the people's adherence, and that is all."

Lord Linwu said, "Not so! In military affairs, what is to be valued is favorable circumstances, and what is to be practiced is shiftiness and deception. One who is good at using military forces creates feelings of confusion and spreads about obfuscation, so nobody knows whence he will launch his attack. Sun and Wu used this approach, and so everywhere they obliterated their enemies.[2] How could it be necessary to wait upon obtaining the people's adherence?"

Xunzi said, "Not so! That of which I speak is the military affairs of someone who is *ren*, and the intentions of a true king. What you pro-

---

[1] Throughout this chapter, Xunzi is referred to as "Sun Qingzi" (孫卿子), but I have substituted "Xunzi" to avoid confusion. For more on this usage, see chapter 8, note 10. Little is known about Lord Linwu, but it is worth noting that Linwu (臨武) literally means "overseeing martial affairs." King Xiaocheng reigned ca. 265 to ca. 244 BCE.

[2] The "Wu" referred to here is the famous general Wu Qi of Wey. The "Sun" who is mentioned is likely Sun Wu, also known as Sunzi, to whom is attributed the famous book *Sunzi Bingfa*, the title of which is often rendered simply as *The Art of War* in English. Many of the ideas expressed by Lord Linwu here are quite similar to what one finds in that text.

30 pose to value is favorable circumstances in scheming after power, and what you propose to practice is shiftiness and deception in offensive invasions, and these are the affairs of mere feudal lords.

"In military affairs, the person who is *ren* cannot be deceived. The ones who can be deceived are those who are indolent and arrogant, who are spent and unsound,[3] and for whom relations among lord and 35 ministers, superiors and subordinates, are disordered and character- ized by a divisive spirit. Thus, for a tyrant Jie trying to deceive an- other tyrant Jie, good fortune may still depend on whether he is cun- ning or inept, but a Jie trying to deceive a Yao can be compared to throwing eggs against a rock or using one's finger to stir a boiling 40 pot. It is like walking into water or fire—he who enters upon it will simply drown or burn!

"And so, when a *ren* person is in charge of those below,ᵃ the hun- dred generals share one heart, and the three armies[4] merge their strengths. The way that ministers treat their lord, the way that subor- 45 dinates treat their superiors, is like a son serving his father, or like a younger brother serving his elder brother. It is like the way that the hands and arms protect the head and eyes and shield the chest and belly. Trying to deceive such a person and ambush him will have the same result as if one first alerted him and then attacked him.

50 "Moreover, if the *ren* person comes to have the use of a state ten *li* in size, then his hearing will cover the area of a hundred *li*.[5] If he has the use of a state a hundred *li* in size, then his hearing will cover the area of a thousand *li*. If he has the use of a state a thousand *li* in size, then his hearing will cover everywhere within the four seas. Such a 55 person will surely have keen hearing, sharp sight, and be on guard. Collecting and harmonizing, he will form a unified force.

"And so, the soldiers of the *ren* person are such that when assem- bled, they form up by companies, and when dispersed, they form up by squads. When extended, they are like the long blade of Moye— 60 those who touch it will be cleaved.[6] When pointed, they are like the sharp tip of Moye—those who confront it will be ruptured. When they encamp in a circle or establish perimeter in a square, they are like a massive boulder—those who charge against it will have their

---

[3] This description is meant to apply in a moral sense.
[4] In ancient China, military forces were divided into three sections on the battlefield, namely left, right, and center, and these were conventionally referred to as the "three armies."
[5] This and the subsequent claims about "hearing" are not to be taken literally. In- stead, the *ren* ruler has great "hearing" in that he will hear *from others* about what happens in the wider area. Compare 12.463–87.
[6] Moye was the name of a famous sword owned by King Helü of Wu.

horns broken. Accordingly, the opposing force, defeated and disgraced, will withdraw.[7]

"Furthermore, who will accompany the lord of a violent state to war? Those who will accompany him will surely be his people. However, his people's love for me will be as enthusiastic as that toward their own parents.[8] Their liking for me will be as keen as that toward the fragrant *jiao* and *lan* plants.[9] In contrast, they will regard their superior as if he had punished them with branding or tattoos, and as if he were a detested enemy. The human disposition is such that even if one were a tyrant Jie or a Robber Zhi, how would one be willing, for the sake of those whom one hates, to do villainy toward those whom one likes? The situation would be like someone commanding people's offspring to personally do villainy toward their own parents—the ones thus commanded would surely inform their parents of his plans, so how could they be deceived?[10]

"Hence, when the *ren* person has the use of a state, day by day he becomes more perceptive. Among the feudal lords, those who early on comply with him will be secure. Those who delay in complying with him will be endangered. Those who think to become a rival to him will have their territory reduced. Those who fight against him will perish. The *Odes* says:

> When our martial king set forth,[11]
> Axe held fiercely in his hand,[12]
> It was like a blazing fire;
> In our way none dared to stand.[13]

This expresses my meaning."

---

[7] The Chinese text of this sentence is barely intelligible. It may be an ancient colloquialism whose meaning is lost, a problem possibly compounded by copying errors. Commentators are at a loss to explain it. I follow a rough consensus among them, but the translation remains highly tentative.

[8] As before (see chapter 9, note 8), the "I" here is spoken from the imaginary perspective of the ideal ruler, and does not refer to Xunzi himself.

[9] The *lan* plant has been mentioned earlier in the text as something worn for its fragrance. See 1.49–53.

[10] See the ending of *Mencius* 2A5 for a sentiment comparable to the idea in these last few lines about the improbability of people attacking their own parents for the sake of their leaders.

[11] Normally, "martial king" is the name for King Wu of the Zhou dynasty, but here it refers to the sage Tang when he campaigned against the tyrant Jie.

[12] *Qian* 虔, rendered here as "fiercely," might also be translated as "respectfully," which would echo the earlier point that military strength comes from being moral. In its original context, "fierce" seems better, but Xunzi may intend the other sense, or he may be playing with both senses.

[13] See Mao #304. The received text of the *Odes* differs slightly from what is quoted here.

90   King Xiaocheng and Lord Linwu said, "Well spoken! May we ask: what are the ways and practices to establish, if one is to be able to achieve the military might of a true king?"

Xunzi said, "Everything that depends upon the generals and commanders who serve you, great king, is a secondary matter. I ask per-
95 mission to follow this up by speaking of the achievements that lead kings and feudal lords to strength or weakness, survival or destruction, and the circumstances that lead them to security or danger.

"If the lord is someone worthy, his state will be well ordered. If the lord is someone incapable, his state will be chaotic. If he exalts ritual
100 and values *yi*, his state will be well ordered. If he belittles ritual and scorns *yi*, his state will be chaotic. A well-ordered state is strong. A chaotic state is weak. These are the roots of strength and weakness.

"When those in the position of superiors can be looked up to, then those who are subordinates can be put to use. When those in the
105 position of superiors cannot be looked up to, then those who are subordinates cannot be put to use. When subordinates can be put to use, the state will be strong. When subordinates cannot be put to use, the state will be weak. These are the constancies of strength and weakness.

110   "To exalt ritual and base success on accomplishments is the highest.[14] To bestow weighty compensation yet also value regulation is next. To esteem accomplishments but scorn regulation is the lowest. These are the overall types for strength and weakness.[15]

"He who is fond of well-bred men will be strong. He who is not
115 fond of well-bred men will be weak. He who cares for the people will be strong. He who does not care for the people will be weak. He whose governmental commands are trustworthy will be strong. He whose governmental commands are not trustworthy will be weak. He whose people are coordinated will be strong. He whose people are
120 not coordinated will be weak. He whose rewards are weighty will be strong. He whose rewards are insubstantial will be weak. He whose punishments inspire awe will be strong. He whose punishments inspire disdain will be weak. He whose equipment, supplies, weapons, and armor are well made, complete, easy to use, and effective will be
125 strong. He whose equipment, supplies, weapons, and armor are rotten, disintegrating, and neither easy to use nor effective will be weak. He who regards using military force as a weighty matter will be strong. He who takes using military force as an insubstantial matter will be weak. Where authority derives from a single source there will

---

[14] The word "accomplishments" (*gong* 功) here is probably intended to refer especially to military exploits.

[15] In what follows, the three types seem to correspond roughly to (1) sages such as Tang and King Wu, (2) hegemons such as Duke Huan of Qi and Duke Wen of Jin, and (3) the contemporary rulers of Qi, Wei, and Qin. See 15.173–79.

be strength. Where authority derives from two sources there will be 130
weakness. These are the constancies of strength and weakness.

"The men atop Qi exalt hand-to-hand fighting.[b] In hand-to-hand
encounters, he who obtains an enemy head is given as recompense
gold in the amount of one zi.[16] There are simply no base rewards.[17]
Thus, when the engagement is small and the enemy is frail, then, 135
scraping by, they can be put to use, but when the engagement is large
and the enemy is firm, then they simply flee, scattering, like flying
birds do. In less than a day's time they are toppled and overturned.
These are the military forces of a state about to perish, and no military
forces are weaker than this! There is hardly any difference between 140
this approach and hiring menial servants in the marketplace then
sending them off to war.

"The combat troops of the Wei clan[18] are chosen according to the
following measure. They wear three-section armor. They wield twelve-
dan crossbows.[19] They carry on their backs a quiver with fifty bolts, 145
and to that is added a halberd. They cover their heads with helmets
and strap swords to their waists. They pack provisions for three days.
Under the midday sun, they charge a distance of one hundred li. For
those who pass this trial, tax exemptions are granted to their households, and increases are made to their fields and homes. Their way of 150
doing things is such that after several years the soldiers go into decline, but these benefits cannot be taken from them. Even when these
soldiers are rotated out of service, no alterations are made to what
they were given.[c] For this reason, although Wei's territory is large, its
income from taxes is sure to dwindle. These are the military forces of 155
an endangered state.

"As for the men atop Qin, the way they rear the common people is
tight and austere, and the way they employ the common people is
harsh and ruthless. They restrain the common people with brute
power, challenge them with austerity, tempt them with prizes and 160
rewards, and bear down on them with penalties and punishments.
They would have it that, except for fighting, there is no route by
means of which any of the common people in the world can acquire
benefits from their superiors. They subject the common people to

[16] The exact weight of one zi 錙 in modern units is difficult to determine, but it was
apparently a fairly small amount by ancient standards, as a zi became a byword for
a paltry sum.

[17] This remark is a little obscure, but as I understand it, the meaning is that no recompense is given to all soldiers merely for serving or fighting; rewards go only to those
who actually succeed in killing the enemy. Contrast this with the procedures of Wei
and Qin described below.

[18] I.e., the state of Wei.

[19] According to commentators, the dan measure refers to the amount of force needed
to cock the crossbow. A twelve-dan crossbow apparently required a great deal of
strength to use, which is the point of the reference here.

165　austerity and then put them to use, and only after the common people have achieved successes do they treat them as having accomplishments. Accomplishments and rewards mutually nurture each other.
He who takes five armored heads receives five families to be his servants. Thus, Qin has been most populous and strong for a long time,
170　and it has much territory that it taxes. Hence, it has been victorious
for four generations, and this is due not to luck, but rather to the arrangements they have made.[20]

　　"And so, the hand-to-hand fighting of Qi could not stand against
the combat troops of the Wei clan. The combat troops of the Wei clan
175　could not stand against the well-honed soldiers of Qin. The well-
honed soldiers of Qin could not counter the regulation and control
instituted by Duke Huan and Duke Wen. The regulation and control
instituted by Duke Huan and Duke Wen could not oppose the *ren*
and *yi* practiced by Tang and Wu. If the former were to try to stand
180　against the latter,[21] the result would be the same as if one took something that had been burned to a crisp and threw a rock against it.[d]
Taking those several states together,[22] all their forces are composed of
soldiers who chase after rewards and stalk after profit; theirs is the
way of menial servants and vendors hawking wares. They do not yet
185　have the orderliness that comes from valuing one's superiors, feeling
at ease with being under their control, and practicing the utmost in
regulation. If among the feudal lords there were one who was able to
refine these soldiers so as to make them regulated, then when he went
into action he would indeed make them even more dangerous.[e]

190　　"Thus, attracting people with incentives and choosing among
them selectively, exalting the use of circumstances and deception,
and esteeming accomplishments and profits—these water down one's
forces. Ritual, *yi*, and transformation through education—these make
one's forces coordinated. And so, in using deception to go up against
195　deception, cunning and ineptitude may still make a difference there,
but using deception to go up against coordination can be compared
to seeking to topple Mount Tai using only the blade of an awl—none
but the stupidest person under Heaven would dare to make such a
trial.

200　　"Hence, the military forces of a true king are not made trial of.
When Tang and Wu executed Jie and Zhòu, these sages merely stood
with hands clasped together and gave directions, and then none of

---

[20]　See the similar description at 16.315–16.

[21]　The Chinese text here is quite ambiguous, and commentators argue about how to
construe it. In light of what follows, "the former" is probably best taken as referring
to the current states of Qi, Wei, and Qin, and "the latter" is probably best taken as
referring to Duke Huan, Duke Wen, Tang, and Wu.

[22]　The states in question are most likely Qi, Wei, and Qin.

the strong and violent states failed to hurry in doing their bidding.[23] Executing Jie and Zhòu was as easy as executing lone individuals.[24] The 'Great Declaration' uses the phrase 'the lone man Zhòu.'[25] This expresses my meaning. And so, if one's military forces are coordinated to the greatest degree, then one will control all under Heaven. If they are coordinated to a lesser degree, then one will restrain one's neighbors and rivals.

205

"As for attracting people with incentives and choosing among them selectively, exalting the use of circumstances and deception, and esteeming accomplishments and profits,

210

> When such are the forces employed on the campaign
> Constant triumphs or defeats they do not obtain.
> In one fight they wax. In another fight they wane.
> In one fight they live. In another they are slain.

215

They simply alternate as the vanquished or as the victor. These are called bandit forces, and the gentleman does not follow this route.

"And so, Tian Dan of Qi, Zhuang Qiao of Chu, Wey Yang of Qin, Miao Ji of Yan—these individuals are all called 'good at using military forces' by the vulgar people of this age.[26] Their respective areas of cunning, ineptitude, strength, and weakness are such that none has ever been able to lord over the others. As for the ways they follow, they are one and the same. Their forces have never been harmonized and coordinated. They practice entrapment, rely on deception, scheme after power, and plot overthrows,[27] and so cannot avoid being mere bandit forces.

220

225

"As for Duke Huan of Qi, Duke Wen of Jin, King Zhuang of Chu, King Helü of Wu, and King Goujian of Yue, theirs were all harmonized and coordinated forces. They can be said to have entered into the right territory indeed, but they never possessed the guiding factor that is fundamental.[28] Hence, they were able to become hegemons, but were unable to become true kings. These are the achievements that lead to strength or weakness."

230

King Xiaocheng and Lord Linwu said, "Well spoken! May we ask about the proper way to be a general?"

235

---

[23] Compare the nearly identical wording at 10.593–96.

[24] See the similar wording at 18.83–84.

[25] The "Great Declaration" is a chapter of the *Documents*. The received edition of that chapter (which most scholars now consider a forgery) differs slightly from what is quoted here. See Waltham (1971, p. 117).

[26] Wey Yang is better known as Shang Yang, the purported author of the *Book of Lord Shang*. For more on Zhuang Qiao, see below, note 53.

[27] Compare the nearly identical wording at 10.189–91.

[28] I.e., the approach based on *ren*, *yi*, ritual, and moral education generally.

Xunzi said, "In terms of wisdom, nothing is greater than to have discarded all that is dubious. In terms of conduct, nothing is greater than to be free of faults. In terms of operations, nothing is greater 240 than to lack any cause for regret.[29] It is simply enough when the operation is such as to give one no cause for regret, because success cannot be ensured.[30]

"In turn, desire that ordinances and orders be strict, so as to inspire awe. Desire that rewards and punishments be certain, so as to 245 be trustworthy.[31] Desire that encampments and stores be carefully planned, so as to be secure. Desire that actions and movements be executed stably, so as to be weighty, and desire that they be prompt, so as to be expeditious. In scrutinizing the enemy and observing changes in his movements, desire to delve beneath the surface, so as 250 to gain a deeper understanding, and desire to compare reports, so as to verify them. In engaging the enemy and deciding the battle, proceed on the basis of what you know clearly, and do not proceed on the basis of what you consider dubious. These are called the six techniques.

255   "Do not be so desirous of being general that you cannot stand to be removed from the position. Do not be so hasty in seeking victory that you forget about the possibilities for defeat. Do not take those within your camp to be so awe-inspiring that you underestimate those outside it. Do not fix your 260   gaze on potential profits so much that you do not look at potential harms. Desire that all deliberations about operations be thorough, and desire that deployment of resources be ample.[32]

These are called the five considerations.
265   "There are three cases in which the general will not accept a command from his ruler:[33] when the general is willing to be executed, but cannot be made to occupy an unsound position; when the general is

---

[29] See *Analects* 2.18.

[30] This comment might seem surprising in light of Xunzi's earlier comments about the invincibility of a true king's forces. However, if we understand him as speaking solely from the perspective of a general, who may or may not have a sage as his ruler, then the remark is perhaps not so surprising.

[31] Both the idea and the wording here are highly similar to what one finds in various places in the *Han Feizi* and the *Book of Lord Shang*.

[32] From the beginning of the paragraph to this point, the passage is rhymed in the original.

[33] The issue of when a general might refuse orders was apparently a popular theme in ancient Chinese military writings. See *Sunzi Bingfa* (*The Art of War*), chap. 8. A modern parallel can be found in debates about unlawful orders and how soldiers should respond to them.

willing to be executed, but cannot be made to assault an unconquer-
able foe; and when the general is willing to be executed, but cannot
be made to mistreat the common folk. These are called the three stop-   270
ping points.

"Every time he accepts a command from his ruler and marches out
the three armies, then when the three armies are set, the hundred officials have each obtained their proper positions, and the assembled
goods are all correctly in place, then his ruler cannot tempt him with   275
delights, and the enemy cannot provoke him with rage. Such a one is
called the ultimate minister.

"Make sure that deliberations precede operations, and augment
them with respect.

> Be as careful at the end as at the beginning: when the end   280
> and beginning are treated with one and the same care, this is
> called great good fortune.[34] Success in all the hundred differ-
> ent kinds of operations surely rests in treating them with re-
> spect. Defeat in them surely rests in treating them casually.
> And so, when respect prevails over laxity, then one will have   285
> good fortune. When laxity prevails over respect, then one
> will be destroyed. When planning prevails over desires, then
> one will proceed with ease. When desires prevail over plan-
> ning, then one will have misfortune.[35]

"Do battle as if one were defending a position. Do marches as if   290
one were engaged in battle. Treat having an accomplishment as if it
were due merely to good luck.[36] Respect planning, without a single
lapse. Respect operations, without a single lapse. Respect functionaries, without a single lapse. Respect the masses, without a single lapse.
Respect the enemy, without a single lapse. These are called the five   295
prohibited lapses.

"Carefully practice these six techniques, five considerations, and
three stopping points, and dwell in them by being reverent and respectful, without a single lapse. Such a one is called the greatest general under Heaven, and he reaches to spirit-like power and under-   300
standing indeed!"

Lord Linwu said, "Well spoken! May I ask about the military ordinances of a true king?"

---

[34] Compare *Daodejing* chap. 64.
[35] These lines are rhymed in the original.
[36] Commentators try to provide these three terse instructions with plausible explanations by saying that the point of the first is that one should not chase down defeated
forces, the point of the second is that one should exercise extreme caution when on
the march, and the point of the third is that one should avoid being overly proud
of one's military achievements.

Xunzi said, "A general is to die at his drums.[37] A charioteer is to die
at his reins. The hundred functionaries are to die carrying out their
official tasks. The well-bred men and grand ministers are to die maintaining their positions among the rank and file.

"When one hears the sound of the drums, advance. When one
hears the sound of the gongs, withdraw. Complying with commands
is most important; gaining an accomplishment is secondary. Advancing when ordered not to advance is just like withdrawing when ordered not to withdraw—as offenses, these two are exactly even.

"Do not kill the old and the feeble. Do not trample down people's
crops. Those who surrender are not to be treated as captives. Those
who maintain resistance are not to be let go. Those who flee over to
one's side to offer their lives before the battle[f] are not to be taken as
prisoners. In all cases of executions, one is not to execute the common people. Rather, one is to execute those who bring disorder to the
common people. However, if among the common people there are
those who protect such villains, then they, too, are villains.

"For this reason, those who yield to one's blade will live. Those
who take on one's blade will die. Those who flee over to one's side to
offer their lives before the battle will join one's camp.[g] Weizi Qi was
enfeoffed as ruler of Song.[38] Cao Chulong was cut to pieces amidst
the army.[39] As for the Shang people who submitted, the means that
the king used to nurture and rear them were no different than what
he used for the Zhou people. And so, singing and chanting, those
who were nearby delighted in him.[40] Exhausted and stumbling, those
who were far away ran to him. Among the isolated and remote states,
all quickly sent envoys and took comfort and delighted in him.[41] All
within the four seas became like one family, and all the men of understanding willingly submitted. This is called being the teacher of the
people. The *Odes* says:

---

[37] In ancient China, drums were used as a means of communicating orders widely
over the din of battle, as is mentioned further below in the main text. (See also the
remark about the hierarchical value of drums at 20.166.) The demand that a general
die "at his drums" thus means that he must not abandon his post and responsibilities as commander.

[38] According to early sources, Weizi Qi was a half brother of the tyrant Zhòu. He realized that Zhòu was in danger of being overthrown and tried to warn him, but was
not heeded, and so he left. Carrying tokens of submission, he met King Wu's army
when it arrived. The mention of Weizi Qi here is apparently intended to illustrate
the sentence immediately prior in the text.

[39] Almost nothing is known about Cao Chulong. Given what Xunzi says about him at
13.174–185, he was apparently a corrupt minister of Zhòu, and judging by Xunzi's
comment here, he refused to surrender to King Wu.

[40] The Chinese text beginning from this sentence on down to the line after the quotation of the *Odes* also appears in an almost identical passage at 8.85–94.

[41] This same sentence appears at 9.258–59, where the idea of the "teacher of the people" is also mentioned.

From the west and from the east,
From the south and from the north,
All submit as they come forth.[42]   335

This expresses my meaning.

"A true king may carry out executions, but will not have to do battle. He will not assault cities that are heavily fortified. He will not attack military forces that are boxed in.[h] If, among the enemy, superiors and inferiors delight in one another, then he congratulates them.[43] He does not slaughter cities. He does not lay his armies in wait for ambushes. He does not station mass occupations. His campaigns do not exceed a single season. And so, the people of chaotic states take joy when he launches war,[i] because they are not at ease with their own superiors, and instead desire his arrival."

Lord Linwu said, "Well spoken!"

Chen Xiao[44] asked Xunzi, "When debating military affairs, you, sir, always take *ren* and *yi* as what is fundamental. One who is *ren* cares for others, and one who is *yi* follows good order. If this is so, then what use does one have for military forces? The reason why one has military forces is for struggle and contention."

Xunzi said, "Things are not as you understand them. The person of *ren* indeed cares for others, but it is because he cares for others that he hates for people to harm them. The person of *yi* indeed follows good order, but it is because he follows good order that he hates for people to throw it into chaos. Indeed, military forces are that by which one prohibits violence and does away with what is harmful. They are not for struggle and contention. Thus, wherever the military forces of a person of *ren* reside, that place enjoys a spirit-like state.[45] Wherever they pass by, that place is transformed, like the falling of a timely rain, and all are pleased with them.

"Thus, Yao attacked the Huan Dou. Shun attacked those who controlled the Miao. Yu attacked the Gong Gong. Tang attacked the one who controlled the Xia. King Wen attacked Chong. King Wu attacked the tyrant Zhòu.[46] These four emperors and two kings all em-

---

[42] Mao #244. These lines are also quoted at 8.91–93 and 11.324–26.

[43] I have translated this sentence as most commentators understand it, but its structure does not fit with the context, and although it can be made intelligible, the thought expressed also does not fit well. I suspect that the sentence has fallen out of place from somewhere else.

[44] Nothing is known about Chen Xiao, but given his respectful address here, most commentators think he is one of Xunzi's students.

[45] I.e., a state that is extremely good. Compare the similar use of this phrase at line 529 below and at 32.142–43.

[46] Concerning this list, early sources give various and sometimes conflicting reports about the Huan Dou, the Miao, and the Gong Gong. Some texts portray them as

ployed a military approach based on *ren* and *yi* in conducting their campaigns throughout the world. And so, those nearby drew close to their goodness, and far away regions admired their virtue. The blades
370 of their weapons were not stained with blood, but people far and near came and submitted to them. Such was the abundance of their virtue, and its effects reached to the limits of all four directions. The *Odes* says:

> As for the noble man and gentleman,
> 375 Their standard does not err or deviate.
> [Their standard does not err or deviate.]
> [On all four sides they correct every state.]⁴⁷

This expresses my meaning."

Li Si⁴⁸ questioned Xunzi, saying, "Qin has been victorious for four
380 generations. Its forces are the strongest in the area between the seas. Awe toward it pervades the feudal lords. But it is not the case that it employed *ren* and *yi* to accomplish this; it merely pursues its affairs according to what is expedient."

Xunzi said, "Things are not as you understand them. The 'expedi-
385 ents' of which you speak are 'expedients' that are inexpedient. The *ren* and *yi* of which I speak are the most expedient of great expedients. Indeed, *ren* and *yi* are that by which one cultivates the government. When the government is cultivated, then the people will love their superiors, delight in their lord, and look lightly upon dying for
390 their sake. Thus I say: everything that depends upon the generals and commanders of the army is a secondary matter. Qin has been victorious for four generations, but full of apprehension, it constantly fears that all under Heaven will unite and combine to roll over it. This is

---

tribes or regions that opposed the sage kings, which is probably how they are conceived here. "The one who controlled the Xia" refers to the tyrant Jie. Chong was a state whose ruler did not behave virtuously.

⁴⁷ Mao #152. Compare the use of this same quotation at 10.554–557 and 24.121–24. The last two lines are omitted from the original Chinese text in this chapter, but they seem necessary to make sense of why Xunzi quotes the *Odes* here. In ancient China, those who were educated were likely to know and be able to recall the missing lines on their own after being given the prompt of the first two lines, so Xunzi could rely on his audience to fill in the missing information to make the argument intelligible. However, since few modern readers are likely to know the *Odes* so well, I have added these two lines.

⁴⁸ According to an early source, Li Si was once a student of Xunzi. Later, he left Xunzi and went to the state of Qin, where he eventually served as prime minister, so his challenge here may be intended to foreshadow Li's future career. Some commentators read this exchange as a part of the conversation with Chen Xiao, rather than being a separate occasion.

what is called the military approach of a reigning house in decline.
Qin has never possessed the guiding factor that is fundamental. Thus,   395
Tang's banishment of the tyrant Jie was not simply a matter of that
one time when he drove him off at Ming Tiao. King Wu's execution
of the tyrant Zhòu was not simply a matter of conquering him on that
one morning of the day *jiazi*.[49] In every case, the sages had practiced
proper conduct beforehand and had made cultivation their habit.   400
This is what is called the military approach based on *ren* and *yi*. Now,
you do not seek for answers in what is fundamental, but rather search
for them in what is secondary.[50] Such behavior is the reason for why
the current age is chaotic."[51]

Ritual is the height of good order and proper distinction. It is the   405
fundamental point for making the state strong. It is the way to inspire
awe pervasively. It is the crucial element for gaining accomplishments and fame. When kings and dukes follow it, that is the means
whereby they obtain the whole world. When they do not follow it,
that is the means whereby they obliterate their own altars of soil and   410
grain.

And so, sturdy armor and sharp weapons do not suffice to make
one victorious. High walls and deep moats do not suffice to make one
solidly defended. Strict orders and profuse punishments do not suffice to make one awe-inspiring. If one follows the proper way, these   415
things will be effective. If one does not follow the proper way, these
things will be ineffective.

The people of Chu use shark skins and rhinoceros hides to make
armor that is as hard as metal or stone. Their steel spears made in
Wan are as cruelly wounding as wasps and scorpions. They are light-   420
footed and agile, moving as swiftly as the gusting wind. Nevertheless,
their forces perished at Chuisha, and Tang Mie died.[52] Zhuang Qiao
instigated rebellion, and Chu was split into a number of pieces.[53]

---

[49] *Jiazi* is the name of the first day in the sixty-day cycle of the traditional Chinese
calendar. Legend had it that Zhòu was conquered on a *jiazi* day.

[50] The text here plays on two senses of the Chinese term *mo* 末 in a way that is untranslatable. On the one hand, *mo* means "derivative" or "secondary." On the other
hand, it means "ending" or "in decline." Xunzi's criticism that Li Si pursues what is
mo thus refers both to Li Si's admiration for the state of Qin (which Xunzi labels as
"in decline") and to his fondness for amoral, technical approaches to warfare
(which Xunzi regards as inferior).

[51] Most commentators think that Xunzi's speech to Li Si ends here. However, ancient
Chinese texts had no markers for the end of a speech, so the paragraphs that follow
could also be part of Xunzi's speech. In fact, some commentators think that Xunzi's
speech goes right to the end of the chapter.

[52] Xunzi is apparently referring to a defeat suffered by Chu when it was attacked by
the combined forces of Qin, Qi, Han, and Wei ca. 301 BCE. Tang Mie (listed by
other texts as Tang Mei) was the Chu general.

[53] It is somewhat unclear to what events Xunzi is referring here. According to some
sources, Zhuang Qiao had been a rebel in Chu, but later served the king as a gen-

How could this be due to a lack of sturdy armor and sharp weapons!
425 Rather, the reason is that the means by which their leaders guided
them was not the proper way.

The people of Chu have the Ru and Yin rivers to serve as traps.
They have the Yangtze and Han rivers to serve as moats. They make
the edge of their state at the forests of Deng, and they surround it with
430 Mount Fangcheng. Nevertheless, when the Qin armies came, Yanying
was upturned as easily as shaking a withered tree.[54] How could this be
due to a lack of solid fortifications, obstructing barriers, blocking
obstacles, and hindering impediments! Rather, the reason is that the
means by which their leaders guided them was not the proper way.

435 The tyrant Zhòu eviscerated Bi Gan and imprisoned Jizi. He in-
vented the punishment of "burning and roasting,"[55] and he engaged
in killing without any appropriate occasion. His ministers and subordinates were terrified, and none could be certain of living. Nevertheless, when the Zhou armies came, his orders had no effect among
440 those below, and he could not employ his people. How could this be
due to orders not being strict and punishments not being profuse!
Rather, the reason is that the means by which he guided them was not
the proper way.

The weapons of ancient times were merely halberds, spears, and
445 bows and arrows. Nevertheless, rival states submitted without making trial of them. There was no separated building of inner and outer
city walls. There was no digging of ditches and moats. There was no
erecting of solid fortifications and obstructing barriers. There was no
setting up of opportune situations and shifty stratagems. Neverthe-
450 less, the state was calm, not fearing those outside its borders, and
instead enlightening those within its borders,[j] and there was no other
reason for this situation than that the ruler guided the people in an
enlightened manner and through allotments balanced them out, and
he employed the people in a timely manner and truly cared for them,
455 so that subordinates harmonized with their superiors as closely as a
shadow or echo. If there were still some who did not follow orders,
only then did he execute them as punishment. And so, he might punish a single person, and all under Heaven would submit to him, and
the culpable person would not blame his superiors, because he knew

---

eral. Other sources report that, when serving as general, Zhuang Qiao was sent to
conquer a certain area for Chu, but when he found his return cut off by Qin (ca. 281
BCE), he established himself as king of the conquered territory; it may be this latter
event to which Xunzi refers as his "rebellion" and the splitting of Chu.

[54] Yanying was the capital of Chu. The defeat of Chu by Qin that Xunzi mentions oc-
curred ca. 278 BCE.

[55] According to early sources, the punishment consisted in laying a bronze pillar
above burning coals. Prisoners were forced to walk across the heated metal and
would fall into the flames below.

that the culpability lay with himself. Hence, punishments and penal- 460
ties were sparsely used, yet awe toward the ruler was overflowing.[56]
There is no other reason for this than that he followed the proper way.

In ancient times, the way that Emperor Yao brought order to all
under Heaven was such that, in sum, he killed one person and executed two others, and all under Heaven submitted.[57] A proverb states, 465
"Awe-inspiring power was honed sharp, but was not made trial of.
Punishments were put in place, but were not made use of."[58] This
expresses my meaning.

Whenever people act, if they do so for the sake of rewards and
prizes, then they will desist if they see that they will be harmed and 470
injured. Thus, rewards, prizes, punishments, penalties, circumstantial conditions, and deception are not sufficient to get the utmost effort out of people to or to make people willing to die. In serving as
people's ruler and superior, if the way that one treats the common
people below is lacking in ritual, yi, loyalty, and trustworthiness, how 475
can one think simply to make thoroughgoing use of rewards, prizes,
punishments, penalties, circumstantial conditions, and deception to
control one's subordinates, subject them to austerity, and reap accomplishments and results from them?[k] In the event that a large raid-
ing force came, then if one were to send them to hold an endangered 480
city, they would surely commit treason.[59] If they were to meet the
enemy and be placed into battle, they would surely turn their backs
and run. If they were tasked with some bitter endeavor or burdened
with some disgraceful undertaking, they would surely flee away.
Quickly they would head off, and thus the subordinates would, on 485
the contrary, put a stop to their superiors.

Thus, the way constituted by using rewards, prizes, punishments,
penalties, circumstantial conditions, and deception is the way of menial servants and vendors hawking wares. It is insufficient for joining
together the great masses or refining the state and its clans. Hence, 490
the people of ancient times considered it shameful and did not take
it as their way.

And so, make great your reputation for virtue so as to stand at the
forefront of the people. Make clear ritual and yi so as to guide the
people. Make yourself loyal and trustworthy so as to make the people 495
care for you. Elevate the worthy and employ the capable so as to
order the people in ranks. Make gifts of positions, emblems, and

---

[56] The idea of using a few select punishments to reduce the overall number of punishments as well as the notion of making people acknowledge their own culpability are
again highly similar to what one finds in various places in the *Han Feizi* and the *Book
of Lord Shang*.

[57] The details of the story to which Xunzi refers here are unknown.

[58] This saying is repeated at 28.90–91.

[59] I.e., the soldiers would hand the city over to the enemy.

other rewards in order to make the people exert themselves. Make the people's works accord with the times and lighten their burdens, in
500 order to harmonize them and coordinate them. Nurture and raise them, as though caring for a newborn.[60]

In this manner, government orders will become settled practice, and people's customs will be unified. Then, should there be anyone who departs from custom and will not comply with his superiors, the
505 common people will all find him odious and hateful, and will all regard him as poisonous and calamitous, just as they do when exorcising something inauspicious. Only then does punishment arise for such a case. His behavior is that to which the greatest punishment is applied, and what disgrace could be greater than that? Will someone
510 think this behavior is profitable? But then the greatest punishment is applied to it. How could anyone who is not crazy, confused, stupid, or boorish look upon this result and not change his behavior!

Thereupon, the common people will all know clearly to cultivate their superior's model and imitate his intentions, and will feel at ease
515 with and delight in this. If on top of this there is someone who can transform himself with goodness, cultivate his person, correct his conduct, accumulate practice in ritual and *yi*, and revere the Way and virtue, then the common people will all value and respect him, and will all love and extol him. Only then do rewards arise for such a case.
520 His behavior is that to which high office and abundant salary are given, and what honor could be greater than that? Will someone think this behavior is harmful? But then he has high office and abundant salary to support and nurture him. Among all people who live, who would not wish for this?

525 If one prominently hangs noble office and hefty rewards in front of people, and hangs conspicuous punishments and great disgrace behind them, then even if they wished not to remain untransformed, could they do it? Thus, the people will return to one like flowing water.[61] Wherever one resides, that place will enjoy a spirit-like state.[62]
530 Wherever one takes action, that place will be transformed and submit.[63] Those who commit violent brutalities and those who are audacious in using force will transform for one and live honestly. Those who are biased for one side and those who are crooked with selfishness will transform for one and avoid prejudice. Those who are arro-
535 gantly disruptive and those who are stubbornly unruly will transform

---

[60] The sentences of this paragraph down to this point also appear in nearly identical form at 11.592–602.

[61] I.e., as naturally as water flows downward.

[62] Compare the similar use of this phrase at lines 359–60 above and at 32.142–43.

[63] Here, the text is odd and may be corrupt. Commentators propose various emendations, but none are appealing. I follow Pan Zhonggui, who presents the most conservative reading, but the translation remains highly tentative.

for one and become concordant. This is called the great transformation leading to unity. The *Odes* says:

> When the king's plan was a true success,
> The lands of Xu came to acquiesce.[64]

This expresses my meaning.   540

Overall, there are three methods for capturing a people. There is capturing a people by means of virtue. There is capturing a people by means of force. There is capturing a people by means of wealth.

In one case, people regard my name and reputation as noble, consider my virtue and conduct to be splendid, and desire to become my   545
subjects. And so, they open up their doors and sweep clear the roads to welcome my entrance. Following along with the ruler's people, one assumes his place, and the common folk are all at ease. One establishes laws, promulgates orders, and none fail to comply with and adhere to them. For this reason, one gains territory, and one's power   550
becomes weightier. One captures a people, and one's forces become stronger. Such is capturing a people by means of virtue.

In another case, people do not regard my name and reputation as noble, and they do not consider my virtue and conduct to be splendid. Others fear my awe-inspiring might, and they are restrained by   555
my authoritative control. And so, even though the people have a mind to desert, they do not dare to engage in deliberations about revolting. When it is like this, then arms and armor will be used in even greater numbers, and the support and provisions involved will surely be expensive. For this reason, one gains territory, but one's   560
power becomes slighter. One captures a people, but one's forces become weaker. Such is capturing a people by means of force.

In yet another case, people do not regard my name and reputation as noble, and they do not consider my virtue and conduct to be splendid. Beset by poverty, they seek to become wealthy. Beset by hunger,   565
they seek to fill their stomachs. With empty bellies and gaping mouths, they come for my food. When it is like this, then one must make distributions from the grain kept by the Overseer of Granaries, in order to feed them. One must provide them with money and goods, in order to make them wealthy. One must establish good supervisors,   570
in order to handle them. Only after completing a period of three years can the people then be trusted. For this reason, one gains territory, but one's power becomes slighter. One captures a people, but one's state becomes poorer. Such is capturing a people by means of wealth.

---

[64] Mao #263. These same lines are also quoted at 12.78–79. The poem from which the quotation comes describes how the land of Xu is attacked and brought to submission by king Xuan of the Zhou dynasty.

575   And so I say: he who captures a people by means of virtue will become a true king, he who captures a people by means of force will become weak, and he who captures a people by means of wealth will become poor. Both ancient times and the present age are one and the same in this.

580   To capture and take over others is something that it is easy to be capable of doing, but it is solidifying and consolidating one's grip on them that is the hard part. Qi was able to take over Song, but was not able to consolidate its grip, and so Wei snatched it away.[65] Yan was able to take over Qi, but was not able to consolidate its grip, and so
585   Tian Dan snatched it back.[66] The territory of Shangdang in Han was several hundred *li* in its area, and it was well preserved, sound, wealthy, and well supplied. It left to become part of Zhao, but Zhao was not able to consolidate its grip, and so Qin snatched it away.[67]

        Thus, if one is able to take over another land, but not able to con-
590   solidate one's grip on it, it is sure to be snatched away. If one is neither able to take over another land nor to consolidate one's grip on one's original holdings, then one is sure to perish. If one is able to consolidate one's grip on one's original holdings, then one will surely be able to take over another land. When one obtains it, then one will
595   consolidate one's grip on that as well, and one's capture and taking over of lands will have no boundaries.[1] Tang used Bo, and King Wu used Hao—these were both territories of merely a hundred *li* in size. But the world became united under them, and the feudal lords became their servants. There is no other reason for this than that they
600   were able to consolidate their grip on their territories.

        And so, one consolidates one's grip on well-bred men by means of ritual. One consolidates one's grip on the people by means of proper government. When ritual is cultivated, the well-bred men will submit. When government is evenhanded, the people will be at ease.
605   When the well-bred men submit and the people are at ease, this is called the great consolidation. If you use it when defending, you will be secure. If you use it when attacking, you will be strong. Orders will be carried out, and prohibited activities will stop. In this, the affairs of a true king are complete.

---

[65] In ca. 286 BCE, Qi took over Song and eliminated it as an independent state, but in ca. 284 BCE, Wei joined with Han, Qin, Yan, and Zhao to attack Qi, which resulted in Qi losing a great deal of its territory, and Wei absorbed what had previously been the state of Song.

[66] In the attack on Qi mentioned in the previous note, Yan played a leading role and nearly eliminated Qi as an independent state. Tian Dan was a general of Qi who managed to save Qi from utter destruction and restore much of its territory, and he became famous for his exploits (see above, lines 219–221).

[67] In ca. 262 BCE, Shangdang surrendered to Zhao, but approximately three years later it was taken by Qin.

CHAPTER 16

The Strong State

If the mold is straight, the metal fine, the craftsmanship skilled, and the heat appropriate, then when you break open the mold you will have a Moye.[1] However, if you do not trim away the excess and sharpen it, then it could not sever even a rope. If you trim away the excess and sharpen it, then it will cut through metal plates and bowls and behead oxen and horses with a single slash. Every state is a strong state just come from the mold. However, if you do not educate and train it, if you do not adjust and unify it, then at home you will not be able to defend yourself, and abroad you will not be able to make war. If you educate and train it, adjust it and unify it, then its soldiers will be vigorous and its fortifications will be solid, and rival states will not dare to touch it.[2] For the state there is also means of sharpening, and that is ritual, *yi*, regulation, and rules. Thus, the fate of a person rests in Heaven, and the fate of a state rests in ritual. If the lord of men exalts ritual and honors the worthy, then he will become a true king.[3] If he relies heavily on law and has concern for the people, then he will become a hegemon. If he cares only for profit and frequently engages in deception, then he will be endangered. If he is scheming, debauched, and unpredictable and dangerous, then he will perish.

There are three kinds of power to inspire awe. There is the power to inspire awe that comes from the Way and virtue. There is the power to inspire awe that comes from being harsh and stringent. There is the power to inspire awe that comes from being wild and reckless. One must not fail to examine thoroughly these three kinds of power to inspire awe.

In one case, ritual and music are cultivated. Social divisions and *yi* are made clear. Government policies and acts are timely. Concern for and benefit toward people are manifest. When things are like this, then the common people will honor their ruler like Shang Di, look up to him like Heaven, love him like their own parents, and fear him like a spirit intelligence.[4] And so, even though rewards are not employed, the people will work hard, and even though punishments are not employed, his power to inspire awe will be pervasive. This is called the power to inspire awe that comes from the Way and virtue.

---

[1] A famous sword.
[2] Compare the similar wording at 20.67–68.
[3] This and the next two sentences also appear at 17.199–202 and 27.2–5.
[4] Compare the similar wording at 10.157–159.

35   In another case, ritual and music are not cultivated. Social divisions and *yi* are not made clear. Government policies and acts are not
timely. Concern for and benefit toward people are not manifest. Nevertheless, the ruler's prohibitions against those who are violent are
stringent. His executions of those who do not submit are thorough-
40   going. The punishments and penalties that he assigns are hefty and
can be trusted to be applied, and the executions and killings that he
commands are fierce and certain to be carried out, falling upon people as swiftly as a clap of thunder striking them or a collapsing wall
crushing them. When things are like this, then if the common people
45   are constrained, they will be extremely fearful, but if their circumstances are relaxed, then they will treat their superiors arrogantly. If
they are held in check, then they will join together, but if they get an
opening, then they will scatter. If they become enemies of those in
central positions, then they will create upheaval.[a] If the ruler does not
50   constrain them by means of arrangements and authority, and if he
does not shake them by means of executions and killings, then he will
have no way to keep hold of his subordinates. This is called the power
to inspire awe that comes from being harsh and stringent.
      In another case, the ruler lacks a heart that is concerned for peo-
55   ple, he makes no effort to benefit people, and instead he daily practices ways that create chaos among people. When the common people
grumble and complain, he then follows it up by seizing and binding
them, punishing and branding them, not harmonizing with people's
hearts at all.[5] When things are like this, then those below will defi-
60   nitely conspire together secretly and move in a surge to abandon their
superior.[b] One can simply stand by and wait for him to be overthrown
and destroyed. This is called the power to inspire awe that comes
from being wild and reckless.
      One must not fail to examine thoroughly these three kinds of
65   power to inspire awe. The power to inspire awe that comes from the
Way and virtue results in security and strength. The power to inspire
awe that comes from being harsh and stringent results in danger and
weakness. The power to inspire awe that comes from being wild and
reckless results in destruction.

70   Gongsunzi[6] said, "When Zifa was general, he went west to attack
Cai.[7] He vanquished Cai and captured the Marquis of Cai. Upon re-

---

[5] Alternatively, the last part of this sentence might be translated as ". . . and he does
not act to make people's hearts harmonious."
[6] There is no reliable historical information to identify who Gongsunzi is, and the
events he relates do not match exactly with other early Chinese historical accounts.
Based on what follows, his speech is presumably intended to present Zifa as a model
to be imitated.
[7] "Cai" (蔡) normally refers to a state located in modern-day Henan province, but
since that Cai was north of Chu (whence Zifa is said to march), some commentators

turning, he rendered account of his mission, saying, 'The Marquis of Cai offered up his altars of soil and grain and assigned them to Chu. Your servant She[8] engaged a few followers and took control of his territory.' Thereafter, when Chu proclaimed his reward, Zifa declined   75
it, saying, 'When the mere issuing of instructions and announcement of commands makes the enemy withdraw, that is due to the ruler's power to inspire awe. When positioning of troops and launching an offensive makes the enemy withdraw, that is due to the general's power to inspire awe. When joining in battle and using brute force   80
makes the enemy withdraw, that is due to the masses' power to inspire awe. Your servant She should not receive a reward for something that is due to the masses' power to inspire awe.'"

[I] criticized this,[9] saying, "Zifa's rendering account of his mission was a case of reverence, but his declining the reward was a case of   85
thick-headedness. In elevating the worthy and employing the capable, when one rewards those who have meritorious accomplishments and punishes those who are guilty of crimes, it is not because the person acted so alone.[c] That is the way of the former kings, the fundamental point for unifying people, and the proper response in treating   90
as good those who are good and treating as bad those who are bad. To achieve order one must follow it, and ancient times and the present are one and the same in this.

"In ancient times, the manner in which enlightened kings undertook great tasks and set up great accomplishments was such that,   95
when the great tasks had been fulfilled and the great accomplishments had been established, then the lord enjoyed their success, the assembled ministers enjoyed their accomplishment, the well-bred men and grand officers received an increase in rank, the officials received an increase in emolument, and ordinary service members re-   100
ceived an increase in salary. Thus, those who did good were encouraged, and those who did what was not good were obstructed. Superiors and subordinates shared one heart, and the three armies merged their strengths. Thus, the hundred tasks were successfully completed, and people's accomplishments and fame were great.   105

"Now, Zifa is alone in not being like that. He went against the way of the former kings, brought disorder to the laws of Chu, degraded ministers who gave rise to meritorious accomplishments, and cast shame on those who had accepted rewards. Though he was not executed in front of his clan and fellow villagers, yet he debased and   110

---

suggest that here "Cai" is shorthand for Gaocai (高蔡), another state that was indeed to the west of Chu.

[8] Zifa here refers to himself in a humble manner by using his personal name.

[9] The sentence lacks an explicit grammatical subject, which is not uncommon in classical Chinese, but based on other cases in the text, most commentators take the speaker to be Xunzi himself.

humiliated his descendants. He was indeed alone in acting thus for the sake of his own personal rectitude. Is this not a great error! Thus I say: Zifa's rendering account of his mission was a case of reverence, but his declining the reward was a case of thick-headedness."

115 Xunzi attempted to persuade the prime minister of Qi, saying, "If one occupies a position of authority that prevails over people, but also practices the way that prevails over people, then nobody under Heaven will regard one with anger—such were Tang and Wu. If one occupies a position of authority that prevails over people, but does
120 not practice the way that prevails over people, then although one might be so generously endowed as to have a position of authority over the whole world, one could not successfully seek even to finish out one's days as a mere commoner—such were the tyrants Jie and Zhòu. That being the case, obtaining a position of authority that pre-
125 vails over people is far inferior to the way that prevails over people.

"As for being in charge of the post of prime minister, that is to prevail over people by means of one's position of authority. Treating what is right as right, treating what is wrong as wrong, treating those capable as capable, treating those incapable as incapable, shutting
130 out selfish desires, making sure to abide by the capacity for inclusiveness that is part of the Way and *yi* that encompass all—this is the way that prevails over people.

"Now you, Prime Minister, are able to have exclusive influence over the ruler above, and are able to have exclusive influence over the
135 state below. With respect to a position of authority that prevails over people, you truly possess this. That being the case, why not ride this position of authority that prevails over people to arrive at the way that prevails over people? Seek out gentlemen who are *ren*, generous, comprehending, and intelligent, and entrust the king to them. To-
140 gether with them participate in the governance of the state, and set straight what is right and what is wrong. If things were like this, then who in the state would dare not to practice what is *yi*? If the lord and the ministers, superiors and subordinates, noble and lowly, senior and junior, right down to the common people, all practiced what is
145 *yi*, then who anywhere under Heaven would not want to conform to what is *yi*? Worthy men would wish to be in your court, capable men would wish to your officials, and all the common people who are fond of benefit would wish to have Qi as the place where they return home. This would be to unify all under Heaven.

150 "If you, Prime Minister, abandon this and do not practice it, instead simply practicing the means adopted by the vulgar people of this age, then the Mistress[10] will create chaos in the palace, deceiving

---

[10] I.e., the ruler's wife.

ministers will create chaos in the court, greedy functionaries will create chaos in the official posts, and the masses and common people
will all adopt being greedy, profit-minded, contentious and grasping   155
as their custom. How can one maintain the state when things are like
this? Now, the gigantic state of Chu looms before us. The massive
state of Yan bears down on us from behind. The forceful state of Wei
puts its hooks in us from the right, and the ability of our western
districts to avoid being cut off is something that hangs by a thread.   160
As for the people of Chu, they hold Xiangfei and Kaiyang so as to
press in on us from the left. Thus, if one of these states formulates a
plot, all three states will surely rise up and climb over us. If things are
like this, then Qi will surely be broken up into a number of pieces.
The state will be as though its cities were merely borrowed,[11] and   165
surely it will be greatly laughed at by all under Heaven. What is one
to do? Of these two options,[12] which is worth practicing?"[13]

As for Jie and Zhòu, each was the descendant of a sage king and the
heir to those who possessed all under Heaven. For each, his power
was seated in the most venerable household under Heaven.[14] The ter-   170
ritory of each was so large that the area within its boundaries was a
thousand *li*, and the people were so numerous as to be counted by the
millions. Yet all of a sudden, everyone under Heaven defiantly de-
serted Jie and Zhòu and ran to the side of Tang and Wu. Rebelliously,
they all hated Jie and Zhòu and honored Tang and Wu. Why was   175
this? How did Jie and Zhòu lose them? How did Tang and Wu obtain
them? I say: there is no other reason for this than that Jie and Zhòu
were good at doing what people hate, and Tang and Wu were good
at doing what people like. What is it that people hate? I say: being
corrupt, arrogant, grasping, contentious, greedy, and profit-minded   180
are just that. What is it that people like? I say: ritual, *yi*, yielding,
deference, loyalty, and trustworthiness are just that. Now as for a lord
of men, if in his analogies and comparisons he desires to place himself alongside Tang and Wu, but in the means he uses to control

---

[11] I.e., the conquest of Qi by the other states would be so easy that it would be as if
Qi's holdings were never really its own, and its dissolution would be like the "returning" of borrowed goods to their rightful owners.

[12] I.e., pursuing the way that prevails over people and hence unifying the whole
world, or forsaking the way that prevails over people and hence becoming an object
of derision for the whole world.

[13] Ancient Chinese provides no marks to indicate the end of direct speech, so it is possible that Xunzi's remarks to the prime minister of Qi continue after this point in
the text. However, given that there are no clear instances of Xunzi addressing the
prime minister after this, I have taken his speech as ending here. Others think it
continues until the question from the Marquis of Ying below at line 288.

[14] See the similar wording at 18.64–65.

185 people he is no different than Jie and Zhòu, yet he seeks to have the accomplishments and fame of Tang and Wu, is that achievable?

Thus, whoever is to obtain victory must have other people as his comrades. Whoever is to obtain other people must have the Way as his comrade. What is the Way? I say: ritual, *yi*, yielding, deference,
190 loyalty, and trustworthiness are just that. Thus, when a state with forty or fifty thousand people or more is strong and victorious, that is not due to strength from its numbers. Rather, the significant point rests in being trustworthy. When a state with an area of several hundred *li* or more is peaceful and secure, that is not due to
195 strength from its size. Rather, the significant point rests in cultivating the government.

Now suppose that one who already has masses of people numbering several tens of thousands engages in behavior that is fraudulent, boastful, cliquish, and factionalist in order to vie for comrades, or
200 suppose that one who already has a state measuring several hundred *li* engages in behavior that is corrupt, arrogant, rapacious, and bandit-like in order to vie for territory. In such circumstances, to act thus is to abandon the means by which one will become secure and strong and instead vie for the means by which one will become endangered
205 and weak. It is to decrease that in which one is not adequately supplied in order to redouble that which one has in abundance. When one is so misguided and mistaken, yet seeks to have the accomplishments and fame of Tang and Wu, is that achievable? To draw an analogy for it, this would be like trying to lick Heaven by bending down,
210 or trying to save someone from hanging to death by pulling on their feet. Such a proposition is sure not to succeed, and the harder one works at it, the further off one gets.[15]

If in serving as someone's minister, one does not care that one's conduct will not succeed, but instead one merely goes about gaining
215 profit by improper means, this is tantamount to driving a siege engine into a cave and seeking benefit from it there. Such behavior is something that a person of *ren* considers shameful and will not do.[16]

And so, there is nothing that people value more than life,[17] and there is nothing that they delight in more than security.[18] Of the
220 means to nurture one's life and secure one's delights, none is greater than ritual and *yi*. If people know to value life and delight in security, but reject ritual and *yi*, then to draw analogy for it, this is like desiring

---

[15] Compare the identical wording at 7.164–168.

[16] This paragraph and the two that follow it do not seem well integrated with the previous three paragraphs or with each other in terms of their topics and language. Perhaps they were not originally meant to go together.

[17] See 22.284–85.

[18] The word *an* 安, translated here as "security," also means "ease" and "comfort," and Xunzi probably has those senses in mind here as well.

longevity but then cutting one's own throat—there is no greater stupidity than this.

And so, if the ruler of men cares for the common people, then he 225
will have security. If he is fond of well-bred men, then he will have
glory. If he does neither of these two things, then he will perish. The
Odes says:

> From the great man comes your palisade.
> From the masses are your ramparts made.[19]   230

This expresses my meaning.

The method based on brute strength reaches an impasse. The
method based on *yi* goes through. How can I say this? I say: The state
of Qin is just what I mean. In its strength and power to inspire awe,
it exceeds Tang and Wu. In its breadth and bulk, it exceeds Shun and 235
Yu. Nevertheless, its worries and troubles are innumerable. Full of
apprehension, it constantly fears that all under Heaven will unite and
combine to roll over it. This is what I mean by saying that the method
based on brute strength reaches an impasse.

How can I say that, in its strength and power to inspire awe, it 240
exceeds Tang and Wu? Tang and Wu were merely able to get those
who were pleased with them to serve in their employ. Now Chu's
patriarch died at the hands of Qin, Chu's capital was upturned by
Qin, and Chu carried away the temple ancestor tablets of its several
kings and took refuge between Chen and Cai.[20] Since then, Chu 245
watches for opportunities and looks for openings, for it desires to
sharpen its foot and stomp on Qin's belly. Nevertheless, when Qin
orders it to the left, accordingly it moves left, and when Qin orders it
to the right, accordingly it moves right. This is a case of making one's
enemies into one's servants. This is what I mean by saying that, in its 250
strength and power to inspire awe, Qin exceeds Tang and Wu.

How can I say that, in its breadth and bulk, it exceeds Shun and
Yu? In the past, when the hundred kings united all under Heaven and
made the feudal lords their ministers, there were never any among
them whose territory exceeded a thousand *li* in area. Nowadays in the 255
case of Qin, to the south it has Shayi to serve as its shared border—
this amounts to possessing the area south of the Yangtze River.[d] To

---

[19] Mao #254. See the earlier quotation of this passage at 12.201–2.

[20] According to commentators, this sentence refers to two separate events. In the first,
ca. 297 BCE King Huai of Chu (here referred to as "patriarch") was captured by
Qin and died in captivity. In the second, ca. 277 BCE the Qin general Bai Qi attacked Chu, sacked its capital Ying, and burned its royal tombs. In ancient China,
ancestral temples were major symbols of a ruling family's authority, so the mention
of how Chu saved its ancestor tablets only by relocating them conveys that it came
very close to utter extinction.

the north, it is neighbors with the Hu and Mo peoples, and to the West, it has the Ba and Rong peoples.[21] To the east, its holdings in
260 Chu lands border on Qi. Its holdings in Han lands go beyond Mount Chang and include Linlü. As for its holdings in Wei lands, it occupies Yujin, which is only a hundred and twenty *li* away from Daliang.[22] As for its holdings in Zhao lands, it sliced off and took possession of Ling, and it occupies the border forests of pine and cedar. Qin backs
265 up against the western sea[23] and uses Mount Chang as a fortification. Thus, its land is everywhere under Heaven. This is what I mean by saying that, in its breadth and bulk, it exceeds Shun and Yu.

Qin's power to inspire awe rattles all within the four seas, and its strength threatens the central states.[24] Nevertheless, its worries and
270 troubles are innumerable. Full of apprehension, it constantly fears that all under Heaven will unite and combine to roll over it. That being the case, what can it do about this? I say: Let it curtail its use of awe-inspiring power and return to good form, and accordingly let it employ gentlemen who are upright, have integrity, possess trust-
275 worthiness, and perfect themselves, and let it bring order to all under Heaven through them. In the course of this, let Qin allow these gen-tlemen to participate in the governance of the state, to set straight what is right and what is wrong, to keep in order what is crooked and what is straight, and to judge the affairs of Xianyang.[25] As for those
280 who are compliant, let it leave them be, and when there are people who are not compliant, let it only then execute them. If things are like this, then without its soldiers going outside its borders again, its or-ders will be carried out everywhere under Heaven. If things are like this, then even if one were to build for Qin a Hall of Light outside its
285 borders and summon the feudal lords to court there, that might suc-ceed.[26] In the current era, working at increasing one's territory is not as good as working at increasing one's trustworthiness.

[21] Commentators note that these four tribes were in fact subjugated to the Qin state, so the description of them as "neighbors" here is euphemistic.

[22] Daliang was the capital of Wei.

[23] The deserts of northwest China (in the modern-day provinces of Xinjiang and Qin-ghai) were sometimes referred to by the Chinese as the "western sea" (i.e., "seas of sand") and that may be the sense of the reference here.

[24] Compare the descriptions of the five hegemons at 11.81–84.

[25] Xianyang was the Qin capital. The point is that such worthy gentlemen should be employed at the highest levels of Qin government.

[26] The *mingtang* 明堂 or "Hall of Light" was a building used by the Zhou kings to conduct official business. The idea here is that, if Qin were to reform itself as sug-gested, then it could effectively assume the mantle of the Zhou dynasty, and it would be so strong and secure in this role that it could even hold court outside its own borders, in places where it would normally be vulnerable to attack and less able to command obedience.

The Marquis of Ying asked Xunzi, "Since you entered Qin, what have you seen?"[27]

Xunzi replied, "It has fortifications and barriers that are formida- 290 ble. It has a configuration and position that are advantageous. It has mountains, forests, rivers, and valleys that are fine. It has plentiful benefit from resources given by Heaven. Thus, its configuration is one that disposes it toward victory.

"When I entered its borders and observed its customs, I saw that 295 its common folk are simple.[28] Their songs and music are not perverse and corrupt. Their clothing is not provocative. They greatly fear those in charge and comply with them. They are the same as the common people in ancient times.[29]

"Coming to its cities and their official bureaus, the hundred func- 300 tionaries behave solemnly. All are reverent, restrained, earnest, re- spectful, loyal, and trustworthy, and free of shoddiness. They are the same as functionaries in ancient times.

"When I entered its capital and observed its officers and grand ministers, I saw that they exit their personal compounds and enter 305 the official compounds; they exit the official compounds and return to their homes—there are no private dealings among them. They do not conspire together. They do not form cliques. Maintaining their distance, all are intelligent, comprehending, and without prejudice. They are the same as officers and grand ministers in ancient times. 310

"When I observed its court, I saw that the way it hears and decides the hundred affairs when court is held[e] is such that no tasks are left over. It has a leisurely manner, as if there were nothing to put in order. It is the same as court in ancient times.

"Thus, Qin has been victorious for four generations, and this is 315 due not to luck, but rather to the arrangements it has made.[30] This is what I have seen. And so I say: To be at ease, yet bring about order; to act with restraint, yet take care of all the details; to be free of worry, yet achieve meritorious accomplishments[31]—such is the ultimate in good government. Qin indeed resembles this, but even so, there is 320 still something it fears. It combines the preceding accomplishments and possesses them fully. Nevertheless, if one hangs it up for com- parison with the accomplishments and fame of true kings, then the

---

[27] The Marquis of Ying, also known as Fan Ju or Fan Sui, was for a time the prime minister of Qin. His question to Xunzi is thus not merely a matter of curiosity about Qin, since the Marquis already knew much about it. Rather, he is presumably asking with the expectation of hearing a glowing report about Qin.

[28] In an interesting echo of the *Daodejing*, here Xunzi uses the word *pu* 樸 ("simple") as a term of praise for the common people.

[29] I.e., they behave the way people did during the reign of the sage kings.

[30] See the similar wording at 15.170–72.

[31] See the description of the ideal ruler at 11.257–60.

distance by which it does not match up is far indeed. Why is this?
325 Might it be because Qin lacks any *ru*? Thus it is said, 'He who possesses them purely will be a true king, he who possesses them in
adulterated form will be a hegemon, and he who does not have even
a single one of them will perish.'[32] This is perhaps something in which
Qin falls short."

330 In accumulating something that is minute, working at it for a time
each month does not surpass working at it for a time each day, working at it for a time each season does not surpass working at it for a
time each month, and working at it for a time each year does not
surpass working at it for a time each season. In general, people like
335 to be disdainful and scorning of small matters; only when big matters
arrive do they then take them up and work at them. When they are
like this, they simply will never surpass those who devotedly apply
themselves to small matters. Why is this? It is because the occurrence
of small matters is frequent, the days over which they spread are
340 many, and their accumulation is big, whereas the occurrence of big
matters is sparse, the days over which they spread are few, and their
accumulation is small.
  And so, he who makes good use of the day will become a true king.
He who makes good use of the season will become a hegemon. He
345 who patches up oversights will be endangered. He who practices
great neglect will perish. Thus, a true king respects each day. A hegemon respects each season. He who barely preserves his state falls into
danger and only then frets over it. He who loses his state reaches the
point of losing it and only then realizes that he has lost it. He reaches
350 the point of dying and only then knows that he is dead. The disaster
and defeat for him who loses his state are more than can be lamented,
while the effectiveness and prominence of a hegemon can be entrusted to seasonal efforts, but for achieving the accomplishments
and fame of a true king, nothing can surpass daily focusing one's
355 intentions on them.[33,f] When it comes to money, assets, goods, and
treasures, great magnitudes are what is important. When it comes to

---

[32] See 11.198–200 and 26.10–13, where this saying is also quoted. In this context, its
meaning is somewhat ambiguous. On the one hand, if the "them" mentioned in the
quotation is something like "the proper methods of government," then since Xunzi
has just said that Qin possesses some features of the best government, the implication would be that Qin can become a hegemon. On the other hand, if the "them"
refers to the *ru*, then since Xunzi has just pointed out that Qin lacks any *ru*, the
implication would be that Qin is heading for destruction. Given what Xunzi is
portrayed as saying to Li Si about Qin at 15.393–94, he may well have meant the
latter. Since the Marquis of Ying was a high-ranking official of Qin, though, Xunzi
may have employed the quotation in a deliberately ambiguous manner, so as to
avoid giving offense.

[33] The Chinese text of this sentence is difficult, and the text may be corrupt, so the
translation is tentative.

government through education and having accomplishments and fame, it is the opposite of this; those who are able to accumulate what is minute will quickly have success. The *Odes* says, "Virtue is as light as a hair, but among the common people, few are able to take it up."[34] 360
This expresses my meaning.

In general, the reason that vile people arise is that those in the position of superiors do not honor *yi* and do not respect *yi*. As for *yi*, it is the means to prevent and forbid people from engaging in what is bad and vile. Now suppose that those in the position of superiors 365
do not honor *yi* and do not respect *yi*. When things are like this, then the personnel and the common folk who are their subordinates will all abandon *yi* in their intentions and hasten toward vileness in their hearts. This is the reason that vile people arise.

Furthermore, superiors are teachers to their subordinates. The way 370
that subordinates harmonize with their superiors is comparable to the way an echo responds to one's sound or the way a shadow resembles one's form.[35] And so, in serving as people's superior, one must not fail to be disciplined.

As for *yi*, it is something that, inside, brings proper regulation to 375
the person, and outside, brings proper regulation to the myriad things. It is something that, above, brings security to the ruler, and below, brings concord to the common people. For inside, outside, above, and below all to be properly regulated is the true disposition of *yi*. 380

That being the case, then of all the things that are crucial for presiding over the world, *yi* is most fundamental, and trustworthiness comes next.[36] In ancient times, Yu and Tang made *yi* their foundation and worked at trustworthiness, and the world was ordered. Jie and Zhòu rejected *yi* and turned their backs on trustworthiness, and the 385
world was chaotic. And so, in serving as people's superior, you must carefully observe ritual and *yi* and work at loyalty and trustworthiness, and only then will you suffice. This is the great foundation for serving as people's lord.

When the area within one's hall is not cleared, then the weeds in 390
the countryside are not expected to be removed.[g] When a bared blade is waved before one's chest, one's eyes do not see onward-rushing arrows. When a brandished halberd is poised above one's head, then one's ten fingers will not refuse to be severed. This is not because one does not regard these latter things[37] as worth working to avoid. 395

---

[34] Mao #260.

[35] See 12.144–45 and 18.2–7 for similar imagery.

[36] Compare this remark with Xunzi's discussion of the true king versus the hegemon at 11.12–14.

[37] I.e., the encroachment of weeds, the threat of arrows, and the severing of one's fingers.

Rather, it is because when it comes to the urgency of distressful events, there are some things that take priority over others.[38]

---

[38] Commentators explain that this paragraph is meant to continue the theme of the previous paragraph about how the "first" task of a ruler is to cultivate *yi* (and ritual).

CHAPTER 17

Discourse on Heaven

There is a constancy to the activities of Heaven.[1] They do not persist because of Yao. They do not perish because of Jie. If you respond to them with order, then you will have good fortune. If you respond to them with chaos, then you will have misfortune.   5

If you strengthen the fundamental works[2] and moderate expenditures, then Heaven cannot make you poor. If your means of nurture are prepared and your actions are timely, then Heaven cannot make you ill. If you cultivate the Way and do not deviate from it, then Heaven cannot ruin you. Thus, floods and drought cannot make you   10
go hungry or thirsty, cold and heat cannot make you sick, and aberrations and anomalies cannot make you misfortunate.

If the fundamental works are neglected and expenditures are extravagant, then Heaven cannot make you wealthy. If your means of nurture are sparse and your actions are infrequent, then Heaven can-   15
not make you sound in body. If you turn your back on the Way and act recklessly, then Heaven cannot make you fortunate. And so, although floods and drought have not yet come, you still will go hungry. Although heat and cold are not yet pressing, you will still become sick. Although aberrations and anomalies have not yet come, you will   20
still be misfortunate. To receive the benefits of the seasons is the same as having an ordered age, but calamities and disasters are incompatible with there being an ordered age. You must not complain against Heaven; its way is simply thus. And so, one who understands clearly the respective allotments of Heaven and humankind can be called a   25
person of utmost achievement.

That which is accomplished without anyone's doing it and which is obtained without anyone's seeking it is called the work of Heaven.[3] With respect to what is like this, even though he thinks deeply, a proper person does not try to ponder it. Even though he is mighty,   30
he does not try to augment it by his own abilities. Even though he is expertly refined, he does not try to make it more keenly honed. This is called not competing with Heaven's work. When

---

[1] This and the next few sentences are rhymed in the original.
[2] The "fundamental works" are agriculture and textile production.
[3] A similar idea is articulated in *Mencius* 5A6.

Heaven has its proper seasons,[4]
35 Earth has its proper resources,
And humankind has its proper order,

—this is called being able to form a triad. To neglect that whereby we form a triad and wish instead for those things to which we stand as the third is a state of confusion. The arrayed stars follow each other
40 in their revolutions, the sun and the moon take turns shining, the four seasons proceed in succession, *yin* and *yang* undergo their great transformations, and winds and rain are broadly bestowed.

Their harmony[5] keeps the myriad things alive.
Their nurturing helps the myriad things to thrive.

45 What is such that one does not see its workings but sees only its accomplishments—this is called spirit-like power. What is such that everyone knows how it comes about, but no one understands it in its formless state—this is called the accomplishment of Heaven. Only the sage does not seek to understand Heaven.
50 When the work of Heaven has been established and the accomplishments of Heaven have been completed, then the body is set and spirit arises. Liking, dislike, happiness, anger, sorrow, and joy are contained therein—these are called one's Heavenly dispositions. The abilities of eyes, ears, nose, mouth, and body each have their respec-
55 tive objects and are not able to assume each other's abilities—these are called one's Heavenly faculties. The heart dwells in the central cavity so as to control the five faculties—this is called one's Heavenly lord.[6] Using what is not of one's kind as a resource for nourishing what is of one's kind—this is one's Heavenly nourishment. To be in
60 accordance with what is proper for one's kind is called happiness, and to go against what is proper for one's kind is called disaster—this is called one's Heavenly government. To becloud your Heavenly lord, disorder your Heavenly faculties, abandon your Heavenly nourishment, go against your Heavenly government, and turn your back
65 on your Heavenly dispositions, so that you lose the accomplishments of Heaven—this is called the greatest misfortune. The sage keeps clear his Heavenly lord, sets straight his Heavenly faculties, makes complete his Heavenly nourishment, accords with his Heavenly government, and nurtures his Heavenly dispositions, so as to keep whole

---

[4] This and the following two lines are rhymed in the original.
[5] I.e., the harmonious operations of the various natural elements that are mentioned in the sentence immediately prior to this remark.
[6] Xunzi is playing on the fact that *guan* 官 (here translated as "faculty") means both "organ" and "official."

the accomplishment of Heaven. A person who is thus is someone who   70
knows what he is to do and what he is not to do. Then Heaven and
Earth will have their proper positions and the myriad things will all
be servants to him. His conduct will be completely ordered, his nourishment will be completely appropriate, and his life will suffer no
harm—*this* is called knowing Heaven.   75

Thus, the greatest cleverness lies in not doing certain things, and
the greatest wisdom lies in not pondering certain things.

> With respect to Heaven, focus only on those manifest phe-
> nomena to which you can align yourself. With respect to
> Earth, focus only on those manifest places which are suitable   80
> for growing. With respect to the four seasons, focus only on
> that manifest order by which work is to be arranged. With
> respect to *yin* and *yang*, focus only on those manifest harmo-
> nies which can be used to order things.[7]

Let the officials keep watch over Heaven and yourself keep watch   85
over the Way.

Are order and disorder due to Heaven? I say: The sun, the moon,
and the stars are wondrous calendrical phenomena. These things
were the same for both Yu and Jie, but Yu used them to bring about
order, while Jie used them to bring about disorder, so order and dis-   90
order are not due to Heaven.

Are order and disorder due to the seasons? I say: In spring and
summer things flourish, blossom, prosper, and grow. In fall and winter they are gathered, piled up, taken in, and stored. These things
were the same for both Yu and Jie, but Yu used them to bring about   95
order, while Jie used them to bring about disorder, so order and disorder are not due to the seasons.

Are order and disorder due to Earth? I say: If one gains use of the
land, one will live, and if one loses use of the land, one will die. These
things were the same for both Yu and Jie, but Yu used them to bring   100
about order, while Jie used them to bring about disorder, so order
and disorder are not due to Earth. The *Odes* says:

> Heaven made the high mountain.
> The Great King opened the land.
> These works were completed,   105
> And King Wen made them more grand.[8]

This expresses my meaning.

---

[7] These lines are rhymed in the original.
[8] Mao #270. See the earlier quotation of this passage at 9.281–84.

Heaven does not stop producing winter because humans dislike cold, Earth does not stop being broad because humans dislike huge distances, and the gentleman does not cease his conduct because of the chatter of petty men. Heaven has a constant way, Earth has a constant measure, and the gentleman has a constant substance. The gentleman makes his way based on what is constant, whereas the petty man calculates what he can accomplish. The *Odes* says, "[I lapsed not from the ways of high antiquity, nor did I deviate from ritual and *yi*.] So why should others' words be of concern to me?"[9] This expresses my meaning.

If the king of Chu has a thousand chariots following behind him, this is not because he is wise. If the gentleman eats only crude greens and drinks only plain water, this is not because he is foolish. It is just because of the circumstances. What is up to me is to cultivate my heart and thoughts, to make my virtue and good conduct abundant, to make my understanding and deliberations enlightened, and to live in the present age but focus my intentions on the ancients. And so, the gentleman respects what rests with himself and does not long for what rests with Heaven. The petty man sets aside what rests with himself and instead longs for what rests with Heaven. Since the gentleman respects what rests with himself and does not long for what rests with Heaven, every day he improves. Since the petty man sets aside what rests with himself and instead longs for what rests with Heaven, every day he loses ground. Thus the factors in why the gentleman improves every day and the petty man loses ground every day are one and the same.[10] The reasons why the gentleman and petty man are so far apart from each other rest with these things.

If stars fall or trees groan, the people of the state are filled with fear and say, "What is this?" I say: it is nothing. These are simply rarely occurring things among the changes in Heaven and Earth and the transformations of *yin* and *yang*. To marvel at them is permissible, but to fear them is wrong. Eclipses of sun and moon, unseasonable winds and rain, unexpected appearances of strange stars—there is no age in which such things do not occur. If the superiors are enlightened and the government is stable, then even if all these things come about in the same age, there is no harm done. If the superiors are benighted and the government is unstable, then even if none of these things comes to pass, it is of no benefit. The falling of stars and the groaning of trees are simply rarely occurring things among the

---

[9] This poem does not appear in the received text of the *Odes*. For the sake of intelligibility, two lines are added here, based on another quotation of this poem at 22.231–33.

[10] I.e., both depend on what one relies upon and longs for.

changes in Heaven and Earth and the transformations of *yin* and *yang*. To marvel at them is permissible, but to fear them is wrong.

Of things that come to pass, it is human ill omens that are to be feared. When poor plowing harms the planting, when the cutting loses control over the weeds, when the government is unstable and loses control over the people, such that the fields are overgrown with weeds and the planting is bad, buying rice is expensive and the people face famine, and there are corpses lying in the roads—these are called human ill omens. When efforts are not exerted in a timely fashion, such that cows and horses will give birth to each other and the six domestic animals produce monstrous offspring,ᵃ when government orders are not clear, when policies are not timely, when the fundamental tasks are not well ordered—these are called human ill omens. When ritual and *yi* are not cultivated, when insiders and outsiders are not properly differentiated, when men and women engage in perverse, disorderly conduct, then fathers and sons are suspicious of one another, superiors and inferiors desert one another, and bandits and other difficulties arrive together—these are called human ill omens. Ill omens thus arise from disorder. If all three are present, then there will be no security for the state. The explanations for these things are very close at hand,[11] and the disasters that follow are most wretched. These are worth marveling at, and also worth fearing.

A saying goes, "As for anomalies among the myriad things, the *Documents* does not explain them."[12] As for unnecessary debates and unimportant investigations, abandon them and do not study them. As for the *yi* of lord and minister, the intimate relations of father and son, and the differentiation of husband and wife, polish and refine them daily and do not let them go.[13]

One performs the rain sacrifice and it rains. Why? I say: there is no special reason why. It is the same as when one does not perform the rain sacrifice and it rains anyway. When the sun and moon suffer eclipse, one tries to save them. When Heaven sends drought, one performs the rain sacrifice. One performs divination and only then decides on important affairs. But this is not to be regarded as bringing one what one seeks, but rather is done to give things proper form. Thus, the gentleman regards this as proper form, but the common people regard it as connecting with spirits. If one regards it as proper form, one will have good fortune. If one regards it as connecting with spirits, one will have misfortune.

---

[11] Commentators note that that these things rest with human beings, and so are "close at hand" compared to falling stars and groaning trees, which rest with Heaven.

[12] The point seems to be that it does not try to explain them because their causes do not rest with human behavior and so cannot be controlled.

[13] See *Analects* 1.15.

Among the features of Heaven, none are more dazzling than the sun and moon. Among the features of Earth, none are more dazzling than water and fire. Among things, none are more dazzling than
190 pearls and jade. Among human beings, nothing is more dazzling than ritual and *yi*.

Thus, if the sun and moon are not high above, their light is not radiant. If water and fire do not accumulate, their gleam and shimmer does not spread far. If pearls and jade are not
195 visible on the outside,[14] then kings and dukes do not treasure them. If ritual and *yi* are not applied to the state and family, then accomplishments and fame do not shine.[15]

And so, a person's fate rests with Heaven. The fate of the state rests with ritual. If the lord of men exalts ritual and honors the worthy, he
200 will become a true king.[16] If he relies heavily on law and has concern for the people, he will become a hegemon. If he cares only for profit and frequently engages in deception, he will be endangered. If he is scheming, debauched, unpredictable and dangerous, he will utterly perish.

205   To exalt Heaven and long for it—[17]
          How can this compare to nourishing things and
             overseeing them?
       To obey Heaven and praise it—
          How can this compare to overseeing what Heaven
210   has mandated and using it?
       To observe the seasons and wait upon them—
          How can this compare to responding to the seasons
             and employing them?
       To follow along with things and increase them—
215   How can this compare to developing their powers
             and transforming them?
       To long for things and appraise them—[b]
          How can this compare to ordering things and never
             losing them?
220   To desire that from which things arise—
          How can this compare to taking hold of that by
             which things are completed?

---

[14] I.e., by remaining hidden in mountains and under water. See 1.125–26.
[15] These lines are rhymed in the original.
[16] This and the following two sentences also appear at 16.14–18 and 27.2–5.
[17] From here down to the word "confusion" in the next paragraph, the original text is rhymed.

Thus, if one rejects what lies with man and instead longs for what lies with Heaven, then one will have lost grasp of the disposition of the myriad things.[18]   225

The unchanging element among the reigns of the hundred kings can serve as the binding thread of the Way.[19] As one thing passes by and another arises, respond to them with this thread. If one has mastered the thread, there will be no chaos. If one does not know the thread, one will not know how to   230 respond to changes. The major substance of the thread has never perished, but chaos arises from falling short of it, whereas order arises from adhering to it meticulously. And so as for what is counted good in light of the Way, courses of action conforming to it may be followed, but those veering   235 from it may not be followed. Those that obscure it will create great confusion.

Those who cross waters mark out the deep places, but if the markers are not clear, people will fall in.[20] Those who order the people mark out the Way, but if the markers are not clear, there will be chaos. The   240 rituals are those markers. To reject ritual is to bemuddle the world, and to bemuddle the world is to create great chaos. And so, when the Way is in no part unclear, and that which is within the bounds and that which is outside the bounds have different markers, and that which is inglorious and that which is illustrious have constant mea-   245 sures, then the pitfalls of the people will be eliminated.

The myriad things are but one facet of the Way. A single thing is but one facet of the myriad things. Foolish people take a single facet of a single thing and think themselves to know the Way—this is to lack knowledge.[21]   250

Shenzi saw the value of hanging back, but not the value of being in the lead.[22] Laozi saw the value of yielding, but not the value of exerting oneself. Mozi saw the value of making

---

[18] The Chinese text of the last part of the sentence is ambiguous between two possible meanings: (1) failing to understand how the myriad things actually operate (because one mistakenly thinks Heaven exercises greater influence over them than it really does), and (2) missing the opportunity to control the condition of the myriad things (because one mistakenly focuses on Heaven's influence over them). Both senses are probably intended, and the translation here is worded to allow both construals.

[19] See *Analects* 4.15. Compare also 11.438–440.

[20] Compare this and the next few sentences with 27.58–65.

[21] This remark and the sentences after it are worth comparing with 21.101–25.

[22] This "Shenzi" is Shen Dao. The text rhymes from here down to the *Documents* quotation.

things uniform, but not the value of establishing differences.
Songzi saw the value of having few desires, but not the value
of having many desires. If there is only hanging back and no
being in the lead, the masses will have no gateway to advancing. If there is only yielding and no exerting oneself, noble
and lowly will not be distinguished. If there is only uniformity and no difference, governmental orders cannot be
given. If there are only few desires and not many desires, the
masses cannot be transformed.

The *Documents* says:

Do not create new likes.
Follow the kings' way.
Do not create new dislikes.
On the kings' path stay.[23]

This expresses my meaning.

---

[23] See *Shujing*, *Hongfan* ("The Great Plan"), translated in Waltham (1971, p. 128). See also the earlier citation of this passage at 2.228–31.

CHAPTER 18

Correct Judgments[a]

The vulgar purveyors of doctrine say, "In the ways of a ruler, it is beneficial to be secretive."[1] This is not so. The ruler is lead singer to his people; the superior is sundial to his subordinates.[2] The people listen for the lead singer and then respond; the subordinates look to the sundial and then move. If the lead singer is silent, then the people 5 will not respond. If the sundial is hidden, then the subordinates will not move. Without response, without movement, superior and subordinates will have no hold on each other. This is the same as there being no superior at all, and nothing is more inauspicious than that.

The superior is root for his subordinates. If he is conspicuous and 10 clear, they will be ordered and regimented. If he is scrupulous and has integrity, they will be conscientious and honest. If he is principled and without prejudice, they will be easy to rectify. If the subordinates are ordered and regimented, then they will be easy to unify. If they are conscientious and honest, then they will be easy to employ. 15 If they are easy to rectify, then they will be easy to know. If one's subordinates are easy to unify, then one will be strong. If one's subordinates are easy to employ, then one will accomplish things. If one's subordinates are easy to know, then one will have clear understanding. This is what order is born from. 20

If the superior is secretive and clandestine, then his subordinates will be hesitant and unclear. If he is unpredictable and dangerous, then they will be sly and deceptive. If he is one-sided and twisted, then they will be cliquish and closed. If the subordinates are hesitant and unclear, then they will be difficult to unify. If they are sly and 25 deceptive, then they will be difficult to employ. If they are cliquish and closed, then they will be difficult to know. If one's subordinates are difficult to unify, then one will not be strong. If one's subordinates are difficult to employ, then one will not accomplish things. If one's subordinates are difficult to know, then one will not have clear 30 understanding. This is what chaos is born from. And so, in the ways of a ruler it is beneficial to be clear. It is not beneficial to be unpredictable. It is beneficial to be outspoken. It is not beneficial to be secretive.

---

[1] Although Xunzi does not identify any particular figures who hold this view, one can find versions of it in statements that are attributed to Guan Zhong, Shen Buhai, and Han Feizi by early texts. This view is also mentioned and criticized at 21.433–436.

[2] Compare 12.144–45 and 16.370–73.

35   Thus, if the ways of the ruler are clear, the subordinates will feel secure. If the ways of the ruler are unpredictable, the subordinates will feel endangered. If the subordinates feel secure, then they will value their superior. If they feel endangered, then they will despise him. If he is easy to know, then they will have affection for him.[3] If
40 he is difficult to know, then they will fear him. If they have affection for him, he will be secure. If they fear him, he will be endangered. Thus, in the ways of a ruler, nothing is worse than being difficult to know, and nothing is more dangerous than to cause one's subordinates to fear oneself. A proverb says, "Those who are hated by many
45 are in danger." The *Documents* says, "He was able to make clear his bright virtue."[4] And the *Odes* says, "It was radiantly bright below."[5] Thus, the former kings made things clear. How could it be that they worked only to make them unclear?

     The vulgar purveyors of doctrine say, "Jie and Zhòu possessed the
50 world. Tang and Wu usurped and snatched it away." This is not so. If one thinks that, in terms of regular procedure,[6] Jie and Zhòu possessed the highest status in the world, then that is so, but if one thinks that, in terms of their own persons, they possessed the highest status in the world, then that is not so. If one says that the world sided with
55 Jie and Zhòu, that is not so.

     In ancient times, the Son of Heaven had a thousand officials, and the feudal lords each had a hundred officials. He who by means of these thousand officials has his orders carried out among the various Xia states is called a king.[7] He who by means of these hundred offi-
60 cials has his orders carried out within his borders, so that even if his state is not secure, he does not reach the point of being deposed, replaced, banished, or perished, is called a lord.

     The offspring of a sage king is successor to one who possessed the world. His power and status rest with the most venerable household
65 in the world.[8] Nevertheless, if he is neither talented nor correct, then within the state, the common folk will hate him, and outside the state,

---

[3] Compare 3.26–27.
[4] See *Shujing, Kanggao* ("The Announcement to the Prince of K'ang"), translated in Waltham (1971, p. 147). Xunzi's quotation is slightly different from the received edition of the *Documents*. In its original context, the remark refers to King Wen.
[5] Mao #236. This line is also quoted at 21.444–45 for similar purposes.
[6] I.e., inheriting the position from their fathers, as was common practice. The Chinese text of this and the following sentence is problematic, and commentators have proposed numerous different emendations to make sense of it. I have adopted a rather conservative approach, but the translation remains tentative.
[7] The Chinese title *wang* 王 ("king") was originally reserved solely for the Son of Heaven, and that is at least part of the sense upon which Xunzi is drawing in contrasting it with the term *jun* 君 ("lord") here.
[8] See the similar wording at 16.169–170.

the feudal lords will turn against him. Among the people nearby him, those residing within his borders will not unite with him, and among those far away from him, the feudal lords will not heed him. His orders will not be carried out within his borders, and in severe cases, the feudal lords will invade and carve off pieces of his state, and they will attack and smite him. When things are like this, then even though he has not yet perished, I say that he simply does not possess the world.

When the sage kings have died and those who possess their power and status are unfit and inadequate to carry the world, so that there is no lord over the world, then if there is one among the feudal lords who is able to have virtue that shines and power to inspire awe that piles up, the common people within the four seas will all want to obtain him as their lord and leader. If nevertheless there is some violent state that alone remains depraved, he is then able to punish it. In doing so, he is sure not to harm the innocent common people, and punishing the lord of the violent state is as easy as punishing a lone individual.[9] When things are like this, then he can simply be called one who is able to put the world to use, and one who is able to put the world to use is called a king.

It is not the case that Tang and Wu snatched away the world. They cultivated their ways and carried out what was *yi* for them, they established benefits for the whole world and eliminated harms to the whole world, and the world then went over to them. It is not the case that Jie and Zhòu abandoned the world. They went against the virtue of Tang and Wu and disrupted the social divisions that come from ritual and *yi*. Their beastly conduct accumulated in them what was ruinous and made complete in them what was bad, and the world then abandoned them. When the world goes over to a person, he is called king, and when the world abandons a person, he is called perished.[10] And so, from this it can be confirmed that Jie and Zhòu did not possess the world, and that Tang and Wu did not commit regicide against their lords.

Tang and Wu were regarded by the common people as their own father and mother. Jie and Zhòu were regarded by the common people as detested villains. Now the vulgar purveyors of doctrine are taking Jie and Zhòu to be lords, and taking Tang and Wu to be regicides. That being the case, they would thus punish the mother and father of the common people and treat as leader those who are detested villains to the common people. Nothing is more inauspicious than that! If one views as the lord him with whom the world joins,

---

[9] See the similar remarks at 15.204.

[10] As elsewhere in the text, here Xunzi plays on the fact that the terms for "king" (王) and "perish" (亡) were close in sound during ancient times.

well, the world never joined with Jie and Zhòu. That being the case,
if one takes Tang and Wu to be regicides, well, no one in the world
110 has ever explained how that could be. It simply amounts to straightforward slander against them.

And so, for the position of Son of Heaven, only the right person
will do. Responsibility for the world is supremely heavy. Nobody
except one who possesses ultimate strength can undertake it. Its size
115 is supremely great. Nobody except one who possesses ultimate ability in making distinctions can divide it up properly. Its people are
supremely numerous. Nobody except one who possesses ultimate
brilliance can harmonize them. As for these three "ultimates," nobody except a sage can possess them fully. And so nobody except a
120 sage is able to reign as a true king. The sage is one who fully equips
himself with the Way and makes complete in himself what is fine—
this is the scales for weighing and balancing out the world.[11]

As for Jie and Zhòu, their understanding and deliberations about
things were shaky to an ultimate degree, the things to which they
125 directed their thoughts were benighted to an ultimate degree, and
their practice of these resulted in chaos to an ultimate degree. Those
who were originally close grew distant from them, those who were
worthy looked down on them, and all the common people living then
detested them. Even though they were the successors to Yu and Tang,
130 they did not get even a single person to stand with them. With acts
like the evisceration of Bi Gan and the imprisonment of Jizi,[12] they
came to die and their states perished. They became the greatest disgraces in the world, and discussions by subsequent generations about
those who are bad are sure to mention them.[13] Theirs is a way of ar-
135 ranging things that will not keep even a wife or child by one's side.

And so, those who are worthy to an ultimate degree will take as
their realm the area within the four seas, and such were Tang and Wu.
Those who are unfit to an ultimate degree will not keep even a wife
or child by their side, and such were Jie and Zhòu.

140 Now the vulgar purveyors of doctrine take Jie and Zhòu as pos-
sessors of the world and make Tang and Wu out to be their ministers—are they not severely mistaken indeed! To draw an analogy for

---

[11] The text here is ambiguous, and perhaps intentionally so, in order to suggest multiple senses. First, the referent of "this" could be the sage, or his actions of cultivating the Way and what is fine. (Other remarks in the text favor the latter reading
somewhat; compare 21.145 and 22.338–47.) Alternatively, the last part might be
rendered as "[doing] this is to hang out [i.e., set up] the greatest scales in the world."
[12] Although the surrounding context is concerned with both Jie and Zhòu, these two
acts belong to Zhòu alone.
[13] See the similar wording at 5.57–59.

it, this would be like a hunchbacked shaman or lame-footed invalid[14] grandiosely thinking of themselves as having true understanding.

And so, it is possible that someone might snatch away a state when 145 it belongs to another, but it is not possible that someone might snatch away the world when it belongs to another. It is possible that someone might steal a state, but it is not possible that someone might steal the world. For one who can snatch away things, it is possible to possess a state, but it is not possible to possess the world. Stealing can 150 get one a state, but it cannot get one the world. Why is this? I say: the state is the lesser instrument.[15] It can be possessed by a petty man. It can be gotten by petty ways. It can be maintained by petty strength. The world is the greater instrument. It cannot be possessed by a petty man. It cannot be gotten by petty ways. It cannot be maintained by 155 petty strength. As for the state, a petty person can possess it, but he will not necessarily avoid perishing. As for the world, its size is supremely great. Nobody except a sage is able to possess it.

The vulgar purveyors of doctrine say, "In the orderly ancient times, there were no corporal punishments, and instead there were symbolic 160 punishments:[16] painted-on tattoos; chin-straps woven from grass; in place of castration, holes cut in the knee-coverings; in place of amputating the feet, hempen shoes; in place of execution, red-brown clothes without a collar. The orderly ancient times were like this."[17] This is not so. Do they think that there was order? If so, then nobody 165 would have been guilty of offenses in the first place, and not only would corporal punishments have gone unused, but also symbolic punishments would have simply gone unused. Or perhaps they think that some people were indeed guilty of offenses, but simply believe that their punishments were slight. That being the case, then those 170 who killed others would not be put to death, and those who injured others would not be punished. When the offense is most weighty but

---

[14] Such people were used as court diviners. See 9.416–22.

[15] Here the text uses the term *xiao* 小 multiple times in a way that is difficult to render consistently in English. The word simultaneously means "small," "lesser," and—as a moral notion—"petty." Compare this discussion of the state as "instrument" with that at 11.1–2 and 11.123–24.

[16] In ancient China, there was a traditional set of "five punishments" for criminals: branding/tattooing the face, cutting off the nose, castration, amputating the feet, and execution. The "symbolic" alternatives presented here in the text are apparently meant to follow this traditional listing.

[17] As elsewhere, Xunzi does not identify who holds this view. However, the Tang dynasty text *Chuxueji* 初學記 contains a quotation that expresses a similar view, which is attributed to Shen Dao. The text of the *Xunzi* here is very difficult and seems corrupted. Most commentators base their reading of it on the *Chuxueji* passage, and I have followed them, with hesitation.

the punishment is most slight, then ordinary people will not know to treat it as bad. Nothing is more chaotic than that.

175 The basis for all cases of punishing people is putting a halt to those who are violent, treating as bad those who are bad, and warning those who have not yet acted. When those who kill others are not put to death, and those who injure others are not punished, this is called showing kindness to those who are violent and being generous to-
180 ward villains—it is not treating as bad those who are bad. And so, symbolic punishments likely were not born during the orderly ancient times, but rather arose together with the chaotic present age.

The orderly ancient times were not thus. In every case, high rank and official employment and rewards and punishments all were be-
185 stowed as requitals; they were things that followed according to kind. If even a single matter missed out on its proper matching response, it was the start of chaos. If virtue was not matched up to position, if ability was not matched up to office, if rewards did not correspond to meritorious accomplishments, if penalties did not correspond to of-
190 fenses—nothing was more inauspicious than that. In the past, King Wu attacked the possessor of the Shang.[18] He executed Zhòu, cut off his head, and hung it from a red banner. Carrying out punitive campaigns against those who are violent and executing those who are brutal is the blossoming of order. Those who kill others are put to
195 death, and those who injure others are punished—this is something in which the hundred kings were the same, though there has never been anyone who knows how these practices came about.

If punishments match up to offenses, there will be order. If they do not match up to offenses, there will be chaos. And so, when there is
200 order, punishments are appropriately weighty, and when there is chaos, punishments are inappropriately slight, for the offenses of those who transgress during times of order are certainly regarded as weighty, and the offenses of those who transgress during times of chaos are certainly regarded as slight. The *Documents* says, "Punish-
205 ments and penalties in some ages are slight and in other ages are weighty."[19] This expresses my meaning.

The vulgar purveyors of doctrine say, "Tang and Wu were not able to enforce their prohibitions and commands." How is that? They say, "Chu and Yue did not accept their regulations." This is not so. Tang
210 and Wu were ones who were absolutely best in the world at enforcing their prohibitions and commands. Tang dwelt in Bo, and King Wu

[18] "The possessor of the Shang" is an alternative way of referring to the ruler of the Shang dynasty, which in this case was the tyrant Zhòu.

[19] See *Shujing, Lüxing* ("The Marquis of Lü on Punishment"), translated in Waltham (1971, p. 235). In its original context, the line appears to have a very different sense than how Xunzi construes it here.

dwelt in Hao—these were both territories of merely a hundred *li* in size. But the world became united under them, the feudal lords were their servants, and among those of penetrating intelligence, all were stirred to submit and follow and thereby became transformed and fully compliant with them. How would it be that Chu and Yue alone did not accept their regulations? 215

The manner in which a true king establishes regulations is that he observes conditions and then establishes regulations for implements. He weighs up distances and then sets gradations in tributes. How could it be necessary that these things be identical? Thus, the people of Lu use the *tang*, the people of Wey use the *ke*, and the people of Qi use the *yige*.[20] For those whose lands and conditions are not the same, their implements and accoutrements cannot but differ. 220

And so, the various Xia states are the same in serving the king, and they have the same standards, while the states of the Man, Yi, Rong, and Di peoples are the same in serving the king, but they do not have the same regulations.[21] The area within the king's borders constitutes the "tillage" zone. Beyond that, the area just outside the king's borders constitutes the "lords" zone. Beyond that, the next region constitutes the "retainers" zone. Beyond that, the Man and the Yi constitute the "controlled" zone. Beyond that, the Rong and the Di constitute the "wilderness" zone. Those in the "tillage" zone provide supplies each day for the *ji* ceremonies. Those in the "lords" zone provide supplies each month for the *si* ceremonies. Those in the "retainers" zone provide supplies each season for the *xiang* ceremonies. Those in the "controlled" zone provide tribute once a year. Those in the "wilderness" zone pay their respects when a king passes away. Making this arrangement for daily provision of the *ji* ceremonies, monthly provision of the *si* ceremonies, seasonal provision of the *xiang* ceremonies, tributes once a year, and paying respects when a king passes away is called observing conditions and establishing regulations for implements, weighing up distances and setting gradations in tributes. Such are the regulations of a true king. 225 230 235 240

As for Chu and Yue, moreover, they are in the category of those who provide supplies each season for the *xiang* ceremonies, provide 245

---

[20] It is not known exactly what the *tang*, *ke*, and *yige* were. Based on other sources, commentators propose that they are different types of containers or vessels that were used in tributes paid to the Son of Heaven.

[21] Here and in what follows, Xunzi references an idealized plan, mentioned in some early texts, that divides the world up into various administrative units (*fu* 服, "zones," lit. "submissions") that radiate outward from the Son of Heaven's state and perform different services for him. The language is rather technical and condensed and very difficult to render into English without extreme awkwardness. I have therefore taken certain liberties with the translation in order to keep it intelligible for a modern reader.

tribute once a year, or pay their respects when a king passes away.[22] Must one make them identical to the ones in the category of those who provide daily for the *ji* ceremonies or provide monthly for the *si*
250 ceremonies and only then say that they "accepted the regulations"? That is a doctrine tantamount to a worn-out compass.[23] Never has an emaciated corpse in a ditch been fit to take part in attaining the regulations of a true king.[24] A saying goes, "One who is shallow is not fit to take part in probing something deep. One who is stupid is not fit
255 to take part in planning something clever. A frog sunk in a well cannot take part in discussing the joys of the eastern sea."[25] This expresses my meaning.

The vulgar purveyors of doctrine say, "Yao and Shun relinquished the throne and yielded it to others."[26] This is not so. As for the Son of
260 Heaven, his power and position are supremely revered, and there is no rival to them in the whole world. To whom could he yield the throne?[27] He follows the Way and virtue purely and completely. His wisdom and kindness are profound and luminous. Facing south, he renders decisions for the whole world, and all those living as com-
265 moners are stirred to submit and follow and thereby become transformed and fully compliant with him. In all the world, there are no well-bred men in hiding, and no good men who have been forsaken.[28]

---

[22] Chu and Yue were located in the far south and thus fell into the three outer zones described above.

[23] I.e., the standard being applied is inaccurate.

[24] Commentators explain that the "emaciated corpse" is a metaphor for someone "starved" of understanding and thus too ignorant to grasp the regulations of a true king. See the similar view expressed at 4.268–84.

[25] The last of these sentences is more fully explained by a story in chap. 17 of the *Zhuangzi*. There, a sea tortoise describes the vastness of the sea to a frog who has never left the confines of his little well, and the frog is dumbfounded by the idea of such a great expanse of water.

[26] The force of this claim is unclear, so interpreters disagree about how to construe Xunzi's reply. In my view, the abdication of Yao and Shun is being presented as a model for imitation, and Xunzi is opposing this model on the grounds that its historical basis is false. Compare *Mencius* 5A5, which likewise displays a critical attitude toward the stories of sage kings abdicating. It is probable that the *Mencius* passage is partly a reaction to a famous incident in which (ca. 316 BCE) the king of Yan attempted to imitate Yao and Shun by turning over power to his minister Zizhi, with disastrous results. Xunzi may also have that incident in mind here.

[27] I take the line of argument here to be as follows. As the passage goes on to explain, the world will accept only the best person as Son of Heaven. So, as long as there is someone successfully serving as Son of Heaven, then there cannot be anyone else as good in the world, and so there is no one else whom the Son of Heaven could cause the world to follow in his place.

[28] In times of bad government, virtuous officials would often resign and live in reclusion, and other virtuous people might be dismissed or might never be employed by the ruler. So, this remark conveys the idea of good order.

That which conforms with him is affirmed, and that which diverges from him is repudiated. How would he come to relinquish the world?

Some say, "At the point of death, Yao and Shun relinquished it."[29] 270 Again, this is not so. When a sage king rules above, he assigns rank by reckoning virtue, awards official positions by assessing ability, and in each case makes it so that the people undertake the right tasks and each gets what is proper for him.[30] Those who are unable to use *yi* to overcome their motives for profit, or who are not able to use deliber- 275 ate effort to beautify their natures, are all relegated to the status of common people. When the sage king has died, if there is no sage left in the world, then certainly there is simply no one adequate to have the world relinquished to him. If there is a sage left in the world, and he is among the king's descendants, then the world does not desert 280 him. The court does not change location. The state does not alter its regulations. The world remains calm, no different from before. One Yao succeeds another Yao, so what switch is there? If the sage is not among the king's descendants, and is instead among the three dukes, then the world goes and sides with him, as if returning and restoring 285 a former ruler to the throne. The world remains calm, no different from before. One Yao succeeds another Yao, so what switch is there? He moves the court and changes the regulations, but only with reluctance.[b] And so, while the Son of Heaven lives, the world exalts this one man, behaves with paramount compliance, and is ordered. 290 He assigns rank by judging virtue, and when he dies, then whoever is able to assume responsibility for the world is sure to take posses- sion of it.[c] When the social divisions according to ritual and *yi* are completely implemented, what use would be served by relinquishing the throne and yielding it to others?[31] 295

Some say, "When Yao and Shun grew old and went into decline, they relinquished the throne." Again, this is not so. In the case of one's blood, *qi*, and the strength in one's tendons, there is decline, but in the case of one's wisdom, deliberations, and choices of what to accept or reject, there is no decline.[32] They say, "But as old men, 300 they could not cope with the required toil and so retired from the

---

[29] The Chinese text could be construed as meaning that Yao and Shun relinquished the throne just as they were about to die, or upon dying.

[30] See the similar wording at 12.234–36.

[31] The point here is rather unclear. As I see it, Xunzi means that the Son of Heaven simply makes sure to follow ritual and *yi* fully, and does not bother to appoint a successor, because in following ritual and *yi*, he has done all that he could do—it is simply not within his power to ensure that any particular person will succeed him, and hence it is wrong to say that Yao and Shun "handed over" the empire at the point of death. Again, compare the claim at *Mencius* 5A5 that the Son of Heaven does not give the empire to his successor.

[32] To modern readers, the common phenomenon of senility may make Xunzi's claim here seem completely implausible. It is important to remember, however, that in his

throne." This is, rather, the sort of contention made by people who are afraid of work. As for the Son of Heaven, his power has the utmost weight, and his body has the utmost ease. His heart has the
305 utmost happiness, and nowhere do his intentions suffer being turned back.

His body does not endure toil, because he receives reverence unsurpassed. For his garments, people clothe him in the five regular colors, intersperse the mixed colors,[33] provide copious patterning
310 and embroidery, and add further adornment to this with pearls and jade. For his meals, they provide copiously the Grand Livestock,[34] prepare precious and unusual dishes, and assemble fragrant and flavorful ingredients.[d] They play assorted instruments as the meal is presented.[e] They beat drums as he eats. They play the *Yong* as the food
315 is withdrawn for the five *si* ceremonies.[35] Serving up these offerings are a hundred people who wait upon him in the western chamber. When he inhabits the palace, they set up a canopy and sheltering screens, he sits with his back to the *yi** screen, and the feudal lords hasten to the foot of his hall.[36,f] When he goes outside the palace, then
320 his shamans and sorcerers set to work, and when he goes outside the capital, then his Master for Ceremonies and Master for Prayers set to work.[37] He rides in the Grand Chariot, in which are placed cushions, as a means to nurture his body.[38] On the sides are carried sweet-smelling angelica, as a means to nurture his nose. In front there is a pat-
325 terned crossbar, as a means to nurture his eyes. The sounds of the attached bells match the tunes *Wu* and *Xiang* when proceeding slowly, and they match the tunes *Shao* and *Hu* when proceeding quickly, as

---

time, the average human life span was much shorter than today, and not many people would have lived to an age where they developed senility.

[33] The "five regular colors" were blue (or green), yellow, red, white, and black. The "mixed colors" were combinations of these.

[34] "The Grand Livestock" (*tailao* 太牢) refers to the trio of an ox, a lamb, and a pig. This trio was often used for important sacrifices (compare the ancient Roman practice of the *suovetaurilia*), and hence given the special appellation of "Grand." In ancient China, because of the efforts required to raise large animals, eating such meat was something of a luxury, which is the point of mentioning it here.

[35] The *Yong* is a piece of music. The Chinese text of this sentence is rather obscure, and commentators disagree greatly about its exact meaning, so the translation is tentative. The exact referent of "the five *si* ceremonies" is equally unclear, but the most plausible candidate seems to be sacrifices conducted to spirits overseeing five areas of the home.

[36] According to commentators, the *yi** was a screen used only in the Son of Heaven's audience chamber, and only the Son of Heaven turned his back to it, while all visitors faced it. Almost the exact same wording occurs at 8.306–8.

[37] Commentators explain that "work" here refers to ceremonies to ward off evil, and prayers for good fortune for the Son of Heaven.

[38] The wording of this and the next few sentences recurs at 19.23–30. Similar wording also appears at 27.252–54.

a means to nurture his ears.[39] The three dukes support the yoke or steady the reins. The feudal lords steady the wheels, flank the car, or go before the horses. Behind are arrayed the greater marquises, and next are the grand ministers. Next are the lesser marquises and the foremost noblemen. Infantrymen wearing armor flank the road. The ordinary people scurry away and hide, with none daring to look upon him. Thus, when he inhabits the palace, he is like a supreme spirit, and when he is on the move, he is like Heavenly Shang Di. 330

335

For holding off old age and fortifying against decline, is there anything better than this? Those who do not suffer from old age are well rested, and for resting, is there anything as comfortable, enjoyable, pleasing, and happy as this? And so I say: There is such a thing as old age for the feudal lords, but there is no such thing as old age for the Son of Heaven.[40] There is such a thing as relinquishing a state, but there is no such thing as relinquishing the world. Ancient times and the present are one and the same in this. As for saying, "Yao and Shun relinquished the throne and yielded it to others"—this is empty talk.[41] It is a rumor circulated by shallow people, a doctrine spoken by boorish people.[42] They are people who do not understand the patterns of what is conflicting and what is agreeable, and do not understand what changes happen to greater and lesser entities, supreme and nonsupreme ones.[43] They are people who have never been able to take part in attaining the greatest order in the world. 340

345

350

The vulgar purveyors of doctrine say, "Yao and Shun were not able to educate and transform people." How is that? They say, "Zhu and Xiang were not transformed."[44] This is not so. Yao and Shun were ones who were absolutely best in the world at educating and transforming people. Facing south, they rendered decisions for the whole world, and all those living as commoners were stirred to submit and 355

---

[39] The *Wu* and *Xiang* were pieces of music associated with King Wu. The *Shao* and *Hu* were pieces of music associated with Shun and Tang, respectively.

[40] Xunzi does not mean this literally. Rather, "old age" here stands more specifically for the *ills* of old age, and Xunzi's point is that the Son of Heaven lives so well that he never experiences any such ills, and hence never has any reason to abdicate.

[41] Despite the strong condemnation of this view here, chapter 25 (25.161–95) seems to endorse it, or at least to use the language normally used to express it. It is not easy to reconcile the two passages, other than perhaps to regard them as reflecting a change of mind on Xunzi's part, or to deny that they were written by the same person.

[42] For more on the term "boorish," see 2.73–74 and note 12 there.

[43] Here, the "greater" and "supreme" entity is the world, and the "lesser" and "nonsupreme" entity is a state. See the discussion earlier in this chapter, lines 145–58.

[44] Zhu was Yao's son. Some early texts portray him as self-indulgent. Xiang was Shun's half brother. According to some early stories, he was an especially bad person and even plotted to kill Shun.

follow and thereby become transformed and fully compliant with them. Nevertheless, Zhu and Xiang alone were not transformed, yet this is not a failing of Yao and Shun, but is rather the fault of Zhu and
360 Xiang. Yao and Shun were the most splendid men in the world. Zhu and Xiang were the most twisted men in the world, and the paltriest men of a whole age. Now the vulgar purveyors of doctrine do not consider Zhu and Xiang aberrant, but instead condemn Yao and Shun. Are they not severely mistaken indeed! This is called a twisted
365 doctrine.

Yi and Peng Men were the best in the world at archery, but even they could not use a warped bow and crooked arrows to hit targets. Wang Liang and Zao Fu were the best in the world at driving, but even they could not use lame horses and a broken chariot to cover
370 great distances rapidly. Yao and Shun were the best in the world at educating and transforming people, but even they could not make such twisted and paltry men become transformed. In what generation are there no such twisted men? In what age are there no such paltry men? From the time of Tai Hao and Suiren,[45] no era has been without
375 such people. And so:

When such men appear,
Auspicious they are not.
Those who learn their ways
Self-ruin will have wrought.
380 Those rejecting that
Have rewards as their lot.

The *Odes* says:

The hardships of us lowly folk
Are not from Heaven bestowed.
385 Those men talked nicely face to face,
Turned their backs, then hate they showed.
The main source of contentiousness
From these human beings flowed.[46]

This expresses my meaning.

[45] "Tai Hao" is another name for Fu Xi, a sage king who supposedly preceded Yao and Shun by several generations and first taught people how to farm, how to fish, and how to raise livestock. Suiren, whose name might be translated as "the Kindler," was another sage king who supposedly came before even Fu Xi and first taught people how to use fire and cook food. These two figures thus represent the very dawn of human civilization.

[46] Mao #193. In the original context, the speaker is apparently someone who has been slandered and is complaining about his mistreatment.

The vulgar purveyors of doctrine say, "The practice of most ancient   390
times was frugal burials. Coffins were only three inches thick. There
were only three sets of burial clothes. Burial sites did not impede
farming. Hence, people did not burrow into them. The practice of the
chaotic present age is lavish burials and ornately decorated coffins.
Hence, people burrow into them."[47] This is something spoken by   395
those who have not attained an understanding of the way to bring
about order, and who have not investigated why people do or do not
dig into tombs.

Whenever people engage in robbery, they surely do it for the sake
of possessing things. If it is not for the sake of furnishing something   400
in which they lack sufficiency, then it is for the sake of multiplying
what they already have in abundance. But the way a sage king rears
the common people is that he makes each of them meet the condition
of being amply supplied and well-off, like those who do not know
when to be satisfied, yet he also makes it so that people do not get to   405
exceed the proper measure in their possession of abundance.[48] And
so, robbers will no longer engage in stealing, and villains will no
longer kill people. Dogs and pigs will pass up on beans and grains,
and farmers and merchants will all be able to yield in matters of
goods and wealth.[49] People's customs will achieve a fine state: men   410
and women will on their own avoid taking up with each other on the
roads, and the common folk will be ashamed to take items that have
been lost. Thus, Confucius said, "When the world acquires the Way,
will not robbers be the first to change?"[50]

In that case, even if the corpse is covered in pearls and jades, the   415
inner coffin filled with patterned and embroidered textiles, and the
outer coffin filled with gold objects; even if one enhances it with cin-
nabar and augments it with malachite;[51] and even if one makes trees

[47] In ancient China, the practice of "frugal burials" was most famously advocated by
the Mohists, though perhaps others held this view, and the text may be attacking
them as well.

[48] The Chinese text of this sentence is odd and appears corrupt. Almost all commentators propose emending it in some way, but the emendations are not very persuasive.
I have adopted a fairly conservative stance and tried to make sense of it without any
emendations, but the translation remains tentative. The main point, at any rate,
should be clear enough: a sage king eliminates any motivation for grave robbing.
On the way in which a sage enriches the common people, see 10.44–61.

[49] Commentators explain the remark about dogs and pigs by saying that it is supposed to convey abundance: food will be so plentiful that even these domestic animals will get to eat until they are full and cannot eat any more, and still there will
be food left over. As for the farmers and merchants, they were often regarded as
especially greedy, so for them to become yielding represents a major transformation.

[50] This quote does not appear in the *Analects*, but it does vaguely resemble what Confucius is reported to have said in *Analects* 12.18.

[51] Commentators note that these materials were used to decorate the coffin.

out of rhinoceros horns and elephant tusks, with *lianggan*, *huajin*, and
420 *longzi* stones for fruit[52]—still no one will dig into the tomb. Why is
that? It is because their yearning to seek profit is slackened,ᵍ and their
shame at going against what has been allotted is great.

It is only with the chaotic present age that things are the opposite
of this. Superiors employ people according to no proper model, and
425 their subordinates behave according to no proper measure. Those
who are intelligent do not get to take part in government deliberations, those who are capable do not get to bring about order, and
those who are worthy do not get to be employed by the ruler. When
things are like this, then above one loses out on Heaven's nature,[53]
430 below one loses out on Earth's benefits, and in the middle one loses
harmony among humankind. And so, the hundred tasks become neglected, wealth and supplies shrink, and disasters and chaos arise.
Above, kings and dukes are troubled by deficiencies. Below, the common folk freeze and starve and waste away.

435 Thereupon, people who are as bad as Jie and Zhòu congregate,
and robbers and villains engage in assaults and thefts, to the point of
endangering even those above. These people thus have the conduct
of birds and beasts, and they are as rapacious as tigers and wolves.
And so, they will even cook infants and make adult victims into dried
440 meat. When there are people like this, then what is there to be aghast
at if they dig into a person's tomb, rummage around in the corpse's
mouth,[54] and seek profit thereby? Even if the person is buried as just
a naked corpse, still they will surely dig him up, and how then would
one get to keep him buried? For, they will eat his flesh and gnaw his
445 bones.

As for saying, "The practice of most ancient times was frugal burials, and so people did not dig up the tombs, but the practice of the
chaotic present age is lavish burials, and so people dig them up"—
this is simply a case of vile people being misled by chaotic doctrines,
450 and using these to deceive and sink the foolish and steal profits from

---

[52] The *lianggan*, *huajin*, and *longzi* were apparently precious stones, but the exact kinds
of stones are unknown, so I have left the names untranslated. A number of artificial
trees, often bronze, have been recovered from inside ancient tombs. Some particularly spectacular examples that survive from the Han dynasty, known as "money
trees," have branches dripping with coins as "fruit." The trees and their "fruits" had
various symbolic meanings, including providing goods for use by the deceased in
the afterlife.

[53] The triad of "Heaven's seasons," "Earth's benefits," and "human harmony" is a common theme in the *Xunzi* (see 10.265–67) and other early texts, so commentators
suggest understanding "Heaven's nature" as referring to its activity in producing
the four seasons. Some even suggest that the word "nature" here is simply a mistake
for "season," but such an emendation does not seem necessary.

[54] As part of ancient Chinese funeral practices, bodies were often buried with precious
stones in the mouth.

them. A proverb states, "They endanger others to get safety for them-selves. They harm others to get profits for themselves." This expresses my meaning.[55]

'Master' Songzi says,[56] "Making clear that being insulted is not dis-graceful will cause people not to engage in brawling. People all take   455
being insulted as disgraceful, and so they engage in brawling. If they understand that being insulted is not disgraceful, then they will not engage in brawling."

I reply:[57] then does he also think that the disposition of people is that they do not hate being insulted?   460

He says, "They do hate it, but it is not disgraceful."

I say: if that is so, then he will surely not obtain what he seeks from them. Whenever people engage in brawling, one must take their ha-tred for something as the explanation, and not take their belief that it is disgraceful as the reason. Now, when entertainers, dwarves, and   465
jesters curse at and insult one another, but do not set to brawling, how would it be because they understand that being insulted is not disgraceful? Rather, the reason they do not engage in brawling is that they do not hate being treated so. Now, if someone were to enter their irrigation channels and steal their pigs, then they would take up   470
swords and halberds and pursue him, avoiding neither death nor injury. How would it be because they regard losing pigs as disgrace-ful? Rather, the reason they do not shy away from brawling then is that they hate being treated so. Even if one regards being insulted as disgraceful, when one does not one hate being treated that way then   475
one will not engage in brawling. And even if one understands that being insulted is not disgraceful, when one hates being treated that way then one is sure to engage in brawling. This being the case,

[55] The sense in which the advocates of the view criticized here are benefitting them-selves at the expense of others is rather ambiguous and could be taken in a number of different ways. The most plausible explanation is perhaps that given in 10.216–73, where Xunzi complains that the Mohist practice of frugality actually makes the world poorer than it would otherwise be. Hence, those who use such proposals to seek employment with a ruler are, in a sense, stealing from him to benefit them-selves.

[56] Xunzi here uses a particularly honorific way of referring to Songzi. Yet, since he criticizes Songzi harshly here, it is unlikely that the honorific sense is genuinely intended, and so I have put "Master" in scare quotes to indicate that it is likely meant ironically.

[57] There is uncertainty about the dates of Xunzi's life (see the introduction, p. xix), and on some reckonings, it would have been possible for Xunzi to have been a contemporary of Songzi. However, most scholars think that Xunzi lived well after Songzi, in which case the "conversations" between them portrayed here should be understood as Xunzi dialoguing with Songzi's views—perhaps through Songzi's writings or his students—rather than speaking directly with Songzi, and this is how I have rendered it here.

whether or not people engage in brawling does not rest with whether
480   or not they regard something as disgraceful, but instead rests with
whether or not they hate it.

Now, 'Master' Songzi cannot undo people's hatred for being insulted, but still works at persuading people not to consider it disgraceful—is he not severely mistaken indeed! Even if he had a metal
485   tongue and wore out his mouth speaking with it, his words would still
be of no help. If he does not know that his words will be of no help,
then he is not intelligent. If he does know that his words will be of no
help, but simply uses them to deceive people, then he is not *ren*. Not
to be intelligent and not to be *ren*—there are no greater disgraces than
490   these. If one thinks it will be of help to people, but then it is of no
help at all to people, and then one merely obtains great disgrace before withdrawing—there is simply no doctrine more flawed than this.

'Master' Songzi says, "Being insulted is not disgraceful."

I reply: whenever one is debating, one must first establish a lofty
495   standard of correctness, and only then may one proceed. Without a
lofty standard of correctness, right and wrong will not be divided up,
and disputes and litigations will not be resolved.[58] And so, what I
have heard is: "That which is most great and lofty in the world, is the
boundary for right and wrong, and is the source from which arise the
500   allotment of tasks and the naming of phenomena—the regulations of
true kings are just that." Thus, whenever one is discussing, debating,
procuring agreement, or naming in relation to right and wrong,[59]
take the sage kings as your teachers—and the way the sage kings divided up honor and disgrace is just such a case.

505   These things have two origins. There is honor in terms of what is
yi. There is honor in terms of one's circumstances. There is disgrace
in terms of what is *yi*. There is disgrace in terms of one's circumstances. When one's intentions and thoughts are cultivated, when
one's virtues and proper conduct are substantial, and when one's un-
510   derstanding and deliberations are brilliant, this is a case where honor
derives from within. This is called honor in terms of what is *yi*. When
one's title and rank are eminent, when one's emoluments and salary
are substantial, and when one's position and circumstances over-
power others—at the greatest, by being the Son of Heaven or a feudal
515   lord, or at the least, by being a councilor, prime minister, officer, or
grand officer—this is a case where honor comes from outside. This is
called honor in terms of one's circumstances. When one is perverse

---

[58] See 21.397–403 for similar remarks about the "lofty standard of correctness."

[59] The last two items in this list, "procuring agreement" (*qi* 期) and "naming" (*ming* 命), are quasi-technical terms for Xunzi that refer to different stages in a progression toward settling the use of language. See 22.171–86.

and corrupt, when one goes against what has been allotted and disrupts the proper order, when one is arrogantly violent and greedy for profit, this is a case where disgrace derives from within. This is called   520
disgrace in terms of what is *yi*. When one is cursed at or insulted, when one is dragged by the hair or pummeled, when one is caned or has one's feet cut off, when one is decapitated or drawn and quartered, or when one's family records are destroyed or one's descendants are eradicated,[60,h] this is a case where disgrace comes from out-   525
side. This is called disgrace in terms of one's circumstances. These are the two origins of honor and disgrace.

And so, it is possible for a gentleman to suffer disgrace in terms of his circumstances, but it is not possible for him to suffer disgrace in terms of what is *yi*. It is possible for a petty man to have honor in   530
terms of his circumstances, but it is not possible for him to have honor in terms of what is *yi*. Suffering disgrace in terms of one's circumstances is no impediment to being a Yao. Having honor in terms of one's circumstances is no impediment to being a Jie. Only a gentleman will have honor both in terms of what is *yi* and in terms of his   535
circumstances. Only a petty man will suffer disgrace both in terms of what is *yi* and in terms of his circumstances.

That is how honor and disgrace are divided up.[61] The sage kings took this as their model, their officers and grand officers took this as their way, their officials took this as what they were to preserve, their   540
people took this as their set custom, and in ten thousand generations it cannot be changed.[62] Now 'Master' Songzi, however, is not like that. Idiosyncratically adopting an acquiescent demeanor and working away at himself, he thinks to change all these things in the space of a single morning. Such a proposition is sure not to succeed. To draw an   545
analogy for it, this is like someone damming the Yangtze River or the whole sea by packing together lumps of mud, or holding up Mount Tai by having a dwarf carry it—without waiting even a moment, he will be turned head over heels, crushed, and broken. Those of you followers who think well of 'Master' Songzi would perhaps do better to put   550
a stop to this, because you will, I fear, wind up harming yourselves.

'Master' Songzi says, "People's inborn disposition is that they desire little, but they all believe that their inborn disposition is to desire

---

[60]   The Chinese text of this clause is quite obscure and is likely corrupted. Commentators have proposed various ways to make sense of it, but none are very persuasive. The translation here is highly conjectural. For details, see endnote h.

[61]   Based on the preceding remarks in the text, the "dividing up" of honor and disgrace is supposed to include both how various kinds of honor and disgrace are to be distinguished and how those kinds of honor and disgrace are distributed among people in the world.

[62]   See the similar description of ritual at 19.567–70.

much. This is a mistake." Thus, he leads about his group of followers,
555   demonstrates his arguments and teachings, and clarifies his terms
and analogies, all in order to cause people to understand the sparse-
ness of the desires deriving from their inborn disposition.

I answer: That being the case, you do take people's inborn disposition to be desirous of things. Do not people's eyes desire the utmost
560   in sights? Do not people's ears desire the utmost in sounds? Do not
people's palates desire the utmost in flavors? Do not people's noses
desire the utmost in fragrances? Do not people's bodies desire the
utmost in comforts? Do you not also believe people's inborn disposition is to desire these five utmosts?

565   He says, "People's inborn disposition is to desire exactly these
things."

I say: If that is so, then his proposition is sure not to succeed. To
believe that people's inborn disposition is to desire these five utmosts
but not to desire much is like believing that their inborn disposition
570   is to desire wealth but not to desire material goods, or is to like beauty
but dislike Xi Shi.[63] The ancients did not do things thus. They believed that people's inborn disposition is to desire much and not to
desire little. Thus, they rewarded people with wealth and abundance,
and they penalized people with cuts and losses. This is something in
575   which the hundred kings were the same. Hence, the most worthy
were given the whole world as their lot, the next worthy were given a
state as their lot, the lowest worthy were given fields and a town as
their lot, and dependable and honest commoners were provided fully
with food and clothing.

580   Now 'Master' Songzi believes that people's inborn disposition is
to desire little and not to desire much, but then did the former kings
reward people with what they did not desire and penalize them with
what they did desire? There would be no greater chaos than that!
Now 'Master' Songzi is serious and fond of arguing. He gathers fol-
585   lowers, establishes teacher-student relationships, and composes written canons. Nevertheless, his propositions cannot avoid turning utmost order into utmost chaos.[64] Is he not severely mistaken indeed!

[63] Xi Shi was a famous Chinese beauty.
[64] Xunzi's reasoning here seems to be that if Songzi were right, then the sage kings
were doing something that should have resulted in chaos. The reader is presumably
to infer that since they did not create chaos, they were not doing the wrong thing.
Hence, their understanding of human psychology was right, and Songzi's was
wrong.

CHAPTER 19

Discourse on Ritual

(1)

From what did ritual arise? I say: Humans are born having desires. When they have desires but do not get the objects of their desire, then they cannot but seek some means of satisfaction. If there is no measure or limit to their seeking, then they cannot help but struggle with each other. If they struggle with each other then there will be chaos, and if there is chaos then they will be impoverished. The former kings hated such chaos, and so they established rituals and *yi* in order to divide things among people, to nurture their desires, and to satisfy their seeking. They caused desires never to exhaust material goods, and material goods never to be depleted by desires, so that the two support each other and prosper. This is how ritual arose.[1]

Thus, ritual is a means of nurture. Meats and grains, the five flavors and the various spices are means to nurture the mouth. Fragrances and perfumes are means to nurture the nose. Carving and inlay, insignias and patterns are means to nurture the eyes. Bells and drums, pipes and chimes, lutes and zithers are means to nurture the ears. Homes and palaces, cushions and beds, tables and mats are means to nurture the body. Thus, ritual is a means of nurture. The gentleman not only obtains its nurturing, but also loves its differentiations. What is meant by "differentiations"? I say: It is for noble and lowly to have their proper ranking, for elder and youth to have their proper distance, and for poor and rich, humble and eminent each to have their proper weights.[2] And so, in the Grand Chariot of the Son of Heaven there are cushions, as a means to nurture his body.[3] On the sides are carried sweet-smelling angelica, as a means to nurture his nose. In front there is a patterned crossbar, as a means to nurture his eyes. The sounds of the attached bells match the tunes *Wu* and *Xiang*[4] when proceeding slowly, and they match the tunes *Shao* and *Hu*[5] when proceeding quickly, as a means to nurture his ears. There is a dragon pennant with nine tassels, as a means to nurture his ability to inspire trust. There are insignias of a crouching rhinoceros and kneeling tiger, serpent-decorated coverings for

5

10

15

20

25

30

---

[1] Compare *Mozi*, chap. 11.
[2] Compare 10.76–78.
[3] The wording of this and the next few sentences also appears at 18.322–328, and similar wording appears at 27.252–54.
[4] The *Wu* and *Xiang* were pieces of music associated with King Wu.
[5] The *Shao* and *Hu* were pieces of music associated with Shun and Tang, respectively.

the horses, silk curtains, and dragon patterns on the chariot hooks, as a means to nurture his awe-inspiring authority. Thus, the horses of the Grand Chariot are repeatedly given training to be obedient, and only then will they be harnessed, as a means to nurture his safety.

Know well that in going out, to abide by the proper measure even at the risk of death is the means to nurture one's life. Know well that to make expenditures is the way to nurture wealth. Know well that reverence, respect, and deference are the way to nurture safety. Know well that ritual, *yi*, good form and proper order are the way to nurture one's dispositions. And so, if a person has his eyes only on living, such a one is sure to die. If a person has his eyes only on benefiting himself, such a one is sure to be harmed. If a person seeks safety only in laziness and sluggishness, such a one is sure to be endangered. If a person takes pleasure only in delighting his inborn dispositions, such a one is sure to be destroyed. And so, if a person puts even one amount of effort into following ritual and *yi*, he will get back twice as much. If he puts even one amount of effort into following his inborn dispositions and nature, he will lose twice as much. And so, the *ru* are those who will cause people to gain twice as much, and the Mohists are those who cause people to lose twice as much. This is the difference between the *ru* and the Mohists.

Ritual has three roots. Heaven and Earth are the root of life. Forefathers and ancestors are the root of one's kind. Lords and teachers are the root of order. Without Heaven and Earth, how would one live? Without forefathers and ancestors, how would one have come forth? Without lords and teachers, how would there be order? If even one of these three roots is neglected, no one will be safe. And so, ritual serves Heaven above and Earth below, it honors forefathers and ancestors, and it exalts lords and teachers. These are the three roots of ritual.

And so, the king sacrifices to the founder of his lineage alongside Heaven. The feudal lords do not dare to spoil [their own founders' ancestral temples].[6] The grand ministers and aristocrats each keep up their own lineage temple. This is the means to distinguish among noble beginnings, for noble beginnings are the root of what one has.

---

[6] The text here is difficult and may be corrupt. Commentators generally agree that its point is that the feudal lords reverently maintain the temples (and sacrifices) dedicated to the respective founders of their ruling lines, but the commentators disagree about exactly what the sentence says. My translation is based on the most straightforward reading of the line, though it remains unclear whether the "spoiling" that is mentioned refers to mere neglect of the temples or to intentional damage (for some unstated reason) to them.

The *jiao* sacrifice[7] is performed by no one lower than the Son of   70
Heaven. The altar of soil sacrifice[8] is performed by no one lower than
the feudal lords. The *tan* sacrifice[9] extends to the aristocrats and
grand ministers. This is the means to distinguish that those who are
lofty pay respect to the lofty, those who are lowly pay respect to the
lowly, what is fitting for those of great station is done on a grand   75
scale, and what is fitting for those of humble station is done on a
small scale.

Thus, he who possesses all under Heaven pays respect to seven
generations. He who possesses a single state pays respect to five generations. He who holds enough land to field five chariots[10] pays re-   80
spect to three generations. He who holds enough land to field three
chariots pays respect to two generations. Those who get to eat by the
labor of their hands are not allowed to establish a lineage temple.
This is the means to mark out those with great merit. For those with
great merit leave a widespread legacy, while those with less merit   85
leave a limited legacy.

In the grand *xiang* sacrifice,[11] one offers up a goblet of dark liquid,
places raw fish on the sacrificial stand, and begins with the grand
broth. This is to honor the fundamentals of food and drink. In the
xiang sacrifice,[12] one offers up a goblet of dark liquid but also uses   90
sweet wine, and one begins with wheat and millet, then follows with
cooked grains. In the *ji* sacrifice,[13] one only touches the grand broth
to one's lips,[14] and one fills oneself with the other various dishes.
These honor the fundamentals of food and drink but also take care
for practical needs. To honor the fundamentals is called good form,   95
and to take care for practical needs is called good order. When the
two combine and form a pattern, so as to return to a great unity, this
is called the great exalted state.[15]

---

[7] A sacrifice to Heaven. Since the Zhou king was considered the Son of Heaven, only
he was allowed to sacrifice to it.

[8] A sacrifice to Earth. The feudal lords performed this, because they had landholdings
for which they were responsible.

[9] A sacrifice that marks the end of mourning.

[10] Apart from the costs of maintaining the horses and equipment, a chariot was usually accompanied by a number of foot soldiers as well, so supporting a single chariot required a substantial amount of land.

[11] According to commentators, this is a sacrifice to the former kings.

[12] This is a quarterly sacrifice, different from the "grand *xiang*."

[13] A monthly sacrifice.

[14] I.e., one does not actually drink it.

[15] This passage and the following one are loaded with technical terms for ritual offices,
objects, and practices, the referents of which are not precisely known and are dis-
puted by commentators. Also, at points the text seems to be corrupt. As a result, the
translation here is tentative.

And so, the offering up of dark wine in the goblet, the offering up
100 of raw fish on the sacrificial stand, and the placing the grand broth
on the sacrificial stand first are unified by a single principle.[16] The
reasons why the officiant does not drain the sacrificial cup, why the
impersonator of the dead does not taste the dishes on the sacrificial
stand when the service is complete, and why the officiants do not eat
105 during the three offerings are unified by a single principle.[17] The time
during the grand wedding ceremony when the greeting party has not
yet been sent, the time during the grand temple sacrifice when the
impersonator of the dead has not yet entered, and the time after a
person has first died when the lesser *lian* has not yet been performed[18]
110 are all unified by a single principle.[19] The plain coverings on the
Grand Chariot of the Son of Heaven, the cap of hemp worn for the
jiao sacrifice, and the loose belt of hemp worn initially as part of
mourning garb are all unified by a single principle.[20] The way that
during the three-year mourning one cries without restraint, the way
115 that during the performance of the "Pure Temple"[21] one person sings
and three others chime in, the way one hangs a single bell and suspends two lutes, stringing them with red threads and putting a sounding hole in them, are all unified by a single principle.

   In every case, ritual begins in that which must be released,[22] reaches
120 full development in giving it proper form, and finishes in providing
it satisfaction. And so when ritual is at its most perfect, the requirements of inner dispositions and proper form are both completely
fulfilled. At its next best, the dispositions and outer form overcome
one another in succession. Its lowest manner is to revert to the dispo-
125 sitions alone so as to subsume everything in this grand unity.

> By ritual, Heaven and Earth harmoniously combine;
> By ritual, the sun and the moon radiantly shine;
> By ritual, the four seasons in progression arise;

[16] Presumably, the unifying point is the way they honor the fundamentals, as the text
indicates earlier.

[17] According to commentators, these things signal the end of the ceremony.

[18] The lesser *lian* was a ceremony in which the deceased's clothing was changed.

[19] According to commentators, these periods all occur at the start of the ceremony.

[20] Commentators suggest that the unifying theme is the idea of simplicity and plain-
ness.

[21] One of the *Odes*, Mao #266.

[22] Xunzi's wording is obscure here, but his point as I understand it is that the initial
impetus for ritual practice is certain inevitable human emotions, such as sorrow and
joy, which are manifestations of (natural or acquired) dispositions. These emotions
must find some external expression (compare the beginning of chapter 20), and as
he goes on to say, proper ritual practice balances these emotions and their outward
expression, whereas the lowest type of ritual practice is that in which the emotions
drive behavior at the expense of good form. Compare *Analects* 3.4 and 6.18.

By ritual, the stars move orderly across the skies;
By ritual, the great rivers through their courses flow; 130
By ritual, the myriad things all thrive and grow;
By ritual, for love and hate proper measure is made;
By ritual, on joy and anger fit limits are laid.
By ritual, compliant subordinates are created.
By ritual, enlightened leaders are generated; 135
With ritual, all things can change yet not bring chaos.
But deviate from ritual and you face only loss.

Is not ritual perfect indeed! It establishes a lofty standard that is ultimate of its kind, and none under Heaven can add to or subtract from it. In it, the fundamental and the secondary accord with each 140 other, and beginning and end match each other.[23] In its differentiations of things, it is the utmost in patterning. In its explanations, it is the utmost in keen discernment. Those under Heaven who follow it will have good order. Those who do not follow it will have chaos. Those who follow it will have safety. Those who do not follow it will 145 be endangered. Those who follow it will be preserved. Those who do not follow it will perish. The petty man cannot fathom it. Deep indeed is the pattern of ritual! Investigations into the hard and the white, the same and the different drown when they try to enter into it.[24] Vast indeed is the pattern of ritual! Those expert in creating in- 150 stitutions and the purveyors of perverse, vulgar doctrines are lost when they try to enter it.[25] High indeed is the pattern of ritual! Those who take violent arrogance, haughty indulgence, and contempt of custom for loftiness fall when they try to enter it.

And so, when the ink-line is reliably laid out, then one cannot be 155 deceived by the curved and the straight. When the scale is reliably hung, then one cannot be deceived by the light and the heavy. When the compass and carpenter's square are reliably deployed, then one cannot be deceived by the circular and the rectangular. The gentleman examines ritual carefully, and then he cannot be deceived by 160 trickery and artifice. Thus, the ink-line is the ultimate in straightness, the scale is the ultimate in balance, the compass and carpenter's square are the ultimate in circular and rectangular, and ritual is the ultimate in the human way. Those who nevertheless do not take ritual as their model nor find sufficiency in it are called standardless com- 165 moners. Those who take ritual as their model and find sufficiency in

[23] Nearly identical wording appears at 27.269–70.
[24] This refers to debates among the so-called *mingjia* 名家 or "sophists" such as Hui Shi, Deng Xi, and Gongsun Long.
[25] This may be a reference to people such as Shang Yang, Shen Buhai, and Shen Dao, who stressed institutional (rather than moral) reform of government, and came to be known as *fajia* 法家 or "Legalists."

it are called men of standards. To be able to reflect and ponder what is central to ritual is called being able to deliberate.[26] To be able to be undeviating in what is central to ritual is called being able to be firm.
170 When one can deliberate and be firm, and adds to this fondness for it, then this is to be a sage. Thus, Heaven is the ultimate in height, Earth is the ultimate in depth, the boundless is the ultimate in breadth, and the sage is the ultimate in the Way. And so, learning is precisely learning to be a sage—one does not learn solely so as to
175 become a standardless commoner.

Ritual takes resources and goods as its implements.[27] It takes noble and lowly as its patterns. It takes abundance and scarcity as its differentiations. It takes elevating some and lowering others as its essentials. When patterning and order are made bountiful, and the
180 dispositions and implements are limited, this is the most elevated state of ritual. When the dispositions and implements are made bountiful, but the patterning and order are limited, this is the lowest state of ritual. When patterning and order, dispositions and implements are in turn central and peripheral, so that they proceed together and
185 are mixed evenly, this is the intermediate course of ritual. And so at his greatest, the gentleman achieves the most elevated state of ritual, and at the least he fulfills completely its lowest form, and when in intermediate circumstances he dwells in its intermediate form. Whether going slowly, quickly, or at full gallop, he never departs
190 from this, for this is the gentleman's home and palace. If a person grasps this, he is a well-bred man or a gentleman. If he departs from this, he is but a commoner. Thus, to be able to travel everywhere in its midst and in every case obtain its proper arrangement is to be a sage. And so, being generous is due to the accumulated richness of
195 ritual. Being great is due to the vastness of ritual. Being lofty is due to the elevated nature of ritual. Being enlightened is due to the exhaustive nature of ritual. The *Odes* says:

> Ritual and ceremony have right measure completely.
> Laugh and speak only in complete accord with propriety.[28]

200 This expresses my meaning.

Ritual is that which takes care to order living and dying. Birth is the beginning of people, and death is the end of people. When the beginning and end are both good, then the human way is complete. Thus, the gentleman is respectful of the beginning and careful about

---

[26] Identical wording appears at 27.267–68.
[27] Identical wording appears at 27.271–73.
[28] Mao #209. See the citation of these same lines at 2.56–57. See note 10 there for further discussion of this translation.

the end. When end and beginning are treated alike,[29] this is the way   205
of the gentleman, and the proper form contained in ritual and *yi*. To
treat people generously while alive but stingily when dead is to show
respect to those with awareness and to show arrogance to those without awareness. This is the way of a vile person and is an attitude of
betrayal. The gentleman considers it shameful to use such a betraying   210
attitude in dealing with servants and children—how much more so in
the case of those he exalts and those he loves!

Thus, the way that death works is that a person dies once and then
cannot get to die again. A minister's opportunity to express utmost
regard for his lord, and a son's opportunity to express utmost regard   215
for his parents, depend completely on this. And so, to serve the living
without loyalty and generosity, without respect and good form, is
called being wild. To send off the dead without loyalty and generosity, without respect and good form, is called being stingy. The gentleman considers it base to be wild and is ashamed to be stingy. There-   220
fore, for the Son of Heaven, the inner and outer coffins are to make
seven layers. For a feudal lord, five layers. For a grand minister, three
layers. For a well-bred man, two layers. Beyond this, in each case
there are different arrangements for the quantity and thickness of
burial clothes and coverings, and in each case there are different   225
grades of emblems and ornaments used for the coffins, in order to
decorate them with respect. Causing life and death and beginning
and end to be treated with one and the same care satisfies what people all wish for. This is the way of the former kings, and the height of
being a loyal minister and filial son.   230

For the funeral of the Son of Heaven, one notifies all within the
four seas and summons the feudal lords. For the funeral of a feudal
lord, one notifies all allied states and summons the grand ministers.
For the funeral of a grand minister, one notifies all within his state
and summons those distinguished among the well-bred. For the fu-   235
neral of a distinguished, well-bred man, one notifies all in his county
and summons his associates. For the funeral of a common person,
one gathers together his family and friends and notifies all within the
neighborhood and district. For the funeral of an executed convict
one is not allowed to assemble his family and friends, but rather sum-   240
mons only his wife and children. The coffin's thickness may be only
three inches.[a] There may be only three layers of burial clothing and
coverings. One is not allowed to decorate the coffin. One is not allowed to have the funeral procession during the day, but must rather
perform the interment at night. One goes out to bury him wearing   245
ordinary clothing, and upon returning, there are to be no periods of

---

[29] I.e., with one and the same care.

crying, no wearing of mourning garb, and no differentiation of mourning periods for closer and more distant relatives. Everyone is to return to their normal ways and revert to their original state. When a person has already been buried, but it is as though there had never been a funeral and the matter has simply come to an end, this is called the greatest disgrace.[30]

250

Ritual takes care that fortunate and unfortunate events do not intrude upon each other. When it comes to the point where one has to place gauze on the person's face[31] and listen for breathing, then the loyal minister and filial son know that the person's illness is serious indeed. Even so, they do not yet seek the items for dressing the corpse and the lying in state. They weep and are filled with fear. Even so, they do not stop in their feelings of hoping that miraculously the person will live, and they do not cease their attempts to maintain the person's life. Only when the person has truly died do they then make and prepare the necessary items.

255

260

Thus, even the best equipped households are sure to pass a day before the lying in state, and three days before the mourning garments are complete. Only then do those sent to notify people far away set out, and only then do those responsible for preparing things get to work.

265

And so, at its longest, the lying in state is not to last for more than seventy days, and at its quickest, it is not to last less than fifty days. Why is this? I say: It is so that those far away can come, so that many needs can be fulfilled, and so that many matters can be accomplished. The loyalty expressed in this is of the highest sort. The proper regulation involved in this is of the greatest type. The good form displayed in this is of the greatest kind.

270

Afterward, as the moon rises one performs divination to determine the burial date, and as the moon sets one performs divination to determine the burial place, and only then does one perform the burial. At this time, who could carry out the funeral in ways that according to *yi* are prohibited? Who could prevent those things that according to *yi* are to be carried out?[32] And so, when the burial occurs in the third month, in its outward appearances it uses the paraphernalia of the living to ornament the dead. Yet, this is not for the

275

280

---

[30] Commentators note that Xunzi's description of this last kind of funeral largely resembles the kind of mourning regulations prescribed by Mozi for everyone, and thus this passage serves as a criticism of Mozi by implying that Mozi would have us treat even our dearest loved ones as no better than executed criminals.

[31] I.e., as a means of detecting breath visually.

[32] These rhetorical questions seem meant to imply that only a truly bad person would dare to violate the norms of *yi* on this most important occasion. Also, as commentators note, the questions echo the idea in this chapter and elsewhere that there is a certain standard of conduct that one should neither fall short of nor overshoot.

sake of simply not letting go of the dead, but is rather for the sake of comforting the living. This is the highest expression of *yi* in longing and remembrance. 285

The standard practice of funeral rites is that one changes the appearance of the corpse by gradually adding more ornamentation, one moves the corpse gradually further away, and over a long time one gradually returns to one's regular routine. Thus, the way that death works is that if one does not ornament the dead, then one will come 290 to feel disgust at them, and if one feels disgust, then one will not feel sad. If one keeps them close, then one will become casual with them, and if one becomes casual with them, then one will grow tired of them. If one grows tired of them, then one will forget one's place, and if one forgets one's place, then one will not be respectful. If one day 295 a person loses his lord or father, but his manner in sending them off to be buried is neither sad nor respectful, then he is close to being a beast. The gentleman is ashamed of this, and so the reason that he changes the appearance of the corpse by gradually adding more ornamentation is to eliminate any disgust. The reason that he moves the 300 corpse gradually further away is to pursue respectfulness. The reason that only over a long time does he gradually return to his regular routine is to properly adjust his life.

Ritual cuts off what is too long and extends what is too short. It subtracts from what is excessive and adds to what is insufficient. It 305 achieves proper form for love and respect, and it brings to perfection the beauty of carrying out *yi*. Thus, fine ornaments and coarse materials, music and weeping, happiness and sorrow—these things are opposites, but ritual makes use of all of them, employing them and alternating them at the appropriate times. And so, fine ornaments, 310 music, and happiness are that by which one responds to peaceful events and by which one pays homage to good fortune. Coarse mourning garments, weeping, and sorrow are that by which one responds to threatening events and by which one pays homage to ill fortune. Thus, the way ritual makes use of fine ornaments is such as 315 not to lead to exorbitance or indulgence. The way it makes use of coarse mourning garments is such as not to lead to infirmity or despondency. The way it makes use of music and happiness is such as not to lead to perversity or laziness. The way it makes use of weeping and sorrow is such as not to lead to dejection or self-harm. This is the 320 midway course of ritual.

Thus, when the changes in disposition and appearance are sufficient to differentiate good fortune and ill fortune and to make clear the proper measures for noble and lowly, close relations and distant relations, then ritual stops. To go beyond this is vile, and even should 325 it be a feat of amazing difficulty, the gentleman will still consider it base. And so, to measure one's food and then eat it, to measure one's

waist and then tie the mourning sash, to show off to those in high positions one's emaciation and infirmity—this is the way of a vile
330   person. It is not the proper patterning of ritual and *yi*, it is not the true disposition of a filial son. It is rather the behavior of one acting for ulterior purposes.

    And so, a joyful glow and a shining face, a sorrowful look and a haggard appearance—these are the ways in which the dispositions in
335   good fortune and ill fortune, happiness and sorrow are expressed in one's countenance. Singing and laughing, weeping and sobbing— these are the ways in which the dispositions in good fortune and ill fortune, happiness and sorrow are expressed in one's voice. Fine meats and grains and wine and fish, gruel and roughage and plain water—
340   these are the ways in which the dispositions in good fortune and ill fortune, happiness and sorrow are expressed in one's food and drink. Ceremonial caps and embroidered insignias and woven patterns, coarse cloth and a mourning headband and thin garments and hempen sandals—these are the ways in which the dispositions in good
345   fortune and ill fortune, happiness and sorrow are expressed in one's dress. Homes and palaces and cushions and beds and tables and mats, a thatched roof and mourning lean-to and rough mat and earthen pillow—these are the ways in which the dispositions in good fortune and ill fortune, happiness and sorrow are expressed in one's dwelling.
350   When people are born, the beginnings of these two dispositions are originally present in them. If you cut these dispositions short and extend them, broaden them and narrow them, add to them and subtract from them, make them conform to their proper classes and fully express them, make them abundant and beautify them, cause root
355   and branch, beginning and end all to go smoothly and fit together, then they can serve as the model for ten thousand ages—and just such is what ritual does! None but a devotedly and thoroughly cultivated gentleman can understand it.[33]

    Thus, I say that human nature is the original beginning and the
360   raw material, and deliberate effort is what makes it patterned, ordered, and exalted. If there were no human nature, then there would be nothing for deliberate effort to be applied to. If there were no deliberate effort, then human nature would not be able to beautify itself. Human nature and deliberate effort must unite, and then the
365   reputation of the sage and the work of unifying all under Heaven are thereupon brought to completion. And so I say, when Heaven and Earth unite, then the myriad creatures are born. When *yin* and *yang* interact, then changes and transformations arise. When human nature and deliberate effort unite, then all under Heaven becomes or-
370   dered. For Heaven can give birth to creatures, but it cannot enforce

---

[33] Compare 4.268–84.

distinctions among creatures. Earth can support people, but it cannot order people. In the world, all members of the myriad things and the human race must await the sage, and only then will they be appropriately divided up. The *Odes* says, "He mollifies the hundred spirits, and extends this to the rivers and towering peaks."[34] This expresses 375 my meaning.[35]

The funeral rites use life to ornament death—they make abundant use of semblances of the person's life to send him off in death. Thus, one treats the dead as if still alive, and one treats the departed as if they survive,[b] in order that end and beginning be given one and the 380 same care. When a person has just died, one washes the hair and the body, binds up the hair and trims the nails, and fills the mouth and covers it, in order to resemble the person's condition during life.[c] If one does not wash the hair, then one takes a wet comb and combs it, using three strokes and then stopping. If one does not wash the body, 385 then one takes a wet towel and wipes it down, using three passes and then stopping. One fills the ears and sets in place the plugs.[36] One fills the mouth with uncooked paddy rice and covers it with dried shells, opposite to the ways of the living. One puts in place the undergarments, but covers them with three layers of clothing. One puts a belt 390 around the waist, but does not close it with the hook. One places a covering over the face and eyes, and binds up the hair but does not cover it with a cap or secure it with a hairpin. One writes out the name of the deceased and places it on a placard, and then the name is not to appear elsewhere, so that it only makes clear to whom the 395 coffin belongs.

For the burial offerings, among the hats there is to be a helmet, but no straps for binding the hair. There are to be various vessels and containers, but they are to be empty and unfilled. There are to be mats, but no bedding materials. The wooden utensils are not to be 400 completely carved, the pottery utensils are not to be finished products, and the utensils woven from reeds are not to be capable of holding things. A set of music pipes is to be prepared, but they are not to be harmonized. A lute and zither are to be laid out, but they are not to be tuned. A chariot is to be included in the burial, but the horse 405 returns home. This is to indicate that these things will not be used.

One prepares the utensils used in life and takes them to the tomb, and this resembles the way one acts when moving house. The burial goods are to be simple and not perfect. They are to have the appearance of the regular items but are not to be functional. One drives a 410

[34] Mao #273.
[35] This paragraph does not fit well with the context. Burton Watson (1963) suggests that it may have fallen out of place from chapter 23. Nonetheless, it expresses very important ideas relating to Xunzi's view of human nature.
[36] The items placed in the ears may have been cloth and/or jade.

chariot out to the tomb and buries it, but the bit ornaments, bridle, and harness are not to be included. This makes clear that these things will not be used. One uses the semblance of moving house, but also makes clear that the things will not be used, and these are all means
415 by which to heighten sorrow. And so, the utensils used in life have their proper form but are not functional, and the burial goods have the appearance of the regular items but are not used.

Overall, ritual works to ornament happiness when serving the living, to ornament sorrow when sending off the dead, to ornament re-
420 spect when conducting sacrifices, and to ornament awe-inspiring power when engaged in military affairs.[37] This is something in which the hundred kings were all alike, and something in which ancient times and the present are one and the same, though there has never been anyone who knows when they began.
425 Thus, the appearance of the tomb resembles a home and dwelling. The inner and outer coffins resemble the front, back, sides, and covering of a chariot. The coverings and decorations for the coffins and funeral cart resemble curtains and canopy. The bracing for the burial pit resembles walls, roofing, fencing, and door and window coverings.[38]
430 And so, the purpose of the funeral rites is none other than to make clear what is *yi* with regard to the living and the dead, to send people off with sorrow and respect, and to put them to rest in a final and comprehensive manner. And so, at the interment, one respectfully buries their bodies. At the sacrifices, one respectfully serves their spir-
435 its. With inscriptions, eulogies, records, and genealogies, one respectfully passes along their names.

To serve the living is to ornament the beginning, and to send off the dead is to ornament the end. When end and beginning are both properly arranged, then the tasks of a filial son are fully realized, and
440 the way of the sage is complete.

Depriving the dead to give to the living is called Mohism.[39]
Depriving the living to give to the dead is called confusion.
Killing the living to send off the dead is called villainy.[40]

To use abundantly the semblances of people's lives to send them off
445 in death, and to cause death and life and beginning and end all to

---

[37] Very similar wording appears at 27.100–3.
[38] As before, this passage is loaded with technical terms and also seems to be partially corrupt, so the translation here is tentative.
[39] This sentence and the two that follow it are rhymed in the original.
[40] The term *zei* 賊, here translated as "villainy," often had the connotation of murder in particular. Xunzi here is criticizing the practice of "accompanying burials," in which people were sacrificed to serve the deceased in death.

match what is fitting and turn out well and good—such is the model
and manner of ritual and *yi*, and the *ru* are just such people.

What is the reason for the three-year mourning period? I say: It
takes measure of people's dispositions and establishes a proper form
for them. It accordingly ornaments the various groups of people,   450
distinguishing different regulations for close and distant relatives and
for the noble and the lowly, such that one can neither add to nor
subtract from it. Thus I say: It is a method that is to be neither adapted
nor changed. When a wound is great, it lasts for many days. When a
hurt is deep, the recovery is slow. The three-year mourning period   455
takes measure of people's dispositions and establishes a proper form
for them. It is the means by which one sets a limit for the utmost hurt.
Wearing the mourning garments, propping oneself on a crude cane,
dwelling in a lean-to, eating gruel, and using a rough mat and earthen
pillow are the means by which one ornaments the utmost hurt. After   460
the twenty-five months of the three-year mourning period, the sorrow
and hurt are not yet done, and the feelings of longing and remembrance are not yet forgotten. Nevertheless, ritual breaks off the
mourning at this time. Surely this is in order that there may be a
proper stopping point for sending off the dead and proper regulation   465
for resuming one's normal life, is it not?

Among all the living things between Heaven and Earth, those that
have blood and *qi* are sure to have awareness, and of those that have
awareness, none fails to love its own kind. Now if one of the great
birds or beasts loses its group of companions, then after a month or   470
a season has passed, it is sure to retrace its former path and go by its
old home. When it does, it is sure to pace back and forth, cry out,
stomp the ground, pause hesitatingly, and only then is it able to leave
the place. Even among smaller creatures such as swallows and sparrows, they will still screech for a moment before being able to leave.   475
Thus, among the creatures that have blood and *qi*, none has greater
awareness than man, and so man's feeling for his parents knows no
limit until the day they die. Will we follow foolish, ignorant, perverse
men? Those who have died that morning they forget by that evening.
If one gives way to this, then one will not even be as good as the birds   480
and beasts. How could such people come together and live in groups
without there being chaos? Will we follow cultivated gentlemen?[41]

---

[41] The passage goes on to imply that, in a sense, one should not follow cultivated
gentlemen, and that suggestion might seem puzzling, since usually gentlemen are
held up as models in the *Xunzi*. As I understand it, the point is primarily about how
the gentlemen *feel*, and not necessarily about how they *act*—their grief is such as to
be never-ending, and the sense in which one should not follow them is that one
should not simply adopt ("acquiesce in") their grief by itself as one's standard for
behavior. The passage leaves open the possibility that the "cultivated gentlemen" in

For them the twenty-five months of the three-year mourning period pass by as quickly as a galloping horse glimpsed though a crack. If
485 one acquiesces in this, then mourning will continue without end. Therefore, the former kings and sages accordingly established a middle way and fixed a proper measure for it, such that once mourning is made sufficient to achieve good form and proper order, then one stops it.

490 That being the case, then how is it divided up? I say: The mourning for those most close is broken off at one year. Why is that? I say: By then, Heaven and Earth have already gone through their alterations, the four seasons have already completed their course, and everything in the world changes and begins again. Thus, the sage kings
495 accordingly took this and made it their image. That being the case, then why the three-year mourning period? I say: To add loftiness to it, they accordingly made the period double, and thus it continues for another year. What about the mourning of nine months and below? I say: They accordingly made it not reach as long. Thus, the three-year
500 mourning period is the most lofty, the *sima* and *xiaogong* mourning periods[42] are the most slight, and the year-long and nine-month mourning periods are in between. The sage kings took an image from Heaven above, they took an image from Earth below, they took a standard from humans in the middle, and then the order by which
505 people are to live together in harmony and unity was complete. Thus, the three-year mourning period is that which gives utmost good form to the human way. This is called the utmost exalted standard. This is something in which the hundred kings are identical, and something in which past and present are one and the same.

510 What is the reason for adopting the three-year mourning period for a lord? I say: The lord is the master overseeing good government and proper social distinctions, the fount of good form and proper order, and the height of proper disposition on the inside and proper display on the outside. Is it not appropriate to lead one another in
515 treating him in the most exalted manner? The *Odes* says, "The contented and tranquil prince is mother and father to the people."[43] Thus there was originally a saying that the prince[d] is mother and father to the people. Their fathers can give them life, but cannot nurture them. Their mothers can feed them, but cannot teach and guide them. The

---

question do not, in fact, let their grief lead them into unending mourning, but rather follow the demands of ritual. Hence, the passage does not necessarily undermine their status as models, but since it contrasts them with the "former kings and sages," here the "cultivated gentlemen" are perhaps conceived as not being morally perfect, while still being superior to most others.

[42] The *sima* lasted for three months, and the *xiaogong* lasted for five months.

[43] Mao #251. This quotation differs slightly from the received version of the *Odes*. The lines are rhymed in the original.

lord is someone who not only can feed them, but who is also good at 520
teaching and guiding them. Is three years' mourning enough?

A wet-nurse gives one food and drink, and one mourns her for
three months. A nanny clothes and covers one, and one mourns her
for nine months. The lord is someone who provides all these things.
Is three years' mourning enough? With him, there is order, and with- 525
out him, there is chaos—he is the ultimate in good form. With him,
there is safety, and without him, there is danger—he is the ultimate in
proper disposition. With these two "ultimates" gathered together in
him, to serve him with three years' mourning is not sufficient, but
there is simply no way to improve on that. And so, for the sacrifice at 530
the altar of soil, one sacrifices to just the spirit of the soil, and for the
sacrifice at the altar of grain, one sacrifices just to the spirit of the
grain, but in the *jiao* sacrifice one combines the hundred kings with
Heaven above and sacrifices to them all.[44]

What is the reason for waiting three months after the lying in state? 535
I say: It is to magnify the event, to emphasize it, because the person
is someone whom one holds in highest esteem, someone whom one
regards with greatest affection. One is going to pick him up and move
him, taking him away from home and palace and consigning him to
the burial mound. The former kings feared lest this become unseemly, 540
so they drew out the period and made it sufficient to fill many days.
Thus, for the Son of Heaven, it is seven months. For the feudal lords,
it is five months. For the grand ministers and aristocrats, it is three
months. In each case, they made it such that the time was sufficient
to allow for the required affairs, the required affairs were of a quantity 545
to allow for their required degree of perfection, their required degree
of perfection was of a kind to allow for the required good form, and
the required good form was of a kind to allow for the preparation of
the required items. When one has made all the proper allowances and
completed all the required items, this is called the Way. 550

The sacrificial rites are the refined expression of remembrance and
longing. To be moved and feel upset are things that cannot but come
upon one at times. And so, on occasions when people are happy and
join together harmoniously, then a loyal minister or filial son will also
be moved and such feelings will come to him.[45] When the feelings 555

---

[44] Commentators debate whether this last sentence is relevant, or whether it might
have fallen out of place from somewhere else. Hao Yixing suggests very plausibly
that it continues the line of thought earlier in the passage by offering a parallel: just
as the lord deserves three years' mourning because he combines the good points of
all other caregivers, so the *jiao* sacrifice to Heaven is especially lavish because
Heaven rules over all other kings.

[45] Xunzi's point is not that the loyal minister and filial son are upset by happy occasions per se, but rather that on happy occasions, the loyal minister will think of his
departed lord, and the filial son will think of his departed parent, either because the

that come to him stir him greatly, but simply play themselves out and
stop, then with regard to the refined expression of remembrance he
feels anguished and unsatisfied, and his practice of ritual and proper
regulation would be lacking and incomplete. And so, the former
560 kings accordingly established a proper form for the situation, and
thereby what is *yi* in venerating those who are esteemed and loving
those who are intimate was set. Thus I say: The sacrificial rites are the
refined expression of remembrance and longing. They are the utmost
in loyalty, trustworthiness, love, and respect. They are the fullest
565 manifestation of ritual, proper regulation, good form, and proper
appearance. If one is not a sage, then one will not be able to understand them. The sage clearly understands them. The well-bred man
and the gentleman are at ease in carrying them out. The officials take
them as things to be preserved. The common people take them as
570 their set customs.[46] The gentleman regards them as the way to be a
proper human being. The common people regard them as serving the
ghosts.

And so, as for bells, drums, pipes, chimes, zithers, and mouth-or-
gans, the *Shao*, *Xia*, *Hu*, *Wu*, *Zhuo*, *Huan*, *Xiao*, and *Xiang*, these are
575 the forms used by the gentleman when he is moved by what he finds
delightful and enjoyable. As for wearing the mourning garments,
propping himself on a crude cane, dwelling in a lean-to, eating gruel,
and using a rough mat and earthen pillow, these are the forms used
by the gentleman when he is moved by what he finds sorrowful and
580 hurtful. As for putting the military in order, arranging the various
grades of punishments, and ensuring that none of them fail to fit the
crime, these are the forms used by the gentleman when he is moved
by what he finds odious and hateful.[f]

For the ritual sacrifices, one engages in divination and determines
585 the appropriate day.

> One fasts and sweeps out the site, sets out tables and food
> offerings, and has the "announcement to the assistant," as if
> the deceased were attending a banquet.[47] The impersonator
> of the dead takes the goods and from each of them makes a

---

happy occasion reminds him of previous happy times spent with that person when
alive, or perhaps (as commentators suggest) because he wishes to share his happiness with those for whom he cares, but then remembers that the departed person
cannot be present to enjoy the occasion, and so feels sad.

[46] See the similar wording at 18.538–42.

[47] The "announcement to the assistant" is a part of the ceremony in which the impersonator of the dead gives blessings to the host of the ceremony. The idea seems to
be that just as guests come with expressions of thankfulness for the host of a feast,
so the spirit of the dead expresses thanks for the sacrifice. Also from here to the end
of the chapter, the text is rhymed in the original.

sacrifice, as if the deceased were tasting them. One does not 590
use a helper to raise a toast, but rather the host himself takes
hold of the cup, as if the deceased were engaging in the toast.
When the guests leave, the host sends them off and bows to
them as they go, then returns and changes his clothing.[48] He
goes back to this position and cries, as if the deceased had 595
left. How full of sorrow! How full of respect! One serves the
dead as if one were serving the living, and one serves the departed as if one were serving a surviving person. One gives a
shape to that which is without physical substance and mag-
nificently accomplishes proper form. 600

---

[48] According to commentators, the host changes from the sacrificial robes back into the robes of mourning.

CHAPTER 20

Discourse on Music

Music is joy, an unavoidable human disposition. So, people cannot be without music; if they feel joy, they must express it in sound and give it shape in movement. The way of human beings is such that changes in the motions of their nature are completely contained in
5   these sounds and movements. So, people cannot be without joy, and their joy cannot be without shape, but if it takes shape and does not accord with the Way, then there will inevitably be chaos. The former kings hated such chaos, and therefore they established the sounds of the *Ya* and the *Song*[1] in order to guide them. They caused the sounds
10   to be enjoyable without becoming dissolute. They caused the patterns to be distinctive without becoming degenerate. They caused the progression, complexity, intensity, and rhythm of the music to be sufficient to move the goodness in people's hearts. They caused perverse and corrupt *qi* to have no place to attach itself to them. This is
15   the manner in which the former kings created music, and so what is Mozi doing denouncing it?

And so, when music is performed in the ancestral temple and the ruler and ministers, superiors and inferiors, listen to it together, none fail to become harmoniously respectful. When it is performed within
20   the home and father and sons, elder and younger brothers listen to it together, none fail to become harmoniously affectionate. And when it is performed in the village, and old and young people listen to it together, none fail to become harmoniously cooperative. Thus, music observes a single standard in order to fix its harmony, it brings to-
25   gether different instruments in order to ornament its rhythm, and it combines their playing in order to achieve a beautiful pattern. It is sufficient to lead people in a single, unified way, and is sufficient to bring order to the myriad changes within them. This is the method by which the former kings created music, and so what is Mozi doing
30   denouncing it?[2]

Thus, in listening to the sounds of the *Ya* and *Song*, people's thoughts and intentions are broadened. In taking up the shield and axe of the war dance and rehearsing its motions, their appearance becomes majestic. In proceeding according to the markings and boundaries of the
35   dance stage and conforming to the rhythm of the accompaniment,

---

[1] These are names of sections of the *Odes*.
[2] The repetition of this sentence here and throughout may be meant to mock Mozi's own repetitive style.

their ranks and formations become ordered, and their advances and retreats become uniform. And so, music is something one uses to conduct punitive military expeditions abroad, and it is something one uses to practice courteous deference and yielding at home. Conducting punitive military expeditions and practicing courteous deference and yielding have one and the same purpose. If one uses music to conduct punitive military expeditions abroad, then there will be none who do not submit. If one uses it to practice courteous deference and yielding at home, then there will be none who do not comply. Hence music brings great uniformity to all under Heaven. It is the key to balance and harmony and something that the dispositions of human beings cannot avoid. This is the method by which the former kings created their music, and so what is Mozi doing denouncing it?

Moreover, music is the means by which the former kings adorned their happiness. Military campaigns and armaments are the means by which the former kings adorned their anger. The happiness and anger of the former kings achieved a uniform measure in these things. Therefore, when they were happy, all under Heaven harmonized with them, and when they were angry, then violent and disorderly people feared them. Ritual and music are precisely the height of the way followed by the former kings, and so what is Mozi doing denouncing them? Thus I say: Mozi's understanding of the Way is like that of a blind person toward black and white, or like that of a deaf person toward high and low sounds, or like someone who wants to go to Chu but seeks it by going north.[3]

Sounds and music enter into people deeply and transform people quickly. Therefore, the former kings carefully made for these things a proper pattern. If music is balanced and peaceful, then the people will be harmonious and not dissolute. If music is solemn and majestic, then the people will be uniformly ordered and not cause chaos. When the people are harmonious and uniformly ordered, then the state's soldiers will be vigorous and its fortifications will be solid, and rival states will not dare to touch it.[4] When the situation is like this, then the common people will all rest secure in their dwellings and delight in their villages, such as to provide sufficiently for their superior. Then their superior's fame will be clear, his glory will be great, and all the people within the four seas will want to have him as their governor. This is the beginning of being a true king.

If music is dissolute and dangerous, then the people will be dissolute, arrogant, vulgar, and base. If they are dissolute and arrogant then they will cause chaos. If they are vulgar and base then they will struggle with each other. If they cause chaos and struggle with each

---

[3] Chu was on the southern end of the Chinese cultural sphere at this time.
[4] See the similar wording at 16.10–12.

other, then the state's soldiers will be weak and its fortifications vulnerable, and rival states will put them in danger. When the situation
80 is like this, then the common people will not rest secure in their
dwellings and not delight in their villages, and will not provide sufficiently for their superior. And so, when ritual and music are discarded and deviant tunes arise, this is the root cause for the superior
being endangered, disgraced, and having his territory diminished.
85 Thus, the former kings valued ritual and music and considered deviant tunes base. As I have already said in "The Proper Order for Officials": The work of the Music Master is to cultivate government regulations and orders, to keep watch over poetry and artistic form, to
prohibit perverse music, and to smoothly cultivate these tasks at the
90 appropriate times, so as to prevent barbarian, vulgar, and deviant
tunes from daring to disorder the refined pieces.[5]

Mozi says: "Music is something that the sage kings denounced.
The *ru* practice it, and this is an error on their part." The gentleman
does not agree. Music is something in which the sages delighted, for
95 it has the power to make good the hearts of the people, to influence
men deeply, and to reform their manners and customs with facility.
Therefore, the former kings guided the people with ritual and music,
and the people became harmonious and congenial. For the people
have dispositions to like and dislike things, but if they are allowed no
100 happy or angry reactions, then there will be chaos. The former kings
hated this chaos, and so they cultivated their conduct and set in order
their music, and all under Heaven became peacefully compliant by
these things.

Thus, the mourning garments and the sounds of weeping make
105 people's hearts sad. To strap on armor, don a helmet, and sing in the
ranks makes people's hearts emboldened. Dissolute customs and the
tunes of Zheng and Wey make people's hearts licentious. Putting on
the ritual belt, robes, and cap, and dancing the *Shao* and singing the
Wu make people's hearts invigorated. And so, the gentleman's ears
110 will not listen to licentious sounds. His eyes will not look upon seductive sights. His mouth will not issue foul doctrines. These three are
things that the gentleman is careful about.

Whenever wanton sounds arouse a person, a perverse qi responds
to them from within. When this perverse qi takes form, then chaos
115 results from it. But when proper sounds arouse a person, a compliant
qi responds to them from within. When this compliant qi takes form,
then good order results from it. Those singing the lead and those
chiming in match each other, and goodness and badness in people
both resemble this. Therefore, the gentleman is careful about what he
120 rejects and what he draws near to.

[5] See 9.385–89.

The gentleman guides his intentions with bells and drums. He delights his heart with the *qin* and *se*.[6] He moves with shield and spear. He decorates his dance with feathers and plumes. He follows it up with stone chimes and pipes. And so, his purity resembles Heaven, his broadness resembles the Earth, and the way he postures and re- 125 volves has resemblance to the four seasons.

Thus:

> When music is played, intentions gain purity.
> When rites are studied, conduct turns out perfectly.
> They make one's ears acute and they make one's eyes sharp; 130
> They give one's blood and *qi* balance and harmony;
> They modify customs and they alter habits,
> So all the people in the world live peaceably,

—and those who are good and fine delight in each other. And so I say: Music is joy. The gentleman takes joy in attaining the 135 Way. The petty man takes joy in attaining the object of his desires. If one takes the Way to regulate one's desires, then one will be happy and not disordered. If one forgets the Way for the sake of one's desires, then one will be confused and unhappy. And so music is the means to guide one's joy. The instruments made of metal, stone, silk 140 string, and bamboo are the means to guide one's virtue. When music proceeds, then the people will turn toward what is correct. Thus, music is the height of ordering people, but Mozi denounces it!

Music, moreover, is unchanging harmony, and ritual is unalterable order. Music unites that which is the same, and ritual distinguishes 145 that which is different. Together the combination of ritual and music governs the human heart.

> To penetrate to the root and encompass all change—this is
> the essential disposition of music.[7] To make clear integrity
> and do away with pretense—this is the guiding principle of 150
> ritual. Mozi denounces these things, and so is deserving of
> punishment. However, the enlightened kings have passed
> away, and so no one corrects him. Foolish people study his
> ways and so endanger themselves. The gentleman clearly understands the value of music, and this is his virtue. Yet, a 155
> chaotic age hates what is good, and so will not heed him.
> Alas, how sad! He cannot succeed. You disciples must work
> hard at your studies and not be confused.

---

[6] These are two types of zithers.
[7] From here to the end of the paragraph, the original text is rhymed.

The phenomena of sounds and music are these:[8] The drum is great and magnificent. The bell is expansive and full. The stone chimes are restrained and orderly. The *yu, sheng, xiao, he, guan*, and *yue*[9] are energetic and vibrant. The *xun* and *chi*[10] are rolling and undulating. The *se* is serene and relaxed. The *qin* is soft and gentle. Song is pure and penetrating.

On the meaning of the dance: The way of Heaven is all-encompassing.[a] The drum is the lord of the music, is it not? Thus, the drum resembles Heaven. The bell resembles Earth. The stone chimes resemble water. The *yu, sheng, xiao, he, guan*, and *yue* resemble the sun, moon, and stars. The *tao, zhu, fu, ge, qiang*, and *qia*[11] resemble the myriad creatures. How does one know the meaning of the dance? I say: The eyes do not themselves see it, and the ears do not themselves hear it. Nevertheless, it controls their postures, gestures, directions, and speed. When all the dancers are restrained and orderly, exerting to the utmost the strength of their bones and sinews to match the rhythm of drum and bell sounding together, and no one is out of step, then how easy it is to tell the meaning of this group gathering![12]

When I observe the village drinking ceremony, I know how easy and carefree the way of a true king is. The host personally goes to greet the guest of honor and the guests of second rank, and all the other guests follow them. When they come to just outside the gate, the host bows to welcome the guest of honor and the guests of second rank, and then all the other guests enter on their own. Thus, what is *yi* for the noble and the lowly is properly differentiated.

As the host thrice gestures politely, they come to the stairs. After the host thrice offers to yield the way, he ascends with the guest of honor. The host bows to him upon arriving at the hall and offers him wine, to which the guest of honor responds with a toast, and here the regulations for deferring and yielding are elaborate, but they are abbreviated for the guests of second rank. When it comes to the rest of the guests, they ascend and receive wine. They sit to offer a sacrifice from it, but stand to drink it. Then, without offering a toast, they descend. Thus, what is *yi* for the exalted and the lesser is distinguished.

---

[8] The Chinese text for this paragraph and the next is somewhat obscure and appears corrupted, so the translation here is tentative.

[9] These are names of wind instruments made of one or more pipes.

[10] The *xun* is a clay, egg-shaped wind instrument (an ocarina). The *chi* is a flute-like instrument.

[11] These are names of various percussion instruments.

[12] I.e., the true meaning of dance lies in the order it brings to a group of people, and this order is not itself a visible object or audible sound, but is nonetheless readily apparent from the performance.

The singers enter, ascend, and sing three songs, and the host offers them wine. The *sheng* players enter, play three pieces, and the host offers them wine. The singers and musicians take turns performing separately three times and then perform together three times. Then, the singers announce that the musical performance is complete, and they depart. Two assistants raise a goblet in toast, and then the Overseer of Decorum is established.[13] From this I know that it is possible to gather in harmony and joy without becoming dissolute.

The guest of honor offers a toast to the host, the host offers a toast to the guests of second rank, the guests of second rank offer toasts to the rest of the guests, and the young and the seniors each drink in turn according to their rank in age, ending with the servants carrying the wash water. From this I know that it is possible to treat appropriately those junior and senior without leaving anyone out.

They descend to remove their shoes and ascend again to sit. Then, the cups are hoisted in toast without counting the rounds, but the regulations for drinking wine are that, if done in the morning, it does not waste the whole morning, and if done in the evening, it does not waste the whole night. When the guest of honor departs, the host bows in sending him off, and then proper regulation and good form have been brought to completion. From this I know that it is possible to enjoy comfort and relaxation without becoming disorderly.

These five kinds of conduct—differentiating noble and lowly, distinguishing exalted and lesser, gathering in harmony and joy without becoming dissolute, treating appropriately junior and senior without leaving anyone out, and enjoying comfort and relaxation without becoming disorderly—these are sufficient to rectify one's person and to settle the state. And when the state is settled, then all under Heaven will become settled. Hence I say: when I observe the village drinking ceremony, I know how easy and carefree the way of a true king is.

The signs of a disordered age are these: Men's clothing is elaborately woven. Their appearances are womanish. Their customs are licentious. Their intentions are set on profit. Their conduct is irregular. Their sounds and music are dangerous. Their emblems and insignias are deviant and ostentatious. The way they nurture the living lacks all proper measure. The way they send off the dead is stingy and Mohist.[14] They denigrate ritual and *yi*, while valuing boldness and strength. When impoverished, they rob others. When wealthy, they become utter villains.

An ordered age is the opposite of all this.

---

[13] The Overseer of Decorum was assigned temporarily as part of the ritual and had the task of presiding over the drinking among the various guests to ensure that no one drank too much or became unruly.

[14] Compare 19.206–12 and 19.441.

CHAPTER 21

Undoing Fixation

In most cases, the problem for people is that they become fixated on one twist and are deluded about the greater order of things.[1] If they are brought under control, then they will return to the right standards. If they are of two minds, then they will be hesitant and confused.[a] There are not two Ways for the world, and the sage is not of two minds. Nowadays the feudal lords have different governments, and the hundred schools have different teachings, so that necessarily some are right and some are wrong, and some lead to order and some lead to chaos. The lords of chaotic states and the followers of pernicious schools all sincerely seek what they consider correct and put themselves into achieving it. They resent what they consider to be erroneous views of the Way, and others are seduced into following their same path.[b] They selfishly favor the approach in which they have accumulated effort and only fear to hear it disparaged. They rely on it when regarding other approaches and only fear to hear those others praised. Therefore, they depart[c] further and further from getting under control and think they are right not to stop. Is this not because they have become fixated on one twist and missed the true object of their search? If the heart does not apply itself to the eyes, then black and white can be right in front of you and the eyes will not see them. If the heart does not apply itself to the ears, then drums and thunder can be right at your side and the ears will not hear them. How much more so in the case of that which is applying[d] itself in the first place![2] The person of true virtue and the true Way is denounced from above by the lords of chaotic states, and denounced from below by the followers of pernicious schools. Is this not lamentable?

Thus, among the cases of fixation, one can be fixated on desires, or one can be fixated on dislikes. One can be fixated on origins, or one can be fixated on ends. One can be fixated on what is far away, or one can be fixated on what is nearby. One can be fixated by broad learning, or one can be fixated by narrowness. One can be fixated on the ancient past, or one can be fixated on the present. In whatever respect the myriad things are different, they can become objects of fixation to the exclusion of each other. This is the common problem in the ways of the heart.

[1] Compare this with the criticism of one-sidedness at 3.201–22. Cf. also 4.230–31.

[2] I.e., just as the heart must apply itself to the sense organs in order for them to perceive correctly, so must it watch over itself in order to avoid fixation and apprehend the truth.

In past times, there were lords of men who were fixated—such were Jie of the Xia dynasty and Zhòu of the Yin dynasty. Jie was fixated on Mo Xi and Si Guan,[3] and so did not recognize the worth of Guan Longfeng. As a result, his heart was confused and his conduct was chaotic. Zhòu was fixated on Dan Ji and Fei Lian,[4] and so did not recognize the worth of Weizi Qi. As a result, his heart was confused and his conduct was chaotic. And so, their assembled ministers forsook loyalty and instead worked for their own personal gain. The common people resented and denounced their rulers and could not be put to use. Good and worthy men withdrew into secluded living and fled into obscurity. This is how Jie and Zhòu came to lose the lands of the Nine Pastures[5] and destroyed their own ancestral states. Jie died at Mount Ting, and Zhòu was hung up on a red banner. They themselves did not see this coming ahead of time, and moreover nobody remonstrated with them. That is the disaster of being fixated and blocked up in one's thinking.

King Tang the Successful took note of the behavior of Jie of the Xia dynasty. Therefore, he mastered his heart and took care to make it well ordered. Thus, he was able to employ Yi Yin for a long time, and he himself did not lose the Way. This is why he could launch a punitive campaign against the king of the Xia and receive the Nine Holdings.[6] King Wen took note of the behavior of Zhòu of the Yin dynasty. Therefore, he mastered his heart and took care to make it well ordered. Thus, he was able to employ Lü Wang for a long time,[7] and he himself did not lose the Way. This is why he could launch a punitive campaign against the king of the Yin and receive the Nine Pastures. Afterward, the outlying areas all paid tributes of precious goods. And so, King Tang's and King Wen's eyes looked upon the greatest sights, their ears listened to the greatest music, their mouths enjoyed the greatest flavors, their bodies dwelt in the greatest palaces, their names received the greatest acclaim. While alive, everyone under Heaven sung their praises. When they died, everyone within the four seas wept for them. This is called the utmost flourishing. The *Odes* says:

Male and female phoenix
To and fro are swaying.
They wave their wings like shields.

---

[3] Mo Xi was a concubine. Nothing is known about Si Guan, though commentators speculate that he was probably one of Jie's ministers.

[4] Dan Ji was a concubine, and Fei Lian was a minister to Zhòu.

[5] This is another name for the empire.

[6] Again, another name for the empire.

[7] Lü Wang is another name for Lü Shang, also known as the "Grand Duke" of the Zhou dynasty.

They sing like pipes playing.
Male and female phoenix
75   Have come here to alight,
Bringing to our king's heart
The greatest in delight.[8]

That is the good fortune that comes from not being fixated.

In past times, there were ministers who were fixated—such were
80   Tang Yang and Xi Qi. Tang Yang was fixated on desire for power and
so banished Zaizi. Xi Qi was fixated on desire to possess the state and
so harmed Shen Sheng.[9] Tang Yang was executed in Song, and Xi Qi
was executed in Jin. One banished a worthy prime minister, and the
other harmed a filial older brother, and as a result they were punished
85   and executed, yet they did not see it coming. That is the disaster of
being fixated and blocked up in one's thinking. And so, from ancient
times to the present, there has never yet been anyone who has used
greed, corruption, and treachery to struggle for power and yet not
suffered danger, disgrace, and destruction.

90   Bao Shu, Ning Qi, and Xian Peng were *ren*, were wise, and were
not fixated. Thus, they were able to support Guan Zhong, and their
reputations, rewards, and fortunes were on a par with Guan Zhong.
Duke Shao and Lü Wang were *ren*, were wise, and were not fixated.
Thus, they were able to support the Duke of Zhou, and their reputa-
95   tions, rewards, and fortunes were on a par with the Duke of Zhou. A
saying goes, "To recognize worthy people is called being clear-
sighted. To assist worthy people is called having ability. Encourage
them, urge them on, and your good fortune is sure to grow." This
expresses my meaning. That is the good fortune that comes from not
100   being fixated.

In past times, there were guest retainers[10] who were fixated—such
were the pernicious schools. Mozi was fixated on the useful and did
not understand the value of good form. Song Xing was fixated on

---

[8] This poem is not contained in the received text of the *Odes*. Commentators speculate
that it refers to an incident during the reign of the sage king Yao when a male and
female phoenix supposedly nested in his territory. Since, according to legend, the
phoenix appears only in times of good government, this was an extremely good
omen, and thus the king was much delighted. In connection with the preceding
lines, the quotation seems meant to illustrate the point that good things come to
virtuous people.

[9] According to traditional records, Xi Qi was the younger brother of Shen Sheng, who
was ahead of him in line to inherit the throne of Jin. However, Xi Qi wanted the state
for himself and so had Shen Sheng slandered, thereby deceiving the ruler into executing him, and thus eliminating him from the line of royal succession.

[10] "Guest retainers" is a term for those who obtained patronage at royal courts and offered assistance to the rulers. This group of people included many whom we might
count as philosophers. Compare this and the next paragraph with 17.247–62.

having few desires and did not understand the value of achieving
their objects. Shen Dao was fixated on laws and did not understand   105
the value of having worthy people. Shen Buhai was fixated on power
and did not understand the value of having wise people. Huizi was
fixated on wording and did not understand the value of what is substantial. Zhuangzi was fixated on the Heavenly and did not understand the value of the human.   110

Thus, if one speaks of it in terms of usefulness, then the Way will
consist completely in seeking what is profitable. If one speaks of it in
terms of desires, then the Way will consist completely in learning to
be satisfied. If one speaks of it in terms of laws, then the Way will
consist completely in making arrangements. If one speaks of it in   115
terms of power, then the Way will consist completely in finding what
is expedient. If one speaks of it in terms of wording, then the Way will
consist completely in discoursing on matters. If one speaks of it in
terms of the Heavenly, then the Way will consist completely in following along with things. These various approaches are all merely one   120
corner of the Way. As for the Way itself, its substance is constant, yet
it covers all changes. No one corner is sufficient to exhibit it fully.

People of twisted understanding observe one corner of the Way
and are unable to recognize it as such. So, they think it sufficient and
proceed to embellish it. On the inside, they use it to disorder their   125
own lives. On the outside, they use it to confuse other people. As
superiors, they use it to transfix their subordinates. As subordinates,
they use it to transfix their superiors. This is the disaster of being fixated and blocked up in one's thinking. Confucius was *ren*, was wise,
and was not fixated, and so through his study of various methods, he   130
was worthy of being one of the former kings. His one line alone
grasped the way of the Zhou and upheld and used it, because he was
not fixated by accumulated deeds. Thus, his virtue equals that of the
Duke of Zhou, and his name ranks with those of the three kings. This
is the good fortune that comes from not being fixated.   135

The sage knows the problems in the ways of the heart, and sees the
disaster of being fixated and blocked up in one's thinking. So, he is
neither for desires, nor for dislikes, is neither for the origins, nor for
the end results, is neither for what is near, nor for what is far away, is
neither for what is broad, nor for what is shallow, is neither for the   140
ancient past, nor is for the present. He lays out all the myriad things
and in their midst suspends his scales. For this reason, the various
different things are unable to become fixating and so disorder his
categories of judgment.

What am I calling his "scales"? I say: it is the Way. Thus, one's   145
heart must not be ignorant of the Way. If the heart does not know the
Way, then it will not approve of the Way, but will rather approve what
is not the Way. For what person would wish to be so dissolute as to

228 • CHAPTER 21

keep to what they disapprove and reject what they approve? If one

150 chooses people using a heart that does not approve of the Way, then
one is sure to accord with people who do not follow the Way, and one
will not know to accord with people who do follow the Way. To use
a heart that does not approve of the Way and to join together with
people who do not follow the Way when judging people who do fol-
155 low the Way—this is the root of chaos.

How will one know [which are the people who follow the Way]? I
say: the heart must know the Way, and only then will it approve of
the Way. Only after it approves of the Way will it be able to keep to
the Way and reject what is not the Way. If one chooses people using
160 a heart that approves of the Way, then one will accord with people
who follow the Way, and one will not accord with people who do not
follow the Way. To use a heart that approves of the Way and to join
together with people who follow the Way when judging what is not
the Way—this is the essential thing for good order. What problem of
165 not knowing [those who follow the Way] could there be? Thus, the
essential thing for good order rests in knowing the Way.

How do people know the Way? I say: with the heart. How does the
heart know the Way? I say: it is through emptiness, single-mindedness, and stillness. The heart is always holding something. Yet, there
170 is what is called being "empty." The heart is always two-fold. Yet,
there is what is called being "single-minded." The heart is always
moving. Yet, there is what is called being "still." Humans are born
and have awareness. With awareness, they have focus.[11] To focus is to
be holding something. Yet, there is something called being "empty."
175 Not to let what one is already holding harm what one is about to receive is called being "empty."[12] The heart is born and has awareness.
With awareness, there comes awareness of differences. These differences are known at the same time, and when they are known at the
same time, this is to be two-fold. Yet, there is what is called being
180 "single-minded." Not to let one idea harm another idea is called being
"single-minded." When the heart sleeps, then it dreams. When it relaxes, then it goes about on its own. When one puts it to use, then it
forms plans. Thus, the heart is always moving. Yet, there is what is
called being "still." Not to let dreams and worries disorder one's un-
185 derstanding is called being "still."

As for those who have not yet grasped the Way but are seeking the
Way, I say to them: emptiness, single-mindedness, and stillness—

---

[11] Reading *zhi* 志 as it appears in the text. Most commentators and translators read it
as *zhi* 誌 "memory."

[12] From this explanation, it is clear that what Xunzi means by "emptiness" is *not* having no thoughts or clearing out one's mind, but rather being able to take up new
ideas and objects of attention. Thus, his "emptiness" is more akin to what nowadays
would be called "receptiveness."

make these your principles.ᵉ If one who would search for the Way
achieves emptiness, then he may enter upon it. If one who would
work at the Way achieves single-mindedness, then he will exhaus-   190
tively obtain it. If one who would ponder the Way achieves stillness,
then he will discern it keenly. One who knows the Way and observes
things by it, who knows the Way and puts it into practice, is one who
embodies the Way. To be empty, and single-minded, and still—this is
called great clarity and brilliance. For such a one, none of the myriad   195
things takes form and is not seen. None is seen and not judged. None
is judged and loses its proper position. He sits in his chamber yet sees
all within the four seas.¹³ He dwells in today yet judges what is long
ago and far away in time. He comprehensively observes the myriad
things and knows their true dispositions. He inspects and examines   200
order and disorder and discerns their measures. He sets straight
Heaven and Earth, and arranges and makes useful the myriad things.
He institutes great order, and the whole world is encompassed
therein.

> So vast and broad is he! Who grasps his true limits?   205
> So lofty and broad is he! Who grasps his true virtue?
> So active and varied is he! Who grasps his true form?¹⁴

His brilliance matches the sun and moon. His greatness fills all the
eight directions. Such a one is called the Great Man. What fixation
could there be in him?   210
    The heart is the lord of the body and the master of one's spirit and
intelligence. It issues orders, but it takes orders from nothing: *it* restrains itself, *it* employs itself; *it* lets itself go, *it* takes itself in hand; *it*
makes itself proceed, *it* makes itself stop. Thus, the mouth can be
compelled either to be silent or to speak, and the body can be com-   215
pelled either to contract or to extend itself, but the heart cannot be
compelled to change its thoughts. What it considers right, one accepts. What it considers wrong, one rejects. And so I say: if the heart
allows its choices to be without restraint, then when it reveals its ob-
jects¹⁵ they will surely be broadly varying.ᶠ Its perfected disposition is   220
to be undivided. The *Odes* says:

¹³ Compare the *Daodejing*, chap. 47.
¹⁴ The first two of these lines are rhymed in the original. The third does not rhyme in
   its current form, and Gu Qianli suggests emending the word "form" to make it
   rhyme. I have not adopted his emendation, but given the parallel structure here, it
   is likely that the third line was supposed to be part of the rhymed set, so I have
   grouped it with the others.
¹⁵ The word here is *wu* 物 (lit. "things"), which in this context could refer to one's
   thoughts and/or to one's purposes; rendering it as "objects" is intended to cover
   both possibilities.

I pick and pick the *juan-er* leaves,
But cannot fill my sloping basket.
Oh for my cherished one!
225 He is stationed on the Zhou campaign.[16]

A sloping basket is easy to fill, and the *juan-er* leaves are easy to get, but one must not be divided with thoughts of the Zhou campaign. And so I say: if the heart is split, it will be without understanding. If it deviates, it will not be expertly refined. If it is divided, then it will
230 be confused. If one guides its examinations, then the myriad things can all be known together, and if the person thoroughly develops his original substance, then he will be truly beautiful.

The proper classes of things are not of two kinds. Hence, the person with understanding picks the one right object and pursues it
235 single-mindedly. The farmer is expert in regard to the fields, but cannot be made Overseer of Fields.[17] The merchant is expert in regard to the markets, but cannot be made Overseer of Merchants. The craftsman is expert in regard to vessels, but cannot be made Overseer of Vessels. There is a person who is incapable of any of their three skills,
240 but who can be put in charge of any of these offices, namely the one who is expert in regard to the Way, not the one who is expert in regard to things.[g] One who is expert in regard to things merely measures one thing against another. One who is expert in regard to the Way measures all things together.[18] Thus, the gentleman pursues the
245 Way single-mindedly and uses it to guide and oversee things. If one pursues the Way single-mindedly, then one will be correct. If one uses it to guide one in examining things, then one will have keen discernment. If one uses correct intentions to carry out discerning judgments, then the myriad things will all obtain their proper station.
250 In the past, the way Shun governed the world was that he did not issue orders for affairs, and myriad things were accomplished of themselves. He dwelt in single-mindedness to the point of precariousness,[19] and his [moral] glory was abundant. He nurtured single-mindedness to the point of sublimeness, and he was glorious without

---

[16] Mao #3. These lines are rhymed in the original.
[17] This sentence also appears at 27.435–36.
[18] See *Analects* 2.12.
[19] The word here is *wei* 危 (lit. "dangerous" or "endangered"). As the discussion of Ji below (lines 288–302) shows, the term refers to a state in which one has an "unsteady" or "precarious" ability in some area, and with respect to morality, it is a state in which one must self-consciously force oneself to act correctly. There is room for debate about what is being described in Shun's case. As I see it, the idea is that his cultivation of single-mindedness first reached the point where his practice of morality was outstanding (and hence glorious) but not effortless and unselfconscious, and later—as described in the next sentence in the text—it became fully effortless and spontaneous, and required no thought of being good.

even being aware of it. Thus, the *Classic of the Way*[20] says, "The human   255
heart is precarious. The heart with the Way is sublime." Only when
one is an enlightened gentleman can one understand the subtle workings of precariousness and sublimeness.

The human heart can be compared to a pan of water. If you set it
straight and do not move it, the muddy and turbid parts will settle to   260
the bottom, and the clear and bright parts will be on the top, and
then one can see one's whiskers and inspect the lines on one's face.
But if a slight breeze passes over it, the muddy and turbid parts will
be stirred up from the bottom, and the clear and bright parts will be
disturbed on top, and then one cannot get a correct view of even large   265
contours. The heart is just like this.[21] Thus, if one guides it with good
order, nourishes it with clarity, and nothing can make it deviate, then
it will be capable of determining right and wrong and deciding what
is doubtful. If it is drawn aside by even a little thing, then on the
outside one's correctness will be altered, and on the inside one's heart   270
will deviate, and then will be incapable of discerning the multifarious
patterns of things.

Thus, those who liked writing were many indeed, but the name of
Cang Jie alone is passed down, because he was single-minded. Those
who liked farming were many indeed, but the name of Hou Ji alone   275
is passed down, because he was single-minded. Those who liked
music were many indeed, but the name of Kui alone is passed down,
because he was single-minded. Those who liked *yi* were many indeed,
but the name of Shun alone is passed down, because he was single-
minded. Chui created the bow, and Fu You created the arrow, but Yi   280
was expert at archery. Xi Zhong created the cart, and Sheng Du created the harnessing of horses, but Zao Fu was expert at driving. From
ancient times to the present, there has never once been one who divides himself between two things and yet is able to be expert at them.
As Zengzi said, "If someone is looking around the room for some-   285
thing with which to strike at a rat he sees, then how can he also sing
along with me?"[22]

In the caves there lived a man named Ji.[23] He was good at guessing
riddles because he was fond of pondering things. However, if the
desires of his eyes and ears were aroused, it would ruin his thinking,   290
and if he heard the sounds of mosquitoes or gnats, it would frustrate
his concentration. So, he shut out the desires of his eyes and ears and

---

[20] This work is lost, and nothing is known of it outside this quotation. However, the
quotation that follows does appear in almost identical form in the *Shujing*, *Dayumo*
("Counsels of the Great Yu"), translated in Waltham (1971, p. 23).

[21] Compare *Zhuangzi*, chap. 5.

[22] Zengzi was a disciple of Confucius.

[23] This person is unattested elsewhere, and the pronunciation of the name is uncertain.

put himself far away from the sounds of mosquitoes and gnats, and by dwelling in seclusion and stilling his thoughts, he achieved com-
295 prehension. But can pondering *ren* in such a manner be called true sublimeness? Mencius hated depravity and so expelled his wife—this can be called being able to force oneself.[24] Youzi[25] hated dozing off and so burned his palm to keep awake—this can be called being able to steel oneself. These are not yet true fondness. To shut out the de-
300 sires of one's eyes and ears can be called forcing oneself. It is not yet truly pondering. To be such that hearing the sounds of mosquitoes or gnats frustrates one's concentration is called being precarious. It cannot yet be called true sublimeness. One who is truly sublime is a perfected person. For the perfected person, what forcing oneself,
305 what steeling oneself, what precariousness is there? Thus, those who are murky understand only external manifestations, but those who are clear understand internal manifestations. The sage follows his de-sires and embraces all his dispositions, and the things dependent on these simply turn out well-ordered. What forcing oneself, what steel-
310 ing oneself, what precariousness is there? Thus, the person of *ren* carries out the Way without striving, and the sage carries out the Way without forcing himself. The person of *ren* ponders it with reverence, and the sage ponders it with joy. This is the proper way to order one's heart.
315   Whenever one's observation of things is doubtful, if on the inside one's heart is not settled, then external things will not be clear. When I deliberate about something unclear, then I cannot determine what is the case and what is not the case. A person who walks in the dark sees a stone lying on the ground and mistakes it for a tiger lying in
320 wait. He see trees standing upright and mistakes them for people fol-lowing behind him. This is because the darkness obscures his clarity of vision. A drunkard tries to leap over a gorge a hundred paces wide, mistaking it for a ditch a half step across. He bends down when exit-ing the city gate, mistaking it for a low doorway. This is because the
325 wine has disordered his spirit. If you press on your eyes and look, you will see one thing as two. If you cover your ears and listen, you will hear silence as if it were chatter. This is because the conditions have disordered your senses. Thus, to people looking down on cows from on top of a mountain, they will look like sheep, but those seeking
330 their sheep do not go down to lead them away, because [they under-stand that] the distance has obscured their true size. To people who from the foot of a mountain look at trees atop it, very tall trees will look like chopsticks, but those seeking chopsticks do not go up to break them off, because [they understand that] the height has ob-

---

[24] For an account of this incident, see Lau (1970, p. 217).
[25] Youzi, also known as You Ruo, was a disciple of Confucius.

scured their true length. When water is stirred up and the reflection 335
on it is shaken, then people do not use it to determine the beautiful
and the ugly, because the condition of the water is blurry. When a
blind person looks up and does not see the stars,[26] people do not rely
on him to establish whether they are there or not, because his vital
energies are muddled. If there is someone among them who uses such 340
occasions to determine things, then he is the most foolish person in
the world. Such a foolish person's way of determining things is to use
one doubtful thing to decide another doubtful thing. In that case, his
decisions surely will not be fitting, and if they are not fitting, then
how can he go without committing errors? 345

In the south of Xiashou there was a man named Juan Shuliang.
His character was such that he was foolish and readily fearful. While
walking under a bright moon at night, he looked down, saw his own
shadow, and mistook it for a ghost lying in wait. He looked up, saw
his own hair, and mistook it for a monster standing over him. He 350
turned about and ran, but as he was about to reach home, he had
completely dissipated his *qi* and died. Is this not sad! Whenever people have experience of ghosts, it is sure to be something they have
determined during a moment when they are disturbed or hurried, or
on occasions when they are confused and unclear. These are the oc- 355
casions when people believe something there is not there, or believe
something not there to be there, and Juan Shuliang[h] had already used
this experience to determine things. And so, if one has become ill
from dampness and beats drums [and sacrifices a pig],[27] then one is
sure to have the expense of wearing out the drums and losing the pig 360
but not yet have the good fortune to recover. Then, even if one is not
living in the south of Xiashou, one is no different from that person.

For everyone, the ability to know comes from human nature, and
what can be known are the underlying patterns of things. If one takes
the human ability to know that comes from human nature and uses 365
it to seek the underlying patterns of things that can be known, but
one has no point at which one will stop, then even with old age and
the end of one's years, one will not be able to cover them all. Even if
the things for which one has managed to string together their patterns are many million in number, it will still not suffice to comprise 370
all the changes of the myriad things, and so one will be the same as a
foolish person. Someone who in pursuing learning becomes old with

---

[26] Although he only mentions "stars" in general here, perhaps Xunzi has in mind the
specific practice of prognosticating by gauging the position of certain heavenly
bodies and constellations in the sky.

[27] The text here seems corrupt, and the addition of these words is based on parallel
texts as well as on what follows in the passage here. Beating drums and sacrificing
pigs was apparently common practice for driving away evil spirits thought to cause
disease.

a grown son, yet who is the same as a foolish person and still does not understand his mistake—such a one is called a reckless person.

375 And so, learning is precisely learning to have a stopping point.[28] Where does one stop it? I say: One stops it when one has reached utter sufficiency. What do I mean by "utter sufficiency?" I say: It is becoming a sage. The sage is one who completely carries out the proper relations, and the true king is one who completely carries out 380 the proper regulations. One in whom these two are complete can be the ultimate standard for all under Heaven. Thus, when the learner takes the sage and the true king as his teacher, he accordingly takes the regulations of the sage and true king as his model. He models himself after their models, so as to seek their guiding categories, and 385 so as to work at resembling their characters.

One who works toward these things is a well-bred man. One who has made himself like these things and is almost there is a gentleman. One who fully understands these things is a sage. And so, one who has intelligence but does not use it to deliberate about these things is 390 called frightening. One who has courage but does not use it to support these things is called villainous. One whose investigations are thorough but does not use it to distinguish these things is called subversive. One who is multitalented but does not use it to cultivate and promote these things is called cunning. One who can argue 395 keenly but does not use it to speak of these things is called an excessive talker.

A saying goes, "There are only two alternatives in the world: using what is wrong to investigate what is right, and using what is right to investigate what is wrong." This refers to whether one does or does 400 not accord with the regulations of a true king. Is there anyone in the world who can fail to take these as his lofty standard of correctness and yet still be able to distinguish between right and wrong and master the crooked and the straight? If one's practice does not distinguish between right and wrong, does not master the crooked and the 405 straight, does not differentiate order and chaos, and does not master the human Way, then being capable of it is of no benefit to people, and being incapable of it is no loss to people. One will simply master strange arguments and toy with bizarre claims so as to disturb and trip up others. Accordingly, such a one will vehemently maintain 410 what is wrong and make his tongue slick, toughen his hide and endure disgraceful conduct, lack any correctness and engage in license and arrogance, argue recklessly and pursue profit. These people do not like deference and yielding, they do not respect ritual and proper measure, but instead they like only to jostle and hassle one another. 415 These are the arguments of vile people and a disordered age, and now

---

[28] See 2.134–51.

the number of those mastering such arguments has become many indeed.

A saying goes, "If one minces words in conducting investigations and makes up statements about things in debating, the gentleman considers such a person base. Even if one is broadly learned and firm 420 in intention, but does not conform to the regulations of a true king, the gentleman still considers it base." This expresses my meaning. If doing these practices is of no help accomplishing things, and seeking these practices is of no help in attaining things, and worrying about these practices is of no help in bringing you closer to success, then 425 distance yourself from them and abandon them. Do not use them to harm yourself. Do not hold them in your breast for even a moment. Do not long for them when they pass before you. Do not care for them when they come your way. Have no pity for them in your heart. Act when the time is fitting. Respond when things come. As affairs 430 arise, distinguish them clearly. Then order and disorder and the permissible and the impermissible will be brilliantly clear.

Success lies in being secretive, and defeat lies in revealing things—an enlightened lord will have none of this attitude. Success lies in being outspoken, and defeat lies in hiding things—a benighted lord 435 will have none of this attitude.[29] Thus, if the lord of men is secretive, then dishonest words will come, and straight talk will be turned back. Petty men will draw near, and gentlemen will be put at a distance. The *Odes* says: "When one mistakes the dark for the bright, then foxes will flourish."[30] This is saying that when the superior is obscure then 440 his subordinates will be dangerous. If the lord of men is outspoken, then straight talk will come, and dishonest words will be turned back. Gentlemen will draw near, and petty men will be put at a distance. The *Odes* says, "It was radiantly bright below. It shone brilliantly above."[31] This is saying that when the superior is clear then his sub- 445 ordinates will be transformed.[32]

---

[29] Apparently, in Xunzi's time various people had argued that the ruler should be secretive and reveal himself as little as possible both to his ministers and to the common people. A very explicit expression of this idea is found in chap. 5 of the *Han Feizi*, though that piece was perhaps written after this one. For similar criticism of views that advocate secrecy for rulers, see 18.1–48 in this work.

[30] The poem does not appear in the received version of the *Odes*. These lines are rhymed in the original Chinese text.

[31] Mao #236. This poem is also quoted at 18.46 for similar purposes.

[32] Throughout this passage, there is an untranslatable play on the fact that the word *ming* 明 means both "clear," as in readily apparent to observation, and "bright," as in "smart" or "enlightened."

CHAPTER 22

Correct Naming[a]

In setting names for things, the later kings followed the Shang in names for punishments, followed the Zhou in names for official titles, and followed their rituals in names for cultural forms. In applying various names to the myriad things, they followed the set customs
5 and generally agreed usage of the various Xia states.[b] Villages in distant places with different customs followed along with these names and so were able to communicate.

    As for the ways the various names apply to people, that by which they are as they are at birth is called "human nature."[c] The close con-
10 nection of stimulus with response, which requires no effort but is so of itself, and which is produced by the harmonious operation of the nature, is also called "human nature." The feelings of liking and disliking, happiness and anger, and sadness and joy in one's nature are called the "dispositions." When there is a certain disposition and the
15 heart makes a choice on its behalf, this is called "deliberation." When the heart reflects and one's abilities act on it, this is called "deliberate effort." That which comes into being through accumulated reflection and training of one's abilities is also called "deliberate effort." Actions performed for the sake of profit are called "work." Actions performed
20 for the sake of *yi* are called "personal conduct." That by which people understand things is called the "understanding." When the understanding connects to things, this is called "knowledge." That by which people are able to do things is called "ability."[d] When ability connects to things, these are also called "abilities."[1] When the nature
25 is injured, this is called "illness." When one encounters unexpected circumstances, this is called "fate." These are the ways the various names apply to people. These are the ways the later kings set names for things.

    So when the kings established names, the names were fixed, and
30 the corresponding objects were thus distinguished. This way was followed, and the kings' intentions were thus made understood. They then carefully led the people to adhere to these things single-mindedly. Thus, they called it great vileness to mince words and recklessly create names such as to disorder the correct names and thereby con-

---

[1] I.e., when the potential to do something is manifested in a certain activity, it is called a particular ability (e.g., one is said to have the *ability* to drive when one performs the activities specific to that skill).

fuse the people and cause them to engage in much disputation and   35
litigation. This wrongdoing was considered to be just like the crime
of forging tallies and measures. Hence, none of their people dared
rely on making up strange names so as to disorder the correct names,
and so the people were honest. Since they were honest, they were easy
to employ, and since they were easy to employ, tasks were accom-   40
plished. Because none of the people dared rely on making up strange
names so as to disorder the correct names, they were unified in following the proper model of the Way and were diligent in following
commands. Because they were like this, the legacy of the kings was
long-lasting. To have such a long-lasting legacy and to achieve such   45
accomplishments is the height of good order. Such is what can be
accomplished by diligently preserving the agreed names.

Nowadays, the sage kings have passed away, and the preservation
of these names has become lax. Strange words have arisen, the names
and their corresponding objects are disordered, and the forms of   50
right and wrong are unclear. As a result, even officers who assiduously preserve the proper models and *ru* who assiduously recite the
proper order are also all thrown into chaos. If there arose a true king,
he would surely follow the old names in some cases and create new
names in other cases.[2] Thus, one must examine the reason for having   55
names, the proper means for distinguishing like and unlike, and the
essential points in establishing names.

When different forms make contact with the heart, they make each
other understood as different things. If the names and their corresponding objects[3] are tied together in a confused fashion, then the   60
distinction between noble and base will not be clear, and the like and
the unlike will not be differentiated. If this is so, then the problem of
intentions not being understood will surely happen, and the disaster
of affairs being thereby impeded and abandoned will surely occur.
Thus, the wise person draws differences and establishes names in   65
order to point out their corresponding objects. Most importantly, he
makes clear the distinction between noble and base, and more generally, he distinguishes the like and the unlike. When noble and base
are clearly distinguished, and like and unlike are differentiated, then
the problem of intentions not being understood will not happen, and   70
the disaster of affairs being thereby impeded and abandoned will not
occur. This is the reason for having names.

---

[2] A noteworthy alternative way of reading this line is proposed by the commentator
Wang Xianqian, who interprets it as saying, "If a true king were to arise, he would
surely follow along with the old names [that are still in use] and change back the
new [i.e., bad] names."

[3] Xunzi's word "object" (*shi* 實) appears to include both the meaning and referent of
a term, as distinguished by modern philosophers.

That being the case, then what does one follow and use to distinguish the same and the different? I say, one follows one's Heaven-given faculties. For all creatures belonging to the same category and having the same dispositions, their Heaven-given faculties cognize things in the same way. Thus, one compares similarities with another party and thereby has communication. This is the means by which one shares agreed-upon names so as to align people with one another. Form, color, and pattern are differentiated by the eyes. Notes, tones, high, low, tunings, pipes, and other strange sounds are differentiated by the ear. Sweet, bitter, salty, bland, piquant, sour, and other strange flavors are differentiated by the mouth. Fragrant, foul, flowery, rotten, putrid, sharp, sour, and other strange smells are differentiated by the nose. Pain, itch, cold, hot, slippery, sharp, light, and heavy are differentiated by the body.ᵉ Persuasions, reasons, happiness, anger, sorrow, joy, love, hate, and desire are differentiated by the heart.

The heart has the power to judge its awareness. If it judges its awareness, then by following along with the ears it is possible to know a sound, and by following along with the eyes one can know a form. However, judging awareness must await the Heaven-given faculties to appropriately encounter their respective kinds and only then can it work. If the five faculties encounter them but have no awareness,⁴ or if the heart judges among them but has no persuasive explanations [for its judgments], then everyone will say that such a person does not know. These are what one follows and uses to distinguish the same and the different. Only after doing this does one then follow it up by naming things.

One treats similar things as similar, and one treats different things as different. When a single word is sufficient to make oneself understood, then one uses a single word. When a single word is not sufficient to make oneself understood, then one combines words.⁵ When the single and combined words in no way contradict each other, then one considers them a group, and even though one groups them together, this will do no harm, for one understands how different objects are named differently.⁶ Thus, one causes different objects all to have different names, and this is something that one must not throw into disorder. Moreover, one causes different objects all to have the same name.⁷

---

⁴ For example, in the case of people who are blind or deaf.
⁵ For instance, when "horse" is not sufficient to indicate what one wants to talk about, then one uses "white horse."
⁶ That is, one groups "white horse" under "horse," and this is not problematic, because according to the senses (which Xunzi takes as the basis for naming above), a white horse still has the form of a horse. This is apparently his answer to the infamous claim by Gongsun Long that "a white horse is not a horse."
⁷ For example, both "horses" and "dogs" are also called "beasts."

Thus, even though the myriad things are very numerous, some- 110
times one desires to refer to them all together, and so one calls them
"things." "Things" is a case of large-scale group naming. By drawing
analogies, one groups things together, grouping and grouping, until
there is nothing more to group, and then one stops. Sometimes one
wishes to refer to them partially, and so one calls them "birds" and 115
"beasts." "Birds" and "beasts" are instances of large-scale differentiated naming. By drawing analogies, one differentiates things, differentiating and differentiating, until there is nothing more to differentiate, and then one stops.[8]

Names have no predetermined appropriateness. One forms agree- 120
ment in order to name things. Once the agreement is set and has
become custom, then they are called appropriate, and what differs
from the agreed usage is called inappropriate. Names have no predetermined objects. One forms agreement in order to name objects.
Once the agreement is set and has become custom, then they are 125
called names of objects.[9] Names do have a predetermined goodness.
If they are straightforward, simple, and do not conflict, then they are
called good names. Some things have a like appearance but reside in
unlike classes, and others have unlike appearances but reside in the
like class, and these two can be differentiated. For those which have 130
a like appearance but reside in unlike classes, even though they could
be combined into one class, they are called two separate objects. If
the appearance changes but the object does not become different so
as to belong to an unlike class, this is called a transformation. When
there is transformation without such difference, it is still called one 135
and the same object. These are what to rely upon in observing the
objects and determining their numbers.[10] This is the essential point
in establishing names, and the names established by the later kings
must not go unexamined.

Claims such as "To be insulted is not disgraceful,"[11] "The sage does 140
not love himself,"[12] and "To kill a robber is not to kill a man"[13] are
cases of confusion about the use of names leading to disordering
names. If one tests them against the reason why there are names, and
observes what happens when they are carried out thoroughly, then

---

[8] As I take it, Xunzi's point is that there are two functions of naming, grouping and
differentiating things, rather than two different kinds of names. This is also part of
his answer to paradoxical claims propounded by Gongsun Long and others.

[9] Xunzi's point seems to be that only after usage is set do the names have any meaning, rather than being mere sound.

[10] Xunzi here seems to be talking about identifying and individuating classes, rather
than identifying and individuating particular entities.

[11] This claim is attributed to Song Xing. See 18.454–551 for discussion.

[12] It is not known who maintained this claim.

[13] This claim was made by the Mohists.

145   one will be able to reject them. Claims such as "Mountains and gorges are level,"[14] "The desires of one's natural dispositions are few,"[15] "Fine meats are not any more flavorful,"[16] and "Great bells are not any more entertaining"[17] are cases of confusion about the use of objects leading to disordering names. If one tests them against the proper means for

150   distinguishing like and unlike, and observes what happens when they are thoroughly practiced, then one will be able to reject them. Claims such as [. . .][18] "Oxen and horses are not horses"[19] are cases of confusion about the use of names leading to disordering the objects. If one tests them against the agreement on names, using the fact that what

155   such people accept goes against what they reject, then one will be able to reject them. In every case of deviant sayings and perverse teachings that depart from the correct Way and recklessly innovate, they will belong to one of these three classes of confusion. Thus, the enlightened lord understands their kind and does not dispute with

160   such people.

    The people can easily be unified by means of the Way, but one should not try to share one's reasons with them. Hence, the enlightened lord controls them with his power, guides them with the Way, moves them with his orders, arrays them with his judgments, and

165   restrains them with his punishments. Thus, his people's transformation by the Way is spirit-like. What need has he for demonstrations[20] and persuasions?[f] Nowadays the sage kings have all passed away, the whole world is in chaos, and depraved teachings are arising. The gentleman has no power to control people, no punishments to restrain

170   them, and so he engages in demonstrations and persuasions.

    When objects are not understood, then one engages in naming. When the naming is not understood, then one tries to procure agreement. When the agreement is not understood, then one engages in persuasion. When the persuasion is not understood, then one en-

---

[14] This claim is attributed to Hui Shi.

[15] This claim is also attributed to Song Xing. See 18.552–87 for discussion.

[16] It is not known who maintained this claim.

[17] It is not known who maintained this claim. Some readers combine it with the previous claim as a single paradox.

[18] Here the text seems very corrupt. I have translated the clearest part of the sentence, and omitted the rest.

[19] It is uncertain who maintained this thesis, but its similarity to the famous claim that "a white horse is not a horse" made by Gongsun Long suggests that it might be his also.

[20] The word here is *bian* 辨, which literally means "to discriminate among things." This character was interchangeable with another, also read *bian* 辯, which means "to argue, dispute." The text seems to play on a fusion of these senses in the idea that true differences between things will be presented and defended through argument. Therefore, I have rendered it "demonstration" to convey the sense both of pointing out differences and of arguing for a position.

gages in demonstration. Thus, procuring agreement, naming, dem-   175
onstration, and persuasion are some of the greatest forms of useful
activity, and are the beginning of kingly works. When a name is heard
and the corresponding object is understood, this is usefulness in
names. When they are accumulated and form a pattern, this is beauty
in names. When one obtains both their usefulness and beauty, this is   180
called understanding names. Names are the means by which one arranges and accumulates objects. Sentences combine the names of
different objects so as to discuss a single idea. Persuasion and demonstration use fixed names of objects so as to make clear the proper
ways for acting and remaining still. Procuring agreement and naming   185
are the functions of demonstration and persuasion. Demonstration
and persuasion are the heart's way of representing the Way. The heart
is the craftsman and overseer of the Way. The Way is the warp and
pattern of good order. When the heart fits with the Way, when one's
persuasions fit with one's heart, when one's words fit one's persua-   190
sions, then one will name things correctly and procure agreement,
will base oneself on the true disposition of things and make them
understood, will discriminate among things without going to excess,
and will extend by analogy the categories of things without violating
them. When listening to cases, one will accord with good form. When   195
engaging in demonstration, one will cover thoroughly all the reasons.
One will use the true Way to discriminate what is vile just like drawing out the carpenter's line in order to grasp what is curved and what
is straight. Thus, deviant sayings will not be able to cause disorder,
and the hundred schools will have nowhere to hide.   200
 One kind of person is brilliant enough to listen to all cases, but has
no combative or arrogant countenance. He has generosity enough to
extend to all sides, but does not make a display of his virtue in his
appearance. If his persuasions are successful, then all under Heaven
is set right. If his persuasions are not successful, then he makes clear   205
his way but lives in obscurity—such are the persuasions and demonstrations of the sage. The *Odes* says:

> Full of refinement and nobility,
> Like a jade tablet or scepter is he,
> So lovely to hear and lovely to see.   210
> The contented and tranquil gentleman
> Serves as a model universally.[21]

This expresses my meaning.
 Another kind of person obtains the proper measure in deference
and yielding. He follows the order of elder and younger. He does not   215

---

[21] See Mao #252. The quotation here is not exactly the same as the Mao text.

speak of forbidden things. He does not issue inauspicious words. He engages in persuasions with a heart that is *ren*. He listens with a heart eager to learn. He engages in demonstrations with a heart that avoids prejudice. He is not moved by the prospect of ill repute among the
220 masses. He is not controlled by the preferences of his audience's eyes and ears. He is not bought out by the power and position of those who are noble. He does not take help from the words of those who spread perverse doctrines. Thus, he is able to dwell in the Way and not be of two minds about it. If he is reviled, he will not be wrested
225 from his purpose. If he is profited, he will not fall into depravity. He values what is unprejudiced and correct and he regards vulgar contentiousness as base. Such are the demonstrations and persuasions of the well-bred man and the gentleman. The *Odes* says:

> As the long night is passing by slowly,
230 > I think long whether I acted wrongly.
> I lapsed not from the ways of high antiquity,
> Nor did I deviate from ritual and *yi*.
> So why should others' words be of concern to me?[22]

This expresses my meaning.
235 The words of a gentleman are far-reaching yet refined. They are fervent but conform to the proper categories. They have gradations and yet are well organized. He is one who sets straight his names and makes fitting his terms in order to work at clarifying his intentions and thoughts. For him, names and terms are the emissaries of his
240 thoughts and intentions. When they are sufficient to communicate with others, then he adopts them. To use them recklessly is vile. Thus, when the names he uses are sufficient to indicate their objects, and the terms he uses are sufficient to make apparent his central standard, then he adopts them. To go beyond this is called being arcane. That
245 is something the gentleman disdains, but the foolish person adopts it as his treasure. Thus, the words of the foolish person are hurried and rough. They are agitated and have no proper categories. They are profuse and jumbled. He is one who makes his words seductive, muddies his terms, and has no deep concern for his intentions and
250 thoughts. Thus, he exhaustively sets out his words yet has no central standard. He works laboriously and has no accomplishments. He is greedy but has no fame.
And so, the teachings of the wise person are such that if one ponders them, it is easy to understand them. If one carries them out, it is
255 easy to be secure. If one upholds them, it is easy to maintain one's

---

[22] This poem does not appear in the received text of the *Odes*. See the quotation earlier at 17.114–16.

stand. When one follows them completely, then one is sure to get what one likes and to avoid what one hates. The teachings of the foolish person are the opposite of this. The *Odes* says:

> If either you were a ghost or you were a *yu*,[23]
> Getting at you would be impossible to do.   260
> But you possess a shameful human face and eyes,
> And you show others a lack of correctness, too.
> So I have now created this good song I sing,
> To correct your ways, which are faithless and untrue.[24,g]

This expresses my meaning.   265

All those who say that good order must await the elimination of desires are people who lack the means to guide desire and cannot handle the mere having of desires. All those who say good order must await the lessening of desires are people who lack the means to restrain desire and cannot handle abundance of desires.[25] Having de-   270 sires and lacking desires fall under two different kinds, namely being alive and being dead, not order and disorder. Having many desires and having few desires also fall under different kinds, namely the numbers of people's dispositions, not order and disorder.

The occurrence of desires does not wait upon the permissibility of   275 fulfilling them, but those who seek to fulfill them follow what they approve of.[26] That the occurrence of desires does not wait upon the permissibility of fulfilling them is something which is received from Heaven. That those who seek to fulfill them follow what they approve of is something which is received from the heart. When a single desire   280 received from Heaven is controlled by many things received from the

---

[23] According to legend, the *yu* was a kind of monster that lived in water and would spit sand with enough force to kill people.

[24] Mao #199. Compare the use of this poem at 8.162–67.

[25] It is not clear exactly whom Xunzi has in mind here. However, the idea that one should eliminate desires appears in the *Daodejing* (e.g., chap. 57), and the idea that one should lessen desires appears in *Mencius* (7B35), so perhaps these are among the intended targets of Xunzi's criticism.

[26] This section is difficult to translate, because the word *ke* 可 is used multiple times in senses that do not always go consistently into English easily, and it is not clear that Xunzi is using it consistently in the first place. When used as a verb, I have rendered it as "approve." When used adjectivally or adverbially in this section, I have usually rendered it as "permissible" (where I take it that Xunzi really intends something like "should be approved"). *Ke* also has the sense of "possible [to do]," and in certain places, it seems necessary to take it this way (which I have rendered as "can" or "cannot"). One could try to use this latter sense throughout, substituting "possible" for "permissible" and "think possible" for "approve," which would give the argument a very different sense, but it seems to me that such a reading is less preferable given the overall context.

heart, then it will certainly be difficult to classify it as something received from Heaven.

285 Life is what people most desire, and death is what people most despise.[27] However, when people let go of life and accomplish their own death, this is not because they do not desire life and instead desire death. Rather, it is because they do not approve of living in these circumstances, but do approve of dying in these circumstances. Thus, when the desire is excessive but the action does not match it, this is 290 because the heart prevents it. If what the heart approves of conforms to the proper patterns, then even if the desires are many, what harm would they be to good order? When the desire is lacking but the action surpasses it, this is because the heart compels it. If what the heart approves of misses the proper patterns, then even if the desires are 295 few, how would it stop short of chaos? Thus, order and disorder reside in what the heart approves of, they are not present in the desires from one's dispositions. If you do not seek for them where they reside, and instead seek for them where they are not present, then even if you should say, "I have grasped them," you have simply missed 300 them.

Human nature is the accomplishment of Heaven. The dispositions are the substance of the nature. The desires are the responses of the dispositions to things. Viewing the objects of desire as permissible to obtain and seeking them are what the dispositions cannot avoid. 305 Deeming something permissible and guiding one are what the understanding must provide. Thus, even were one a gatekeeper, the desires cannot be eliminated, because they are the necessary equipment of the nature. Even if one were the Son of Heaven, one's desires cannot be completely satisfied. Even though the desires cannot be com- 310 pletely satisfied, one can get close to complete satisfaction. Even though desires cannot be eliminated, one's seeking can be regulated. Even though what is desired cannot be completely obtained, the seeker can approach complete fulfillment. Even though desires cannot be eliminated, when what is sought is not obtained, one who is 315 reflective desires to regulate his seeking. When the Way advances, then one approaches complete fulfillment. When it retreats, then one regulates one's seeking. In all under Heaven there is nothing like it. Among all people, no one fails to follow that which they approve and to abandon that which they do not approve. For a person to know 320 that there is nothing as great as the Way and yet not follow the Way— there are no such cases. Suppose there were a person who did not have much desire for heading south, but did have no little dislike for heading north. How would it be that because of the impossibility of going completely south, he would depart from the south and instead

[27] See 16.218.

go north? Now in the case of people who have not much desire for 325
something, but do have no little dislike for something else, how
would they, because of the impossibility of completely fulfilling their
desires, depart from the way of obtaining their desires and instead
take what they dislike? Thus, if one approves of the Way and follows
it, how would lessening things lead to disorder? If one does not ap- 330
prove of the Way and departs from it, then how would increasing
things lead to order? Thus, those who are wise judge the Way and that
is all, and the things the lesser schools wish for in their prized doctrines will all decline.

In every selection that people make, the object of their desire does 335
not come pure.[28] In what they reject, their object of dislike does not
go away pure.[29] Thus, for every action people make, they must come
prepared with a balance. If a set of scales is not correct, then what is
heavy will hang in the raised position, and people will think it is
light. Or what is light will hang in the low position, and people will 340
think it is heavy. This is how people become confused about light and
heavy.[30] If people's balance is not correct, then disaster may be attached to what they desire, but people will think it is good fortune.
Or good fortune may be attached to what they dislike, but people
will think it is disaster. This is likewise how people become confused 345
about disaster and good fortune. The Way is the correct balance from
ancient times to the present. If one departs from the Way and instead,
looking within, chooses based on himself alone, then he will not
know to what disaster and good fortune are attached.

When a person who engages in trade exchanges one for one, peo- 350
ple say he has neither gained nor lost. If he exchanges one for two,
people say he has not lost, but has rather gained. If he exchanges two
for one, people say he has not gained, but has rather lost. Those who
calculate take what they consider to be the greater, and those who
plan follow what they approve of. People do not exchange two for 355
one, because they understand the numbers. If one goes forth following the Way, then it is like exchanging one for two—what loss would
there be? If one departs from the Way and instead, looking within,
chooses based on oneself alone, then this is like exchanging two for
one—what gain would there be? Given the chance to exchange the 360
fulfillment of a hundred years' accumulated desires for a moment's
satisfaction, if one nevertheless does it, this is because one does not
understand the numbers. Let us try to look deeper into the hidden
and difficult-to-uncover aspects of this.

---

[28] I.e., it also brings things they dislike.
[29] I.e., it also takes it with things they desire.
[30] The words "heavy" (*zhong* 重) and "light" (*qing* 輕) were also used in classical Chinese to mean "important" and "unimportant," so this line has broader implications.

365   Anyone who in his intentions thinks little of good order will greatly value material goods. Anyone who greatly values material goods on the outside will be worried on the inside.[31] Anyone whose conduct departs from good order will be endangered on the outside. Anyone who is endangered on the outside will be fearful inside. If one's heart

370 is worried and fearful, then even if one's mouth is stuffed with grass-fed and grain-fed meats, one will not know their flavor. Even if one's ears hear bells and drums, one will not know the sound. Even if one's eyes see beautifully embroidered emblems, one will not know their shape. Even if one wears light and warm clothing and sits on sumptu-

375 ous mats, one will not know their comfort. Thus one can be confronted with the finest of the myriad things and yet not be able to feel satisfaction. Even supposing someone gets to ask about it and the person claims to be satisfied, still the feeling will not depart. Thus, one may be confronted with the finest of the myriad things and yet

380 will be full of worry. One may possess all the most beneficial of the myriad things and yet be full of hurt. Is this the way to seek goods? To nourish life? To foster longevity?

    Thus, such a one wants to nourish his desires but abandons fulfilling his dispositions. He wants to nourish his nature but endangers

385 his body. He wants to nourish his happiness but attacks his heart. He wants to nourish his fame but makes his conduct chaotic. As for one who is like this, even if he is enfeoffed as a feudal lord or given the title of lord, he is no different than a common robber. Even if he rides in a chariot and wears a ceremonial cap, he is no different than a

390 convict with feet amputated.[32] This is called making oneself a servant to things.[33]

    If one's heart is peaceful and happy, then even if the sights are inferior to what is simply plain, they are still enough to nourish the eyes. Even if the sounds are inferior to what is simply plain, they are

395 enough to nourish the ears. Greens for food and vegetable stew are still enough to nourish the palate. Clothes made from coarse cloth and shoes made with coarse thread are still enough to nourish one's body. A thatched hut or storehouse for one's home and dwelling, dried reeds for one's bedding, and at most a single low table and mat

400 are still enough to nourish one's physical form.[34] Thus, even while lacking the finest of the myriad things, one can still nourish one's joy, and even while lacking a position of power and eminence, one can

---

[31] This is presumably so because external goods are not under one's complete control, and in the process of getting them one may have made certain enemies, about whose vengeance one now has to worry.

[32] I.e., because he must live in constant fear and worry, he lives the life of a punished criminal.

[33] Compare this and the following paragraphs with Xunzi's remarks at 2.95–100.

[34] The text here seems corrupt and the translation is tentative.

still nourish one's fame. If one takes a person like this and gives him the whole empire in addition, his actions on behalf of all under Heaven will be numerous, while his pursuits of his own individual joy 405 will be few. This is called valuing oneself and making things one's servants.

Speeches without proof, untested actions, and unprecedented plans—the gentleman is careful of all such things.

CHAPTER 23

Human Nature Is Bad

People's nature is bad. Their goodness is a matter of deliberate effort. Now people's nature is such that they are born with a fondness for profit in them. If they follow along with this, then struggle and con-tention will arise, and yielding and deference will perish therein. They are born with feelings of hate and dislike in them. If they follow along with these, then cruelty and villainy will arise, and loyalty and trust-worthiness will perish therein. They are born with desires of the eyes and ears, a fondness for beautiful sights and sounds. If they follow along with these, then lasciviousness and chaos will arise, and ritual and *yi*, proper form and order, will perish therein. Thus, if people fol-low along with their inborn dispositions and obey their nature, they are sure to come to struggle and contention, turn to disrupting social divisions and order, and end up becoming violent. So, it is necessary to await the transforming influence of teachers and models and the guidance of ritual and *yi*, and only then will they come to yielding and deference, turn to proper form and order, and end up becoming controlled.[1] Looking at it in this way, it is clear that people's nature is bad, and their goodness is a matter of deliberate effort.

Thus, crooked wood must await steaming and straightening on the shaping frame, and only then does it become straight. Blunt metal must await honing and grinding, and only then does it become sharp.[2] Now since people's nature is bad, they must await teachers and proper models, and only then do they become correct. They must obtain ritual and *yi*, and only then do they become well ordered. Now without teachers or proper models for people, they will be deviant, dangerous, and not correct. Without ritual and *yi*, they will be unruly, chaotic, and not well ordered. In ancient times, the sage kings saw that because people's nature is bad, they were deviant, dangerous, and not correct, unruly, chaotic, and not well ordered. Therefore, for their sake they set up ritual and *yi*, and established proper models

---

[1] Here and elsewhere, this chapter deploys two terms in rapid succession, *li* 理 and *zhi* 治, which both mean "order" or "well ordered," and their close proximity makes it difficult to translate the text without making it sound as if Xunzi is simply repeating himself. In such cases, I have kept *li* 理 as "order," while rendering *zhi* 治 as "con-trolled," in the sense of disciplined restraint. *Zhi* 治 can also carry the connotation of good government in particular, though that sense seems less relevant in the instances where *li* 理 and *zhi* 治 are closely juxtaposed. When not so juxtaposed, both *li* 理 and *zhi* 治 have been rendered here as "order" or "well ordered," depending on context.

[2] See 1.7–9. Also compare Gaozi's metaphors in *Mencius* 6A1.

and measures. They did this in order to straighten out and beautify people's inborn dispositions and nature and thereby correct them, and in order to train and transform people's inborn dispositions and nature and thereby guide them, so that for the first time they all came to order and conformed to the Way. Among people of today, those 35 who are transformed by teachers and proper models, who accumulate culture and learning, and who make ritual and *yi* their path, become gentlemen. Those who give rein to their nature and inborn dispositions, who take comfort in being utterly unrestrained, and who violate ritual and *yi*, become petty men. Looking at it in this way, it is 40 clear that people's nature is bad, and their goodness is a matter of deliberate effort.

Mencius says: When people engage in learning, this manifests the goodness of their nature. I say: This is not so. This is a case of not attaining knowledge of people's nature and of not inspecting clearly 45 the division between people's nature and their deliberate efforts. In every case, the nature of a thing is the accomplishment of Heaven. It cannot be learned. It cannot be worked at. Ritual and *yi* are what the sage produces. They are things that people become capable of through learning, things that are achieved through working at them. 50 Those things in people which cannot be learned and cannot be worked at are called their "nature." Those things in people which they become capable of through learning and which they achieve through working at them are called their "deliberate efforts." This is the division between nature and deliberate effort.[3] 55

Now people's nature is such that their eyes can see, and their ears can hear. The brightness by which they see does not depart from their eyes, and the acuity by which they hear does not depart from their ears. Their eyes are simply bright, and their ears are simply acute. One does not learn this brightness. Mencius says: people's nature is 60 good, but they all wind up losing their nature and original state. I say: if it is like this, then he is simply mistaken. People's nature is such that they are born and then depart from their original simplicity, depart from their original material; they are sure to lose them. Looking at it in this way, it is clear that people's nature is bad. The so- 65 called goodness of people's nature would mean for one not to depart from one's original simplicity and instead beautify it, not to depart from one's original material and instead make use of it. It would be to cause the relation of one's original simplicity and original material to beauty, and the relation of the heart's thoughts to goodness, to be 70 like the way the brightness by which one sees does not depart from one's eyes, and the acuity by which one hears does not depart from

[3] See Xunzi's explanations at 22.8–18.

one's ears. Thus I have said: "The eyes are simply bright and the ears are simply keen."

75 Now people's nature is such that when hungry they desire satiety, when cold they desire warmth, and when tired they desire rest. This is people's inborn disposition and nature. Now if people are hungry and see food but do not dare to eat first, that will be because there are some to whom they will give way. If people are tired but do not dare 80 to seek rest, that will be because there are some for whom they will substitute themselves. When a son gives way for his father, a younger brother gives way for his older brother, a son stands in for his father, or a younger brother stands in for his older brother, these two kinds of conduct both go against one's nature and are at odds with one's 85 inborn dispositions. Nevertheless, they are the way of a filial child, and the proper form and order contained in ritual and *yi*. Thus, if one follows along with one's inborn dispositions and nature, then one will not defer and give way. If one defers and gives way, then one is at odds with one's inborn dispositions and nature. Looking at it in 90 this way, it is clear that people's nature is bad, and their goodness is a matter of deliberate effort.

Someone asks: if people's nature is bad, then from what are ritual and *yi* produced? I answer: In every case, ritual and *yi* are produced from the deliberate effort of the sage; they are not produced from 95 people's nature. Thus, when the potter mixes up clay and makes vessels, the vessels are produced from the deliberate efforts of the craftsman; they are not produced from people's nature. Thus, when the craftsman carves wood and makes utensils, the utensils are produced from the deliberate efforts of the craftsman; they are not produced 100 from people's nature. The sage accumulates reflections and thoughts and practices deliberate efforts and reasoned activities in order to produce ritual and *yi* and in order to establish proper models and measures.[4] So, ritual and *yi* and proper models and measures are produced from the deliberate efforts of the sage; they are not produced 105 from people's nature.

As for the way that the eyes like pretty colors, the ears like beautiful sounds, the mouth likes good flavors, the heart likes what is beneficial, and the bones and flesh like what is comfortable—these are produced from people's inborn dispositions and nature. These are 110 things that come about of themselves in response to stimulation,

---

[4] There is a noteworthy alternative way of reading this line, which construes it as being in the past tense, and with a plural subject: "Sages accumulated reflections and thoughts and practiced deliberate efforts and reasoned activities. . . ." This reading would fit well with the suggestion of Nivison (1996) that Xunzi's view can allow for a series of sages to produce ritual and *yi* by working in a piecemeal fashion over time, perhaps without even being fully aware of what they were doing. See also Van Norden (2011, pp. 169–70).

things that do not need to await being worked at before being produced. Those things that are not immediate responses to stimulation, that must await being worked at before they are so, are said to be produced from <u>deliberate effort</u>. These are the things that nature and deliberate effort produce, and their different signs.   115

So, the sage transforms his nature and establishes deliberate effort. In establishing deliberate effort, he produces ritual and *yi*. In producing ritual and *yi* he institutes proper models and measures. Thus, ritual and *yi* and proper models and measures are produced by the sage. Thus, that in which the sage is like the masses, that in which he   120
is no different than the masses, is his nature. That in which he differs from and surpasses the masses is his deliberate efforts.

Liking what is beneficial and desiring gain are people's inborn dispositions and nature. Suppose there were brothers who had some property to divide, and that they followed the fondness for benefit   125
and desire for gain in their inborn dispositions and nature. If they were to do so, then the brothers would conflict and contend with each other for it. However, let them be transformed by the proper form and order contained in ritual and *yi*. If so, then they would even give it over to their countrymen. Thus, following along with inborn dis-   130
positions and nature, even brothers will struggle with each other. If transformed by ritual and *yi*, then they will even give it over to their countrymen.[5]

In every case where people desire to become good, it is because their nature is bad. The person who has little longs to have much. The   135
person of narrow experience longs to be broadened. The ugly person longs to be beautiful. The poor person longs to be rich. The lowly person longs to be noble. That which one does not have within oneself, one is sure to seek for outside. Thus, when one is rich, one does not long for wealth. When one is noble, one does not long for power.   140
That which one has within oneself, one is sure not to go outside oneself for it. Looking at it in this way, people desire to become good because their nature is bad.

Now people's nature is originally without ritual and *yi*. Thus, they must force themselves to engage in learning and seek to possess them.   145
Their nature does not know of ritual and *yi*, and so they must think and reflect and seek to know them. So, going only by what they have from birth, people lack ritual and *yi* and do not know of ritual and *yi*. If people lack ritual and *yi*, then they will be chaotic. If they do not know of ritual and *yi*, then they will be unruly. So, going only by   150
what they have from birth, unruliness and disorder are within them.

---

[5] This seems to be a reference to the story of Bo Yi and Shu Qi, brothers and heirs to the throne. They could not settle who should rule, though both were willing to give up their claim to rule, so they fled the state altogether.

Looking at it in this way, it is clear that people's nature is bad, and their goodness is a matter of deliberate effort.

Mencius says: people's nature is good. I say: this is not so. In every
155   case, both in ancient times and in the present, what everyone under Heaven calls good is being correct, ordered, peaceful, and controlled. What they call bad is being deviant, dangerous, unruly, and chaotic. This is the division between good and bad. Now does he really think that people's nature is originally correct, ordered, peaceful, and con-
160   trolled? Then what use would there be for sage kings? What use for ritual and *yi*? Even though there might exist sage kings and ritual and *yi*, whatever could these add to its correct, ordered, peaceful, and controlled state? Now that is not the case, because people's nature is bad. Thus, in ancient times the sage kings saw that because their na-
165   ture is bad, people were deviant, dangerous, and not correct, unruly, chaotic, and not well-ordered. Therefore, for the people's sake they set up the power of lords and superiors in order to oversee them. They made ritual and *yi* clear in order to transform them. They set up laws and standards in order to make them well ordered. They multi-
170   plied punishments and fines in order to restrain them. As a result, they caused all under Heaven to come to order and conform to goodness. Such are the ordering influence of the sage kings and the transformative effects of ritual and *yi*.

Now suppose one were to try doing away with the power of lords
175   and superiors, try doing without the transformation from ritual and *yi*, try doing away with the order of laws and standards, try doing without the restraint of punishments and fines, then relying on these things and observing how all the people of the world treat each other. If it were like this, then the strong would harm the weak and take
180   from them. The many would tyrannize the few and shout them down. One would not have to wait even a moment for all under Heaven to arrive at unruliness and chaos and perish. Looking at it in this way, it is clear that people's nature is bad, and that their goodness is a matter of deliberate effort.

185   So, those who are good at speaking of ancient times are sure to have some measure from the present. Those who are good at speaking of Heaven are sure to have some evidence from among mankind. For any discourse, one values it if things conform to its distinctions, and if it matches the test of experience. Thus, one sits and propounds
190   it, but when one stands up then one can implement it, and when one unfolds it then one can put it into practice. Now Mencius says: people's nature is good. Nothing conforms to his distinctions, and this does not match the test of experience. He sits and propounds it, but when he stands up then he cannot implement it, and when he unfolds
195   it then he cannot put it into practice. Is his error not great indeed! Thus, if human nature is good, then one may do away with the sage

kings and put ritual and *yi* to rest. If human nature is bad, then one simply must side with the sage kings and honor ritual and *yi*.

Thus, the press frame originated because of crooked wood. The ink-line arose because of things that are not straight. Lords and supe- 200 riors were established and ritual and *yi* were made clear because of the fact that human nature is bad. Looking at it in this way, it is clear that people's nature is bad, and that their goodness is a matter of deliberate effort. Straight wood does not await the press frame in order to become straight, because its nature is to be straight. Crooked 205 wood must await the press frame and steaming and bending and only then will it be straight, because it is by nature not straight. Now people's nature is bad, and so they must certainly await the ordering influence of sage kings and the transformative effects of ritual and *yi* and only then will they all come to order and conform to goodness. 210 Looking at it in this way, it is clear that people's nature is bad, and that their goodness is a matter of deliberate effort.

Someone asks: ritual and *yi* and the accumulation of deliberate effort are people's nature, and that is why the sage is able to produce them. I answer: this is not so. The potter mixes clay and produces 215 tiles. Yet, how could the clay of the tiles be the potter's nature? The craftsman carves wood and makes utensils. Yet, how could the wood of the utensils be the craftsman's nature? The relationship of the sage to ritual and *yi* can be compared to mixing up clay and producing things. So, how could ritual and *yi* and the accumulation of deliber- 220 ate effort be people's original nature? In every aspect of human nature, the nature of Yao and Shun was one and the same as that of Jie and Robber Zhi. The nature of the gentleman is one and the same as that of the petty man. Now will you take ritual and *yi* and the accumulation of deliberate effort to be a matter of human nature? Then 225 for what do you value Yao and Shun? For what do you value the gentleman? Everything that one values in Yao and Shun and the gentleman is due to the fact that they were able to transform their nature and to establish deliberate effort. In establishing deliberate effort, they produced ritual and *yi*. Thus, the relationship of the sage to rit- 230 ual and *yi* and the accumulation of deliberate effort is like mixing up clay and producing things. Looking at it in this way, then how could ritual and *yi* and the accumulation of deliberate effort be people's nature? What one finds base in Jie and Robber Zhi and the petty man is due to the fact that they follow along with their inborn dispositions 235 and nature and take comfort in utter lack of restraint, so that they come to greed for profit and to struggle and contention. Thus, it is clear that people's nature is bad, and that their goodness is a matter of deliberate effort. Heaven did not favor Zengzi, Minzi Qian, and Xiao Yi and exclude the masses. Then why is it that only Zengzi, 240 Minzi Qian, and Xiao Yi were rich in the true substance of filial

piety and were perfect in their reputation for filial piety? It is because they exerted themselves to the utmost in ritual and *yi*. Heaven does not favor people of Qi and Lu and exclude the people of Qin. Then
245 why is it that with regard to the *yi* between father and son, and the distinction between husband and wife, the people of Qin are not as good at filial reverence and respectful good form as those of Qi and Lu? It is because the people of Qin follow along with their inborn dispositions and nature, take comfort in utter lack of restraint, and
250 are lax in regard to ritual and *yi*. How could it be because their nature is different?

Anyone on the streets can become a Yu. How do I mean this? I say: that by which Yu was Yu was because he was *ren*, *yi*, lawful, and correct. Thus, *ren*, *yi*, lawfulness, and correctness have patterns that can
255 be known and can be practiced. However, people on the streets all have the material for knowing *ren*, *yi*, lawfulness, and correctness, and they all have the equipment for practicing *ren*, *yi*, lawfulness, and correctness. Thus, it is clear that they can become a Yu. Now if *ren*, *yi*, lawfulness, and correctness originally had no patterns that could be
260 known or practiced, then even Yu would not know *ren*, *yi*, lawfulness, and correctness and could not practice *ren*, *yi*, lawfulness, and correctness. Shall we suppose that people on the streets originally do not have the material to know *ren*, *yi*, lawfulness, and correctness, and that they originally do not have the equipment for practicing *ren*, *yi*,
265 lawfulness, and correctness? If so, then within the family, people on the streets could not know the *yi* of father and son, and outside the family, they could not know the proper relations of lord and minister. This is not so. Now it is the case that anyone on the streets can know the *yi* of father and son within the family, and can know the proper
270 relations of lord and minister outside the family. Thus, it is clear that the material for understanding these things and the equipment for practicing them is present in people on the streets. Now if people on the streets were to use their material for understanding these things and the equipment for practicing them to base themselves upon the
275 knowable patterns and practicable aspects of *ren* and *yi*, then is it clear that anyone on the streets could become a Yu. Now if people on the streets were to submit themselves to study and practice learning, if they were to concentrate their hearts and make single-minded their intentions, if they were to ponder, query, and thoroughly investi-
280 gate—then if they add to this days upon days and connect to this long period of time, if they accumulate goodness without stopping, then they will break through to spirit-like powers and understanding, and will form a triad with Heaven and Earth.

Thus, becoming a sage is something that people achieve through
285 accumulation. Someone says: sageliness is achieved through accumulation, but why is it that not all can accumulate thus? I say, they can

do it, but they cannot be made to do it. Thus, the petty man can become a gentleman, but is not willing to become a gentleman. The gentleman can become a petty man, but is not willing to become a petty man. It has never been that the petty man and gentleman are incapable of becoming each other. However, the reason they do not become each other is that they can do so but cannot be made to do so. Thus, it is the case that anyone on the streets can become a Yu, but it is not necessarily the case that anyone on the streets will be able to become a Yu. Even if one is not able to become a Yu, this does not harm the fact that one could become a Yu. One's feet can walk everywhere under Heaven. Even so, there has not yet been anyone who has been able to walk everywhere under Heaven. It has never been that craftsmen, carpenters, farmers, and merchants cannot do each other's business. However, none have ever been able to do each other's business. Looking at it in this way, then one is not always able to do what one can do. Even if one is not able to do it, this is no harm to the fact that one could do it. Thus, the difference between being able and unable, and can and cannot is far indeed. It is clear, then, that [the gentleman and petty man] can become one another.

Yao asked Shun, "What are people's inborn dispositions like?" Shun answered, "People's inborn dispositions are most unlovely! Why ask about them? When one has a wife and son, then one's filial piety to one's parents declines. When one's appetites and desires are fulfilled, then one's faithfulness to friends declines. When one's rank and salary are full, then one's loyalty to one's lord declines. People's inborn dispositions? People's inborn dispositions? They are most unlovely. Why ask about them? Only the worthy man is not like that."

There is the understanding of the sage, there is the understanding of the well-bred man and gentleman, there is the understanding of the petty man, and there is the understanding of the slavish man. For one sort of person, even when he speaks much, he displays proper form and accords with the proper categories of things. He can debate all day long the basis for his claims, and throughout numerous twists and myriad changes his guiding categories remain one and the same—such is the understanding of the sage.

For another sort of person, even when he speaks only a little, he is straightforward yet reserved in his use of words. When he debates, he conforms to the proper model as surely as though being regulated by a carpenter's ink-line—such is the understanding of the well-bred man and the gentleman.

For another sort of person, his speech is careless, and his conduct is disorderly. In his handling of affairs there is much that is cause for regret—such is the understanding of the petty man.

Another sort of person is hasty and reckless and abides by no proper categories. He has assorted abilities and wide experience but

does not put them to good use. He is quick with analysis and refined and easy in speech, but does not worry about what he says. He takes no care for right and wrong and does not judge between the straight
335 and the crooked. He takes only putting himself on the side of those who beat out others as his intention—such is the understanding of the slavish man.

There is the highest kind of courage, there is the middle kind of courage, and there is the lowest kind of courage.[6] For one kind of
340 person, there is a central standard for the whole world, and he dares to establish himself upon it. The former kings had a certain way, and he dares to carry out his understanding of it. Above, he does not follow along with the lords of a chaotic age. Below, he does not conform to the people of a chaotic age. He considers no impoverishment or
345 hard times to follow from affairs involving *ren*. He considers no wealth or honor to follow from affairs lacking *ren*. If the world recognizes him, then he wishes to share the world's pain and joy over things. If the world does not recognize him, then independently he stands alone between Heaven and Earth and does not fear. Such is
350 the highest kind of courage.

Another kind of person practices the rituals reverently, and his thoughts are restrained. He values following and being faithful to this, and he takes material goods and wealth lightly. He dares to promote and elevate those who are worthy. He dares to pull out and
355 dismiss those who are unworthy. Such is the middle kind of courage.

Another kind of person takes his own character lightly but gives much weight to material goods. He takes comfort in what leads to disaster and then seeks widely to free himself and improperly evades
360 the consequences. He takes no care for how right and wrong and what is so and what is not so are truly disposed. He makes it his sole intention to put himself on the side of those who beat out others— such is the lowest kind of courage.

Fanruo and Jushi were great bows of ancient times. However, if
365 they had not been set on the bow maker's press frame, then they would not have been able to become straight on their own. The sword Cong which belonged to Duke Huan, Jue which belonged to the Grand Duke, Lu which belonged to King Wen, Hu which belonged to Lord Zhuang, Ganjiang and Moye which belonged to Helü, along
370 with Jujue and Pilü—these were all great blades of ancient times. However, if no one had honed them, then they would not have been able to be sharp. If no one wielded them, then they would not have been able to slice anything. Hua Liu, Qi Ji, Xian Li, and Lü'er—these were all great horses of ancient times. However, one had to have the

[6] Compare the discussion of courage at 4.62–77.

control of bit and bridle in front, and the threat of whip and prod   375
behind, and add to that the driving of Zao Fu, and only then could
they go a thousand *li* in a single day.

As for people, even if they had a fine nature and inborn substance
and their hearts were keenly discriminating and wise, they would still
need to seek worthy teachers to serve, and choose worthy friends to   380
befriend. If you obtain a worthy teacher to serve, then what you hear
will be the ways of Yao, Shun, Yu, and Tang. If you obtain a worthy
friend to befriend, then what you see will be conduct that is loyal,
trustworthy, respectful, and deferential. Then you will make daily
progress toward *ren* and *yi* and you will not even realize it. That is due   385
to what you rub up against. Now if you live alongside people who are
not good, then what you hear will be trickery, deception, dishonesty,
and fraud. What you see will be conduct that is dirty, arrogant, perverse, deviant, and greedy. Moreover, you will suffer punishment and
execution, and you will not even realize it is upon you. That is due to   390
what you rub up against. A saying goes, "If you do not know your
son, observe his friends. If you do not know your lord, observe his
companions." Everything depends on what you rub up against! Everything depends on what you rub up against!

CHAPTER 24

The Gentleman

The Son of Heaven has no partner.[1] That is to say, he has no equal. Within the four seas he practices no guest rituals. That is to say, there is no other home for him to visit.[2] His feet can walk, but he awaits his prime minister before going forward. His mouth can talk, but he
5   awaits his officials before issuing summons. He sees things without looking upon them, and hears things keenly without listening to them. He is trusted without speaking, knows things without having to ponder them, and accomplishes things without moving. That is to say, everything is perfectly arranged for him. The power of the Son of
10   Heaven is utterly overwhelming, his body is utterly at ease, and his heart is utterly joyful. His intentions are frustrated in nothing, and his body labors at nothing, because he is given unsurpassed honor. The *Odes* says:

Everywhere underneath the skies,
15   There the king's royal domain lies.
Those on the shores of every land
Are all his servants to command.[3]

This expresses my meaning.
When a sage king is above, and social divisions and *yi* are carried
20   out below, then the officers and grand ministers will have no deviant or perverse conduct, the hundred functionaries and officials will have no instances of neglectfulness or laziness, the masses and common people will have no vile and abnormal customs, nor any crimes of robbery or murder. None will dare to violate the prohibitions of their
25   grand superior. All under Heaven will clearly know that people engaging in theft and robbery cannot be wealthy. They will all know that murderous and harmful people cannot be long-lived. They will all know that if they violate the prohibitions of the superior, they cannot be safe. If they follow his ways, then people will obtain things
30   they like from him. If they do not follow his ways, then they are sure

---

[1] Chapter titles usually come from the first words of the text, but here it begins with "the Son of Heaven." Therefore, some commentators have thought the title is mistaken, but since Xunzi believes only a morally cultivated person can become the true Son of Heaven, the two names are almost the same.

[2] I.e., as Son of Heaven, the whole world properly belongs to him, so everywhere is his home.

[3] Mao #205. This quotation differs slightly from the received version of the *Odes*.

to meet with things they hate from him. For this reason, his penalties and punishments are very few, and his awe-inspiring authority spreads like a rushing torrent. The world knows clearly that if one engages in vile acts, even though one tries to cover it up, hide, or flee, this will not be sufficient to escape. Thus, all who have committed crimes will themselves come seeking leniency. The *Documents* says, "In all cases, people bring guilt for their crimes upon themselves."[4] This expresses my meaning.

Thus, if punishments fit the crimes, then one will have awe-inspiring authority. If they do not fit the crimes, then one will be considered disgraceful. If official salaries fit the worthiness of the recipients, then one will be considered noble. If they do not fit the worthiness of the recipients, then one will be considered base. Among the ancients, penalties did not exceed the crimes, and official salaries did not outstrip the recipient's virtue. Thus, they might kill a father and yet employ his son as a minister. They might kill an older brother and yet employ the younger brother as a minister. In meting out punishments and penalties, they did not rage against the crime,[5] and giving out rewards and salaries, they did not exceed the recipient's virtue. Each case was carefully processed according to the truth of the matter. Thus, those who did good were encouraged, and those who did bad were stopped. Their punishments and penalties were extremely sparse, yet their awe-inspiring authority proceeded like a great river flowing. Governmental orders were extremely enlightened, and they changed and transformed the people as though they had the power of spirits. A saying goes, "When there is goodness in the one right person, then the myriad common folk will rely upon him." This expresses my meaning.

In a disordered age, things are not like this. Punishments and penalties are acts of rage against the crime, and rewards and salaries exceed the recipient's virtue. Whole clans are included in the judgment of guilt, and people are held up as worthies because of deeds of former generations. Thus, one person is guilty, but all three clans are extinguished,[6] and even if the others' virtue is like that of Shun, they

---

[4] See *Shujing, Kanggao* ("The Announcement to the Prince of K'ang"), translated in Waltham (1971, p. 149). Xunzi's quotation is slightly different from the received version of the *Documents*, and he seems to be using this sentence out of line with its original context.

[5] I.e., they acted out of careful regard for the wrong done, rather than simply lashing out in anger at the wrongdoer.

[6] Commentators disagree about to whom the "three clans" refers. Some say that it refers to everyone in the wrongdoer's father's family, mother's family, and wife's family. Others say it refers to the wrongdoer and all his brothers, the wrongdoer's father and his brothers, and the wrongdoer's son and his brothers (i.e., three generations). The practice of extending punishment to other members of the criminal's family was supposedly a common practice of the Qin regime during Xunzi's time.

65   cannot avoid sharing in the punishment—this is for whole clans to be included in the judgment of guilt. When the ancestors were worthies, then their sons and grandsons are sure to be well-known. Yet if the descendants are unfailingly given honored positions among the ranks of followers even though their conduct is like that of the tyrants Jie

70   and Zhòu, then this is for people to be held up as worthies because of deeds of former generations. When whole clans are included in the judgment of guilt, and people are held up as worthies because of deeds of former generations, then even if one wished for no disorder, could one achieve this? The *Odes* says:

75

> The hundred rivers are roiled out of their banks,
> And mountain peaks crash down precipitously.
> High cliffs become valleys,
> Deep chasms become crests.
80 > Alas for the people of today!
> Why will none of them cease this?[7]

This expresses my meaning.

   If in one's judgments one takes the sage kings as one's model, then one will know what to value. If one uses *yi* to regulate one's affairs,
85   then one will know wherein true profit lies. If in one's judgments one knows what to value, then one will know what to regard as nurturing. If in one's affairs one knows wherein true profit lies, then in one's actions one will know whence to start out. These two are the root of right and wrong, the source of gain and loss. Thus, in his relationship
90   with the Duke of Zhou, there was nothing King Cheng did without listening to his advice, because he knew what to value. In his relationship with Guan Zhong, there were no affairs of state for which Duke Huan did not use him, because he knew wherein true profit lay. The state of Wu had Wu Zixu but could not put him to good use. As a
95   result, the state perished, because it turned its back on the Way and lost its worthy men. Thus, he who venerates sages becomes a true king. He who values the worthy becomes a hegemon. He who respects the worthy will be preserved. He who treats the worthy with arrogance will perish. In this both ancient times and the present are
100   one and the same.

   Thus, to elevate the worthy and employ the capable, to give appropriate ranking to the noble and the lowly, to divide the more intimate from the more distant, to give proper ordering to elders and the young—this is the way of the former kings. And so, if one elevates the
105   worthy and employs the capable, then the ruler will be venerated and those below him will be peaceful. If the noble and the lowly are ap-

---

[7] Mao #193. These lines are rhymed in the original.

propriately ranked, then orders will be carried out without deviation. If the more intimate are properly divided from the more distant, then kindness will be practiced without giving rise to strife. If elders and the young have their proper ordering, then work will quickly be accomplished and there will be time for rest. And so, one who is *ren* is 110 *ren* according to these things. One who is *yi* makes divisions according to these things. One who is properly regulated lives and dies following these things. One who is loyal is faithful and circumspect according to these things. To combine all of these things and add ability on top of them is to be complete. To be complete and yet not be 115 haughty, but single-mindedly work at making oneself good—this is called being a sage. He is not haughty, and so no one in the world tries to compete with his abilities, but rather all do their utmost to put their accomplishments to good use. What he has, he does not flaunt having,[8] and so he is valued by the whole world. The *Odes* says: 120

> As for the noble man and gentleman,
> Their standard does not err or deviate.
> Their standard does not err or deviate.
> On all four sides they correct every state.[9]

This expresses my meaning. 125

---

[8] This line is somewhat ambiguous. It could mean that the sage does not flaunt his possession of virtue. However, the sentence is very similar to a line found in chaps. 2, 10, and 51 of the *Daodejing*, which talks about how the Way "gives birth to things but does not treat them as its possessions." For that reason, Xunzi's remark could also be meant to describe how a sage king possesses the whole world (going back to the beginning of the chapter) but does not lord it over others.

[9] Mao #152. Compare the use of this same quotation at 10.554–557 and 15.374–77.

CHAPTER 25

Working Songs

Allow me to sing you a working song[1]
To recount this era's calamity.
People's stupidity and ignorance
Have cast down men who are good and worthy.
5   The rulers of men have no worthy aides.
They are like the blind lacking guides to see;
Oh, how they blunder about helplessly!

Allow me to set out fundamentals.
Listen to these words very carefully.
10   Stupid men who monopolize power
Will not make affairs come out orderly.
To rulers jealous and overbearing,
Ministers will not speak out warningly.
Such rulers meet disaster certainly.

15   To judge if ministers have gone astray,
Go back and look at their activity.
To honor the ruler and guard the state,
They will value worthies and men of *yi*.
But if they stop warnings,[2] keep wrongs hidden,

---

[1] There is controversy over how to construe the two characters *chengxiang* 成相, from which the title of this chapter comes. Following a number of commentators, I take it as referring to a kind of syllable and rhyme pattern that was apparently used for songs sung during farm labor. However, the contents of the chapter are best understood as an adaptation of this pattern by Xunzi, rather than songs actually sung by farmers. The pattern in the original Chinese is divided into seven groups of syllables as follows (with "x" as a nonrhyming syllable and "R" as a rhyming syllable):

X X R, X X R, X X X X, X X R, X X X X, X X X X, X X R

For the translation, I have retained the seven syllable groups as seven lines, but the lines are of ten syllables each and do not match the rhyme scheme exactly. In addition, I have occasionally taken liberties with the text for the sake of poetic effect, but I tried to keep these departures to a minimum. Commentators disagree about how to group the stanzas. This issue is addressed in note 22 below.

[2] This remark is ambiguous and could refer to any or all of the following: a bad minister (1) does not offer criticism when his lord errs, (2) prevents others from offering such criticism, or (3) does not accept criticism himself.

And with those above comply foolishly,[3]   20
Then the state surely has catastrophe.

What do I mean by the term "depleted"?
A state where many men act selfishly.
They form cabals encircling the ruler.
They play partisans and work cliquishly.   25
They drive off worthies, draw slanderers near,
And block ministers who act loyally.
The ruler's power then ebbs rapidly.

What do I mean by the term "worthy man"?
He knows lord and minister roles clearly.   30
This man can honor his ruler above.
Toward the folk below he acts caringly.
If the ruler truly listens to him,
All under Heaven attain unity,
And he has as guests the lands ringed by sea.[4]   35

A ruler's downfall comes about like this:
When slanderers advance successfully,
Worthies and able men run off and flee,
Then the state tumbles precipitously.
The stupid ruler grows yet more stupid.   40
Benighted, he acts more benightedly,
And becomes a tyrant Jie finally.

The disasters befalling the era[5]
Came from hating those able and worthy.
Fei Lian was in charge of the government.   45
Wu Lai held official authority.[6,a]
The lord lowered his thoughts and intentions,

---

[3] Here the phrase *shangtong* 上同 (lit. "agree with those above") is used in a disparaging fashion. This phrase figures prominently in certain passages in the *Mozi*, and so there may be a subtle criticism of that text implied here.

[4] The ancient Chinese believed that the world was surrounded by seas on all four sides, so the reference to the "lands ringed by sea" (lit. "the area within the seas") means the world as a whole. The point is that all lands will send emissaries to this ruler's court as "guests" to submit and pay tribute to him.

[5] Given what follows, the era in question seems most specifically to be the final years of the Shang dynasty. This era is, however, also being held up as a mirror for Xunzi's own age.

[6] Fei Lian and Wu Lai were bad ministers who served the tyrant Zhòu, and it is Zhòu to whom the next few lines refer.

Expanding his parks and preserves greatly,
And building pavilions high and lofty.

50 When King Wu of Zhou was stirred to anger
To the fields of Mu he brought his army.
The soldiers of Zhòu changed their direction.[7]
One laying down his arms was Weizi Qi.[8]
Since King Wu thought very well of this man,
55 He gave him Song as his territory,
And raised a temple for his family.[9]

The degeneration of the era[10]
Came from slanderers' accumulation.
Bi Gan was eviscerated alive.
60 And Jizi suffered incarceration.
Then King Wu came and executed Zhòu.
Lü Shang waved the pennants at his station.[11]
Both were embraced by Yin's population.

The catastrophe of a whole era[12]
65 Comes from detesting men who are worthy.
So Wu Zixu thus suffered being killed.[13]
Baili Xi had to move unwillingly.[14]
Duke Mu of Qin obtained this latter man,
Then matched the five hegemons' potency,
70 And used "six-minister" bureaucracy.[15]

[7] This same line appears at 8.330–31. A more detailed account of the events before and after the battle is given there.

[8] See the discussion at 15.322–24 and note 38 there.

[9] Each state's ruling house had a temple to honor its lineage, so this action signifies the establishment of Weizi Qi as a lord.

[10] As before, the "era" mentioned here is the final years of the Shang (Yin) dynasty.

[11] Lü Shang, also known as "the Grand Duke," was an important minister for King Wen and King Wu. The "pennants" mentioned here were used to control troop movements from afar, so the point is that he served as general.

[12] Unlike the two previous mentions of an "era," this one seems to have no particular referent, as the lives of Wu Zixu and Baili Xi (and the "catastrophes" suffered by the states of Wu and Yu, respectively), used by the text as examples, were more than a century apart.

[13] For the story of Wu Zixu, see chapter 13, note 4.

[14] According to various stories, Baili Xi served the Duke of Yu, but the duke did not appreciate his advice, and as a result Yu was destroyed by the state of Jin (ca. 654 BCE) and Baili Xi was forced into exile.

[15] The "six-minister" (liu qing 六卿) system was a bureaucratic arrangement reserved for use by the Son of Heaven. Duke Mu's action thus amounts to an assertion of power.

In the present era's stupidity,
Great *ru* are by many people hated.
Opposed, reviled, they are denied success:
Confucius's movements were frustrated,[16]
Zhan Qin's official post was thrice cut short,[17]   75
Chunshen's ways wound up eliminated.[18]
Fundamentals[19] are all devastated.

Allow me to look at fundamentals:[b]
Let matters be pondered by the worthy.
Then though ten thousand eras passed since Yao,   80
It will be like viewing Yao presently.[20]
But since slanderous men know no limits,
Behaving crooked and dangerously,
They make men view these things suspiciously.

Fundamentals must be implemented: 85
Distinguish the unfit and the worthy.
In this, the ways of King Wen and King Wu
Were the same as that practiced by Fu Xi.[21]
Those who follow this will be well ordered.
Those who do not will be disorderly.   90
What is there to regard suspiciously?[22]

Each of my working songs marks distinctions—
Of proper models and methods each sings.
Reaching extremes of ultimate order
Comes from returning to the later kings.   95

---

[16] Famously, Confucius was surrounded in Kuang by soldiers who supposedly mistook him for a criminal, and on another occasion he was trapped between the states of Chen and Cai and left short of provisions.

[17] Zhan Qin, also known as Liuxia Hui, was a famous personage of Lu.

[18] Lord Chunshen was a high-ranking minister in Chu, who at one point employed Xunzi as a magistrate. After Lord Chunshen was assassinated ca. 238 BCE, Xunzi lost his position. It is these events to which he refers here.

[19] I.e., the fundamentals necessary for good government, foremost of which is the employment of good men.

[20] I.e., if worthy ministers are allowed to take part in the government, they will help make the ruler a modern-day Yao.

[21] Fu Xi was one of the earliest sage kings, preceding even Yao.

[22] Commentators disagree about how to group the stanzas in this chapter. There are two main camps: some divide them into five sections, and some into three. Convinced by neither, I have not marked sections in the main text, and have chosen instead to mark the proposed sections in the footnotes. With the five-section grouping, the first section ends here.

The words of those men Shen, Mo, Ji, and Hui[23]
And the hundred schools' various sayings
Truly are very inauspicious things.

For order, return to the one right thing.[24]
100 Cultivate this to live auspiciously.
The gentleman firmly takes hold of it.
His heart is as though tied to it tightly.[25]
The masses are of two minds about it.
And slanderers reject it completely;
105 They treat its realized form reproachfully.[26,c]

Water is utmost in being level.
It lies straight and does not lie slantingly.
If the course of one's heart is just like this,
Then one will resemble a sage closely.[27]
110 One who . . . but has official station,[28]
Who is upright but can show leniency,[d]
Will be a partner to Heaven surely.

The present era has not one true king.
It puts the good and worthy in dire woe.
115 Violent people feast upon fine meats.
Those who are *ren* have mere dregs to swallow.
Ritual and music are smashed and cease.

[23] Of the four names mentioned here, three are easily identified: "Shen" refers to Shen Dao, "Mo" to Mozi, and "Hui" to Hui Shi. However, concerning "Ji" there is no certainty, and speculation abounds. Perhaps the most plausible explanation is that of Liu Shipei, who proposes that "Ji" is an error for "Wei" and refers to Wei Mou, who is criticized at 6.6–12, alongside the other figures mentioned here.

[24] I.e., the Way. Some commentators read the "one thing" more specifically as the practices of the later kings, as mentioned in the previous stanza.

[25] The Chinese text here is almost identical to a line from the *Odes*, Mao #152, which is quoted at 1.119. (There the words are translated differently, due to different rhyme patterns.)

[26] This line could mean one or both of the following: (1) these people disapprove of what the Way would look like when manifested, and hence they do not follow it, or (2) these people disapprove of those who manifest the Way (i.e., gentlemen and sages) and hence treat them badly. Some commentators read the line very differently, as meaning roughly "Punishment will bring these people under control."

[27] Compare the analogy between the heart and a pan of water drawn at 21.259–72.

[28] Based on the number of syllables per stanza up to this point, and the grammar of this line, there appears to be a lacuna in the text here. Commentators have proposed various candidates to fill in the one character that seems to be missing, but I find none of them particularly convincing and so have opted to leave a blank space instead. The same applies to other lacunae further below in this chapter.

Sages go into hiding and lie low
While the methods of Mozi spread and grow.

There are warp threads for weaving good order: 120
Rites and punishments are exactly these.
The gentleman takes and cultivates them.
The common folk are thereby put at ease.
Make virtue bright. Treat penalties with care.
This orders the state and its families,   125
And peace comes to all within the four seas.

The intention to achieve good order
Ranks wealth and station as secondary.
Gentlemen have integrity in it,
And so they are good and wait patiently.[29]   130
They dwell in it amply and with firmness.
They also store it in themselves deeply.
Hence, they can ponder things far-reachingly.

When your ponderings reach a refined state,
Glorious intentions you will attain.   135
With fondness, be single-minded in them,
A spirit-like state will thereby obtain.
Merging these refined and spirit-like states,
Deviate not. Single-minded remain.
Becoming a sage is what you will gain.[30]   140

The way that will bring about good order
Is beautiful and is also ageless.
A gentleman will follow it closely.
He will thus live nobly and with goodness;
Below, teach his sons and younger brothers;   145
Above, serve his forbears with faithfulness.[31]

[29] Exactly what the gentlemen await is not stated. Many commentators take it as awaiting employment by a ruler who appreciates their worthiness, an idea expressed elsewhere in this chapter as meeting with the right time (see below, lines 168–74). Perhaps what gentlemen await includes, moreover, the achievement of good order in society.

[30] The language of this stanza is highly reminiscent of two other passages in the text, namely 8.274–80 and 21.226–55.

[31] Although the Chinese text of this stanza has the number of syllables that is the norm for this chapter, the grammar of the lines does not fit with the seven-unit pattern described in note 1 above. Instead, the syllables break into six units, which I have therefore rendered as six lines.

Though this working song now comes to an end,
What I have said will not prove unsteady.
A gentleman will take it as his way
150   And thus act smoothly and insightfully.
He will revere the worthy and the good,
Recognize downfall and calamity,
. . .[32]

Allow me to sing you a working song
155   To speak of many a sage and true king.
Yao and Shun elevated worthy men
Yet remained deferential and yielding.
For the two figures Xu You and Shan Juan,
Yi weighed heavily, but not profiting.[33]
160   Their behavior stood out and was shining.

Yao tried to yield rule to a worthy man.[34]
This was for his people's prosperity.
He spread benefits, showed inclusive care.[35]
He practiced virtue evenhandedly.[36]
165   He marked out and ordered the high and low.
Noble and humble were ranked properly.
He set lord and minister roles clearly.

[32] Based on the normal number of syllables per stanza, there appears to be a lacuna here, and the entire last line is missing. With the five-section grouping of the stanzas, the second section ends here. With the three-section grouping, this is the end of the first section.

[33] Little is known about Xu You and Shan Juan, but according to some early stories, they were wise and worthy men. Yao tried to cede his throne to Xu You, who refused, and Shun likewise tried to cede his throne to Shan Juan, who similarly refused. It may be these events to which the text refers in speaking of how *yi* weighed more with them than profit.

[34] Although the text does not name the person, the most likely candidate is Xu You (see the previous note). Regardless, this and the following couple of stanzas seem to conflict with the denial at 18.258–350 that Yao and Shun handed off their thrones.

[35] Here the text uses the two characters *jian'ai* 兼愛. This phrase was famously used in the *Mozi*—where it is perhaps best translated as "impartial care"—to designate the view that people should not give preferential treatment to others with whom they share what we might call "special" ties, e.g., children should not privilege their own parents over the parents of others. With so little surrounding context, it is hard to determine the exact sense in which the phrase is used here. However, nowhere else does the text endorse the sort of view espoused in the *Mozi*, so it is more likely that the phrase is used in the weaker sense of referring to care that is "comprehensive" or "inclusive," rather than being "impartial" with regard to "special" ties between people.

[36] Here the word *de* 德 ("virtue") has the more specific sense of "kindness."

When Yao gave his throne to that able man,[37]
Shun happened to meet with the right moment.
Yao raised worthies, boosted men of virtue,   170
And thus gave the world ordered government.
So though there was one worthy and sagely,
If for him the right time were not present,
Who would have recognized this man's talent?

Yao did not make a show of his virtue.[38]   175
Shun did not decline what Yao was giving.
Yao made his two daughters the wives of Shun
And assigned Shun the tasks of governing.
Shun was a magnificent man indeed!
When he stood in position, south-facing,[39]   180
Properly arranged was everything.

In turn Shun did give away unto Yu
Rule over the world's every denizen.
Shun raised men of virtue, boosted worthies
And on order was never mistaken.   185
Among nonkin, he did not shun old foes,[40]
Neither did he favor his own kinsmen.[41]
Those who were worthy sided with him then.

Of those who labored by means of their hearts[42]
Yao was one in possession of virtue.   190
Without making use of his shields and spears,
Submission by the San Miao did ensue.[43]
He raised up Shun from the fields where he worked
Gave him rule of the world as his purview
Then into rest and retirement withdrew.   195

---

[37] I.e., Shun.

[38] I.e., in giving his throne to Shun.

[39] In ancient China, the king faced south in holding court, so this remark refers to Shun's ascension to the throne.

[40] Commentators explain that this line refers to a story, according to which Shun executed Yu's father Gun, and was thus Yu's foe in a sense, but still employed him as a minister.

[41] Commentators explain that this line refers to Shun's passing over his own son, Shang Jun, and handing the throne to Yu instead.

[42] The text here seems corrupt. I follow Liu Shipei's emendation of this line (but not his suggestion to switch its place with the line below). The translation nonetheless remains tentative. The wording here is reminiscent of wording in *Mencius* 3A4.

[43] The San Miao (lit. "Three Miao") were "barbarian" peoples. Their submission to Yao without the compulsion of war is mentioned as a testament to the greatness of his virtue.

Yao obtained Hou Ji as a minister.
Then the five grains grew quite flourishingly.
With Kui serving as Music Director
The birds and beasts behaved submissively.[44]
200   When Xie was the Director of Workers[45]
Folk knew to be filial, brotherly
And treat men of virtue reverently.

Yu accomplished feats meritorious.
He stopped the floodwaters and made them wane,
205   Eliminated harms to the people,
And banished the Gong Gong from the domain.[46]
To the north he dredged the nine waterways,
Made passable the twelve islands' terrain,
And dug routes to let the three rivers drain.[47]

210   Yu did bring the land back under control.[e]
He restored normal life the whole world through.[48]
For the people, he worked his own body.
Laborious, bitter toils he did do.
He enlisted Yi, as well as Gao Yao,
215   He also got Heng Ge, and Zhi Cheng, too,
As . . . assistants in his retinue.[49]

Xie was named with the title of "Dark King."[50]
He begot a son. Zhao Ming was his name.

---

[44] According to some stories, Kui's music could charm even animals.

[45] For more on Xie, see below, lines 217–23, and note 50 there.

[46] Early sources give various and sometimes conflicting reports about the Gong Gong, with some portraying the Gong Gong as an individual, while others portray the Gong Gong as a tribe. The latter seems to be the case in the only other place where the *Xunzi* mentions the Gong Gong, at 15.364, so perhaps the same applies here as well.

[47] The referents of the "nine waterways," "twelve islands," and "three rivers" are difficult to determine. However, Hao Yixing suggests plausibly that the "twelve islands" are the same as the twelve main regions into which the world was divided by Shun, in which case the point would be that Yu reclaimed the world's habitable land from the floodwaters.

[48] The word *ping* 平, translated here as "normal," can also mean "calm" or "balanced," and those connotations are likely intended here as well.

[49] There seems to be a lacuna of one character/syllable in the last section of the stanza, but its meaning remains clear. Of the four figures mentioned here, almost nothing is known of Heng Ge and Zhi Cheng. Early texts contain many references to Yi (not the same as Archer Yi) and Gao Yao, on the other hand, and they are portrayed as virtuous ministers who played key roles in the administrations of Shun and Yu (see, e.g., *Mencius* 3A4).

[50] "Dark" here does not imply anything sinister. Rather, the epithet comes from the story that Xie was conceived when a dark-colored bird laid an egg, which was swal-

Originally, they lived at Di Shi,
Later, they moved and unto Shang they came.   220
This line, in its fourteenth generation,
Had one Tian Yi as its member to claim.
He and Tang the Successful are the same.[51]

Tian Yi, who is also known as King Tang,
Properly judged things and chose appointees.   225
To Bian Sui, he once tried to yield his throne;
To Mou Guang, hand responsibilities.[52]
. . .[53]
All talk of ancient sages and worthies
Must unfold fundamental policies.[54]   230

I would like to set out some words for you.
. . .[55]
Since this chaotic era hates good men,
They do not get to make it orderly.
Those who hide transgressions and loathe worthies,   235
And do vile, deceptive acts skillfully,
Can avoid disaster only rarely.

What troubles and difficulties there are!
In leading positions crooked men sit.[f]
Those with sagely wisdom are not employed;   240
Government plans are made by the stupid.
Though the cart ahead has already flipped,

---

lowed by Xie's mother, who then became pregnant. An early reference to the story
appears in the *Odes*, Mao #303. Xie was made a "king" when Yao enfeoffed him in
return for his good service as a minister.

[51] I.e., this is King Tang who overthrew Jie and founded the Shang dynasty.

[52] Little is known of Bian Sui and Mou Guang. A story in the *Zhuangzi* (chap. 28) depicts them as worthies who declined Tang's offer of the throne. That story, though,
casts Tang in a bad light, so it is probably not that particular version of history that
is being referenced here.

[53] There appears to be a lacuna in the text here. Following commentators, I view it as
occurring in place of the fifth syllable group in the stanza, but it is also possible that
the missing characters are the sixth syllable group, in which case this line should be
swapped with the one below it.

[54] With the five-section grouping of the stanzas, the third section ends here.

[55] There appears to be a lacuna in the text here, but the missing characters could be
either the first or the second syllable group in the stanza. It seems more probable to
me that what is missing is the second syllable group, so that is how I have rendered
it here, but the possibility remains that this line should be swapped with the one
above it.

Those behind still do not know they should quit.[56]
At what time will these men awake to it?

245   Those who are neither awake nor aware,
Do not know their oncoming bitter plight.
Lost and confused, they lack all direction,
Reversing what is low and what has height.
Those loyal don't get through to them above.
250   They have blocked up their hearing and their sight.
Their windows and their gates have been shut tight.[57]

Shut tight are the windows and gates of some.
They are quite lost; their confusion is great.
Their chaotic acts and benightedness
255   Neither have a limit nor terminate.
They reverse right and wrong; they form cabals;
Those above they trick and manipulate;
And toward correct and upright men have hate.

Some have hate for correct and upright men;
260   Their hearts lack proper measure totally.
They are crooked, warped, perverse, and twisted;
They have lost proper ways and paths wholly.
Without a person who gives one rebukes,[g]
One will only think of oneself finely,
265   But how could such a one act blamelessly?

Those who do not know to heed forewarnings
Are certainly by bad outcomes beset.[h]
Obstinately, they proceed with mistakes,
Nor are willing to change based on regret.
270   Slanderers then will attain much progress;
Words and language they pervert and upset;
Lies and deception are what they beget.

In these people's practice of deception
They never know a lack of energy.[i]
275   They contend for favor, resent worthies,
And gain from acting badly and vilely.

[56] The "cart ahead" seems to be a metaphor for previous people; the point is that history shows clearly that those who are morally corrupt court disaster.

[57] "Windows" and "gates" here are probably intended both literally and figuratively. Literally, these people shut out those who, out of loyalty, try to warn them away from error. Figuratively, the "windows" and "gates" refer to points of access to their hearts, e.g., their hearing and sight.

Envious of merit, smearing worthies,
Below, they form cliques and grow their party;
Above, spread blindness and obscurity.[58]

When those above are blocked up and blinded,   280
They lose true helpers and authority.
Employing and trusting slanderous men,
Ruling then escapes their ability.
Thus the Duke of Guo, Zhang Fu, caused troubles,
And off to Zhi did King Li of Zhou flee.[59]   285

As for the two kings You and Li of Zhou,[60]
The reason that they suffered dethronement
Is their not heeding reproofs and warnings,
And giving loyal men harmful treatment.
Alas, how could I be the sole person   290
Who happens not to meet the right moment
But faces an age that is turbulent?

Though one desires to answer in earnest,[j]
If none will follow one's words willingly,
One may, I fear, become a Wu Zixu,   295
And meet with misfortune similarly:
He submitted warnings, was not heeded,
Cut his own throat with Zhu Lou by decree,[61]
Then his corpse was thrown into the Yangtze.

If one observes happenings from the past   300
In order to give oneself forewarning,
Then order and chaos and right and wrong
Are within reach of one's recognizing.
. . .[62]

---

[58] The word translated here and in the next stanza as "blindness" (*bi* 蔽, lit. "covered")
is the same word that is translated as "fixation" in chapter 21.

[59] King Li, a disastrous king (r. ca. 878–841 BCE) of the Zhou dynasty, was forced out
of power and into exile at the end. Early texts make only passing references to
Zhang Fu, so his role in these events is not clear. On the six-line structure here, see
note 31 above.

[60] During the reign of King You (r. ca. 781–771 BCE), who—like King Li—was a bad
king, the Zhou dynasty suffered a terrible military defeat that effectively destroyed
the dynasty's ruling power and resulted in a relocation of the capital eastward. The
reign of King You (who was killed by the attackers) thus constitutes the end of the
Western Zhou dynasty.

[61] Zhu Lou was the name of a sword. Wu Zixu was commanded by his lord to commit
suicide, which he did. See chapter 13, note 4.

[62] There appears to be a lacuna in the text here. Following commentators, I view it as

305   I trust them to this working song I sing,
        For the sake of making plain my thinking.[63]

        Allow me to sing you a working song.
        Of methods to bring order it will tell.
        In explaining lordship there are five points[64]
310   That are condensed yet enlightened counsel.
        If the lord keeps careful watch over these,
        All below in peace and uprightness dwell.
        And then the state does prosper and excel.

        From ministers on down, let each have tasks.
315   Let none gain food by drifting in action.[65]
        Work at basics, restrain expenditures,
        Then wealth will grow in boundless profusion.[66]
        If, in their work, they heed just those above,
        And cannot give each other direction,
320   Then the people's strength will be joined as one.[67]

        If people do keep up their assigned tasks,
        Provide them sufficient food and clothing.
        When having more or less follows fit grades
        This shows high rank and dress have a grounding.[68]
325   Let them look above to have profit come;[k]
        But let none usurp control of giving.[69]
        Then who can gain from personal dealing?

---

occurring in place of the fifth syllable group in the stanza, but it is also possible that the missing characters form the sixth syllable group, in which case this line should be swapped with the one below it.

[63] With the five-section grouping of the stanzas, the fourth section ends here. With the three-section grouping, the second section ends here.

[64] A number of commentators take the "five points" as referring to the next five stanzas.

[65] The sense of "drifting" (*you* 游) is ambiguous here. Some commentators take it as referring to "laziness," while others take it more specifically as referring to "straying" away from one's assigned task.

[66] The "basics" (*ben* 本) are the tasks of agriculture. The language and ideas here are very close to what one finds at 9.498–502 and 10.44–61.

[67] See 9.67–83, on the problems that result when each person tries to command everyone else, and the need for a clear hierarchy.

[68] Due to the condensed character of the text here, the meaning is somewhat unclear, but I take the thought to be this: if greater or lesser degrees of wealth are distributed according to a hierarchy of merit in terms of performing one's assigned role, people will understand that only by fulfilling their tasks well can they attain greater positions and benefits.

[69] The point is apparently that the ruler should retain exclusive control over how certain goods are distributed, as a means of preventing threats to his rule. A very similar idea is found in several places in the *Han Feizi*.

If the lord institutes laws that are clear,
And for judgments puts constancy in place,
Then when markers and standards are set out,   330
Folk will know the right direction to face.
If promotions and demotions have rules,
And others can't make men noble or base,
Then who will seek the king's personal grace?

If the laws and standards set by the lord   335
Prevent those actions one is to forswear,
Then none will not delight in his teachings,
Nor will any alter their assigned share.[70,1]
Those cultivating them will have glory.
Those leaving them will have disgrace to bear.   340
Then who will seek for a teacher elsewhere?

Have punishments be evenly laid out.
Of their boundaries maintain oversight.
Don't let those below get to employ them;
Thus keep their personal influence slight.[71]   345
If offenses and sentences have rules,
And none can make them more heavy or light,
You can keep whole your awe-inspiring might.

Allow me to look at what's propitious,
And show how to have a good foundation.   350
A ruler fond of debates and discussions
Surely excels in deliberation.
If he heeds these five[72] to refine his reign,
And all are done with coordination,[m]
He will have a firm grasp on his station.[73]   355

This is crucial for one hearing cases:
Things' true disposition you must discern.
Check, verify, get clear, and be careful.
Apply rewards and punishments in turn.
Obvious things then surely get noticed,   360

---

[70] I.e., people will diligently fulfill their roles and not try to arrogate to themselves what is not properly theirs.

[71] For a similar warning about how rulers should not let subordinates use administration of punishments as a means to gain power, see the "Two Handles" chapter of the *Han Feizi*.

[72] The "five" here appears to refer back to the five points mentioned in line 309 above.

[73] I.e., the ruler both will be secure in his position and will exercise effective control over the state.

Hidden ones become obvious to learn,
And to integrity folk will return.

Let there be a measure for people's words;
Investigate their actuality.
365   Thus divide those trustworthy and those false.
Ensure them a reward or penalty.
Then those below won't deceive those above;
All will tell how things are disposed truly,
And, like the sun, matters will shine clearly.

370   To one penetrating and keen above
News of things far and hidden will carry.
Watching for legal and illegal deeds,
Even without looking, still he does see.[74]
Since his eyes and ears are so perceptive,
375   Officials respect his law and decree,
And none dare to act irresponsibly.

When the lord's teachings are promulgated,
Over behavior will rules then extend.
If officials carefully uphold them,
380   And to harshness or leniency don't tend,[n]
Those below won't ask personal favors,
Each will by what's appropriate . . . fend,[75]
And bring cheating the inept to an end.[o]

Let ministers diligently follow.
385   Let the lord manage change in policy.[76]
Unprejudiced probing and good thinking
Keep judgments from being disorderly.
If by means of them one orders the world,
They will form models for posterity,
390   And a binding thread for rules will they be.

[74] See 12.316.
[75] There appear to be a lacuna of one character/syllable in this section of the stanza, but its location cannot be determined. The meaning remains clear enough, though.
[76] The "change" here is most likely changes to the government, so I have added "in policy" here, but it may also refer to "changing circumstances" in the world generally.

CHAPTER 26

Fu

Here there is an object magnificent.
Though it is neither silk thread nor fabric,
Its forms and patterns make an arrangement.
Though it is neither the sun nor the moon,
Of all the world's things it is most brilliant.   5
Through it, the living gain longevity.
Through it, the dead are given interment.
Through it, city walls are well fortified.
Through it, the three armies become potent.
He who possesses it in its pure form[1]   10
Will accomplish a true king's government.
If it's impure, he'll be a hegemon.
He'll perish if it is wholly absent.
I, your dumb minister, do not know it.
So I dare ask Your Majesty's judgment.   15

The King said, "Is it the sort of thing that
Has good form yet is not just flowery?
Is it something simple, easily known,
Yet does it also make things orderly?
Is it something the gentleman respects,   20
Yet is rejected by a man petty?
Is it such that if our nature lacks it,
Then we do wind up becoming beastly,
But if human nature does obtain it,
Then one behaves extremely gracefully?[a]   25

The title of this chapter, *fu* 賦, is the name of a genre, sometimes translated as "rhapsody" or "rhyme-prose" in English. The genre was very popular during the Han dynasty, but the pieces here have features that do not match the "canonical" form of *fu* from the Han era, which has spurred much discussion about the relation of this chapter to the development of the *fu* genre. However, the title *fu* may have been added by the first editor, Liu Xiang, so the classification might be an entirely later artifact. Although the Chinese text rhymes, the length of the rhyming units varies quite a bit, as does the rhyme scheme itself. In the translation, rather than follow the irregular pattern of the original, I have adopted a format of ten-syllable lines. Neither the line divisions nor the rhyme scheme correspond to the Chinese exactly. Knechtges (1989) provides a very useful discussion of this chapter.

[1] This and the following three lines also appear at 11.198–200 and 16.325–28, though in reference to different objects. The translation here differs somewhat from those occurrences, in order to fit the rhyme scheme.

Is it something that, if he exalts it,
Makes a common man into one sagely,
Or lets a feudal lord who exalts it
Give all within the four seas unity?
30   It is most brilliant and also condensed.
It makes deportment proper, quite smoothly.
Ritual let us conclude it to be."

Ritual[2]

August Heaven made exalted a thing
35   So to show direction to folk lowly.
In some, it's abundant; in others, thin.
Sovereigns do not have it evenly.
By means of this, Jie and Zhòu made chaos.
By means of this, Tang and Wu were worthy.
40   Though it is sometimes muddied, sometimes clear,
It is an august and fine entity.[3]
It completes a circuit round all four seas
Without spending even a day fully.
With it, gentlemen cultivate themselves.
45   With it, Zhi cut into homes an entry.[4]
Though at its greatest, it matches Heaven,
Refined and subtle, there's no form to see.
With it, one's practice of *yi* is correct.
With it, one's work turns out successfully.
50   It can put a stop to violent men
And give impoverished men sufficiency.
The common people await its coming
And only then have peace and rest calmly.
I, your dumb minister, do not know it.
55   So I would like to ask its name of thee.

---

[2] In this chapter, the answers to this riddle and to others are given as labels that appear after the riddles. These labels may have been intended as section titles. On ancient Chinese manuscripts, section titles usually come at the end of the section, rather than at the beginning. However, in our received version of the *Xunzi*, other labels that likely were originally section titles now appear at the head of their respective sections (e.g., "The Proper Order for Officials" at 9.379; see Knoblock's 1988 discussions of "embedded titles" in vol. 1, pp. 107, 121, and 123–24). Perhaps the labels that appear in this chapter were placed (or were left) at the end to avoid spoiling the riddles by giving the answers at the beginning.

[3] This and the previous line are rather awkward and difficult to construe. Commentators propose various emendations to make it more sensible, but I do not find the proposals very compelling. I have translated the lines roughly as they stand, but the translation remains tentative.

[4] This Zhi is Robber Zhi, who (according to some stories) broke into homes by literally cutting through walls in some cases.

He said,[5] "Is it that which regards as safe
Things that are expansive and lie even,[6]
But treats things risky and hard to pass through
As dangerous conditions that threaten?
Is it such that: cultivate and cleanse it,   60
And affection will to you be given,
But if you do defile and pollute it,
Into barbarity you have fallen?
Is it what is hidden quite deep within,
Yet on the outside overcomes foemen?   65
Is it what takes Yu and Shun as models
And on their tracks is able to fasten?
Is it what one's deeds and movements await
And only then is fittingness gotten?
It's a state where blood and *qi* are refined,   70
Where one's intentions and thoughts have thriven.
The common people await its coming
And only then does peace for them happen.
All under Heaven await its coming
And enjoy tranquility only then.   75
Brilliant, penetrating, pure, and pristine,
It is not with any defects laden.
This is called the knowledge of gentlemen."[7]

Knowledge

There are some objects here I shall narrate: 80
Whenever these objects dwell in a place,
Dense and still, in low spots they situate,
But then when these objects are on the move,
They are huge and to great heights levitate.
They match the compass with their rounded shape,   85
Match the square with their rectangular state,
Rival Heaven and Earth with their grandness.
And top Yao and Yu with virtue more great.[8]
So fine, they are slighter than a thin hair.

---

[5] The speaker is not identified in the text, but it is most likely the king.
[6] The language of this and the next line is spatial, referring to broad and level or risky and narrow *places*, but given the answer to the riddle below, the descriptions are also meant to apply to *courses of action*, so I have used the word "things" here to capture the ambiguity.
[7] Here "knowledge" translates *zhi* 智, which is elsewhere usually translated as "wisdom." Since the answer to the riddle is supposed to explain, among other things, what Robber Zhi used to commit crimes (see above, line 45 and note 4), the more neutral rendering as "knowledge" seems better here.
[8] Here, "virtue" more specifically refers to "kindness" or "generosity."

90   So grand, through the Grand Vault they permeate.[9]
    Oh so indistinct do these things become,
    As off to great distances they migrate.
    Oh so swirling, they chase one another
    And back through their positions they rotate.
95   Lofty, oh so lofty, do they rise up,
    And round the whole world they perambulate.[10,b]
    Their virtue is profuse and unstinting.[11]
    Set with five hues, lovely forms they create.
    Their comings and goings are dark and dim;
100   Unto great spirithood they penetrate.[12]
    They enter and exit very swiftly,
    And there is nobody who knows their gate.[13]
    Without them, all under Heaven would die.
    With them, life endures and does not abate.
105   I, your disciple, am not quick-witted,
    Thus these objects here I wish to relate.
    May you, oh gentleman, set forth some words.
    These things, I ask, please gauge and estimate.

    He said, "Are these things that are grand in size,
110   Yet things whose movements one cannot stymie?
    Do they fill and permeate the Grand Vault
    Without leaving any spaces empty,
    Yet also enter crevices and cracks
    And are not constricted even slightly?
115   Are they things that travel far with great speed
    But can't be given reports to carry?[14]
    Are their comings and goings dark and dim
    But they cannot serve as screens fixedly?[c]
    Are they things whose violence hurts and kills,
120   But do not mean to behave hatefully?
    Are they things whose good deeds blanket the world

[9] The "Grand Vault" refers to the sky or the cosmos. The idea of filling the Grand Vault thus connotes vastness.

[10] The meaning of this line is quite obscure, and the translation is tentative.

[11] See note 8 above.

[12] The meaning of this remark is quite ambiguous and difficult to determine with any certainty. However, in light of the surrounding lines, I take it to mean that the workings of the things in question are invisible, like a great spirit entity. See the discussion of "spirit-like power" at 17.45–46.

[13] I.e., nobody knows whence they come or to where they depart.

[14] The Chinese text of this line seems to depart from the rhyme scheme of the poem. Commentators are unsure what to do with it, and some propose emending it to make it rhyme. I do not find their proposals compelling, so I have translated it as it stands, with the caveat that the line may be corrupt.

And are not implemented privately?
They attach themselves close unto the earth
But in the Vault, too, they wander idly.
They take the blowing winds to be their friends.   125
They have the rainfall as their progeny.
In the winter days, they make things frigid.
In the summer days, they make them sultry.
They are broad, grand, refined, and spirit-like.
Clouds let us conclude these objects to be."   130

Clouds

Here is a thing with the following traits:
Its figure is oh so completely bare,
Yet repeatedly, spirit-like, mutates.
Its good deeds blanket all under Heaven.   135
With forms, myriad eras it decorates.
Rituals and music it makes complete.
The noble and lowly it separates.
Nurturing the old and raising the young—
Upon this thing their continuance waits.   140
The name it is called is quite unlovely;
To violence as neighbor it relates.[15]
With good deeds done, its body is wasted.
Works completed, its home disintegrates.
Its aged and elderly, one discards;   145
New generations one accumulates.
It is something that humankind assists
And something a flying bird devastates.
I, your dumb minister, do not know it.
I ask to divine it from the Five Greats.[16]   150

The sovereign divines and then conveys,[d]
"Is it a thing with a girlish torso,
Yet a head like a horse's it displays?
Is it that which repeatedly mutates,
Yet lacking long life, it but briefly stays?   155
Is it a thing good at living its prime,

---

[15] This clue is based on features of the Chinese language. Since it cannot be explained here without giving away the answer to the riddle, I have placed the explanation at the very end of this section. The same applies to the other clues here that modern readers will likely find puzzling.

[16] The identity of the "Five Greats" is mysterious and a subject of dispute among commentators. In early China, rulers often performed divinations for the purpose of consulting spirits to acquire answers to various questions. It appears that some such practice is being referenced here.

Yet is clumsy at its elderly phase?
Is it that which has father and mother,
Yet is not male or female in its ways?
160   During the wintertime, it lies in wait.
In the summertime, it wanders and strays.
This thing does eat of the mulberry tree
And after that spits out silken thread sprays,
Which in the beginning are chaotic
165   But later fall into ordered arrays.
It is born during summer but hates heat.
It's fond of dampness but hates rainy days.
For pupae, this thing acts as a mother,[e]
And for moths, the role of father it plays.
170   Three times does this thing lie down to take rest,
And thrice, from resting, itself does it raise;
Its work then comes to a great completion.
These are called patterns a silkworm obeys."[17]

Silkworm

---

[17] Even with the answer to the riddle in hand, readers unfamiliar with silkworm farming (sericulture) may still find various aspects of the poem puzzling, so here is further explanation of the clues that may seem mysterious. Line 133: the silkworm is "bare" in the sense that it has no fur, feathers, or scales. Line 134: the silkworm "mutates" or "transforms" from an egg, through a series of intermediate stages, to become a moth. Line 136: silk is used for embroidered patterns, and in that sense the silkworm "decorates" myriad generations with "forms." Line 137: silk is used for ritual garments, and also as strings for instruments, so that is how the silkworm "completes" ritual and music. Line 138: this refers to how different types of silk clothing and embroidery mark differences in status. Lines 139–40: the point is that people's lives are dependent upon having clothing, such as the silkworm helps produce. Lines 141–42: the word for "silkworm" in ancient Chinese, *can* 蠶, was close in sound to words that mean "cruelty" (*can* 慘, or *can* 殘), and hence the silkworm's name is a "neighbor" to "violence" phonetically. Lines 143–44: this refers to the fact that silk is obtained by boiling or steaming the silkworm's cocoon before the insect breaks out of it; its body is thus destroyed and its "home" ruined. Lines 145–46: in sericulture, one does not strive to keep the mature animals (moths), as one would with other forms of animal husbandry, but rather focuses on harvesting its eggs. Line 147: though the silkworm is killed in the process of obtaining silk, humans may be said to "assist" it, in the sense of helping it to propagate. The word *li* 利, translated as "assist," can also mean "make use of" or "consider useful," and these other senses are probably implied as well. Lines 152–53: "girlish" here may be intended in the sense of "soft" or "supple." Alternatively, these two lines might refer to the Chinese legend of *ma tou niang* 馬頭娘 (lit. "the horse-headed maiden"), in which a girl became wrapped in a horse skin and was magically transformed into a silkworm; she was later conceived as the goddess of sericulture, and in some parts of China silkworms are referred to as *ma tou niang*. Line 155: the entire life cycle of silkworms is only a few months long. Lines 156–57: the meaning of these lines is somewhat unclear, but I take them to refer to the fact that the mature silkworms (i.e., moths) live for only a few days, whereas they occupy a caterpillar form for a period several

There is an object that is here present:
It is born from mountains and from hillsides.   175
In people's rooms and halls it's resident.
It has neither knowledge nor cleverness,
Yet it is good at sewing a garment.
Though it neither robs nor steals from people,
Drilling and boring, it makes its movement.[18]   180
Day and night it links things separated
So to make a form or an arrangement.
With it, one can link things vertically
And craft well horizontal attachment.[19]
Below, to common folk, it gives cover;   185
Above, to kings and sov'reigns, adornment.
It has great works and deeds very widespread,
But flaunts not its good, worthy achievement.
If frequently used, then it is well-kept.[20]
If it is not used, then it goes absent.   190
I, your dumb minister, do not know it.
So I dare ask Your Majesty's judgment.

The king said, "Is it what's big when first born
Yet when doing great deeds, small size it shows?
Is it that which develops a long tail   195
Yet also has a keen-honed tip at its nose?

---

times longer; they are thus "good at" maintaining themselves in their "prime age," but falter when it comes to being old. Lines 164–65: this apparently refers to how silk is obtained from a cocoon (a "chaotic" bundle) by unraveling the strands and spinning them into thread, which is then woven into cloth (an ordered arrangement). Line 167: the exact meaning is unclear, but one possible meaning, as explained by Yang Liang, is that the silkworm eggs need to be washed at the beginning, but once hatched, the silkworms need to be kept dry. Alternatively, it may refer to the fact that silkworms require high humidity, but excessive humidity can lead to mold and disease. Lines 168–69: though in one sense the silkworm *becomes* a pupa and then a moth, in another sense it might be said to "give birth" to these later forms, like a parent. Lines 170–71: these lines refer to the three (or in some cases, four) molting stages the silkworm undergoes before spinning its cocoon. During these periods, it is inactive and does not eat.

[18] Thieves and robbers would often drill or bore through walls in order to gain access to a home stealthily, so the fact that the object works by drilling and boring, but is not a criminal, is meant to be puzzling.

[19] As with many riddles, in this and the preceding line the text employs language that provides a clue yet can also mislead an audience, but the play is hard to render in English. The terms translated as "vertical" (從) and "horizontal" (衡) were often used in the Warring States period to refer to north-south or east-west strategic alliances of states. Thus, an early Chinese audience might be tempted to think of the answer to the riddle in terms of something political.

[20] For further explanation of this and the following clue, see the note that follows the answer to the riddle.

Is it that whose head sharply moves forward
Yet whose tail in a winding motion flows?
200   Though it proceeds, now hither, now thither,
To use it for work, tie the tail it tows.[21]
Though it neither has feathers nor has wings,
Rapid back-and-forth moves it does compose.[22]
Its work commences when a tail it grows.
205   Its work ends when its tail back around goes.
This thing is the father unto hairpins
And mother whence shuttle-bobbins arose.[f]
With it, one both stitches outer layers
And attaches inner linings of clothes.
210   These are called patterns a needle follows."[23]

Needle

The world is lacking its proper order;
Let me sing a song of its oddity.[24]
Heaven and Earth have switched their positions.
215   Seasons have switched directionality.

---

[21] The word "tie" (*jie* 結) here can mean either "tie on" or "tie up," and the poem is probably playing intentionally on the ambiguity (see note 23 below). However, the latter sense seems most relevant to the kind of puzzling contrast that the text appears to aim at presenting here: one makes use of the to-and-fro motion of the thing by tying up its tail and thereby restricting its movement.

[22] The Chinese text here is somewhat ambiguous on the exact type of movement envisioned, but given the comparison with flying creatures in the previous line, and in light of the answer to the riddle, it is presumably a kind of up-and-down motion (like the flapping of wings) that is meant.

[23] As with the riddle on the silkworm, I here add explanation of some clues that may seem puzzling even after the answer is revealed. Line 176 refers to the mining of metal from which needles are made. Line 187 refers to embroidery. Line 191 refers to the experience of losing a needle. Lines 194–95 refer to how the needle, a small thing, originally comes from a large chunk of metal ore. From line 196 onward, the "tail" refers to the thread. Line 204 refers to the initial knot one makes in the thread to anchor it, and line 205 refers to the final loop or knot one makes with the thread to end the stitching. Lines 206–207: a hairpin is like a larger version of needle, and in that sense the needle is "father" to the hairpin. The shuttle-bobbin is a long, thin stick around which thread is wound. As the shuttle is passed back and forth on a loom, it lays down a long tail of thread, and thus likewise resembles a larger version of a needle, so the needle may be said to be a "mother" to it.

[24] From here onward, the text no longer presents riddles, and the form of poetry shifts. Accordingly, some scholars have thought that this final section was not originally intended to go with the preceding poems, and that it was added here during the process of editing. The poetry here is divided mostly into units of four characters, with rhymes on the final character of every other unit. I have rendered each unit as a separate line of ten syllables, but as before, the rhyme scheme in the translation does not match the rhyme scheme in the Chinese exactly.

The arrayed stars have perished and fallen.[25]
Both day and night it is dark and gloomy.[g]
Dimness and dark ascend to prominence.
Sun and moon sink into obscurity.
Unprejudiced, upright, unselfish men   220
Are thought to practice factionality.[26]
Those who intend and love the public weal[27,h]
Stack buildings and raise halls for royalty.[28]
Those who without selfishness sentence men
Bring out armor and double weaponry.[29,i]   225
Those pure and whole in the Way and virtue
Are denounced by slanderous mouths many.
People of *ren* are dismissed and held back.
Haughty, violent men take charge strongly.
The world is so dark and precarious,   230
I fear it will lose its best men wholly.
Chi dragons are reduced to mere lizards.[30]
Owls assume phoenixes' identity.[31]
Bi Gan underwent evisceration.
In Kuang, Confucius was a detainee.   235
So radiant, so very radiant!
Such was their wisdom's luminosity!
Lamentable, oh how lamentable![j]
Their meeting such times was so unlucky!
So corrective were the great acts they did[k]   240
In their desire for ritual and *yi*!
Yet how benighted was the entire world
In its condition so dark and gloomy!

---

[25] Here, "stars" is a metaphor for virtuous people. So, too, with the reference to "sun" and "moon" a few lines later.

[26] More literally: "Are thought to practice Vertical and Horizontal [politicking]." On the Vertical and Horizontal alliances, see note 19 above.

[27] The Chinese text of this and the following three lines is very difficult and perhaps corrupt. Not content with the proposals of previous commentators, I present my own understanding of their meaning, but the translation remains tentative. See textual note h for further explanation.

[28] I.e., these good people are assigned tasks for the selfish benefit of the ruler, and are not allowed to act in ways that benefit people more broadly.

[29] I.e., the enactment of due punishments winds up increasing hostility from the people (because they mistakenly think the judge is acting oppressively).

[30] The *chi* is a type of dragon, but commentators disagree over what its distinctive features were. As with the references to astronomical bodies, here the dragon—as a noble creature—is a metaphor for a virtuous person, and its being reduced to a lizard is a metaphor for social and political setbacks.

[31] The owl was often regarded in early China as an inauspicious bird. Here it is a metaphor for a bad person, and its taking on the identity of the phoenix (an auspicious bird) represents social and political success.

       While that once-bright Heaven does not return,

245   Our sorrowfulness has no boundary.

       A thousand years done, it's sure to come back;[32]

       This is a constant from antiquity.

       So, disciples, work hard at your learning,

       And Heaven will not act divergently.[33,l]

250   The sage folds his hands in patient waiting;

       Soon will arrive his opportunity!

       Some join with fools, and confusion possess;[34]

       I wish to sound words of their backwardness.[m]

       The little song goes:

255   I think of that location far away.

       Oh how it is in such difficulty!

       People of *ren* are dismissed and held back.

       Violent men advance successfully.[n]

       Loyal ministers face dangers and threats

260   While slanderous people live happily.

       A beautiful jade or a lovely pearl[35,o]

       Some don't know to make their accessory.

       Miscellaneous cloth and silk brocade[36]

       They don't know how to tell apart rightly.

265   As for the likes of Lüju and Zishe[37]

---

[32] The "it" here is "bright Heaven" (i.e., the proper state of the world). A number of early Chinese texts report the view that order and disorder go in cycles of several centuries. See *Mencius* 2B13, which predicts a true (i.e., sage) king every five hundred years, and *Han Feizi*, chap. 8, which remarks that sages appear once every thousand generations.

[33] I.e., "bright Heaven" will not break its thousand-year cycle.

[34] From here to the end of the chapter, there is a great deal of uncertainty about how to group the lines of the text and, therefore, how to construe their meaning. The approach adopted in the translation is largely my own (tentative) attempt to make good sense of the text, and it differs from those of the majority of commentators. Further explanation is provided in the endnotes.

[35] The section of the poem from this line to the end is quoted in other early texts, where it is said to be a poem that Xunzi wrote to Lord Chunshen, declining the lord's invitation to return to serve him after one of his retainers had persuaded him to send Xunzi away. For that reason, many editors treat this section as separate from the previous lines, but I dissent from that view. The person who does not know to wear jades and pearls as accessories is a metaphor for a person (e.g., a lord) who does not know to employ worthy men.

[36] Here, "miscellaneous cloth" and "silk brocade" are metaphors for inferior and superior men.

[37] Lüju was a famously beautiful woman. Nothing is known of Zishe, but some identify him as Zidu, who was a famously beautiful man (see *Mencius* 6A7). Here, peo-

None are willing to assist to marry.
Instead, the likes of Momu and Lifu[38]
Are what these people treat delightedly.
Blindness they take to be sharp-sightedness.
Deafness they regard as hearing keenly.					270
Dangerous things they consider as safe.
Auspicious things they view as unlucky.
Alas! Alack! Oh Heaven high above!
How could I keep such people's company?

---

ple's unwillingness to serve as their matchmakers stands for a lord's unwillingness
to put worthy people in positions of power.

[38] Momu was a famously ugly woman. Nothing is known of Lifu, but the contrast
with the preceding lines suggests that he was a famously ugly man. Here they stand
for people who are inferior, yet win the ruler's favor.

CHAPTER 27

The Grand Digest

THE GRAND DIGEST[1]

If the lord of men exalts ritual and honors the worthy, he will become
a true king. If he relies heavily on law and has concern for the people,
he will become a hegemon. If he cares only for profit and frequently
5 engages in deception, he will be endangered.[2]

•

If one wishes to be close to all four sides at once, no place is better
than the absolute center. And so according to ritual, the true king is
sure to dwell at the center of the world.

•

According to ritual, the Son of Heaven sets up screens outside his
10 gates, and the feudal lords set up screens within their gates. The reason for setting up screens outside the gates is that one does not want
to show off what is outside them. The reason for setting up screens
inside the gates is that one does not want to show off what is inside
them.[3]

•

15 According to ritual, when a feudal lord summons his minister, the
minister does not wait for his chariot to be harnessed, but goes off
running,[4] making a shambles of his clothing. The *Odes* says:

> In shambles, off he is going;
> Him the Duke's man is summoning.[5]

---

[1] Because of the wide variety of topics covered here, this chapter is thought to be a
compilation of Xunzi's teachings that was done by his students. Many pieces of it
appear in identical or nearly identical form in earlier chapters. I have generally followed earlier commentators' divisions of the text into numerous small paragraphs,
but readers should be aware that in many cases there is room for debate over how the
sentences should be grouped.

[2] These same words appear at 16.14–18 and 17.199–202.

[3] These lines are extremely ambiguous in the Chinese. Commentators are divided
over how to take them, and the translation is tentative. Perhaps the idea is that although the Son of Heaven owns the whole world, he should avoid becoming arrogant about this, so he sets up screens outside his gates to prevent a view of his territory, whereas even though the feudal lord has great possessions and power, he
should not be arrogant about this, either, so he sets up screens within his gates to
avoid flaunting his possessions.

[4] Compare *Analects* 10.20.

[5] Mao #100.

According to ritual, when the Son of Heaven summons a feudal lord, 20
the feudal lord rides his chariot, pulled by men, out to the horses.[6]
The *Odes* says:

> I now take my chariot out,
> Out into the meadows thither;
> One from the Son of Heaven's place 25
> Declares unto me: "Come hither."[7]

•

According to ritual, the Son of Heaven wears a garment with a mountain decoration and a high ceremonial cap. A feudal lord wears black
garments and a cap. A grand officer wears lesser garments and a high
ceremonial cap. A regular officer wears leather garments and a cap of 30
hide.[8]

•

According to ritual, the Son of Heaven has as his accoutrement a *ting*,
a feudal lord has as his accoutrement a *shu*, and a grand officer has as
his apparatus a *hu*.[9]

•

According to ritual, the Son of Heaven wields a carved bow, a feudal 35
lord wields a vermillion bow, and a grand officer wields a black bow.[10]

•

When feudal lords meet with one another,[11] they are to have their
councilors act as intermediaries, they are to take along trained officers
for the duration of their journey, and they are to employ people of *ren*
to stay behind and keep watch over things. 40

•

When inquiring after a person, one is to use a *gui*. When asking questions of a well-bred man, one is to use a *bi*. When summoning a person, one is to use a *yuan*. When dismissing a person, one is to use a
jue. When reversing a dismissal, one is to use a *huan*.[12]

•

---

[6] I.e., as opposed to waiting for someone to bring the horses in to be harnessed and
then mounting the chariot. Again, this expresses haste in responding to the summons.

[7] Mao #168. The received version of the *Odes* differs slightly from the version quoted
here.

[8] Nearly identical wording appears at 10.78–82.

[9] *Ting* 珽, *shu* 荼, and *hu* 笏 are ritual implements of varying materials and shapes.
They were used as insignias of rank.

[10] Besides warfare, occasions for the use of bows included hunts and archery contests,
and it may be one or all of these contexts that is at issue here.

[11] The particular kind of "meeting" envisioned here appears to be a formal summit
conducted outside the feudal lord's capital, and is not simply a matter of one feudal
lord visiting or happening upon another.

[12] The text does not specify who is the subject doing all these things, but in context, it
is most likely the Son of Heaven or a feudal lord. Accordingly, the "inquiry" men-

45 As for the ruler of men, when a heart that is *ren* is set up within him, then understanding is its servant, and ritual is its completion. And so, a true king puts *ren* first and puts ritual behind, because the Heavenly given order of implementation is thus.[13]

•

The *Register of Rituals of Inquiry* says, "When the money spent be-
50 comes copious, it harms virtue. When the resources utilized become lavish, it disrupts ritual."[14] Talk of ritual, talk of ritual—is it talk of just jades and silks?[15] The *Odes* says:

> These things, they are so lovely;
> Only, let them match rightly.[16, a]

55 If it is neither timely nor fitting, if it is neither respectful nor good form, if it is neither cheerful nor joyful, then even though it is lovely, it is not a case of ritual propriety.[17]

•

---

tioned here is probably a diplomatic mission sent to foster ties with a feudal lord. *Gui, bi, yuan, jue,* and *huan* were all jade tokens of various shapes that were shown or given to the person at whom these acts were directed. In the case of at least the last three, there seems to be a linguistic or symbolic rationale for their use. In ancient Chinese, the name *yuan* 瑗 sounds close to another word, *yuan* 援, which means "to wave the arm" or "to assist," so using the *yuan* token signaled a wave or call for assistance. The name *jue* 玦 sounds like the words "to part" (*jue* 訣) or "to release" (*jue* 决). (In modern Mandarin, it also has the same pronunciation as the word translated here as "dismiss" [*jue* 絕], though in ancient times they were apparently more distant in sound.) Furthermore, the *jue* token was shaped like a circle, but with a section missing. Thus, it symbolized the "breaking off" of relations involved in dismissal from office. The name *huan* 環 sounds like "to return" (*huan* 還), and the token itself was shaped like a loop, i.e., a "circling back," so it symbolized being recalled to office.

13 The meaning of this passage is obscure, but I take its point to be this: the orientation of one's heart sets the direction for the rest of one's abilities (i.e., this is the "Heavenly given" or "natural" order of implementation in human psychology), and so it is most important to prioritize achieving *ren*, because then ritual will bring it to its full fruition, as is appropriate. Prioritizing ritual over *ren*, by contrast, might lead to empty formalism in which the caring for others that is constitutive of *ren* is improperly sacrificed for ritual correctness.

14 In the ancient ritual compendium, the *Yili*, there is a chapter titled "Rituals of Inquiry," a section of which is a "Record" containing statements that are close to, but not identical to, what is quoted here.

15 This sentence also appears in *Analects* 17.11, where it is presented as a saying of Confucius.

16 Mao #170. The received text of the *Odes* differs slightly from what is quoted here. However, Xunzi seems to read the lines quite differently from how they are commonly understood in their original context.

17 Though Xunzi elsewhere recognizes that rituals are used for sad occasions, here he demands that the practice of ritual be "cheerful" and "joyful" for the reason that the particular ritual in question, namely inquiring after another person, is meant to express goodwill toward that person.

Those who cross waters mark out the deep places, to make it so that people will not fall in. Those who order the people mark out what is chaotic, to make it so that people will not err. The rituals are their   60
markers. The former kings used rituals to mark out what would make the whole world chaotic. Now if one discards the rituals, this is getting rid of the markers. And so, the people become lost and confused and fall into disasters and troubles. This is why punishments and penalties become profuse.[18]   65

•

Shun said, "It is the case that I follow my desires yet attain order."[19,b] Thus, the genesis of rituals is for the sake of worthies on down to the common people, not for the sake of the perfected sage. Nevertheless, they are also the means by which one achieves sagehood. If one does not study them, one will not achieve it. Yao studied under Jun Chou,   70
Shun studied under Wucheng Zhao, and Yu studied under Xi Wangguo.[20]

•

After the age of fifty, one is not to perform the mourning ritual in its entirety.[21] After the age of seventy, it is only the wearing of the mourning garments that is to be kept.   75

•

In the ritual for "personal welcoming,"[22] the father stands, facing south. The son kneels, facing north. The father performs a libation and commands him: "Go and welcome your helpmate, to accomplish our ancestral tasks.[23] Reverently guide her to serve respectfully as the successor to your mother. Thus may we have constancy." The son   80
says, "Yes. I only fear that I may not be capable of this. How would I dare forget your command?"

•

As for "proper conduct," it means conducting ritual. As for ritual, through it those who are noble are treated with respect. Through it those who are elderly are treated with filiality. Through it those who   85
are senior are treated with deference. Through it those who are young

---

[18] Compare 17.238–42.

[19] A line very similar to this appears in the *Dayumo* chapter of the *Documents* (see "The Counsels of the Great Yü" in Waltham 1971, p. 22). See also *Analects* 2.4.

[20] Ancient texts provide few details about these teachers of the sages.

[21] The Tang commentator Yang Liang explains that parts of the ritual to be foregone are those that involve vigorous wailing and hopping about.

[22] This ritual is part of the wedding process. The groom (here referred to as "the son") personally goes to the home of the bride to lead her back to his household. The part of the ritual described here takes place as he sets off.

[23] "Ancestral tasks" here refers both to carrying on the line of one's ancestors and to the continuance of sacrifices to them, tasks that are accomplished by producing offspring.

are treated with kindness. Through it those who are lowly are treated with generosity.

•

90 Giving gifts to the members of one's household is like employing commendations and rewards toward the state and its clans. Showing anger to one's servants and concubines is like employing punishments and penalties on the myriad common people.[24]

•

The way a gentleman treats his children is that he loves them but is not besotted with them, he assigns them tasks but is not demeaning 95 toward them, and he guides them with the Way but does not force them.[25,c]

•

Ritual has making people's hearts agreeable as its root. And so, those things that are not in the *Classic of Rituals* yet make people's hearts agreeable are still things that carry ritual propriety.[d]

•

100 The major, overall works of ritual are to ornament happiness when serving the living, to ornament sorrow when sending off the dead, and to ornament awe-inspiring power when engaged in military affairs.[26]

•

To treat relatives as is appropriate for relatives, to treat old friends as 105 is appropriate for old friends, to treat servants as is appropriate for servants, to treat laborers as is appropriate for laborers—these are the gradations in *ren*.[e]

To treat those noble as is appropriate for those noble, to treat those venerable as is appropriate for those venerable, to treat those worthy 110 as is appropriate for those worthy, to treat those elderly as is appropriate for those elderly, to treat those with seniority as is appropriate for those with seniority—these are the classings in *yi*.

To attain proper regulation in carrying these out is the ordering in ritual.

115 *Ren* is care, and so it makes for affection. *Yi* is good order, and so it makes for proper conduct. Ritual is proper regulation, and so it makes for completion [of these].

---

[24] By itself, this section is obscure. Nearly identical wording appears in the early text *Da Dai Liji*, where it is attributed to Confucius's disciple Zengzi. There the surrounding lines argue that one who is a good family member will serve well in government, for the reason that the tasks of family life are like the tasks of government. I have translated the line as expressing that reason, in accordance with that context, since the context here gives one no other hints about how to construe it.

[25] Like the previous passage, this statement is also attributed to Zengzi in the *Da Dai Liji*. For similar remarks about restraint between father and son, see *Mencius* 4A18.

[26] Very similar wording appears at 19.418–21.

For being *ren*, there is a proper neighborhood.[27] For being *yi*, there is a proper gateway. If in attempting to be *ren* one dwells in what is not its proper neighborhood, then it is not *ren*. If in attempting to be   120
yi one proceeds by what is not its proper gateway, then it is not *yi*.[28]

To extend kindness without good order does not constitute *ren*. To follow good order without proper regulation does not constitute *yi*.[f] To observe proper regulation without harmoniousness does not constitute ritual propriety. Harmoniousness without external expression   125
does not constitute musicality. And so I say: as for *ren*, *yi*, ritual propriety, and musicality, their achievement is united.

The gentleman dwells in *ren* by means of *yi*, and only then is it *ren*. He carries out *yi* by means of ritual, and only then is it *yi*. In implementing ritual, he returns to the roots and completes the branches,   130
and only then is it ritual.[29] When all three are thoroughly mastered, only then is it the Way.

•

The goods and money [given for a funeral] are called "donations."[30] The carts and horses are called "contributions." The clothes and garments are called "presents." The paraphernalia are called "gifts." The   135
jades and shells are called "offerings." The donations and contributions are what are used to assist the living. The presents and gifts are what are used to send off the dead. If one's send-off for the dead does not arrive while the corpse is still lying in repose, or if one's condolences for the living do not arrive while they are still grieved and sad,   140
that is not ritual propriety. And so, going fifty *li* a day when traveling to participate in auspicious events, going a hundred *li* a day when rushing to participate in mourning, and having one's contributions and gifts arrive in time for the undertakings—these are major points in ritual propriety.   145

•

Ritual is what tows government. When engaging in government, if one does not employ ritual, then the government will not go.

•

When the Son of Heaven ascends to the throne, the Upper Councilor comes forward and says, "What will you do about this? So expansive

---

[27] Here and in the paragraph below, the wording is reminiscent of both *Analects* 4.1 and *Mencius* 5B7.

[28] The text of this and the next paragraph appears to be corrupt; following commentators, I have adopted a number of emendations here.

[29] Commentators offer different suggestions about how to construe the "roots" and "branches." Perhaps the most plausible is the Tang commentator Yang Liang's view that "roots" refers to *ren* and *yi*, and "branches" refers to particular regulations of ritual.

[30] This passage employs a number of technical terms for funeral offerings, for which there are no ready English equivalents. The words in brackets are added here to convey the context implied by the technical terms.

150   are the things to worry over! If you are able to eliminate troubles, then you will be counted as a blessing. If you are not able to eliminate troubles, then you will be counted as a villain." He gives the Son of Heaven this first memorandum.[31]

155   The Middle Councilor comes forward and says, "You who are partner to Heaven and possessor of the lands below:[32]

> May you deliberate about undertakings before pursuing them and deliberate about troubles before they arrive. To deliberate about undertakings before pursuing them is called taking hold of things. If one takes hold of things, then undertakings will be accomplished splendidly. To deliberate about troubles before they arrive is called anticipating things. If one anticipates things, then disasters will not happen. To deliberate about undertakings after they have come about is called following after things. If one follows after things, then undertakings will not be handled properly. To deliberate about troubles after they have come about is called being trapped. If one is trapped, then disasters cannot be averted."

160

165

He gives the Son of Heaven this second memorandum.

170   The Lower Councilor comes forward and says, "Be respectful and vigilant without slacking. Though celebrants may be in your hall, those offering condolences are at your door. Disasters and blessings are neighbors, and no one recognizes their respective gates.[33] Anticipate them! Anticipate them! The myriad common people look to this." He gives the Son of Heaven this third memorandum.

•

175   Whenever the sage Yu saw people plowing in pairs, he stood leaning on the crossbar of his chariot.[34] Whenever he passed through a village of ten households, he was sure to descend from his chariot.[35]

•

If one holds hunts excessively early, or if one holds court excessively late, that is not ritual propriety.

•

---

[31] Since the minister is said to give the Son of Heaven this "memorandum" (*ce* 策, literally a "bundle" of bamboo strips on which something is written), the minister is apparently reciting his speech from this text.

[32] Apart from this opening remark, the remainder of the memorandum is rhymed in the original.

[33] Commentators note similarity between this thought and *Daodejing* chap. 58.

[34] A gesture of respect, resembling a bow.

[35] The purpose of this act is unclear, but Yang Liang's commentary proposes that "in any village of ten households there was sure to be someone loyal and trustworthy," so Yu got down to search out this person.

In bringing order to the people, if one does not employ ritual, actions   180
will then succumb to pitfalls.[36]

     •

When one bows even with the horizontal, this is called "paying obeisance." When one bows lower than the horizontal, this is called "tapping the head." When one goes all the way to the ground, this is
called "tapping the forehead."[37]   185

     •

The ministers of a grand officer are to pay obeisance to him, but are
not to tap their heads for him. This is not a matter of exalting his
household's ministers, but is rather a means of showing deference to
the lord.[38]

     •

With those at the first level, the arrangement is to be by order of their   190
age among their fellow villagers.[39] With those at the second level, the
arrangement is to be by order of their age among their clansmen.
With those at the third level, even though their clansmen may include
people in their seventies, those people are not to dare to take precedence over them. [Upper grand officers, middle grand officers, lower   195
grand officers.][40]

     •

In undertakings for good fortune,[41] treat as highest those who have
exalted status. In undertakings for mourning, treat as highest those
who are close relatives.

     •

---

[36] The text does not express clearly whose actions are at issue. It could be those of the
ruler and/or the people. The language here is also quite reminiscent of the earlier
passage in lines 58–65.

[37] The commentator Hao Yixing explains that these types of bows are all performed
while kneeling. In the first, neither one's hands nor head touches the ground. In the
second, one's hands are clasped together and touch the ground, and one's head
then touches one's clasped hands. In the third, both one's hands and head touch
the ground.

[38] I.e., since the lord is supreme in the state, the more reverent gesture of "tapping the
head" is done only for him.

[39] Here, "level" (ming 命, more literally, "commission") refers to a governmental rank,
with the "first" as lowest. The context is not specified, but commentators suggest
that the "arrangement" in question refers to the order of drinking at a drinking
ceremony, or perhaps the order of seating at some other kind of ceremony. The
basic point of the passage is that age is given precedence over official rank, but only
up to a certain point.

[40] The bracketed words appear in the original, but do not constitute a coherent syntactic unit. The text may be corrupt, or, as the commentator Yu Chang suggests,
these words may be an early gloss on the words "third level," "second level," and
"first level," respectively, that has mistakenly been incorporated into the main text.

[41] E.g., sacrifices.

200 Without him,[42] relations between lord and minister will not be reverent. Without him, relations between father and son will not be close. Without him, relations between brothers will not be smooth. Without him, relations between husband and wife will not be happy.

205   Through him, the young grow and mature.
    Through him, the old obtain nurture.

Thus, Heaven and Earth produce them, but the sage completes them.

•

At the "inquiry," one asks about the person. At the "banquet," one presents offerings. At the "private audience," one has a private meeting with the person.[43]

•

210   Beauty in words and speeches
    Is talking finely and augustly.
    Beauty in a royal court
    Is its being full and orderly.

•

In serving as another's minister or subordinate, you may remonstrate
215 with him, but you may not disparage him. You may leave him, but you may not simply run off.[g] You may be upset at him, but you may not rage against him.

•

The way a lord is to treat a grand officer of his is to ask after him thrice if the man is sick, and to make condolence calls thrice if the man dies.
220 The way a lord is to treat a regular officer of his is to ask after him once, and to make a condolence call once. Except for asking after one who is sick or mourning one who has died, feudal lords are not to visit the homes of their ministers.

•

After the burial [of one's father], if one's lord or the friends of one's
225 father provide food for the occasion, then indeed eat it, and do not avoid the fine grains and meats, but if there is regular or sweet wine, then decline that. •

[42] The text here does not specify the thing that is lacked. However, this section is almost identical to a passage at 10.176–82, and there it is clear that the passage is referring to the gentleman/sage. Also, like that passage, the text here ends with the claim about the sage. Hence, it seems most reasonable to take the missing referent in this case as some particular person (the "him" used in the translation), who turns out to be the gentleman/sage.

[43] The point of this passage is to explain stages and terms of diplomatic protocol. When an emissary from one state visits another, he first "inquires" after the well-being of the ruler, as a matter of ritual politeness. A feast is then given in the emissary's honor, at which he presents gifts sent by his own ruler. The emissary then has a "private summit" with the ruler.

According to ritual, one's sleeping quarters are not to outdo a temple, and garments for feasts[44] are not to outdo those for sacrifices.

·

The *xian* hexagram of the *Book of Changes* presents the proper rela-   230
tions for husband and wife.[45] The way of husband and wife must be
correctly followed, for it is the root of relations between lord and
minister, father and son.[46] *Xian* is stimulus [and response]:[47] the lofty
places itself beneath the lowly, the male places himself beneath the
female, what is soft and yielding is above and what is hard and firm   235
is below.[48]

·

The *yi* of recruiting an officer[49] and the way of personal welcoming[50]
are instances of laying weight upon beginnings.[51]

·

Ritual is something upon which people stand.[52] Just as one who loses
that upon which he stands is sure to tumble, stumble, fall, and drown,   240

---

[44] The text seems corrupt here. I have followed an emendation suggested by commentators, but the emendation can still result in different readings. Instead of "garments for feasts," an alternative would be "garments for ordinary wear."

[45] Hexagram 31 of the *Changes* is *xian* ䷞. Its name literally means "all," and it is composed of the trigram *dui* above the trigram *gen*. *Dui* is taken to represent a young
female, while *gen* is taken to represent a young male, hence the connection with
marital relations.

[46] An early commentary on the *Book of Changes* (the *Xu Gua*) elaborates on this point
in a helpful way: "Only after there are Heaven and Earth will there be the myriad
things. Only after there are the myriad things will there be man and woman. Only
after there are man and woman will there be husband and wife. Only after there are
husband and wife will there be father and son. Only after there are father and son
will there be lord and minister."

[47] Here the text is playing with the fact that the name of the hexagram, 咸, when combined with the word "heart" 心, becomes the word *gan* 感, meaning "feeling" or
"stimulus." The words "and response" are not in the original text, but in early Chinese thought, a "stimulus" was supposed to engender a proper "response" from
things, and that half of the interaction seems presupposed in the discussion here.

[48] Apart from describing the position of the trigrams, as well as possible sexual connotations, the point of this claim seems to be that those occupying the stronger or
higher position must also be humble and to that extent put themselves "beneath"
the other party.

[49] Lords were supposed to follow specific rituals in requesting the service of a worthy
person. The phrase rendered awkwardly here as "the *yi* of recruiting an officer"
might thus be rendered more perspicuously as (roughly) "the right conduct seen in
the rituals for properly recruiting an officer."

[50] On the ritual of "personal welcoming," see note 22 above.

[51] I.e., beginnings of important relationships.

[52] The word translated here as "stand" is *lü* 履, which also frequently has the sense of
"walking," as opposed to merely standing still. There may also be a phonetic word
play involved here, as the pronunciation of 履 at various times and places has been
very close to that of *li* 禮 ("ritual").

so ritual is something where even a slight loss brings about great chaos.

•

The role of ritual in setting the state aright is like that of scales in relation to the light and the heavy, or like the ink-line in relation to the
245 curved and the straight. And so,

    If their lives are without ritual,
    Then people cannot survive.
    If affairs are without ritual,
    In them success does not thrive.
250   If state and clan are without ritual,
    For them peace does not arrive.[53]

•

The sounds of the attached bells [on the chariot of the Son of Heaven] match the tunes *Wu* and *Xiang* when proceeding slowly, and they match the tunes *Shao* and *Hu* when proceeding quickly.[54]

•

255 The gentleman heeds proper standards, practices proper deportment, and only then takes office.[55,h]

•

The "descending frost"[56] is the time to welcome new brides [into the home]. When the ice melts, then such receptions are to decrease.[i] "Riding"[57] is to happen only once every ten days.

•

260 When he is sitting, look at his knees. When he is standing, look at his feet. When responding to his words, look at his face.[58]

•

---

[53] The Chinese text of this rhyme is not quite identical to that which appears 2.48–53, but the difference between them is so slight that it makes no difference to the translation, so I have used the same rendering here.

[54] These lines are nearly identical to ones found at 18.325–28 and 19.27–29. Regarding the one character that differs here, I follow the emendation suggested by a number of commentators to make it the same as in those other passages.

[55] Many commentators group this sentence with the previous line and (with an emendation) arrive at a very different reading: "The gentleman [i.e., the ruler] hears the notes [i.e., of the bells], practices his deportment, and only then goes out [i.e., to ride the chariot to court]."

[56] A traditional name for a period of time, around the last part of October.

[57] Most commentators regard this word, which more literally means "driving" (e.g., a chariot), as a euphemism for sexual intercourse.

[58] The referent of "he" is not clear from the text. Based on parallels with the *Liji*, commentators take the "he" to be a father, and take these sentences to be directed at the son, as descriptions of proper deference. However, since commentators take the following section to be a minister's behavior toward his lord, this section might be taken in that vein, too.

When he is standing, then look at him from a distance of six *chi*, or increase it up to six sixes, which is thirty-six, or three *zhang* and six *chi*.[59]

•

Patterning and seemliness, dispositions and implements are in turn   265
central and peripheral.[60]

•

To be able to reflect and ponder what is central to ritual is called being able to deliberate.[61]

•

In ritual, the fundamental and the secondary accord with each other, and beginning and end match each other.[62]   270

•

Ritual takes resources and goods as its implements. It takes noble and lowly as its patterns. It takes abundance and scarcity as its differentiations.[63]

•

An inferior minister serves his lord with material goods. A mediocre minister serves his lord with his body.[64] A superior minister serves his   275
lord with his person.[65]

•

The *Book of Changes* says, "If one returns and follows the Way, what blameworthiness is there?" The *Spring and Autumn Annals* treats Duke Mu as being worthy, because he was able to change.[66]

•

---

[59] As noted above, commentators take the "he" in this passage as referring to a lord, and they view these words as directed to a minister. Some also combine this section with the previous one. A *chi* was roughly nine inches (approximately twenty-three centimeters), and a *zhang* was the equivalent of ten *chi*. So, according to the text, the minimum respectful distance from which to engage the person would be about four and half feet, and the maximum would be about twenty-seven feet.

[60] This wording is nearly identical to wording at 19.183–84. However, there it is not a freestanding sentence, and moreover the situation it describes appears (in context) *not* to be something that Xunzi is strongly endorsing. The discrepancies between that passage and this line, along with the lack of further context here, make it extremely difficult to know how best to understand the sentence in this location, and I strongly suspect that this portion of text is corrupt. I have rendered the line in a way that best reflects its similarity to the earlier passage, but the translation remains highly tentative.

[61] Identical wording appears at 19.167–68.

[62] Nearly identical wording appears at 19.140–41.

[63] Identical wording appears at 19.176–78.

[64] I.e., he is willing to die for his lord.

[65] I.e., with his character, namely through being good. An alternative construal of the last part, favored by some commentators, is ". . . with people," where this is taken as meaning that the superior minister serves his lord by recommending good and worthy persons for office.

[66] The quotation from the *Changes* is from hexagram 9, *xiaoxu* (☴), and in particular

If a man has a friend who is jealous, then worthy acquaintances will
280 not draw near to this man. If a lord has a minister who is jealous, then
worthy people will not come to this lord. To block out those who are
unprejudiced is called obfuscation. To keep unseen those who are
good is called jealousy. To recommend those who are jealous and
obfuscating is called promoting acquaintance with deceivers. People
285 who promote acquaintance with deceivers, and ministers who are
jealous and obfuscating—they are ruin and calamity for a state.

•

One whose mouth can speak it[67] and can personally practice it is a
treasure for the state. One whose mouth cannot speak it, but who can
personally practice it, is a precious vessel of the state. One whose
290 mouth can speak it, but who cannot personally practice it, is an implement for the state. One whose mouth speaks what is good, but
who personally practices what is bad, is an abomination for the state.
One who brings order to a state respects its treasures, cares
for its precious vessels, employs its implements, and eliminates its
295 abominations.

•

If you do not enrich the people, you will lack the means by which to
nurture their dispositions.[68] If you do not teach the people, you will
lack the means by which to bring order to their nature.[69] And so, let
families have a plot of five *mou* for their residence, and a plot of one
300 hundred *mou* for their farmland. Set them to work at their tasks, and
do not snatch the proper times away from them.[70] That is how to enrich them. Set up Grand Academies. Establish provincial and village

---

from a "line statement" explaining the bottom line. The original sense of the quotation is ambiguous, and here it is perhaps being read out of context. It is not clear
exactly what aspect of the *Spring and Autumn Annals* is being mentioned, but commentators propose that it refers to how Duke Mu of Qin ignored the advice of his
ministers Baili Xi and/or Jian Shu, leading to a major military defeat at Yao 殽 ca.
627 BCE. He admitted his error, learned to take advice, and so became successful.

[67] The referent of "it" is not specified in the text, but in light of the later part of the
passage about one who "speaks what is good," the referent seems likely to be "what
is good." The "it" might also refer more generally to the Way. Compare the wording
of *Analects* 6.20.

[68] Commentators explain "nurturing" the "dispositions" as providing for people's
natural desires for food and other essentials. However, given Xunzi's discussions of
human "dispositions" elsewhere (e.g., chapters 19 and 20), it may include providing
means of satisfaction for people's natural dispositions to feel joy, sorrow, and other
emotions as well.

[69] The advice here to enrich and teach the common people is reminiscent of *Analects*
13.9.

[70] I.e., do not call people away from farming to do military service or other compul-
sory service during times when their presence in the fields is required for a good
harvest.

schools. Cultivate the six rituals.[71] Make clear the ten teachings.[72]
That is how to guide them. The *Odes* says: 305

> Give to them drink. Give them food sustaining.
> Give to them teaching. Give to them training.[73]

In this the affairs of a true king are complete.

•

When King Wu first entered Yin,[74] he erected a laudatory marker at
the entrance to the neighborhood of Shang Rong,[75] he released Jizi   310
from imprisonment, and he wept at the tomb of Bi Gan, and then all
under Heaven turned toward goodness.

•

Throughout the world, each state has men who are outstanding, and
each generation has people who are worthy. Those who do not inquire after the route are the ones who wind up getting lost, those who   315
do not inquire after the ford are the ones who wind up drowning, and
those who are fond of behaving autocratically are the people who
wind up perishing. The *Odes* says:

> My remarks are serious business.
> May you not use them for a guffaw.   320
> The people of old had a proverb:
> "Ask gatherers of kindling and straw."[76]

This is telling one to inquire widely.

•

[71] Commentators explain the "six rituals" as those concerning cappings, weddings,
funerals, sacrifices, village drinking ceremonies, and meeting people.

[72] Commentators disagree about this remark. Quoting one section of the *Liji*, Yang
Liang explains the "ten teachings" as "A father is to be kind. A son is to be filial. An
elder brother is to be good. A young brother is to have brotherly respect. A husband is to be *yi*. A wife is to be obedient. A senior is to be generous. A junior is to
be compliant. A lord is to be *ren*. A minister is to be loyal." Quoting a different section of the *Liji*, Wang Niansun argues that "ten" here is a mistake for "seven" (the
characters are similar and can be confused), and the seven teachings are those that
govern the following pairs: father and son, elder brother and younger brother, husband and wife, lord and minister, friend and friend, and primary guest and secondary guest. However, since Wang's view requires an emendation, it seems somewhat
less preferable than Yang's.

[73] Mao #230. Xunzi may be taking the lines slightly out of context.

[74] I.e., after defeating the Shang forces and overthrowing the tyrant Zhòu.

[75] According to commentators, Shang Rong was a virtuous minister whom Zhòu had
dismissed because of his remonstrances.

[76] Mao #254. The received text of the *Odes* differs slightly from what is quoted here. In
their original context, these lines are apparently spoken by one government officer
to another, warning him about impending disaster. The proverb may originally
have applied to finding one's way in unfamiliar territory, thus connecting nicely
with the earlier remark about the importance of asking about the route to take.

In cases for which there is a model, act according to the model.[77] In
325 cases for which there is no model, handle them according to their
proper category. By means of the root, know the branches. By means
of the left, know the right.

•

All the hundred affairs follow different patterns but maintain each
other.[78,j] When prizes, rewards, punishments, and penalties have in-
330 terlinked categories, only then are they appropriate responses.[79,k]
When government regulations and teachings and people's habits and
customs conform to each other, only then are they successful.

•

With those over eighty, one child is to be excused from service.[80] With
those over ninety, the entire family is to be excused from service. With
335 those who are disabled or ill and who cannot obtain nurture without
the help of others, one family member is to be excused from service.
Those in mourning for a parent are to be excused from service for
three years. Those performing the *zishuai* or *dagong* mourning[81] are to
be excused from service for three months. Those who have just come
340 from the territory of another feudal lord, as well as those who are
newly married, are to be excused from service for one year.

•

The Master remarked:[82] Zijia Ju was a grand officer who behaved
solemnly,[l] but he was not the equal of Yanzi. Yanzi was a minister who
achieved great accomplishments and service, but he was not the equal

---

[77] This and the following sentence also appear at 9.57–60.
[78] This meaning of this sentence is difficult to construe, and a number of commentators append it to the end of the previous section, as an explanation of the last two
sentences there. Some commentators also take this section and the previous one as
a single unit.
[79] I take the text to mean roughly the following. Prizes and rewards are to be given to
those who do good, and not to those who do bad, while punishments and penalties
are to be applied to those who do bad, and not to those who do good. However, if
the categories of "good" and "bad" used in applying or withholding prizes and rewards are not the same as ("interlinked with") the categories of "good" and "bad"
used in applying or withholding punishments and penalties, then these practices
will be contradictory and will not achieve their intended results. Thus, these practices need to be mutually adjusted so as to "maintain" each other.
[80] There is some dispute among commentators as to whether "service" here refers to
corvée labor, or to work as a government official. It seems to me that both sorts are
probably intended.
[81] The *zishuai* and *dagong* are mourning regimens named after particular kinds of
mourning garments. The *dagong* lasted for nine months, and the *zishuai* ranged from
a year down to three months.
[82] It is not made clear who the "Master" is. Based on linguistic parallels with the *Analects*, many commentators take it to be Confucius. In the current context, though, it
might refer to Xunzi instead.

of Zichan. Zichan was a kind person, but he was not the equal of   345
Guan Zhong. As for the way Guan Zhong was as a person, he put his
efforts toward great accomplishments, but not toward *yi*, and he put
his efforts toward cleverness, but not toward *ren*. He was a vulgar
person, and could not have been a grand officer for a true Son of
Heaven.[83]   350

⊙

Three times Mencius had an audience with King Xuan, but did not
once speak of official matters. His disciples said, "Why is it that you
met with the king of Qi three times and did not once speak of official
matters?"
    Mencius said, "I was first assailing his vile heart."[84]   355

⊙

When Gongxing Zizhi was traveling to Yan, he encountered Zeng
Yuan[85] on the road, and said, "What is the lord of Yan like?"[86]
    Zeng Yuan said, "His intentions are lowly. One whose intentions
are lowly makes light of things, and one who makes light of things
does not seek help. If such a one does not seek help, how can he raise 360
himself up? When members of the Di and Qiang are taken as prisoners of war, they do not fret over their captivity, but instead fret over
not being cremated.[87] If the profit to be gained from a course of action is trifling, but the associated harm will obliterate one's state and
family, yet a person nevertheless does it, how could he be knowledge- 365
able about planning?"

⊙

[83] Zijia Ju (also called Zijia Ji) was a grand officer in the state of Lu in the sixth century
    BCE. Yanzi, or Yan Ying, was a famous minster of Qi in the sixth century BCE. He
    is also mentioned later in this chapter, at lines 500–13 below. For a similar remark
    about Zichan and Guan Zhong, see 9.118–21.

[84] It is unclear what this story is supposed to illustrate. Nowhere else in the text is
    Mencius held up for praise, so perhaps the point is critical: Mencius acted in a way
    that was strange (and ineffectual?), which was perhaps a reflection of his (mis-
    guided) views. On the other hand, the idea of getting rid of the king's bad inclina-
    tions before leading him to correct behavior is reminiscent of what Xunzi says at
    3.100–6.

[85] Zeng Yuan is the son of Zengzi, who was a disciple of Confucius.

[86] It is not known who Gongxing Zizhi is. (In fact, it is unclear how to parse the text,
    and some commentators read it differently, rendering the subject as "Gongxingzi"
    instead, an equally uncertain personage.) The commentator Wang Tianhai pro-
    poses that this Zizhi is the same as the infamous Zizhi who, as a minister to King
    Kuai of Yan, duped the king into handing power over to him and led Yan to ruin.
    Such an identification, though, remains speculative.

[87] The Di and Qiang were "barbarian" tribes. According to some early texts, they
    practiced cremation of the dead. Since the custom in Chinese areas was to bury the
    dead, this explains why the prisoners would fret over not receiving a proper funeral.
    Here they are mentioned as an example of people who, like the lord of Yan, focus
    on the wrong sorts of problems.

Now in the case of a man who has lost a needle, he may search for it a whole day without finding it. If he does eventually find it, it is not because his eyesight has grown keener. Rather, it is because he has
370 looked closely and spotted it. The way the heart works in deliberations is also like this.[88]

•

Yi and profit are two things that humans have.[89] Even Yao and Shun could not get rid of the common people's desire for profit. However, they were able to cause their desire for profit not to overcome their
375 fondness for *yi*. Likewise, even Jie and Zhòu could not get rid of the common people's fondness for *yi*. However, they were able to cause their fondness for *yi* not to defeat their desire for profit. And so, when *yi* defeats profit, it is an ordered age. When profit overcomes *yi*, then it is a chaotic age.
380   If superiors give great weight to *yi*, then *yi* will overcome profit. If superiors give great weight to profit, then profit will overcome *yi*. And so, the Son of Heaven is not to discuss things in terms of "much" and "little." Feudal lords are not to discuss things in terms of "profit" and "harm." Grand officers are not to discuss things in terms of "gain"
385 and "loss." Regular officers are not to traffic in goods and wealth. A lord in possession of a state is not to breed oxen and sheep. A minister who has submitted tokens of fidelity[90] is not to breed chickens and pigs. A high councilor is not to cultivate money. A grand officer is not to set up threshing grounds and growing plots. From regular officers
390 on up, all are to be ashamed to practice profit-mongering, and they are not to compete with the common people for business; all are to delight in sharing and making distributions, and they are to regard as disgraceful the accumulation of hoards. Thus and for this reason, the common people will not face difficulties with regard to wealth,
395 and those who are poor and needy will have opportunities to which they can set their hands.[91]

•

King Wen launched four punitive campaigns. King Wu launched two. The Duke of Zhou finished their work, and by the time of King

---

[88] I.e., successfully figuring out what to do is not a matter of growing smarter, but rather comes from carefully sifting through possible courses of action.

[89] The language and ideas here make for interesting comparisons and contrasts with both 9.316–19 and 23.144–48.

[90] In ancient China, a person taking up a ministerial position submitted tokens of servitude to his lord as part of a "swearing-in" ceremony.

[91] More literally, the last part of the sentence says that the poor and needy will have "someplace to burrow their hands," which commentators explain as meaning that they will have a way to make a living.

Cheng and King Kang, accordingly there were simply no more puni-
tive campaigns.[92]   400

·

Massively accumulating wealth and being ashamed to lack it, making
heavier the burdens of the common people and sentencing those unable to bear them—these are how perverse practices arise and how
punishments and penalties become numerous.

·

If superiors are fond of a sense of shame, then the common people   405
will quietly make themselves decorous.[m] If superiors are fond of
riches, then the common people will struggle to death for profit.
These two are the fork in the road where chaos lies. A saying of the
common people states, "Do you want to be rich? Then endure what
is disgraceful. Incline toward what is extreme.[n] Forsake your old   410
friends and acquaintances. Depart from and turn your back on *yi*."[93]
If superiors are fond of riches, then the people's behavior will be like
this, so how could one avoid chaos?

·

During the reign of King Tang, there was a drought,[94] and he offered
a prayer, saying:[95]   415

> Has my rule not been well regulated?
> Have I caused the people to suffer ills?
> Why has the lack of rain reached such extremes?

> Are my halls and chambers extravagant?
> Have women's pleadings influenced too much?   420
> Why has the lack of rain reached such extremes?

> Has giving of presents been going on?[96]
> Have slanderous men been rising higher?
> Why has the lack of rain reached such extremes?

·

Heaven's birthing of the common people was not for the sake of their   425
lords, but Heaven's establishing of lords was for the sake of the common people. And so, when the ancients divided up lands and established states, it was not simply to honor the feudal lords. When they

---

[92] Nearly identical wording appears at 7.58–60. King Kang was the successor to King
Cheng.

[93] This saying may originally have been rhymed.

[94] According to some early accounts, the drought lasted seven years.

[95] The prayer that follows is partly rhymed in the original.

[96] The words rendered here as "presents" more literally mean "packages," but in this
context the reference is to bribes.

430 divided up official posts and established differences in ranks and salaries, it was not simply to exalt grand officers.

•

Understanding people is the proper way of a ruler. Understanding
tasks to be done is the proper way of a minister. And so, when Shun
was in charge of the world, he did not summon people to assign them
tasks, yet myriad things were accomplished.[97]

•

435 The farmer is expert in regard to the fields, but cannot be made Overseer of Fields. Craftsmen and merchants are also like this.[98]

•

When you use those who are worthy to replace those who are unworthy, then you need not wait for divination to know whether you will
have good fortune. When you use those who are well-ordered to at-
440 tack those who are in disarray, then you need not wait for battle to
know whether you will conquer.

•

The people of Qi wanted to attack Lu, but they dreaded Zhuangzi of
Bian, so they did not dare to pass through Bian.[99] The people of Jin
wanted to attack Wey, but they feared Zilu, so they did not dare to
445 pass through Pu.[100]

•

"If you do not know it, then ask it of Yao and Shun.[101] If you lack it,
then seek it from the Heavenly repository."[102] I say: the way of the

---

[97] See *Analects* 15.5.

[98] Nearly identical wording appears at 21.235–39. In that context, the point is that
ruling requires knowledge of the Way, rather than mere technical expertise, which
is presumably also the point here.

[99] Zhuangzi of Bian—not to be confused with the thinker Zhuangzi discussed elsewhere in this text—was famous for his courage.

[100] Zilu was a disciple of Confucius. Exactly why the people of Jin feared him is unclear. Some early stories depict him as fond of courage (see *Analects* 5.7), while
others depict him as skillfully governing Pu, and either or both of these may have
awed the people.

[101] The text of this section is extremely terse and also seems to be partially corrupt. It
is thus quite difficult to understand, and the translation here is tentative. The word
"it" in the translation is not explicit in the Chinese, and is supplied here based on
the context. Its referent appears to be "the proper way to rule" or something of the
sort.

[102] The phrase "Heavenly repository" is odd, especially for the *Xunzi*, and has puzzled
commentators. It appears in a number of other early texts, where it has several different meanings. In this case, though, it seems best to take its sense as close to one
that appears in the *Zhuangzi* (chap. 2), namely as describing a kind of limitless resource: "Though you pour into it, it does not become filled up. Though you draw
from it, it does not become depleted." (Perhaps the *Xunzi* is responding to the
Zhuangzi here.) The notion of the "Heavenly repository" also appears later in this
chapter. See below, line 525.

former kings is just this "Yao and Shun," and the broad contents of the Six Masterpieces are just this "Heavenly repository."[103]

•

The gentleman's process of learning is like molting—continually it changes him.[o] And so, in walking, he works on it. In standing, he works on it. In sitting, he works on it. In arranging the expression on his face and voicing his words and tone, he works on it. He never neglects to do what is good. He never hesitates to ask questions.

•

Those who are good at learning plumb exhaustively the patterns of things. Those who are good at action overcome completely the difficulties in things.

•

A gentleman settles his intentions such that it is as if he had no alternatives. Even if the Son of Heaven or the three dukes question him, he responds exactly according to his judgments of right and wrong.

•

A gentleman, though he be obstructed and thwarted, does not become lost. Though he be weary from toil, he does nothing improper. When he confronts troubles and difficulties, he does not forget those doctrines that he has set out in detail.[p]

•

If the year never turned cold, we would have no occasion to appreciate the pine and cypress.[104] If matters were never difficult, we would have no occasion to appreciate the gentleman.

•

Let there be no day not spent on what is right.[105]

•

With the raining down of little droplets, the Han River thereby becomes deep.[q] Thus, one who exhaustively takes in what is little becomes great. One who accumulates what is subtle becomes eminent. One whose virtue is perfect has a countenance that is kind and congenial. His conduct is flawless and his reputation is heard far and

[103] I.e., one should search for the way to rule in the ways of the former kings and in the canonical bodies of lore. The "Six Masterpieces" (*liu yi* 六藝, "Six Arts" or "Six Classics") are usually identified as the *Documents*, *Odes*, *Rituals*, *Music*, *Changes*, and the *Spring and Autumn Annals*.

[104] See *Analects* 9.28. Some commentators group this section with the previous one.

[105] Many commentators group these words with the previous section, translating thus: "There is no day that he [the gentleman] does not spend on what is right." Some append them to the last sentence there: "If matters were never difficult, we would have no occasion to realize that there is no day that the gentleman does not spend on what is right." However, neither the wording nor the thought fits well with what precedes or follows, so I have treated these words as an independent line (as does Yang Liuqiao).

wide.ʳ The petty man lacks integrity on the inside and instead seeks
475 these things from the outside.[106]

•

When one's doctrines do not match those of one's teacher, this is
called rebelling. When one's teachings do not match those of one's
teacher, this is called betrayal. As for people who are betraying and
rebellious, an enlightened lord will not include them in his court, and
480 his officers and grand officers will not talk with them if they encounter them on the roads.

•

It is people who prove inadequate when it is time to take action that
discourse excessively. It is people who prove inadequate when it is
time to behave faithfully that stress the integrity of their words. And
485 so the *Spring and Autumn Annals* commends exchanging directives,
while the *Odes* condemns the repeated making of formal covenants,
because they are of one mind with this.[107] Those who are good at the
Odes do not make a show of discoursing on it, those who are good at
the *Changes* do not make a show of divining with it, and those who
490 are good at rituals do not make a show of conducting them, because
they are of the same mind as this.ˢ

•

Zengzi said, "As for a filial son, his words are fit to be heard, and his
actions are fit to be seen. Having words that are fit to be heard is the
means to please those who are far away. Having actions that are fit to
495 be seen is the means to please those who are nearby. When those
nearby are pleased, they treat one with affection. When those far
away are pleased, they become one's allies. To have the affection of
those nearby and the allegiance of those far away is the way of a filial
son."

•

500 Zengzi was leaving. Yanzi followed him to the suburban districts and
said, "I have heard it said that the gentleman gives people gifts of
words, while the commoner gives people gifts of material wealth. I

---

[106] The referent of "these things" is not entirely clear. Most likely, it refers to the greatness, eminence, inviting appearance, and high reputation mentioned previously.

[107] Commentators explain the remark about the *Spring and Autumn Annals* as follows.
One of the entries in the text for Duke Huan, reign year 3, reads, "In the summer,
the Marquis of Qi and the Marquis of Wey exchanged directives at Pu." The *Gongyangzhuan* comments, "What is this 'exchange of directives'? It is giving directives
to each other. Why does it speak of giving directives to each other? Because that
approaches what is correct. How does it approach what is correct? The ancients did
not make formal covenants. They merely concluded their discussions and withdrew." In the *Odes*, the criticism of repeatedly making of formal covenants can be
found in Mao #198.

am poor and have no material wealth, so allow me to borrow from the gentleman and give you, my good sir, a gift of words. The wheels of chariots and carriages were once trees on great mountains. Expose   505
them to the shaping frame for three to five months, and the trees become wheel rims, and even if the spokes break, they will not return to their once-usual shape.ᵗ The shaping frame of the gentleman is something one must diligently pursue. Carefully attend to it! The *lan*, *chai*, and *gaoben*, if steeped in sweet spirits, are worth a jade pendant   510
in trade.[108] An otherwise upright lord, if steeped in fragrant wine, can be told slander and won over. That in which the gentleman steeps himself is something one must carefully attend to!"[109]

•

Culture and learning are to people as carving and grinding are to jade. The *Odes* says: 515

> He's like a thing chiseled, like a thing someone shined.
> He's like a thing carved, like a thing someone did grind.[110]

This is speaking of learning and inquiry. The *bi* disc of He was a stone dug out from a well,ᵘ but after a jade worker carved it, it became a treasure for the Son of Heaven.[111] Zigong and Ji Lu were originally   520
bumpkins, but after they attired themselves with culture and learning and clothed themselves with ritual and *yi*, they were among the world's outstanding men.

•

To pursue learning and inquiry insatiably, and to treat well-bred men with fondness tirelessly—this is to be a Heavenly repository.[112]   525

•

---

[108] *Lan*, *chai*, and *gaoben* are fragrant plants. The point is that the steeping makes them even more valuable.

[109] For more on Yanzi, see above, note 83. Yanzi follows Zengzi to the suburbs (of the state of Qi, presumably) as a polite gesture to see him off. It was also common practice to give those leaving a parting gift, which is why Yanzi feels obliged to make a present of words. Commentators note, though, that there was a sizable gap in time between the life of Yanzi and Zengzi, so this story is likely an anachronistic invention.

[110] Mao #55. In their original context, these lines refer to an aristocratic "gentleman" who is being praised. They are also famously quoted in *Analects* 1.15.

[111] The jade *bi* disc of He was a famous treasure. According to early stories, a commoner named He presented the uncarved stone to two different rulers, and when their jade workers dismissed it as worthless, he was punished for trying to cheat the ruler. Eventually, though, a jade worker saw its potential and transformed it into a beautiful object. In Chinese, the "*bi* disc of Mr. He" has become a byword for people (and things) that have high value, but whose merits are unappreciated by those of inferior understanding.

[112] On the notion of the "Heavenly repository," see note 102 above.

If a gentleman considers something to be doubtful, then he will not speak for it.[113] If he has not inquired into something, then he will not take a stand on it. Though his road is long,[114] daily he improves!

•

530 People who know many things but have no particular affections among them; people who pursue wide-ranging learning but have no direction; and people who like many things but have no fixity—these the gentleman will not take as his associates.

•

If a person does not recite [the classics] when young, and if he does not discuss and debate things when in his prime, then even if he turns 535 out acceptably, he remains incomplete.

•

If the gentleman is single-minded in teaching, and if the disciple is single-minded in learning, then they will quickly achieve completion.[115]

•

If the gentleman obtains advancement,[116] then he is able to augment 540 the good reputation of those above and reduce the worries of those below. To be incapable of this yet occupy his position is to engage in deceit. To have nothing to contribute in this yet receive the bounty of his position is to engage in theft. Those who pursue learning will not necessarily undertake to serve in office, but those who serve in office 545 must engage in learning.

•

Zigong made a request of Confucius, saying, "I am worn out from learning. I wish to rest and serve a lord."
Confucius said, "The *Odes* says:

Day and night, with warmth and reverently,
550 They performed their tasks assiduously.[117]

Serving a lord is difficult. In serving a lord, where can one find rest!"
"In that case, I wish to rest and serve my parents."
Confucius said, "The *Odes* says:

Those filial sons will be untiring.
555 They will grant to you blessings unending.[118]

---

113 Wording that is nearly identical to the first two sentences of this section appears below at lines 659–661.
114 Compare *Analects* 8.7.
115 I.e., of the task of moral cultivation.
116 I.e., within or to government service.
117 Mao #301.
118 Mao #247. The way Xunzi uses these lines differs from what they appear to mean in their original context. The second line is particularly ambiguous, and so I have

Serving one's parents is difficult. In serving one's parents, where can one find rest!"

"In that case, I wish to rest and have a wife and child."

Confucius said, "The *Odes* says:

> He served as a model to his wife-mate,   560
> Then to his elder and younger brothers;
> He thereby brought order to clan and state.[119]

Having a wife and child is difficult. In having a wife and child, where can one find rest!"

"In that case, I wish to rest and carry on friendships."   565

Confucius said, "The *Odes* says,

> A thing in which friends do help each other:
> They help with awe-inspiring deportment.[120]

Carrying on friendships is difficult. In carrying on friendships, where can one find rest!"   570

"In that case, I wish to rest and do farming."

Confucius said, "The *Odes* says:

> In the day thatch-reeds you go gathering.
> At night you bind them together with string.
> Up top to patch the roof, hasten to go.   575
> Soon the hundred grains you'll begin to sow.[121]

Doing farming is difficult. In doing farming, where can one find rest!"

"In that case, is there nothing in which I can find rest?"

Confucius said, "Behold the grave: so final, blocked up, and cut   580 off!ᵛ With this, one knows where to find rest."

Zigong said, "How great is death! The gentleman finds rest in it. The petty man comes to an end in it."

•

As for the depictions in the *Guofeng* of fondness for someone good-looking,[122] a tradition states, "There is fulfillment of one's desires   585

---

rendered it in a way that best fits the point here. The first line is also quoted at 29.29–30.

[119] Mao #240. In its original context, this line refers to King Wen. The translated rhyme scheme here does not match the pattern in the Chinese.

[120] Mao #247.

[121] Mao #154.

[122] The *Guofeng* ("Airs of the States") is the first section of the *Odes*. Many commentators take this remark to refer specifically to the poem "Guanju" ("The Cry of the

without leading one's deportment to excess.[123] Their integrity can be compared to precious metals and stones. Their sounds can be taken into the ancestral temple." The "Lesser *Ya*" do not take the approach of smearing superiors.ʷ They draw themselves back and stay humble.
590 They hate the contemporary government and think longingly of past times. Their words have good form to them. Their sounds have sorrow in them.

•

A state that is going to flourish is sure to honor teachers and give great weight to instructors. If one honors teachers and gives great
595 weight to instructors, then proper models and measures will be preserved. A state that is going to decline is sure to belittle teachers and regard instructors lightly. If one belittles teachers and regards instructors lightly, then people will be careless. If people are careless, then proper models and measures will be wrecked.

•

600 In ancient times, commoners served in office only after age fifty. As for the Son of Heaven and the feudal lords, their sons would undergo the capping ceremony at age nineteen. After being capped they would hear administrative cases, because their education had reached its end.

•

605 One who is fond of what pertains to being a gentleman is the right person. If you have someone who is the right person but do not educate him, this is inauspicious. One who is fond of what does not pertain to being a gentleman is not the right person. If you have someone who is not the right person and yet you educate him, this is
610 to offer provisions to a robber, to lend weapons to a villain.

•

Those who do not themselves take a humble view of their own actions will make claims that are extravagant and exaggerated.

•

As for the worthies of ancient times, when they were as lowly as peasants or as poor as commoners, for food they had gruel that was not
615 even sufficient, and for clothing they had coarse garments that were not even whole. Nevertheless, whatever was not in accordance with ritual, they would not advance, and whatever was not in accordance

---

Ospreys"), which is the first poem in that section, and which Confucius famously praises (in *Analects* 3.20) for its depiction of restrained romance.

[123] Here the text seems to be playing on the fact that this sentence can have two meanings: the romance of people in the *Guofeng* is such that *their* desires are fulfilled without going to excess, or the romances depicted in the *Guofeng* are such that the *audience* listening to the account can have *its* desires fulfilled (perhaps through imaginatively identifying with the characters) without going to excess. A similar ambiguity affects the word "their" in the subsequent two sentences.

with *yi*, they would not accept, and they comfortably chose this behavior.

•

Zixia was poor. His clothes were full of patches.[124] A person said, "Why don't you take an official position?" He replied, "I will not serve as minister for any feudal lord who has treated me arrogantly, nor will I meet again with any grand officer who has treated me arrogantly. Liuxia Hui had the same clothes as the keepers of the city's back gate but was not considered doubtful, because he rejected momentary fame.ˣ Contesting for profit is like clutching one's fingernail yet losing one's hand."[125]   620

                                                                                                           625

•

A lord of men must choose his ministers carefully, and a commoner must choose his friends carefully. Friendships are how people hold to each other, and if people did not share the same ways, how would they hold to each other?[126] If you spread out firewood evenly and apply fire to it, the fire will seek out the dry pieces.[127] If you level the earth and irrigate it with water, the water will flow to the wet places. Since the way in which the classes of things follow each other is so evident as this, if one observes a person based on his friends, wherein will there be anything left to doubt?[128] In choosing friends and deeming people to be good, one must be careful, for this is the foundation of virtue. The *Odes* says, "Do not push the big wagon; the dust makes things dark."[129] This is telling one not to dwell in the company of petty people.   630

                                                                                                           635

                                                                                                           640

---

[124] The Chinese text of this sentence deploys an analogy that is hardly intelligible in English, so I have used a very loose rendering to convey the sense here. Literally, the line says that Zixia's clothes were "like strung-up quail" (i.e., quail that have been brought back by a hunter and hung up in preparation for cooking). Commentators disagree about exactly how to construe the analogy, with some suggesting that it means that the holes in the clothes have been tied shut such that they bunch up and stick out like the stub tail of a (plucked?) quail, while others think the comparison is with the multiple knots in the string used to tie up the quail. Either way, it is clear enough from the context that it refers to shabbiness of clothing.

[125] The last two sentences of this quotation are very difficult to understand, and commentators dispute their meaning and whether they belong here as part of the quotation or should be broken off as a separate passage. The translation is, therefore, rather tentative.

[126] Compare *Analects* 15.40.

[127] Wording nearly identical to this and next sentence also appears at 1.69–71.

[128] Compare 23.391–93. See also *Analects* 2.10 for an idea that is similar, but not quite the same as this.

[129] Mao #206. The sense of the line is somewhat ambiguous between saying that the dust kicked up by the wagon dirties those helping to push it and saying that the dust obscures the vision of those pushing. Since both senses are equally applicable in this context, perhaps the text is playing on both.

Laying wily traps and plotting deceptive strategies[130] resemble wisdom but are not it.[y] Being meek and soft and being easily prevailed upon resemble *ren* but are not it. Being violent and loutish and having a fondness for brawling resemble courage but are not it.

•

645 *Ren, yi*, ritual, and goodness are to people like goods, wealth, millet and grain are to families—those who possess them abundantly are rich, those who possess them sparsely are poor, and those who utterly lack them are in dire straits. And so, if one neither is capable of the greater instances of them nor practices the smaller instances of them,
650 this is a way that will throw away one's state and one's life.

•

In every case, there is that upon which the coming of a thing depends. To regard the result as what is depended upon is getting it backward.[131,z]

•

When it comes to wayward talk, eliminate it. When it comes to mate-
655 rial goods and lovely faces, keep a distance. As for that from which disaster is born, it is born from little things. For this reason, the gentleman acts early to break it off.

•

Talk that is trustworthy rests between what is empty and what is overstated.[aa] If you consider something to be doubtful, then do not speak
660 for it. If you have not inquired into something, then do not take a stand on it.[132]

•

Those with understanding are clear-headed in regard to affairs and are penetrating in regard to arrangements. One cannot serve them with what lacks integrity. And so I say: gentlemen are hard to per-
665 suade.[133] If in trying to persuade them, one does not do so by means

---

[130] In the Chinese text, the first few words of this sentence are incomprehensible. Commentators have proposed numerous solutions, none of which are entirely convincing. The translation here is modeled on Liu Shipei's reading, but remains highly tentative.

[131] The Chinese text here is extremely terse and oddly worded, making it difficult to understand. Many commentators want to emend it to make it more sensible. The translation here is my own attempt to make sense of it as it stands. The point, as I understand it, is that when, for example, one is treated well or badly by others, this is (usually) a reaction to one's previous conduct (see 1.57–60), but people mistakenly take this treatment simply as an incitement to which they must react, and the text is warning against that mistake.

[132] The last two sentences of this section are nearly identical to an earlier section of this chapter, at lines 526–28 above.

[133] In this and the following sentence, the character translated as "persuade" might also be translated as "please," and the text may intentionally be playing on the two possible meanings of the character, though it seems to me that the former meaning

of the Way, they will not be persuaded. A saying goes, "A wayward ball comes to a stop when it reaches a hollow. Wayward talk comes to a stop when it reaches those with understanding." This is why talk by other schools and doctrines that are deviant both speak badly of the *ru*. When something's rightness or wrongness is in doubt, then measure it by means of far-off affairs,[134] examine it by means of things nearby, and consider it with a balanced heart. Wayward talk will come to a stop at this, and talk that is bad will die at this.   670

•

Zengzi ate fish, and there were leftovers. He said, "Use rice-water to keep them." His disciples said, "When kept in rice-water, they become harmful to people. It is better to pickle them." Zengzi cried and said, "How could my heart be so aberrant!" He was aggrieved that he was late in learning this.[135,bb]   675

•

Do not use those things where you fall short to go against those things where others have excelled. Thus, inhibit and avoid those things where you fall short, but shift to and follow those things to which they applied themselves.[cc] Being thoroughly clever yet not adopting proper models, being acute in debate yet upholding things that are deviant,[dd] being boldly decisive yet lacking ritual propriety—these are what a gentleman detests and hates.   680   685

•

He who speaks much but whose words match the proper categories of things is a sage. He who speaks little but conforms to the proper model in everything is a gentleman. He who speaks much but does not follow the proper model, and whose words are perverse and twisted,[ee] even if he argues keenly, is nothing but a petty man.[136]   690

•

The reason why the laws of the state prohibit the taking of items that have been left lying about is to express a dislike for the common people becoming accustomed to obtaining things without following social divisions. If there are social divisions and *yi*, then one can take possession of everyone under Heaven and there will be order. If there   695

---

is likely the primary one here. See *Analects* 13.25, which uses nearly identical wording, with the same ambiguity of meaning.

[134] I.e., affairs that are far off in time, in the past and/or perhaps in the future (i.e., long-range consequences).

[135] This passage is difficult to understand, because the text is quite terse and uses terms in an unusual fashion. Commentators explain that Zengzi, who was known for being highly filial, is upset because he had probably served fish soaked in rice water to his parents at some point and thus done something harmful to them, and his exclamation is thus an expression of self-rebuke for such negligence.

[136] A nearly identical passage appears at 6.103–8.

are no social divisions and *yi*, then even in acquiring just a wife and a concubine there will be disorder.[137]

•

With regard to all people in the world, it is indeed the case that they each have their own particular ideas. Nevertheless, there are some
700 people to whom they accede in common. Those who discourse on flavor accede to Yi Ya. Those who discourse on tones accede to Music Master Kuang. Those who discourse on order accede to the three kings. Since the three kings have already fixed models and measures and established rituals and music and handed them down, then if
705 there should be some who do not use them and instead change and create these themselves, how would this be any different from changing Yi Ya's blends of flavors and altering Music Master Kuang's musical scales? When the models of the three kings are absent, the empire will be lost without even a moment's delay, and a state will perish
710 without even a moment's delay.

•

That which drinks but does not eat is the cicada. That which neither drinks nor eats is the mayfly.[138]

•

Shun from Yu and Xiao Yi were filial, but their parents did not love them.[139] Bi Gan and Zixu were loyal, but their lords did not heed
715 them. Confucius and Yan Yuan were knowledgeable, but were put in dire straits by their era.[140]

•

If you are constrained and forced to live in a violent state and there is no way to avoid it, then extol what is good about it, praise what is fine in it, speak of its strong points, and do not mention its
720 shortcomings.[141]

•

---

[137] Compare 9.316–39.

[138] The point of these two sentences is exceedingly obscure. The Tang dynasty commentator Yang Liang appends them to the previous passage with the explanation that they emphasize its point: since human beings must both drink and eat in order to live, they have even greater need of resources than these insects, and hence especially need the models of the three kings. That explanation, however, seems very forced, and I know of no other attempts to explain the purpose of these remarks.

[139] "Shun from Yu" is an alternative way of referring to the sage king Shun, based on the fact that his original home was said to be the state of Yu. According to early stories (see *Mencius* 5A2), Shun's father hated him and even tried to kill him. Little is known of Xiao Yi.

[140] Yan Yuan, also known as Yan Hui, was Confucius's favorite disciple. He was impoverished and died young.

[141] See the nearly identical wording that appears at 13.114–18. Many editors append this paragraph to the end of the previous one and interpret it as a description of how the people mentioned there behaved, but that parsing seems rather strained,

Vilifying others will cause you to perish, even though you are very obedient. Slandering others will cause you to face impasses, even though you are broadly learned. An uncontrolled mouth will cause you to be stained all the more, even though you try to purify yourself.[142]   725

•

The gentleman can make himself honorable, but he cannot ensure that others will honor him. He can make himself useful, but cannot ensure that others will employ him.[143]

•

The practice of making official proclamations and swearing oaths does not go as far back as the five lords. The practice of making for-   730
mal covenants and pacts does not go as far back as the three kings. The practice of exchanging sons as hostages does not go as far back as the five hegemons.[144]

---

    since "living in a violent state" would not apply in the case of Shun, who lived under the reign of the sage Yao.

[142] See the nearly identical wording that appears at 4.16–19.

[143] See the nearly identical wording that appears at 6.184–88.

[144] Regarding the last sentence, a common practice among early Chinese states was for the rulers to send sons to other states to serve as hostages, as a way of discouraging hostilities between states. Commentators explain that the overall point of this passage is to describe a decline in morality over time, with rulers resorting to increasingly drastic measures in order to secure the trust of others.

CHAPTER 28

The Right-Hand Vessel

Confucius was observing things in the temple of Duke Huan of Lu. There was a tilting vessel there, and Confucius asked the keeper of the temple, "What vessel is this?"

The keeper of the temple said, "This is the right-hand vessel."[1]

5 Confucius said, "I have heard of the right-hand vessel. When empty it tilts, when halfway full it stands correctly, and when full it overturns."[2] Confucius looked to a disciple and said, "Pour water in it." The disciple drew off some water and poured it in. When halfway full the vessel stood correctly, when poured full it overturned, and 10 when empty it tilted. Confucius said with a sigh, "Ah, who would not likewise be overturned when full of himself!"

Zilu said, "May I ask if there is a way to hold oneself steady even when one is becoming filled up?"

Confucius said, "If one has keen perception and sagely under-15 standing, then guard them by awareness of one's own foolishness. If one's accomplishments extend over all under Heaven, then guard them by deference. If one's courage and strength move the whole world, then guard them by timidity. If one is so rich as to possess everything within the four seas, then guard this by humility. This is 20 called the way of 'drawing it off and decreasing it.'"

•

Confucius was acting as prime minister for Lu. After holding court for seven days, he executed Shao Zhengmao. The disciples entered and asked, "Shao Zhengmao was a well-known person in Lu. For the Master to conduct government and begin by executing him, is this 25 not an error?"

Confucius answered, "Wait. I will tell you the reason. There are five worst traits for people to have, and being a robber or thief is not among them. The first is having a heart with penetrating insight and using it for dangerous things. The second is carrying out deviant acts 30 and doing so with resoluteness. The third is speaking falsely and arguing well. The fourth is memorizing foul things and presenting them as broad learning. The fifth is following along with what is wrong and making it seem smooth. If there is merely one of these five in a person, then he cannot avoid execution by the gentleman, but 35 Shao Zhengmao had them all! Thus, his dwelling could gather fol-

---

[1] So named because, like the lord's "right-hand man," the vessel is there to warn him against excesses that constitute vice.

[2] The whole passage plays on the fact that the word *man* 滿 means both "full" and "full of pride," i.e., arrogant.

lowers to the point of forming crowds. His words could disguise what is perverse and draw along the masses. His strength could oppose what is right and allow him to stand independently. Such a one is an outstanding hero for petty men. I could not but execute him.

"For such reasons, Tang executed Yin Xie, King Wen executed Pan   40
Zhi, the Duke of Zhou executed Guan Shu, the Grand Duke executed Hua Shi, Guan Zhong executed Fu Liyi, and Zichan executed Deng Xi and Shi Fu. These seven all lived in different times but had the same kind of heart, and so one could not but execute them. The *Odes* says:

> My heart is aching and aching with worry: 45
> I am resented by crowds of men petty.[3]

When petty men form crowds, that is indeed cause for worry."

•

When Confucius was acting as Minister of Justice for Lu, a father and son were engaged in a legal dispute. Confucius detained them together for three months. Eventually, the father asked to cease the legal   50
dispute, and Confucius released them. Ji Sun heard of this and was not pleased. He said, "This old man has deceived me. He once said to me, 'In managing the state and family, one must rely on filial piety.' Now in that case, he should kill a man to wipe out someone who is not filial, but instead he released him." Ranzi[4] told Confucius of this.   55

Confucius sighed heavily and said, "Alas! To kill the subordinates when it is their superiors who have gone astray—is this permissible? To fail to teach the people and then judge their crimes is to kill the innocent. When the three armies suffer a great defeat, it is not permissible to behead them, and when criminal cases cannot be brought   60
under control, it is not permissible to penalize them, because the fault does not lie with the people. When one is careless with government orders but stringently executes people, then this is being a murderous villain. Now the production of things has its proper times, but if the collection of taxes is not confined to the proper times, then this   65
is being tyrannical. To fail to teach the people and yet hold them responsible for achieving meritorious works is being cruel. It is only when one has put a stop to these three practices that it is permissible to apply punishments. The *Documents* says:

> Even when it is in accordance with *yi* to punish or kill people,   70
> have no haste to do so. Allow yourself to say only, 'I have not yet been able to make matters go smoothly.'[5]

---

[3] Mao #26.

[4] This "Ranzi" is Ran Qiu, a disciple of Confucius.

[5] No section of the received text of the *Documents* matches this quote exactly. For more discussion of this quotation, see the nearly identical version that appears at 14.90–92, which is also followed by the same remark about teaching.

This is saying that one is to use teaching first.[6]

"And so, when the former kings had set it out in accordance with the Way, the superiors first submitted to it. When some people still did not approve of it, the former kings raised up those who were worthies, as a means to educate them.[a] When some people still did not approve of it, the former kings discarded those who were incapable, as a means to frighten them. The former kings educated them for three years, and the common folk indeed went over to them. When some wicked people did not follow along, only then did the former kings meet them with punishment, and then the people indeed understood what was criminal. The *Odes* says:

O you Mister Yin, Grand Master!
For the Zhou, serve as a mainstay.
Uphold peacefulness for the state:
Bind all four sides under one sway.
Give aid to the Son of Heaven.
Then humble folk won't go astray.[7]

Thus, 'Awe-inspiring power was honed sharp, but was not made trial of. Punishments were put in place, but were not made use of.'[8] This expresses my meaning.

"Today's generation[9] is not like that. They have made their teachings disorderly and have made their punishments profuse.[10] When their people, being lost and confused, fall down in this regard, they then follow up by disciplining them. Thus, punishments are increasingly profuse, yet wickedness is still not overcome. Where there is a bluff that is merely three feet high, even an empty cart cannot climb

---

[6] Since classical Chinese texts usually lack marks indicating the end of a quotation, there is disagreement over where Confucius's speech ends. Some editors think it stops here, and treat the next few paragraphs as Xunzi speaking in his own voice. However, given the structure of the other sections of the chapter, it seems more likely to me that the subsequent paragraphs are intended to be read as parts of Confucius's speech, which is how I have presented them here.

[7] Mao #191. The quotation here differs slightly from the received text of the *Odes*. In its original context, the poem is actually criticizing the Grand Master Yin for failing to behave well, rather than holding him up as a model, so in using this section Confucius seems to be ignoring (or ignorant of?) that context.

[8] The two sentences of this quotation also appear at 15.465–67, where they are presented as a traditional saying.

[9] I.e., of rulers.

[10] The first part of this sentence is ambiguous. It could mean that the rulers teach things that lead to disorder rather than order, or it could mean that the teaching done by the rulers is itself carried out in a disorderly (and ineffective) fashion. Perhaps both senses are intended.

up it, but with mountains a hundred fathoms high, even fully loaded carts climb up them. How can they do that? It is because the moun- 100 tains slope downward gradually. When there is a wall a few fathoms tall, the people will not trespass against it, but with mountains a hundred fathoms high, even young lads will ascend and wander about them, because the mountains slope downward gradually. Now since the gradual downward sloping of this generation has been 105 going on for quite a long time, can they get the people not to trespass against them? The *Odes* says:

> The roads of Zhou were smooth as a whetstone.[11]
> Their straightness was like that of an arrow.
> They were once walked upon by gentlemen. 110
> They were admired by the common fellow.
> When I now look back and behold these things,
> I well up with tears and out they then flow.[12]

Is this not sad indeed?"

•

The *Odes* says: 115

> I watch the sun and moon go by
> And think of him most forlornly.
> The road he travels is so far!
> How can I have him come to me?[13]

The Master said,[14] "If she but tapped her head,[15] then would not he 120 come back?"[16]

•

---

[11] On its surface, the poem laments the state of neglect into which the roads built by the great Zhou rulers have fallen, but since the word *dao* 道 ("road") also means a "way" of doing things, the poem is simultaneously lamenting contemporary neglect for the past ways (i.e., of governing) of the great Zhou rulers. It is this latter sense that is relevant to the context here.

[12] Mao #203. The quotation here differs slightly from the received text of the *Odes*.

[13] Mao #33. These lines are traditionally understood as being spoken by a woman longing for her husband (or suitor), who is away for some task.

[14] Given the context, the "Master" here is most likely Confucius (the passage is also reminiscent of *Analects* 9.31), but it could also be Xunzi's way of referring to his own teacher, or even Xunzi's disciple referring to Xunzi.

[15] On "tapping the head," see chapter 27, note 37.

[16] The Master's remark here is so terse and worded so peculiarly as to be extremely unclear, and a variety of interpretations are possible. As I understand it, the point is that if the woman shows respect (by tapping her head when the man departed), this will ensure that the man wants and tries to return, an interaction that in turn is an image for the attractive power of virtue.

Confucius was gazing intently at a waterway flowing eastward.[17] Zigong asked Confucius, "Why is it that whenever a gentleman sees a large waterway, he is sure to gaze intently at it?"

125   Confucius said, "When the waterway is large, it provides for the various living things in an all-encompassing fashion, without any ulterior motive—this resembles virtue. Its flow is toward sunken and low places, and even through curves and bends it is sure to follow this pattern—this resembles *yi*. Its gushing current is never depleted or

130   exhausted—this resembles the Way. If someone opens a channel for it to go through, its response is as swift as an echo, and it rushes at crevasses a hundred fathoms deep without fear—this resembles courage.[18] When it pours into a basin, it is sure to achieve a balanced, level state—this resembles following proper models. When it fills up a

135   place, one does not need a leveling stick—this resembles adhering to correctness.[19] Being soft and supple, it reaches into even minute spaces—this resembles keen discernment. By going into and out of it, one uses it to become fresh and clean—this resembles being transformed to goodness. Even through ten thousand turns, it is sure to

140   head east—this resembles having settled intentions. For these reasons, whenever a gentleman sees a large waterway, he is sure to gaze intently at it."

•

Confucius said, "There are things that I consider shameful.[20] There are things that I consider vulgar. There are things that I consider

145   dangerous. Not being able to devote one's strength to learning when one is young, and so having nothing to teach others when one is old—this I consider shameful. After leaving one's hometown to serve one's lord and having become successful, yet upon running into a former acquaintance, to speak not even once of the past—this I con-

150   sider vulgar. Living together with a petty person—this I consider dangerous."

•

Confucius said, "If a person's learning is like a mere ant mound but he works to advance it, then I will join him. If a person's learning is like a hill but he ceases working at it, then I will simply stop also.

---

[17] Compare *Analects* 9.17.

[18] The first half of the sentence is rather obscure, especially the way that it fits into the analogy with courage. Perhaps the point is that the swiftness with which the water flows into a new channel is like the unhesitating readiness to take on challenges that is displayed by courageous people. (Compare the way that brave soldiers who are ready to rush at an enemy are sometimes praised as "hard-charging" in English.)

[19] In ancient China, after a measuring cup was dipped into grain, a stick would be used to level off the top and get rid of excess, thereby ensuring an accurate measure. The point here is that any excess water simply drains away, so that the way water fills up a place is "self-correcting."

[20] This sentence and the two that follow it are rhymed in the original.

Nowadays, some people's learning has never even been as big as a   155
pimple and yet, behaving as though they were perfected, they desire
to be the teacher of others."[21]

•

Confucius was heading south to go to Chu, but became trapped
between Chen and Cai.[22] For seven days there was no cooked food,
and what stew they made from pigweed did not even have grain   160
mixed in. The disciples all had starving countenances. Zilu entered
and asked Confucius, "I have heard that those who do good are
rewarded by Heaven with good fortune, and those who do bad are
rewarded by Heaven with misfortune. Now, a long time indeed are
the days that you, Master, have spent amassing virtue, accumulat-   165
ing *yi*, and embracing fine conduct, so why do you live in such dismal circumstances?"

Confucius said, "Zhong You,[23] you do not understand. I will tell
you. Do you think that those who are knowledgeable are sure to be
heeded? But did not Prince Bi Gan have his heart cut out? Do you   170
think that those who are loyal are sure to be heeded? But did not
Guan Longfeng undergo punishment? Do you think that those who
remonstrate are sure to be heeded? But did not Wu Zixu wind up
with his corpse displayed outside the east gate of Gusu? What one
encounters or does not encounter depends on the times. Whether a   175
person is worthy or unworthy depends on his material. Gentlemen
learn broadly and consider things deeply, but those among them who
have not encountered the right times are many indeed! Looking at it
in this way, those who have not encountered the right age are numerous indeed, so how could I be alone in this?   180

"The angelica plant grows deep in the midst of forests, but it does
not stop being fragrant just because there are no people around to
smell it. The gentleman undertakes learning, not so that he will become successful, but rather so that when in dire straits, he will not be
at a loss, so that when he faces troubles, his thoughts will not sink,   185
and so that he will understand how misfortune and good fortune end
and begin, without his heart becoming confused. Whether one is
worthy or unworthy depends on one's own material. What a person
does or does not do depends on the person himself. What one encounters or does not encounter depends on the times. Whether one   190
dies or lives depends on fate. Now if there is the right person, but he

---

[21] See *Analects* 9.19. Some editors treat the last sentence here as being a comment
added by Xunzi, rather than being part of the quotation from Confucius.

[22] See *Analects* 15.2. There are different stories told about exactly why Confucius became trapped between Chen and Cai. One story says that the ministers of Chen and
Cai feared that if Confucius helped Chu, Chu would become a threat to their states,
and so they sent soldiers to block his way.

[23] Zhong You is Zilu's personal name. "Zilu" is an alternative, more formal name.

does not encounter the right time, then even if he is worthy, can he get somewhere? And if he does encounter the right time, then what difficulties will there be for him? Thus, gentlemen learn broadly, con-
195 sider things deeply, cultivate themselves, and straighten their conduct, so as to await the right time."

Confucius said, "Zhong You, stay! I will tell you. In the past, the heart that made Prince Chong'er of Jin a hegemon was born from his experiences at Cao. The heart that made King Goujian of Yue a he-
200 gemon was born from his experiences at Kuaiji. The heart that made Xiaobai, Duke Huan of Qi, a hegemon was born from his experiences in Ju. Thus, those who have not lived in dismal circumstances do not have far-reaching ideas, and those who have not personally fled for their lives do not have broad-ranging intentions. How do you know
205 that I will not go on to gain from here, under the falling mulberry leaves?"[24]

•

Zigong was looking around the north hall of the ancestral temple of Lu. He went out and asked Confucius, "Just now I was looking around the north hall of the Grand Temple. I looked continuously,
210 going back and forth inspecting the nine doors. Each of them has been patched together. Is there some explanation for this? Did the carpenters originally cut off too much?"[25]

Confucius said, "When it comes to the halls of the Grand Temple, there should be some explanation. The officials brought in excellent
215 craftsmen, who accordingly executed motifs and patterns. It is not that there were no good materials. We may perhaps say that it is because they simply valued these patterns."[26,b]

---

[24] The wording of this last sentence is ambiguous and also contains four characters that are very unclear in meaning and have provoked tremendous speculation among commentators. I have adopted a fairly straightforward reading of the line, but the translation remains tentative.

[25] Zigong's question is rhymed in the original.

[26] The text of most of this story appears to be seriously corrupt. Commentators rely on a parallel version in the text *Kongzi Jiayu* to try to reconstruct it, but much remains uncertain, including the main point of the anecdote. The translation here is highly tentative.

CHAPTER 29

The Way to Be a Son

To be filial upon entering and to be a good younger brother upon going out is lesser conduct. To be compliant to one's superiors and devoted to one's inferiors is middle conduct. To follow the Way and not one's lord, to follow *yi* and not one's father is the greatest conduct. If one's intentions are at ease in ritual, and one's words are put forth in accordance with the proper classes of things, then the Way of the *ru* is complete. Even Shun could not improve on this by so much as a hair's breadth.

There are three cases in which the filial son does not follow orders. When following orders will endanger one's parents, but not following orders will make them safe, then the filial son will not follow orders, and this is having scruples. When following orders will disgrace one's parents, but not following orders will bring them honor, then the filial son will not follow orders, and this is being *yi*. When following orders requires a beastly act, but not following orders requires cultivation and decorum, then the filial son will not follow orders, and this is being respectful. And so, not following orders when it is permissible to do so is to behave as though one is not a son. Following orders when it is not permissible to do so is to lack any scruples. If one understands the proper purposes of following and not following orders, and if one can be reverent, respectful, loyal, trustworthy, scrupulous, and honest so as to carry these out vigilantly, then this can be called the greatest filial piety. A proverb states, "Follow the Way, not your lord. Follow *yi*, not your father."[1] This expresses my meaning. And so, to face hard labor and physical exhaustion without losing one's respectfulness, to face calamities and difficulties without losing one's regard for *yi*, so that even in the unfortunate case of unsmooth relations and being hated one still does not lose one's love for one's parents—none but the person of *ren* can do this. The *Odes* says, "Those filial sons will be untiring."[2] This expresses my meaning.

•

Duke Ai of Lu asked Confucius, "Does filial piety consist in a son's following his father's orders? Does fidelity consist in a servant's following his lord's orders?" Three times he asked, but Confucius did not answer him.

---

[1] Compare this with the partial quotation of this proverb at 13.92.
[2] Mao #247. This line is also quoted at 27.554.

35   Confucius left quickly and told Zigong about it, saying, "Just now,
our lord asked me, 'Does filial piety consist in a son's following his
father's orders? Does fidelity consist in a servant's following his lord's
orders?' Three times he asked, but I did not answer him. What do you
think about this?"

40   Zigong said, "Filial piety consists indeed in a son's following his
father's orders. Fidelity consists indeed in a servant's following his
lord's orders. What response do you have to this, Master?"

Confucius said, "What a petty man you are, Duanmu Si! This is
because you do not understand. In the past, if a state that could field

45   ten thousand chariots had merely four contentious ministers, its territories and boundaries would not be reduced. If a state that could
field a thousand chariots had merely three contentious ministers, its
altars of soil and grain would not be endangered. If a state that could
field a hundred chariots had merely two contentious ministers, then

50   its ancestral temple would not be destroyed. A father who has a contentious son will not act in ways that lack ritual propriety. A well-bred
man who has a contentious friend will not do what is not *yi*. Thus, if
a son simply obeys his father, how would that son be filial? If a minister simply obeys his lord, how would that minister be exercising

55   fidelity? To be careful about the cases in which one obeys another—
this is called filial piety, this is called fidelity."

•

Zilu asked Confucius, "Here is a man who rises early in the morning
and retires late in the evening, plowing, weeding, planting, and gardening, until his hands and feet are rough and calloused, all in order

60   to nourish his parents. Yet, he has no reputation for being filial. Why
is that?"

Confucius said, "Perhaps you mean that in conducting himself he
is not respectful? Or his speech is not humble? Or the expression on
his face is not compliant? The ancients had a saying, 'You may clothe

65   me and outfit me, but I still will not rely on you.' "[3]

Zilu said,[a] "But now in the case of a man who rises early in the
morning and retires late in the evening, plowing, weeding, planting,
and gardening, until his hands and feet are rough and calloused, all
in order to nourish his parents, and who has none of those three

70   faults, what must he have done to lack a reputation for being filial?"

Confucius said, "Zhong You, pay attention to this. I tell you: Even
if one has the strength of a top warrior for the state, one may not be
able to raise oneself up, and not because one lacks strength, but
rather because one's position does not permit it. For this reason, if

_____

[3] The point of the saying seems to be that if one offers others material goods such as
clothing, but without the proper attitude of respect, one will not be able to win them
over. See *Analects* 2.7.

within the home one's conduct is not cultivated, this is one's own   75
mistake. If outside the home one's reputation is not renowned, this is
the fault of one's friends. Thus, within the home the gentleman makes
his conduct honorable, and outside the home he befriends the worthy. How would he not have a reputation for being filial then?"

                                    •

Zilu asked Confucius, "Is the way that the grand ministers of Lu sleep   80
in their beds after performing the *lian* sacrifice in keeping with
ritual?"[4]

   Confucius said, "I do not know."

   Zilu went out and told Zigong, "I thought there was nothing the
Master did not know, but there is indeed something the Master does   85
not know."

   Zigong said, "What did you ask?"

   Zilu said, "I asked, 'Is the way that the grand ministers of Lu sleep
in their beds after performing the *lian* sacrifice in keeping with ritual?' The Master said, 'I do not know.'"   90

   Zigong said, "I will ask on your behalf." He asked [Confucius], "Is
sleeping in one's bed after performing the *lian* sacrifice in keeping
with ritual?"

   Confucius said, "It is not in keeping with ritual."

   Zigong went out and told Zilu, "You said there was something the   95
Master does not know, didn't you? There is indeed nothing the Master does not know. Rather, your question was wrong. According to
ritual, when staying in a certain locale, one does not denigrate the
grand ministers there."

                                    •

Zilu was dressed in splendid clothes when he met with Confucius.   100
Confucius said, "Zhong You, what is the reason for this fanciness?
Early on, when the Yangtze emerges from Mount Min, at its point of
origin its flow is barely enough to overflow a goblet. But when it
reaches the crossing point,[5] then without tying together boats and
avoiding the winds, you would not be able to cross it. Is this not sim-   105
ply because of the vast amount of water flowing down? Now your
clothes are splendid and your countenance is puffed up. Who in the
world would be willing to remonstrate with you like this?"[6]

---

[4] The *lian* is a sacrifice performed after the first year of the three-year period of mourning for a parent. Mourners were supposed to sleep in a hut away from their normal
residence, and they were to resume sleeping in their regular beds only at the end of
the full period of mourning. In returning to their beds after only a year, the grand
ministers of Lu would thus seem to be in clear violation of ritual protocol, which is
why Zilu asks about it.

[5] Although it is not specified where the crossing point is, presumably it is far down the
river from its origin.

[6] The point of Confucius's analogy seems to be that, just as people are intimidated by

Zilu quickly went out, changed his clothing, and came back in, but
he still had the same manner as before. Confucius said, "Zhong You,
pay attention to this. I tell you: Those who are aggressive in their
words embellish things, and those who are aggressive in their conduct show off to others. One who makes a display of wisdom and
lords his ability around is a petty man. Thus, when a gentleman
knows something, he says he knows it, and when he does not know
something, he says he does not know it—this is the key point in
speaking.[7] When he is capable of something, he says that he is capable, and when he is not capable of something, he says that he is not
capable—this is the perfection of conduct. When one has grasped the
key point in speaking, then one is wise, and when one has perfected
one's conduct, then one is *ren*. When one is both wise and *ren*, what
shortcomings could one have?"

•

Zilu entered. Confucius said, "Zhong You, what is a wise person like?
What is a person of *ren* like?"
Zilu answered, "A wise person gets others to know him, and a per-
son of *ren* gets other people to love him."
Confucius said, "Zhong You can be called a well-bred man."
Zigong entered. Confucius said, "Duanmu Si, what is a wise per-
son like? What is a person of *ren* like?"
Zigong answered, "The wise person knows others, and the person
of *ren* loves others."
Confucius said, "Duanmu Si can be called a well-bred man and a
gentleman."
Yan Yuan entered. Confucius said, "Yan Hui, what is a wise person
like? What is a person of *ren* like?"
Yan Yuan answered, "The wise person knows himself, and the per-
son of *ren* loves himself."
Confucius said, "Yan Hui can be called an enlightened
gentleman."

•

Zilu asked Confucius, "Does a gentleman have worries?"[8]
Confucius said, "When the gentleman has not yet succeeded,[9] then
he takes joy in his ideals, and when he has succeeded, then he takes
joy in bringing good order to affairs. Thus, he has joy to the end of

---

an imposing river, people are also intimidated by a person's imposing appearance.
By putting on such airs, Zilu risks scaring away people who might correct him, and
thus the point of Confucius's criticism is that Zilu is not displaying the conduct appropriate to a would-be student.

[7] Compare *Analects* 2.17.

[8] This issue is frequently discussed in early Confucian texts. Compare the discussion
here with *Analects* 7.3, 9.29, 12.4, and 14.28, as well as *Mencius* 4B28.

[9] "Success" here is somewhat ambiguous. It may refer to success just in getting some-

his life, without a single day of worry. As for the petty man, when he has not yet succeeded, then he worries that he will never succeed, and 145 when he has succeeded, then he fears that he will lose it. Thus, he has worry to the end of his life, without a single day of joy."

thing desired, but more likely it refers to success in achieving a government position.

CHAPTER 30

The Proper Model and Proper Conduct

Gongshu[1] could not improve on the plumb line, and none of the sages can improve on ritual. The common people take ritual as their model but do not understand it. The sage takes ritual as his model and does understand it.

•

5 Zengzi said, "Do not distance those in your innermost circle and yet draw close to outsiders. Do not resent others while you yourself are not good. Do not cry out to Heaven when punishment has already arrived. To distance those in your innermost circle and draw close to outsiders—is this not far off the mark? To resent others while you 10 yourself are not good—is this not getting things backward? To cry out to Heaven when punishment has already arrived—is this not acting too late?[2] The *Odes* says:

> When the fount's waters were still flowing slowly,
> You did not stop or block them up.
15 > When the wheel's hub has already broken,
> You increase the size of the spokes.
> When affairs have already been ruined,
> You redouble your great sighs.[3]

Is there any advantage to behaving this way?"

•

20 Zengzi was ill, and Zeng Yuan[4] clasped his legs. Zengzi said, "Yuan, pay attention to this. I tell you: the fish, turtles, and crocodiles consider the watery depths as too shallow, and so they dig even further into them. The eagles and kites consider the mountains as too low, and so they build their nests [in trees] above them. Thus, when they 25 are captured, it is surely by means of some bait. So, if the gentleman can avoid harming *yi* because of a desire for profit, then for him there

---

[1] A master craftsman of antiquity.

[2] In the original, the entire passage is rhymed up to this point.

[3] This poem does not appear in the received text of the *Odes*. Because of this fact, it is not entirely clear whether the poem ends at this line or the one that follows. The lines are rhymed in the original up to this point, and the next line does not rhyme, so most editions of the *Xunzi* do not include it in the quotation, which I have followed.

[4] Zeng Yuan is Zengzi's son.

will be no source from which dishonor and disgrace might come upon him."

•

Zigong asked Confucius, "Why is it that the gentleman honors jade yet considers *min*[5] of low value? Is it because jade is rare, and *min* is common?"   30

Confucius said, "Ah, Duanmu Si, what words are these? How would a gentleman consider something to be of low value merely because it is common, and honor something merely because it is rare! As for jade, the gentleman compares it with virtue. The way it is   35 warm, smooth, and lustrous resembles *ren*. The way it has structure and contains patterns resembles wisdom. The way it is firm and un-yielding resembles *yi*. The way it is sharp but does not cut resembles proper conduct. The way it can be broken but does not bend resem-bles courage. The way that even its flaws are visible resembles genu-   40 ineness. In the way that when struck, its sound is pure, rises high, and can be heard far away, but when it stops, it finishes completely, it resembles proper speech. Thus, though there is ornately decorated *min*, it is not as good as the elegance of jade. The *Odes* says, 'Oh how I long for my gentleman! So warm is he, like jade!'[6] This expresses   45 my meaning."

•

Zengzi said, "If I travel with people but am accorded no care from them, I must have failed to be *ren*. If in my interactions with others I am not accorded respect, I must have failed to treat my elders prop-erly. If when dealing with money matters I am not accorded trust, I   50 must have failed to be trustworthy. When these three faults are pres-ent in my person, how could I complain against others? Those who complain against others in such a situation are bankrupt. Those who complain against Heaven in such a situation are witless. To be lack-ing something in oneself yet blame it on others—is this not far off the   55 mark?"

•

Nanguo Huizi asked Zigong, "Why is there such a motley assortment of people at your Master's gate?"[7]

---

[5] According to commentators, *min* is another kind of stone that looks like jade.

[6] Mao #128. In context, the speaker is a woman longing for her husband, who is away on a military campaign.

[7] It is not clear exactly what Nanguo Huizi is asking about, but the term *za* (here translated as "motley assortment") often has a disparaging connotation, implying mixing of bad in with the good. Nanguo Huizi's relation to Zigong and Confucius is not known, and the question may be meant as a slight, by implying that there must be something wrong with Confucius to have attracted such people of inferior quality.

Zigong said, "The gentleman rectifies his person and awaits the
60   right opportunity. He does not refuse those who desire to come to
him, nor does he stop those who desire to leave him. Moreover, at the
gate of a good doctor you will find many sick people, and beside a
press frame you will find many crooked pieces of wood. That is why
they are a motley assortment."

•

65   Confucius said, "There are three things in which the gentleman strives
to exercise *shu*.[8] If one has a lord but fails to serve him well, then if
one has a minister and requires him to perform well in one's employ,
this is not *shu*. If one has parents but fails to repay their love, then if
one has a son and requires him to be filial, this is not *shu*. If one has
70   an elder brother but fails to treat him with respect, then if one has a
younger brother and requires him to obey one's orders, this is not
shu.[9] If a well-bred man is clear about these three occasions for *shu*,
then he can rectify his person."

•

Confucius said, "There are three things for which the gentleman takes
75   thought, and you must not fail to take thought for them. If you do
not study when young, then when grown you will have no abilities. If
you do not teach when old, then when you are dead no one will think
of you. If you do not exercise generosity when you possess the means,
then when you are impoverished no one will give to you. For these
80   reasons, when the gentleman is young he takes thought for when he
is grown and so he studies. When old, he takes thought for when he
is dead and so he teaches. When he is possessed of means, he takes
thought for impoverished times and so he exercises generosity."

---

[8] The virtue of *shu* is difficult to translate into English. According to Confucius's statement in *Analects* 15.15, it involves not doing to others what one would not want for
oneself. Thus, it can be understood as a kind of "sympathetic understanding" or
"reciprocity."
[9] In the original, the whole passage is rhymed up to this point.

CHAPTER 31

Duke Ai

Duke Ai of Lu asked Confucius, "I desire to judge among the well-bred men of my state, so that together with them I may order the state. May I ask how to go about choosing them?"

Confucius answered, "To live in today's world but focus one's intentions on the way of the ancients, to dwell in today's customs but   5
dress in the clothes of the ancients—those who abide by these and still do wrong are few indeed, are they not?"[1]

Duke Ai said, "If so, then is anyone who dons court robes and court shoes and tucks an official tablet into his sash a worthy?"

Confucius answered, "Not necessarily so. But one who wears the   10
ceremonial robes and hat and rides in the ceremonial cart does not focus his intentions on eating savory foods.[2] One who wears the robes and shoes of mourning, leans on a cane, and eats gruel does not focus his intentions on wine and meat. To live in today's world but focus one's intentions on the way of the ancients, to dwell in today's cus-   15
toms but dress in the clothes of the ancients—even if there should be some who abide by these and still do wrong, they would be few indeed, would they not?"

Duke Ai said, "Well spoken!"

•

Confucius said, "There are five grades of people. There is the vulgar   20
man, the well-bred man, the gentleman, the worthy, and the great sage."

Duke Ai said, "May I ask what sort of person can be called a vulgar man?"

Confucius answered, "As for the one called a vulgar man, his   25
mouth cannot speak good words, and his heart does not know to control the expression on his face.[a] He does not know to choose worthy people and good men and entrust his person to them, so that they will worry on his behalf. When vigorously exerting himself, he does not know what to work at, and when limiting his interactions, he does   30
not know where to take a fixed stand. In his daily choices among things, he does not know what to value. He simply follows along with things like flowing with a current and does not know where to re-

---

[1] Compare 12.180–81.
[2] Such foods were prohibited in the period of fasting preceding sacrifices.

turn.[3] His five senses govern him, and his heart obeys them and is
35 ruined. One who is like this can be called a vulgar man."

Duke Ai said, "Well spoken! May I ask what sort of person can be
called a well-bred man?"

Confucius answered, "As for the one called a well-bred man, even
though he is unable to practice the Way and its methods completely,
40 he is certain to have a proper model for his actions, and even though
he is unable to be completely fine and good, he is sure to have places
where he does achieve these things. For this reason, he does not work
at knowing many things, but rather works at being careful about
what he understands. He does not work at saying many things, but
45 rather works at being careful about what he means. He does not work
at practicing many things, but rather works at being careful about the
standard that he follows. Thus, when he knows something, he has
already understood it. When he says something, he has already meant
it. When he practices something, he has already followed his stan-
50 dard. As a result, he does all these things with a constancy like the
way one's nature, life, and flesh cannot be traded for another's. Thus,
wealth and noble station are insufficient to add anything to him.
Humble and lowly station are insufficient to detract from him. One
who is like this can be called a well-bred man."

55 Duke Ai said, "Well spoken! May I ask what sort of person can be
called a gentleman?"

Confucius answered, "As for the one called a gentleman, his words
are trustworthy and loyal, yet his heart does not flaunt his virtue. He
has *ren* and *yi* in his person, yet his countenance is not arrogant. His
60 reflections and deliberations are clear and penetrating, yet his speech
is not contentious. Thus one who is hesitant, as though he were about
to be able to reach it[4] is a gentleman."

Duke Ai said, "Well spoken! May I ask what sort of person can be
called a worthy?"

65 Confucius answered, "As for the one called a worthy, his actions
conform to compass and ink-line, but he brings no harm upon the
fundamentals.[5] His words are sufficient to serve as a model for all
under Heaven, but he brings no harm upon his person.[6] He can be

---

[3] I.e., he lacks a guiding standard to which he "returns" over and over again in his judgments.

[4] I.e., the great goal, the Way.

[5] The meaning of this rather obscure sentence seems to be that the worthy man's actions match the dictates of ritual (and so can be said to conform to compass and ink-line), yet he is not so rigid and inflexible as to follow ritual protocol strictly when doing so would go against the spirit of the rites (because doing so would "harm the fundamentals").

[6] This is in contrast with other people (especially rulers) whose actions would, if widely emulated, lead to their own downfall.

wealthy enough to possess the whole world yet will not be resented
for his riches. He can spread his beneficence over the whole world yet   70
not worry about becoming poor. One who is like this can be called a
worthy."

Duke Ai said, "Well spoken! May I ask what sort of person can be
called a great sage?"

Confucius answered, "The one called a great sage is one whose   75
understanding comprehends the great Way, who responds to changes
appropriately without cease, and who correctly distinguishes among
the inborn dispositions and natures of the myriad things. The great
Way is that by which he changes, transforms, employs, and perfects
the myriad things. Their inborn dispositions and natures are that by   80
which he sets in order what is right and what is not, what is to be
adopted and what is to be rejected. For this reason,[7] in his works he
brings about great distinctions over Heaven and Earth, he looks
keenly into [the movements of] the sun and the moon, and grasps
and masters the myriad things amidst the wind and rain.   85

> Mixed up and jumbled,[8,b]
> His works cannot be followed.
> Like a true descendant of Heaven,
> His works cannot be recognized.[9]
> The common people are shallow;   90
> They do not even recognize him as their neighbor.

One who is like this can be called a great sage."

Duke Ai said, "Well spoken!"

•

Duke Ai of Lu asked Confucius about the cap worn by Shun. Confucius did not answer. After asking three more times without receiving   95
an answer, Duke Ai said, "I asked you about the cap worn by Shun.
Why do you not speak?"

Confucius replied, "The kings of ancient times were men who,
when there were tasks to be done, kept to leadership, and that is all.[c]
In their government, they valued life and hated killing. For this rea-   100
son, there were phoenixes among the rows of trees, and there were
unicorns in the suburbs and the wilds.[10] One could look upon the
nests of crows and sparrows just by bending down.[11] My lord, though,

---

[7] From this point to the end of the paragraph, the text seems to be corrupted, and the
translation here is tentative.

[8] This and the next few lines are rhymed in the original.

[9] Compare 17.27–28 about the inscrutability of Heaven's works.

[10] According to legend, the phoenix and the unicorn were beasts that appeared only
in times of sagely government.

[11] The point seems to be that the times were so peaceful that even the birds felt safe
enough to make their nests on the ground.

did not ask about these things, but instead asked about the cap worn
105 by Shun. That is why I did not answer."

•

Duke Ai of Lu asked of Confucius, "I was born deep within the palace and I grew up at the hands of women. I have never known sorrow.
I have never known worry. I have never known labor. I have never
known fear. I have never known danger."

110   Confucius said, "That which my lord asks about is a question worthy of a sage ruler. I am a nobody. How would I be capable of knowing it?"

Duke Ai said, "But if not you, there is no one from whom I might
hear it."

115   Confucius said, "When my lord enters the ancestral temple and
ascends from the stairs on the right, looking up, you see the beams
and rafters, looking down, you see the tables and mats. The implements remain, but the people who owned them are no more. If my
lord uses this to ponder sorrow, then how would understanding of
120 sorrow not come?

"At daybreak, my lord combs his hair and dons his cap. During the
day, my lord hears cases at court. If even one matter does not meet
with the proper response, it is the start of chaos. If my lord uses this
to ponder worry, then how would understanding of worry not come?

125   "During the day, my lord hears cases at court. When the sun goes
down, my lord retires, but among the sons and grandsons of the feudal lords there are sure to be some who remain at the margins of the
chamber.[12] If my lord uses this to ponder labor, then how would understanding of labor not come?

130   "When my lord goes out from the four gates of the Lu capital in
order to gaze upon the four suburbs of Lu, there are sure to be several
structures left from among the ruins of perished states. If my lord
uses this to ponder fear, then how would understanding of fear not
come?

135   "Moreover, I have heard it said that the lord is like a boat, and the
common people are like water. The water may support the boat, but
the water may also overturn the boat. If my lord uses this to ponder
danger, then how would understanding of danger not come?"

•

Duke Ai of Lu asked Confucius, "Are ceremonial belts and caps of use
140 in becoming *ren*?"

---

[12] According to commentators, these are nobility whose states have been destroyed
and who therefore sought refuge in Lu as retainers for the ruler. Thus, their lot
symbolizes the kind of labor to which Duke Ai might be subject should he govern
badly and lose his own state as a result.

Confucius was startled and said, "Why does my lord speak like this? One who takes up the garments and cane of a mourner does not listen to music, not because his ears cannot hear it, but because his accoutrements make him so. One who wears the sacrificial robes does not eat meat, not because his mouth cannot taste it, but because his   145
accoutrements make him so. Moreover, I have heard it said that those who are fond of business do not preserve the sacrificial grounds, while elders do not act for the sake of the market.ᵈ If one examines what things are of use or are of no use, my lord will surely know the answer."   150

•

Duke Ai of Lu asked Confucius, "May I inquire about how to choose people?"¹³
Confucius answered, "Do not choose those who are self-important. Do not choose those who are domineering. Do not choose those whose mouths talk excessively.¹⁴ Those who are self-important are   155
greedy. Those who are domineering create disorder. Those whose mouths talk excessively engage in deception. Thus, only when bows are properly strung does one then seek for the strongest among them. Only when horses are tame does one then seek for the best among them. Only when men are trustworthy and honest does one then seek   160
for the most intelligent and capable among them. If a man is not trustworthy and honest but has much intelligence and ability, one can compare him to a wolf—one must not allow oneself to get close.¹⁵ A saying goes, 'Duke Huan employed someone who tried to do him villainy. Duke Wen employed someone who stole from him.'¹⁶ And so,   165
an enlightened ruler relies on careful calculation and does not trust in his anger. The benighted ruler trusts in his anger and does not rely on careful calculation. He in whom calculation wins out over anger will be strong. He in whom anger wins out over calculation will not last long."   170

•

¹³ I.e., select people for official positions in the government.
¹⁴ The first part of the quotation from Confucius is possibly corrupt, and the translation here is tentative.
¹⁵ Some editions of the *Xunzi* break the quotation from Confucius off here and treat the following saying as a separate passage. However, since the topic of the saying and the subsequent analysis also concern how to choose one's subordinates, it seems plausible that the saying belongs with the preceding sentences.
¹⁶ Duke Huan of Qi employed Guan Zhong, even though Guan Zhong had once almost killed him in battle. Guan Zhong was extremely capable, and by employing him Duke Huan became very powerful (see 7.16–36). Duke Wen of Jin employed Tou Xu (or according to some versions, Lifu Xu), who had stolen from him. However, Tou Xu's exact contribution to Duke Wen's government is not known. At any rate, both cases are supposed to illustrate how lords who overcame personal enmity became more powerful by not acting on anger and seeking revenge.

Duke Ding asked Yan Yuan, "Is Master Dongye good at chariot driving?"

Yan Yuan answered, "He is good as good goes, but even so, he will lose his horses."

175 Duke Ding was not pleased. He went in and said to his aides, "Is it originally the case that a gentleman slanders people?"

Three days later, the keeper of the stables came in and reported, "Dongye Bi has lost his horses. The two outer steeds[17] have broken away, and the two center steeds have entered the stables."

180 Duke Ding left his mat and stood up. He said, "Quickly send a chariot to summon Yan Yuan." Yan Yuan arrived, and Duke Ding said, "Previously when I questioned you, you said, 'Dongye Bi's chariot driving is good as good goes, but even so, he will lose his horses.' I do not understand how you knew this."

185 Yan Yuan answered, "I knew it from the way governing works. In the past, Shun was skilled at employing the people, and Zao Fu was skilled at employing horses. Shun did not reduce his people to dire straits, and Zao Fu did not reduce his horses to dire straits. Thus, Shun did not lose any of his people, and Zao Fu did not lose any of 190 his horses. Now as for the way Dongye Bi drives, in mounting the chariot and taking up the reins, he has the body of the bit correctly aligned. In walking, trotting, and galloping, he performs the court rituals completely. In overcoming obstacles and going far distances, he exhausts the strength of the horses. Yet, he still requires that the 195 horses do not stop. This is how I knew what would happen."

Duke Ding said, "Well spoken. Can I get you to elaborate a little further?"

Yan Yuan answered, "I have heard it said that when birds are reduced to dire straits, they bite, when beasts are reduced to dire straits, 200 they lash out, and when people are reduced to dire straits, they engage in deception. From ancient times to the present, there has never been someone who reduces his subordinates to dire straits and yet can be free of danger."

---

[17] Dongye Bi was apparently driving a four-horse chariot where the horses were yoked together in a single row.

CHAPTER 32

Yao Asked

Yao asked Shun, "I desire to make everyone under Heaven come to my side. How may I do so?"

Shun replied, "Hold to single-mindedness without fail. Attend to what is minute without laziness. Have loyalty and faithfulness without tiring. Everyone under Heaven will then come on their own. If you hold to single-mindedness like Heaven and Earth, if you attend to what is minute like sun and moon,[1] if loyalty and integrity fill you up on the inside, pour forth on the outside, and manifest themselves to all within the four seas, then all under Heaven will be as though already in the corner of your room. What more could you need to make them come?"

•

Marquis Wu of Wei was planning affairs and hitting on exactly the right course, and none of his various ministers could keep up with him. He withdrew from court with a happy look on his face. Wu Qi entered and said, "Have you ever heard the tale of King Zhuang of Chu from your aides?"

The Marquis said, "How does the tale of King Zhuang of Chu go?"

Wu Qi replied, "King Zhuang of Chu was planning affairs and hitting on exactly the right course, and none of his various ministers could keep up with him. He withdrew from court with a worried look on his face. Duke Wu Chen of Shen entered and asked, 'Why does your majesty have a worried look after holding court?' King Zhuang said, 'I was planning affairs and hitting on exactly the right course, and none of my various ministers could keep up with me. That is why I am worried. A saying of Zhong Hui[2] goes:

> A feudal lord who on his own obtains a teacher will become a true king. He who obtains true friends will become a hegemon. He who obtains people to question his policies will survive. He who plans affairs on his own with nobody else as good as himself will perish.

Now given my own unworthiness, and that none of my own ministers can keep up with me, isn't my state close to perishing? That is why I

---

[1] The sun and moon symbolize thoroughness because they shine on big and small alike.

[2] A famous minister of the sage king Tang.

am worried.' King Zhuang of Chu took this as a reason to worry, but you, my lord, take it as a reason to be happy."

35 Marquis Wu of Wei took a step backward and bowed repeatedly, saying, "Heaven has sent you to shake out my faults."

•

Bo Qin was going to return to Lu.[3] The Duke of Zhou addressed Bo Qin's teacher, saying, "You are about to go. Might you report on my son's fine points and virtues?"

40 He answered, "His character is magnanimous. He likes to rely on himself and is cautious. These three things are precisely his fine points and virtues."

The Duke of Zhou said, "Alas! You have taken a person's failings for fine points and virtues! The gentleman likes to rely on the Way

45 and virtue, and so his people return to the Way. As for my son's 'magnanimity,' it comes from acting indiscriminately. Yet you praise him!

"As for his 'fondness for relying on himself,' this is why he is narrow and petty. Even if the gentleman's strength is comparable to that of an ox, he does not contest with the ox to show off his strength.

50 Even if his running is comparable to that of a horse, he does not contest with the horse to show off his running. Even if his understanding is comparable to that of a well-bred man, he does not contest with the well-bred man to show off his understanding. My son contests with others because he has an attitude of wanting to prove that he is equal

55 to them. Yet you praise him!

"As for his 'cautiousness,' this is why he is shallow. I have heard it said, 'If one does not cross boundaries, one will not get to meet with well-bred men.' When one meets a well-bred man, one asks, 'Is there something I have failed to look into?' If one does not hear them out,

60 then important things will less frequently come to one's attention. If important things less frequently come to one's attention, then one will be shallow. My son's shallowness is due to the way he has low regard for people. Yet you praise him! Let me tell you: with my relation to King Wen as his son, my relation to King Wu as his younger

65 brother, and my relation to King Cheng as his uncle, I am not lowly compared to anyone under Heaven. Nevertheless, there are ten people with whom I consulted after presenting them greeting gifts. There are thirty people with whom I consulted after reciprocating their greeting gifts. There are more than a hundred well-bred men whom I

70 have treated courteously [in order to gain their advice]. There are more than a thousand people whom I have wished to speak and asked to give a complete account of affairs. From among all these

---

[3] Bo Qin is the son of the Duke of Zhou. According to commentators, on the occasion of this story he is returning to Lu to take up a ruling position, which is why the Duke of Zhou is concerned to learn about his virtue first.

people, I obtained only three well-bred men to set straight my person
and put right all under Heaven. The source from which I obtained
these three well-bred men was not among the ten or the thirty, but   75
rather among the hundred and the thousand. For this reason, I treat
high-ranking men with less courtesy, and low-ranking men with more
courtesy. People all regard me as overstepping boundaries and being
fond of well-bred men. Thus and for that reason, well-bred men come
to me. When well-bred men come, then one truly sees things. When   80
one truly sees things, then one knows where right and wrong lie. You
be careful about this!

"Using the state of Lu to treat people arrogantly is risky. Men who
highly regard an official salary may be treated arrogantly, but men
who can correct one's person may not be treated arrogantly. Men   85
who can correct one's person abandon noble status and live lowly.
They abandon wealth and live poorly. They abandon ease and do
hard labor. Their faces are dark,[4] but they do not lose their proper
position. For this reason, the guiding principles for all under Heaven
are not extinguished, and good culture and proper form are not   90
destroyed."

•

According to a story, a border official from Zengqiu[5] met Sunshu Ao,
the prime minister of Chu, and said, "I have heard it said, 'Those who
occupy official positions for a long time incur the jealousy of the well-
bred men,[6] those who have a generous official salary are resented by   95
the common people, and those who hold exalted status are hated by
the lord.' Now you have been prime minister for Chu these three
times but have not offended the well-bred men and the common people of Chu. How is that?"

Sunshu Ao said, "I have been prime minister three times, and each   100
time my heart has been more unpresumptuous. For each addition to
my official salary, my exercise of generosity has been more broad. For
each greater exaltation of my status, my practice of the rituals has
been more reverent. Thus, I have not offended the well-bred men and
the common people of Chu."   105

•

Zigong posed a question for Confucius, saying, "I will be someone's
subordinate, but I do not yet know how to conduct myself."

Confucius said, "Being a person's subordinate? Is this not like the
ground? If one digs deeply into it, one will obtain a sweet spring from

[4] I.e., from doing manual labor under the sun.
[5] This place is not known, and therefore commentators have suggested different readings. Perhaps the most plausible is that of Liu Shipei, who suggests it is Qinqiu, a
land that belonged to Sunshu Ao.
[6] The reference here is probably to aristocrats in general, rather than morally cultivated people.

110   it. If one plants on it, the five grains will grow from it. Grasses and trees multiply upon it, and birds and beasts are nourished upon it. When one lives, one stands upon it. When one dies, one enters into it. It provides bountiful merits without cease. To be a person's subordinate, is this not like the ground?"

•

115   In the past, the state of Yu[7] did not employ Gongzhi Qi, and so Jin swallowed it up. The state of Lai did not employ Zi Ma, and so Qi swallowed it up. The tyrant Zhòu eviscerated Prince Bi Gan, and so King Wu succeeded him. These people did not draw near to the worthy and employ the wise, and so they died and their states were
120   destroyed.

•

The purveyors of doctrines say: "Xunzi[8] was not as good as Confucius." This is not so.

Xunzi was coerced by a chaotic age and threatened with severe punishment.[9] Above, there were no worthy rulers.
125   Below, he encountered the violence of Qin. Ritual and *yi* were not being practiced. Teaching and transformation were not being accomplished. People of *ren* were held back and constrained. All under Heaven were living in darkness. Those with perfect conduct were attacked. The feudal lords were all
130   highly deviant.

At that time, the wise did not get to deliberate, and the capable did not get to govern. The worthy did not get to be employed. Thus, lords and superiors were fixated and had no clear vision. Worthy people were rejected and not accepted. However, Xunzi held a heart intent
135   on becoming a sage, but feigned the appearance of madness[10] in order to present the world with a façade of stupidity. The *Odes* say, "He was enlightened and wise, and used this to protect his person."[11] This is the reason why his reputation is not clear, his followers and allies are few, and his brilliance is not widely known.

140   When scholars of today obtain Xunzi's remaining words and the teachings he left behind, they are sufficient to be models

---

[7] This is the name of a particular state, not the sage king Yu.

[8] The name given in the text is actually "Sun Qing" (孫卿), which is an alternate, honorific way of referring to Xunzi. To avoid any confusion for readers, though, I have simply substituted "Xunzi" here. This passage was probably written by Xunzi's students.

[9] From this sentence down to the word "deviant," the original text is rhymed.

[10] Nothing is known of this incident beyond the report here.

[11] Mao #260.

and standards for all under Heaven.[12] Wherever they reside, that place enjoys a spirit-like state.[13] Wherever they pass by, that place becomes transformed. If one observes his good conduct, Confucius did not surpass him. The world does not look into things carefully, and so they say he was not a sage. Why? The world was not ordered then, and Xunzi did not meet with the right times. His virtue was like that of Yao and Yu, but few in the world understood him. His methods and techniques were not used, and he was viewed with suspicion by people. Yet his understanding was extremely clear, he cultivated the way and corrected his conduct, and he made himself a guiding standard. Alas for such a worthy person! He was fit to be a sovereign king. Those between Heaven and Earth did not understand him, but rather praised Jie and Zhòu and killed good and worthy men. Bi Gan was eviscerated. Confucius was trapped in Kuang. Jie Yu avoided the world. Jizi feigned madness. Tian Chang created chaos.[14] Helü monopolized brute force. Those who were bad obtained good fortune, while the good suffered catastrophes. Now the purveyors of doctrine once more do not look into the truth of the matter but rather believe the reputations. Now that times are different, where will Xunzi's fame come from? Since he did not get to engage in government, how would his merits have been accomplished? Yet his intentions were cultivated and his virtue was abundant. Who would say he was not worthy?

[12] From here to the end of the paragraph, the original text is rhymed. This and the following two sentences are somewhat ambiguous. The "they" could refer to either Xunzi's teachings themselves or the scholars who have obtained (and practice) Xunzi's teachings.

[13] I.e., a state that is extremely good. Compare the similar use of this phrase at 15.359–60 and 15.529.

[14] Tian Chang, also known as (Lord) Meng Chang, the Duke of Xue, was an infamous minister of Qi who helped other states overthrow the ruler of Qi. See 11.96–118 and 13.38–39.

Important Terms and Names

This appendix is for the benefit of readers who have no previous knowledge of Chinese thought and/or who are reading this text without the aid of an instructor to explain items that are not explained elsewhere in the footnotes. Readers should keep in mind that, as with all other renderings in this work, the translations chosen for particular terms are *not* to be taken as exact semantic equivalents for any Chinese word. Rather, they are intended as stand-ins for (and approximations to) the Chinese terms, and so readers should base their understanding of the Chinese concepts on how they are actually deployed in the text, rather than simply on the English words chosen to represent them.

Documents (*Shu* 書): The *Documents* is a collection purporting to record the speeches and deeds of past sage kings. Following the practice of Confucius, the *Xunzi* treats it as a source of moral and political wisdom and quotes from it in support of its claims, but also relegates it to a secondary place in the process of moral development (see 8.395–96).

gentleman (*junzi* 君子): This term originally meant "the son of a lord," that is, a prince. In archaic Chinese, it is often used to refer to aristocrats generally. Traces of these earlier meanings appear in the *Xunzi*, but in this text (as in most other Confucian texts), the term usually designates a kind of morally ideal person, one that potentially anyone can become. Sometimes, the text ranks the gentleman as the second highest level of moral achievement, just beneath sagehood (e.g., 2.167–70), but sometimes the text also speaks in ways that would equate the gentleman and the sage (compare chap. 9.295–301 with 19.370–74). The translation "gentleman" is intended to capture the idea that the *junzi* is someone who is highly cultivated and abides by ritual (see the entry on "ritual" below), as well as echoing the term's earlier aristocratic connotations. In many other English translations of early Chinese texts, *junzi* is also rendered as "gentleman."

Odes (*Shi* 詩): The *Odes* is a collection of poems (originally songs) dating from very ancient times. Confucius used it as part of his moral curriculum, believing that it contained insights from and illustrations of the lives of past sages. The *Xunzi* follows this view, frequently citing the *Odes* in support of its claims. However, it is clear in relegating the *Odes* to a secondary place in the process of moral development (see 8.395–96).

ren (仁): In Xunzi's thought, *ren* is a major virtue, and arguably *the* most important virtue, as it is for many other early Confucian thinkers. In the context of the *Xunzi*, its most salient component is concern for the well-being of others (e.g., 15.353–55), with greatest concern being reserved for one's parents (e.g., 27.104–5). In other texts, one commonly sees *ren* translated as "benevolence" or "humaneness."

ritual, rites (*li* 禮): As with *yi* (see the entry on *yi* below), the term *li* has two main senses in the *Xunzi*. First, it refers to a set of standards for behavior that were created by the sage kings in order to bring order to people (e.g., 19.1–11). These standards range from what we nowadays think of as etiquette all the way up to grand ceremonies for special occasions. For this reason, "ritual" and "rites" are the conventional translations for *li*. It is worth noting that the text treats ritual as distinct from both law (e.g., 17.198–201) and common custom (e.g., 8.239–62). The *Xunzi* repeatedly stresses adherence to ritual as the primary means by which to improve one's moral character. Second, the text uses the term *li* to refer to a person's tendency to adhere to ritual, that is, as a virtue, and in those cases it is rendered as "ritual propriety."

Spring and Autumn Annals (*Chunqiu* 春秋): The *Spring and Autumn Annals* is a very terse chronological history of the Chinese state of Lu during the eighth to fifth centuries BCE. Like the *Odes* and *Documents* (see entries above) the *Xunzi* treats it as an important source of moral and political knowledge (e.g., 8.280–86), but draws on it much less frequently than those other works.

virtue (*de* 德): The term *de* refers primarily to a kind of power to sway others, win them over to one's side, and have them do one's bidding. In the *Xunzi*, as in many other Confucian texts, this power is conceived as arising (almost) exclusively from being a good person, and so *de* comes, by extension, to refer as well to those good traits that give rise to this power, which is why *de* is translated here as "virtue." *De* is commonly rendered as "virtue" in many other translations, but sometimes "power" or "inner power" is also used.

Way (*Dao* 道): In the *Xunzi*, the Way is the highest normative standard, and constitutes the guide both for how individuals should live and for how the world as a whole should be managed. The notion of the *Dao* is sometimes mistakenly equated with the view found in "Daoist" texts such as the *Daodejing* and the *Zhuangzi*. In fact, the term was common property among all early Chinese thinkers, who all used it to designate the ideal way to live, while disagreeing about what was involved in following the Way. The *Xunzi* explicitly criticizes other major early Chinese thinkers' understandings of the Way (see 17.247–262 and 21.101–22). It also explicitly rejects any attempt to identify the Way with the ways of Heaven and Earth (see 8.101–2).

well-bred man (*shi* 士): In early China, the term *shi* referred to members of a certain socioeconomic class, who often served as civilian and/or military officials. Membership in this class was originally hereditary, but by Xunzi's time it could be acquired in various ways. Like *junzi* (see "gentleman" above), the *Xunzi* often treats *shi* as the label for a person with a noteworthy level of moral cultivation—one that potentially anyone could attain—with the *shi* being a step below the gentleman (e.g., 2.167–69). To reflect both the moral and earlier aristocratic senses of the term, it is rendered as "well-bred man" when used in this way. However, the other uses of *shi* in the *Xunzi* are so varied that it is impossible, without being extremely awkward or misleading in places, to render it consistently with a single English word. For that reason, here *shi* is also rendered as "officer" or simply "man," as the context demands. Other translations of early Chinese texts use "knight," "scholar-official," and "a/the noble[man]."

yi (義): In the *Xunzi*, *yi* has two main meanings. On the one hand, it refers to a certain set of ethical *standards* that were created by the ancient sage kings to bring order to people (e.g., 23.27–31). These standards delineate proper social roles and the privileges and responsibilities attached to them (e.g., 27.691–97). On the other hand, *yi* also refers to a *virtue*, namely the tendency to adhere to these standards and the order they contain (e.g., 15.355–57). In other texts, one commonly sees the latter sense of *yi* translated as "righteousness," and the former sense is sometimes translated as "duties."

Cross-Reference List

Because there is no standard numbering system for the text of the *Xunzi*, here I have provided a list that will help those who are comparing Knoblock's translation or who are checking references in the secondary literature (based on concordance numbers) to find the corresponding passage in this volume. References are given in the following formats:

Knoblock:
chapter number.paragraph number (volume number.page number)

Hutton:
chapter number.line number

Harvard-Yenching Index Series Concordance to the *Xunzi* (HYIS):
page number/chapter number/line number

Chinese University of Hong Kong Institute of Chinese Studies Ancient Chinese Texts Concordance Series Concordance to the *Xunzi* (HKCS):
chapter number/page number/line number

Chapter	Knoblock	Hutton	HYIS	HKCS
1. *Quanxue* 勸學	1.1 (I.135)	1.1	1/1/1	1/1/3
	1.2 (I.136)	1.12	1/1/3	1/1/7
	1.3 (I.136)	1.27	1/1/6	1/1/12
	1.4 (I.136)	1.39	1/1/9	1/1/17
	1.5 (I.137)	1.57	1/1/13	1/2/3
	1.6 (I.138)	1.80	2/1/17	1/2/9
	1.7 (I.139)	1.121	2/1/24	1/3/3
	1.8 (I.139)	1.128	2/1/26	1/3/7
	1.9 (I.140)	1.145	2/1/30	1/3/14
	1.10 (I.140)	1.159	2/1/30	1/3/20
	1.11 (I.140)	1.168	3/1/35	1/3/23
	1.12 (I.141)	1.186	3/1/39	1/4/6
	1.13 (I.142)	1.206	3/1/43	1/4/12
	1.14 (I.142)	1.217	3/1/46	1/4/16

Chapter	Knoblock	Hutton	HYIS	HKCS
2. *Xiushen* 修身	2.1 (I.151)	2.1	3/2/1	2/5/3
	2.2 (I.152)	2.30	4/2/6	2/5/11
	2.3 (I.153)	2.59	4/2/11	2/5/18
	2.4 (I.153)	2.78	4/2/14	2/6/6
	2.5 (I.154)	2.95	4/2/19	2/6/12
	2.6 (I.154)	2.108	5/2/22	2/6/16
	2.7 (I.155)	2.128	5/2/26	2/7/5
	2.8 (I.155)	2.134	5/2/27	2/7/8
	2.9 (I.156)	2.162	5/2/34	2/7/17
	2.10 (I.156)	2.167	5/2/35	2/7/18
	2.11 (I.157)	2.175	5/2/37	2/8/1
	2.12 (I.157)	2.194	5/2/41	2/8/7
	2.13 (I.158)	2.212	6/2/45	2/8/12
	2.14 (I.158)	2.214	6/2/45	2/8/12
3. *Bugou* 不苟	3.1 (I.173)	3.1	6/3/1	3/8/20
	3.2 (I.174)	3.26	6/3/6	3/9/7
	3.3 (I.174)	3.34	6/3/7	3/9/10
	3.4 (I.175)	3.48	6/3/10	3/9/15
	3.5 (I.175)	3.55	6/3/12	3/9/19
	3.6 (I.176)	3.72	6/3/16	3/10/6
	3.7 (I.176)	3.94	7/3/20	3/10/12
	3.8 (I.177)	3.109	7/3/24	3/10/18
	3.9a (I.177)	3.118	7/3/26	3/11/4
	3.9b (I.178)	3.128	7/3/28	3/11/6
	3.9c (I.178)	3.142	7/3/31	3/11/9
	3.10 (I.179)	3.157	8/3/35	3/11/14
	3.11 (I.179)	3.175	8/3/39	3/11/20
	3.12 (I.180)	3.201	8/3/44	3/12/3
	3.13 (I.180)	3.207	8/3/45	3/12/6
	3.14 (I.180)	3.223	8/3/48	3/12/11
4. *Rongru* 榮辱	4.1 (I.186)	4.1	8/4/1	4/12/17
	4.2 (I.186)	4.14	8/4/3	4/12/21
	4.3 (I.187)	4.29	9/4/6	4/13/1
	4.4 (I.188)	4.62	9/4/16	4/13/13
	4.5 (I.188)	4.78	9/4/20	4/13/19
	4.6 (I.189)	4.87	9/4/22	4/14/3
	4.7 (I.189)	4.102	9/4/25	4/14/8
	4.8 (I.190)	4.136	10/4/32	4/14/17
	4.9 (I.191)	4.176	10/4/42	4/15/7
	4.10 (I.192)	4.202	11/4/49	4/15/14
	4.11 (I.193)	4.244	11/4/60	4/16/5
	4.12 (I.194)	4.294	12/4/72	4/16/18

Chapter	Knoblock	Hutton	HYIS	HKCS
5. *Feixiang* 非相	5.1 (I.203)	5.1	12/5/1	5/17/10
	5.2 (I.204)	5.53	13/5/13	5/17/26
	5.3 (I.205)	5.81	13/5/19	5/18/7
	5.4 (I.206)	5.104	13/5/23	5/18/13
	5.5 (I.207)	5.139	13/5/32	5/18/24
	5.6 (I.208)	5.173	14/5/40	5/19/10
	5.7 (I.208)	5.193	14/5/45	5/19/17
	5.8 (I.209)	5.217	14/5/50	5/20/7
	5.9 (I.210)	5.227	14/5/53	5/20/12
	5.10 (I.210)	5.249	14/5/59	5/21/1
6. *Fei shi'erzi* 非十二子	6.1 (I.222)	6.1	15/6/1	6/21/10
	6.2 (I.223)	6.6	15/6/2	6/21/13
	6.3 (I.223)	6.13	15/6/3	6/21/16
	6.4 (I.223)	6.22	15/6/4	6/21/19
	6.5 (I.223)	6.31	15/6/6	6/21/22
	6.6 (I.224)	6.41	15/6/8	6/22/4
	6.7 (I.224)	6.51	15/6/10	6/22/8
	6.8 (I.225)	6.66	16/6/14	6/22/13
	6.9 (I.225)	6.98	16/6/21	6/23/4
	6.10 (I.226)	6.131	16/6/27	6/23/13
	6.11 (I.227)	6.163	16/6/33	6/24/4
	6.12 (I.228)	6.184	17/6/38	6/24/12
	6.13 (I.228)	6.198	17/6/42	6/24/17
7. *Zhongni* 仲尼	7.1 (II.57)	7.1	17/7/1	7/25/7
	7.2 (II.59)	7.71	18/7/17	7/26/6
	7.3 (II.60)	7.102	19/7/24	7/26/14
	7.4 (II.61)	7.143	19/7/32	7/27/3
	7.5 (II.62)	7.158	19/7/35	7/27/8
8. *Ruxiao* 儒效	8.1 (II.68)	8.1	19/8/1	8/27/14
	8.2 (II.69)	8.39	20/8/10	8/27/26
	8.3 (II.71)	8.99	20/8/23	8/28/15
	8.4 (II.72)	8.132	21/8/31	8/29/4
	8.5 (II.73)	8.169	21/8/39	8/29/14
	8.6 (II.74)	8.193	21/8/46	8/29/21
	8.7 (II.75)	8.239	22/8/56	8/30/12
	8.8 (II.77)	8.298	23/8/70	8/31/12
	8.9 (II.78)	8.345	23/8/80	8/32/4
	8.10 (II.79)	8.386	24/8/89	8/32/16
	8.11 (II.81)	8.443	24/8/102	8/33/11
	8.12 (II.83)	8.528	25/8/119	8/34/14
	8.13 (II.83)	8.549	25/8/124	8/34/20

Chapter	Knoblock	Hutton	HYIS	HKCS
9. *Wangzhi* 王制	9.1 (II.94)	9.1	25/9/1	9/35/3
	9.2 (II.95)	9.26	26/9/6	9/35/10
	9.3 (II.96)	9.67	26/9/15	9/35/22
	9.4 (II.97)	9.84	26/9/19	9/36/5
	9.5 (II.97)	9.116	27/9/25	9/36/15
	9.6 (II.98)	9.139	27/9/30	9/36/22
	9.7 (II.98)	9.147	27/9/32	9/36/23
	9.8 (II.99)	9.179	27/9/39	9/37/6
	9.9 (II.100)	9.202	27/9/44	9/37/14
	9.10 (II.100)	9.216	28/9/47	9/37/19
	9.11 (II.101)	9.221	28/9/48	9/38/1
	9.12 (II.101)	9.233	28/9/51	9/38/5
	9.13 (II.101)	9.246	28/9/54	9/38/9
	9.14 (II.102)	9.261	28/9/57	9/38/14
	9.15 (II.103)	9.286	28/9/63	9/39/1
	9.16a (II.103)	9.316	28/9/69	9/39/9
	9.16b (II.105)	9.354	29/9/77	9/39/18
	9.16c (II.105)	9.369	29/9/81	9/39/22
	9.17 (II.106)	9.379	29/9/82	9/40/1
	9.18 (II.108)	9.451	30/9/96	9/40/18
	9.19a (II.109)	9.491	30/9/106	9/41/9
	9.19b (II.110)	9.526	30/9/113	9/41/18
	9.19c (II.111)	9.555	31/9/121	9/42/2
	9.19d (II.111)	9.576	31/9/125	9/42/6
10. *Fuguo* 富國	10.1 (II.120)	10.1	31/10/1	10/42/12
	10.2 (II.121)	10.44	32/10/10	10/42/23
	10.3a (II.122)	10.76	32/10/16	10/43/1
	10.3b (II.123)	10.99	32/10/21	10/43/6
	10.4 (II.123)	10.105	32/10/22	10/43/9
	10.5 (II.124)	10.139	33/10/29	10/43/18
	10.6 (II.126)	10.168	33/10/36	10/44/5
	10.7 (II.127)	10.200	33/10/43	10/44/15
	10.8 (II.127)	10.216	33/10/47	10/44/20
	10.9 (II.129)	10.274	34/10/60	10/45/16
	10.10 (II.131)	10.331	34/10/71	10/46/12
	10.11 (II.133)	10.407	35/10/85	10/47/4
	10.12 (II.133)	10.421	35/10/88	10/47/9
	10.13 (II.134)	10.458	36/10/96	10/47/19
	10.14 (II.136)	10.508	36/10/107	10/48/7
	10.15 (II.137)	10.559	36/10/117	10/48/21
11. *Wangba* 王霸	11.1a (II.149)	11.1	37/11/1	11/49/12
	11.1b (II.150)	11.33	37/11/8	11/49/20

Chapter	Knoblock	Hutton	HYIS	HKCS
	11.1c (II.151)	11.57	38/11/13	11/50/4
	11.1d (II.152)	11.88	38/11/19	11/50/10
	11.2a (II.153)	11.123	38/11/26	11/50/20
	11.2b (II.153)	11.143	38/11/30	11/51/4
	11.2c (II.154)	11.170	39/11/36	11/51/11
	11.3 (II.155)	11.202	39/11/42	11/51/19
	11.4 (II.156)	11.212	39/11/44	11/51/23
	11.5a (II.157)	11.246	39/11/52	11/52/7
	11.5b (II.157)	11.264	39/11/56	11/52/14
	11.6 (II.158)	11.302	40/11/63	11/52/23
	11.7a (II.159)	11.328	40/11/69	11/53/8
	11.7b (II.160)	11.348	40/11/73	11/53/12
	11.7c (II.161)	11.383	41/11/81	11/53/20
	11.7d (II.161)	11.403	41/11/86	11/53/25
	11.8 (II.161)	11.411	41/11/87	11/54/3
	11.9a (II.162)	11.440	41/11/94	11/54/11
	11.9b (II.163)	11.481	42/11/103	11/54/19
	11.9c (II.164)	11.503	42/11/106	11/54/23
	11.10 (II.165)	11.526	42/11/111	11/55/7
	11.11 (II.165)	11.538	42/11/113	11/55/11
	11.12 (II.166)	11.581	42/11/121	11/55/21
	11.13a (II.168)	11.633	43/11/131	11/56/7
	11.13b (II.169)	11.665	43/11/138	11/56/16
12. *Jundao* 君道	12.1 (II.175)	12.1	44/12/1	12/57/3
	12.2 (II.176)	12.30	44/12/7	12/57/11
	12.3 (II.178)	12.81	44/12/17	12/57/23
	12.4 (II.180)	12.142	45/12/29	12/58/10
	12.5 (II.180)	12.153	45/12/32	12/58/14
	12.6 (II.181)	12.204	46/12/43	12/59/11
	12.7 (II.184)	12.271	46/12/57	12/60/10
	12.8a (II.185)	12.324	47/12/65	12/60/20
	12.8b (II.185)	12.338	47/12/68	12/60/25
	12.8c (II.186)	12.357	47/12/73	12/61/6
	12.9 (II.187)	12.386	47/12/78	12/61/13
	12.10 (II.189)	12.463	48/12/94	12/62/12
	12.11 (II.190)	12.531	49/12/108	12/63/3
13. *Chendao* 臣道	13.1 (II.197)	13.1	49/13/1	13/63/16
	13.2 (II.199)	13.47	50/13/10	13/63/28
	13.3 (II.200)	13.108	50/13/22	13/64/16
	13.4 (II.201)	13.124	50/13/25	13/64/21
	13.5 (II.201)	13.152	51/13/31	13/65/4
	13.6 (II.202)	13.166	51/13/33	13/65/8

Chapter	Knoblock	Hutton	HYIS	HKCS
	13.7 (II.202)	13.186	51/13/37	13/65/14
	13.8 (II.203)	13.218	51/13/43	13/65/22
	13.9 (II.203)	13.225	51/13/44	13/66/1
14. *Zhishi* 致士	14.1 (II.205)	14.1	52/14/1	14/66/10
	14.2 (II.206)	14.23	52/14/5	14/66/17
	14.3 (II.207)	14.60	52/14/13	14/67/1
	14.4 (II.207)	14.64	52/14/14	14/67/3
	14.5 (II.208)	14.77	52/14/17	14/67/8
	14.6 (II.208)	14.94	52/14/20	14/67/13
	14.7 (II.209)	14.105	53/14/22	14/67/17
	14.8 (II.209)	14.112	53/14/23	14/67/20
	14.9 (II.209)	14.126	53/14/25	14/67/24
15. *Yibing* 議兵	15.1a (II.218)	15.1	53/15/1	15/68/3
	15.1b (II.219)	15.20	53/15/5	15/68/9
	15.1c (II.221)	15.90	54/15/19	15/69/11
	15.1d (II.222)	15.132	54/15/27	15/69/21
	15.1e (II.225)	15.235	55/15/46	15/70/24
	15.1f (II.226)	15.302	55/15/57	15/71/10
	15.2 (II.228)	15.348	56/15/66	15/72/21
	15.3 (II.228)	15.379	56/15/72	15/72/1
	15.4 (II.229)	15.405	56/15/78	15/72/9
	15.5 (II.231)	15.468	57/15/91	15/73/11
	15.6a (II.233)	15.541	57/15/104	15/74/9
	15.6b (II.234)	15.580	58/15/112	15/74/19
16. *Qiangguo* 強國	16.1 (II.238)	16.1	58/16/1	16/75/6
	16.2 (II.239)	16.20	58/16/5	16/75/12
	16.3 (II.240)	16.70	59/16/14	16/76/1
	16.4 (II.241)	16.115	59/16/23	16/76/12
	16.5 (II.244)	16.232	60/14/49	16/77/16
	16.6 (II.246)	16.288	61/16/61	16/78/10
	16.7 (II.247)	16.330	61/16/69	16/78/20
	16.8 (II.248)	16.362	62/16/75	16/79/3
	16.9 (II.249)	16.390	62/16/81	16/79/11
17. *Tianlun* 天論	17.1 (III.14)	17.1	62/17/1	17/79/16
	17.2a (III.15)	17.27	62/17/6	17/80/1
	17.2b (III.15)	17.39	62/17/8	17/80/5
	17.3a (III.16)	17.50	62/17/10	17/80/9
	17.3b (III.16)	17.76	63/17/16	17/80/17
	17.4 (III.17)	17.87	63/17/19	17/80/21
	17.5 (III.17)	17.108	63/17/22	17/80/27
	17.6 (III.17)	17.118	63/17/24	17/81/4

Chapter	Knoblock	Hutton	HYIS	HKCS
	17.7 (III.18)	17.136	63/17/29	17/81/10
	17.8 (III.19)	17.176	64/17/38	17/82/6
	17.9 (III.20)	17.187	64/17/40	17/82/10
	17.10 (III.20)	17.205	64/17/44	17/82/15
	17.11 (III.21)	17.226	64/17/45	17/82/20
	17.12 (III.22)	17.247	64/17/50	17/83/3
18. *Zhenglun* 正論	18.1 (III.32)	18.1	65/18/1	18/83/11
	18.2 (III.34)	18.49	65/18/10	18/83/23
	18.3 (III.36)	18.159	66/18/35	18/85/5
	18.4 (III.38)	18.207	66/18/44	18/85/17
	18.5a (III.39)	18.258	67/18/53	18/86/6
	18.5b (III.40)	18.270	67/18/56	18/86/8
	18.5c (III.41)	18.296	67/18/62	18/86/15
	18.6 (III.42)	18.351	68/18/72	18/87/7
	18.7 (III.43)	18.390	68/18/80	18/87/17
	18.8 (III.45)	18.454	69/18/93	18/88/10
	18.9 (III.46)	18.493	69/18/102	18/88/21
	18.10 (III.47)	18.552	70/18/114	18/89/11
19. *Lilun* 禮論	19.1a (III.55)	19.1	70/19/1	19/90/3
	19.1b (III.55)	19.12	70/19/3	19/90/5
	19.1c (III.56)	19.19	70/19/5	19/90/10
	19.1d (III.56)	19.38	70/19/9	19/90/14
	19.2a (III.58)	19.55	71/19/13	19/90/20
	19.2b (III.59)	19.87	71/19/19	19/91/7
	19.2c (III.60)	19.119	71/19/25	19/92/3
	19.2d (III.61)	19.147	71/19/30	19/92/12
	19.3 (III.62)	19.176	72/19/37	19/92/21
	19.4a (III.62)	19.201	72/19/42	19/93/6
	19.4b (III.63)	19.220	72/19/47	19/93/11
	19.4c (III.64)	19.253	72/19/54	19/93/19
	19.5a (III.64)	19.286	73/19/60	19/94/3
	19.5b (III.65)	19.304	73/19/63	19/94/8
	19.6 (III.66)	19.359	73/19/75	19/95/1
	19.7a (III.67)	19.377	73/19/79	19/95/6
	19.7b (III.68)	19.418	74/19/87	19/95/13
	19.8 (III.68)	19.441	74/19/91	19/96/1
	19.9a (III.69)	19.448	74/19/93	19/96/4
	19.9b (III.69)	19.467	74/19/97	19/96/10
	19.9c (III.70)	19.478	75/19/100	19/96/15
	19.10 (III.70)	19.510	75/19/108	19/97/7
	19.11 (III.72)	19.551	75/19/117	19/97/20

Chapter	Knoblock	Hutton	HYIS	HKCS
20. *Yuelun* 樂論	20.1 (III.80)	20.1	76/20/1	20/98/14
	20.2 (III.82)	20.61	76/20/15	20/99/15
	20.3 (III.83)	20.98	77/20/23	20/99/25
	20.4 (III.85)	20.159	77/20/36	20/100/19
	20.5 (III.85)	20.177	78/20/40	20/101/6
	20.6 (III.87)	20.224	78/20/49	20/101/24
21. *Jiebi* 解蔽	21.1 (III.100)	21.1	78/21/1	21/102/5
	21.2 (III.100)	21.27	78/21/6	21/102/12
	21.3 (III.101)	21.79	79/21/16	21/103/1
	21.4 (III.102)	21.101	79/21/21	21/103/8
	21.5a (III.103)	21.136	79/21/27	21/103/16
	21.5b (III.103)	21.145	79/21/29	21/103/18
	21.5c (III.104)	21.156	80/21/32	21/103/21
	21.5d (III.104)	21.167	80/21/34	21/103/25
	21.5e (III.105)	21.195	80/21/41	21/104/7
	21.6a (III.105)	21.211	80/21/44	21/104/10
	21.6b (III.106)	21.235	80/21/50	21/104/16
	21.7a (III.106)	21.250	81/21/53	21/105/3
	21.7b (III.107)	21.259	81/21/54	21/105/5
	21.7c (III.107)	21.273	81/21/58	21/105/8
	21.7d (III.108)	21.288	81/21/61	21/105/14
	21.8 (III.108)	21.315	81/21/67	21/106/3
	21.9 (III.110)	21.363	82/21/78	21/106/18
	21.10 (III.111)	21.433	82/21/93	21/107/14
22. *Zhengming* 正名	22.1a (III.127)	22.1	83/22/1	22/107/21
	22.1b (III.127)	22.8	83/22/2	22/107/22
	22.1c (III.128)	22.29	83/22/6	22/108/4
	22.2a (III.128)	22.48	83/22/9	22/108/8
	22.2b (III.128)	22.58	83/22/13	22/108/12
	22.2c (III.129)	22.73	83/22/15	22/108/14
	22.2d (III.129)	22.80	83/22/17	22/108/16
	22.2e (III.129)	22.88	83/22/19	22/109/1
	22.2f (III.130)	22.96	83/22/21	22/109/5
	22.2g (III.130)	22.120	83/22/25	22/109/10
	22.2h (III.131)	22.128	84/22/27	22/109/11
	22.3a (III.131)	22.140	84/22/29	22/109/16
	22.3b (III.131)	22.145	84/22/31	22/109/17
	22.3c (III.131)	22.151	84/22/32	22/109/19
	22.3d (III.132)	22.156	84/22/33	22/109/20
	22.3e (III.132)	22.161	84/22/34	22/110/1
	22.3f (III.132)	22.171	84/22/36	22/110/3
	22.4a (III.133)	22.201	84/22/43	22/110/10

Chapter	Knoblock	Hutton	HYIS	HKCS
	22.4b (III.133)	22.214	84/22/45	22/110/14
	22.4c (III.134)	22.235	85/22/49	22/110/20
	22.5a (III.135)	22.266	85/22/55	22/111/4
	22.5b (III.136)	22.301	85/22/63	22/111/14
	22.6a (III.136)	22.318	85/22/67	22/111/20
	22.6b (III.137)	22.335	85/22/71	22/111/24
	22.6c (III.137)	22.350	86/22/74	22/112/4
	22.6d (III.137)	22.363	86/22/78	22/112/9
	22.6e (III.138)	22.392	86/22/84	22/112/18
	22.6f (III.138)	22.408	86/22/88	22/112/23
23. *Xing'e* 性惡	23.1a (III.150)	23.1	86/23/1	23/113/3
	23.1b (III.151)	23.19	87/23/5	23/113/9
	23.1c (III.152)	23.43	87/23/10	23/113/13
	23.1d (III.152)	23.56	87/23/13	23/113/19
	23.1e (III.153)	23.75	87/23/18	23/114/2
	23.2a (III.153)	23.92	87/23/22	23/114/8
	23.2b (III.154)	23.134	88/23/32	23/114/18
	23.3a (III.155)	23.154	88/23/36	23/115/1
	23.3b (III.156)	23.185	88/23/44	23/115/10
	23.3c (III.157)	23.204	88/23/48	23/115/16
	23.4a (III.157)	23.213	88/23/50	23/115/20
	23.4b (III.158)	23.239	89/23/58	23/116/1
	23.5a (III.158)	23.252	89/23/60	23/116/6
	23.5b (III.159)	23.285	89/23/69	23/116/17
	23.6a (III.160)	23.306	90/23/75	23/116/25
	23.6b (III.160)	23.314	90/23/77	23/117/1
	23.7 (III.161)	23.338	90/23/82	23/117/5
	23.8 (III.161)	23.364	90/23/86	23/117/12
24. *Junzi* 君子	24.1 (III.164)	24.1	91/24/1	24/118/5
	24.2 (III.165)	24.19	91/24/4	24/118/10
	24.3 (III.166)	24.39	91/24/9	24/118/17
	24.4 (III.166)	24.59	91/24/12	24/19/3
	24.5 (III.167)	24.83	91/24/16	24/119/8
25. *Chengxiang* 成相	25.1 (III.172)	25.1	92/25/1	25/120/3
	25.5 (III.173)	25.29	92/25/4	25/120/6
	25.10 (III.174)	25.64	92/25/7	25/120/10
	25.15 (III.176)	25.99	92/25/12	25/120/14
	25.20 (III.177)	25.134	92/25/16	25/121/2
	25.25 (III.179)	25.168	93/25/19	25/121/8
	25.30 (III.180)	25.203	93/25/23	25/121/12
	25.35 (III.182)	25.238	93/25/27	25/122/1

Chapter	Knoblock	Hutton	HYIS	HKCS
	25.40 (III.183)	25.273	93/25/31	25/122/6
	25.45 (III.185)	25.307	93/25/35	25/122/12
	25.50 (III.186)	25.342	93/25/39	25/123/1
	25.55 (III.188)	25.377	94/25/42	25/123/5
26. *Fu* 賦	26.1 (III.194)	26.1	94/26/1	26/123/11
	26.2 (III.195)	26.34	94/26/5	26/123/17
	26.3 (III.197)	26.80	94/26/10	26/124/7
	26.4 (III.199)	26.132	95/26/17	26/124/16
	26.5 (III.200)	26.175	95/26/22	26/125/6
	26.6 (III.202)	26.212	95/26/27	26/125/13
	26.7 (III.203)	26.254	95/26/33	26/125/19
	26.8 (III.204)	26.261	95/26/34	26/126/1
27. *Dalüe* 大略	27.1 (III.207)	27.1	96/27/1	27/126/7
	27.10 (III.209)	27.45	96/27/7	27/126/27
	27.20 (III.211)	27.100	96/27/18	27/127/24
	27.30 (III.215)	27.197	97/27/34	27/128/29
	27.40 (III.216)	27.239	97/27/41	27/129/22
	27.50 (III.218)	27.280	98/27/47	27/130/18
	27.60 (III.221)	27.356	98/27/61	27/131/22
	27.70 (III.224)	27.435	99/27/77	27/132/22
	27.80 (III.226)	27.482	99/27/86	27/133/22
	27.90 (III.229)	27.539	100/27/97	27/134/20
	27.100 (III.233)	27.645	101/27/118	27/136/15
	27.110 (III.235)	27.698	101/27/128	27/137/16
28. *Youzuo* 宥坐	28.1 (III.244)	28.1	101/28/1	28/138/10
	28.2 (III.245)	28.21	102/28/5	28/138/17
	28.3 (III.246)	28.48	102/28/12	28/139/1
	28.4 (III.247)	28.115	103/28/24	28/140/1
	28.5 (III.248)	28.122	103/28/25	28/140/4
	28.6 (III.248)	28.143	103/28/29	28/140/11
	28.7 (III.248)	28.152	103/28/31	28/140/14
	28.8 (III.249)	28.158	103/28/32	28/140/17
	28.9 (III.250)	28.207	103/28/43	28/141/12
29. *Zidao* 子道	29.1 (III.251)	29.1	104/29/1	29/141/19
	29.2 (III.251)	29.9	104/29/2	29/141/20
	29.3 (III.252)	29.31	104/29/8	29/142/7
	29.4 (III.253)	29.57	104/29/14	29/142/15
	29.5 (III.253)	29.80	104/29/19	29/142/22
	29.6 (III.254)	29.100	105/29/23	29/142/28
	29.7 (III.254)	29.123	105/29/28	29/143/8
	29.8 (III.255)	29.140	105/29/31	29/143/14

Chapter	Knoblock	Hutton	HYIS	HKCS
30. *Faxing* 法行	30.1 (III.256)	30.1	105/30/1	30/143/20
	30.2 (III.256)	30.5	105/30/1	30/143/23
	30.3 (III.256)	30.20	105/30/4	30/144/1
	30.4 (III.257)	30.29	105/30/6	30/144/5
	30.5 (III.257)	30.47	106/30/11	30/144/11
	30.6 (III.258)	30.57	106/30/13	30/144/15
	30.7 (III.258)	30.65	106/30/14	30/144/18
	30.8 (III.258)	30.74	106/30/16	30/144/22
31. *Aigong* 哀公	31.1 (III.259)	31.1	106/31/1	31/144/27
	31.2 (III.259)	31.20	106/31/5	31/145/7
	31.3 (III.261)	31.94	107/31/20	31/146/13
	31.4 (III.262)	31.106	107/31/23	31/146/17
	31.5 (III.262)	31.139	107/31/31	31/147/9
	31.6 (III.263)	31.151	107/31/33	31/147/14
	31.7 (III.263)	31.171	108/31/37	31/147/20
32. *Yaowen* 堯問	32.1 (III.265)	32.1	108/32/1	32/148/13
	32.2 (III.265)	32.12	108/32/3	32/148/17
	32.3 (III.266)	32.37	108/32/8	32/149/1
	32.4 (III.267)	32.92	109/32/21	32/149/16
	32.5 (III.268)	32.106	109/32/23	32/149/21
	32.6 (III.268)	32.115	109/32/26	32/150/1
	Eulogy (III.269)	32.121	109/32/27	32/150/4

These notes are intended for those who have advanced skills in classical Chinese and are familiar with commentaries on the *Xunzi*, and no attempt has been made to render the information here intelligible to nonspecialists. As stated in the introduction, my base text for the translation is Wang Xianqian's *Xunzi Jijie*, and in order to minimize the number of technical notes, I have generally added notes only for those cases where I am not following any of the commentaries cited by Wang. Commentaries referenced here that are not listed in the bibliography may be found in Yan (1979).

CHAPTER 1: AN EXHORTATION TO LEARNING

a Wang Niansun recommends reading the character 柱 as 祝, in turn understood as 折 "break." The meaning would then be "The strong brings itself to be broken. The soft brings itself to be bound." I prefer the commentary of Zhong Tai, taking 柱 in the sense of 拄, because it stays closer to the received text, and because it fits the analogy with building materials implied by 束 in the next line.

b This line is puzzling. It literally states, "The *teng* snake has no feet but flies. The *wu* rodent has five talents but is exhausted." In the context of Xunzi's remarks about single-minded devotion to self-cultivation, it makes little sense. How is having no feet an impediment to flying that is overcome by single-mindedness, and how is this opposed to having five talents? I propose we view 飛 as hyperbole for running fast. In that case, having no feet poses an obvious challenge. I further suggest we read 技 as 支, which can mean "limb." In this case, the contrast between limbless snake and the rodent's five limbs (legs and tail) is now obvious, and it is also parallel to the earlier comparison between worm and crab. I presume the reason for juxtaposing snake to rodent is that snakes eat rodents, and so the point of 窮 is that the rodent exhausts all its means trying to escape but fails. In sum, the snake overcomes its natural disadvantage through concentrated effort, while the rodent's natural advantages do it no good because it is frenetic, like the crab.

c Many editors and translators take the characters 禮 and 樂 in this and the surrounding passages to be *names* of works or texts. However, I think we need to be cautious in attributing such references to *Xunzi*. While there were extensive bodies of lore about ritual and music in Xunzi's time, the extent to which they were organized into distinct works (or more concretely, written texts) with the specific titles 禮 and 樂 is somewhat uncertain and still under investigation by historians. Therefore, here and elsewhere in the translation, I have generally avoided taking 禮 and 樂 as titles, unless context absolutely demands it. I think that very little turns on the issue philosophically, since even if 禮 and 樂 are taken as titles, presumably what matters to Xunzi is the actual content of those works, i.e., the rituals and music themselves, rather than their form as organized works or texts.

d Most commentators take 尊 and 周 as referring to the student. However, the previous lines stress that one needs a teacher precisely because the various texts and practices alone will not give one correct understanding. Therefore, for Xunzi to speak of the student becoming honored and famous throughout the world (or alternatively, gaining all-encompassing knowledge) seems abrupt and out of place. I read 尊 and 周 as having an implied object, namely the principles and precepts underlying the materials studied, which are made clear by the teacher.

e The words 經緯 normally refer to the warp and woof of a loom. However, they can also refer to the main streets running north-south and east-west through a city (see 周禮, 考工記). Understood thus, these two words fit better with 蹊徑, which also refer to roads, and in translating I simplify all four to "highways and byways."

f I follow Wang Niansun in understanding 頓 as 引. He further claims 順者不可勝數 refers to the hairs of the fur collar. This is not implausible, but then the analogy does not fit so easily with the description of rituals as the right roads. I suggest that the fur collar image is intended to demonstrate the ease with which learning will proceed if done according to ritual, and the last sentence is meant to summarize by saying that all will go smoothly. Read thus, this section then forms a nice parallel with the rest of the paragraph, which gives first a condition (以詩書為之), then illustrations by analogy, and last a summation (不可以得之) that applies both to the analogies and to the point about learning.

g The switch from 見 to 貴 has puzzled many commentators. Perhaps it was motivated by the thought that while Heaven and Earth proudly display their most valuable qualities, the gentleman is ideally somewhat humble.

CHAPTER 2: CULTIVATING ONESELF

a I follow Wang Niansun in understanding 存 as 察, because it preserves the parallel use of 自 as object of the verb in each line. Commentators disagree about how to understand 脩然. The uses of 脩 in the paragraphs right after this line suggest a way of reading it that I follow here, namely taking 脩 in its sense as "cultivating," and so taking 脩然 as describing the manner of someone trying to cultivate himself.

b Harbsmeier (1997) rightly points out that in many cases, these first-person pronouns have an impersonal sense. However, in English, first-person pronouns can also have an impersonal sense, and therefore *pace* Harbsmeier I do not think it necessary always to render such instances with the impersonal "one." Accordingly, I have retained the first-person expressions in the translation in many places.

c I follow Wang Niansun in understanding 扁 as 遍. Commentators disagree about whether 後 is to be taken as "live longer" or "come second to." Since Xunzi rejects physiognomy and belief in ghosts, it seems unlikely he would believe ritual could really ensure such long life, and so the latter reading appears preferable. Yet, he does mention how following ritual is good for one's health. This supports the first reading, and so I have chosen to follow it. Last, 自名 apparently troubled commentators because in chapter 1, for example, Xunzi says the student should not use his learning to seek fame. However, here he may just be speaking of the results of self-cultivation, rather than the intentions involved in it. Thus, his point would be that while one should not seek recognition for being learned, if one winds up being renowned for morality, then one's accomplishments will equal those of Yao and Yu. See 以為名則榮 at 4.290–91.

d The word 之 makes this sequence difficult to translate because it could refer to the person possessing the faults or the faults themselves. The passage is easier to render if 之 is the person, but then Xunzi sounds as though he is advising us on how to treat others. The method, however, is supposed to be for *self*-cultivation, so I have taken 之 as the faults. Commentators reject 通之以思索 because it is not parallel with the other sentences. Yet, Xunzi is not so rigidly confined by parallelism, and since he mentions simple-minded (愚) goodness, it is quite natural that he advises correcting it with reflection.

e My reading of this line combines the readings of Zhang Jue and Li Disheng. Like Zhang (and before him, Yang Liang), I take 學 to refer to a learner and regard 曰 as the beginning of a quotation. Also like Zhang, I take 遲 to mean "slow" (unlike Yang, who explains it as 待) and take this to be something the learner says about himself. However, whereas Zhang takes 彼 to refer to a person, I follow Li in taking 彼 to refer to the object of learning. On the reading where 彼 refers to a person, the quote describes how slower learners can catch up with faster learners, if the faster learners wait for them. However, the immediately preceding lines stress that there is a proper limit or stopping point for the gentleman's learning (and not that he patiently waits for slower learners or relies on faster learners to wait for him), so Li's reading seems preferable in this context.

CHAPTER 3: NOTHING IMPROPER

a The text here seems corrupt, since it is not parallel with the proceeding lines. As it stands, 吟口 is hard to make sense of, and various emendations have been proposed. The most promising is that of Hao Yixing, who replaces 吟口 with 貪凶 on the basis of a parallel in the *Shuo Yuan*. Wang Xianqian valiantly tries to keep the original text. He points out a case in the *Hou Han Shu* where 吟 means "stutter." Wang then argues that, despite the reversal of the two characters here, the text is to be read as saying Robber Zhi was a stutterer. This move is unsatisfying, since Xunzi clearly wants to point out that his fame was acquired through viciousness, and his stuttering could have nothing to do with that. However, taking a clue from Wang, I suggest that since the text reads 吟口, the meaning is causative, i.e., Robber Zhi caused people to stutter (because he was such a frightening villain). Thus we can preserve the original text while still conveying the contrast Xunzi wants to draw.

CHAPTER 4: ON HONOR AND DISGRACE

a Leaving out the next twenty-two characters.

CHAPTER 5: AGAINST PHYSIOGNOMY

a Here 有 cannot mean simply "have," since Xunzi immediately goes on to describe how physiognomy was something that the ancients did indeed have. Instead, 有 can have a stronger sense of "master," or "be in control of." (See the use of 有之 in quote from the *Shijing* at 3.69, for a clear example in the *Xunzi*. Compare also the use of 有 in passages such as the following from the "Ba Jian" 八姦 chapter of the *Han Feizi*: 所謂亡君者，非莫有其國也，而有之者，皆非己有也. The sense of the last instance of 有 must clearly be something more like "control.") I therefore read this sentence in chapter 5 as saying that physiognomy was an art that the ancients did not "take up" or "embrace" in the sense of seeking to cultivate it.

b Some read 目可瞻馬 as being about the king's ability to see, but this does not make any sense in context, which clearly concerns people's appearance. Others claim 馬 is 焉, a variant for 顏, so the text says the king's face was such that he could see his own forehead. This is better, but a linguistic stretch. I propose that 瞻 is interchangeable with 詹, which can mean 給 or 足 (as 澹). The point in saying that the king's eyes "could supply a horse" is, I take it, that they were as big as those of a horse, and I have translated the line with this more idiomatic phrasing.

c Following Long Yuchun (1987).

d Most commentators take 曲直 as referring to talent, and read the sentence as saying that the person's abilities are far behind those who are worthy. However, in the *Xunzi* 曲直 is more frequently a synonym for wrong and right, so I take it to refer to his views. Also, commentators take 仁人 and 知士 as the objects of 推 and 明, but this seems a strained reading of the grammar. Instead, I take 仁人 and 知士 as the grammatical subjects of 推 and 明, similar to Wang Tianhai's treatment, though I understand 推 and 明 differently than he does.

e Following the reading of John Knoblock.

f Following Liang Qixiong, taking 世 as 抴.

g Here 抴 is puzzling and does not seem to fit the context. Commentators take it as 枻, which is 楫 (oar) or 檠 (instrument for adjusting or protecting a bow), meaning that the gentleman guides others to what is right. However, the passage emphasizes tolerance, not instruction. I propose 抴 is a mistake for 貰, which means 赦 or 弛 (see the 中文大辭典, citing the *Guoyu* and the *Han Shu*); it was originally 世, and a copyist wrongly added the "hand" radical, probably because of the earlier 世, which Liang Qixiong is likely right in taking as 抴. In parallel to 繩 one would expect a noun, as Wang Niansun points out, but even though 貰 is not a noun, it still seems closest to what Xunzi intends.

CHAPTER 6: AGAINST THE TWELVE MASTERS

a There is disagreement about how the last seven characters are to be read, and commentators suggest various emendations. In all the previous X 而 Y constructions in this segment of the text, the Xs and Ys seem meant to be contrastive, so I take it that here 離 and 跂 are here likewise meant to be opposed. Among the meanings for 跂 attested in dictionaries (e.g., the 中文大辭典) are 行 or 進, which (as indicating movement toward something) seem like appropriate contrasts for 離 (as indicating movement away from something). Accordingly, I read the text as it stands and take 離縱 as meaning that the person literally "goes away" from unrestrained behavior (at least in the ordinary sense), and take 跂訾 as meaning that the person "goes toward" slandering others.

b The wording here is very difficult to understand. Many readers take 逢 as "large." Since the corresponding defect is described a few lines later as 其纓禁緩, where 緩 seems clearly to refer wearing clothes loosely, reading 逢 as "large" does not make a sensible contrast. Instead, a common meaning for 逢 is "to meet," where this moreover implies a kind of conformity or fitting with the thing met (see *Mengzi* 6B7: 逢君之惡，其罪大). Applied to clothing, then, an extended sense might be that it is "form-fitting," i.e., not worn slackly or loosely. Such a construal allows us to make better sense of the contrast with 緩, and I have translated to convey this sense, but the reading remains tentative.

c Taking 罔 here as a loangraph for 亡.

d Commentators are divided over how to make sense of the two characters 神禪. Yang Liang suggests taking 神 as 沖, and 禪 as 澶. However, it seems more consistent to take 禪 as 潭, keeping the phonetic the same for both. Both 沖 and 潭 can mean "deep," and that provides a sensible reading of the line that accords with the traditional understanding of the line; these Confucians try to dress up their words, much as they do their appearance and gait, but lack the true substance of sagehood.

CHAPTER 7: ON CONFUCIUS

a The words 徒處 are difficult to interpret. I take them to mean literally "dwelling while on the move," i.e., having no fixed residence.

b Commentators disagree on how to parse this line, resulting in different readings. I take it as 以爸嗇而不行施道。乎上為重，招權於下，以防害人。I then take 乎 as 呼 "call," in which case it forms a nice parallel with 招 "summon."

c Following Guo Qingfan's reading, but taking 炊 as 吹.

CHAPTER 8: THE ACHIEVEMENTS OF THE *Ru*

a Following the construal of 屏 given by Sun Yirang and Ikai Hikohiro.

b Commentators argue that 罔不分 should be read as 罔罘分 "they share the contents of their nets." However, 罔 itself can mean 無, and I follow that reading, as more conservative textually.

c The expression 僂指 is odd, but commentators seem to give it relatively little discussion. Yang Liang recommends reading 僂 as "quickly," so that the point would be that even a sage cannot quickly resolve such issues. However, given what Xunzi says at 2.135–38, it seems he believes that such issues are simply irresolvable, so that neither could a sage answer them. For that reason, I follow Liu Shipei in understanding 僂 as 曲.

d The poem is difficult, and the traditional commentaries on the *Xunzi* do not seem to make good sense of how it relates to the context. I instead follow the commentary of Qu Wanli (1983). I take the point to be that the purveyors and followers of vile doctrines are also just human beings and can be corrected if shown their faults, as Xunzi is trying to do in the passage.

e There is a problem with understanding 詔 that most commentators seem not to notice. In the previous comparisons in the passage, the emphasis has been on how easy it is for the sage to do something hard. The literal meaning of 詔, however, is "summon," and summoning the four seasons is hardly a human task at all. Some commentators take 詔 as "announce," and announcing the four seasons is certainly easier than summoning them. However, it is then unclear what the basis of comparison is. For announcing the four seasons involved elaborate rituals, and was not practiced very consistently. Therefore, I instead take 詔 in its meaning of 致 "make come," with the idea being that the seasons reliably come on their own, independently of human intervention, and the sage's knack for acting at the right time and in the right way is as reliable as this process.

f For explanation of my approach to treating 禮 and 樂 as titles, see note c for chapter 1. This is one instance where it seems clear that the words are being used as titles.

g Commentators suggest changing "sat" to "stood," on the grounds that there are no records of the Son of Heaven sitting while having an audience with the feudal lords. However, the rest of the passage does not fit with certain standard historical accounts, and so it should be no surprise if this detail does not agree with the records, either. Hence, there seems little reason to emend the text.

h Following Wang Tianhai on the meaning of 選.

i The characters 解果 are problematic. Commentators recommend understanding them as saying the vulgar *ru* wears a cap of particular shape, implying somehow that he "forces himself to dress as the *ru*, but lacks the true substance." However, this line seems intended to justify the claim a few sentences later that the vulgar *ru* is hardly any different from vulgar people. The fact that he wears a different cap than they do is not enough to support such a claim, but the idea that he wears it in a similarly uncultivated manner would be. For that reason, the rendering here follows Yang Liuqiao, though with hesitation.

j Most modern editors of the *Xunzi* want to emend 情 to 積, on the basis of recommendations by Wang Niansun. I think the emendations are not necessary and that the passage can be read as it stands. The translation and notes reflect my view of how it makes sense without the emendations.

k For this understanding of 有 as "have mastery of," see note a for chapter 5.

CHAPTER 9: THE RULE OF A TRUE KING

a Traditional commentaries argue that 繆 should be read as 穆. The phrase 昭穆 refers to the ranking of father and son within the ancestral temples, and they take this as standing for such ranking and division of roles generally, so that the last part of the sentence is urging one to make such divisions, if they are not already clear. However, it seems quite strange for Xunzi to speak in such an elliptical fashion. We can instead arrive at more or less the same point and still make sense of the text as it stands, by taking 繆 in its sense of a binding, i.e., social bonds. The character 昭 can then be read with its primary sense of "illumination," so that the text is recommending one make clear the proper social bonds within society.

b Commentators tend to take 累 as "worries," but since the previous sentence contrasts apparent gains with actual losses, and this sentence is clearly meant to parallel that one, it seems better to take 累 as "accumulations," likewise intended as merely apparent or short term.

c This phrase has puzzled commentators. I take 愿 as shorthand for 鄉愿, behavior that Xunzi elsewhere clearly dislikes (see 3.223–29).

d The authors of the Beida Zhexuexi commentary emend 室律 to 質律 on the basis of a parallel in chapter 18, which they read as referring to "the prices of goods." However, if 律 is taken in this way, then we can keep 室 as it is and instead read the words as referring to the rates for (temporary) dwelling charged to travelers, etc.

e Reading 抃 as is, but emending 急 to 愿, as Yang Liang suggests. For the reading of 愿, see note c above.

f Following Wang Zhonglin's suggestion to read 殷 as 慇.

g Taking the sense of 殷 here as 當, instead of as 盛, as most commentators do.

CHAPTER 10: ENRICHING THE STATE

a Reading 掩 as 淹.

CHAPTER 11: THE TRUE KING AND THE HEGEMON

a Most commentators and editors want to read 憚 as some other character, most usually 禪. However, this seems unnecessary to me, since I think it is possible to make sense of the line while retaining the original reading 憚 (as per my translation), and since 憚 occurs earlier in the chapter, there is good reason for thinking that the 憚 here is not just a mistake.

b Following Ikai Hikohiro.

c There is some controversy about how best to understand 以是. I take the 是 as referring back to the 執業 of the 天子 in the previous line.

d The text is somewhat odd here, and commentators have wanted to emend it by dropping the 在 after 安. However, if one is willing to allow some nonparallel structure, much the same reading can be achieved without emendation, by adopting the following punctuation of the lines: 兩者並行而國在.上偏而國安在. 下偏而國危.

e Commentators have wanted to drop the second 適 from this line or emend it to 是. Both of these seem unnecessary, because the same meaning that these emendations aim at can be achieved by leaving the line as it is and instead reading the second 適 as a causative verb meaning "to make match."

CHAPTER 12: THE WAY TO BE A LORD

a Following Wang Xianqian in reading 爍. This seems preferable to 落, because 落 seems to imply that such a ruler will necessarily be *destroyed*, whereas the previous lines make it clear that such a ruler may merely have some of his territory taken away. The weaker force of 爍, by contrast, seems more consistent with the previous lines.

b Following Yu Yue's emendation of 六 to 大.

c Following Long Yuchun (1987) in preference to the common reading of 齫 as "toothless," on the grounds that the common reading makes the phrase 齫然而齒墮 seem overly repetitive.

d There is much controversy about how to understand the six characters 不還秩不反君. Li Disheng notes that the opening of the following sentence, 然而, is contrastive, and so whatever 不還秩不反君 means, it ought to be such that one would not expect what follows the 然而. On this basis, Li rejects the reading of Wang Niansun, but a similar worry applies to his own preferred reading. My reading starts from Li's argument against Wang, which I find persuasive. That is to say, 不還秩不反君 should be the kind of conduct on the part of an emissary that one would not usually think of as conducive to protecting his own state. Next, most commentators read the 君 as referring to the emissary's *own* lord, but in fact nothing in the Chinese makes this necessary, and it seems a little unlikely, given that everywhere else in the surrounding context the emissary's *own* lord is referred to as 人主. So instead, I take 君 here as referring to the lord of *the state that the emissary is visiting*. It is then possible to read 反 straightforwardly in its sense of "oppose" (i.e., act confrontationally toward), instead of needing to read it as 返 or 叛, as most commentators do. Obviously, if the emissary does not (seem to) oppose the hostile lords whose court he visits, then it would be surprising that he would still succeed in protecting his own state. Li notes (quoting Zhong Tai) that 還 and 反 have similar meanings, but whereas he reads 反 as 返 and so takes 還 as likewise meaning 返, I read 還 as having the original sense of 反, namely "oppose," a sense for 還 also attested to in dictionaries (see the entry for 還 in 中文大辭典). Parallel to 君, I take 秩 as referring to order in *the state that the emissary is visiting*. Again, one would not expect an emissary who acts in a very restrained and compliant manner to be able to protect his own state. So, this construal sets up very nicely the contrast with what follows 然而. Regarding that portion of the sentence, most commentators read 薄 as 迫, but this seems unnecessary, since 薄 can originally have the meaning "to treat derogatorily," which fits this context quite well.

Chapter 13: The Way to Be a Minister

a Most commentators understand 入其道 as (roughly) "cause him to enter upon the proper way." However, such a reading of 其 here is not plausible, given that the 其 in 改其過 two sentences earlier clearly refers to the violent lord's own mistakes. Instead, parallel to 其過, I construe 其道 as referring to the violent lord's own (bad) ways, and I understand the sense of 入 as roughly the same as 納, like the use of 內 in the previous paragraph.

b Following Long Yuchun (1963) in reading 正 for 直.

Chapter 14: On Attracting Men of Worth

a Following the argument of Wang Niansun in the *Ruxiao* chapter: 譽 is equivalent to 與, which means 類.

b It seems unnecessary to accept Wang Yinzhi's suggestion to understand 當 as 實. The text makes sense if taken as saying that the gentleman determines what merits what response, and then applies the right response to the right case.

c Commentators suggest reading other characters for 士, but this seems unnecessary since one can take it simply as a verb, "treat as one's 士," i.e., employ.

Chapter 15: A Debate on Military Affairs

a The phrase 仁人上下 is awkward, and most commentators suggest emending the sentence. However, that is not necessary, since we can make sense of the construction as it stands, if we read 上 as a verb and 下 as its object, i.e., "to be superior over those below." Such a reading is supported by the parallel construction of the two subsequent four-character clauses, where 一心 in 百將一心 and 同力 in 三軍同力 both have a verb-object structure.

b Here and below, I follow Wang Tianhai, who reads 技 *pu* instead of 技 *ji*, based on the appearance of 技 in multiple editions of the text.

c Following Zhang Jue and Wang Tianhai in reading 周 as 賙.

d Most readers understand the grammar of the line as being the same as the phrase 以卵投石 that occurs a little earlier in the chapter, but the presence of the particle 焉 at the end of this sentence seems to demand the different construal I give in the translation.

e This sentence is problematic, but nearly all commentators seem to overlook the problem. There are two occurrences of 之 in the sentence. The first is generally ignored entirely, while the second is taken as referring to the "states" mentioned in the previous sentence. However, if the first 之 does not refer to those states (and it seems impossible to take it that way), then it is implausible grammatically to take the second 之 as switching referents to point those states. Looking at what follows in the text, in the subsequent phrases 是漸之 and 是齊之, the unexplained 之 pretty clearly refers to "the soldiers," and this, I suggest, is accordingly the most plausible referent for the two preceding occurrences of 之. In order to accommodate this reading, I take 殆 as "make dangerous" instead of "endanger," as most read it. For a use of 殆 as "dangerous" as opposed to "endangered," see the use of 殆物 in the 忠孝 chapter of the *Han Feizi*.

f Following Kubo Ai's understanding of the sense of 犇命.

g I find the proposals offered by commentators for how to read 貢 unsatisfying. One of the attested meanings of the character is 進入 (see *Ciyuan*, citing 書經, 顧命篇:「爾無以釗冒貢于非幾」), and that is how I propose to understand it, where the sense of "enter" is roughly that of "join with." This notion also seems to be what the example of Weizi Kai (Qi) in the main text demonstrates.

h Wang Tianhai gives good reason for dissenting from most other commentators and not taking 格 here in the same sense as it appears earlier, as "resist." Rather than read 格 as 潞, as he suggests, a simpler solution is available. A common meaning of 格 is "stop" or "block," and I take it as referring to soldiers who are "blocked" from fleeing, which makes them especially dangerous. This seems to fit better with the context, since most commentators take Xunzi's point to be that a true king will not pursue a fight that would involve heavy casualties. (Cf. the contrasting advice given in chap. 11 of the *Sunzi Bingfa* to block avenues of retreat: 圍地吾將塞其關.)

i Following Hoashi Banri and Wang Tianhai in reading 政 as 征.

j Here I follow Tsukada Taiho's argument for not emending the text.

k Most commentators do not take this sentence as a question, perhaps because it does not end with a particle expressing a question. However, such constructions are not impossible. See the phrases 哀將焉而不至矣, 憂將焉而不至矣, 勞將焉而不至矣, and 懼將焉而不至矣 at 31.118–34, which in context all demand to be taken as questions and are usually read so. It seems to me that this reading is preferable to the construal that most commentators take, on which the sentence says (roughly) that rulers without virtue usually adopt such means to control their people, because that seems simply to state the obvious, and does not fit with the general point made by the passage, which is that such an approach will fail. Also, most commentators emend 除 to 險. However, this is not really necessary, and we can make sense of the sentence as it stands by taking 除 in the sense of 修治, one of its attested meanings (see 易經, 萃卦:「君子以除戎器, 戒不虞」).

l Following Tsukada Taiho in reading 彊 as 疆, on the grounds that it best fits with the subsequent sentences.

CHAPTER 16: THE STRONG STATE

a The sentence 敵中則奪 is difficult, and commentators have made numerous proposals. Most of them seem inadequate, because they require reading the subjects of 敵中 and 奪 as something other than 百姓, which breaks the parallel with the preceding two sentences, where 百姓 seems clearly to be the grammatical subject for both what precedes and what follows the 則. My reading here is inspired by Yang Liuqiao. However, whereas Yang seems to take 中

as a locative expression (i.e., 於中), I read it as the direct object of 敵, to maintain the parallel with 得間 from the preceding sentence. Yang cites Li Xian's commentary to the *Hou Han Shu* for his reading of 奪:「奪,謂易其常分也。」Support for a similar understanding of 奪 can be found in Zheng Xuan's gloss on the phrase 給奪慈仁 in the 仲尼燕居 chapter of the *Liji*:「奪猶亂也。」

b Following Ikai Hikohiro's reading of 賁潰.

c Many commentators read this line—and the argument of the passage—differently. They understand it roughly as follows: "As for honoring the worthy and employing the capable, rewarding those who have meritorious accomplishments, and punishing those who are guilty of crimes, it is not that [the king of Chu] was alone in doing so." They also take the point of Xunzi's criticism to be that Zifa was rejecting the whole practice of rewarding accomplishments. However, Zifa's stated reason for declining the reward is that he cannot take credit for the accomplishment alone as general, and accordingly I take the thrust of Xunzi's argument to be aimed at such a narrow conception of merit; great accomplishments require joint efforts, so reward should still be given for shared achievements. On this reading, Xunzi's repeated references in the passage to how Zifa acted "alone" (獨) stand out as instances of sarcastic emphasis.

d Following Wang Tianhai on the construal of 與俱.

e Most commentators read 閒 as 閑. I think this unnecessary and take 閒 in the sense of "time" or "period" instead.

f Almost all commentators want to emend the text here in one way or another. However, I find most of the proposed emendations not very plausible. Furthermore, almost all of them take the sentence 王者之功名不可勝日志也 as saying roughly "The accomplishments and fame of true kings are more than can be remembered in a day" and try to make their reading of 霸者之善著焉可以時託也 parallel to that, so that it also concerns how memorable the works of the hegemons are. However, such an interpretation seems to me to make the text suddenly switch topics in an implausible way; it has been emphasizing that daily cultivation is needed, and now it switches to talking about the issue of remembering or recollecting accomplishment. The end of the passage clearly returns to the topic of the need for daily cultivation, so I have tried to read the Chinese here in a way that fits more smoothly with the overall theme of the paragraph, though it may be strained in other ways. My parsing and understanding of 霸者之善著焉可以時託也 follow Wang Tianhai, but I read 焉 as equivalent to 案, rather than as the interrogative 安, as he does.

g Like Yang Liang, I understand the meaning of 曠 as 空, but unlike him, I take this 空 in a verbal sense, i.e., "to empty," so that it pairs as a verb with the 芸 that follows it, and I render the pair as "remove" for the sake of simplicity. See *Mencius* 4A10「曠安宅而弗居」for such a verbal use of 曠.

CHAPTER 17: DISCOURSE ON HEAVEN

a Following the emendations suggested by Wang Niansun.

b The second 物 here is difficult, and commentators are divided. I favor Liu Shipei's reading of it as 慮度, because that seems more consistent with Xunzi's use of 物 as a verb elsewhere. See the use of 物 at 21.242–44.

CHAPTER 18: CORRECT JUDGMENTS

a I follow Yang Liang, Zhang Jue, and Liao Jilang in taking the title 正論 as an "adjective + noun" construction rather than a "verb + noun" construction. They do not explain their reasons for doing so, but my reason is the parallel with the title 正名, which I also read as an "adjective + noun" construction (see note a for chapter 22 for explanation).

b This sentence is difficult to understand, especially the last character, 難. Many readers seem to construe the 徙朝改制 as referring to the case where the throne goes to someone other than a sage, with the implicit assumption that 徙朝改制 is not something that a sage rising from among the three dukes would do. For example, Knoblock renders it "Only when there is the removal of a dynasty and the creation of new regulations are difficulties engendered." However, the way that the passage repeats the lines 天下厭然與鄉無以異也 。以堯繼堯 。夫又何變之有矣, while omitting the part 朝不易位，國不更制, seems to me to suggest precisely that 朝不易位，國不更制 is a point of contrast between the sage who is the descendant of the Son of Heaven and the sage who rises from among the three dukes, and that 徙朝改制 is thus intended to refer to the latter kind of sage. The problem is then how to construe 難, because if the sentence refers to the sage, it seems implausible to take it as saying literally that it is hard for him to accomplish. Instead, I take it in a psychological sense, i.e., that he finds it difficult to do (but does it anyway).

c I follow Tao Hongqing's parsing of this and the previous sentence. In addition, many readers take the 之 in 死則能任天下者必有之矣 as referring back to the 能任天下者, and so construe it as saying, "When he dies, there is sure to be someone who can take responsibility for the world." However, given that a few lines earlier the text clearly recognizes the possibility that there might be no sage to succeed the Son of Heaven (天下無聖), and given that the decline of the Xia, Shang, and Zhou dynasties was a widely recognized historical fact, such a reading seems extremely implausible. Instead, I take the 之 to refer back to 天下, and to take 有 as "possess" rather than as an existential verb. This reading also gains support from the discussions of how Tang and Wu took control of the empire that appear earlier, 18.87–99 and 16.168–86.

d Following Long Yuchun (1999) on the meaning of 期.

e Following Kubo Ai on the meaning of 曼.

f See note g for chapter 8.

g Following Wang Tianhai on the reading of 詭.

h Through various methods, most commentators read this clause as meaning roughly "when one is bound and tied." While such approaches manage to make sense of the four characters 藉靡舌縲 by themselves, they all have a substantial shortcoming: the twelve characters that precede these four present a list that is clearly arranged in order of increasing severity of treatment, ending with being drawn and quartered, so reading these four as referring to being bound and tied breaks this structure in a way that looks very awkward and is, thus, implausible. Hence, the alternative I adopt reads these four characters in a way that makes them refer to even more severe punishment, namely when it extends to beyond an individual to the individual's other family members, which was sometimes done in ancient China. The basis for this alternative is as follows. First, 藉 is to be read as 籍, with which it is interchangeable, and 籍 in turn is to be taken as referring to "family records." Second, 靡 is to be read as it stands, but taken in the sense of "destroy"; see 方言, 十三: 「靡, 滅也」. Third, according to Duan Yucai's commentary on the *Shuowen Jiezi*, 舌 and 后 were sometimes substituted for each other in ancient texts. Sun Yirang, commenting on this passage in the *Xunzi*, thus reads 舌 as standing in for 后, and further reads 后 as 後, with which it was interchangeable. He reads 後, however, in the literal sense of "behind" (i.e., bound behind one's back). I propose to follow him in reading 舌 as 後, but take 後 in the sense of "descendants." Finally, Liao Jilang proposes reading 繹 as 舉, which he further takes in the sense of 捕 ("captive"). I follow him in reading 繹 as 舉, but propose to take 舉 as 拔 ("uproot" or "overturn"), a sense that is well attested in dictionaries.

Chapter 19: Discourse on Ritual

a Following Kubo Ai.

b Following Yu Yue's suggestion to reverse *cun* and *wang*, but without following the rest of his suggested emendation.

c Reading 執 as 勢, following Yu Xingwu.

d Because the subject of the preceding and subsequent sentences is the 君, some commentators suggest changing the 君子 here to just 君. However, the quote from the *Odes* clearly does refer to the 君子, and since 君子 is originally an aristocratic title, it seems to me that no emendation is necessary, and rather we can make sense of the passage in its context by taking 君子 here as "the prince," rather than "the gentleman."

e The character 情 has caused debate, because it does not seem to fit well with the context, and this has led some commentators, such as Wang Niansun, to suggest emending it to 積. Instead, I propose emending it to 精, which is much closer to the character as it currently stands and which also fits well with the implied parallel among 情, 至, and 盛 in the lines 志意思慕之情也. 忠信愛敬之至矣. 禮節文貌之盛矣 a little later in the passage. I thank P. J. Ivanhoe for this suggestion.

f Following Kubo Ai.

Chapter 20: Discourse on Music

a Most commentators read 舞意 and 天道 as dual main subjects governing the single main verb 兼, and thus understand the sentence roughly as "The meaning of the dance and the way of Heaven are united." While sensible in the context, such a reading seems rather implausible, because it requires 兼 to be used either as an active intransitive verb or as a passive transitive verb, but 兼 is, as far as I know, never used that way elsewhere in early classical Chinese, especially for a dual-subject construction. In the *Xunzi*, it is mostly used as an active transitive verb, when it is used as a verb. Therefore, I think a different reading is called for. My proposal is, first, to treat this line as the beginning of a new section, rather than merely a continuation of the previous sentences, especially since it seems to have more in common (the issue of dance) with what follows than what precedes it. Second, instead of taking 舞意 and 天道 as dual main subjects, I propose to read 舞意 as a paragraph heading much like the use of 序官 at 9.379 (also quoted at 20.86–87), rather than as part of the rest of the sentence. That leaves 天道 as the single subject of the sentence, with 兼 as the main verb. It is much easier to make sense of this sentence, because we can take 兼 as an active verb, in a manner it is used elsewhere in the *Xunzi*. In particular, Xunzi sometimes uses 兼 by itself as an active verb, meaning "to take in" or "encompass," as in swallowing up another ruler's state. The sense of the sentence is then that the way of Heaven "takes in" (i.e., rules over) other things, and then the subsequent parallel with the drum is a natural one to make.

CHAPTER 21: UNDOING FIXATION

a Transposing 疑 and 則, based on the argument of Long Yuchun (1987).

b The traditional interpretation of 妬 as "jealous" is strange. How can one be jealous of the Dao? Or if 妬 here means jealously of people, then it seems out of place. Therefore, I take it in its more general sense as "resent," and take 繆於道 as its object. The traditional reading of the latter half of the sentence is "Others mislead them through what they are inclined to." This is also strange, because 誘 is usually followed by its object. The clause 其所迨 is not in the right place to express instrumentality with an active verb (i.e., one would expect 人以其所迨誘之). Instead, I suggest reading it as having a suppressed 於 (i.e., 人誘於其所迨), which makes 誘 passive and 其所迨 the agent of change; literally, "Others are drawn off by the place where they approach."

c Reading 離 instead of 雖.

d The traditional reading suggests 蔽 instead of 使. I reject this as unnecessary. See chapter 21 footnote 2 for what I take to be the right construal. This passage foreshadows the remarks about the heart later in the chapter, which likewise stress that the heart must apply itself to itself in order to know the Dao.

e Here I follow Ogyu Sorai and Xiong Gongzhe on the punctuation and construal of this difficult sentence.

f The more popular reading of this section is, "The condition of the heart is such that its choices are without [external] restraint—rather, it is sure to show itself through them. And even though its objects are broadly varied, at the utmost of its refinement, it is undivided." I reject this reading because it seems an unusually strained way of reading the sentence, and instead I follow Yang Liang's reading.

g Following Yu Yue.

h Most commentators seem to take this sentence as referring to people in general, rather than Juan Shuliang in particular. However, most of them seem to emend or otherwise read the 已 which appears in Wang Xianqian as 己. If we read it as 己, though, it does not make sense as a general (and therefore temporally neutral) statement, which perhaps explains why the others read it as 已. Yet, we can read it as 已, if we take it as referring to Juan Shu-liang in particular. Also, since he is referred to at the end of the passage, it is not impossible that he is mentioned at this juncture as well.

CHAPTER 22: CORRECT NAMING

a Although many readers interpret 正名 as "verb + object" on the basis of the doctrine of "rectifying names" found in the *Analects*, it seems to me that a more proximate source for the title is the occurrence of 正名 at 22.34, where it is clearly an "adjective + noun" construction, so that is how I have rendered the chapter title, though I translate 名 in the title as "naming" (instead of as "names") in order to reflect the fact that the chapter discusses both the correct naming that was done by the sage kings in the past and the correct way to do naming in the present.

b Here I follow Long Yuchun (1987) for the punctuation and reading of 曲期, though with hesitation.

c For a partial defense of this reading of the sentence, see my 2011 essay.

d Dropping the initial 智 as accidentally repeated.

e Most commentators emend 鈹 to 鈒 (which they in turn take as a loan for 澀). However, this seems to me unnecessary. One of the regular meanings of 鈹 is a type of needle, and it is sometimes used in combination with other words as an adjective, meaning "needle-like." It can be so understood in this context, as referring to the feeling one gets from a needle, i.e., sharpness, and in this context that meaning works just as well as a contrast with 滑 as does 澀.

f Following the emendation of 埶 to 說 suggested by commentators.

g See note d for chapter 8.

CHAPTER 25: WORKING SONGS

a Some readers take Fei Lian as the subject of 任, and they then take Fei Lian and Wu Lai together as the subjects for 卑, 大, and 高, reading 卑 causatively as "caused to lower." However, in all known discussions of Fei Lian and Wu Lai of which I am aware, there is no mention of Fei Lian being the one who employed Wu Lai, and rather all the references to Wu Lai state merely that he served Zhòu. For this reason, it seems more plausible to take Zhòu as the subject of 任 and of the subsequent lines of this stanza. (This is not reflected in the translation of 任惡來, however, due to the framework of syllables and rhymes employed there.) While this amounts to a rather sudden change of grammatical subject, that such a switch in referents is possible is clearly demonstrated by the line 武王誅之, two stanzas later, in which 之 clearly cannot refer to either of the subjects of the two immediately preceding sentences (Bi Gan and Jizi), but must refer to another person, which again would seem clearly to be Zhòu, since when the *Xunzi* speaks of King Wu's engaging in 誅, Zhòu is most frequently mentioned as the object.

b Following Yang Liuqiao on the construal of 牧.

c Here I follow the broad outlines of Yang Liang's understanding of this line, since it adopts a more conservative stance toward the text and does not read 形 as a loan for 刑. *Pace* Knoblock, Yang's gloss of 詰 as 詰問 means not simply "inquire about" but rather "to question" in an accusing and reproachful tone (i.e., 責問).

d For the reading of 抵, see note g for chapter 5.

e Most commentators read 傅 (or as it appears in some editions, 溥) as 敷, and following Ma Rong understand 敷 as 分 ("divide"). However, an alternative sense of 敷 is 治, as attested in dictionaries and commentaries: see Zhao Qi's commentary on 敷 in *Mencius* 3A4. This sense seems more appropriate to the context here, so I have followed this reading instead. (In some cases, 分 can imply a sense of "order," too, though it is not clear to me that this is how the commentators take it in the current case.)

f Following Liang Qixiong on the meaning of 阪.

g I follow Kubo Ai on the meaning of 無尤人, and I follow Ikai Hikohiro's understanding of the meaning of the last three lines of the stanza.

h Here I follow Li Zhongsheng's understanding of 後必有.

i I follow Ikai Hikohiro in reading 備 as 憊.

j Following Yu Yue, I reverse the order of 衰對 to 對衰. However, I see no need to understand 對 as 遂, as he does. Since the following line mentions 言, reading 對 in its common sense of "answer" (verbally) is perfectly fitting.

k Following Liao Jilang and Wang Tianhai in taking 往 in the sense of 至.

l Following Tsukada Taiho in understanding 名 as 名分.

m Most commentators take the 莫 in 莫不理續 as referring to the ruler's *subordinates*, parallel to the phrases 莫得相使, 莫得擅與, 莫得貴賤, and 莫得輕重 that occur earlier in the chapter. However, given that the phrasing of this line is not the same (莫不 instead of 莫得), it seems to me that the case for the parallel construal is not that strong. Instead, I take the referent of 莫 as the 五 of the previous line. Following Wang Niansun, I take 續 as a substitute for 績, but instead of understanding 績 in the sense of 事, as many do, I understand it in the sense of 成. The literal meaning is thus "none of the five [guidelines for the ruler] are not put in order and accomplished."

n Here I follow Yu Xingwu on the general sense of this line, though I do not accept his emendation of 鈹 to 鈒. On 鈹, see note e for chapter 22. Here I take the sense of "sharpness" as "harshness" or "cruelty."

o Here I understand 巧拙 in a fashion roughly similar to Zhu Xi, namely as referring to people contesting over cleverness and ineptness, i.e., struggling for advantage by trying to outwit one another.

CHAPTER 26: *Fu*

a Following Liu Shipei's understanding of 似.

b Here I follow Yang Liuqiao, though with reservations.

c Following Yang Liuqiao on the reading of 固塞.

d Following the manuscript traditions which read 帝.

e Commentators appear uniformly to read the grammar of this and the following line in an inverted fashion, i.e., 蛹以為母 as 以蛹為母 and 蛾以為父 as 以蛾為父. Such inversions are not uncommon in Chinese poetry, but choosing this reading over a more straightforward reading of the grammar must ultimately be justified by the fact that the inverted reading gives one a more sensible construal of the text, and in this case it does not. Since the "thing" under discussion is the silkworm (i.e., the larval form), the pupa clearly "gives birth" not to that form of the animal but rather to the moth. Some commentators explain that, since the moth comes from the pupa and then lays the eggs that become the silkworm, the pupa could still count as the "mother" of the silkworm, in an indirect sense. However, that explanation seems very strained, especially since on the inverted reading, the text says that the moth is the "father" of the silkworm, and the idea of the pupa generating the father of the silkworm would be better described as the pupa being the "grandmother" of the silkworm. For these reasons, I reject the inverted reading, and instead take the grammar as it stands, with an implied object following 以, i.e., 蛹以為母 is really 蛹以(之)[i.e., 蠶]為母, and the same for the following line. That the silkworm is "mother" to the pupa is easy enough to understand, since the larva "produces" the pupa (more specifically, the cocoon) directly, and since in a sense it is the larva that, inside the cocoon, gives birth to the moth, it also makes sense to say that the larva "fathers" the moth. Many commentators are perhaps inclined to adopt the inverted reading because the cocoon might be seen as womb-like, hence fitting the idea of pupa as mother. However, ancient Chinese descriptions of the ruler as "mother and father to the people" (民之父母) show that to say that X is the "mother" of Y need not always be understood to imply such a close analogy between X and the womb nurturing performed by mothers. Finally, additional support for this way of taking the text is to be found earlier at 26.126. There, a clue in the third riddle points to the clouds by *identifying the rain as their children*.

f As before (see note e above), commentators seem uniformly to adopt an inverted reading of the grammar of these two lines, and I again reject that reading, on the grounds that it does not succeed in making better sense of the text than the more straightforward reading of the grammar. Its shortcomings are especially apparent in the reading of the line 管以為母. Following Yang Liang, commentators understand this as saying that "the tube [i.e., needle case] is its [i.e., the needle's] mother," on the grounds that the needle case holds the needles inside itself (like a womb). Again, though, this is imposing a very strained analogy, since the needle case does not really "generate" the needles (also certainly not in any sense that would parallel generation by the "hairpin" in the previous line), and furthermore, the poem early on says that when not used, needles go missing, so for the poem to talk about having needles in needle cases contradicts its earlier clue. (Some commentators—perhaps trying to reconcile this tension away—read the earlier 亡 in a weaker sense, namely as "be hidden away," but it seems to me that such a weak sense is clearly undermined by 27.367, which similarly uses 亡 in relation to needles, but clearly refers to the needle going *missing*, and not merely being stored away.) It thus seems to me that a different interpretation is needed. In relation to the problematic line 管以為母, commentators have overlooked the following. Dictionaries commonly note that the characters 管 and 筦 were used interchangeably (e.g., sometimes 管子 appears as 筦子). In turn, one meaning of 筦 is the "spindle" on to which silk threads are wound

during the process of spinning, and the *Shuowen* glosses it even more specifically as 筅, which refers to the "bobbin" or spool of thread that was attached
to the weaver's shuttle, and which thus unwound the weft threads as the
shuttle passed back and forth through the warp threads (see also Needham
and Kuhn 1988, p. 207); Dieter Kuhn, who authored this volume, sometimes
seems even to translate 筅 as "shuttle" (e.g., Needham and Kuhn 1988, p.
218). So understood, the 筅 is very much like a needle, in that it has a long
and thin shape, it has thread tied to it, and it lays down a long tail (i.e., the
weft) as it moves. In light of this resemblance, the needle might be said to be
"mother" to the 筅 in a metaphorical sense, namely that it inspired the 筅, or
that the 筅 was modeled after it. The same could also be said of the "father-
son" relation between the needle and the hairpin. This seems to me a much
more satisfactory explanation of the passage.

g Here I understand 盲 as 冥, following Yang Liuqiao.

h The source of the difficulty with 志愛公利，重樓疏堂 is that, based on a
parallel with the previous sentence 公正無私，反見從橫, one would expect
that 志愛公利 describes good people, while 重樓疏堂 describes something bad
that happens to them, but it is hard to see how 重樓疏堂 could be something
bad that happens to them, especially if these same good people are taken as
the grammatical subject of the verbs 重 and 疏—in that case, they would be
doing something bad, which seems nonsensical. Zhu Xi tries to get around
the difficulty by taking 愛 in a negative sense, as "greedy," so that 志愛公利
refers to *bad* people, and 重樓疏堂 refers to something good that they acquire
(unjustly), in keeping with the poem's theme of how the world is turned
upside down. However, given that the parallel phrases 公正無私, 無私罪人,
and 道德純備 in the surrounding sentences are all unmistakably about good
people, Zhu's reading seems implausible. The alternative, adopted by many
commentators, is to read 志愛公利 as describing good people, but carry the
sense of 反見 from the previous sentence over to the line 重樓疏堂, i.e., these
good people "*are accused of* [selfishly] stacking up buildings and raising halls
[for themselves]." However, carrying 反見 over in this way is a big stretch. My
proposal is that we need to reconceive the contrast between the first and
second halves of the sentences. Namely, rather than thinking of the second
half as something bad that happens to the good people mentioned in the first
half, we should think of the second half as just *something opposite of what one
would expect* in relation to good people. In the case of 重樓疏堂, this is opposite of what one would expect good people to do, but it need not imply
any fault on their part, if we take it that their activity of construction work is
not, as many commentators assume, for their own benefit, but is rather ordered by the ruler for his own benefit. In fact, since both the preceding and
the subsequent two sentences are primarily concerned with people in the
position of minister, it makes more sense to understand 重樓疏堂 as construction for the ruler, rather than for the minister himself. In the translation I add
the words "for royalty" to make this explicit, and to bring out the contrast in
the idea of people who are devoted to the public good but are made to serve
the personal interests of the few.

i A difficulty similar to 志愛公利，重樓疏堂 also affects this sentence. See
my discussion in the previous note. Here I follow Yang Liang's understanding of 憼, and Liao Jilang's understanding of 貳. However, I understand the

overall import of 愨革貳兵 differently than they do. See chapter 26 note 29 for the explanation of its sense.

j Here I follow Yang Liuqiao's suggestion to read 郁郁 as a loan for 鬱鬱, which I understand in the sense of 愁, on the grounds that this is a more conservative approach to the text than Yang Liang's suggested emendation, which is what most commentators seem to follow.

k Here I again follow Yang Liuqiao in reading the line as it stands, with the character 拂. I also follow his understanding of the sense of that character. However, I depart from him and most other commentators in my construal of the grammar. Most readers seem to take the 拂 (or 郁郁, if they adopt Yang Liang's emendation) as modifying 其欲, and they take the entire phrase 禮義之大行 as the object of 欲. However, surrounding sentences clearly have a parallel construction, and in the cases of 昭昭乎其知之明也 and 闇乎天下之晦盲也, it is clear that 昭昭乎 modifies 明 and 闇乎 modifies 晦盲. (My translation of the latter case, though, does not fully reflect my understanding of the grammar because of the restrictions imposed by the rhyme scheme and syllable count.) Accordingly, by parallel, the 拂 should modify just 大行, which leaves the object of 欲 as simply 禮義. I thus read 其欲禮義之大行 as "the great acts of (i.e., done from) their desire for (i.e., to follow) ritual and *yi*."

l Here I follow the excellent suggestion of Chow Tse-tsung (apud Knechtges 1989, p. 13n60) to read 忘 in the sense of 妄 "deviate," based on the line in the *Odes*, 不愆不忘 (Mao #249). It is unclear whether Chow intends to read 忘 as a loangraph for 妄 (which it apparently was in some instances in ancient texts), or whether he is suggesting this as a way for understanding 忘 in light of Zheng Xuan's commentary on the *Odes*, which glosses 忘 as 遺失. In either case, 忘 on this reading has the sense of "fail," "err," or "stray." Given the preceding remark about how every thousand years order will prevail and the following remark about how the sage awaits the approaching opportunity to right the world, this construal of 忘 makes very good sense in the context, and better sense than the more straightforward sense of "forget" that most commentators take it to have, especially since chapter 17 of the *Xunzi* presents a view of Heaven on which it does not seem to have any particular interest in humans.

m First, regarding the grouping of lines here, it is important to note the reference to 遠方 in line 255. Given the mention of this "distant place" that becomes the subject of discussion, it seems implausible to me to take the lines that follow it as simply a reprise or coda of the 佹詩, as many commentators do, for in contrast the 佹詩 repeatedly makes its remarks about 天下. Thus, I take the 小歌 to be a free-standing poem (but on a similar theme). On this view, it also seems implausible to think that the 小歌 ends with 讒人服矣, because it would be a startlingly abrupt ending. As Yu Yue points out, it is more plausible to take everything from line 255 to the end of the chapter as a single poem. The only reason that I can see for separating off the section from 琁玉瑤珠，不知佩也 onward as a separate piece is that it is only that section that is quoted in the *Zhan Guo Ce* and *Hanshi Waizhuan*. Such a reason assumes, though, that the quotations in those texts were supposed to be complete in the first place. Yet, there are no good grounds for such an assumption; just as Xunzi himself quotes piecemeal from the *Odes*, it is quite possible that the *Zhan Guo Ce* and *Hanshi Waizhuan* left out lines of Xunzi's original poem.

Accordingly, though I agree with commentators that the lines 與愚以疑，顧聞反辭 serve as the introduction to the 小歌 follows, I do not think they should be grouped with the lines that precede it, since the 小歌 is not a reprise or coda. In turn, that then requires a very different construal of 與愚以疑，顧聞反辭 than the common one of taking these words to be spoken by disciples requesting further instruction on the 佹詩. Also, in trying to make sense of them, they need to introduce *everything* that follows, all the way to the end of the chapter. With that assumption in mind, my interpretation is this. The clearest theme in the 小歌 is how *backward* everything is, and that provides a perfectly sensible way to understand the meaning of 反辭. Indeed, 反辭 thus seems to be a kind of parallel to the 佹詩 (a "song of anomaly"). On that basis, I suggest that the lines 與愚以疑，顧聞反辭 should be taken as a kind of parallel to the earlier lines 天下不治，請陳佹詩, namely that the first line describes some bad condition, and in the second line Xunzi proposes to sing about it. Starting with 顧聞反辭, the line can be read in the manner just described by taking 聞 causatively, as "make heard," a sense that it has in some cases (Yang Liuqiao adopts a similar reading of 顧聞反辭, though he has a different view of 反辭 than I). As for 與愚以疑, almost every commentator wants to emend it, but on my view, no emendations are necessary. I take 與 and 以 as transitive verbs ("make associations with" and "adopt, grasp") with 愚 and 疑 as their respective objects. The subject of these verbs I take to be an implicit "some [people]," a construction that occurs elsewhere in the *Xunzi*; see the beginning of chapter 6, where the lines 忍情性，不知壹天下建國家之權稱，尚法而無法，不法先王, and 略法先王而不知其統 each introduce a new group of people (who are identified later) without an explicit subject. In the present case, if we accept the idea that the poem was written on the occasion of Xunzi's being ousted due to slanderers who turned the lord against him, then it is perfectly fitting that he should introduce the poem by speaking of "[those who] associate with the foolish and take up confusion."

n Here I follow Lu Wenchao's suggested emendation of the surrounding lines to make them rhyme with 衍. As for 衍 itself, I understand its meaning as 達 or 行, as attested in the 中文大辭典, citing the *Guangya*, the *Hou Han Shu*, the *Jiyun*, and the *Taixuan Jing*.

o Following Wang Tianhai, I take 琁玉瑤珠 as two objects, instead of four. Wang does not give an explicit defense of this reading, but to judge from the use of 琁 and 瑤 in other early Chinese texts, when they are put in parallel as they are here, they usually function descriptively (see 琁室瑤台 in the *Huainanzi*, and 琁瑰瑤碧 in the *Shanhaijing*). Also, when Xunzi puts 玉 and 珠 in a list of four elsewhere in the text, he usually lists them together as 珠玉. The contrast between that construction and the one here likewise suggests in this case we do not have a list of four items.

CHAPTER 27: THE GRAND DIGEST

a Even in its original context, the meaning of the line 唯其偕矣 is not very clear. Many take it as explaining the preceding line, i.e., the things are fine *because* they (the things themselves, or the people who own them) are orderly. However, the comment in the main text that immediately follows the quotation ("even if it is lovely . . .") clearly supposes that the practice might be lovely *without* being appropriate, so that understanding of the line does not seem to fit here. For the same reason, the other common understanding of the line, namely that it simply adds to the previous line (e.g., Zheng Xuan's gloss on the two: 魚既美又齊等), likewise does not fit here. In the *Xunzi*, some quotes from the *Odes* are intended to illustrate what follows, and so I base my reading of the quote on the comment in the main text. The point of the comment is that the practice of the ritual needs to be appropriate both in the circumstances and in expressing certain attitudes; perfunctory performance of ritual is not acceptable. Thus, in order to convey the idea that the "things" (i.e., the ritual) *should* be fitting, I read 唯其偕矣 in a hortatory sense, as reflected in the translation.

b Rather than understand 維 as "only," as many commentators do, I take it in the sense in which 維/惟/唯 often appears at the beginning of bronze inscriptions, namely as meaning, "It is (or was). . . ." To the extent that the text is quoting (an alternative version of) the *Dayumo* chapter of the *Documents*, this reading makes better sense than taking 維 as "only," especially because there is no implication in the *Documents* context that Shun is claiming this accomplishment as unique to him.

c Following Gao Heng and Wang Tianhai on 面 and 貌.

d Here I follow the older manuscript tradition that reads 背禮者也 instead of 皆禮也. The latter looks to be an emendation introduced by those who could not make sense of the former, but I think it is in fact possible to make sense of the former, so the emendation is not necessary. (Indeed, as my translation indicates, the former version can be seen as expressing the same thought as the latter.) My understanding of 背 is inspired by, but not the same as, that of Wang Tianhai. Also, most readers seem to take 順 as meaning roughly "agree with." However, given that the text in many places stresses that people's hearts may be misguided and that ritual acts as a corrective to such cases, reading 順 this way makes the passage say that whatever follows along with people's hearts is ritually appropriate, which risks introducing a serious contradiction into the text. To avoid such a contradiction, I choose instead to read 順 causatively, as "make agreeable." For an example of a similar, causative use of 順 in the text, see the phrase 足以順服好利之人 at 11.314–15.

e Here I read 庸 as a loan for 備.

f Here I follow Ikai Hikohiro in taking as 敢 an error for 節.

g Most commentators seem to take 疾 as a loan for 嫉, meaning "hate." However this seems to me somewhat out of character with surrounding lines (especially the preceding one), which are clearly permitting a certain kind of reaction, but forbidding a more extreme form of it. Taking 疾 as a loan for 嫉 seems to break the parallel, because "hating" is not merely a more extreme form of "leaving." (Also, understanding 疾 as "hate" seems to make the subsequent sentence about anger rather redundant.) For that reason, I instead take 疾 in its well-attested sense of "hurry," understanding this to mean "rushing off" or "storming away" from the lord's service.

h Although commentators are inclined to group this line with the previous ones about music, the fact that those other lines also appear in chapters 18 and 19 *without* being followed by this line calls into question whether they are really supposed to be a group. Furthermore, given the difficulty in reading them as a single group without taking this line in a rather unusual way (i.e., reading 君子 as referring to the ruler and emending 土, as discussed below), it seems to me that there is greater reason *not* to group them together, unless there is some compelling evidence for doing so. As for the emendation of 土 to 出, this seems motivated by the desire to have this line fit with the previous ones, or by parallel with the *Liji* line 既服習容觀玉聲乃出. However, the wording of the *Liji* passage is not very close to this one (it is only the two characters 習容 that are shared). Also, as just noted, the motivation to try to link this line with the lines about the music made by the chariot is dubious. For these reasons, it seems to me that there is no need to emend 土 to 出. Instead, taking the line as a freestanding sentence, it is more natural to read 土 in a verbal sense, as 仕, a character with which 土 was often interchangeable in classical Chinese.

i Here I follow the reading of Liu Shipei on the understanding of 內 and its place in the sentence.

j The tendency of many commentators to append 凡百事異理而相守也 to the end of the previous sentence seems not well grounded to me. First, the syntactic structure of this grouping is much more similar to the sentences that follow it than to the sentences that precede it, which argues for reading it with the subsequent claims. Second, the point of the two sentences preceding this remark is very clear: because of a shared (hierarchical) structure, it is possible to use one thing *to make inferences* about another thing. Yang Liang, whom most commentators seem to be following, tries to tie these remarks together by glossing 凡百事異理而相守也 with the explanation: 其理雖異，其守則一. However, this is a very forced (and to my mind, implausible) way to understand 相守. A far more plausible explanation of those two characters is Yang Liuqiao's gloss of them as 相待. In that case, though, the point—which is about mutual *influence*—is very different from the point about *a shared structure underwriting inferences*, so in terms of the meaning of the remark, 凡百事異理而相守也 does not fit especially well what comes before it. (To his credit, Yang Liuqiao does not treat 凡百事異理而相守也 as simply part of the preceding sentence, perhaps because he sees that there is a significant difference here. On the other hand, he does not group it with the subsequent sentences, so maybe he did not fully appreciate the possibilities for reading the text opened up by his own interpretation.)

k The two characters 通類 are difficult to construe. My understanding of them is based on two points. First, insofar as the sentence is supposed to be an elaboration on the two characters 相守 in the previous sentence (see the previous note), they should have a meaning that is analogous both to 相守 in that sentence and to 相順 in the following sentence. Second, the particular sense of 通類 as "interlinked categories" is attested by a passage in the *Chunqiu Fanlu* 55 (四時之副) with a close parallel in terms of its subject matter: 天之道，春暖以生，夏暑以養，秋清以殺，冬寒以藏。暖暑清寒，異氣而同功，皆天之所以成歲也。聖人副天之所行以為政，故以慶賞副暖而當春，以賞副暑而當夏，以罰副清而當秋，以刑副寒而當冬。慶賞罰刑，畢事而同功，皆王者之所以成德也。慶賞罰刑與春夏秋冬，以類相應也，如合符。故曰王者配天，謂

其道。天有四時，王有四政，四政若四時，通類也，天人所同有也。 Here the "interlinking" is of the four government activities and the four seasons, which is not what the *Xunzi* is discussing, but the use of 通 here to designate linking among the categories is the kind of meaning that seems called for in the context of the *Xunzi*.

l Here I follow Wang Tianhai's suggestion to read 續 as a (phonetic) loan for 肅.

m Though many commentators emend 羞 to 義, this seems to me unnecessary. They seem to be motivated by the problem of making sense of 好羞, and how this contrasts with 好利. However, I suggest that there is no need to be puzzled by the contrast. In the saying from the people that follows in the main text, the person who pursues riches is told to 忍恥, and in this case, the 恥 clearly refers to *things at which one properly ought to be ashamed*. Since 羞 and 恥 are very close in meaning (see the remark a few lines earlier in the main text: 從士以上皆羞利而不與民爭業，樂分施而恥積藏), we can understand the 羞 in 好羞 in a way similar to 恥, namely as referring to *a proper sense of shame*. See also the line in *Analects* 2.3 有恥且格, where it is clear that what is being said is not that the common people will commit shameful acts, but that they have the proper response of shame to inappropriate behavior.

n I take 絕 in the sense of 極, where this designates some kind of excessive behavior.

o Following Yang Liuqiao, I take 幡 as 翻 in the sense of 反覆. Many commentators seem to understand 翻 instead as "quickly," but speed does not seem to be the relevant issue for this context.

p The words 細席 are puzzling, and most commentators suggest emending 細 to something else. However, this is not really necessary, especially if we take 席 as a verb. Commenting on the line 「儒有席上之珍以待聘」in the 儒行 chapter of the 禮記, Zheng Xuan explains, 「席，猶鋪陳也.」 We can apply a similar verbal understanding of 席 in this case to arrive at much the same meaning as the commentators endorse, without emending 細.

q Here I follow Liang Qixiong.

r Here I follow the manuscript tradition that reads 聞 instead of 問.

s A number of commentators break the last sentence off from the preceding ones as a separate section. This seems less preferable to me, on the grounds that the similar constructions 其心一也 and 其心同也 seem to tie the last two sentences together grammatically, and on the grounds that, when broken off by itself, the sentence does not make a lot of sense to me, especially the way that most commentators seem to construe it. Furthermore, most commentators seem to take 不說, 不占, and 不相 literally, as "not speak," "not practice divination," and "not play the role of assistant." However, when so construed, the remarks seem to have little to do with the preceding sentences, which stress how truly good people do not make a show of their abilities or virtue. Also, to claim that the expert in ritual never plays the role of ritual assistant seems so odd as to make it implausible. (Why would the ritual expert refuse to be anything less than the lead ritual practitioner?) For these reasons, I prefer to take 不說 and 不占 in the sense of not *making a show* of doing these things, rather than literally not doing them. (Compare the use of 不德 in *Daodejing* chap. 38: 上德不德.) Also, instead of taking 相 in the sense of "assistant," it seems preferable, and more parallel in meaning to 不說 and

不占, to take it in the sense of "guide," or "conduct," which are also well-attested senses of the term.

t For the reading of this difficult sentence, I follow the Beida Zhexuexi commentary, but with hesitation.

u Many commentators follow Yang Liang in taking 井里 as a place name. However, Yang provides no citation for this claim, nor do there seem to be any references to such a place in other early texts. A number of other commentators take 井 as meaning 鄉, and construe the two characters together as meaning roughly "a village." However, the whole point of the line would seem to be to emphasize the *humble origins* of the jade of He, as shown by the parallel with the subsequent sentence about Zigong and Ji Lu. As a place name, 井里 does not convey this sense, especially since—to judge from the evidence of other texts—it was not especially known as a backwater. Nor does the reading of 井里 as 鄉里 accomplish this sense, since the mere fact that it comes from a village would not convey lowliness. Those adopting this latter reading often take 厥 as 橛, a doorstop, which does convey the right point, but the problem is that, so understood, the story of its discovery is further removed from accounts, e.g., in the *Han Feizi*, that tell us that Bian He obtained the jade from the *mountains* of Chu. (It also makes for a rather strange story in itself—how did the stone come to be a doorstop and then be discovered by Bian He?) Instead, taking 井里 as "in a well" makes better sense here, and makes for a more sensible story that is more compatible with the other accounts: it would be no surprise that such a stone might be discovered in the process of digging a well.

v For the understanding of this very difficult sentence, I follow Wang Tianhai's suggestion to read 鬲 as 隔 and 嵮 as 填, though I take the latter in a somewhat different sense than he does. As for 皋如, based on the fact that parallel texts have 睪如 instead of 皋如, Wang takes 皋 as 睪, and in turn reads 睪 as a loan for 澤. However, 睪 is sometimes a loan for 繹, and one meaning of 繹 attested in the dictionaries is 終, which makes better sense here than 澤, so that is how I propose to understand it.

w Here I follow Zhong Tai's reading of 不以於汙上.

x Many commentators read 非一日之聞也 as meaning (roughly) ". . . and this is not a single day's news" (i.e., this has been known for a long time). However, such a construal seems to me to make little sense in this context, because it leaves the relevance of the reference to Liuxia Hui unexplained, and it also makes mysterious the transition from talking about refusing to serve those who are arrogant to the remark about the self-defeating nature of struggling for profit. The construal adopted in the translation solves these problems by making explicit that Liuxia Hui was not someone to seek a trifling gain, which then connects naturally with the sentence that follows, and also conveys the idea—which is presumably Zixia's point—that he is not willing to take a quick and easy (but debased) way out of his predicament.

y Liu Shipei's proposal to read 藍苴路作 as 濫狙略詐 seems most plausible to me, especially since 狙詐 occurs in a number of texts as a binomial for deceptiveness. However, I take 濫 somewhat differently than he does. The problem is that 濫 in its normal sense of "overflow" does not seem to be a proper parallel verb for 略. However, one sense attested in the 中文大辭典

(citing the *Wen Xuan* and the *Shuowen Tongxun Dingsheng*) is "to set out a net," as a loangraph for 檻. This seems to me a better way to make sense of 濫 as a parallel verb for 略 here.

z Most readers take the second occurrence of 乘 as a verb in the exact same sense of the earlier 乘, which is hard to make sense of. I propose instead to take the second 乘 as a verb in a different sense, namely "treat as 乘 (i.e., as 所乘)." Second, I take the 其 to refer back to whatever is referred to by 有乘 in the first part of the sentence. I read 是其反者也 as "This is its opposite" (i.e., this is the opposite of how the cause-result process goes), but have rendered it more colloquially in the translation. Such a reading makes better sense to me than any of the alternatives I have seen, and has the advantage of not needing to emend the text.

aa The expression 區蓋 has puzzled commentators. One of the senses of 區 attested in dictionaries is "empty," which I follow here. The word 蓋 literally means to "cover," but in early texts it is sometimes used figuratively to mean "cover over" or "surpass" (see the expression 功蓋五帝 in the *Shi Ji*). That is the sense in which I construe it here. The point, as I understand it, is that in order to establish one's trustworthiness, one must avoid saying both things that have no basis in fact (i.e., are "empty") and things that have some basis in fact but "surpass" what is actually the case (i.e., are "overstated").

bb Here I follow Wang Tianhai's explanation of 汗 and 奧.

cc Following commentators, I take 仕 as a loangraph for 事. Most commentators seem to treat this 事 as having the same grammatical subject as the verb 短 in the preceding parallel construction 所短, namely "you." However, given the earlier contrast between 吾之所短 and 人之所長, it seems more likely to me that the grammatical subject of 所事 is 人. On this construal the referent of 所事 is the accomplishments of those others who are or were superior, and thus this reading also seems to fit better with the remarks that follow, especially the criticism of those who do not follow a proper model (不法).

dd Here I follow the manuscript tradition that reads 察辯.

ee The character 喆 has caused consternation for commentators. Here I follow Ikai Hikohiro's suggestion that it is a loan (or perhaps more accurately, an error) for 詰, since dictionaries say that the two characters were confused with each other at times. Ikai in turn understands 詰 as 爭辯貌. However, on the parsing of the line I adopt (taking 流詰然 as a unit, instead of breaking after 流), such a reading would be unnecessarily repetitive. Another sense of 詰 that is attested in dictionaries is 屈曲 "twisted" or "bent" (詰 often appears in texts in compounds with 屈, 詘, and 曲), which fits this context and line parsing better, so that is how I read it here.

CHAPTER 28: THE RIGHT-HAND VESSEL

a Following Kubo Ai in reading 綦 as 甚.

b My reading here mostly follows that of Liao Jilang, with two exceptions. Whereas he emends 九蓋 to 北蓋, I follow Zhang Jue's reading of 九蓋, and I read 蓋曰貴文 more literally than Liao does.

CHAPTER 29: THE WAY TO BE A SON

a The original Chinese text does not clearly indicate that Zilu says these words, and so commentators have assumed they are uttered by Confucius. However, the text subsequently states quite clearly that Confucius responds to these words, and it would be odd for the text to note this unless it were taking these words to have been spoken by Zilu, so I have inserted this in the translation. Switches in speaker without any indication are not uncommon in classical Chinese (see, e.g., *Mencius* 1B1), so this is a fairly plausible way of construing the passage.

CHAPTER 31: DUKE AI

a Most commentators emend 色色 to 邑邑 and take 邑邑 as 悒悒, reading, "His heart does not know to worry [about bad consequences of his actions]." This seems unnecessary. The word 色 can be a verb (see 列子，天瑞篇：有色色者). I read 色色 literally as "to make one's countenance a certain countenance," i.e., to control one's expression. This reading contrasts better with the subsequent remarks about 色不伐.

b Reading 忳 for 肫 here.

c Most commentators take this line very differently. Reading 務 as 鍪 (or 冒, or 帽), they understand this line as "The kings of ancient times were men with (simple) hats and round collars," the point being that they did not even wear (fancy) ritual caps, but merely crude headgear, yet were nonetheless able to rule the whole world (i.e., clothing is not such an important issue). While this reading is certainly possible, it seems to me unnecessary and even somewhat at odds with the point of the passage. Confucius is upbraiding Duke Ai for asking about the sages' clothing rather than their conduct, so it seems odd for him to start his answer by talking about their clothing, and more natural to understand him as pointing out that the sages worried about their government first, not their dress.

d The interpretation of this passage suggested by commentators is "Those fond of business do not let their goods go to waste, and elders do not engage in selling." However, not only does the contrast between "those fond of business" and "elders" seem odd, but also it seems irrelevant to Confucius's point, which is that putting oneself in certain circumstances influences one's feelings and behavior. For this reason, it seems best to consider alternate ways of reading the line. According to the *Ciyuan*, 折 can refer to a sacrificial ground, and this makes better sense of the first Chinese sentence; those who spend their time in the marketplace are not concerned with the rites. The point of the contrast with the elders would then be that the elders are not especially concerned with market activities, and are rather concerned with something else. (It is not clear exactly who the "elders" are, but if they are taken to be the supervisors of some ritual or leaders in government, then it would be natural that they would not be concerned with the markets.)

BIBLIOGRAPHY

This bibliography lists only texts used in preparing the present translation and certain secondary works mentioned in the introduction and notes. More general bibliographies covering a wide range of primary and secondary sources are available in the volumes by Knoblock and the anthology by Kline and Ivanhoe listed below.

Beida Zhexuexi 北大哲學系. 1979. *Xunzi Xinzhu* 荀子新注. Beijing: Beijing Daxue.

Berkson, Mark. 2014. "Xunzi's Reinterpretation of Ritual: A Hermeneutic Defense of the Confucian Way." In T. C. Kline III and Justin Tiwald, eds., *Ritual and Religion in the Xunzi*. Albany: State University of New York Press.

Dubs, Homer H. 1928. *The Works of Hsüntze*. London: A. Probsthain.

Harbsmeier, Christoph. 1997. "Xunzi and the Problem of Impersonal First Person Pronouns." *Early China* 22: 181–220.

Hou Zongcai 侯宗才. 1999. *Xunzi* 荀子. Lanzhou: Gansu Minzu Chubanshe.

Hutton, Eric. 2011. "A Note on the Xunzi's Explanation of Xing 性." *Dao* 10, no. 4: 527–30.

Ikai, Hikohiro 豬飼彥博. 1983. *Junshi Hoi* 荀子補遺. Reprint in *Zengbu Xunzi Jijie* 增補荀子集解. Taibei: Lantai Shuju.

Kjellberg, Paul. 1996. "Sextus Empiricus, Zhuangzi, and Xunzi on 'Why be skeptical?'" In Philip Ivanhoe and Paul Kjellberg, eds., *Essays on Skepticism, Relativism, and Ethics in the Zhuangzi*, 1–25. Albany: State University of New York Press.

Kline, T. C., III, and P. J. Ivanhoe, eds. 2000. *Virtue, Nature, and Moral Agency in the Xunzi*. Indianapolis: Hackett.

Knechtges, David. 1989. "Riddles as Poetry: The '*Fu* Chapter' of the *Hsüntzu*." In Chow Tse-Tsung, ed., *Wen-Lin, vol. 2: Studies in the Chinese Humanities*, 1–31. Madison: University of Wisconsin Press.

Knoblock, John. 1982–83. "The Chronology of Xunzi's Works." *Early China* 8: 28–52.

———. 1988–94. *Xunzi: A Translation and Study of the Complete Works*, vols. 1–3. Stanford: Stanford University Press, vol. 1, 1988; vol. 2, 1990; vol. 3, 1994.

Kubo, Ai 久保愛. 1983. *Junshi Zōchū* 荀子增注. Reprint in *Zengbu Xunzi Jijie* 增補荀子集解. Taibei: Lantai Shuju.

Lau, D. C. 1970. *Mencius*. New York: Penguin.

Li Disheng 李滌生. 1979. *Xunzi Jishi* 荀子集釋. Taibei: Xuesheng Shuju.

Li Zhongsheng 李中生. 2001. *Xunzi Jiaogu Conggao* 荀子校诂丛稿. Guangzhou: Guangdong Gaodeng Jiaoyu Chubanshe.

Liao Jilang 廖吉郎. 2002. *Xinbian Xunzi* 新編荀子. Taibei: Guoli Bianyiguan.

Long Yuchun 龍宇純. 1963. "Xianqin Sanwen zhong de Yunwen" 先秦散文中的韻文. *Chung Chi Journal* 2, no. 2: 137–68; and 3, no. 1: 55–87.

———. 1999. "Xunqingzi Ji Yu" 荀卿子記錄. *Zhongguo Wenzhe Yanjiu Jikan* 中國文哲研究集刊 15: 199–262.

———. 1987. *Xunzi Lunji* 荀子論集. Taibei: Xuesheng Shuju.

Machle, Edward J. 1993. *Nature and Heaven in the Xunzi: A Study of the Tian Lun*. Albany: State University of New York Press.

Mei Y. P. 1961. "Hsün-tzu's Theory of Education." *Tsing Hua Journal of Chinese Studies* 清華學報 2, no. 2: 361–79.

Needham, Joseph, and Dieter Kuhn. 1988. *Science and Civilisation in China: Volume 5, Chemistry and Chemical Technology: Part 9, Textile Technology: Spinning and Reeling*. Cambridge: Cambridge University Press.

Nivison, David. 1996. "Critique of David B. Wong, 'Xunzi on Moral Motivation.'" In Philip J. Ivanhoe, ed., *Chinese Language, Thought, and Culture: Nivison and His Critics*, 323–31. Chicago: Open Court.

Qian Mu 錢穆. 2008. *Xianqin Zhuzi Xinian* 先秦諸子繫年. Taibei: Dadong Tushu Gongsi.

Qu Wanli 屈萬里. 1983. *Shijing Quanshi* 詩經詮釋. Taibei: Lianjing Chubanshe.

Van Norden, Bryan. 2011. *Introduction to Classical Chinese Philosophy*. Indianapolis: Hackett.

Waltham, Clae. 1971. *Shu Ching: Book of History*. London: George Allen and Unwin.

Wang Sen 王森. 1992. *Xunzi Baihua Jinyi* 荀子白话今译. Beijing: Zhongguo Shudian.

Wang Tianhai 王天海. 2005. *Xunzi Jiaoshi* 荀子校釋. Shanghai: Shanghai Guji Chubanshe.

Wang Xianqian 王先謙. 1983. *Xunzi Jijie* 荀子集解. Reprint in *Zengbu Xunzi Jijie* 增補荀子集解. Taibei: Lantai Shuju.

Wang Zhonglin 王忠林. 1972. *Xunzi Duben* 荀子讀本. Taibei: Sanmin Shuju.

Watson, Burton. 1963. *Hsün Tzu: Basic Writings*. New York: Columbia University Press.

Xiong Gongzhe 熊公哲. 1975. *Xunzi Jinzhu Jinyi* 荀子今註今譯. Taibei: Shangwu Yinshuguan.

Yan Lingfeng 嚴靈峰, ed. 1979. *Wuqiu Beizhai Xunzi Jicheng* 無求備齋荀子集成. Taibei: Chengwen Chubanshe.

Yang Liuqiao 楊柳橋. 1987. *Xunzi Guyi* 荀子詁譯. Xinzhu: Yangzhe Chubanshe.

You Guo'en 游國恩. 1982. "Xunqing Kao" 荀卿考. In Luo Genze 羅根澤, ed., *Gushi Bian* 古史辨, vol. 4, 94–103. Shanghai: Shanghai Guji Chubanshe.

Zhang Jue 张觉. 1995. *Xunzi Yizhu* 荀子译注. Shanghai: Shanghai Guji Chubanshe.

INDEX

(Numbers in bold indicate pages where notes explaining names and terms can be found.)

accumulation of cultivation, 3, 5, 27, 58, 65–66, 68, 81, 103, 127, 160, 172–73, 236, 249–50, 253–54, 307, 323
allotments, xxvii, 59, 106, 110, 112, 125–26, 131, 158, 175, 196, 198–99. *See also* differentiations; distinctions; divisions
Analects, xv, xxiii, 1nn. 3 and 7, 2n. 11, 5n. 23, 7n. 28, 8n. 32, 9n. 1, 11n. 12, 63n. 44, 76n. 16, 136n. 10, 152n. 29, 179n. 13, 181n. 19, 195n. 50, 204n. 22, 230n. 18, 288n. 4, 290n. 15, 291n. 19, 293n. 27, 300nn. 67 and 69, 302n. 82, 306nn. 97 and 100, 307n. 104, 309n. 110, 310n. 114, 312n. 122, 313nn. 126 and 128, 315n. 133, 321n. 14, 322n. 17, 323nn. 21 and 22, 326nn. 3, 328nn. 7 and 8, 332n. 8, 373n. a (chap. 22), 381n. m. *See also* Confucius
animals: as affectionate toward their own kind, 213; as different from humans, 24, 35, 76
approval, 34, 83, 227–28, **243**–45, 320
Archer Yi, 62, 107, 117, 145, 194, 231
Art of War, The. See Sunzi Bingfa

Ba (people), 170
ba (霸). *See* hegemon
Bai Qi, 169n. 20
Baili Xi, **264**, 300n. 66
Bao Shu, 226
benefit, 17, 22, 24–28, 42, 58, 76, 85, 87, 89–90, 113–14, 121, 134, 139, 144–45, 149, 163–64, 171, 183, 185, 196, 202, 250–51, 268. *See also* profit
bi (蔽). *See* fixation
Bi Gan, **61**, 135, 158, 186, 264, 285, 301, 316, 323, 342–43, 373n. a (chap. 25)
Bian (place), 306
bian (辨). *See* distinctions
Bian He, 309, 382n. u
Bian Sui, **271**
Bo (place), 100, 110, 162, 188
Bo Le, **127**
Bo Qin, **340**
Bo Ya, 5
Bo Yi, 251n. 5

Book of Changes, 78n. 22, 297, 307n. 103, 308; quotations from, 37, 299
Book of Lord Shang, xxv, 152n. 31, 159n. 56. *See also* Shang Yang
boorishness, **11**, 28–29, 36, 160, 193
brothers: relations of, 15–16, 26, 34, 44–45, 47, 53–54, 75–76, 78, 87, 119, 128–29, 134, 146, 218, 226, 250–51, 267, 270, 296, 311, 325, 332
buxiao (不肖). *See* unworthy person(s)

Cai (state), 164–65, 169, 265n. 16, 323
Cang Jie, 231
Cao (place), 324
Cao Chulong, 138, 154
chaos and disorder, 12, 14, 18–19, 28–29, 36, 40, 56, 58–59, 63, 65, 69, 70, 75–76, 79, 85–86, 89, 94, 97, 104–5, 109, 111, 114, 116–17, 120, 124, 127–28, 130, 132, 136–40, 142–44, 146, 148, 155, 157, 164–65, 166–67, 173, 175, 177, 179, 181, 183, 186, 188, 195–96, 200–201, 205, 213, 215, 218–21, 223–24, 228, 234, 237, 240–41, 243–45, 248, 251–52, 259–60, 271–72, 291, 298, 304–5, 316, 336–37. *See also* order
Chen (state), 169, 265n. 16, 323
Chen Xiao, **155**, 156n. 48
Chen Zhong. *See* Tian Zhong
cheng (誠). *See* integrity
Chong (place), 155, 156n. 46
Chu (state), xix–xx, 27, 33, 66, 100–101, 107, 121n. 22, 134, 151, 157–58, 164n. 7, 165, 167, 169–70, 178, 188–89, 190n. 22, 219, 265n. 18, 323, 339–41, 369n. c, 382n. u
Chui (person), 231
Chuisha, 157
Chunqiu (春秋). *See Spring and Autumn Annals*
Chunqiu Fanlu, 380n. k
Chuxueji, 187n. 17
Confucians. *See ru* (儒)
Confucius, xxiii, xxv, 32–33, 41n. 6, 42, 46n. 15, 47–48, 53n. 9, 54, 61, 63, 99, 227, 231n. 22, 232n. 25, 265, 285, 290n.

Confucius (*cont.*)
 15, 292n. 24, 302n. 82, 303n. 85, 306n.
 100, 312n. 122, 316, 342–43, 344, 384n.
 a (chap. 29), 384nn. c and d (chap.
 31); quotations from, 50, 60, 70, 112,
 114, 195, 310–11, 318–29, 331–37,
 341–42. See also *Analects*
courage, 11, 15, 23–25, 43, 234, 256,
 306nn. 99 and 100, 314, 318, 322, 331
craftsmen, 27–28, 30, 55–56, 66–67, 74,
 76, 78, 95, 106, 110, 116, 123, 230, 250,
 253, 255, 306, 324, 330n. 1

Da Dai Liji, 292nn. 24 and 25
Daliang, 170
Dan Ji, 225
dao (道). *See* Way, the
Daodejing, xv, xx, xxvi, xxix, 10n. 9,
 126n. 30, 153n. 34, 171n. 28, 229n. 13,
 243n. 25, 261n. 8, 294n. 33, 345, 381n.
 s. *See also* Laozi
Daoism, 345
de (德). *See* virtue
death, 25, 206–7, 209, 211–12, 244, 311.
 See also funerals; mourning
deliberate effort, xxvi, 191, 210, 236,
 248–53
Deng (place), 158
Deng Xi, 13n. 18, 16, 40n. 1, 41, 56,
 205n. 24, 319
desire, 27, 83, 104, 126, 128, 153, 182,
 199–200, 201, 221, 224, 227, 231–32,
 238, 240, 243–45, 248, 250–51, 291, 304
Di (people), 189, 303
Di Shi, 271
differentiations, 35, 38, 179, 201, 205. *See
 also* allotments; distinctions; divisions
disorder. *See* chaos and disorder
dispositions, 12, 14, 19–22, 29–30, 36,
 40, 59, 65–67, 81, 104, 108, 147, 176,
 197, 199–200, 202, 204, 206, 209–10,
 213–15, 218–20, 232, 236, 243–44, 246,
 248–51, 253–55, 299–300, 335
distinctions, 35, 40, 59, 86, 105–7, 111,
 115–16, 119, 124, 157, 186, 211, 214,
 222–23, 236, 238, 252, 335. *See also* allotments; differentiations; divisions
divisions, 5, 21, 25, 29–30, 35, 38, 40–41,
 57, 59n. 25, 68–70, 76, 83–85, 88, 106,
 109, 111–13, 119, 124, 163–64, 185–86,
 191, 198–99, 201, 211, 214, 248, 258,
 260–61, 305–6, 315–16, 365n. a (chap.
 9). *See also* allotments; differentiations;
 distinctions

Documents, 5–6, 29–30, 60, 63, 179, 291n.
 19, 307n. 103, **344**–45, 379n. b; quota-
 tions from, 15, 70, 84, 92, 117, 125,
 137, 143, 151, 182, 184, 188, 259, 319
Dongye Bi, 338
drinking ceremony, 222–23
Duan Yucai, 371n. h
Duanmu Si. *See* Zigong (子貢)
Duke Ai of Lu, 325, 333–37, 384n. c
Duke Bai, 33
Duke Ding, 338
Duke Huan of Lu, 308n. 107, 318
Duke Huan of Qi, 47–48, 72, 100, 112,
 138, 148n. 15, 150–51, 256, 260, 324,
 337
Duke Ling of Wey, 32
Duke Mu of Qin, 264, 299
Duke of Guo. *See* Zhang Fu
Duke of Shao, 111
Duke of Xue, 101. *See also* Meng Chang;
 Tian Chang
Duke of Yu, 264n. 14
Duke of Zhou, xxiv, xxxi, 1n. 5, 21n. 20,
 32–33, 37n. 21, 48, 52–53, 60–62, 81,
 112, 138, 143n. 5, 226–27, 260, 304,
 319, 340–41
Duke Si of Wey, 70
Duke Wen of Jin, 100, 148n. 15, 150–51,
 337
Duke Wu Chen of Shen, 339
Duke Zhuang of Lu, 72
Duke Zigao of Ye, 33

Earth, 1, 8, 16–17, 20–21, 44, 55, 63, 65,
 69, 74–75, 77, 87, 89–90, 108, 116,
 120–21, 140, 145, 176–80, 196, 202,
 203n. 8, 204, 206, 210–11, 214, 221–22,
 229, 254, 279, 284, 296, 297n. 46, 339,
 346, 360n. g
emotions. *See* dispositions
emptiness, xxx, 228–29

fa (法), 117n. 1. *See also* law; models
Fan Sui, 171
Fanruo (bow), 256
farmers, 12, 27–28, 30, 55, 66–67, 74, 76,
 78, 83, 95n. 24, 106, 110, 116, 123, 195,
 230, 255, 306, 311
fathers, 45, 119, 143, 214, 292; relations
 with sons, 20, 26, 34–35, 66, 75–76, 87,
 146, 179, 209, 218, 250, 254, 291, 296–
 97, 319, 325–26
Fei Lian, **61**, 140, 225, 263, 373n. a (chap.
 25)

fen (分). *See* allotments; divisions

Feng (section of *Odes*), 60, 311, 312n. 123

Feng Yang, 134

feudal lords, xiii, **25–26**, 42, 48, 61–62, 64, 67, 71–72, 79, 85, 99–100, 106–8, 110, 112, 122–24, 129, 131, 133, 146–48, 150, 156, 162, 169–70, 184–85, 189, 192–93, 198, 202–3, 207, 215, 224, 246, 278, 288–89, 290n. 12, 296, 302, 304–5, 312–13, 336, 339, 342, 364n. g

filial piety, 50, 54, 70, 76, 78, 207–8, 210, 212, 215, 226, 250, 253–55, 270, 291, 301n. 72, 308, 310, 315n. 135, 316, 319, 325–27, 332

fixation, 22n. 21, 141, 224–29, 273n. 58, 342

former kings, **1**, 6, 21n. 20, 28–30, 37, 41, 43, 53, 55 63, 70, 85, 90, 91n. 16, 93, 120, 165, 184, 200–201, 203n. 11, 207, 214–16, 218–20, 227, 256, 260, 291, 307, 320. *See also* later kings; sage king(s)

Fu Liyi, 319

Fu Xi, **194n. 45**, 265

Fu You, 231

Fu Yue, 33

funerals, 73, 75, 111, 195–96, 207–9, 211–12, 215, 293, 301n. 71, 303n. 37. *See also* mourning

Ganjiang (sword), 256

Gao Heng, 379n. c

Gao Yao, 33, 270

Gaocai (state), 165

Gaozi, 1n. 2, 248n. 2

gentleman, xxiv, 1–9, 12–32, 35–39, 41, 43, 45–48, 51, 55–59, 66–67, 69–70, 74–75, 84, 87, 97, 103, 107, 111, 117–18, 120, 128, 138–39, 141–42, 144, 151, 156, 166, 170, 178–79, 199, 201, 205–7, 209–10, 213, 214n. 41, 216, 220–21, 230–31, 234–35, 240–42, 247, 249, 253, 255, 258n. 1, 261, 266–68, 277–80, 292–93, 296, 298, 307–12, 314–15, 317–18, 321–24, 327–28, 330–34, 338, 340, **344**, 346, 360n. g, 361n. d, 362n. g, 367n. b (chap. 14), 371n. d

Gong (mountain), 61

Gong Gong, **155**, 270

Gong Shen, 54

Gongshu, 330

Gongsun Long, 13n. 18, 56n. 18, 205n. 24, 238n. 6, 239n. 8, 240n. 19

Gongsun Lü, 32

Gongsunzi, 164

Gongxing Zizhi, 303

Gongyangzhuan, 308n. 107

Gongzhi Qi, 342

government, 5, 20, 25, 36, 48, 68, 70–71, 74, 77, 79–80, 84–85, 93, 94, 98, 100–101, 108, 110, 114–16, 119, 122, 126, 133, 141, 143, 148, 156, 160, 162–4, 168, 173, 178–79, 182, 224, 259, 294, 302, 312, 318, 335, 343. *See also* chaos and disorder; lords; ministers; order; rulers

Grand Duke (office), 79

Grand Duke (person). *See* Lü Shang

grand *xiang* (大饗) sacrifice, 203

Gu Fu lance, 24

Gu Qianli, 95n. 26, 229n. 14

Guan Longfeng, 225, 323

Guan Shu, **52**, 319

Guan Zhong, **47**, 48n. 6, 71, 112, 134, 138, 183n. 1, 226, 260, 303, 319, 337n. 16

Guanzi, 47

Gubu Ziqing, 32

Gun (Yu's father), 269n. 40

Guo Qingfan, 363n. c (chap. 7)

Guofeng. See *Feng* (section of *Odes*)

Gusu, 323

Han (dynasty), xx, xxxi, 196n. 52, 277n.

Han (people), **1**

Han (river), 158, 307

Han (state), 134, 157n. 52, 162, 170

Han Feizi (person or text) xix, 121n. 18, 183n. 1; references to text of, xxv n. 16, 10n. 9, 15n. 24, 36n. 19, 152n. 31, 159n. 56, 235n. 29, 274n. 69, 275n. 71, 286n. 32, 362n. a (chap. 5), 368n. e, 382n. u

Han Shu, 135n. 3, 362n. g

Han Yu, xx

Hanshi Waizhuan, xxi, 377–78n. m

Hao (place), 100, 110, 162, 189

Hao Yixing, 215n. 44, 270n. 47, 295n. 37, 361n. a

Harbsmeier, Christoph, 360n. b

harm, 15, 22, 24–27, 28n. 12, 29, 35, 42, 83, 85, 113, 129, 139, 144, 152, 155, 159–60, 185, 197, 202, 258, 270, 304

He (river). *See* Yellow River

heart, xxx, 3–5, 8–9, 11–12, 18–20, 28, 32, 43, 45, 48, 51, 62, 66, 72, 80, 83, 90, 98–101, 108, 118, 126, 131, 137, 146, 164–65, 173, 176, 178, 192, 218, 220–

heart (*cont.*)
    21, 224, 225–32, 235–38, 241–44, 246,
    249–50, 254, 257–58, 266, 269, 272,
    290, 292, 297n. 47, 303–4, 315, 318–19,
    323–24, 333–34, 341–42, 372nn. d and
    f, 379n. d, 384n. a (chap. 31)
Heaven, xxix–xxx, **1**, 8, 15–18, 20–21,
    25, 34, 44, 51, 55, 58, 63, 65–66, 68–69,
    74–75, 77, 79, 84, 87–91, 108, 116,
    120–21, 140, 142, 145, 163, 168, 171,
    175–81, 193–94, 196, 202, 203n. 7, 204,
    206, 210–11, 214–15, 221–22, 227, 229,
    238, 243–44, 249, 252–54, 266, 278–79,
    284, 286–87, 290, 294, 296, 297n. 46,
    305–7, 309, 323, 330–31, 335, 339, 340,
    346, 360n. g, 371–72n. a (chap. 20),
    377n. l. *See also* Son of Heaven
hegemon, xxv, xxviii, **33**, 47–48, 71–73,
    79, 82, 99–104, 111–12, 117, 126, 132,
    148n. 15, 151, 163, 170n. 24, 172, 173n.
    36, 180, 260, 264, 277, 288, 317, 324,
    339, 369n. f. *See also* Duke Huan of Qi;
    Duke Wen of Jin; King Goujian of
    Yue; King Helü of Wu; King Zhuang
    of Chu
Heng Ge, 270
Hoashi Banri, 368n. i
Hong Yao, 33
honor and disgrace, 3, 23–27, 30, 44, 58,
    73, 99, 109, 126, 133, 160, 198–99, 256
Hou Han Shu, 361n. a, 369n. a (chap.
    16), 378n. n
Hou Ji, 231, 270
Hu (music), 62, 192, 193n. 39, 201, 216,
    298
Hu (people), 170
Hu (sword), 256
Hu Ba, 5
Hua Liu, 256
Hua Shi, 319
Huai (river), 61
Huainanzi, 378n. o
Huan (music), 216
Huan Dou, 155
Hui Shi, 13n. 18, 16, 40n. 1, 41, 56, 205n.
    24, 227, 240n. 14, 266n. 23
human nature, xxv–xxviii, 14, 20n. 18,
    26–27, 40, 41n. 6, 59, 65–67, 81, 191,
    202, 210, 211n. 35, 218, 233, 236, 244,
    246, 248–54, 257, 277, 300, 334
hundred kings, 21, 59–60, 106, 110–11,
    169, 181, 188, 200, 212, 214–15. *See also*
    sage king(s)
Huo Shu, 61

Ikai Hikohiro, 363n. a (chap. 8), 365n. b
    (chap. 11), 369n. b (chap. 16), 374nn.
    g and i, 379n. f, 383n. ee
integrity, 12, **19**–20, 38, 103, 130, 170,
    183, 221, 267, 276, 308, 312, 314, 339
Ivanhoe, P. J., xxvi n. 17, 371n. e

Ji (clan), **52**, 61, 129
Ji (guesser of riddles), 230n. 19, 231–
    32
Ji (star), 97
Ji (thinker), 266
Ji Lu, 309, 382n. u
Ji Sun, 319
Jiang (clan), 129
Jian Shu, 300n. 66
Jie (tyrant), xxxi, **7**, 22, 27–29, 33, 35, 49,
    63, 79, 81, 110, 126, 135n. 2, 136, 137n.
    13, 146–47, 150–51, 156n. 46, 157, 166–
    68, 173, 175, 177, 184–86, 196, 199, 225,
    253, 260, 263, 271n. 51, 278, 304, 343
Jie Yu, 343
Jin (state), 100, 134, 148n. 15, 151, 226,
    264n. 14, 306, 324, 337n. 16, 342
jing (靜). *See* stillness
Jiu Fan, 134
Jixia, xix
Jizi, **61**, 135, 158, 186, 264, 301, 343,
    373n. a (chap. 25)
Ju (state), 47, 324
Juan Shuliang, 233, 372–73n. h
Jue (sword), 256
Jujue (sword), 256
Jun Chou, 291
junzi (君子). *See* gentleman
Jushi (bow), 256

Kaiyang (place), 167
ke (可). *See* approval
King Cheng of Zhou, 32n. 1, 49, 50n. 12,
    52–53, 61, 111, 138, 260, 304–5, 340
King Fuchai of Wu, 135n. 4, 138
King Goujian of Yue, 100, 151, 324
King Helü of Wu, 100, 146n. 6, 151, 256,
    343
King Huai of Chu, 169n. 20
King Kang of Zhou, 305
King Kuai of Yan, 303n. 86
King Li of Zhou, 273
King Ling of Chu, 121n. 22
King Min of Qi, 72, 99, 101
King Wen of Zhou, xxiv, xxxi, 1n. 5,
    21n. 20, 32, 37n. 21, 44n. 11, 48–49,
    52–53, 75, 86n. 8, 111, 117, 129, 131,

155, 177, 184n. 4, 225, 256, 264n. 11, 265, 304, 311n. 119, 319, 340
King Wu of Zhou, xxiv, xxxi, 1n. 5, 7n. 30, 21n. 20, 29, 32n. 1, 37n. 21, 48, 50n. 12, 52–53, 61–62, 100, 110–11, 113–14, 140, 145, 147n. 11, 148n. 15, 150, 154nn. 38 and 39, 155, 157, 162, 166–69, 184–86, 188, 193n. 39, 201n. 4, 264–65, 278, 301, 304, 340, 342, 370n. c, 373n. a (chap. 25)
King Wuding of Shang, 33n. 11
King Xian of Song, 99
King Xiaocheng of Zhao, 145, 148, 151
King Xuan of Qi, 303
King Xuan of Zhou, 119n. 8, 161n. 64
King Yan of Xu, 33
King You of Zhou, 273
King Zhao of Qin, 53–55
King Zhuang of Chu, 100, 121, 151, 339–40
Kjellberg, Paul, 2n. 13
Kline, T. C. III, xxvi n. 17
Kongzi. See Confucius
Kongzi Jiayu, xxi, 324n. 26
Kuaiji, 324
Kuang (state), 265n. 16, 285, 343
Kubo Ai, 368n. f, 370n. e, 371nn. a and f (chap. 19), 374n. g, 383n. a
Kuhn, Dieter, 376n. f
Kui, 231, 270

Lai (state), 342
Laozi, xx, xxiii, xxv–xxvi, 181. See also Daodejing
later kings, 21, 35, 63–64, 67, 73, 236, 239, 265, 266n. 24. See also former kings
Lau, D.C., xvii, 232n. 24
law, 24–26, 41, 54, 56, 79–80, 99, 115–16, 119, 161, 163, 165, 180, 227, 252, 254, 275–76, 288, 315, 345. See also punishments
learning, 1–2, 5–8, 14, 56–57, 63–64, 66, 68, 206, 224, 233–34, 249, 251, 254, 286, 291, 307, 309–11, 322–23, 332
li (禮). See ritual
Li Disheng, 361n. e, 366n. d
Li Si, xix, **156**, 157nn. 50 and 51, 172n. 32
Li Xian, 369n. a (chap. 16)
Li Zhongsheng, 374n. h
Liang (place), 32
Liang Qixiong, 362nn. f and g, 374n. f, 381n. q

Liao Jilang, 370n. a, 371n. h, 374n. k, 383n. b
Lifu, 287
Lifu Xu. See Tou Xu
Liji, xxi, xxvii n. 18, 298n. 58, 301n. 72, 369n. a (chap. 16), 380n. h
Ling (place), 170
Lingyin Zixi, 33
Linlü, 170
Liu Shipei, 266n. 23, 269n. 42, 314n. 130, 341n. 5, 364n. c, 369n. b (chap 17), 374n. a, 380n. i, 382n. y
Liu Xiang, xviii, xix, 277n.
Liuxia Hui, 265n. 17, 313, 382n. x
Long Yuchun, 18n. 14, 362n. c, 366n. c, 367n. b (chap. 13), 370n. d, 372n. a (chap 21), 373n. b (chap. 22)
Lord Chunshen, **265**, 286n. 35
Lord Linwu, 145, 148, 151, 153, 155
Lord on High. See Shang Di
Lord Pingyuan, **135**
Lord Xinling, **135**, 139
Lord Zhuang, 256
lords, 20, 34–35, 53, 55, 70, 75–76, 79, 81, 83, 85, 88, 90, 96–97, 104–5, 108–9, 110–13, 117, 119, 121, 123, 132, 134–36, 143, 147–48, 163, 165–68, 173, 180, 184–86, 202, 214–15, 224–25, 235, 240, 246, 252–53, 263, 274–76, 288, 296–97, 300, 303–5, 308–9, 313, 316, 341–42. See also feudal lords; rulers
lou (陋). See boorishness
loyalty, 9, 12, 26, 39, 51, 54, 58, 92–93, 96, 107, 109, 114, 116, 118, 119–20, 133–34, 136–39, 140nn. 21 and 22, 141, 159, 167–68, 171, 173, 207–8, 215–16, 225, 248, 255, 257, 261, 263, 272–73, 286, 294n. 35, 301n. 72, 316, 323, 325, 334, 339
Lu (state), 5n. 21, 54, 72, 189, 254, 265n. 17, 303n. 83, 306, 318–19, 324–25, 327, 333, 335–37, 340–41, 345
Lu (sword), 256
Lü Shang, 111, 129, 134, 225, 256, 264, 319
Lu Wenchao, 378n. n
Lü'er, 256
Lüju, 286

Ma Rong, 374n. e
markers, 67, 93, 181, 275, 291
Marquis Cheng of Wey, 70
Marquis of Ying. See Fan Sui
Marquis Wu of Wei, 339–40

Mei, Y.P., 2n. 9

Mencius (person or text), xi, xv, xx, xxv–xxvi, 40n. 1, 41, 232, 249, 252, 303; references to text of, 1n. 2, 8n. 34, 10n. 5, 28n. 13, 34n. 14, 37n. 23, 77n. 20, 109n. 22, 121n. 17, 135n. 2, 147n. 10, 175n. 3, 190n. 26, 191n. 31, 243n. 25, 248n. 2, 269n. 42, 270n. 49, 286nn. 32 and 37, 292n. 25, 293n. 27, 316n. 139, 328n. 8, 369n. g, 374n. e, 384n. a (chap 29)

Meng Chang, 134. See also Duke of Xue; Tian Chang

Meng Ke. See Mencius

Mengzi. See Mencius

merchants, 24–25, 30, 66–67, 74, 85, 95, 106, 110, 116, 123, 195, 230, 255, 306

Miao (people), 155. See also San Miao

Miao Ji, 151

military affairs. See war and military affairs

mind. See heart

Ming Tiao, 157

ministers, 26, 30, 34, 42–44, 53–54, 58–59, 62, 67–68, 71, 75–76, 81–83, 88, 94–95, 99–101, 105–6, 109–10, 112–13, 115–16, 118–19, 121, 123–24, 126, 128–37, 146, 153–54, 158, 165–68, 171, 192–93, 198, 202–3, 207–8, 215, 218, 225–26, 258, 262–64, 274, 276, 286, 288, 295–97, 299–300, 302, 304, 306, 313, 326–27, 332, 339, 341

Minzi Qian, 253

Mo (people), 1, 170

Mo Di. See Mozi (person or text)

Mo Xi, 225

models, 5–6, 14–15, 18, 28, 35, 37–38, 41–43, 53, 59, 63–65, 67, 69, 73–74, 84, 94, 98, 102–3, 106–7, 109–11, 113, 115, 117n. 1, 123–24, 127, 131–32, 139, 142, 160, 196, 199, 205, 213, 234, 237, 248–251, 255, 260, 265, 276, 279, 302, 312, 315–16, 322, 330, 334, 342, 383n. cc

Mohism, xxv, xxix, 195n. 47, 197n. 55, 202, 212, 223, 239n. 13. See also Mozi (person or text)

Momu, 287

mothers, 214, 291

Mou Guang, 271

Mount Chang, 170

Mount Fangcheng, 158

Mount Min, 327

Mount Tai, 150, 199

Mount Ting, 225

mourning, xxvii, 203n. 9, 204, 208–10, 213–16, 217n. 48, 220, 291, 293, 295–96, 302, 327n. 4, 333, 337. See also funerals

Moye, 146, 163, 256

Mozi (person or text), xxv, xxvii–xxviii, 12, **13n. 16**, 40, 56, 63, 88–91, 106, 109n. 22, 181, 208n. 30, 218–21, 226, 266n. 23, 267; references to text of, 201n. 1, 263n. 3, 268n. 35. See also Mohism

music, 5–6, 12, 13n. 16, 29–30, 37, 47, 60, 62, 73, 77–79, 85, 89, 91, 108, 112, 139, 163–64, 171, 209, 211, 218–23, 225, 231, 266, 270, 281, 282n. 17, 293, 307n. 103, 316, 337, 359–60n. c, 380n. h. See also Hu (music); Shao (music); Wu (music); Xiang (music); Yong (music)

Music Master Kuang, 316

naming, 198, 236–43, 373n. a (chap. 22)

Nanguo Huizi, 331

nature: of Heaven, 196; of humans (see human nature); of myriad things, 335

Needham, Joseph, 376n. f

Ning Qi, 226

Nivison, David, xxviii n. 19, 250n. 4

Odes, xv–xvi, 5–6, 29–30, 60, 63, 204n. 21, 266n. 25, 271n. 50, 307n. 103, 308, **344–45**, 371n. d, 377nn. l and m, 379n. a; quotations from, 1, 4, 7, 9, 11, 14, 16–18, 31, 35, 38, 44–45, 49–50, 55, 57–59, 66, 74–75, 86–88, 90–91, 97, 104, 107, 119, 122, 126, 131, 136, 138–42, 144, 147, 154, 156, 161, 169, 173, 177–78, 184, 194, 206, 211, 214, 225–26, 229–30, 235, 241–43, 258, 260–61, 288–90, 301, 309–11, 313, 319–21, 325, 330–31, 342. See also Feng (section of Odes); Song (section of Odes); Ya (section of Odes)

Ogyu Sorai, 372n. e

order, 19, 21, 26, 28–29, 36, 55–57, 59–60, 68–70, 75–76, 86, 88, 94, 97, 100, 104–6, 109–12, 114, 117–18, 120, 123–24, 128, 132, 142, 144, 148, 150, 155, 157, 159, 170–71, 173, 175–77, 181, 183, 187–88, 191, 200, 202, 205, 210–11, 215, 220–21, 223–24, 228, 237, 241, 243–45, 248–49, 252–53, 265–69, 274, 276, 291, 295, 300, 304, 306, 315–16. See also chaos and disorder

Pan Zhi, 319
Pan Zhonggui, 160n. 63
parents, 24, 54, 76, 207, 213, 255, 310–11,
316, 325–26, 332. *See also* fathers;
mothers
Peng Men, 107, 194
Peng Zu, 10
persuasion, 23, 37–38, 43, 114, 125, 131,
238, 240–42, 314–15
petty man, 5–6, 9, 12, 17–18, 21–28, 32,
39, 43, 48, 56, 63, 66, 69, 87, 103–4, 115,
126, 139, 142, 144, 178, 187, 199, 205,
221, 235, 249, 253, 255, 277, 308, 311,
313, 315, 319, 322, 326, 328–29, 340
Pilü (sword), 256
Prince Bi Gan. *See* Bi Gan
Prince Chong'er of Jin. *See* Duke Wen of
Jin
profit, 1, 11–12, 15, 48–49, 63, 83, 93,
95–97, 101, 103, 108, 115, 118, 127,
150–52, 160, 163, 167–68, 180, 191,
196–97, 199, 223, 227, 236, 242, 248,
253, 260, 268, 274, 288, 303–5, 313,
330, 382n. x. *See also* benefit
Pu (place), 306, 308n. 107
punishments, 25–26, 44, 48–49, 68, 72–
74, 78, 80–81, 89–90, 92–93, 99–100,
108, 115, 119, 125, 135–36, 141, 143–
44, 147, 149, 152, 157–60, 163–65, 185,
187–88, 216, 221, 236, 240, 252, 259–
60, 267, 275, 291–92, 302, 305, 319–20,
370–71n. h

Qi (戚, place), 61
Qi (齊, state), xix, 16, 47, 99–101, 112,
133–34, 148n. 15, 149–51, 157n. 52,
162, 166–67, 170, 189, 254, 303, 306,
308n. 107, 309n. 109, 324, 337n. 16, 342
qi (氣), **10**–12, 15, 76, 121, 191, 213, 218,
220–21, 233, 279
Qi Ji (horse), 3, 13, 256
Qi Si, 33
Qiang (people), 303
Qin (dynasty), xix–xx, xxxi
Qin (state), xix, 16, 53, 80n. 25, 98n. 33,
101, 107, 134, 135nn. 5 and 6, 148n. 15,
149–51, 156–58, 162, 169–72, 254,
259n. 6, 264, 300n. 66, 342
qing (情). *See* dispositions
Qinqiu, 341n. 5
Quedang, 54

Ran Qiu, **319**
Ran Yong. *See* Zigōng (子弓)

rectification of names, 373n. a (chap. 22)
ren (仁), xiii, xxiv, 6–7, 15, 19, 22, 27–30,
33, 35, 39, 41–43, 48, 51, 55, 57, 64, 73,
80, 84, 86–87, 96–97, 99, 101–3, 107,
111, 121, 126, 138–40, 145–47, 150,
151n. 28, 155–57, 166, 168, 198, 226–
27, 232, 242, 254, 256–57, 261, 266,
285–86, 289–90, 292–93, 301n. 72, 303,
314, 325, 328, 331, 334, 336, 342, **345**
ritual, xxiv–xxv, xxvii–xxix, 5–7, 10–12,
13n. 16, 14, 16, 19, 21, 28–30, 35, 37,
41, 43–45, 52nn. 4 and 6, 53–55, 59,
60, 62–64, 66–68, 70–71, 73, 75–76, 79,
84–85, 93–94, 96, 98–99, 101, 102n. 5,
103–4, 106, 108, 110–11, 114–15, 118–
21, 124, 127, 132, 139, 141, 143, 148,
150, 151n. 26, 157, 159–60, 162–64,
167–68, 173, 174n. 38, 178–81, 185,
191, 199n. 62, 201–2, 204–13, 214n. 41,
216, 219–21, 223, 234, 236, 242, 248–
54, 256, 258, 266–67, 278, 281, 282n.
17, 285, 288–95, 296n. 43, 297–99, 301,
307n. 103, 308–9, 312, 314–16, 325–27,
330, 334n. 5, 338, 341–42, 344–**45**,
359–60n. c (chap. 1), 360n. f, 361n. c,
364n. e, 377n. k, 379nn. a and d, 381n.
s, 384nn. c and d; as markers, 181, 291.
See also drinking ceremony; funerals;
mourning; sacrificial rites
Robber Zhi, 7, 16, 27–28, 63, 81, 147,
253, 278, 279n. 7, 361n. a
Rong (people), 170, 189
Ru (river), 158
ru (儒), xxiv–xxvi, xxix–xxx, **6**, 37, 41, 46,
52–55, 62–64, 67, 90, 106, 115–16, 172,
202, 213, 220, 237, 265, 315, 325, 364n. i
rulers, 43, 49, 58, 64, 67, 71, 88, 92, 94–
96, 98–99, 101–3, 105–15, 117, 122,
126–32, 135–36, 139, 142–43, 158–59,
164–65, 169, 173, 183–84, 218, 262–63,
275, 290, 306, 337. *See also* feudal
lords; lords

sacrificial rites, 54n. 11, 73, 75, 77, 91n.
16, 111, 179, 192nn. 34 and 35, 202–4,
212, 215–17, 222, 233, 291n. 23, 295n.
41, 297, 301n. 71, 327, 333n. 2, 337,
384n. d
sage(s), xxiv–xxvii, xxviii n. 19, 3, 5, 14,
20, 30, 33nn. 8 and 11, 34n. 14, 36, 39,
41n. 6, 42–43, 46, 51, 53, 56–57, 59–60,
64, 66, 77, 80, 84, 87, 102n. 5, 121, 128,
133, 157, 176, 186–87, 191, 206, 210–
12, 214, 216, 220, 224, 227, 232, 234,

sage(s) (*cont.*)
239, 241, 249–51, 253–55, 260–61, 266–69, 271, 278, 286, 291, 296, 315, 318, 330, 333, 335, 342–44, 363n. d, 364nn. c and e, 370nn. b and c, 377n. l, 384n. c. *See also* Confucius; sage king(s); Zigōng (子弓)
sage king(s), xxiv–xxv, xxviii, xxxi, 5n. 20, 10n. 7, 16n. 3, 21n. 20, 24, 33n. 12, 35, 39, 42–43, 74n. 12, 77, 106, 108, 124, 137n. 13, 156n. 46, 167, 171n. 29, 184–85, 190n. 26, 191, 194n. 45, 195, 198–99, 200n. 64, 214, 220, 226n. 8, 237, 240, 248, 252–53, 258, 260, 261n. 8, 265n. 21, 286n. 32, 316n. 139, 339n. 2, 344–46, 373n. a (chap. 22). *See also* Duke of Zhou; former kings; King Wen of Zhou; King Wu of Zhou; later kings; Shun (sage); Tang (sage); true king(s); Yao (sage); Yu (sage)
San Miao, 269. *See also* Miao (people)
Shan Juan, 268
Shang (dynasty), xxxi, 7n. 30, 14n. 22, 33nn. 11 and 12, 44, 52, 61, 134, 135n. 2, 154, 188, 236, 263n. 5, 264n. 10, 271n. 51, 301n. 74, 370n. c. *See also* Yin (dynasty)
Shang (place), 271
Shang Di, **14**, 44, 87, 114, 163, 193
Shang Jun (son of Shun), 269n. 41
Shang Rong, 301
Shang Yang, 205n. 25. See also *Book of Lord Shang*; Wey Yang
Shangdang, 162
Shangjun Shu. See *Book of Lord Shang*
Shanhaijing, 378n. o
Shao (music), **62**, 192, 201, 216, 220, 298
Shao Zhengmao, 318
Shayi, 169
Shen (place), 339
shen (神). *See* spirits; spirit-like power; spirit-like state
Shen Buhai, 183n. 1, 205n. 25, 227
Shen Dao, 40n. 1, 41, 56, 181n. 22, 187n. 17, 205n. 25, 227, 266n. 23
Shen Gui, 54
Shen Sheng, 226
Shen You, 54
sheng (聖). *See* sage(s)
Sheng Du, 231
sheng wang (聖王). *See* sage king(s)
Shentu Di, 16
shi (士). *See* well-bred man

Shi (詩). See *Odes*
Shi Fu, 319
Shi Ji, 383
Shi Qiu, 22, 40
shu (恕), 332
Shu Qi, 251n. 5
Shun (sage), xxiv, xxxi, **16**–17, 21n. 20, 32–33, 36n. 18, 42, 46, 62n. 40, 80, 97, 109, 155, 169–70, 190–91, 193–94, 201n. 5, 230–31, 253, 255, 257, 259, 268–69, 270nn. 47 and 49, 279, 291, 304, 306–7, 316, 317n. 141, 325, 335–36, 338–39, 379n. b
Shuo Yuan, 361n. a
Shuowen Jiezi, 371n. h, 376n. f
Si (river), 61
Si Guan, 225
Sima Ziqi, 33
single-mindedness, xxx, 4, 7, 12, 19n. 17, 49, 60, 63–64, 228–31, 236, 254, 261, 267, 310, 339, 359n. b
Son of Heaven, **7**, 25, 26n. 8, 30, 52, 61, 67, 85, 106, 108, 111, 123–24, 126, 184, 186, 189n. 20, 190–93, 198, 201, 203–4, 207, 215, 244, 258, 264n. 15, 288–89, 293–94, 298, 303–4, 307, 309, 312, 320, 364n. g, 370nn. b and c
Song (section of *Odes*), **60**, 218
Song (state), 99, 101, 154, 162, 226, 264
Song Xing. *See* Songzi
Songzi, 40, 182, 197–200, 226, 239n. 11, 240n. 15
sons. *See* fathers: relations with sons; filial piety
spirits: of the dead and other entities, xxix, 2, 4n. 16, 91n. 16, 163, 179, 192n. 35, 193, 211–12, 216n. 47, 233n. 27, 280n. 12, 281n. 16; as parts of human psychology, 176, 229, 232
spirit-like power, 2n. 10, 3, 12, 19, 22, 43, 65, 74, 75n. 12, 77, 142, 153, 176, 240, 254, 259, 280n. 12, 281. *See also* spirit-like state
spirit-like state, **2**, 38, 60, 155, 160, 267, 343. *See also* spirit-like power
Spring and Autumn Annals, 5–6, 60, 299, 300n. 66, 307n. 103, 308, **345**
stillness, 44, 228–29
study. *See* learning
Su Qin, 133
Suiren, **194**
Sun Wu. *See* Sunzi
Sun Yirang, 363n. a (chap 8), 371n. h
Sunshu Ao, 33, 134, 341

Sunzi, 145n. 2
Sunzi Bingfa, 145n. 2, 152n. 33, 368n. h

Tai Hao. *See* Fu Xi
Tang (sage), xxiv, xxxi, **7n. 30**, 29, 31n.
    19, 33, 36, 62n. 40, 95, 100, 110–11,
    113–14, 135n. 2, 137n. 12, 140, 145,
    147n. 11, 148n. 15, 150, 155, 162,
    166–69, 173, 184–86, 188, 193n. 39,
    201n. 5, 225, 257, 271, 278, 305, 319,
    370n. c
Tang Ju, 32
Tang Mie, 157
Tang Yang, 226
Tao Hongqing, 370n. c
teachers, 9, 11–12, 14, 28, 55, 65, 74–75,
    144, 154, 173, 198, 202, 234, 248–49,
    257, 275, 291n. 20, 308, 312, 323, 339–
    40, 360n. d
tian (天). *See* Heaven
Tian Chang, 343. *See also* Duke of Xue;
    Meng Chang
Tian Dan, 151, **162**
Tian Pian, 40n. 1, 41
Tian Yi. *See* Tang (sage)
Tian Zhong, 22, 40
Tou Xu, 337n. 16
true king(s), 48, 68–69, 71–74, 75n. 13,
    79–82, 86, 99–100, 102–4, 107–9, 111,
    113, 117, 132–33, 141, 145, 148, 150–
    51, 152n. 30, 153, 155, 162–63, 171–72,
    173n. 36, 180, 186, 189–90, 198, 219,
    222–23, 234–35, 237, 260, 266, 268,
    277, 288, 290, 301, 339, 368n. h, 369n.
    f. *See also* sage king(s)
trustworthiness, xxviii, 12, 21–23, 26, 42,
    45, 51, 54, 58, 92–94, 96, 99, 101, 102–
    3, 107, 114, 116, 118, 137, 139, 142,
    144, 148, 152, 159, 167–68, 170–71,
    173, 216, 248, 257, 276, 314, 325, 331,
    334, 337, 383n. aa
tyrant. *See* Jie; Zhòu
Tsukada Taiho, 368nn. j and l, 374n. l
Tuo Xiao, 40

unworthy person(s), 2, 15, 43–44, 48, 51,
    56, 58, 68, 89–90, 114, 126, 134, 138–
    39, 142, 256, 306, 323, 339

Van Norden, Bryan, 250n. 4
Vertical and Horizontal alliances, **80**,
    283n. 19, 285n. 26
villainy, 9, 11, 15, 18, 39, 44, 65, 81, 93,
    123–24, 127, 134–36, 138–39, 147, 154,

185, 188, 195–96, 212, 223, 234, 248,
    294, 312, 319, 337
virtue, xxiv, 2n. 10, 3, 5, 8, 17, 19n. 16,
    20, 22n. 23, 25, 38n. 29, 43–45, 49, 51,
    56, 58–59, 67–68, 72–73, 79, 83–88, 92,
    100, 106, 114, 123, 125–26, 129, 137–
    38, 143–44, 156, 159–64, 173, 178,
    184–85, 188, 190–91, 198, 221, 224,
    227, 229, 241, 259, 267–70, 279–80,
    285, 290, 307, 313, 321n. 16, 322–23,
    331, 334, 340, 343, **345**

Wan (place), 157
Wang Liang, 107, 194
Wang Niansun, 301n. 72, 359n. a, 360n. f
    (chap. 1), 360nn. a and c (chap. 2),
    362n. g, 364n. j, 366n. d, 367n. a
    (chap. 14), 369n. a (chap. 17), 371n. e,
    374n. m
Wang Tianhai, 303n. 86, 362n. d, 364n.
    h, 367nn. b and c (chap. 15), 368nn. h
    and i, 369nn. d and f, 370n. g, 374n. k,
    378n. o, 379nn. c and d, 381n. l, 382n.
    v, 383n. bb
Wang Xianqian, xiv, 237n. 2, 359, 361n.
    a, 366n. a, 372n. h
Wang Zhonglin, 365n. f
war and military affairs, 31, 48–49, 61–
    62, 71–72, 80–81, 94, 96, 98, 100, 115–
    16, 121, 136, 145–65, 170, 188, 219–20,
    264, 277, 306, 319
Watson, Burton, xii, xv, xvii, 211n. 35
Way, the, xxiv–xxvi, 2, 5, 7, 12–13, 15,
    18, 20–21, 36, 45, 49, 52, 54, 58–60, 79,
    99, 105, 124, 127, 133, 135, 137, 142,
    160, 163–64, 166, 168, 175, 177, 186,
    190, 195, 206, 215, 218–19, 221, 224–
    25, 227–32, 234, 237, 240–42, 244–45,
    249, 260, 285, 292–93, 299, 306n. 98,
    315, 320, 322, 325, 334–35, 340, **345–
    46**; as distinct from the ways of
    Heaven and Earth, 55; marked out by
    ritual, 181; as the way of a true lord,
    123
wei (偽). *See* deliberate effort
Wei (魏, state), 32n. 3, 135, 148n. 15,
    149–50, 157, 162, 167, 170, 339–40
Weizi Qi, **154**, 225, 264, 368n. g
well-bred man, 3, 5, 12–14, 24–25, 37, 39,
    44–45, 57, 67, 70, 122, 127, 131–33,
    142, 145, 148, 154, 162, 165, 169, 190,
    206–7, 216, 234, 242, 255, 289, 309,
    326, 328, 332–34, 340–41, **346**
Wen, Duke of Jin. *See* Duke Wen of Jin

Wey (衛, state), 32, 145n. 2, 189, 220, 306, 308n. 107
Wey Yang, 151. See also *Book of Lord Shang*; Shang Yang
wisdom, 11, 19–20, 24, 29–30, 38, 41n. 6, 43, 47, 48n. 7, 50, 55–57, 67, 80, 83–84, 86, 112, 114, 121, 126–27, 130–31, 152, 177–78, 190–91, 226–27, 237, 242, 245, 257, 271, 279n. 7, 314, 328, 331, 342
wives, 54, 75, 84, 120, 166n. 10, 179, 186, 207, 232, 254–55, 291n. 22, 296–98, 301n. 72, 311, 316
women, 16, 34–35, 84, 108, 114, 179, 195, 297, 305, 336. *See also* mothers; wives
worthy person(s), 9, 15, 27, 34, 38, 42, 44, 48, 50–51, 55–56, 58, 64, 68, 70, 73–74, 77, 80, 88–90, 93–94, 103, 107, 109, 114, 118, 124, 126, 132, 134, 136, 138–39, 142, 148, 159, 163, 165–66, 170, 180, 186, 196, 200, 225–27, 255–57, 259–60, 262–66, 268–69, 271–73, 278, 283, 286, 288, 291–92, 299–301, 306, 312, 320, 323–24, 327, 333–35, 342–43, 369n. c
Wu (music), **62**, 192, 193n. 39, 201, 216, 220, 298
Wu (state), 100, 135n. 4, 146n. 6, 151, 260, 264n. 12
Wu Huo, 98
Wu Lai, **61**, 140, 263, 373n. a (chap. 25)
Wu Qi, **145**, 339
Wu Zixu, **135**, 138, 260, 264, 273, 316, 323
Wucheng Zhao, 291

Xi Qi, **226**
Xi Shi, **200**
Xi Wangguo, 291
Xi Zhong, 231
Xia (Chinese) states, 66, 184, 189, 236
Xia (dynasty), xxxi, 7n. 30, 10n. 7, 117, 155, 156n. 46, 225, 370n. c
Xia (music), 216
xian (hexagram), 297
xian (賢). *See* worthy person(s)
Xian Li, 256
Xian Peng, 226
Xiang (music), 62, 192, 201, 216, 298
Xiang (person), **193**–94
xiang (享) ceremony, 189
xiang (饗) sacrifice, 203
Xiangfei (place), 167
Xianyang (place), 170
xiao (孝). *See* filial piety
Xiao Yi, 253, 316

Xiaobai (person). *See* Duke Huan of Qi
xiaoren (小人). *See* petty man
Xie, **270**–71
xin (心). *See* heart
xin (信). *See* trustworthiness
xing (性). *See* human nature; nature
xu (虛). *See* emptiness
Xu (place), 38, 119, 161
Xu Gua, 297n. 46
Xu You, 268
Xunzi: as not inferior to Confucius, 342–43; shown debating, 53–55, 145–57, 171–72

Ya (section of *Odes*), 60, 218, 312
Yan (state), 101, 151, 162, 167, 190n. 26, 303
Yan Hui, **316n. 140**, 328, 338
Yan Ying. *See* Yanzi
Yan Yuan. *See* Yan Hui
Yang Liang, xviii, 87n. 10, 283n. 17, 291n. 21, 293n. 29, 294n. 35, 301n. 72, 316n. 138, 361n. e, 363n. d, 364n. c, 365n. e, 369n. g, 370n. a, 372n. f, 374n. c (chap. 25), 375n. f, 376n. i, 377nn. j and k, 380n. j, 382n. u
Yang Liuqiao, 307n. 105, 364n. i, 368n. a, 373n. b (chap. 25), 374nn. b and c (chap. 26), 376n. g, 377nn. j and k, 378n. m, 380n. j, 381n. o
Yang Zhu, **109**
Yangtze river, 158, 169, 199, 273, 327
Yanying (city), 158
Yanzi, **302**–3, 308–9
Yao (sage), xxiv, xxxi, **10**, 16n. 3, 21n. 20, 27–28, 32–33, 36n. 18, 57, 79–80, 97, 105, 146, 155, 159, 175, 190–91, 193–94, 199, 226n. 8, 253, 255, 257, 265, 268–70, 271n. 50, 279, 291, 304, 306–7, 317n. 141, 339, 343
Yellow River, 138
Yellow Springs, **4**
Yi (archer). *See* Archer Yi
Yi (minister), 270
Yi (people), 1
Yi (star), 97
yi (一, 壹). *See* single-mindedness
yi (義), xiii–xxiv, 6–7, 11–12, 15–19, 21, 25, 27–30, 33, 37, 41–44, 49, 51–55, 57, 63–64, 66, 68, 70, 73, 75–76, 80, 84, 93–94, 96, 99–101, 103, 107, 113–15, 118, 120–21, 124–25, 127, 132–33, 136–37, 139, 141, 143, 148, 150, 151n. 28, 155–57, 159–60, 163–64, 166–69, 173, 174n.

38, 178–80, 185, 191, 198–99, 201–2,
207–10, 212–13, 216, 222–23, 231, 236,
242, 248–54, 257–58, 260–62, 268, 278,
285, 292–93, 297, 301n. 72, 303–5, 309,
313–16, 319, 322–23, 325–26, 330–31,
334, 342, **346**, 377n. k
Yi Ya, 316
Yi Yin, **33**, 111, 134–35, 225
Yijing. See *Book of Changes*
Yili, xxvii n. 18, 290n. 14
Yin (dynasty), 7n. 30, 225, 264n. 10. *See
also* Shang (dynasty)
Yin (river), 158
yin and *yang*, 78, 176–79, 210
Yin Xie, 319
Yong (music), **192**
You Ruo. *See* Youzi
Youzi, **232**
Yu (sage), xxiv, xxxi, **10**, 16–17, 21n. 20,
22, 27–28, 33, 35–36, 42, 46, 57, 95,
105, 109, 117, 126, 155, 169–70, 173,
177, 186, 254–55, 257, 269–70, 279,
291, 294, 343, 361n. c
Yu (state), 264n. 12, 264n. 14, 316n. 139,
342
Yu Chang, 295n. 40
Yu Xingwu, 371n. c, 374n. n
Yu Yue, 366n. b, 371n. b, 372n. g, 374n.
j, 377n. m
Yue (people or state), 1, 27, 66, 100,
135n. 4, 151, 188–90, 324
Yujin, 170

Zaizi, 226
Zao Fu, 62, 107, 145, 194, 231, 257, 338
Zeng Yuan, **303**, 330
Zengzi, **231**, 253, 292nn. 24 and 25,
303n. 85, 308, 309n. 109, 315, 330–31
Zhan Guo Ce, 377–78n. m
Zhan Qin. *See* Liuxia Hui
Zhang Fu, 273
Zhang Jue, 361n. e, 367n. c (chap. 15),
370n. a, 383n. b
Zhang Quji, 134
Zhang Yi, 134
Zhao (state), xx, 101, 134–35, 145, 162,
170
Zhao Ming, 270
Zhao Qi, 374n. e (chap. 25)
Zheng (state), 220
Zheng Xuan, 369n. a (chap. 16), 377n. l,
379n. a, 381n. p
zhengming (正名). *See* rectification of
names

zhi (智). *See* wisdom
Zhi (place), 273
Zhi (robber). *See* Robber Zhi
Zhi Cheng, 270
zhong (忠). *See* loyalty
Zhong Hui, **339**
Zhong Tai, 359n. a, 366n. d, 382n. w
Zhong You. *See* Zilu
Zhongyong (中庸), 41n. 6
Zhou (dynasty), xix, xxiv, xxxi, 1n. 5,
7nn. 29 and 30, 21n. 20, 32n. 1, 33n.
5, 36, 37n. 21, 48–49, 52–53, 61, 75n.
13, 119n. 8, 129, 134, 147n. 11, 154,
158, 161n. 64, 170n. 26, 203n. 7,
225n. 7, 227, 230, 236, 273, 304–5,
320–21, 370n. c; Duke of (*see* Duke
of Zhou). *See also* King Cheng of
Zhou; King Wen of Zhou; King Wu
of Zhou
Zhòu (tyrant), xxxi, **7**, 29, 33, 49, 61,
110, 135n. 3, 136, 138, 150–51, 154nn.
38 and 39, 155, 157–58, 166–68, 173,
184–86, 188, 196, 225, 260, 263n. 6,
264, 278, 301nn. 74 and 75, 304, 342–
43, 373n. a (chap. 25)
Zhou Hou, 133–34
Zhu (son of Yao), **193–94**
Zhu (state), 47
Zhu Lou, 273
Zhu Xi, 374n. o, 376n. h
Zhuang Qiao, 151, **157**
Zhuangzi (thinker or text), xvii, xx,
xxiii, xxv–xxvi, xxix, 227, 306n. 99;
references to text of, 2n. 13, 12n. 14,
13n. 17, 34n. 14, 36n. 18, 190n. 25,
231n. 21, 271n. 52, 306n. 102, 345
Zhuangzi of Bian, 306
zhuhou (諸侯). *See* feudal lords
Zi Ma, 342
Zichan, 71, 303, 319
Zifa, 164–66, 369n. c
Zigōng (子弓), **32**, 42, 63
Zigong (子貢), **32n. 2**, 309–11, 322, 324,
326–28, 331–32, 341, 382n. u
Zijia Ju, 302, **303n. 83**
Zilu, **306**, 318, 323, 326–28, 384n. a
(chap. 29)
Zishe, **286**
Zisi, 40n. 1, **41–42**
Zixia, **46**, 313, 382n. x
Zixu. *See* Wu Zixu
Ziyou, **46**
Zizhang, **46**
Zizhi, **190n. 26**, 303n. 86